AN INTRODUCTION TO CONTEMPORARY INTERNATIONAL LAW

An Introduction to Contemporary International Law

A POLICY-ORIENTED PERSPECTIVE

THIRD EDITION

Lung-chu Chen

OXFORD
UNIVERSITY PRESS

OXFORD
UNIVERSITY PRESS

Oxford University Press is a department of the University of Oxford. It furthers the University's objective of excellence in research, scholarship, and education by publishing worldwide.

Oxford   New York
Auckland   Cape Town   Dar es Salaam   Hong Kong   Karachi   Kuala Lumpur   Madrid
Melbourne   Mexico City   Nairobi   New Delhi   Shanghai   Taipei   Toronto

With offices in
Argentina   Austria   Brazil   Chile   Czech Republic   France   Greece   Guatemala   Hungary
Italy   Japan   Poland   Portugal   Singapore   South Korea   Switzerland   Thailand
Turkey   Ukraine   Vietnam

Oxford is a registered trademark of Oxford University Press in the UK and certain other countries.

Published in the United States of America by
Oxford University Press
198 Madison Avenue, New York, NY 10016

Library of Congress Cataloging-in-Publication Data
Chen, Lung-chu, author.
   An introduction to contemporary international law : a policy-oriented perspective / Lung-chu Chen.—
Third edition.
      pages cm
   Includes bibliographical references and index.
   ISBN 978-0-19-022798-2 (hardback) : alk. paper)—ISBN 978-0-19-022799-9 (pbk.) : alk. paper)
1. International law. I. Title.
   KZ3110.C48 2015
   341—dc23
                                                                                    2014026011

9 8 7 6 5 4 3 2 1

Printed in the United States of America on acid-free paper

Note to Readers
This publication is designed to provide accurate and authoritative information in regard to the subject matter covered. It is based upon sources believed to be accurate and reliable and is intended to be current as of the time it was written. It is sold with the understanding that the publisher is not engaged in rendering legal, accounting, or other professional services. If legal advice or other expert assistance is required, the services of a competent professional person should be sought. Also, to confirm that the information has not been affected or changed by recent developments, traditional legal research techniques should be used, including checking primary sources where appropriate.

(Based on the Declaration of Principles jointly adopted by a Committee of the American Bar Association and a Committee of Publishers and Associations.)

> **You may order this or any other Oxford University Press publication by visiting the Oxford University Press website at www.oup.com**

In Affectionate Memory of
Myres S. McDougal (1906–1998)
and
Harold D. Lasswell (1902–1978)
Proponents of an International Law of Human Dignity

Contents

About the Author

DR. LUNG-CHU CHEN is an internationally recognized scholar and Professor of Law at New York Law School, specializing in international law, human rights, and the United Nations. He previously served as Research Associate, Senior Research Associate, and Senior Research Scholar at Yale Law School. He received his LL.B. with first-place honors from National Taiwan University, his LL.M. from Northwestern University, and his LL.M. and J.S.D. from Yale University. While still a junior at the National Taiwan University, he ranked first of some four thousand participants in Taiwan's national examination for judgeship and other high governmental posts—a unique distinction in Taiwan's history.

He is founder and chairman of the Taiwan New Century Foundation, founder and president of the New Century Institute (New York), and charter president and honorary president of the Taiwan United Nations Alliance (TAIUNA). He is a board member of the Policy Sciences Center, a former president of the Taiwanese Society of International Law, and a former national policy adviser to the president of Taiwan.

Formerly he was also chairman of the section on international law of the Association of American Law Schools, a member of the executive council of the American Society of International Law, a director of the American Society of Comparative Law, and a member of the editorial board of its journal (*American Journal of Comparative Law*). He was chief editor of *Human Rights*, published by the American Bar Association Section on Individual Rights and Responsibilities. In addition, he served as vice president and a member of the governing council of the International League for Human Rights and president of the North America Taiwanese Professors' Association. He was a principal lecturer at the International Institute of Human Rights in Strasbourg, a training center for human rights experts founded by Nobel Peace Prize winner René Cassin.

His publications include *Membership for Taiwan in the United Nations: Achieving Justice and Universality* (editor), *An Introduction to Contemporary International Law, Human Rights and World Public Order* (with Myres S. McDougal and Harold D. Lasswell), and *Formosa, China, and the United Nations* (with Harold D. Lasswell). In addition, he has written and edited numerous books and articles in Chinese. Currently he is general editor of a series of books relating to the U.N. system published under the auspices of the Taiwan Institute for U.N. Studies, a project of the Taiwan New Century Foundation. He is also editor in chief of *New Century Think Tank Forum*, a quarterly in Chinese published jointly by the Taiwan New Century Foundation and the New Century Institute.

Preface to the Third Edition

THE PURPOSE OF the third edition of *An Introduction to Contemporary International Law: A Policy-Oriented Perspective* is to propose to readers an answer to the question: What is international law? The answer given follows in the tradition of the New Haven School, whose policy-science approach to international law has its origins in the works of Professors Myres S. McDougal and Harold D. Lasswell of Yale Law School. Beginning in the mid-twentieth century, Professors McDougal and Lasswell and their collaborators sought to understand and to describe the forces rapidly reshaping the global landscape after the end of World War II. According to them, international law is not static but is a *process* by which members of the world community attempt to clarify and secure their *common interests* through *authoritative decisions* and *controlling practices*. For students wishing to understand international law, I submit that there is no better place to start than with the New Haven School's systematic approach to world events and its accompanying set of intellectual tools for identifying and describing the factors that underlie international legal order.

With the twenty-first century well underway, every feature of this decision process is impacted by the ever-quickening pace of globalization, technological change, and interactions among the world's peoples. Through the use of contemporary examples, the third edition aims to build on the previous editions by contextualizing and dramatizing these changes with reference to seven features that characterize the New Haven approach to international law: *participants, perspectives, arenas of decision, bases of power, strategies, outcomes*, and *effects*. As explained in chapter 1, these elements make up what the New Haven School terms the *world constitutive process of authoritative decision*. It is this process that is the ultimate subject of this book.

By *participants* we mean both the states and non-state actors who take part in the process of authoritative decision. Traditionally, scholars believed that only states could properly participate in international law. However, this view has given way to a more nuanced perspective. The third edition aims to enlighten readers to the many ways in which states, non-state entities, and even individual people can take part in the international legal process. Chapter 2 explores the complex relationships among the concepts of statehood, self-determination, recognition, and international politics that animate the creation of new states, as dramatized by the example of Taiwan. Chapter 3 describes the increasingly important roles played by intergovernmental organizations such as the United Nations and its specialized agencies in the pursuit and maintenance of *minimum world order* and *optimum world order*—two outcomes by which the effectiveness of international legal processes may be measured. As of today, the United Nations has grown to include 193 member states, compared to 189 in 2000, owing to the inception of new states such as Timor-Leste (East Timor), Montenegro, Serbia, and South Sudan.

Chapter 4 describes the establishment of transnational nongovernmental organizations and associations and their growing influence in international arenas. These bodies include civil society organizations that promote human rights and other important objectives as well as multinational corporations, whose power to influence world order has increased tremendously as an outgrowth of the global pursuit and distribution of wealth. Meanwhile, individuals—acting on their own and as representatives of territorial communities or functional groups—have taken on new prominence globally. In chapter 5, individuals are presented as the ultimate actors in the international legal process. Furthermore, the third edition of this book places greater emphasis on the centrality of human beings in international law, as evidenced by an increased recognition of human rights and the expansion of individual criminal responsibility.

The term *perspectives* refers to the diverse viewpoints of members of the world community viewed in light of the pursuit of their common interests. The New Haven School posits that all individuals share an interest in both minimum world order—the minimization of unauthorized coercion and violence—and optimum world order—the widest possible shaping and sharing of values. As such, chapter 6 of the third edition emphasizes the notion of "human security," a term that embraces both minimum and optimum world order.

Chapter 7 explores the various *arenas* of the international legal process. The term *arena* denotes the establishment of, and access to, international structures of authority. The trend in recent decades has been toward a higher degree of institutionalization as demonstrated by agencies such as the World Trade Organization (WTO). International bodies provide a forum where participants may deliberate and coordinate actions across borders. International bodies may also provide access to third-party decision making, as exemplified by the dispute settlement procedures under the Law of the

Sea Convention and the WTO. The introduction of international criminal tribunals, such as the International Criminal Tribunals for the former Yugoslavia and for Rwanda, represent the world community's condemnation of egregious human rights abuses. The International Criminal Court, established in 2002, now serves as a forum for the prosecution of individuals accused of perpetrating certain crimes under international law.

Bases of power, as outlined in chapters 8 to 14, encompass both nonhuman and human resources. Nonhuman resources include territory, the use and control of the sea, and other shareable and nonshareable resources. Since the Law of the Sea Convention went into effect in 1994, controversies have arisen over competing claims to the use of exclusive economic zones and ownership of territories in the South China Sea and other regions. Global warming has introduced a new dimension to such issues, as de-icing in the polar regions leads to geopolitical tensions, while some island nations face probable extinction from rising sea levels. Meanwhile, the overall well-being of the global environment has emerged as a focal concern, as leaders struggle to reach agreements necessary to limit pollution amid a rush toward industrialization and to deal with the growing problem of climate change.

Globalization and the effects of the attacks of September 11, 2001, have altered our thinking about human resources and the transnational movement of people. Simultaneously, the protection of people has taken on greater importance. Traditional notions of state sovereignty are giving way to the more urgent responsibility to protect human rights, and the number of issues that are of "international concern" is increasing as people recognize their deepening interdependence.

The term *bases of power* also refers to the authority held by states and non-state actors to make decisions within defined realms. Authority may be distributed vertically, as between the general community of states and individuals, or horizontally across groupings of states. The horizontal allocation of authority is becoming increasingly common as participants face challenges that defy the jurisdiction of singular nations.

The term *strategies* refers to the four primary instruments of policy: diplomacy, ideology, the economy, and the military. These instruments are employed alone or in various combinations in the pursuit of values, as explored in chapters 15 to 19. Issues arising under the diplomatic instrument—for example, the protection of nationals abroad—highlight the interplay of international law and domestic law. International agreements, which are the outcome of diplomatic interactions, deserve special attention and study in recognition of their traditional role as a source of international law. In light of this importance, the third edition offers the reader a more detailed analysis of international agreements in relation to domestic law and U.S. constitutional principles. The ideological instrument has been enhanced by the dissemination of science-based technologies such as personal computers and mobile phones. Communications technologies, including the worldwide Internet, permit us to be better informed more quickly and to interact easily with counterparts everywhere. The emerging information society presents both challenges and opportunities and highlights the conflict between the desire for the free flow of information and governmental control of media. Use of the economic instrument is oriented pragmatically to the goal of human development, as exemplified by the Millennium Development Goals (MDGs). The recent global economic crisis has brought with it new challenges and dynamics among the developed and developing nations. Finally, the aftermath of 9/11 has forever changed our understanding of the military instrument. The resulting "preemption doctrine" and the proliferation of weapons such as unmanned aerial drones have pushed the boundaries of the law of war as traditionally understood. At the same time, the desire and necessity for increased humanitarian intervention has led many to accept a larger role for militaries in the defense and protection of mass human rights.

Outcomes refer to the seven functions that make up the international process of authoritative decision. These functions, which are highlighted in chapters 20 to 26, are divided into *intelligence, promotion, prescription, invocation, application, termination*, and *appraisal*. Information gathering and dissemination has been strengthened by the impact of technology and by the fact-finding activities of both officials and nonofficials. Promotion by nongovernmental organizations and individuals plays an increasingly influential role in the international decision-making process and the prescriptions adopted by both domestic and international bodies. Chapter 24 acknowledges the difficulties of ensuring compliance with international norms, while putting such challenges in perspective by reference to six sanctioning goals: *prevention, deterrence, restoration, rehabilitation, reconstruction*, and *correction*. The appraisal function has evolved democratically thanks to the dissemination of technologies that permit a wide range of participants to assess the outcomes of various actions.

The cumulative effects of the decision functions, described in chapters 27 to 29, can be observed in a trend toward greater accountability for states and individual decision makers under international law. As highlighted in chapter 28, events such as the Arab Spring must be understood in relation to the right to self-determination and states' responsibility for promoting the well-being of their peoples. In the realm of individual criminal responsibility, the importance of the establishment and operation of the International Criminal Court cannot be overemphasized. The third edition includes a new chapter 29 that explores the vital role individual responsibility plays in the emerging field of international criminal law. Individuals—notably representatives of states—can and must be held accountable for conduct that is inimical to fundamental human rights and dangerous to world order.

Chapter 30 of the third edition ends with a call for a "grand strategy of simultaneity." International law matters because it can help us build a stronger world community based on the notion of human dignity for all people. Individuals are the driving force behind this positive change. However, individuals must be educated about how international law shapes the world around them in order to serve effectively as citizens and decision makers. I hope that this fresh edition of *An Introduction to Contemporary International Law: A Policy-Oriented Perspective* supplies a new generation of students with the interest, insights, and intellectual tools needed to do their part.

Where possible, contemporary examples have been used to illustrate key principles, with many examples current as of 2013. In some cases, references are made to events taking place in 2014. The treatment is admittedly brief, as the purpose of the text is not to provide a history of world events, but to help readers understand the nature of international authoritative decision. Therefore, readers are encouraged to consider these examples in light of more recent events and to notice new examples on their own in the years to come.

I remain indebted to my mentors—Myres S. McDougal and Harold D. Lasswell. In writing the third edition of this book, I hope to contribute, however modestly, to their ongoing legacies as founders of the New Haven School of international law, from which countless scholars, students, practitioners, and other members of the world community have benefited and will continue to benefit.

Throughout my years at New York Law School, I have received much support from both the faculty and student body. I wish to thank Dean Anthony Crowell, former Dean Richard Matasar, former Interim Dean Carol Buckler, and Associate Dean Deborah Archer for their continued support of my scholarly works, as well as the colleagues who have offered their assistance and generous feedback over the years. I am also indebted to the staff of the New York Law School library, especially Associate Dean Camille Broussard, Senior Reference Librarian Michael McCarthy, and their teams. From the student body, I would like to acknowledge my research assistants, Manny Alicandro, Eduardo Blount, Vanessa Craveiro, Joshua Eidsvaag, Corey Gaul, Neil Giovanatti, Timothy Han, Jennifer Lin, Jeffrey Liu, Rebecca Eunhye Moon, Samuel Newbold, Joan O'Hara, Agata Ratajczyk, Halina Schiffman-Shilo, James Tai, and Jessie Tang for their help and diligence throughout the researching, writing, and editing process. In particular, I would like to thank Matthew Goodro, whose efforts contributed significantly to the first draft of the third edition, and Nicholas Turner, who remained dedicated to the project to the end and whose editorial and organizational skills were instrumental to its completion.

At Yale Law School, I am thankful to Dean Robert C. Post and former Dean Harold H. Koh for encouragement and support. At Oxford University Press, I wish to extend sincerest thanks to Blake Ratcliff, whose efforts were essential to the publication of the third edition. I also wish to thank John Louth for his support. The production team, Alden Domizio, Balamurugan Rajendran, and Mary Rosewood, deserve special praise for their superlative expertise and efficiency.

I also extend my appreciation to the New Century Institute for support and to the board members and staff of the Taiwan New Century Foundation for their professional assistance. In particular, I wish to thank Dr. Lung-Fong and Joanne Chen and Dr. Wen-Hsien Chen for their encouragement and support.

And last but not the least, I wish to thank my dear wife, Judy, our children, our children-in-law, and our grandchildren for their affection, patience, and enduring support.

Preface to the Second Edition

INTERNATIONAL LAW IS a continuing process of authoritative decision by which members of the world community identify, clarify, and secure their common interests. These common interests consist of minimum world order and optimum world order. *Minimum world order* refers to the minimization of unauthorized coercion and violence—in other words, the maintenance of international peace and security. *Optimum world order* refers to the widest possible shaping and sharing of values, for example, respect, power, enlightenment, well-being, wealth, skill, affection, and rectitude, popularly expressed in terms of human rights, self-determination and self-governance, education and global communication, health and environmental protection, trade and development, transfer of technology, human solidarity and diversity, and social justice.

The end of the Cold War did not put international law out of business. On the contrary, although the threat of a nuclear holocaust might have been reduced for the time being, the need for maintaining minimum world order and for securing optimum world order has become ever more pressing.

As humankind ushers in a new millennium and a new century of knowledge and power, the degree of global interdependence has deepened, and the amazing frequency of transnational interactions continues to accelerate. The global village is real in fact and in perception. "Globalization" has become a catch word of the new era. As an ongoing process of authoritative decision, international law is as dynamic as ever and constitutes a distinct part of the globalizing process. Taking one another into account, all actors—nongovernmental as well as governmental—have intensified their transnational interactions, generating ever-increasing and interpenetrating transnational effects.

Since the publication of the first edition in 1989, there have been many changes in the world, and so many significant events have happened in the field of international law. Just to name a few: the fall of the Berlin Wall and the end of the Cold War; the disintegration of the Soviet Union and the formation of the Commonwealth of Independent States; the breakup of Yugoslavia and the conflicts in the Balkans; the establishment of the International Criminal Tribunals for the former Yugoslavia and for Rwanda; the transition from apartheid government to a nonracial democracy in South Africa; the Rio Earth Summit and the adoption of Agenda 21, a comprehensive plan for global action in all areas of sustainable development; the entering into force of the U.N. Convention on the Law of the Sea and the concomitant establishment of the International Seabed Authority and the International Tribunal for the Law of the Sea; the establishment of the World Trade Organization to replace the General Agreement on Tariffs and Trade (GATT) as the only international body overseeing international trade; the creation of the office of the U.N. High Commissioner for Human Rights and the operation of the U.N. Convention on the Rights of the Child; the adoption of the Rome Statute of the International Criminal Court; and U.N. and U.S. responses to the Iraqi invasion of Kuwait and the continuing struggle with Iraq over enforcing the U.N. ceasefire resolutions.

All these and other developments are reflected in this edition. In updating and preparing the second edition, I benefited a great deal from the comments and suggestions received from many people who have used the first edition of the book and from the assistance and support rendered by many. My deep appreciation to all of them.

The inspiration of my mentors—Myres S. McDougal and Harold D. Lasswell—was as present for this edition as for the original edition. The recent passing of Professor McDougal meant the loss of a great mentor, counselor, and friend to me. It also meant the loss of one of the great international legal scholars of all time, but his legacy to humankind will live forever. Both Mac and Harold will be missed dearly.

W. Michael Reisman was wonderful and helpful in many ways. Jordan J. Paust was thorough in reviewing an early draft of the entire revised manuscript and was generous in offering numerous and invaluable suggestions and comments.

Throughout the years my students at New York Law School have been, in the practical sense, participants in the ongoing enterprise and have offered many helpful suggestions. I especially wish to thank Maria-Alana Recine and Stephanie McQueen for outstanding research assistance. Thanks also go to Ken Ayers, Susan Hennigan, Celena Mayo, and Cliff Scott for their assistance.

At New York Law School I am indebted to Dean Harry H. Wellington and Associate Dean Ellen Ryerson for their strong and continued support, including summer research grants. Professor Joyce Saltalamachia and her library staff were consistent and efficient in rendering profession service; Reference Librarian Marta Kiszely, my faculty library liaison, was ever cheerful, diligent, and efficient in meeting a flow of requests for assistance.

At Yale Law School, I am grateful to Dean Anthony T. Kronman for encouragement and support. At Yale University Press, Jane Zanichkowsky was excellent in her role as copy editor.

In Taiwan, I wish to thank Law Professor Chao-Yuan Huang of Taiwan University and Dr. Yann-huei Song of Academia Sinica for their invaluable suggestions and assistance. At the Taiwan New Century Foundation, my thanks go to En Wei Lin, Hsueh Chin Chen, Su Mei Chiu, and Chien Shou Lu for their assistance.

For this edition, as for the first, the affection, patience, and support of Judy and our family were a constant source of comfort and strength.

Preface to the First Edition

INTERNATIONAL LAW IS perhaps the most dynamic area of law today and one of the most important, as global interdependence deepens and the transnational movement of people, ideas, goods, and services continues to grow. It is an ongoing process of decision through which the members of the world community identify, clarify, and secure their common interests—both minimum world order (in the sense of minimizing unauthorized coercion and violence) and optimum world order (in the sense of fostering the widest possible shaping and sharing of all values). In this process, nation-states have played and continue to play the dominant role. But non-state participants—international governmental organizations, nongovernmental organizations, and private associations—are playing increasingly significant roles. The individual, in particular, acting both alone and as a group representative, is the ultimate participant, performing all the functions relevant to making and applying law.

As one who is identified with the policy-oriented approach developed by Myres S. McDougal and Harold D. Lasswell and their associates (dubbed by some the New Haven School), I have sought as author to bring the essence and insights of the approach to bear on major international legal problems in the rapidly changing context of the earth-space arena.

Unlike conventional works in international law, this book is organized and structured in terms of the process of decision by reference to participants (nation-states, international governmental organizations, nongovernmental organizations and associations, and the individual), perspectives (minimum world order and optimum world order), arenas of decision (establishment and access), bases of power (authority and effective control over people, resources, institutions, and events), strategies (diplomatic, ideological, economic, and military), outcomes, and effects.

As humankind grapples with a host of transnational problems—armed conflicts and the control of armaments, trade and investment, the use and control of the sea and outer space, global environment, illicit drug trafficking, transnational flows of information, technology transfer, human rights, refugees, religious warfare, and so on—it becomes evident that international law is too important to be left to international lawyers and decision makers alone. Individual citizens must rise to the challenge of contemporary international law in the search for a world public order of human dignity. They must:

- Think globally to meet the ever-present challenge of global interdependence and interdetermination.
- Think temporally not only about the present generation but about posterity.
- Think contextually to relate decision making to all community levels and all value sectors of social interaction.
- Think and act creatively in the common interest, mobilizing all available problem-solving skills and resources in the pursuit of both minimum and optimum order.

I hope that not only students of international law but other citizens concerned with law and world affairs will find this book helpful. As an introductory treatise, it seeks to be comprehensive in scope yet selective in emphasis; and the notes are kept to an absolute minimum.

My debts to Professors McDougal and Lasswell, long proponents of an international law of human dignity, are enormous and apparent—the book is dedicated to them. As a member of the New Haven School, I have drawn freely on prior collaborative work with them (especially *Human Rights and World Public Order*, published by Yale University Press in 1980) and also, in the words of McDougal, "on a great variety of past contributions, jointly planned, discussed, and written by members of a large group who regard their work as common property." I am most grateful to Mac, who, with his characteristic generosity, has read the entire manuscript and made many valuable criticisms and suggestions.

I am also deeply grateful to Professors Richard A. Falk of Princeton University, Rosalyn Higgins of the London School of Economics and Political Science, and Jordan J. Paust of the University of Houston Law Center for having read the entire manuscript and offered numerous valuable criticisms and suggestions for improvement. My thanks also go to Professor Gunther F. Handl of Wayne State University Law School and Siegfried Wiessner of St. Thomas University School of Law for helpful comments and suggestions in connection with chapters 27 and 11, respectively.

Thanks are also due my students at New York Law School, especially my outstanding research assistants Raymund Johansen and Gary Gross. The assistance of Frances

Civardi, Carmen Giordano, Sylvia Ospina, Christopher Portelli, and Erik Strangeways at an earlier stage is also gratefully acknowledged.

Esther J. Chen, the fourteen-year-old in-house word processing expert of my family, has been indispensible throughout the preparation of various drafts and the final manuscript. Words are inadequate to express professional appreciation and parental pride.

At New York Law School I am indebted to Dean James F. Simon and Associate Dean Randolph N. Jonakait for strong and consistent support (financial and other). Professor Joyce Saltalamachia and her library staff were instrumental in maintaining a flow of books and other documentation. My appreciation for support and encouragement also goes to colleagues E. Donald Shapiro, B. James George, Jr., Arnold H. Graham, Jane P. Helm, Gerald Korngold, and Edward B. Samuels.

I thank the Dana Fund for International and Comparative Legal Studies for a summer research grant at an early stage of this project, for which I especially thank Professor Richard W. Edwards, Jr., of the University of Toledo College of Law. A grant from the Ernst C. Stiefel Fund, for which I wish to thank Dr. Ernst Stiefel, was helpful in seeing the book through the press.

At Yale Law School I am grateful to Deans Guido Calabresi and Harry H. Wellington for continued support. Professor Morris L. Cohen and his library staff were immensely helpful.

The officers of Yale University Press have been generous in encouragement and support. I owe a special debt of gratitude to Marian N. Ash and John G. Ryden. Laura J. Dooley was perceptive, understanding, and skillful in her role as manuscript editor.

Finally, I wish to thank my parents, parents-in-law, and extended family for all their encouragement and support. My wife, Judy, and children, Ellie, Harold, and Esther, cheerfully bore the brunt of my absorption in this work and lovingly endured the pressure. Without their affection, patience, and support this book would never have been completed.

I Delimitation of the Task

1 International Law in a Policy-Oriented Perspective

EVERY CITIZEN OF the world should have some basic understanding of international law, whatever his or her station or profession may be. In the contemporary world of increasingly complex interdependencies, almost all social problems are transnational in nature, requiring a global or regional solution. These problems include armed conflicts and control of armaments; civil strifes; energy crises; trade, investment, and capital flows; exploration of ocean resources and the use of outer space; environmental problems (for example, radioactive fallout, acid rain, air and marine pollution); control of epidemics and of illicit traffic in narcotics and persons; flows of information and data technology transfer; deprivations of human rights (apartheid, discrimination, genocide, and so on); religious warfare and strife; flows and resettlements of refugees; and reunions of families broken by oppression, conflicts, or disasters—just to name a few. One cannot deal with local and national problems effectively without adequate orientation to the global context. Particular legal problems must be approached in light of the whole.

International law is developing at an ever greater pace as the world community becomes increasingly interdependent, owing in part to the growing movement of people, ideas, goods, and services across national boundaries. This area of law has become recognizably much broader than law governing the relationships between governments, although such law has regulated individuals and groups in the past. Individual human beings, the ultimate participants in any legal process, interact with increasing frequency and intensity across nation-state lines in a host of group forms. But nation-states have historically played, and continue to play, a predominant role as actors at the international level. International governmental organizations, proliferating rapidly in recent years and manifesting varying degrees of comprehensiveness and specialization, also participate in decision making and help to shape attitudes and behavior. Nongovernmental associations and organizations of all kinds, such as multinational corporations and human rights organizations, are increasingly transnational in membership, goals, areas of activity, and impacts.

Although the particular aspects of international law may appear to be quite stable, it is perhaps the most dynamic area of law today, as well as one of the most important. It is made through international agreements (multilateral and bilateral) and through customary behavior and expectations. Compared to national legal systems, international law is decentralized; yet without international law, a basic stability in world order would not be possible. International law and national law sometimes conflict, and in general it is international law that should prevail. States (and the individuals who compose the state) ought to be held to international standards. This is the essence of the supremacy of international law that is so indispensable to maintaining world order. For hundreds of years the relations between international and national law have been intimate and interpenetrating, and those relations continue to grow and become more evident.

International law, like all law, is a continuing process through which the common interests of the members of the world community are clarified and secured. It seeks to attain a minimum order, in the sense of minimizing unauthorized coercion, and to achieve an optimum order, in the sense of the widest possible shaping and sharing of all values (respect, power, enlightenment, well-being, wealth, skill, affection, and rectitude).

As global interdependencies deepen, what happens in one country increasingly affects others, and communities must take one another into account when making choices and decisions. International law brings a distinct and vital dimension to citizenship education. Citizens of the world must be taught to think globally, to think contextually, and to think creatively for the common interest. The ultimate goal should be the establishment of a world community of human dignity. Toward this goal, education in the broadest sense is crucial. We cannot be content with the status quo. We must think about new ways to build a better world.

Myths and Realities about International Law

In spite of the profound importance of international law, misconceptions abound. Sometimes it is not taken seriously. Those who do this exhibit a range of perceptions about international law:

- There is no international law as such, because the world community is a jungle where naked power counts.
- International law is not really law but a form of international morality or a political doctrine.

- International law is a sham, a political facade used to justify the expediency of national policy; international law provides a convenient justification or pretext for certain conduct of states.
- International law is made to be broken at will when the vital interests of a sovereign state are involved.
- International law is weak, without centralized institutions of lawmaking and law enforcement (that is, there is no world legislature, no world police or jails).
- International law is for specialists and is irrelevant to ordinary people.

International law undeniably has not always functioned as effectively and perfectly as desired, but this may also be said of national laws. No social process is free from the law violator. The difference is a matter of degree. Gross violations of international law do occur—and often with seeming impunity. But on the whole, compliance with norms of international law is a cardinal fact of contemporary life in our world community of inter-determination and reciprocity. International law does matter. Otherwise, nation-state officials would not take pains to justify the "lawfulness" of their conduct by recourse to norms of international law.

For instance, after Korean Airlines Flight 007 was shot down by the Soviet Union in September 1983, killing all 269 people on board, the Soviet government, although it gave evasive, inconsistent accounts, did not flatly assert: "Yes, we shot down the airplane and violated international law. So what?" On the contrary, it sought to justify the lawfulness of its action by asserting that the Korean airliner had intruded into Soviet airspace and was engaged in a spy mission, even though it was leaving Soviet territory. A nation-state does not lightly dismiss the relevance of international law.

Take the Iranian hostage seizure case. This episode, which involved the seizure of American diplomats and the takeover of the American embassy in Tehran in 1979 and related efforts to secure the hostages' release, raised a staggering range of international legal issues. For example, what international legal norms were violated by the hostage takers when they seized the embassy? Just who in Iran was responsible for these events—the Iranian government or the militant students? Did the United States act lawfully when President Carter froze all Iranian assets in American banks, cut off oil imports from Iran, and collectively deported Iranian students unlawfully present in the United States? What role did the United Nations play in freeing the hostages? Was the United States' abortive military attempt to rescue the hostages lawful, or did it violate the territorial integrity of Iran? Did the International Court of Justice have jurisdiction over the case, and how did the contending parties react to its decision? Was the agreement of settlement achieved through Algeria's mediation valid, or was the agreement made under duress?

Or consider a more recent example. There were scores of issues raised for international law following the terrorist attacks of September 11, 2001. The September 11 attacks were carried out by Al Qaeda, a non-state actor. Do the laws of war apply to a conflict with a non-state actor? What are the responsibilities of states with respect to non-state actors operating within their borders? Can a state be held responsible for the actions of non-state actors that it allows to operate within its borders? If so, how should this be done? Is a state that has been injured by a non-state actor justified in using force against the state that has harbored the non-state actor?

The U.S. invasion of Afghanistan and the toppling of the Taliban government following the September 11 attacks raised even more questions about the use of force by a state to overthrow a repressive government. When, if ever, is the use of force for such a purpose as regime change justifiable? If the use of force is ever justifiable, who decides whether it is justified in a certain instance? By what criteria are such determinations made? Is there a limiting principle? What distinguishes one repressive government from another and makes that government subject to the will of outside actors?

The overthrow of the Taliban also raised questions about the responsibility of a state to its own people. What are these responsibilities? Are these responsibilities absolute or culturally relative? What is the appropriate response when a state is not fulfilling these obligations? Does this call for sanctions? The use of force?

The "War on Terror" that followed the September 11 attacks raised yet more questions for international law. Are the United States' actions in prosecuting its War on Terror justified as a matter of self-defense? What about the use of waterboarding and other so-called "enhanced" interrogation techniques by the United States? What should the ramifications be when a state is found to have tortured? Where is the appropriate forum for resolving such claims? More fundamentally, who makes international law, and who applies it? Who decides whether activities are lawful? Who reviews such decisions, and how? What role is there for the news media in the making of international law? International law experts? Nongovernmental organizations and associations? Concerned citizens of the world? Does international law mean anything at all if powerful states such as the United States can violate it with impunity? Or alternatively, are we still operating under a system in which "might makes right" and international law is just a façade to be discarded by the wealthy and the powerful?

The U.S.-led invasion of Iraq, which was initially justified in part by the 9/11 attacks, raised many more questions. Before invading Iraq, the United States unsuccessfully sought authorization from the U.N. Security Council. Should nation-states be bound by the decisions of the Security Council? Or, because the U.N. Charter is not a "suicide pact," do nation states retain the right to act unilaterally (or, in the case of Iraq, with a "coalition of the willing") to protect their interests?

The invasion raised the issue of the preemptive use of force. At what point, if any, does an external threat become sufficiently concrete to justify the preemptive use of force in the name of self-defense? How imminent must the threat be? Is there a minimum threshold of proof that must be satisfied?

One might inquire as to the criteria used to determine whether the activities involved are lawful. For example, what international legal norms were violated? The nonviolation of territorial integrity? Norms governing state responsibility to protect its own citizens? Norms governing the use of force for self-defense? Perhaps others?

Regardless of whether the initial invasion was justified or legal under international law, these events raise questions about what obligations, if any, are imposed on an occupying force. Is there an obligation to rebuild? If so, to what extent? How long can an occupying force justify its continued presence? By what criteria can we determine that an occupation is no longer justified?

This array of legal questions underscores how prominently and pervasively international law figures into the entire episode. The aftermath of the September 11 attacks offers an excellent example through which many of the major aspects of international law can be explored and studied.

Globalization is another issue that raises a plenitude of issues. One of the most important trends in recent human history has been the increasingly free movement of people, goods, services, capital, information, and ideas across national boundaries. Along with this freer movement across borders has been a corresponding increase in interdependence across national borders. Greater interdependence, in turn, has led decision makers to expand the scope of their asserted authority so as to account for those beyond their own borders. The trends towards a more globalized world raises many international legal questions.

Are current institutions sufficient to meet the demands of our increasingly globalized world? What are the consequences of the global financial crisis that erupted in 2008 and whose disruptive impacts continue? Given the increasingly free flow of capital across borders, and the interconnectedness of national economies, should there be greater international financial regulation? If so, are the current regulatory bodies sufficient or are new agencies necessary? Given the impact that one national economy can have on others, can a voluntary regulatory system be sufficient, or should there be some requirement that all states participate? What if some states refuse to do so?

With the rise of globalization, there has also been a corresponding shift in the types of participants in international law. No longer are state actors the exclusive makers of international law; multinational corporations, intergovernmental and nongovernmental organizations, and other such actors play an increasingly important function in the shaping of international law. These actors are increasingly international in the scope of their concern. This shift, however, raises some fundamental questions. If the state monopoly on authoritative decision making is over, how should this power be shared with non-state actors? Should non-state actors be afforded greater participation in formal decision making, or should their influence be limited to an informal role?

Free trade in goods and services across borders has brought prominence, as well as some criticism, to institutions such as the International Monetary Fund, the World Bank, and the World Trade Organization. Are these institutions doing enough to promote the free exchange of goods and services? Are they doing too much at the expense of people and the environment? Is enough being done to protect the interests of developing economies? Would regional organizations be more effective at achieving the objectives of international trade law?

Technological advances in recent decades have revolutionized the movement of information across borders. Advances have greatly increased the speed of interaction across borders, with both positive effects (e.g., the free flow of information) and negative ones (e.g., the spread of the financial downturn). Technology was instrumental in organizing and disseminating information about political uprisings during the Arab Spring that began in 2011. Social networking sites and mobile phones were used to organize demonstrations and to share information among protesters as well as a global audience. People around the world were able to view images and receive updates from within countries in North Africa and the Middle East including Tunisia, Egypt, Libya, Bahrain, Syria, and Yemen almost instantaneously as the protests unfolded. These events demonstrate the power of individuals everywhere to use new means to demand greater participation in decisions affecting their well-being.

Advances in information and communication technology have also resulted in a "digital divide." In many parts of the developing world, especially in rural areas, access to technology such as the Internet and mobile communications is sparse or prohibitively expensive for many. These barriers make it difficult, if not impossible, for people to participate in the sharing of knowledge and the economic development that technology promises. The United Nations has played an integral role in promoting efforts to bridge the digital divide in countries around the world. What role can or should international law play in addressing this disparity?

Globalization raises numerous questions about the movement of people. As businesses and jobs cross borders, so too must people. Restrictions on movement, which invite restrictive measures from other states, prevent the free flow of people across borders. Are these matters of domestic or international concern, or both? How do we distinguish between the two in an increasingly interconnected world?

In the aftermath of the Cold War and in response to conflicts such as those in the former Yugoslavia, Iraq, Rwanda, Sudan, and Côte d'Ivoire, the U.N. Security Council has taken an increasingly active role in global peacekeeping and peacemaking, raising even further questions for international law. How relevant and effective is the policy of prohibiting the use of force proclaimed by Article 2(4) of the U.N. Charter? Should U.N. member states provide the Security Council with increased peacekeeping or peacemaking powers? Should a standby peacekeeping fund be established, or should national troops be earmarked for call-up by the Security Council? Should the Security Council have a small, multinational force on standby, ready for dispatch to hot spots? What about joint training exercises between designated national forces?

Aside from such dramatic cases as KAL 007, the Iranian hostage incident, the terrorist attacks of 9/11, and the many events brought on by globalization, the issue of lawfulness arises in a myriad of other contexts. Recent examples include:

- the claims of Israel to launch missiles into southern Lebanon following the kidnapping of Israeli soldiers in 2006;
- the claims of the ousted Honduran president, Manuel Zelaya, against his successor Roberto Micheletti after that nation's coup d'état in 2009;
- the claims by Georgia against Russia that led to an armed conflict in South Ossetia in 2008;
- the claims of those detained at Guantanamo Bay against the United States;
- the claims of the United States and other countries as well as private actors against Somali pirates;
- the claims by the United Kingdom to use force in response to the forcible seizure of the Falkland Islands by Argentina in 1982;
- the claims by Israel of the right to destroy nuclear capabilities in Iran;
- the claims of Palestinians for the ongoing settlement of their territory by Israel;
- the counterclaims by Israel against the targeting of civilians by Hamas and other Palestinian groups;
- the claims to independence by Québec against Canada;
- the claims by the United States to assist the government in El Salvador and the contras in Nicaragua during the Reagan administration;
- the claims of refugees from recent armed conflicts in Africa (Sudan, Rwanda, Côte d'Ivoire, Democratic Republic of Congo, for example) to protection in various nation-states;
- the claims by various states to expropriate the property of foreign nationals and corporations;
- the claims by the United States to extend the application of its financial, antitrust, and intellectual property laws beyond its borders;
- the claims by Russia to intervene forcibly in Chechnya;
- the claims by NATO powers to engage in humanitarian interventions in Bosnia, Kosovo, and Libya;
- the claims by China to use force to annex Taiwan in the name of reunification.

These claims and activities raise the issue of lawfulness. But who decides whether they are lawful? And how is lawfulness determined? Does it really matter whether certain activities are lawful? If unlawful, so what? What can be done to the violator, and by whom?

These and similar questions not only reaffirm the relevance of international law in world affairs but also point to the limitations inherent in the contemporary international legal system.

Unlike domestic legal systems, the international legal system is essentially decentralized; effective power is centered on territorial communities known as nation-states. Many power centers exist, not just one. No centralized institutions have sufficient authority and resources to make, apply, and enforce law globally and to adjudicate disputes. We do have the United Nations, but the United Nations is far from being a world government. The U.N. General Assembly is not a world parliament that makes law and imposes taxes on member states. The secretary-general is not the chief executive of a world government. The United Nations is not somehow distinct from member states but belongs to all of its members, with all the advantages, problems, and, most important, responsibilities of ownership. Only the member states have the power to undertake the task of renewing the framework of global cooperation to shape a new world order.

The present order (or disorder) sprung from the collapse of communism and the end of the Cold War and has been characterized in large part by vicious internal conflicts. Nationalistic and ethnic tensions have become a predominant feature in conflicts around the globe. The relaxation of authoritarian regimes and the destructive effects of civil conflicts have strained fragile state structures, leading in cases such as Somalia, Rwanda, and Bosnia to the dissolution of states into regions controlled by competing factions, to widespread violence, and to egregious human rights violations.

There is no single institution with the power to mediate such disputes around the globe. The most powerful office in the world, in popular perception, is the presidency of the United States, and yet the United States will not, and cannot, be a "world policeman." The International Court of Justice (ICJ), although commonly known as the World Court, lacks the authority of compulsory jurisdiction. Because its jurisdiction is contingent on the consent of states, few international disputes come before the ICJ for adjudication. Its light caseload stands in stark contrast to the heavy caseload of the U.S. Supreme Court.

When an unlawful act is alleged, a counterclaim usually follows. Such competing claims raise important questions about who decides which party is right and which party is wrong in a decentralized legal regime. In the general absence of a centralized authoritative decision maker, it falls on individual nation-states, through their officials, to decide, although all of us are involved as reviewers and ultimate participants in shaping attitudes and behavior: your claims against mine, and my characterizations against yours. Here nation-state officials perform what is known as the "double function": They act simultaneously as claimants and as judges. They engage in "auto-interpretation"— they are judges of their own acts and they interpret the legal implications of their own conduct. The cumulative effect of such individual assertions and characterizations often leads to a sense of confusion, uncertainty, and frustration. An observer may rightfully ask, why are disputing states unwilling to submit their disputes to a third-party decision maker?

The contemporary international legal system is still state-centered and places an inordinate emphasis on "national sovereignty" and "equality of states." Effective power is still overwhelmingly concentrated in individual states, though obviously some states wield far greater power than others, and even some private groups wield more effective power, control more wealth, and enjoy more respect in the community than some nation-states. Thus, even after a determination is made about the unlawfulness of certain conduct, effective sanctions in the form of centralized command and the federal marshal, familiar in a domestic legal order, are generally not forthcoming. International law is especially fragile in its inability to impose effective sanctions against gross violations of international law. One need only look to the decades-long conflict in Sudan. Many, including the U.S. government, have categorized violence against black African Sudanese as genocide. Nonetheless, the international community has struggled to mount an effective response to the atrocities. It remains to be seen whether peace negotiations in the Darfur region of Sudan or the establishment of the Republic of South Sudan following a referendum in 2011 will succeed in quelling the violence in the long term. Confronted with dramatic cases of this kind—gross violations met with seeming impunity—concerned citizens naturally wonder where international law is and how good it is, and this explains a lot about some of the popular myths regarding international law in a crisis.

It is worth noting that several sanctioning measures are available, though not in the form of centralized sanctions. In a decentralized legal order, securing compliance with authoritative norms depends largely on reciprocity, retaliation, and relevant expectations. If you scratch my back, I will scratch yours. If you twist my arm, I will twist yours. If you claim a continental shelf along your coastal lines, we will do the same. If you claim a two-hundred-mile fishery zone, we will do the same—we might even claim five hundred miles. In the final analysis, the real policing and stabilizing power comes from the shared perception of common interest. This is the keystone of international law, as in all forms of law. When effective elites and officials realize that they have more to gain through cooperation than through arbitrary claims that provoke excessive counterclaims and even anarchy, they learn, sooner or later, how to act with self-restraint.

International law may have its weaknesses and limitations, but it makes an important contribution to world order. International law, like all law, is a continuing process of authoritative decision through which the common interests of the members of the world community are identified, clarified, and protected.

Inadequacies of Traditional Approaches to International Law

The difficulties and limitations inherent in a state-centered, decentralized system are compounded and exacerbated by the inadequacies associated with traditional approaches to international law.

International law has its origins in the natural law school and has been influenced in varying degrees by all major schools of jurisprudence. The past influence of the positivist (analytical) school lingers, despite recent signs of growing receptivity to new, more pragmatic theories. The late nineteenth- and early twentieth-century approaches to international law, as dominated by the positivist school, were rule-oriented, conceiving international law as a body of rules—indeed, often unrealistically as rules merely between states.

The rule-oriented approaches tend to view international law dogmatically as a static body of auto-operational rules—rules that are given and self-contained and operate automatically. The judicial task is said to be to discover and enforce, in particular cases, extant "correct rules." Logical derivation is the intellectual task stressed; when behavior can be sustained by statements logically derived from existing rules, it is regarded as "legal" or "lawful." In this perspective, international law operates automatically within its autonomous realm of self-contained rules, with its own internal logical mechanism.

Such rule-oriented approaches to international law have several inadequacies: (1) they fail to grasp the notions of decision (choice) in the legal process; (2) they pay insufficient attention to the goals (policies) for which rules are devised and to value consequences of particular applications of rules; (3) they fail to relate rules to the dynamic context of interaction involving the international and domestic social processes and to the ongoing process of decision making; (4) they fail to grasp the normative ambiguity involved in rules; (5) they fail to come to grips with the generality and complementarity involved in rules; and (6) they fail to develop and employ adequate intellectual skills in problem solving.

The underlying assumption of the rule-oriented approaches is that law is "rules" and nothing more. But law *is* more. The nature of the judicial task is not confined to impartial discovery and application of supposedly neutral rules, and no application of a rule can be neutral in terms of social consequences. International law is a continuing process of authoritative decision and cannot be adequately described by mere reference to the derivations from past decisions that are termed rules. Rules are not self-applicatory and do not change by themselves. Rules are made and applied by human beings. The task of applying law is not merely to discover correct rules but to make choices, to make decisions.

Making choices (decisions) inevitably involves policy considerations (what are the policy purposes for which certain rules are developed and maintained?) and involves considerations of alternatives (what are alternative value consequences of making one choice or another?). This the rule-oriented approaches are unwilling to acknowledge openly. In the guise of impartial discovery of correct, neutral rules, rule-oriented observers refuse to concede that applying rules involves choice and instead dismiss policy considerations and alternative thinking as beyond the realm of law. But whether they acknowledge it or not, rule-orienters cannot escape the necessity and burden of choice in their purported impartial search for correct rules in concrete cases. They may disguise the element of choice, but they cannot escape it. Decisions (choices) cannot be made by neutral decision makers (neutral human beings) neutrally applying neutral rules that are neutrally derived. Rules simply do not decide cases: people decide, and rules may provide only minimal guidance in decision making.

Indeed, rules are not autonomous absolutes and do not exist in a vacuum. Divorced from policy and context, rules are skeletons without body and soul. Rules cannot make much sense without reference to policy or the purposes for which they are created and maintained. Rules cannot be meaningfully understood without reference to the context of interaction that gives rise to legal controversies and to the ongoing process of decision making in which rules are made and remade, applied and reapplied, by human decision makers in response to changing demands and expectations under an ever-changing context of conditions. The dynamism of the law in real life cannot be grasped by mere reference to law in the abstract. Law in the social process is dynamic and based on what real human beings think and do. The fact that the relatively peaceful dissolution of the Soviet Empire or the overturning of the Egyptian government in 2011 caught most international legal scholars completely by surprise indicates the extent to which rule-oriented approaches fail to anticipate the element of human, dynamic choice in response to changing conditions and perceptions of value consequences.

Traditional approaches to international law, with their obsession with inherited rules, also fail to grasp the normative ambiguity involved in their reference to rules. Rules are perceived as given, rigid, self-contained, and automatic in application. Their doctrinal concepts purport to refer simultaneously to the events that precipitate decision, to the factors that affect decision, and to the outcomes of decision. A simple statement that "this is law" ("this is the rule") may be loaded with ambiguity; it may refer to patterns of past decision, to probable future decision, or to a preferred future decision. This approach fails to distinguish past decision from probable future decision and from preference for future decision. It even confuses statements of past trends in decision with scientific inquiry concerning factors affecting decision.

Rules not only have normative ambiguity but are commonly phrased in general and abstract ways and manifest complementarity—rules travel as pairs of complementary opposites, for example, domestic jurisdiction versus international concern, aggression versus self-defense, impermissible coercion versus permissible coercion, or the conclusions "murder" versus "self-defense." When a legal claim is matched by a counterclaim, it is certain that the application of relevant rules is neither clear nor autonomous but requires interpretation and selection. Rigid rules cannot be relied on automatically to resolve a controversy without consideration of context and function. Consider whether a particular form of violence leading to the death of a human being is "murder" or "self-defense" in a domestic context. The two conclusions, tied to black-letter rules (that is, one cannot "murder" but one can kill in "self-defense"), are easy to identify, but they are not self-applying.

Creative thinking about new solutions is impaired by the overemphasis of past decisions by the rule-oriented approaches. Inherent in their preoccupation with past decision is the assumption, conscious or unconscious, that what has been done in the past will, and should, be repeated in the future. Under this assumption, a study of a set of self-contained or given rules in terms of syntax and logic is considered sufficient. This ignores the changing contexts in which new problems arise and particular decisions are made. This completely fails to take into account the dynamic character of the legal process—especially the international legal process. It fails to mobilize relevant intellectual skills to solve ever-emerging problems.

The Policy-Oriented Approach of the New Haven School

In an effort to remedy the inadequacies inherent in the traditional approaches, Myres S. McDougal and Harold D. Lasswell pioneered a policy-oriented approach. This approach, occasionally called a configurative or policy science approach, has been dubbed the approach of the New Haven School, or the Yale School of International Law. Many of McDougal and Lasswell's associates have gone on to achieve great distinction in their work as scholars and practitioners, applying the New Haven School to a vast range of international legal problems.[1]

Building on the insights of American legal realism, the New Haven School has moved beyond the basic insights and horizon of legal realism. It seeks not only to demolish the traditional approaches of rigid rule orientation, unrealistic as they often are, but also to provide a constructive jurisprudence of problem solving.

Recognizing that law is a continuing process of authoritative decision for clarifying and securing the common interest of community members, the policy-oriented approach stresses that law serves not only as a limit on effective power but also as a creative instrument in promoting both order and other values. Inherited rules are to be interpreted and applied not as autonomous absolutes but in light of the fundamental community policies they are intended to serve in contemporary contexts.

To grasp the dynamics of international law in the contemporary global context, the policy-oriented approach identifies international law as an ongoing process of authoritative decision in which many decision makers continually formulate and reformulate policy. These decision makers formulate policies projecting desired consequences into living contexts, as well as respond to words describing what prior decision makers have done in earlier contexts. Its design is not merely to offer a dynamic concept of what is meant by international law but also to detail the role of decision processes at all community levels and to mobilize and integrate appropriate intellectual skills to maximize the utility of international law. It is a theory *about* international law rather than a theory *of* international law. It projects and relates international law to the living context of the contemporary world rather than to the inner or unreal world of autonomous rules and logical exercises. Function and context, goals and expectations, trends, conditions, projections, and alternatives are properly within its domain of concern and inquiry.

In sum, this policy-oriented approach is contextual, problem-solving, and multi-method in nature. It is contextual in the sense of viewing the role of law in society dynamically, by relating it to relevant social, community, and decisional contexts and variables. It is problem-solving in the sense of recognizing the intrinsic function of law as an instrument of policy for promoting a preferred social order and in the sense of providing an effective tool to optimize the function of law. It is multi-method in the sense of seeking to mobilize and integrate relevant intellectual skills to facilitate effective problem solving toward the establishment of a more peaceful, abundant, and just world—a world community of human dignity.

The student of the New Haven School of international law should be forewarned that this school of thought is necessarily complex. Dynamic, complex realities of transnational interaction cannot be reduced to simple, rigid formulas. International law in action cannot be insulated from the dynamics of international politics and relations. Profound insights require laborious efforts to absorb. The broad outlines of the policy-oriented approach of the New Haven School include: (1) the establishment of an observational standpoint; (2) the formulation of problems; (3) the delimitation of the focus of inquiry; (4) the explicit postulation of public order goals; and (5) the performance of intellectual tasks.

1. *The establishment of the observational standpoint.* In approaching international legal problems on a global scale, it is essential to make manifest the standpoint of the observer. An observer's standpoint needs to be kept as distinct as humanly possible from the process under scrutiny so that appropriate criteria for appraisal can be developed.

The appropriate observational standpoint, as stressed by the New Haven School, is that of citizens of the world community who are identified with the future of humankind as a whole rather than with the primacy of any particular group. This standpoint is especially vital in international law—operating as it does in a generally decentralized legal system without centralized institutions of lawmaking and application, in which nation-states in general serve simultaneously as claimants and decision makers—if the common interests are to be clarified, identified, and secured. The responsibility of the scholar who is concerned with enlightenment as well as of the decision maker who is concerned for all the consequences of his or her decisions through time is to ascertain and specify the common interests of all peoples in their transnational interaction—in all their interpenetrating communities, both territorial and functional. It is imperative that both the scholarly inquirer and the established decision maker acquire an observational standpoint that is as free as possible from parochial interests and cultural biases, which will enable them to ascertain and clarify for the active participants in the different communities common interests that these participants are otherwise unable to perceive. The clarity and fidelity with which this standpoint is maintained affects every other feature of inquiry: how problems are defined, what goals are postulated, and what intellectual skills are employed.

2. *The formulation of problems.* Recognizing the important bearing of the formulation of problems on the outcome of inquiry, the New Haven School has developed an economical and comprehensive way of categorizing problems to ease study through time and across community boundaries. It seeks formulations that are acceptable as matters of taste to different cultures but that can also be made to transcend differences in culture,

community, and time so as to foster comparisons in goals, trends, and conditions. It stresses that particular problems are most effectively and economically formulated in terms of disparities between demanded values and their achievement in community processes.

It seeks to make problems operational and manageable by adopting a set of value categories borrowed from ethical philosophers and other normative specialists: respect, power, enlightenment, well-being, wealth, skill, affection, and rectitude. Values are preferred events—what people cherish. And these eight values can be defined succinctly:

- Respect: freedom of choice, equality, and recognition;
- Power: making and influencing community decisions;
- Enlightenment: gathering, processing, and disseminating information and knowledge;
- Well-being: safety, health, and comfort;
- Wealth: production, distribution, and consumption of goods and services; control of resources;
- Skill: acquisition and exercise of capabilities in vocations, professions, and the arts;
- Affection: intimacy, friendship, loyalty, positive sentiments;
- Rectitude: participation in forming and applying norms of responsible conduct.

The aggregate of all these values may be described as *security*.

This set of values is supplemented by a set of institutional practices taken from cultural anthropologists: participation, perspectives, situations, base values, strategies, outcomes, and effects. Through these operational indices, value categories can be made comprehensive and inquiry can be made as detailed as required. Problems in authoritative decision, as integral components of effective power processes, are generally described in terms of decision makers, basic policies, structures of authority, bases of power, strategies, and decision outcomes. Such an explicit and economic categorization aids the performance of relevant intellectual tasks. It facilitates a detailed clarification of basic community policies in relation to particular problems and allows one to analyze past trends in decision in terms of their approximation to preferred policies, to identify the important factors affecting decisions and outcomes, to assess the probable costs and benefits of the different options to common interests, and to develop better alternatives to implement preferred community policies.

3. *The delimitation of the focus of inquiry.* In delimiting the focus of inquiry, the policy-oriented approach seeks to be both comprehensive and selective. It establishes a focus on authoritative decisions in their context, placing dual emphasis on the conception of law to be deployed and the larger context to be studied.

The New Haven School characterizes law not as rules only but as a continual process of authoritative decision by which people identify, clarify, and secure common interests. It is concerned with decision that embodies both perspectives and operations. It is concerned with what people do as well as what people say and expect. It is especially concerned with authoritative decision—that is, decision in which elements of authority and control are properly balanced. Authority refers to the normative expectations of relevant social actors—expectations of community members about who is to make what decisions, in what structures, by what procedures, and in accordance with what goals and criteria. Control refers to effective participation in the choices that are put into community practice. The key to a viable conception of law is to incorporate both authority and control so that legal scholarship will not drift into the fantasy lands of naked power or semantic law. In the absence of decision characterized by authority, international law is an expression of naked power. When control does not accompany decision, international law or at least decisional outcome may become mere illusion and mockery.

The processes of authoritative decision within any community must be related to the larger social process that envelops such decision making. In international law, the New Haven School orients itself to the most comprehensive context of the earth-space arena, as punctuated by global interdependence, in which people interact.

Viewed comprehensively, humanity today presents the fact of a global community, wholly comparable to the internal communities of lesser territorial groupings, in the sense of interdetermination and interdependence in the shaping and sharing of all values. Vital within this larger community process is an ongoing process of effective power, also global in its reach, in which decisions are taken and enforced by severe deprivations or high indulgences, regardless of the wishes of any particular participant. Operating within this globally effective power process is a comprehensive process of authoritative decision in which a continual flow of decisions are made by those who are expected to make them, in accord with criteria expected by community members, in established structures of authority, by those with enough bases of power to secure necessary control, and by authorized procedures.

The comprehensive process of authoritative decision consists of two distinct, though interrelated, kinds of decisions: *constitutive decisions*, which establish and maintain the ongoing process of authoritative decision, and *public order decisions*, which emanate from the constitutive process to regulate all other community value processes. In other words, "constitutive process" refers to those decisions that identify and characterize authoritative decision makers, identify and project basic community policies, establish appropriate structures of authority, allocate bases of power for sanctioning purposes, authorize procedures for making different kinds of decisions, and perform all the various decision functions (intelligence, promotion, prescription, invocation, application, termination, and appraisal) essential to maintain and administer general community policy. In brief, these seven decision functions may be defined as follows:

- Intelligence: gathering, processing, and disseminating information essential to decision making;
- Promotion: advocacy of general policies and the urging of proposals;

- Prescription: projecting authoritative community policies about the shaping and sharing of values;
- Invocation: provisional characterization of events in terms of community prescriptions;
- Application: final characterization and execution of prescriptions in concrete situations;
- Termination: ending a prescription or arrangement within the scope of a prescription;
- Appraisal: evaluating performance in decision process in terms of community goals.

"Public order" decisions refer to those decisions emerging as outcomes of the established constitutive process that shape and maintain the protected features of the community's value processes. To illustrate this principle, an analogy can be drawn between constitutive and public order decision processes and the legislative processes familiar to students of the American system of constitutional law. Constitutive decisions are those that shape the way power is distributed vertically between the federal and state government and horizontally among the three branches of the U.S. government. Public order decisions refer to the constant flow of decisions of those entities and their outcomes relative to each value sector.

Both processes of effective power and of authoritative decision must be studied closely if the dynamics of international law are to be grasped. In an interdependent and globalized world, the degree of effectiveness of international law does not depend merely on the social and decision processes within any single territorial community. It depends also on the operation of such processes within a whole hierarchy of interpenetrating communities—from local or national to regional and global. It requires a firm grasp of the dynamic interplay between transnational and national processes of decision and their reciprocal impacts.

4. *The explicit postulation of public order goals.* In any process of authoritative decision, policy choices and consequences are inescapable, whether one cares to admit it or not. The insistent question for every decision maker or other evaluator is to what basic policy goals he or she, as a representative of the larger community of humanity and of its various component communities, will ascribe as the primary postulates of public order for inspiring and fashioning particular choices.

The New Haven School confronts this question squarely by articulating and appraising policy considerations openly and explicitly in terms of the common interest. The comprehensive set of public order goals it recommends for postulation, clarification, and implementation are those which today are commonly characterized as the basic values of human dignity or of a free society. This is not an idiosyncratic or arbitrary choice but the product of many heritages.

The contemporary image of people as capable of respecting themselves and others and of constructively participating in shaping and sharing all human dignity values is the culmination of many trends in thought. These trends are secular as well as religious; their origins extend far back into antiquity and come down through the centuries with vast cultural and geographical reach. The postulate of human dignity can no longer be regarded as the eccentric doctrine of lonely philosophers and peculiar sects. This postulate, in the sense of demands for the greater production and wider sharing of all values and a preference for persuasion over coercion, has been incorporated, with varying completion and precision, into a great cluster of global and regional prescriptions, both conventional and customary, and into the constitutional and legislative codes of many national communities.

The emphasis is on the postulation and clarification of public order goals rather than their derivation by the exercise of logical, syntactic skill. It contributes precious little to rational decision to engage in the syntactic exercises in infinite regress. Peoples subscribing to different styles in derivation have long demonstrated that they can cooperate to promote the values of human dignity regardless of the faiths or creeds they employ for justification. The shared demands for human dignity values can be given effective expression through different institutional practices and cultural adaptations.

The recommended postulation of basic goal values differs from a mere exercise in faith. The New Haven School does not expect to acquire new knowledge by postulation alone. Acquisition of new knowledge requires the systematic and disciplined exercise of all relevant intellectual skills.

5. *The performance of intellectual tasks.* The intellectual tasks essential to rational decision and effective inquiry extend beyond exercises in logical derivation and restrictive conceptions of science to a whole series of distinct, yet interrelated, activities. These tasks include:

a. The clarification of goals. This involves detailed specifications of postulated goals, whatever the level of abstraction of their initial formulation, to be disciplined by empirical observation and analysis in particular social contexts.

b. The description of past trends in decision. This historical task emphasizes not anecdotal treatment of isolated tidbits of doctrine and practice but systematic inquiry in terms of degrees of approximation to clarified goals and policies for constitutive process and public order.

c. The analysis of factors affecting decision. Trends in past decision are useful to project probable future developments and invent alternatives only if the factors affecting those decisions are identifiable. The scientific task employed here is concerned especially with the interplay of the multiple factors affecting prior decision, the complex of predispositional and environmental factors, not with dogmatic determinations of causality.

d. The projection of future trends. Problem solving is oriented toward the future, and the policy-oriented approach seeks to anticipate the future as much as humanly possible. The futuristic task seeks to anticipate and project expectations about the future as an aid to problem solving. The method is not one of dogmatic prophecy of inevitability but one of developmental constructs, embracing a spectrum of futures, from the most to the least desirable in terms of human dignity values, to be tested in the light of all available knowledge and information.

e. The invention and evaluation of policy alternatives. The policy-oriented approach explicitly encourages the cultivation of creativity and the invention of new alternatives in policy, norms, institutional structures, and procedures for the optimal realization of preferred goals. Particular alternatives are to be evaluated in terms of gains and losses in relation to all clarified goals and to be disciplined by the available knowledge concerning trends, conditioning factors, and future probabilities. All the other intellectual tasks will be synthesized and brought to bear on the search for integrated solutions with promise of optimum gains and minimum costs.

These intellectual tasks are distinct yet interrelated. Each affects and is affected by the others. It is crucial that all of these tasks be performed systematically and contextually in relation to specific problems.

The foregoing are the basic features associated with the New Haven School of international law. With the passage of time, a new generation of international legal scholars, especially represented from the ranks of Yale Law School, have come to reappraise the classic New Haven School. Thus, we have seen the appearance in recent years of what is known as the "New" New Haven School. This New New Haven School has reaffirmed the core beliefs and practices of the classic New Haven School, but with a greater emphasis on transnational legal processes amid ever-growing globalization and on the role of policy makers and legal practitioners in addition to scholars. Harold Koh, the former dean of Yale Law School and former legal adviser to the U.S. State Department, has identified these beliefs and practices as:

- continuing the investigation of theory and interdisciplinary work in international law;
- a commitment to studying transnational law;
- a commitment to studying the transnational legal process;
- a renewed commitment to normativity; and
- a commitment to connecting law to policy.[2]

The new generation of thinkers is continuing the ongoing process of applying and adapting the work of McDougal, Lasswell and other New Haven School scholars to fit the ever-changing context in which they find themselves.[3] While holding to the original tenets of the New Haven School, these scholars are exploring new topics related to globalization and information technology that are shaping and defining the world as we know it today. They are also active in a range of fields, from government policy to economic development to human rights to trade and business. All the while, though, these New New Haven School scholars reaffirm the ongoing significance and relevance of the classic New Haven School.

The American Society of International Law characterized McDougal and Lasswell's work as "one of the most significant contributions of our time to international law. . . marked by boldness of imagination, originality and depth of insight, and scrupulous adherence to a comprehensive conceptual framework." Looking back at the international law literature of the past half century, one cannot help but marvel at how significant and far-reaching the McDougal-Lasswell contributions have been—there has not been total adoption and incorporation, to be sure, but, in the favorite lexicon of Lasswell, diffusion through partial restriction and incorporation.

A comprehensive exposition of international law in the grand fashion of the New Haven School would indeed take many volumes, as witness those volumes that have been published to date. As an introduction to orient the reader to international law generally, such is beyond the scope of the present task. In dealing with various aspects and problems of international law, however, the essence of the special concerns of policy-oriented jurisprudence will be, it is hoped, significantly reflected.

To examine the contemporary global constitutive process of authoritative decision, with special emphasis on the role played by, and the protections afforded, nation-states, I propose to explore in succession each of the basic features of the process: participants, perspectives, arenas, bases of power, strategies, outcomes, and effects.

Notes

1. Some of McDougal and Lasswell's major collaborative works include: MYRES MCDOUGAL ET AL., STUDIES IN WORLD PUBLIC ORDER (1960); MYRES MCDOUGAL & FLORENTINO FELICIANO, LAW AND MINIMUM WORLD PUBLIC ORDER: THE LEGAL REGULATION OF INTERNATIONAL COERCION (1961); MYRES MCDOUGAL & WILLIAM T. BURKE, THE PUBLIC ORDER OF THE OCEANS: A CONTEMPORARY INTERNATIONAL LAW OF THE SEA (1962); MYRES MCDOUGAL, HAROLD LASSWELL, & JAMES MILLER, THE INTERPRETATION OF AGREEMENTS AND WORLD PUBLIC ORDER: PRINCIPLES OF CONTENT AND PROCEDURE (1967); MYRES MCDOUGAL, HAROLD LASSWELL, & LUNG-CHU CHEN, HUMAN RIGHTS AND WORLD PUBLIC ORDER: THE BASIC POLICIES OF AN INTERNATIONAL LAW OF HUMAN DIGNITY (1980); MYRES MCDOUGAL & W. MICHAEL REISMAN, INTERNATIONAL LAW ESSAYS: A SUPPLEMENT TO INTERNATIONAL LAW IN CONTEMPORARY PERSPECTIVE (1981). For more examples, please consult the bibliography at the end of this book.

2. Harold Hongju Koh, *Is There a "New" New Haven School of International Law?*, 32 YALE J. INT'L. L. 559 (2007), *available at* http://digitalcommons.law.yale.edu/fss_papers/1683.

3. *See, e.g.*, LOOKING TO THE FUTURE: ESSAYS ON INTERNATIONAL LAW IN HONOR OF W. MICHAEL REISMAN (Mahnoush Arsanjani et al. eds., 2011); Oona A. Hathaway, *The Continuing Influence of the New Haven School*, 32 YALE J. INT'L L. 553 (2007); Paul Schiff Berman, *A Pluralist Approach to International Law*, 32 YALE J. INT'L L. 301 (2007); Rebecca Bratspies, *Rethinking Decisionmaking in International Environmental Law: A Process-Oriented Inquiry into Sustainable Development*, 32 YALE J. INT'L L. 363 (2007); Laura Dickinson, *Toward a "New" New Haven School of International Law?*, 32 YALE J. INT'L L. 547 (2007); Janet Koven Levit, *Bottom-Up Transnational Lawmaking: Reflections on the New Haven School of International Law*, 32 YALE J. INT'L L. 393 (2007); Hari Osofsky, *A Law and Geography Perspective on the New Haven School*, 32 YALE J. INT'L L. 421 (2007); Melissa A. Waters, *Normativity in the "New" Schools: Assessing the Legitimacy of International Legal Norms Created by Domestic Courts*, 32 YALE J. INT'L L. 455 (2007); TAI-HENG CHENG, WHEN INTERNATIONAL LAW WORKS: REALISTIC IDEALISM AFTER 9/11 AND THE GLOBAL RECESSION (2011).

II   Participants

IN RECENT DECADES, participation in the global constitutive process of authoritative decision has been greatly democratized. All participants—conveniently categorized as nation-states, international governmental organizations, nongovernmental organizations and associations (including political parties, pressure groups, and private associations), and individual human beings—now openly or recognizably play important roles and perform numerous functions. The role of nation-states has been, and continues to be, predominant at the international level. International governmental organizations, now recognized as appropriate "subjects" of international law, participate in all functions. Political parties, though often receiving no formal recognition, exert effective influence on many authoritative decisions. Pressure groups actively seek to promote and influence decision making. Multiplying hosts of private associations, dedicated to values other than power, are increasingly transnational in membership, goals, organizational structure, spheres of activity, and influence. Individuals, acting both alone and as representatives of groups, have ample opportunity to participate in all the activities that comprise the making, invocation, application, and termination of law. Indeed, individuals are the ultimate participants in the international legal process and in each organization or association mentioned above. Such a realistic role has been recognized at various times but appears to be increasingly evident in the latter part of the twentieth century.

2 Nation-States

SINCE THE RISE of the nation-state system in the seventeenth century, nation-states have played, and continue to play, a predominant role in the global processes of decision. With their control of unique territorial bases, nation-states remain the overwhelmingly dominant participants in the world arena, although each is not equally dominant and some participants wield more effective power, wealth, and other values. The officials of nation-states are still by far the most important participants in the performance of all decision functions at the international level. They make and apply, or participate in making and applying, all aspects of international law.

Statehood

The term nation-state, though not altogether satisfactory, has gained wide acceptance. In common usage, it refers to a territorially organized community that achieves, or makes claim to, the highest degree of effective power and authority in the global power process. It is distinct from "nation" in the anthropological sense. Nation-states, enjoying the greatest degrees of freedom in decision, as traditionally expressed in degrees of "independence" and "sovereignty," are in contrast to lesser entities, including protectorates, mandated territories, trust territories, non-self-governing territories, and associated states, which are neither fully independent nor sovereign. The component unit of a federation, often known as a state, is distinguishable from the nation-state. In popular usage, the nation-state is variously referred to as nation, state, country, or body politic. The relevant context will help clarify what is meant when equivalent terms are used.

What criteria, then, distinguish nation-states from non-state entities? In other words, how does one identify a nation-state? The traditional prescription is expressed in the Montevideo Convention on Rights and Duties of States of 1933: "The State as a person of international law should possess the following qualifications: (a) a permanent population; (b) a defined territory; (c) government; and (d) capacity to enter into relations with other States." This formulation, with slight refinements and nuances here and there, has been widely accepted in theory.

In practice, some unusual situations may present considerable difficulty in relation to each condition. A permanent population, together with a defined territory, is meant to signify a reasonably stable territorial community. The frontiers of a nation-state need not be fully settled and defined. In arguing that Israel should be recognized as a state despite an ongoing dispute as to Israel's precise boundaries, the U.S. representative to the United Nations, Philip Jessup, argued that a precise delimitation of borders was never a prerequisite to statehood under international law. To illustrate his point, Ambassador (formerly Professor) Jessup pointed to the United States' own experience; at the time the United States achieved its independence from Britain, its precise territory was unclear, with ongoing ambiguity as to where American, French, British, and Spanish claims began and ended. Nonetheless, there was widespread acceptance and recognition that the United States satisfied the traditional criteria for statehood. The requirement that a state possess a defined territory, according to Jessup, means only that "there must be some portion of the earth's surface which its people inhabit and over which its Government exercises control."[1]

Similarly, with respect to the requirement that a state have a government, international law generally does not require a nation-state to adopt a particular form of government but expects its government to be authoritative, effective, and capable of conducting international relations with other nation-states. This issue has become more complicated however, as will be discussed further in this chapter, as recognition of states and governments has become an increasingly political act. Traditionally, however, the issue of recognition was treated as separate from approval of a particular government; so long as the requirement that a state have a government capable of conducting relations with other states was satisfied, a state was considered to exist under international law.

This last point raises the difficult question of the declarative theory of statehood versus the constitutive theory (discussed in greater detail below). Under the declarative theory, which is widely accepted, recognition by other states has no bearing on the determination of whether a state exists or not. Rather, so long as the four traditional criteria for statehood are satisfied, a state exists. One state's act of recognizing another state has no legal effect; it is merely a declaration of the legal fact that the other state exists. This is the view taken in the Montevideo Convention. Under the minority constitutive view, statehood is judged only in terms of recognition, although the constitutive theory presumes that states will apply the traditional criteria in determining whether to recognize a state.

In addition to the widely accepted traditional criteria for statehood, states and scholars have suggested that additional criteria be imposed. For example, James Crawford, in his text *The Creation of States in International Law*, appears to suggest an additional requirement that a state assert its statehood. Statehood, Crawford argues, "is a claim of right. Claims to statehood are not to be inferred from statements or actions short of explicit declaration...."[2] This argument will be discussed in more detail below with respect to the issue of Taiwan's statehood.

The nation-state formed as a response to demands for better protection and security for the individual in the chaos of declining feudalism. Since then, the nation-state has been the major framework within which demands for shaping and sharing values (power, wealth, respect, enlightenment, and so on) are expressed and fulfilled. Because nation-states represent both the symbol and the fact of accumulated value assets, individuals have sought many of their values through close identification with the nation-state of which they are members. When the degree of transnational interdependence was relatively low, this emphasis on the nation-state as a principal instrument of value shaping and sharing and decision making was easily understandable.

Our epoch is marked by nationalism—yet it is also marked by global interdependence. Though the nation-state, with its inherited perspectives and institutions, continues to command the primary loyalty of peoples about the globe, the functional imperative of transnational cooperation has become more evident and pressing. The past role of the nation-state cannot be taken for granted without a critical reappraisal in light of the changing demands, expectations, and conditions of the present. Indeed, many have begun to argue that we may be living in an age of transition in which the nation-state may well have come to outlive its usefulness. Adjusting the role of the nation-state to the functional needs of global interdependence is vital.

In the contemporary world scene, nation-states of varying sizes and strengths—superpowers, major powers, intermediate powers, small states, and mini-states—coexist. They differ widely in population, territory, resources, science-based technology, defense capabilities, institutions, and projected public order systems. Nominal equality in law is one thing, and the actual discrepancy in effective power is something else.

In recent decades the number of nation-states has multiplied greatly, thanks to the disintegration of empires and the transformation of ex-colonies into independent states. This is most vividly reflected in the relatively recent and dramatic expansion of membership in the United Nations, from the original 51 in 1945 to 193 by 2013.

The proliferation of new nation-states has brought a considerable measure of democratization to the global processes of decision making. With the massive increase of non-European states, the contemporary international legal system has moved from a Eurocentric, Christian order toward one of universal participation. Virtually all the territorial communities—with all the richness of their diverse religious and cultural heritages—in the different continents are represented. Guided by the fundamental principles of sovereign equality and one-state-one-vote, all nation-states, large and small, new and old, have become active participants in the global process of decision making. In recent decades, with the addition of newly independent Soviet bloc countries to the community of independent states, the Cold War has had to make way for new global perspectives in economics, peace and security, and the sharing of information and cooperation between states. It is a relative democracy in action on a global scale, giving effective expression to the aspirations and interests of the peoples around the world, although the one-state-one-vote formula does not fully represent the world's people, resources, institutions, and so forth.

New states located throughout Asia and Africa, together with Latin American countries, have imparted a distinctive character to participation in the world arena. As a group, they have been loosely and variously labeled as newly independent, developing, underdeveloped, nonaligned, Afro-Asian, emerging and Third World countries. Although these nations are far from homogeneous in terms of history, geography, economic development, and political orientation, they do share certain perspectives toward the global process of decision making and some special concerns because of their past experiences with the colonial powers and their present preoccupation with nation-building and modernization.

The predominance of European states in the nineteenth century, during which many rules of international law were developed, has not unnaturally aroused suspicion and reservations among newly independent states. Many new states ask whether they can reasonably be expected to abide by rules they played little or no part in formulating and that were the product of what they regard as an alien civilization. In the words of Oliver J. Lissitzyn:

> International law is a heritage of the Christian West. In the age of expansion of Europe it was largely imposed on the rest of the World. More often this was a matter of Western self-interest rather than a matter of Christian morality.... Can a body of principles and precedents exclusively Western in origin be successfully transmuted into a world law which is freely accepted by nations of widely different historical backgrounds?[3]

Although no wholesale rejection of international law has been seriously voiced, the new nation-states have challenged the authority of inherited customary rules in several key sectors. Their challenge is particularly vehement in the following areas:

1. Customary law of state responsibility for injury to aliens. The problem of state responsibility arising from injury to aliens, as will be discussed in later chapters, vividly exemplifies the cleavage between the new states and the old Western

states. In the perspectives of the new states, customary law in this area is colored by the unequal relationship between great powers and small powers, and for too long "state responsibility" was a frequent excuse for coercion against the weaker states.

Controversy has centered especially on customary rules governing nationalization and expropriation. The newly independent states generally find themselves in the position of debtor upon their birth into the family of nations. Resentful of past subordination and deprivations and determined to achieve the goal of national development, they challenge the customary law of providing "prompt, adequate, and just compensation" for expropriated foreign property within their borders. They often feel, because of past colonial exploitation, that they should receive, rather than pay, compensation for nationalization measures to further the public purpose of national development.

2. State succession. The rapid proliferation of new states has raised serious problems in the field of state succession: whether a new state is bound by some or all of the international legal obligations incurred by its predecessor. Can it simply pick and choose, beyond the right to participate in the ongoing process of law formation? As discussed in chapter 27, divergent views have been in contention, ranging from universal succession through selective succession to outright rejection based on a clean-slate theory.

3. Unequal treaties. The dilemmas of state succession are especially acute in relation to treaties. The concept of unequal treaties has been developed and invoked to repudiate all those international agreements that are found to unduly burden new states. Though the concept remains highly controversial, unequal treaties generally refer to treaties having the character of inequality (unequal in bargaining power, in relative benefits and burdens, and so on) or the element of coercive imposition.

4. Compulsory third-party decision making. Nation-states as a whole are notorious for being unwilling to submit to compulsory third-party decision, which allegedly might compromise their "sovereignty." The general distrust of the inherited norms of international law has made the new states even more reluctant to have their hands tied. Hence, their initial disposition was to avoid running the risks of third-party adjudication according to a traditional law that they feel generally favors powerful creditor states and to keep their options open.

Because of their discontent with rules inherited from the past, these nations generally favor revision so that specific norms can be formulated or reformulated, with all deliberation and explicitness, in light of new demands and expectations and contemporary conditions. This is exemplified by the final implementation of the U.N. Convention on the Law of the Sea, a comprehensive treaty adopted in 1982 after some ten years of intense negotiation by more than one hundred fifty delegations and implemented in 1994 after another twelve years of negotiations over provisions disputed between newer nation-states and the developed powers.

In addition to the law of the sea, the insistent demands of new states to change and reform international law have been propagated in recent decades in connection with movements, such as the New International Economic Order and the New World Information and Communication Order. These demands for new orders, comprehensive in scope, extended far beyond the sectors of wealth and enlightenment. In a profound sense, they represented enormous attempts to reshape the entire global process of decision making—both authoritative decision and effective power. Though highly controversial, the issues raised by these movements cannot be ignored.

In the drive to codify and reform international law in general and to establish new orders in particular, these new nations have mustered impressive voting strength. Known as the Group of Seventy-Seven within the framework of U.N. bloc politics (though the number now exceeds 130), the Third World countries command a two-thirds majority in the parliamentary arena of the United Nations (the General Assembly) or its equivalent forum (for example, a specially convened conference) to pass one resolution after another. Their numerical unity is especially apparent in response to issues perceived as part of the global North-South confrontation. This automatic overwhelming majority has led to a mounting tension between numerical strength and effective power. In a real world where the effective power process is constantly operating, genuine support of community members must be measured in terms of effective power as well as numerical strength. The conjunction of numerical strength and effective power is crucial. Democracy and responsibility go hand in hand. Without effective power, sheer numerical strength is hollow. Without popular support, effective power can be sheer arrogance.

The agonizing process in which claims and counterclaims—at times exaggerated, radical, and even absurd—are pressed reflects how international law evolves in response to the changing demands and expectations of the active participants.

As eloquently articulated by B. V. A. Roling, the emergence of the new states in the contemporary world arena strikingly resembles the rise to power of the working classes in the national communities of the West.[4] With democratization, the previously deprived and submerged groups were able to demand greater participation in the processes of authoritative decision and effective power and in other value sectors. Their demands for legal protection of organized labor first seemed radical and dangerous but eventually gained acceptance by the dominant and opposing elements, thanks to a process that sought the common interest by accommodating competing demands. Where the common interest in orderly change and reform fails to take hold, where all-or-nothing attitudes persist in polarizing struggling classes, the outcome can be violent upheaval.

This historic lesson from national development is no less cogent for humanity and the world community as a whole. International law, like all law, is far from static. It is a continuing process of identifying, clarifying, and securing the common interest in response to the changing demands and expectations of all participants (not merely nation-states) in the decision processes under constant change.

The key is common interest—the common interest of all participants from both short-term and long-term perspectives. The search for the common interest is a continuous and laborious process. There is no room for one-sided nonnegotiable demands that disregard the common interest. It is obvious that the demands of the new states for change and reform need to be, and are, tempered by their keen perception that international law serves the interests of all participants, especially the weaker ones that require special protection. It is equally apparent that in a world of growing interdependence, the security and prosperity of the few cannot endure in a sea of miseries.

Today all nation-states share a common destiny of survival on spaceship earth. In common parlance, "We are all in this together." Nation-states, like living organisms, are born, grow, mature, decline, and eventually die. The developing life cycle brings challenges and opportunities. The changing role of nation-states will be as promising as nation-states seize new opportunities to communicate and collaborate in the face of formidable new challenges in an age of transition.

The Principle of Self-Determination

The driving force behind the rapid and vast proliferation of new states after World War II is the principle of self-determination. This precept has been asserted with increasing vigor and frequency in recent decades, and the number of peoples involved in claims to self-determination has greatly expanded.

The demand for self-determination is an important dimension of the demand for freedom in our world. It is the demand of human beings to form groups and to identify with groups that can best promote their pursuit of values in both individual and aggregate terms.

The new era of self-determination can be symbolized by the contrasting fates of Biafra in the late 1960s and Bangladesh in 1971—the former failed to achieve secession from Nigeria; but the latter achieved secession from Pakistan. As former colonial peoples and territories substantially disappear, attention to claims of self-determination has shifted from colonial to noncolonial contexts. Despite some contemporary doubts as to the viability of some new nation-states, it is undeniable that self-determination played a leading role in accelerating the emancipation of millions of people from colonial shackles. It was the driving force behind postwar decolonization.

The demands of humanity to secure an optimum freedom and wide sharing of power have been made under a variety of legalistic labels and contexts. Self-determination may be invoked singly or in combination with other labels, such as sovereignty, independence, and nonintervention.

Comprehensively formulated, claims to self-determination can be divided into two basic categories:

1. Claims involving establishment of a new state—that is, claims by a group within an established state to form a new state from part of the preexisting state (external self-determination);
2. Claims not involving establishment of a new state, notably:
   a. Claims of a state to be free of external coercion and interference;
   b. Claims of a state to control its own natural resources (that is, economic self-determination);
   c. Claims of a people to overthrow their effective rulers and establish a new, authoritative government in the whole of a state (that is, the right of revolution, or more currently known as the right for "regime change");
   d. Claims of a group within a state to enjoy autonomy; and
   e. Claims of a group to enjoy such special protections as language rights, religious rights, and land rights.

The present focus relates primarily to claims of external self-determination—namely, claims of a group within an established state to form a new state from part of an existing state and hence to establish and maintain its own internal decision processes and external relations.

The modern principle of self-determination originated in the sixteenth century when nation-states first emerged. It was deeply rooted in the contemporary concept of nationality. The principle of national self-determination crystallized at the end of World War I under the strong championship of President Woodrow Wilson. In his words, "No peace can last, or ought to last, which does not recognize and accept the principle that governments derive all their just powers from the consent of the governed, and that no right anywhere exists to hand people about from sovereignty to sovereignty as if they were property."[5]

Because of its universal appeal rooted in the concept of human dignity and human rights and linked to the maintenance of world order, self-determination was enshrined in the Charter of the United Nations, as sustained by the systems of international trusteeship and non-self-governing territories. A major purpose of the United Nations, according to Article 1(2) of the charter, is to "achieve friendly relations among nations based on respect for the principle of equal rights and self-determination of peoples, and to take other appropriate measures to strengthen universal peace."

Both the International Covenant on Civil and Political Rights and the International Covenant on Economic, Social, and Cultural Rights accord a prominent place to the principle of self-determination. In identical words, both covenants proclaim in their first article that "[a]ll peoples have the right of self-determination. By virtue of that right they freely determine their political status and freely pursue their economic, social and cultural development." This principle has been affirmed and reaffirmed by the landmark Declaration on the Granting of Independence to Colonial Countries and Peoples (1960),[6] the Declaration on Principles of International Law Concerning Friendly Relations and Co-operation Among States in Accordance with the Charter of the United Nations (1970),[7] and many other U.N. resolutions, such as the proclaiming of the International Decade for the Eradication of Colonialism (1990–2000). The impressive record of the United Nations in facilitating independence of former trust territories and non-self-governing territories is common knowledge. The application of self-determination in the colonial context has done much to change today's world map and to affect the world constitutive process of authoritative decision.

Without going into detail, the U.N. practice in the colonial context can be highlighted in terms of "who gets self-determination, when, and how." First, let us look at the question of who is eligible for self-determination. The charter stipulates "self-determination of peoples," not states, and hence leaves the door wide open to arguments over who is entitled to self-determination—who constitutes a proper self-determining "unit." In ascertaining the basic unit of "nation" or "peoples" to exercise self-determination, the sociological, geographical, historical, psychological, and political factors of a social context have been recognized as relevant in U.N. practice. Thus, reference is generally made to the distinct features of population concerned in terms of race, language, religion, or cultural heritage. It is also considered pertinent to discuss whether territory is involved and whether the territory is identifiable or sufficiently contiguous to constitute one geographical unit. The wishes of the people—their demands, expectations, and identifications—are commonly conceded to have great weight.

After a provisional identification of who is entitled to self-determination, decision makers face the problem of when and under what conditions self-determination is to be realized. In terms of timing, whereas most member states favor self-determination for all dependent peoples without undue delay, they generally agree that cases differ too much from one another to warrant the adoption of blanket timing. Nevertheless, the overall pace of decolonization has been breathtaking.

The plebiscite has become a useful device to determine political self-determination. The key standard of authority of any government recognized by international law is that based on the "will of the people" (as enunciated in Article 21[3] of the Universal Declaration of Human Rights), a will best expressed in free and genuine elections, but a will that is a dynamic process in which individuals freely participate. The importance of effective and impartial international supervision of every phase of the plebiscite process has been clearly demonstrated as in the case of East Timor in August 1999 and the Republic of South Sudan in 2011. Persuasion is obviously a desirable alternative to violence and coercion. But international law also acknowledges (or bows to the reality) that on occasion armed struggle may be the last resort open to a people oppressed under systematic subjugation. During apartheid in South Africa, for example, some resolutions of the General Assembly recognized the propriety of self-determination assistance to those who sought to overthrow the government, and were instrumental in producing the radical reforms in that country that led to the abolition of apartheid and South Africa's readmittance to the U.N. fold in 1994.

In terms of outcomes, although self-determination is commonly equated with independence, it is not necessarily so. Arrangements other than independence, when freely chosen by the people concerned, are also acceptable. Viewed in terms of U.N. practice and the context of world politics, self-determination ranges from considerable self-government inside an existing state, through an autonomous status within an established state, to complete independence. The fundamental requirement inherent in the concept of self-determination is a process or procedure, not a preset outcome. Whether the choice in a particular case is independence or otherwise is less important than whether it is genuinely and freely made by the people concerned. If the freedom of choice of the people is sustained, the policy objective of self-determination is fulfilled, although self-determination is actually a continual process. The decisions of the United Nations manifest the flexibility that is realistically adapted to the contextual complexities of world affairs.

Viewing U.N. practice as a whole, it appears that the world community has as much interest as the people directly concerned in seeing that solutions to self-determination problems will benefit everyone. Hence, in dealing with a claim to self-determination, the United Nations is concerned with: (1) the prospect of the territory or peoples concerned becoming a viable state; (2) the present stage of advancement toward self-government; and (3) the effect of granting or refusing the exercise of self-determination in terms of regional and international peace, the effectuation of authoritative governmental processes and human rights, and impacts on all regional and global value processes. It is considered essential that the people directly concerned have a reasonable prospect of becoming a viable entity—politically, economically, and so on—in this increasingly interdependent world.

The accelerating pace of decolonization in the post–World War II era brought about the radical multiplication of many more smaller units—now called mini-states—and compounded by the breakup of the Soviet Union into a multitude of republics, has resulted in much international concern about the viability of the existing mini-states and the desirability of adding potential mini-states. Although no formula has been worked out to determine how small is too small for the purposes of self-determination, the point that a new entity should be capable of developing itself as a viable entity and capable of acting responsibly in the external arena is widely appreciated. It is increasingly recognized that the very existence and function of a new entity have value consequences far beyond its own borders. An increased awareness of the relation of respect for human rights to optimum world order may lead to new perspectives on the role of the nation-state entity as a vehicle for the attainment of human dignity.

Will the experience gained from the past six decades be relevant for the future? Will the experience gained from the accelerated independence of former trust territories and non-self-governing territories be relevant for the future? Will self-determination be relevant to the case of secession? Yes, indeed! This is so even though national elites understandably have approached the subject with great caution and skepticism. Self-determination is an ongoing process for people to forge and express their shared identity and destiny under ever-changing conditions in the collective pursuit of power, respect, and other values.

So long as social process moves on, human beings will continue to search for individual and group identities in an attempt to associate or dissociate with certain groups. Self-determination is not a "one-shot affair." The attainment of independence from dependency does not foreclose human aspirations to search for appropriate group identification and affiliation in the defense and fulfillment of all important values.

External Self-Determination in Practice: The Cases of Québec and Kosovo

Until the birth of Bangladesh as an independent state in 1971, it was generally assumed that in the contemporary world self-determination did not include the right of secession in the sense of a group breaking off from an established nation-state. The success of Bangladesh has significantly changed people's expectations. Indeed, change is a cardinal principle in human affairs. Change occurs to groups as well as individuals. It is critical that demands for change in value fulfillment through group identification, association, and expression in the name of self-determination are effected to serve the common interest of the world community. The recent experiences of the former Yugoslavia and the former Soviet Union emphasize the need for careful scrutiny of each claim to determine whether its fulfillment would promote security and foster human dignity values.

Two of the most prominent claims of a right to secession in recent decades have been those of the people of Québec to secede from Canada and of the people of Kosovo to secede from Serbia. Both claims have been argued and decided on their merits in court (at least in part) and thus provide an interesting insight into the practice of secession.

The right of Québec to secede from Canada was decided by the Supreme Court of Canada in 1998.[8] Of relevance here is the court's decision of whether Québec had a basis in international law to unilaterally secede from Canada. In reaching its decision that international law did not afford Québec a right to unilaterally secede, the court emphasized the tension between territorial integrity and the right of self-determination:

> [I]nternational law expects that the right of self-determination will be exercised by peoples within the framework of existing sovereign states and consistently with the maintenance of the territorial integrity of those states. Where this is not possible, in [certain] exceptional circumstances..., a right of secession may arise.[9]

The court then discussed those narrow circumstances under which international law recognizes a right of secession may arise: (1) where a people has been colonized, and (2) where a people is otherwise subject to alien domination outside of the colonial context. The court also recognized, without deciding the issue, that there is debate as to whether international law recognizes a third circumstance that may give rise to a right of secession, that is, where a people is denied a meaningful right to internal self-determination, a right of secession may arise as a last resort. The common denominator among these two or three bases of the right of secession, the court recognized, is the frustration of a people to exercise its right to internal self-determination within the framework of an existing state.

The court went on to apply these standards to determine whether Québec had a proper basis to assert its claim to external self-determination and quickly rejected all three possible grounds. With regard to the third possible basis of a right to secede, the denial of any meaningful form of internal self-determination, the court pointed to Québécois access to participation in a democratic political process, their representation in all branches of government, and their ability to pursue economic, social, and cultural advancements. Having found that the Québécois have a meaningful ability and opportunity to participate in domestic political processes, the court concluded that, under the circumstances, a right for Québec to effect unilateral secession would not arise under international law.

A second prominent claim of secession is that of Kosovo to secede from Serbia, for which the International Court of Justice (ICJ) rendered an advisory opinion in July 2010.[10] Although the opinion, in which the court held that Kosovo's February 2008 declaration of independence was legal under international law, has been widely celebrated by those who favor independence for Kosovo, the actual scope of the court's opinion was quite narrow. The court emphasized the narrowness of the scope of the question posed to it by the U.N. General Assembly. "Is the unilateral declaration of independence by the Provisional Institutions of Self-Government of Kosovo in accordance with international law?" The court was careful to point out issues that were outside the scope of the General Assembly's query:

> It does not ask about the legal consequences of that declaration. In particular, it does not ask whether or not Kosovo has achieved statehood. Nor does it ask about the validity or legal effects of the recognition of Kosovo by those states which have recognized it as an independent state.[11]

The court was also careful to contrast the narrowness of the question before it, the legality of Kosovo's declaration of independence, with the much broader question considered by the Supreme Court of Canada in the Québec case, the right of Québec to unilaterally secede from Canada, by pointing out that "it is entirely possible for a particular act—such as a unilateral declaration of independence—not to be in violation of international law without necessarily constituting the exercise of a right conferred by it."[12] Given the narrowness of the opinion, its significance should not be overstated for what it means about the scope of a right of secession.

What the court did hold in its opinion on the legality of Kosovo's declaration of independence was that the practice of states, taken as a whole, has never suggested that the mere act of declaring independence is contrary to international law. Although the court recognized several instances in which the U.N. Security Council condemned specific declarations of independence, such condemnations were made in reference to the specific factual contexts of each case and did not reflect a general condemnation on unilateral declarations of independence.

Perhaps the most significant aspect of the court's opinion was its rejection of the argument that the right of territorial integrity implies a prohibition on declarations of independence. The right of a sovereign state to control its territory does not include the right to prevent a people from expressing their desire for political independence. The court rejected this proposition, finding that state practice over the course of centuries provided no basis for outlawing such declarations. Furthermore, the court distinguished its opinion from the Québec case, noting that the Canadian decision was specific to whether a people may *effect* a unilateral secession, a question which was not before the ICJ.

Self-Determination and World Order

Though the basic community policy of self-determination has been affirmed and reaffirmed, a key problem remains: how to make its application relevant in particular instances to facilitate optimum achievement of the common interests—both minimum order (in the sense of minimizing unauthorized coercion) and optimum order (in the sense of the widest possible shaping and sharing of all values). Although the decision of the Supreme Court of Canada touched on the ability of the Québécois to control their political, economic, social, and cultural lives, the court did not squarely confront these issues and the International Court of Justice did not have the opportunity to do so in its decision on Kosovo. To do so is a pressing challenge.

In a decentralized world in which the effective power of state participants is patently discrepant, decision in support of or in rejection of particular claims for self-determination will remain essentially decentralized, in the absence of effective collective decisions. Hence, it is essential that appropriate criteria be articulated and formulated to guide rational decision making, unilateral or otherwise. Any serious review of a demand for self-determination from general community perspectives requires a careful contextual scrutiny, a systematic and rigorous appraisal of many features of the situation. Whether to support a claim must depend on the answers to many questions about each feature of the context, with the significance of any one feature being dependent on the total configuration.

The test from a New Haven School perspective for determining whether to grant or reject a demand for self-determination is not whether a given situation is colonial or noncolonial but whether granting or rejecting the demands of a group would move the situation closer to goal values of human dignity, considering in particular the aggregate value consequences for the group directly concerned and the larger communities affected. Self-determination should be viewed in the context of interdetermination. In other words, the basic question is whether separation or unification would best promote security for the people concerned and facilitate effective shaping and sharing of power and of all the other values. A proper balance between freedom of choice and the viability of communities must be maintained.

It is essential to examine alternative consequences of either granting or rejecting claims for separation or unity. Specific consideration should be given to the following: (1) the degree to which the demanding group can form a viable entity, in terms of both its internal processes and its capacity to function responsibly in its relations with other entities; (2) the probable consequences of independence (separation) for the remaining people in the entity of which it has been a part; and (3) the consequences of demanded independence (separation) or unity (unification) for the aggregate pattern of value shaping and shaping for the peoples of the surrounding communities and for the world at large. All these probable consequences must be ascertained and tested in a given context by a careful analysis of the factors involved: participants, perspectives, situations, base values, strategies, outcomes, and effects.

Some of the more important points about these relevant features are briefly indicated as follows.

In terms of perspectives, it is critical to ascertain the intensity of demands in a population, observing the degree and intensity of support on the part of the elite and the rank and file, respectively. Identifications are crucial, especially the intensity and inclusivity of identification with a territorial community and the range and degree of identification with regional and global communities. Hence, it is vital to ascertain: (1) the degree to which the elite and the rank and file of the aspiring group identify with an existing or projected territorial community; (2) the extent to which members of the aspiring group associate themselves with all members of an existing or projected territorial community; (3) the degree to which members of the aspiring group identify with a class or ethnic or political or linguistic group; (4) the degree of territorial inclusivity; and (5) the range and degree of identification with regional and global communities and the degree of conformity to regional and global public policies. Another component is the matter-of-fact expectations about the past, present, and future entertained by the different participants. It is important to explore in which direction and to what extent alternative courses of action will affect these expectations.

In terms of participation, attention should be directed to observe how a particular group that makes a demand for separation fits in with the territorial and functional groups in the contemporary world and to compare what changes in participation are being sought by demanders and by those who oppose the demand.

It is important to ask: Do the people concerned actively participate in making the demand? What choices were available to these people in the past? What choices would be open to them in the future? Would granting the demand lead to significant value shaping and better distribution of values? Would participation in the relevant value processes be effectively widened?

Regarding situations, one must compare the present and proposed structures of authority, both functional and territorial, and ascertain the degree of sharing of a common destiny in reference to the larger community. One must also note the length of time over which previous factors have been integrated and consider alternative time intervals for future integration and consolidation, crisis circumstances, and so forth.

With regard to base values, consideration should be given to consequences of accepting or denying a particular demand in terms of values. What are the present distributions of values of different groups? What changes are demanded in terms of authority and controlling values? What are the available alternatives and the probable consequences for people, territory, institutions, and resources?

In terms of viability of a political community, inquiry can be directed in terms of consideration for security, power, wealth, and other values. The most important of all the features are the outcomes in terms of the impact on different values expected to attend each option for the aspiring group, the old entity to which the aspiring group belongs, and the larger surrounding communities, including the global community. Hence, the critical test in considering a claim to self-determination is to evaluate the aggregate value consequences for all those communities, potential as well as existing, in honoring or rejecting the claim and to honor the option that will promote the largest net aggregate of common interest by fully estimating the relative costs and benefits of the different options for each of those communities.

In making this recommendation, I do not mean to oversimplify or underestimate the enormous complexity and difficulty attending many of the seemingly intractable controversies about self-determination. Notice, for example, the claims for self-determination made by the following peoples: the Palestinians, Lebanese, and Kurds; the Koreans, Taiwanese (Formosans), Tibetans, the Uighurs living in China, East Timorese, and Tamil people in Sri Lanka; the Serbs, Croats, Slovenians, and Bosnian Muslims in the former Yugoslavia; the Albanians in Kosovo; the Chechens in Russia, Armenians, and the Germans of Romania; the Ossetians in South Ossetia in Georgia; the Catalans and Basques of Spain, the Scots, the Welsh, the Catholics of Northern Ireland, and the French Canadians of Québec; the Ibos, Somalis, and the non-Muslim peoples in Southern Sudan; and various indigenous groups. (For many years, indigenous groups have been existing on lands over which they have little or no control and have suffered various deprivations, including conquest, actual and cultural genocide, forced expulsion from their land and dwellings, and compulsory taking of their natural resources. The demands inherent in their claims for self-determination range from the classic sense of establishing a new state to a high degree of autonomy within the existing state to special protection of land rights, cultural rights, religious rights, and so on.)

Although the trend of past decisions indicates that the United Nations, in dealing with issues relating to self-determination, often stresses the basic distinction between colonial and noncolonial issues, this distinction need not be conclusive, particularly when colonialism is narrowly understood to be the domination by whites of non-whites. The essence of self-determination is human dignity, human rights, and authority of the people. Underlying the concept of human dignity is the insistent demand of the individual to form groups freely and to identify with groups that can best promote and maximize the pursuit of values in both individual and aggregate terms. The formation and reformation of groups are ongoing.

Legal doctrines operate in pairs of complementary rules, herein exemplified by the interplay between self-determination and territorial integrity. Is the seeming conflict between territorial integrity and self-determination irreconcilable? And how about territorial integrity: for whom or what purpose and with what social consequences?

As will be shown in chapters 12 and 19 regarding states' responsibility to protect, it has become increasingly apparent that absolute adherence to territorial integrity is no virtue. Rather, it is self-defeating when the people who demand freedom are subject to systematic deprivations on a vast scale. The principle of territorial integrity must not serve as a shield for tyrants, dictators, or totalitarian rulers; it must not become a screen behind which human deprivations are justified, condoned, and perpetuated. Today the world is too interdependent, humanity is living too closely together, to permit the doctrines of domestic jurisdiction or territorial integrity to become an instrument of oppression, politicide, and deprivation. Moreover, new perspectives on human rights have opened the possibility that artificial political entities based on territorial integrity alone may someday have to be replaced by institutions more realistically reflecting human dignity values.

Empires rise and fall; nation-states and territorial boundaries come and go. But the demands of humanity for freedom and human dignity will remain strong. An ongoing process in the search of the self in relation to others, self-determination is profoundly associated with the essence of human dignity. When decisions regarding self-determination are rationally and adequately made, they will greatly contribute to the common interest of humankind in achieving both minimum and optimum world order.

The Theory and Practice of Recognition

The application of the principle of self-determination has led to the establishment of many new states in recent decades. But when does a territorial community come into formal existence as a nation-state, as a full member of the world community? Does it come about automatically when a territorial group meets the widely accepted conditions of statehood: control over a group of people, control over a defined or definable territory, and a government capable of interacting with other entities and assuming international responsibility? If so, who decides whether a group has met such traditional conditions of statehood, and who reviews those decisions? If not, what else will be required? Does a new body politic come into being as a result of self-proclamation and effective control or as a consequence of recognition by other existing entities? This raises the issue of recognition in international law.

Recognition in international law is a highly confusing topic both in theory and in practice. In an interdependent world of constant change, recognition problems are many. The term "recognition" itself gives ambiguous reference simultaneously to both facts and legal consequences. Is *de facto* recognition different from *de jure* recognition? Is recognition, with its inherited ambiguity and confusion, merely a ritual, or does it possess considerable significance? What impact should human rights, the precept of authority, and self-determination have on the process of recognition?

In the most comprehensive sense, recognition choices are made in response to the dynamics of change in the world social process. Within a nation-state such changes may relate to patterns of participation; patterns of demands, expectations, and identification; aggregate situations in time, space, institutions, and crises; authority and control patterns; the overall distribution of value assets; strategies and procedures for the employment of value assets; and the aggregate outcomes in the shaping and sharing of all values. Such changes, though internal, inevitably generate effects external to the group concerned, due to the interactive nature of the global system—a system of growing interdetermination and interdependence in which participants act and react by taking one another into account.

Recognition problems that particularly vex international and national decision makers arise in a number of contexts, notably the emergence of new states, changes of government, retention of effective power through extraconstitutional means, territorial changes resulting from use of force, and the rivalry (belligerency or insurgency) in a civil strife. The post–Cold War era has been characterized by violent civil wars that have led to the creation of a number of new states. The particular need for recognition arises when the birth of a new nation-state or the seizure of power by a new government of an existing state is an extraordinary political event. In the case of recognizing an entity as a new state, what is extraordinary usually involves a revolutionary separation from another state. Though every new state holds out for recognition, the process of recognition is routine if the new entity results from peaceful separation from an existing state, as is the case with most of the new states under decolonization.

In the case of recognition of a new government, if the transfer of power from one government to another results from the ordinary and authoritative constitutive process, the question of recognition poses no difficulty. Only when the change of government is extraconstitutional, such as by a revolution, a coup d' état, martial law, or a radical departure from the prescribed line of succession, is a decision called for as to whether the new or newly changed regime should be recognized as authoritative. The great majority of recognition problems involve recognition of regimes as the governments of already recognized states without affecting the continuity of legal identity of the states. This problem is explored further in chapter 27 in regard to state succession.

Our principal concern here is with the emergence of a new state—that is, the question of recognizing the state. In this sense, recognition refers to the authoritative decision by one nation-state to signify its willingness to accept another territorial community as a nation-state, as a full participant, for a wide range of purposes, in the global processes of authoritative decision. The question of recognizing a particular government will be dealt with insofar as it relates to this question.

A wide consensus exists among international lawyers that the minimum conditions of statehood requisite to recognition consist of territory, people, political institutions, and the capacity to fulfill international obligations. They disagree, however, on the modalities for applying these criteria to concrete cases, as manifested in the basic difference in their perspectives regarding the nature of recognition. Much ink has been spilled over the question of whether recognition is declaratory or constitutive in nature. The declaratory theory holds that recognition merely declares, and is automatic upon, the "objective" existence of the conditions of statehood. The constitutive theory maintains that the presence of objective conditions of statehood is itself insufficient to endow formal statehood on a new entity—formal recognition by other existing states is essential to making a new entity a full member of the community of nations. The declaratory-constitutive controversy relates primarily to recognition of states and only incidentally to recognition of governments.

The practice of recognition lies somewhere between the two theories. The declaratory theory, in its search for objective pronouncement of factual existence, cannot escape the element of subjective appreciation in determining whether a particular territorial community has demonstrated all the required conditions. Of the requisite conditions of statehood, determining whether there exists a government capable of responsible interaction with other territorial communities is particularly challenging. Nothing is automatic or objective about making such a determination. By contrast, constitutive theorists and practitioners cannot really operate in a vacuum without regard for relevant legal precepts and for factual situations concerning people, territory, and institutions.

Closely related to recognition of states is the recognition of government. This question becomes acute when an extraconstitutional change in government takes place without affecting the continuity of legal identity of the established state. If a governmental change results from ordinary constitutional procedures, recognition by others is automatic and implicit, through such communications as messages of felicitation. But when a governmental change results from extraconstitutional means, the questions of authority and recognition take on special significance: Is the claiming government to be recognized as the government representative of the state it purports to represent? Do other states (governments) have the duty to extend recognition to such a claiming government? Under what conditions? Does such recognition signify approval of the recognized government and its practices? Or does it simply acknowledge effective control by the claiming government in the state involved? The tenor of the questions thus raised, though somewhat akin to the constitutive-declaratory controversy, is distinct.

Again, practice varies widely, and the practice and the theory are far from congruent. Decision makers have made use of recognition in various ways, depending largely on the context of political conditions and their perception of the national interest involved in a change of government. Take, for instance, the practice of the United States. Early in its history, recognition was tied to standards of authority and democratic values. Throughout most of the nineteenth century, it was a general U.S. policy to accord recognition to stable governments without attempting to confer approval. But the recognition policy became more complex as various administrations introduced different policy considerations, including popular support, free elections, ability and willingness to honor international obligations, sound political orientation, positive attitude toward foreign investment, and proper treatment of U.S. citizens. The United States has employed recognition as a deliberate instrument to support antimonarchical governments under George Washington, to foster economic expansion under Theodore Roosevelt, to promote constitutional democracy under Woodrow Wilson, to check the spread of communism under Dwight D. Eisenhower, and to encourage the growth of market economies and democracy in the newly independent states of the former Soviet Union. The net effects are to create the impression that recognition signifies approval of a government and its practices, whereas nonrecognition means disapproval and causes considerable confusion regarding the legal implications of recognition and considerable practical difficulties. In recent years the United States has sought to separate the element of approval or disapproval from an act of recognition and has approached the problem of recognizing a government in terms of willingness to establish diplomatic relations to facilitate direct mutual interaction. What impact does such a policy have on self-determination? Is it likely that human dignity, the precept of authority found in the Universal Declaration of Human Rights, and other human rights can be realistically and rationally served by ignoring legal policies at stake and the details of context?

In theory and in practice, a distinction is often made between *de jure* and *de facto* recognition. Generally speaking, when a government is recognized as *de facto*, its effective control is recognized; if a government is deemed *de jure*, recognition is extended to the permanency of its effective control and formal authority. Though *de facto* recognition is often regarded as a prelude to *de jure* recognition, the distinction is often blurred. Furthermore, the modality of recognition may be either express or implied (for instance, through conclusion of a bilateral treaty of a general nature).

In an interactive world, the value consequences of bestowing or withholding recognition are far from trivial. In the words of Kaplan and Katzenbach:

Recognition of a new government normally results in increased prestige and stability at home; access to state funds on deposit in other states; access to private and governmental loans because of legal ability to pledge the state's credit; diplomatic and consular status for its agents in the recognizing entity; access to foreign courts and immunity from foreign process; establishment of normal trade relations; a capacity to request assistance from the recognizing government in the form of financial assistance, supplies, and even military aid; respect in other states for its laws and decrees; and benefits of existing treaty arrangements. The absence of formal recognition has the effect of suspending most or all of these rights insofar as the non-recognizing state controls them. They may be accorded to another claimant, or they may simply be suspended.[13]

Hence, controversy arises as to the permissibility of premature recognition or deliberate nonrecognition. During a civil strife, premature recognition bestowed on the rebellious group can be used as a means of influencing the outcome of the strife. Customarily, as long as the duly constituted government or mother state commands effective control of the substantial part of territory and exercises its authority, it is presumed to represent the state. Unless there are indications beyond reasonable doubt that the rebellious group has effective control over a substantial part of the territory with reasonable expectations of stability and permanency, and the parent state or duly constituted government has discontinued effective efforts to reestablish its control and authority over the lost territory, other nation-states are obligated to refrain from recognizing the new regime. Premature recognition of a rebellious group as either a new state or a new government is traditionally frowned on as impermissible "intervention." The real difficulty, given the highly decentralized nature of recognition, is to determine the appropriate timing for recognition of a new regime as effected unilaterally by individual states.

In 1903, when Panama seceded from Colombia, the United States lost no time in recognizing Panama as an independent state, with a view to preventing Colombia from reasserting its authority and control over the rebellious territory. Though the U.S. government justified its action by citing security interests in the Caribbean and inclusive interests for the construction of the Panama Canal, this has frequently been cited as a classic example of premature recognition. In modern times, premature recognition is increasingly justified in terms of support for self-determination or for "wars of national liberation." Some commentators have suggested that the premature recognition of the breakaway Yugoslav republics in large part precipitated the war in the former Yugoslavia. Others criticized NATO for intervening in what was perceived as a civil war in Libya in 2011.

Deliberate nonrecognition, like premature recognition, can have a devastating effect on a target regime. If a state or a government meets those criteria that are commonly accepted by international law, are other nation-states obligated to recognize this state or government? Or is recognition of a state or government a matter of discretion, to be granted or withheld as a state sees fit? The impact of withholding recognition is particularly keen when preponderant differences in bases of power exist between the recognizing and the target state or government. As indicated, recognition by a powerful nation-state usually carries with it not only increased access to the international arena of authority but also advancement of external position. Conversely, a denial of recognition can deprive and adversely affect the relative influence of the target regime in international affairs. At times the protracted refusal of recognition by a powerful state may even adversely affect the internal position of the target regime.

"Recognition" and "derecognition," "official" and "unofficial" relations, *de jure* or *de facto*, and what have you—it would be quite a nightmare to attempt to dissect this complex picture neatly in terms of a pure theory of recognition. Complex realities, as confounded by conflicting dogmas and politics, do not lend themselves to neat theory. In the long run pragmatism prevails, and old rhetoric continues to flourish. To paraphrase Justice Oliver Wendell Holmes, Jr., the practice of recognition is more a matter of life experience than of pure logic. The confusion in the theory and practice of recognition stems in no small measure from the highly decentralized and discretionary nature of recognition. Individual, unilateral action, rather than collective action, prevails.

To minimize confusion in the field, international lawyers have made a variety of suggestions: eliminate the practice of recognition; take "politics" out of recognition decisions; define the duty of recognition; prohibit premature recognition; distinguish *de jure* from *de facto* recognition, or simply obliterate the distinction; distinguish recognition from establishment of diplomatic relations; limit recognition problems to recognition of states and deal with governmental change in terms of willingness to establish diplomatic relations; substitute collective recognition for individual recognition; focus on the question of "representation" of an entity in transnational arenas of authority instead of the question of recognition of states and governments, and so on. In addition to the traditional criteria for statehood, U.S. Secretary of State James Baker, heralding a new policy on the recognition of states in response to the dissolution of Yugoslavia, indicated five relevant principles. Recognition is to be granted in accordance with a new state's adherence to the following:

1. Determination of the future of the country peacefully and democratically;
2. Respect for all existing borders, both internal and external, with change only through peaceful and consensual means;
3. Support for democracy and the rule of law, emphasizing the key role of elections in the democratic process;
4. Safeguarding of human rights, based on full respect for the individual and including equal treatment of minorities; and
5. Respect for international law and obligations, especially adherence to the Helsinki Final Act and the Charter of Paris.[14]

The European Community has affirmed that its member states will grant recognition to new states under guidelines resembling those set forth by the secretary of state.[15]

Though the frustrations and considerations behind these thoughtful suggestions are well taken, the problem of recognition, in its varied forms and contexts, is unlikely to disappear, given the continuation of a decentralized and dynamic international system of nation-states. The real-life problems cannot be waved away. The important point is to realize what is at stake in a recognition decision and to seek to enhance the degree of rationality in making recognition decisions individually and collectively by taking seriously the legal policies and common interests involved, with specific reference to the demands, expectations, and interests of the aspiring group or community, neighboring communities, and regional and world public order.

Problems of Self-Determination and Recognition in Practice: The Evolution of Taiwan Statehood

As the preceding discussion has made clear, questions of statehood, the right of a people to self-determination, and recognition are difficult, and necessarily fact- and context-specific. The question of Taiwan is highly illustrative and instructive in this regard. In fact, a world-renowned professor of international law in a leading law school once told me he had often used the Taiwan-China case to illustrate various aspects of international law throughout his international law course. An analysis of the complex issues concerning Taiwan requires a careful consideration of the history of Taiwan in relation to the principle of self-determination and the practice of recognition under contemporary international law.

Taiwanese statehood is best understood in the context of an ongoing process of evolution propelled by the desire of the Taiwanese people for self-determination and democracy. Unlike in bygone eras, international law no longer conceives of territories as mere pieces of property to be traded or conquered. To the contrary, in today's world, human beings are properly held to be at the center of international law. As will be explained, the legal status of Taiwan remained undetermined at the conclusion of the San Francisco Peace Treaty with Japan after World War II. And its situation was further clouded by the period of martial law that followed. However, recent decades have witnessed a profound and persistent movement of democratization—and Taiwanization—that runs counter to the unfounded claims of ownership over the island and its people by China. This theory of the evolution of Taiwan's statehood is firmly rooted in contemporary principles of international law.

The People's Republic of China (PRC) is variously known as China, mainland China, and Communist China. The Republic of China (ROC) is variously known as Taiwan, Formosa, and Nationalist China. Both before and after the ROC was replaced by the PRC in the United Nations in 1971—and both before and after relations between the United States and China were "normalized" and the ROC was derecognized in 1979—a number of knotty legal questions persisted. Are there two successor states—Communist China and Nationalist China—as a result of the Chinese civil war of 1949? If so, which is new, which is old, and which represents the authentic state of China? By what criteria would one determine this authenticity? If there is only "one China" and "Taiwan is a part of China," as claimed by the ruling elites in Beijing, what are the respective statuses of the PRC and the ROC? Does the PRC represent a state or only a government? Does the ROC represent a state or only a government? Do the PRC and the ROC each fulfill the traditional requirements of statehood? What are the legal effects of the normalization of U.S.-China relations and the derecognition of the ROC? What is the international legal status of Taiwan? Who owns Taiwan? Since its formation in 1949, the PRC has never extended its effective control over Taiwan; what, then, is the basis of its legal claim over Taiwan? Which of the following labels most aptly describes the current situation: "one China," "one China, two governments," "one China—but not now," "two Chinas," or "one China, one Taiwan?" Will the future of Taiwan be determined by peaceful "reunification" with "the motherland" (mainland China), through negotiation by "the Chinese on both sides of the Taiwan Straits," through forcible "liberation" by China, or by all twenty-three million inhabitants of Taiwan as a right of self-determination? Answers to these questions will not be easy, even for experts in this area.

The continuing controversies about "one China," "one China—but not now," "two Chinas," and "one China, one Taiwan" stem from the basic uncertainty of Taiwan's status in international law after World War II. The competing governments asserted in their struggle for control over the Chinese mainland that Taiwan has always been part of China. The PRC continues to maintain this. The reasoning behind this assertion remains less than persuasive, although its claims are often taken at face value.

The original inhabitants of Taiwan, formerly known as Formosa, were the indigenous Austronesian peoples who settled there thousands of years ago. The first meaningful contact between China and Taiwan began in the late fifteenth and early sixteenth centuries, when dissident Chinese began to settle in Taiwan in substantial numbers. When, during the seventeenth century, both the Dutch and Spanish established settlements on Taiwan, the Ming dynasty in China offered no resistance. It was not until 1662, when the Manchu overthrew the Ming dynasty, that there was any significant contact between China and Taiwan, following the expulsion of the Dutch and Spanish from the island by the exiled Koxinga (Cheng Cheng-kung). And even then, the relationship was not one of Chinese sovereignty over Taiwan, but was more akin to a self-proclaimed regime-in-exile operating from Taiwan. Finally, in 1683, the Manchu (Ching) sent an expedition force to Taiwan which succeeded in establishing some authority in Taiwan, although the Chinese control over Taiwan was merely nominal, as the indigenous peoples retained a large degree of autonomy from the Chinese.

The period of loose Chinese control over Taiwan continued for more than two hundred years. In 1871, for example, when the crew of a wrecked Okinawan ship was murdered by a group of aboriginal people on Taiwan, the Ching government in Peking (now called Beijing) disclaimed responsibility on the ground that the atrocity was committed in a barbaric territory beyond its jurisdiction. It was not until 1887 that the Ching dynasty formally made Taiwan a province of China. Formal Chinese control over Taiwan was tenuous and short-lived, lasting only eight years. Following the Chinese defeat in the Sino-Japanese War of 1895, China and Japan executed the Treaty of Shimonoseki, under which China ceded in perpetuity Formosa (Taiwan) and the Pescadores (Penghu) to Japan. Under the *intertemporal* principle, meaning that the applicable law in determining the validity of that transfer is the international law in effect at the time the transfer was made, this was a legal transfer of territory. Thus from 1895, Japan had formal sovereignty over Taiwan under international law.

At the end of the war in the Pacific in 1945, under the terms of Japan's surrender to the Allies, Japan surrendered control over Taiwan to the Allied forces, which delegated responsibility for occupying Taiwan to the army of the Republic of China (ROC), led by Chiang Kai-shek. Notably, the three heads of state of the Allies had previously signaled that Taiwan would be returned to China, in the Cairo Declaration of 1943 and the Potsdam Proclamation of 1945. In actuality, this was not carried out when the Japanese relinquished control of Taiwan in 1945. Thus, from 1945 until 1952 (when Japan and the Allies finally executed a peace treaty) Taiwan remained Japanese territory, although it was under military occupation by the Allied forces, under the guise of the ROC.

In 1949, major military hostilities in the Chinese civil war ended. The Chinese Communist Party (CPC) established the People's Republic of China on mainland China. Chiang Kai-shek's Chinese Nationalist Party (the Kuomintang, or KMT) was exiled to Taiwan, where it imposed the governmental structure and personnel of the Republic of China by virtue of martial law. Despite the relatively clear territorial separation of the PRC and the exiled ROC, both sides continued to maintain that both Taiwan and mainland China were a single unified state, with each side claiming sovereignty over "one China." The ROC's exile to Taiwan did not change Taiwan's legal status. Taiwan remained Japanese territory, while the ROC continued to exist as a military occupier (acting with Allied authorization in accordance with the Japanese surrender) and took on the additional role as a government-in-exile. The ROC did not and could not acquire sovereignty over Taiwan under international law, whether as a military occupier or as a government-in-exile. Taiwan remained a Japanese territory until the Treaty of Peace with Japan took effect in 1952.

Japan did not formally renounce its sovereignty over Taiwan until 1952, when the Treaty of Peace with Japan, commonly referred to as the San Francisco Peace Treaty, went into force. The Treaty, which was signed in 1951 by 48 nations, is the authoritative document concerning the status of Taiwan and superseded wartime declarations such as the Cairo Declaration and the Potsdam Proclamation. Under Article 2(b) of the San Francisco Treaty, "Japan renounce[d] all right, title and claim" to Formosa (Taiwan) and the Pescadores (Penghu). (When reference is made to Taiwan in this book it includes

Penghu.) The San Francisco Peace Treaty was deliberately silent as to whom Japan was ceding Taiwan.

When negotiating the San Francisco Peace Treaty, it was the shared expectation of the Allies that the legal status of Taiwan, though temporarily left undetermined because of current exigencies, would be decided in the future in light of the purposes and principles of the U.N. Charter. That Taiwan's legal status remained undetermined was the shared expectation of the international community in the years following the San Francisco Peace Treaty. In 1954, for example, U.S. Secretary of State John Foster Dulles stated:

> [T]echnical sovereignty over Formosa and the Pescadores has never been settled. That is because the Japanese peace treaty merely involves a renunciation by Japan of its right and title to these islands. But the future title is not determined by the Japanese peace treaty, nor is it determined by the peace treaty which was concluded between the Republic of China and Japan. Therefore, the juridical status of these islands, Formosa and the Pescadores, is different from the juridical status of the offshore islands [Quemoy and Matsu] which have always been Chinese territory.[16]

The British position was represented by Prime Minister Sir Anthony Eden (then the Deputy Prime Minister and Foreign Secretary) in February 1955 as follows:

> [The Cairo] Declaration was a statement of intention that Formosa should be retroceded to China after the war. This retrocession has, in fact, never taken place, because of the difficulties arising from the existence of two entities claiming to represent China, and the differences amongst the Powers as to the status of these entities.[17]

Eden succeeded Churchill as prime minister two months later, in April 1955.

Because of this long-held position, these former Allied powers (except the United Kingdom, which extended recognition to the PRC shortly after its birth in 1949) simply "took note of," or "acknowledged," rather than "recognized," China's position that Taiwan was part of China when they established diplomatic relations with the PRC in the 1970s. The words were chosen with all deliberateness and help explain the constant controversy about Taiwan's status and the continuing, insistent demands on the part of the Taiwanese people for self-determination.

It is a historical fact that the San Francisco Peace Treaty was silent as to whom Japan was ceding Taiwan. It is this fact—combined with the continued insistence by both the PRC and the ROC that Taiwan is a part of "one China" and the demands for self-determination and independence by the Taiwanese people—that has made Taiwan's international legal status such a difficult question. While the question of sovereignty over Taiwan will be discussed at greater length below, it is important to reiterate here the fundamental principle of international law that peoples are entitled to self-determination and that sovereignty lies ultimately with the people. Accordingly, the perhaps ambiguous question of formal legal sovereignty over Taiwan in the wake of the San Francisco Peace Treaty should not overshadow the fact that it is the Taiwanese people who ultimately have the right to determine Taiwan's sovereignty in the era of the U.N. Charter.

Before the PRC gained a seat in the United Nations, the question of Chinese participation came before the United Nations year after year, generating the bitter debate over whether the question was one of "credentials," "representation," or "admission" of a new member state. When the United Nations acted to seat the PRC on October 25, 1971, the General Assembly adopted Resolution 2758 to "restore all its rights to the People's Republic of China and to recognize the representatives of its Government as the only legitimate representatives of China to the United Nations, and to expel forthwith the representatives of Chiang Kai-shek from the place which they unlawfully occupy at the United Nations and in all the organizations related to it."[18] Overnight, the ROC, which had gained respectable recognition as "the only legitimate government of China" within the United Nations and elsewhere for two decades, by more states than the PRC, suddenly found itself an international outcast. The trend toward formal recognition of the PRC thus accelerated in the 1970s, culminating in the recognition of the PRC as the sole legitimate government of China by an overwhelming majority of the representatives of the world's nations.

The dramatic change of U.S. policy toward China and Taiwan is in line with this overall trend. Before President Richard Nixon's journey to China in February 1972, the United States recognized the ROC as the only legitimate government of China, supported it in the form of a mutual defense treaty, and adopted the policy of nonrecognition of the PRC to "hasten the passing of the Communist regime on mainland China."[19] After Nixon's journey and until the end of 1978, the United States and the PRC developed their economic and cultural ties and maintained "unofficial relations" through the establishment of "liaison offices" in each other's capitals while the official relations between the ROC and the United States continued. On January 1, 1979, the United States and the People's Republic of China agreed to "recognize each other and to establish diplomatic relations": the United States "recognizes" the government of the PRC as "the sole legal Government of China" and "*acknowledges* the Chinese position that there is but one China and Taiwan is part of China"; meanwhile, "the people of the United States will maintain cultural, commercial, and other unofficial relations with the people of Taiwan."[20] With this about-face, the liaison offices located in Washington, D.C., and Beijing were elevated to embassies, whereas the "unofficial relations" between the United States and Taiwan were carried forward through new institutions in lieu of old-fashioned embassies—the American Institute on Taiwan and the Coordinating Council for North American Affairs, both staffed by foreign service officers on loan. To fill the security gap created by President Jimmy Carter's termination of the mutual defense treaty with Taiwan, the U.S. Congress in April 1979 adopted the Taiwan Relations Act (TRA), declaring, among other things, that "peace and stability" in the

"Western Pacific area" are "matters of international concern," that "the United States decision to establish diplomatic relations" with the PRC "rests upon the expectation that the future of Taiwan will be determined by peaceful means," that "any effort to determine the future of Taiwan by other than peaceful means" will constitute "a threat to the peace and security of the Western Pacific area" and be "of grave concern to the United States," and that "the preservation and enhancement of the human rights of all the people on Taiwan are hereby reaffirmed as objectives of the United States."[21] The act stipulates: "The absence of diplomatic relations or recognition shall not affect the application of the laws of the United States with respect to Taiwan.... Whenever the laws of the United States refer or relate to foreign countries, states, governments, or similar entities, such terms shall include and such laws shall apply to Taiwan."[22] The Taiwan Relations Act specifies further that treaty relations at the time of derecognition of the ROC—fifty-nine international agreements were in force between the United States and Taiwan (excluding the mutual defense treaty)—remain essentially unchanged, as do Taiwan's standing to sue and be sued, the choice of law rules, rights and obligations, and ownership of property.

It is important to note that the TRA is framed in terms of the United States' relationship with the people of *Taiwan*, not the ROC. This was the first instance of the United States interacting with Taiwan as a distinct entity, rather than as the subject of a dispute between dueling sovereigns. The TRA's treatment of Taiwan—treating Taiwan as a state for all practical purposes—is compelling evidence of Taiwan's distinct international character, apart from the claims of "one China" made by the PRC and the ROC. This conclusion is reinforced by the fact that if it is accepted that Taiwan is part of China, the TRA would constitute an unlawful interference in Chinese internal affairs by the United States.

The effect of the derecognition of the ROC (and corresponding recognition of the PRC) by the United Nations, the United States, and others, must also be put into perspective. In derecognizing the ROC, all that was meant was that the derecognizing state no longer recognized the ROC's claims to be the legitimate government of China. This was to state a rather obvious conclusion, since the ROC had not exercised any control over mainland China for more than twenty years at the time of "expulsion" by the United Nations in 1971. Thus, derecognition had the effect of discrediting the ROC's claims to sovereignty over China, but did not affect Taiwan's undetermined international legal status. In fact, statements of derecognition of the ROC and recognition of the PRC were carefully deliberate to withhold judgment on the question of Taiwan, by acknowledging the PRC's claims that Taiwan is part of China, without conceding this assertion. In this context, the difference between "acknowledging" and "recognizing" is highly significant. To acknowledge a claim is to say simply that one has heard it and is aware of the speaker's position. To recognize, however, is to accept the validity of the speaker's claim. The PRC's assertions against Taiwan have generally not been recognized, but only acknowledged.

After derecognition of the ROC, what is Taiwan? Do recognition of the PRC and derecognition of the ROC involve recognition of state or recognition of government? *De jure* or *de facto* recognition? What has taken place and what changes have occurred? Although the United States may be constrained from calling Taiwan a government or a state, it continues, for all practical purposes, to treat Taiwan as a *de facto* government or state with virtually all the attributes characteristic of such entities. Furthermore, there is widespread consensus that, judged by the long-established requirements of statehood, both China and Taiwan—existing as separate political entities for more than six decades—fulfill such requirements.

Still, some international legal scholars reject the conclusion that Taiwan has achieved statehood. This is the position taken by Professor James Crawford, for example, perhaps the most prominent scholar on the subject of the creation of states under international law. Crawford's argument against Taiwan's statehood is useful as an illustration of the argument put forth by those who conclude that Taiwan is not a state, but rather is a territory of China.

Crawford begins his argument by considering the possible effects of the Japanese renunciation of Taiwan.[23] For this purpose, Crawford assumes that Taiwan is not a state. If this is so, Crawford continues, there are three possible conclusions as to Taiwan's territorial status. The first theory, which Crawford quickly rejects, is that Taiwan had been returned to China by 1949, either as a result of the Chinese pronouncement to abrogate the Treaty of Shimonoseki or as a result of the transfer of administrative authority to the ROC. Crawford is right to reject this argument, as Taiwan's legal status was not changed by either of these events and Taiwan's legal status continued to be that of a Japanese territory until Japan renounced its interest by the San Francisco Peace Treaty.

Instead, Crawford concludes that if Taiwan is not a state (which he later concludes it is not), then it is part of China. Crawford reaches this conclusion based on the circumstances surrounding the Japanese relinquishment of Taiwan, that is, the intention to return Taiwan to China that was stated in the Cairo Declaration and Potsdam Proclamation, coupled with the occupation of Taiwan by a recognized government of China (the ROC). Thus, Crawford argues that the effect of the San Francisco Peace Treaty was to return sovereignty over Taiwan to China, regardless of whether it was the PRC or the ROC that had the right to exercise that sovereignty. Crawford recognizes that, "[a]s a mode of transfer this may be unique," but goes on to argue that it is more likely than the alternative, namely that the Japanese renunciation had the effect of making Taiwan a condominium of the forty-eight Allied powers that were parties to the San Francisco Peace Treaty.[24]

The shortcoming with Crawford's conclusion is that he ignores a third, much more plausible explanation of the legal effect of Japan's renunciation on Taiwan's international legal status: that Taiwan's international legal status was left undetermined in the wake of Japan's relinquishment of the territory. Although Crawford recognizes this as a potential explanation, and indeed recognizes that it was the view taken by both the United Kingdom and the United States in the years following the treaty, he does not offer any argument against this view. Rather, he rejects this argument only implicitly, by accepting that circumstances surrounding the Japanese renunciation had the effect of returning Taiwan to China. As will be set forth below, however, the better conclusion is that Taiwan's international legal status was left undetermined by the 1952 Japanese renunciation. Moreover, Taiwan has undergone subsequent evolution and transformation toward democracy that has led to its effective self-determination and thus statehood.

Crawford's conclusion that sovereignty over Taiwan was restored to China in 1952 rests on his conclusion that Taiwan is not a state. Crawford points to three "difficulties" that lead him to this conclusion:

1. If by 1952 the ROC had lost its claim to being the legitimate government of China, then ceding Taiwan to the ROC would have breached the terms of the peace agreement and would have constituted an intervention in the Chinese civil war;

2. If Taiwan became a part of China in 1952, then the American patrolling of the Straits of Taiwan (following the outbreak of the Korean War) would have constituted an intervention in the Chinese civil war and an attempted encroachment on China's territorial integrity;

3. "Claims to statehood are not to be inferred from statements or actions short of explicit declaration; and in the apparent absence of any claim to secede the status of Taiwan can only be that of a part of the state of China under separate administration."[25]

The first two problems Crawford sees with Taiwanese statehood can be easily dealt with. Both depend upon Crawford's assumption that Taiwan became a part of China in 1952. As has already been suggested and as will be discussed in greater detail below, the preferable view is that Taiwan's international legal status was left undetermined in 1952. If one does not assume that Taiwan became a part of China in 1952, as one must, given the deliberate omission of China as the successor state in the San Francisco Peace Treaty, neither of these problems arises. The third problem Crawford points to, the lack of a formal declaration of independence, which Crawford views as "determinative" on the issue of Taiwanese statehood, is somewhat more difficult. The response to this point will be discussed in more detail below, but the short answer is that Taiwan has clearly asserted that it is a separate state that is not a part of China, and that to require a more explicit declaration of independence is to ignore the reality on the ground, that is, China's ongoing threat to respond with military force to any such declaration.

Rather than inferring from the surrounding circumstances that the effect of the San Francisco Peace Treaty was to transfer Taiwan to China, a means of transferring authority that Crawford himself recognizes would be "unique," the more plausible view is that the only effect of the treaty was for Japan to renounce its interest in Taiwan, leaving Taiwan's international legal status undetermined. This was the consensus view among the signatory states, which were in agreement that Taiwan's international legal status would be determined in the future and in accordance with the principles of the U.N. Charter, especially the principles of peaceful settlement of disputes and self-determination. The Cairo Declaration, in which Roosevelt and Churchill, along with Chiang Kai-shek, unilaterally expressed their wartime intention that Taiwan be returned to China, and the Potsdam Proclamation, in which this intention was reaffirmed, are superseded by the San Francisco Peace Treaty, the only instrument in which Japan, the then-owner of Taiwan, participated. The San Francisco Peace Treaty was the only legally effective and authoritative instrument, and it did not name China as the successor to Japan's interest in Taiwan. As explained in chapter 8, parties have traditionally deferred to peace treaties as superseding provisional pronouncements made during hostilities.

Nor was the continued military occupation of Taiwan by the KMT exile regime sufficient to cede sovereignty over Taiwan to either the PRC or the ROC. Chiang Kai-shek had declared martial law in Taiwan in 1949 and martial law remained in effect in 1952 when Japan renounced its title to Taiwan, without ceding its interest to the ROC. Thus, in 1952, the KMT's presence in Taiwan was no longer a lawful military occupation pursuant to the terms of the Japanese surrender; rather, it became an illegal and illegitimate military occupation of Taiwan without the consent of the Taiwanese people. The ROC's unlawful military occupation of Taiwan at the time of the Japanese renunciation cannot form the basis of a claim to sovereignty over Taiwan by either the PRC or the ROC. (The martial law imposed by Chiang Kai-shek's exiled KMT regime in 1949 lasted until 1987.)

Thus, Crawford's basis for arguing that in 1952 Taiwan became a territory of China, the unilateral expressions made by the Allies in the Cairo Declaration and Potsdam Proclamation and the ongoing occupation of Taiwan by an exiled regime recognized as a government of China, must be rejected. Neither, individually or taken together, is a legitimate basis for China to claim sovereignty over Taiwan. Rather, as of 1952, Taiwan's international legal status remained undetermined, with the understanding that it would be determined in the future in accordance with the principles of the U.N. Charter.

Given that Taiwan's legal status remained undetermined in 1952, there are two possibilities as to Taiwan's legal status today. First, it is possible that Taiwan's legal status remains undetermined. Alternatively, it is possible that developments and evolution since 1952 have given Taiwan the character of statehood and that Taiwan should be recognized as such. This theory of the evolution of Taiwan's statehood is the more sound and preferable view. In light of the dynamic nature of international law, and applying fundamental principles of international law, especially the right to self-determination, Taiwan's legal status must not be allowed to remain indefinitely in limbo. To treat Taiwan's legal status as perpetually unresolved is to reduce the island of Taiwan to a mere piece of property, rather than as the homeland of twenty-three million inhabitants, all of whom are entitled to basic human rights of respect and dignity. Instead, it should be recognized that developments in Taiwan since 1952, and particularly since 1988, indicate that the Taiwanese people are engaged in the ongoing process of self-determination. Accordingly, Taiwan's status should be seen as having evolved from being undetermined to that of statehood.

The period of martial law, declared by the KMT regime in 1949, lasted until 1987. Finally, in 1987, martial law was lifted and the exiled ROC's illegal military occupation of Taiwan began a gradual process of transformation. The presidency of Lee Teng-hui, which began in 1988, saw great strides in democratization and Taiwanization. In 1991, the original members of the Legislative Yuan and of the National Assembly were forced to retire as a result of the "Wild Lily" student movement. These original members, known as the "Old Thieves," had been elected in 1947 to represent constituencies on the Chinese mainland and had not stood for reelection in Taiwan since that time. In 1996, Lee Teng-hui became the first president in Taiwan to be elected by popular vote. Four-years later, Chen Shui-bian of the Democratic Progressive Party (DPP), was elected president and power was peacefully transferred. Thus, for the first time in fifty-five years, the KMT no longer controlled Taiwan against the will of the Taiwanese people and the modern era of democratic representation began. In addition to this remarkable transformation from authoritarian rule to democratic representation, Taiwan has made enviable economic progress and developed a unique national sociocultural identity. It is these developments that lead to the undeniable conclusion that the Taiwanese people have begun to exercise effective self-determination over political, economic, social, and cultural developments. Of course, self-determination is an ongoing process of continuing action, but the process is well underway in Taiwan. Likewise, there can be no doubt that Taiwan satisfies the conditions of statehood: a permanent population, effective control over a territory, a government, and the capacity to interact with other states. Furthermore, there is no requirement for statehood that a territory have an official title and, in fact, states are very flexible in their use of titles, for example, often having different official titles than their commonly used name. Thus, while Taiwan's international legal status was unresolved for a number of years, it is clear that in the years since 1988, Taiwan has evolved into statehood.

But since the ruling Kuomintang (Nationalist) regime in the past persisted in professing that the ROC represents China, and that Taiwan is only part of China (in order to perpetuate and legitimize its authoritarian power structure in Taiwan), Crawford and other have suggested that "claiming statehood" be added as the fifth requirement of statehood.[26] On July 9, 1999, Taiwan's president, Lee Teng-hui, responded to this claim unequivocally. He stated that the relationship between Taiwan and China is a "special state-to-state relationship."[27] He clearly expressed Taiwan's reality as a state and the shared conviction of the people of Taiwan that their state was independent of the PRC, thereby satisfying fully the suggested fifth requirement. President Chen Shui-bian went even further in 2002, declaring that there are two distinct countries, one on either side of the Taiwan Strait.[28]

This position was made even more explicit in 2007, when President Chen officially applied for membership in the United Nations under the name "Taiwan." (In returning Taiwan's application for U.N. membership, Secretary-General Ban Ki-moon asserted that the United Nations had recognized that Taiwan was a part of China in Resolution 2758, which recognized the PRC as the lawful government of China and expelled the representatives of Chiang Kai-shek from the General Assembly. The United States and Japan protested against Moon's assertion because General Assembly Resolution 2758 made no reference whatsoever to Taiwan and, indeed, did not recognize Taiwan as a part of China. Although the United States and Japan have adopted a "one-China policy," they distinguish between this policy and the question of Taiwan sovereignty.)[29]

While this was not a formal declaration of independence, it is difficult to imagine a more forceful assertion that Taiwan is a separate state from China. Furthermore, to require Taiwan to formally declare its independence misses two other important points. First, the PRC has made clear that it will respond with military force to any Taiwanese declaration of independence. More important, there is no need for Taiwan to formally assert its independence from China because, as the preceding discussion has made clear, Taiwan has not been a part of China since 1895. The key question here is "effective control" over Taiwan. Militant rhetoric of claim does not constitute a form of effective control. For more than six decades since the founding of the PRC in October 1949, it has not governed or extended effective control over Taiwan for a single day. Taiwan has indeed existed as a country independent of the PRC. Thanks to the common efforts of the Taiwanese people, Taiwan has evolved from a territory under military occupation and thirty-eight years of martial law rule into a sovereign, independent state. This is a great success story of self-determination. The principle of self-determination is a fundamental principle of international law having the character of *jus cogens* under the Charter of the United Nations.

When the international legal status of a territory is in dispute, a U.N.-sponsored plebiscite by all its inhabitants provides an ideal means of resolving the dispute peacefully. A plebiscite is not the only way of achieving self-determination, however. All the inhabitants of a disputed territory, through collective effort, can develop their distinct political, economic, social, and cultural system. That is effective self-determination— self-determination in action. As stated above, both international covenants on human rights accord the principle of self-determination a prominent place, stating that "all peoples have the right of self-determination. By virtue of that right they freely determine their political status, and freely pursue their economic, social and cultural development." There can be no doubt that, in the case of Taiwan, the Taiwanese people have exercised their right to freely determine their political status, and freely pursue their economic, social, and cultural development. In effect, a perpetual plebiscite, not just a one-shot ratification, has been in progress. By the people of Taiwan exercising their right to self-determination, Taiwan has evolved from a territory with an undetermined legal status to a state, both sovereign and independent.

Frustrated by the ongoing uncertainty of Taiwan's international legal status, in 2009 some Taiwanese turned to U.S. courts for relief, but were met there only with further frustration. In *Lin v. United States*, brought initially in the U.S. District Court for the District of Columbia and affirmed on appeal by the U.S. Court of Appeals, members of the "Taiwan Nation Party" sought a judicial declaration of their legal status.[30] Specifically, they argued that Taiwan's legal status was left unresolved following the San Francisco Peace Treaty, that Taiwan's legal status remained undetermined, and that as a consequence of Article 23 of the San Francisco Peace Treaty, under which the United States assumed the role of "principal occupying power" of Taiwan, the United States held temporary *de jure* sovereignty over Taiwan, until such time as Taiwan's international legal status is resolved. Accordingly, the plaintiffs in *Lin* argued that they should be recognized as noncitizen U.S. nationals and accorded all rights associated therewith.

The District Court dismissed the complaint, finding that it lacked subject matter jurisdiction to hear the case because it presented a nonjusticiable political question. The court found that resolution of the case would require it to determine who is sovereign over a specific territory, a determination the court said would require it "to address a quintessential political determination and trespass into the extremely delicate relationship between and among the United States, Taiwan and China." On appeal, the Court of Appeals expressed sympathy for the plaintiffs' ambiguous legal status:

> America and China's tumultuous relationship over the past sixty years has trapped the inhabitants of Taiwan in political purgatory. During this time the people on Taiwan have lived without any uniformly recognized government. In practical terms, this means they have uncertain status in the world community which affects the population's day-to-day lives.[31]

Despite its sympathy for the plaintiff-appellants, the Court of Appeals agreed with the District Court that the case presented a nonjusticiable political question. Although the Court of Appeals agreed with plaintiffs' assertion that the case turned on interpretation of treaties and statutory interpretation, which the court recognized as within its competence, the court found that the prudential considerations of the Political Question Doctrine required the court to refrain from exercising its authority to hear the case. The U.S. Supreme Court declined to hear an appeal of the Court of Appeals' decision.

Taiwan's sovereignty belongs to neither the ROC, the PRC, nor the United States, but rather rests with all the inhabitants of Taiwan. This is the very essence of "popular sovereignty" in the contemporary era. The transfer of a territory is not a property transaction; a transfer affects the human rights, the well-being, and even the survival of the territory's inhabitants. Over decades, endowed with their inherent sovereignty, the people of Taiwan have worked together day in and day out to redefine their own political status and to develop their distinct economic, social, and cultural system. Their remarkable achievements in these spheres are testimony to their effective self-determination. Taiwan fulfills all the conditions of statehood under international law.

Taiwan is Taiwan, and China is China, and there are stark contrasts between these two separate states. Taiwan's history has been marked by indigenous patterns of political, economic, social, and cultural development stretching back for centuries. Taiwan, in recent years, has undergone a transition to democracy from authoritarian rule under perpetual martial law, holding its first democratic presidential election in 1996 despite Beijing's unlawful attempts to intimidate and coerce voters. The Taiwanese people today enjoy human rights and freedoms, as well as a remarkable level of economic growth. China, in contrast, continues to be under the dictatorship of the Chinese Communist Party. It has fallen back upon authoritarian practices to silence political dissent, routinely denying its citizens human rights and freedoms that are taken for granted in Taiwan.

That Taiwan has existed as an independent, sovereign state is a reality. There is no need for Taiwan to make a formal declaration of independence in the manner of the American Declaration of Independence. Yet the continued use of "Republic of China" as the official title of Taiwan has caused a great deal of confusion, both internally and externally. How to make Taiwan a "normalized" state both in name and in fact is a continuing concern of the people of Taiwan. As it should be: self-determination is a continuing process of decision and nation-building.

Notes

1. U.S. Ambassador Jessup, UNSCOR 383rd meeting (Dec. 2, 1948).

2. JAMES CRAWFORD, THE CREATION OF STATES IN INTERNATIONAL LAW, 2ND ED., 211 (2006).

3. Oliver J. Lissitzyn, Introductory remarks, 47 AM. SOC'Y INT'L L. PROC. 48, 48 (1953).

4. Bernard V. A. Roling, INTERNATIONAL LAW IN AN EXPANDED WORLD 56–67 (1960).

5. 54 Congressional Record 1742 (Jan. 22, 1917).

6. G.A. Res. 1514, 15 U.N. GAOR Supp. (No. 16) at 66, U.N. Doc. A/4684 (1960).

7. G.A. Res. 2625, 25 U.N. GAOR Supp. (No. 28) at 121, U.N. Doc. A/8028 (1970).

8. Reference re Secession of Quebec, [1998] 2 S.C.R. 217 (Can.).

9. *Id.* at ¶ 121.

10. Accordance with international law of the unilateral declaration of independence in respect of Kosovo, Advisory Opinion, 2010 I.C.J. 141 (July 22).

11. *Id.* at ¶ 51.

12. *Id.* at ¶ 56.

13. MORTON KAPLAN & NICHOLAS DEBELLEVILLE KATZENBACH, THE POLITICAL FOUNDATIONS OF INTERNATIONAL LAW 121 (1961).

14. Testimony of Ralph Johnson, Deputy Assistant Secretary of State for European and Canadian Affairs, Oct. 17, 1991, Vol. 2, No. 3, Foreign Policy Bulletin 39, 42n (Nov.–Dec. 1991).

15. European Community: Declaration on Yugoslavia and on the Guidelines on Recognition of New States (Dec. 16, 1991), *reprinted in* 31 I.L.M. 1485 (1992).

16. *Purpose of Treaty with the Republic of China*, 31 Dep't State Bull. 896 (1954).

17. 536 Parl. Deb., H.C. (5th ser.), Written Answers, 159 (1955).

18. G.A. Res. 2758, 26 U.N. GAOR Supp. (No. 29) at 2, U.N. Doc. A/8429 (1971).

19. United States Policy on Non-recognition of Communist China, Department of State Memorandum to Missions Abroad, 39 DEP'T STATE BULL. 385 (1958).

20. Joint Communiqué on the Establishment of Diplomatic Relations Between the United States and the People's Republic of China, 79 DEP'T STATE BULL. 25–26 (1979).

21. Taiwan Relations Act, 22 U.S.C. § 3301 et seq. (1979).

22. *Id.* §3303(a).

23. CRAWFORD, *supra* note 2, at 207.

24. *Id.* at 209.

25. *Id.*

26. RESTATEMENT (THIRD) OF THE FOREIGN RELATIONS LAW OF THE UNITED STATES §201, comment f.

27. Shirley A. Kan, *China/Taiwan: Evolution of the "One China" Policy—Key Statements from Washington, Beijing, and Taipei*, Congressional Research Service at 63 (Aug. 26, 2013).

28. *Id.* at 69–70.

29. *UN Rejects Taiwan Application for Entry*, N.Y. TIMES, July 24, 2007, *available at* http://www.nytimes.com/2007/07/24/world/asia/24iht-taiwan.1.6799766.html.

30. Roger C.S. Lin, et al. v. United States, 561 F.3d 502 (D.C. Cir. 2009), *cert. denied*, 130 S. Ct. 202 (2009).

31. *Id.* at 192.

3 International Governmental Organizations

INTERNATIONAL GOVERNMENTAL ORGANIZATIONS, created by nation-states to promote common purposes through agreement among themselves, serve a dual function in the global constitutive process: they act as distinctive participants in decision making and provide necessary structures of authority for other participants. Because of the increasing complexity and interdependence evident in international relations, such organizations have proliferated even more rapidly than nation-states in recent years, and they manifest varying degrees of comprehensiveness and specialization. They engage in or facilitate the collective performance of many decision functions. They may be concerned generally with all values or specialized to particular values, and they may be global, regional, or local in geographic reach.

Nation-states, to enhance cooperation, have moved from ad hoc, occasional conferences toward establishing permanent, continuous structures of cooperation. Understandably, such cooperative enterprises began on a limited scale with respect to particular subject matters. Many of the organizations that came into being in the nineteenth century, such as the various European river commissions, the International Telegraph Union (1864), and the Universal Postal Union (1874), addressed specific areas of concern. A comprehensive, multipurpose organization, the League of Nations, came into being following World War I. The International Labour Organization was also created during the same period. The League of Nations, which continued to be centrally focused on Europe, was less than universal and fell far short of achieving its goals of maintaining world minimum order.

The United Nations, which celebrated its sixty-fifth anniversary in 2010, has built on the experience of the League of Nations and is the most comprehensive general purpose organization in the world. As the keystone of the contemporary system of international governmental organizations, it provides the backbone structures of authority for the global constitutive process in order to secure both minimum and optimum world order. Since its creation, the United Nations has undergone significant constitutive development, including greatly expanded membership and activities. The U.N. Charter established six principal organs (the General Assembly, the Security Council, the Economic and Social Council, the Trusteeship Council, the International Court of Justice, and the Secretariat). The General Assembly has become a worldwide forum for expressing the intense aspirations for change demanded by both developed and developing states and has greatly expanded its base of authority. Similarly, the Security Council has been transformed, through broad conceptions of minimum order, into an agency for the more general application of policies and has taken on a greatly expanded role with preventive diplomacy and increasingly multifunctional operations. The Economic and Social Council, with its expanding concern for economic, social, cultural, and humanitarian affairs, is carrying forward its formidable work toward creating conditions for optimum fulfillment of values around the globe. The Trusteeship Council, having completed its historic mission concerning trust territories, now meets where occasion may require. The International Court of Justice, another major organ of the United Nations, plays an important judicial role and has experienced an increasingly busy caseload, although it is hampered by a lack of compulsory jurisdiction. The Secretariat of the United Nations, headed by the secretary-general, is the permanent executive arm, providing a corps of international civil servants.

The United Nations undertook a series of reforms in the 1990s under the leadership of then-Secretary-General Kofi Annan. The reforms focused on the revitalization and restructuring of the U.N. intergovernmental machinery, with, for example, the creation of a deputy secretary-general and the U.N. Development Group in 1997. These efforts were aimed at creating more dynamic and effective relations among the major intergovernmental organs and were a crucial component of the reform process. More recently, Secretary-General Ban Ki-moon has boosted efforts to create a reform agenda that will streamline the organization and create greater accountability and efficiency in the United Nations' wide-ranging operations.

The U.N. System

The United Nations is fortified by a network of fifteen international governmental organizations known as Specialized Agencies and other entities and committees that specialize in particular values or subjects. These functional organizations play specialized roles in the world arena, and their activities contribute significantly to the attainment and maintenance of optimum world order as part of the U.N. system. The fifteen Specialized Agencies are: the Food and Agriculture Organization (FAO); International Civil Aviation Organization (ICAO); International Fund for Agricultural Development (IFAD); International Labour Organization (ILO); International Maritime Organization (IMO); International Monetary Fund (IMF); International Telecommunication Union (ITU); U.N. Educational, Scientific, and Cultural Organization (UNESCO); U.N. Industrial Development Organization (UNIDO); Universal Postal Union (UPU); World Bank Group (WBG); World Health Organization (WHO); World Intellectual Property Organization (WIPO); World Meteorological Organization (WMO); and the U.N. World Tourism Organization (UNWTO).

The World Trade Organization (WTO), technically not one of the fifteen Specialized Agencies, has become an extremely vital and important part of the U.N. system. The WTO is sometimes known as "the United Nations of Economy and Trade." It provides a critical function in facilitating international commerce and trade and contributing to the attainment of optimum order in our globalizing world.

The cooperation of nation-states occurs not only at the global level but also at the regional level. Interdependence requires that cooperation of nation-states be carried forward at all community levels. The U.N. Charter envisages and encourages the development of regional organizations so that collaborative arrangements can be made to fit particular needs of specific regions. These regional organizations, dealing with defense, trade, human rights, dispute settlement, and other matters, are highly diverse; and in the post–Cold War era, multilateral regional organizations have been playing an unprecedented role in many fields, forming part of the tension between what have been called the new regionalism and the new globalism.[1] Most operate independently without formal ties to the central organization—the United Nations. Notable among the regional organizations of general scope are the Organization of American States (OAS), the African Union (AU), the European Union (EU), the League of Arab States, the Association of Southeast Asian Nations (ASEAN), the Asia-Pacific Economic Cooperation (APEC), the Pacific Islands Forum (PIF), the Union of South American Nations (USAN), and the Commonwealth of Independent States (CIS), made up of former Soviet republics. Each projects a program of broad concern and seeks to employ local resources to pursue regional cooperation for established goals.

The North Atlantic Treaty Organization (NATO) and the now defunct Warsaw Treaty Organization (Warsaw Pact), two rival alliances arising from the Cold War, once symbolized the postwar East-West conflict, but the collapse of the Soviet Union and subsequent dissolution of the Warsaw Pact have altered the balance of power in Europe. NATO has been transformed into a peacekeeping alliance aimed at combating regional instability and based on mutual cooperation with non-NATO countries, including those of the former Soviet bloc, some of which have even joined NATO. The Euro-Atlantic Partnership Council allows the former Soviet nuclear power Ukraine to consult with NATO in times of regional crisis, creating a new security council that spans the European continent.[2] The council's membership numbers fifty, including both NATO and non-NATO member states. Beginning in late 2001, NATO members engaged in security operations in Afghanistan after taking command of the United Nations' International Security Assistance Force (ISAF) and cooperated on the enforcement of a no-fly zone in Libya in 2011 to limit the ability of Muammar Gaddafi's government to carry out human rights abuses against its own people. This issue is discussed further in chapter 19.

The development of the European Union is particularly noteworthy. Beginning with the European Coal and Steel Community (formed by France, West Germany, Italy, Belgium, the Netherlands, and Luxembourg) and later joined by the European Economic Community and the European Atomic Energy Community, the European Union has come a long way. The European Union's regional prominence has continued to grow following the end of the Cold War as new member states have joined and expanded Europe's influence into areas that were once the domain of the Soviet Union. As of 2013, there were twenty-eight EU member nations. The European Union's institutions manifest certain distinct features—often characterized as "supranational"—notably the important authority in policy making and execution conferred on commissioners to act on behalf of the community independently of their governments, and the competence of community organs to deal directly with individuals and business enterprises within member states. The European Union has adopted a leadership role in a number of international issues such as global warming and peacekeeping in regions such as the Middle East. In 2008, the European Union undertook its first maritime operation to protect ships from pirate attacks off the coast of Somalia. Together, EU members continue to strive for greater integration and monetary union as they come to grips with the challenges posed by the recent financial crisis, with national leaders seeking cooperative solutions to ensure the ongoing economic stability of the region.

The Association of Southeast Asian Nations (ASEAN) was founded in 1967 and has grown to include ten member nations: Brunei, Burma (Myanmar), Cambodia, Indonesia, Laos, Malaysia, the Philippines, Singapore, Thailand, and Vietnam. Throughout the twentieth century, ASEAN focused much of its energies on economic growth in its region as well as increased peace and stability. More recently, it has begun to pursue environmental concerns related to air pollution, the protection of wildlife, and global warming. In recent years, ASEAN has sought greater cooperation with the United Nations. The U.N. General Assembly granted ASEAN observer status in 2006, and the United Nations has pledged to support ASEAN in its efforts to achieve integration and stability and to reduce economic and social disparities across Southeast Asia.

Established in 1989, the Asia-Pacific Economic Cooperation (APEC) offers a forum for its twenty-one Pacific Rim member economies, including the United States, to cooperate on issues related to regional trade and investment. APEC's self-stated mission is to support sustainable economic growth and prosperity in the Asia-Pacific region through free and open trade and investment. Its members account for a significant portion of the world's population and economic activity. Its objectives include promoting regional economic integration and growth and enhancing security through initiatives on subjects such as food security, emergency preparedness, public health, and terrorism.

International Organizations as Subjects of International Law

Although today it is taken for granted that international governmental organizations, forming an expanding global network, are appropriate "subjects" of international law, this recognition did not come about without a legal battle. For a long time it was widely held that nation-states—and only nation-states—were the exclusive subjects of international law. The question of the legal status of the League of Nations, though widely discussed, was never judicially determined. The issue of the United Nations' international legal personality was faced squarely by the International Court of Justice in 1949 in the landmark case *Reparations for Injuries Suffered in the Service of the United Nations*.[3] After Count Bernadotte of Wisborg, the U.N. mediator in Palestine, was murdered in 1948, the United Nations, while considering whether to bring a claim against Israel (then not yet a member of the United Nations) for its failure to prevent or punish the murderers, was confronted with the question of whether it was legally competent to file such a claim. The General Assembly directed the following question to the court for an advisory opinion:

> In the event of an agent of the United Nations in the performance of his duties suffering injury in circumstances involving the responsibility of a State, has the United Nations, as an Organization, the capacity to bring an international claim against the responsible *de jure* or *de facto* government with a view to obtaining the reparation due in respect of the damage caused (a) to the United Nations or (b) to the victim or to persons entitled through him?[4]

To answer that question, the court considered it necessary to examine first whether the United Nations possesses an international personality. In words ringing and comprehensive, the court stated:

> The subjects of law in any legal system are not necessarily identical in their nature or in the extent of their rights, and their nature depends upon the needs of the community. Throughout its history, the development of international law has been influenced by the requirements of international life, and the progressive increase in the collective activities of States has already given rise to instances of action upon the international plane by certain entities which are not States. This development culminated in the establishment in June 1945 of an international organization whose purposes and principles are specified in the Charter of the United

Nations. But to achieve these ends the attribution of international personality is indispensable.[5]

The court then proceeded to note the wide range of U.N. functions, those it actually performed as well as those authorized by its charter. Stressing that such functions could be explained only in terms of the international personality of the United Nations, the court stated:

> The Organization was intended to exercise and enjoy, and is in fact exercising and enjoying, functions and rights which can only be explained on the basis of the possession of a large measure of international personality and the capacity to operate upon an international plane. It is at present the supreme type of international organization, and it could not carry out the intentions of its founders if it was devoid of international personality. It must be acknowledged that its Members, by entrusting certain functions to it, with the attendant duties and responsibilities, have clothed it with the competence required to enable those functions to be effectively discharged.[6]

Accordingly, the court has come to the conclusion that the organization is an "international person."[7]

What does it mean for the United Nations or any other organization to possess an international personality? It means, in the words of the court, "that it is a subject of international law and capable of possessing international rights and duties, and that it has capacity to maintain its rights by bringing international claims."[8] These international claims can be brought against a nonmember as well as a member of the United Nations.

In this unprecedented opinion, the court also sounded a cautionary note, stating that to say the United Nations is an international person "is not the same thing as saying that it is a State, which it certainly is not, or that its legal personality and rights and duties are the same as those of a State. Still less is it the same thing as saying that it is a 'super-State,' whatever that expression may mean."[9]

With this bold stroke the court made it perfectly clear that states are not the only subjects of international law. Many other international governmental organizations, like the United Nations, with their own objectives, structures, and functions in the world arena, similarly possess international personality and are subjects of international law.

Membership in international governmental organizations is generally open only to nation-states, with further restrictions as may be imposed by the constitutive agreement involved. Membership in the United Nations, for example, is stipulated in Article 4 of the charter:

> Membership in the United Nations is open to all other peace-loving states which accept the obligations contained in the present Charter and, in the judgments of the Organization, are able and willing to carry out these obligations.

The admission of any such state to membership in the United Nations will be effected by a decision of the General Assembly upon the recommendation of the Security Council.

As expounded by International Court of Justice in two of its advisory opinions, a member cannot predicate its consent to the admission of a state on conditions not specified in Article 4(1), and a recommendation for admission by the Security Council must precede a General Assembly decision.[10] This means that admission of a new member is subject to veto by a permanent member of the Security Council.

Obviously, for most international governmental organizations, the most important base of power is formal authority granted by member states to the organization. The formal authority thus granted varies widely from organization to organization in terms of area of concern, the degree of decision-making authority, the scope of people to be affected, and the applicable constitutive instrument. Particular grants of legal capacity and of certain privileges and immunities are especially noteworthy because of their importance in affording proper access and protection and in securing the independent and effective performance of official duties. Such grants again differ from organization to organization and are communicated through constitutive instruments, agreements between organizations and member states, or national legislation.

Article 104 of the U.N. Charter states: "The Organization shall enjoy in the territory of each of its Members such legal capacity as may be necessary for the exercise of its functions and the fulfillment of its purposes." And Article 105 stipulates in part:

1. The Organization shall enjoy in the territory of each of its Members such privileges and immunities as are necessary for the fulfillment of its purpose.
2. Representatives of the Members of the United Nations and officials of the Organization shall similarly enjoy such privileges and immunities as are necessary for the independent exercise of their functions in connection with the Organization.

Note the emphasis on functional necessity as the basis for and extent of privileges and immunities. These privileges and immunities, though often compared to those customarily enjoyed by national diplomats, are more limited in scope and nature. Understandably, nation-state elites are reluctant to accord the functionaries of international governmental organizations more privileges and immunities than necessary. The Convention on the Privileges and Immunities of the United Nations (1946) reiterates that the United Nations has juridical personality and spells out its legal capacity to contract, to acquire and dispose of property, and to sue.

International governmental organizations increasingly perform many of the functions traditionally discharged through bilateral diplomacy. They also perform many innovative functions generated partly by global interdependence and partly by the wide-ranging goals projected by the world community.

For many organizations the intelligence function is not only an activity but a raison d'être. In fact, the initial stimulus to form international organizations stemmed from the recognition that, in certain specialized or technical areas, sharing information and knowledge among nations was essential to the growth of the field. Organizations whose formation was motivated by such considerations include the Universal Postal Union and the International Telecommunication Union, which traces its history to the founding of the International Telegraph Union in 1865. Information gathering and dissemination is today the principal focus of some international organizations, such as the International Meteorological Organization (IMO). For other organizations it forms an essential part of their prime mission, as exemplified by reports prepared for the U.N. Security Council, which are instrumental in the council's efforts to maintain international peace and security.

The promotion of goals and policies thought to be desirable is a highly visible function of international governmental organizations. The numerous resolutions passed by the U.N. General Assembly, though generally hortatory in nature, have had a clear influence on the conduct of nations. Designating a particular time to study and act on an issue, such as International Women's Year (1975), the International Year of the Child (1979), the International Year of the Family (1994), the International Year of Volunteers (2001), the International Year of Freshwater (2003), the International Year of Biodiversity (2010), and the International Year of Cooperatives (2012), exemplifies another aspect of the promoting function.

The expansion of the prescribing function by international governmental organizations, though not without controversy, has been remarkable. As discussed in chapter 22, international governmental organizations assist in the development of authoritative prescriptions in both the public and private sectors. The preeminent role of the General Assembly has been especially striking. Although few have questioned that organizations can prescribe for their own members through internal decision processes, the competence of organizations to conclude agreements with states or other entities has been disputed, a problem reminiscent largely of the lingering myth that states are the only proper subjects of international law. In practice, however, international governmental organizations do enter into various agreements—for example, agreements conferring privileges and immunities on the organization. A keen observer of the work of the U.N. specialized agencies has noted the emerging trends as follows: "While the obsession with the paramount nature of sovereignty still reigns supreme in power politics, the law of Specialized Agencies, in so far as it follows in the wake of scientific and technical progress, has tended to intensify methods of functional co-operation and promote a measure of world integration."[11] This cooperation and integration have been advanced by the acceptance of the doctrine of implied powers expressly granted in their constitutive documents but also those implied from the documents and those developed in practice.

The prescribing function, at least as practiced by the United Nations, can extend to nonmember nations. Article 2(6) of the U.N. Charter provides: "The Organization shall ensure that States which are not Members of the United Nations act in accordance with these Principles so far as may be necessary for the maintenance of international peace and security." This deviation from the general principle that only the parties to a treaty are bound by it rests on the special character of the United Nations as the paramount organization endowed with the task of maintaining international peace and security and characterized by virtual universality in membership.

The invoking and applying functions, like the prescribing function, have expanded in scope despite perceived encroachments on "national sovereignty." The sanctions attempted by the United Nations against the old apartheid regime of South Africa on the Namibia question and then more generally with respect to domestic apartheid provide a notable example. Clearly the prescribing function would be an empty exercise if the prescriptions could not be invoked and applied. The expansion in the area of human rights enforcement is a particularly remarkable development. Although some structures, such as the former European Commission on Human Rights and the European Court of Human Rights, both of which began operating in the 1950s, have been in place for some time, others are of more recent vintage, such as the adoption of an individual petition system by the United Nations for redress of violations of the International Covenant on Civil and Political Rights. International tribunals for the former Yugoslavia and Rwanda have been established by the U.N. Security Council to prosecute grave violations of the 1949 Geneva Conventions and international humanitarian law. The United Nations was also instrumental in the formation of a tribunal to try members of Cambodia's Khmer Rouge for crimes against humanity.

The terminating function may operate by various mechanisms. The agreements concluded by international governmental organizations, like those concluded by states, may provide for denunciation or other means of withdrawal from the agreement. Such agreements may also be for a limited period and may expire of their own force if not renewed. The organizations may by exercise of their internal processes suspend or expel a noncomplying member. Suspension has generally been used only for nonpayment of dues. Expulsion is rarely used and, as mentioned above, may be counterproductive.

Finally, international governmental organizations are continually appraising their roles and performance and refining their approach. The important role of international governmental organizations as participants in the international legal process has greatly expanded in the past several decades and will likely continue to expand for the foreseeable future. Specialized organizations will become ever more important as scientific, technological, and cultural interdependence increases. The United Nations, given its broad mission of maintaining international peace and security, as well as advancing the welfare of all peoples, has continued to retain its position as a paramount participant in international law.

The sustained growth of international governmental organizations reflects not merely the increasing vigor of transnational interactions but also the shared perception of participants that many of their preferred values can be obtained only through or in conjunction with collaborative transnational action. In dealing with problems of transnational magnitude and impact, such organizations dilute the importance of historic, somewhat arbitrary and unnatural, national boundaries. They may gradually provide alternatives to the overweening power of nation-state officials and may help open the internal activities of nation-states to external observation and scrutiny. They begin to constitute, in a manner of speaking, an organized conscience of the world and to bring a world public opinion to bear on world affairs. Additionally, the international civil servants who staff such organizations increasingly develop loyalties to the organizations themselves and seek, in various ways, to fortify their viability as instruments of inclusive goals.

Though the proliferation of international governmental organizations has been impressive, the aggregate contribution of such organizations to global decision making has been less so. The resources, independent of state control, made available to such organizations have been far from adequate. The structures of the organizations remain somewhat primitive, lacking proper regional or functional balance. Their technical procedures are largely unsystematized and uneconomical. Too often particular national elites still view such organizations as instruments of their own national policy rather than as instruments to clarify and protect genuine common interests. In theory, international governmental officials (international civil servants) are required to perform their functions independently of outside influence, including that of their home state. But in practice such independence is often compromised. A careful balance among member states is maintained in staffing international governmental organizations; and, under a reward system having to do with the support of the home state, an international official often feels compelled to maintain ties with his or her home state, giving rise to the problem of multiple or divided loyalties.

The United Nations and World Order

When the United Nations marked its fortieth anniversary in 1985, it was characterized as an organization that, though still alive, had failed to maintain world peace and security.[12] The United Nations was perceived as "drowning in a sea of paperwork and suffocating under an avalanche of paper," as an organization of double standards, with the General Assembly seen "less and less as a forum which expresses the decent opinion of mankind."[13] These popular perceptions, though at the time painfully true to a considerable extent, must be contrasted to the United Nations' achievements today.

At its fiftieth anniversary in 1995, massive institutional reform was under way in response to widespread criticism; yet since then the United Nations has enjoyed a dramatic resurgence in popularity. Today the United Nations is seen by many as an institution which, at this stage in history, "provides the most realistic opportunity for developing reasonable rules" in the area of humanitarian intervention and the achievement of a just world order.[14] With the demise of the bipolar world hopes have reemerged for a new world order where the dictates of ideological competition may give way to greater political, social, and economic cooperation. The new world order envisioned is to be built on the twin pillars of international law and international institutions. A renewed, resurgent United Nations, a dramatic reduction in nuclear and conventional weapons, and an increase in the number of new democracies are presenting new opportunities for enhancing global cooperation.[15]

A widespread lament has always been that the United Nations has fallen far short of the shared expectations of its founders. It has failed, by and large, in its role as preserver of minimum world order. Though World War III has not come to pass thus far, nuclear terror, previously maintained under a precarious system of superpower deterrence, continues as nuclear weapons and technology fall into the hands of unstable, fragmented states. Armed conflicts of lesser magnitudes, many stemming from long-suppressed ethnic, religious, and cultural differences that have emerged with the thawing of the Cold War, and the continuation of oppressive regimes have sustained and heightened expectations of violence. According to varying estimates, sizable interstate armed force was used about two hundred times in the four decades following World War II. Since 1989, there have been roughly one hundred armed conflicts in the world, the majority of which were internal. The helplessness and frustration people have felt in dealing with governmental and private terrorism have generated a pervasive sense of international anarchy and personal insecurity.

The original plan of establishing a standing U.N. force has never come into being. The unity of the major powers in the maintenance of world order, as contemplated by the framers of the U.N. Charter, long proved illusory as the veto power accorded the five permanent members of the Security Council became a tool of obstruction rather than one of big-power cooperation. But the collapse of the Soviet Union, with Russia assuming the former Soviet seat on the Security Council, seemed to have freed the council to intervene in disputes around the globe for a time, and the council was able to become increasingly interventionist in the handling of regional conflicts. Given the fluidity of the post–Cold War order, however, nothing can be taken for granted. The invocation of the inviolability of "national sovereignty" is by no means a thing of the past.[16] Nevertheless, the expansion of peacekeeping missions around the world has transformed the United Nations' role in global security.[17]

The enhanced authority of the General Assembly to cope with crises of peace and security in the event of the paralysis of the Security Council, as authorized by the Uniting for Peace Resolution, has proved less than effective. The incongruity between voting numbers and effective power, as exacerbated by bloc interests and politics, is such that many of the assembly's numerous resolutions simply cannot, and do not, command serious attention and effective support. (The total contribution of half its membership amounts to about 2 percent of its total budget.) The raw, reflexive display of automatic numerical majority, without adequate consideration of the merits of each resolution, has often resulted in double standards and has done much to alienate "the minority" whose effective support (and financial support) really counts. The democratic principle of one-state-one-vote, when divorced from the realities of population, wealth, power, and respect and from the principle of responsibility, becomes hollow and self-defeating. For many years, bypassing, rather than turning to, the United Nations in times of crisis was the norm, in contrast to the last decade.

Other shortcomings of the United Nations already alluded to or to be added include the festering issue of split loyalties among international officials and civil servants; an overblown and inefficient bureaucracy; the tendency of the organization to be a paper mill, long on rhetoric and short on action; and the tendency to be "an octopus walking in every direction at once."[18]

And after marking its fiftieth anniversary in 1995, the United Nations has continued to come under criticism. Some, believing it is supposed to be an international superforce, have imagined the United Nations "to be like the Great Oz, a lot of sound and fury but nothing behind the show."[19] In the post–Cold War world, there is a sense that the United Nations is overstretched, in search of missions, and without clear priorities.[20]

Much can be criticized in terms of both the past record and the current shape of the United Nations. But would the world community be better off without it? Definitely not! Its achievements, given the constraints of reality, have been substantial and significant. In the area of maintaining minimum world order, the United Nations has taken on an increasingly important role. The last sixty-five years have seen an evolution of U.N. peacekeeping to embrace preventive diplomacy, peacemaking, and peacebuilding. Since 1945, more than sixty U.N. peacekeeping operations have been instrumental in preventing the escalation of armed conflicts, terminating hostilities, preventing the recurrence of fighting, and facilitating conflict resolution in areas such as India and Pakistan, Central America, the Middle East, Haiti, Africa, and, since the breakup of the former Soviet Union, in Eastern and Central Europe. For example, U.N. peacekeepers facilitated the withdrawal of Soviet troops from the Baltics. Between 1988 and 1997 alone thirty peacekeeping forces were created, and, as of 2013, there were fifteen peacekeeping operations under way in places such as Afghanistan, Cyprus, Kosovo, East Timor, Liberia, southern Lebanon, the Democratic Republic of the Congo, and Haiti. In 1988, U.N. peacekeeping forces were awarded the Nobel Peace Prize.

In addition, the United Nations, in pursuit of peaceful resolution of conflicts, continues to undertake various peacemaking efforts, not only in the Security Council and the General Assembly but through the good offices of the secretary-general and his special representatives. Such efforts are currently directed to areas of protracted conflict, including the Middle East, Cyprus, Central Africa, and Central America. Thanks to the U.N.-mediated Agreement on Afghanistan, signed in Geneva in April 1988, the phased withdrawal of Soviet troops from Afghanistan was completed by February 15, 1989, as scheduled. The eight-year Iran-Iraq war was ended in 1991, with a ceasefire and withdrawal of all troops to internationally recognized boundaries called for by the Security Council. In the Persian Gulf crisis of 1990–91, the basis for international action in the form of economic sanctions and military action against Iraq lay in Security Council resolutions, rather than in unilateral action. In 1995, after four years of U.N. supervision, the U.N. Protection Force (UNPROFOR), which were deployed in Bosnia-Herzegovina for aid distribution and the protection of "safe areas," formally transferred power to international NATO-commanded forces who would oversee implementation of the Dayton peace accord.

In spite of slow and halting progress, the United Nations has persisted in its original effort toward the elimination and control of weapons of mass destruction and the peaceful use of nuclear energy. Disarmament has been part of the mission of the United Nations since its inception. Indeed, the U.N. Charter itself specifies that the Security Council should facilitate disarmament among its members consistent with its mission to maintain international peace and security. Slowing the escalation of deadly weaponry has come within reach in the decades since the founding of the International Atomic Energy Agency (IAEA) in 1957 and the end of the Cold War in the 1980s. Both the United States and the Russian Federation have reached unilateral moratoriums on nuclear testing. There are currently more than twenty major global and regional arms control and disarmament treaties in place, controlling or prohibiting the production, storage, and use of conventional, nuclear, biological, and chemical weapons.

Since September 11, 2001, there has been increasing international concern not just with regard to nuclear weapons being used by certain governments or nations but with regard to nuclear weapons being acquired and used by non-state actors posing terrorist threats. Stemming from this concern, the Security Council adopted Resolution 1540: Non-Proliferation of Weapons of Mass Destruction in 2004, which calls on member states to "renew and fulfill their commitment to multilateral cooperation... as part of pursuing and achieving their common objectives of non-proliferation and of promoting international cooperation for peaceful purposes."[21] In 2009, the General Assembly adopted Resolution 63/60 entitled "Measures to prevent terrorists from acquiring weapons of mass destruction," urging all member states to "take and strengthen national measures, as appropriate, to prevent terrorists from acquiring weapons of mass destruction, their means of delivery and materials and technologies related to their manufacture."[22]

In an effort to revive the United States' arms control efforts in the twenty-first century, and to strengthen the world's non-proliferation system, U.S. President Barack Obama hosted a Nuclear Security Summit in April 2010 as a precursor to the United Nations' Nuclear Non-proliferation Treaty (NPT) Conference later that year. The summit resulted in forty-seven nations signing onto a plan which would keep the world's nuclear material out of the hands of terrorist groups through means such as locking down all loose nuclear material and instituting measures against smuggling. Perhaps the most significant achievement of the summit was securing commitments from regions that had a history of failing to prioritize nuclear security, such as Latin America and the Middle East. The United Nations' NPT Review Conference, which convened a week later in May 2010, resulted in the adoption of a twenty-two-point Action Plan on Nuclear Disarmament. The conference underscored the importance of resolving all cases of noncompliance with safeguards in full conformity with the IAEA statute and member states' respective legal obligations.

The United Nations' vital role in accelerating decolonization and emancipation is historic. At the end of World War II, more than 750 million people lived in colonial and other dependent territories. Today, all eleven trust territories have either become independent states or have voluntarily chosen to associate with a state. The non-self-governing territories under the jurisdiction of the Special Committee of 24 on Decolonization dwindled to seventeen territories as of 2013.

The United Nations has been the driving force behind the contemporary global human rights movement (see chapter 12). From the development of a global bill of human rights and a host of ancillary instruments to the crusade against apartheid and racial discrimination, the United Nations has been indispensable. It has afforded special protection and assistance to millions of refugees and to countless children around the world. It has promulgated and passed many resolutions dealing with the prevention of human rights abuses and the protection of certain classes of people, such as children or the disabled. The United Nations is poised to continue to provide human beings with relief, refuge, and development far into the twenty-first century.

Its work in the codification and development of international law ranges from the law of treaties and the law of diplomatic relations to the law of the sea and the law of outer space and includes important documentations of customary prescription and clarification of U.N. Charter obligations.

Finally, in its pursuit of optimum world order, the United Nations has also dealt, and at times more effectively, with manifold problems relating to economic, social, humanitarian, and cultural development: trade, monetary systems, environment, population, agriculture and food, hunger, disease, poverty, industry, science and technology, transnational corporations, social development, financial assistance, education, communications and transportation, technical cooperation, and emergency relief.

Accordingly, despite "unfulfilled dreams," the United Nations has filled and continues to fill a vital role in facilitating transnational cooperation. As former Secretary-General Javier Perez de Cuellar once pointed out, without "the safety net" that the United Nations provides, "the world would certainly be a much more dangerous and disorderly place."[23] And to echo a popular sentiment: if the United Nations did not exist today, humankind would have to invent something like it. The dreams of the founders were visionary and inspiring. It is up to each succeeding generation to experience and express contemporary dreams in light of the legacy, a legacy which, fortunately for humankind, has reached into the new century. As the Independent Working Group on the Future of the United Nations stated in 1993, the United Nations did not come through its first fifty years unscathed; and "like any good vessel, it needs refitting, weak timbers replaced, compasses reset."[24] The United Nations can only be as effective as its members make it. The United Nations has proven that in times of human calamity, it is instrumental in coordinating international humanitarian efforts to bring aid to those in need, such as after the 2004 tsunami in Indonesia or extensive flooding in Pakistan in 2010. This level of coordination will be necessary to tackle the world's emergencies, big and small. Recent U.N. reports on the status of the Millennium Development Goals (discussed further in chapter 18) and the state of the world economy, such as the World Economic Situation and Prospects reports, indicate that many countries and peoples are in need.[25] The members of the United Nations are capable of addressing these needs and have an opportunity, made available by sweeping technological, social, and political change, to face the twenty-first century with a new spirit of global cooperation and commitment to the common interest of humankind.

Notes

1. *See* Anthony Clark Arend, *The United Nations, Regional Organizations, and Military Operations: The Past and Present*, 7 DUKE J. COMP. & INT'L L. 3 (1996).

2. *See* THE BOSTON GLOBE, July 10, 1997, at A1.

3. Advisory Opinion, 1949 I.C.J. 173 (Apr. 11).

4. *Id.* at 175.

5. *Id.* at 178.

6. *Id.*

7. *Id.* at 175.

8. *Id.*

9. *Id.*

10. Conditions of Admission of a State to the United Nations (Charter Article 4), Advisory Opinion, 1948 I.C.J. 57 (May 28); Competence of the General Assembly for the Admission of a State to the United Nations, Advisory Opinion, 1950 I.C.J. 1 (Mar. 3).

11. CHARLES HENRY ALEXANDROWICZ, THE LAW-MAKING FUNCTION OF THE SPECIALIZED AGENCIES OF THE UNITED NATIONS 161 (1973).

12. Tommy T. B. Koh, *The United Nations: Is There Life After Forty?*, 21 STAN. J. INT'L L. 1 (1985).

13. *Id.*

14. SEAN D. MURPHY, HUMANITARIAN INTERVENTION: THE UNITED NATIONS IN AN EVOLVING WORLD ORDER 1–3 (1996).

15. *Id.*

16. N.Y. TIMES, Mar. 8, 1993, at 1–10, col. 1.

17. Uniting for Peace Resolution (Nov. 3, 1950), G.A. Res. 377A(V), 5 U.N. GAOR Supp. (No. 20) at 10, U.N. Doc. A/1775 (1951).

18. Sadruddin Aga Khan & Maurice F. Strong, *Proposals to Reform the U.N., "Limping" in Its 40th Year*, N.Y. TIMES, Oct. 8, 1985, at A31, col. 1.

19. SAN DIEGO UNION-TRIB., Aug. 3, 1997, at G1.

20. N.Y. TIMES, Oct. 22, 1995, at 1-1, col. 5, http://www.nytimes.com/1995/10/22/world/the-un-at-50-the-challenges-the-un-at-50-facing-the-task-of-reinventing-itself.html?src=pm&pagewanted=1.

21. S.C. Res. 1540, S/RES/1540 (Apr. 28, 2004).

22. G.A. Res. 63/60, A/RES/63/60 (Jan. 12, 2009).

23. N.Y. TIMES, Sept. 10, 1984, at A13, col. 1.

24. THE UNITED NATIONS IN ITS SECOND HALF-CENTURY: A REPORT OF THE INDEPENDENT WORKING GROUP ON THE FUTURE OF THE UNITED NATIONS 3 (1995).

25. UNITED NATIONS, DEVELOPMENT POLICY AND ANALYSIS DIVISION, WORLD ECONOMIC SITUATION AND PROSPECTS, http://www.un.org/en/development/desa/policy/wesp/.

4 Nongovernmental Organizations and Associations

AS THE WORLD constitutive process of authoritative decision becomes increasingly democratized, the role of nongovernmental groups in transnational interactions has continued to grow enormously. In this chapter nongovernmental groups include, and go beyond, those associated with NGOs, nongovernmental organizations known within the circles of the United Nations and other international governmental organizations. Nongovernmental actors can be conveniently divided into two categories: political parties and nongovernmental organizations and associations (including pressure groups and private associations). Political parties, though often not formally recognized, exert effective influence on many transnational decisions. Pressure groups, which attempt to influence both formal and effective decisions, are increasingly transnational in operation and reach. Multiplying hosts of private associations, which include multinational corporations, are primarily concerned with values other than power and manifest their growing transnational character in membership, objective, structure, activity, and impact.

Political Parties

Political parties are organized groups that present comprehensive programs of policy and seek to place their candidates in government positions through election or other means. They play an important part in global processes of effective power and affect the performance of many functions in authoritative decisions.

Political parties make their strongest impact in the organization and management of particular nation-states. Party representatives gain access to the public organs of the nation-state through election, appointment, and integration into executive, legislative, judicial, and administrative institutions at all levels of government. The same person may be a key actor both within a political party and within a state's structures of authority. In addition, political parties often provide unofficial channels for policies to be initiated and communicated.

The way any particular state is shaped by political parties naturally has its external impact. Modern techniques of mass communication and transportation enable political parties to become highly organized and to centralize their command, coordinate national and international operations, and participate effectively in power processes, both in and out of government and within and beyond the boundaries of any nation-state. Although international governmental organizations may make no formal provision for access by political parties as such, representatives of parties do gain access through other identifications, especially those of the state. In the transnational parliamentary arenas, such as the Consultative Assembly of the Council of Europe, the participants, being parliamentarians conditioned by domestic party politics, often find themselves torn by the clashes between transnational party groupings and loyalties and their national identifications.

Some political parties deliberately seek transnational effects and play roles in intelligence, recommending, prescribing, invoking, and appraising functions, having significant effects on the formulation and application of global policies. In recent decades, four major transnational political party movements—Communist, Socialist, Christian Democratic, and Liberal International—have operated with varying degrees of effectiveness. These transnationals differ significantly in projected goals and platforms, formal structures and official staffs, internal factions, available resources, strategies employed, and overall influence as measured by affiliated groups and external relations.

The greatest threat to shared power in global decision making posed by political parties is that they may degenerate into "political orders," which are characterized by monopoly of power and the claim of exclusive legality. The Communist Internationale once typified such a transnational political order. After the Comintern and Cominform were dismantled in 1943 and the mid-1950s, respectively, the International Department of the Communist Party of the Soviet Union was often regarded as their successor embodiment, until the collapse of the Soviet system left communism largely discredited across the globe. The Chinese Communist Party, however, remained and has achieved increasing prominence in recent decades. The party exercises a monopoly over political power in China and actively suppresses dissent that may threaten is legitimacy, although ideological shifts have allowed some free-market reforms ostensibly to take place. A lesser threat is that political parties may be so parochial and nationalistic as to have little identification with the range of humanity.

Nongovernmental Organizations

A salient trend in contemporary global politics and relations is the phenomenal growth of nongovernmental organizations (NGOs), as contrasted with international governmental organizations (IGOs). Since its creation in 1907, the Union of International Associations at Brussels has maintained a central registry and information service for all international organizations, nongovernmental as well as governmental. Its *Yearbook of International Organizations* lists more than 66,000 nongovernmental and intergovernmental organizations of all types.[1] The numbers of nongovernmental organizations in the broadest sense are staggering, and the days when NGOs adopted a low profile are gone. The activity of NGOs has become an essential dimension of all levels of public life around the world.

Nongovernmental organizations differ greatly in membership, size, objective, structure, geographical reach, available resources, strategy, and overall effectiveness. They are increasingly transnational in each of these features and play a growing role in transnational decision making, affecting various value sectors. Today NGOs are assuming functions that previously had been considered the responsibility of states, for example, the provision of public services such as education and health; in this process, NGOs have become a significant source of development and relief assistance alongside the United Nations.[2] The values pursued by nongovernmental organizations and associations extend to each of the basic values: power, respect, enlightenment, well-being, wealth, skill, affection, and rectitude.

Those that relate to power are exemplified by various groups devoted to peace, disarmament, and national liberation movements. The status of national liberation movements, aimed at establishing authority and control over particular territory, has been controversial under international law. African liberation movements have been accorded observer status and occasionally full membership in many intergovernmental organizations. Pursuant to U.N. resolutions, they have participated in U.N. bodies in the specialized agencies and in international conferences under the aegis of the United Nations. One such movement, the African National Congress, now heads the South African government, brought to power by democratic elections. The Palestine Liberation Organization (PLO), in particular, has achieved a high international profile, achieving special observer status in the United Nations since 1974, ties to regional organizations, and recognition by many states, including Israel. In 1994, the PLO assumed authority over the West Bank when Palestinian self-rule was established in portions of the occupied territories by the Oslo peace agreement. In 2011, the Palestinian National Authority—the territories' governing body—petitioned the U.N. Security Council to recognize Palestine as a state following years of failed negotiations with Israel. The Security Council rejected the bid; however, the Palestinian Authority was successful in securing membership in the U.N. Educational, Scientific, and Cultural Organization (UNESCO) soon after. The move prompted the United States and other nations to suspend funding to UNESCO in protest, insisting that the question of Palestinian statehood ought to be settled through bilateral negotiations between the Palestinian National Authority and Israel.

Those that relate to wealth, as exemplified by the International Chamber of Commerce, trade associations, and multinational corporations, establish and maintain a global economy, affecting the production and distribution of goods and services everywhere. Those that relate to enlightenment, as exemplified by the International Press Institute and the International Law Association, gather, process, and disseminate information transnationally. Those that relate to well-being, as exemplified by environmental groups and the International Red Cross, seek to enhance health, safety, and comfort transnationally. Those that relate to skill, as exemplified by labor unions and various professional associations, attempt to maintain professional ties and collaboration transnationally. Those that relate to affection, as based on ethnic, religious, linguistic, kinship, and other ties, seek to establish and maintain congenial relationships, group identifications, and collaboration transnationally.

Those that relate to rectitude, as symbolized by the Roman Catholic Church, the World Council of Churches, the World Jewish Congress, the World Muslim Conference, and other religious organizations, formulate and communicate norms of responsible conduct transnationally. The Roman Catholic Church continues to be the religious organization with the highest degree of cohesion, leadership, and hierarchy. Unique in its internal and external relations, the Vatican maintains a diplomatic corps and possesses a recognized competence to make international agreements, although the legal status of the church remains controversial in the literature. The leader of the Roman Catholic Church is a recognized international figure who performs important decision functions in the world arena. The late Pope John Paul II, through his numerous pilgrimages to many lands, was recognized as the most traveled, most talked about, and most televised pope in history.

The organizations concerned with respect include human rights organizations, dedicated to the defense and fulfillment of human rights, and honorific societies (for example, the Nobel Foundation) that recognize and bestow honor for preeminent contributions to the common interest. Human rights organizations have proliferated so much that a "human rights industry" has emerged. Among the important human rights organizations are Amnesty International, the International Commission of Jurists, the International League for Human Rights, Anti-Slavery International (formerly known as the Anti-Slavery Society), Human Rights Watch, the International Service for Human Rights, and the Open Society Institute. Amnesty International, a winner of the Nobel Peace Prize, seeks to protect both prisoners of conscience and all other prisoners from torture and execution. The International Commission of Jurists is dedicated to fostering the understanding and observance of the rule of law and the legal protection of human rights throughout the world. The International League of Human Rights, one of the oldest human rights NGOs, is concerned with all human rights, taking as its platform the Universal Declaration of Human Rights. Anti-Slavery International has long been in the forefront of campaigns to eradicate slavery and slavery-like practices from the earth. Human Rights Watch was originally an organization dedicated to monitoring the Union of Soviet Socialist Republics' (USSR) compliance with the Helsinki Accords. Today it serves as an advocate and watchdog for addressing human rights abuses around the world. The International Service for Human Rights provides education and training for human rights advocates. The Open Society Institute was founded by billionaire George Soros to promote reforms in support of democratization and human rights as well as the development of other NGOs.

Organizations that seek particular power objectives are sometimes known as pressure groups, whereas those dedicated primarily to shaping and sharing values other than power are called private associations. Pressure groups, unlike political parties, do not present comprehensive political programs and candidates for elective office. The difference between pressure groups and private associations is often a matter of emphasis or degree, because even private associations often seek power outcomes in the sense of influencing decision making (both national and transnational) in areas of special concern.

The influence of pressure groups and private associations on decision making has grown tremendously in recent years. Such organizations circulate the globe and employ all media of communication in pursuit of their power purposes or other values. They can operate with minimal regard for national boundaries, and the communications revolution affords them practically unlimited geographic reach. Many such organizations have acquired consultative status or comparable relations with the United Nations (notably with the Economic and Social Council) or other international governmental organizations (ILO, UNESCO, WHO, FAO, and so on). Indeed, with the phenomenal growth of the NGO sector over the past twenty years, an understanding of U.N. politics would be incomplete without making an appraisal of the impact of NGOs collectively responsible for far-reaching changes to the U.N. system. Questions concerning their role in U.N. politics are assuming new importance and complexity.

The importance of nongovernmental organizations (sometimes called civil society organizations) is formally recognized by the U.N. Charter. Article 71 of the charter stipulates: "The Economic and Social Council may make suitable arrangements for consultation with nongovernmental organizations which are concerned with matters within its competence. Such arrangements may be made with international organizations and, where appropriate, with national organizations after consultation with the Member of the United Nations concerned." Effective power thus obtains a formal voice in the processes of authoritative decision, enabling nongovernmental organizations to use their expertise to serve the common interest.

The Economic and Social Council (ECOSOC) has created three categories of consultative status for NGOs: general category, special category, and roster. General category organizations are concerned with most of the activities of the council and have demonstrated capabilities to make marked and sustained contributions toward U.N. objectives.

They are closely involved with the economic and social life of the peoples of the areas they represent, and their broad membership represents major segments of populations in many countries. Special category organizations are more limited, having special concern and competence in areas of activity covered by the council. The third category, officially designated "roster," refers to other organizations that lack general or special consultative status but, in the views of the council or the U.N. Secretary-General, are capable of making occasional contributions to the work of the council or its subsidiary bodies or other U.N. bodies within their competence. The council has taken steps to increase participation of NGOs in the council's work. In 1996, ECOSOC approved Resolution 1996/31 following an in-depth review of the arrangements under which the council consults with NGOs. The resolution spelled out a number of changes to how consultative relationships would be established and operated.

The NGOs may send representatives to sit as observers and to speak at public meetings of the Economic and Social Council and its subsidiary bodies. They may submit memorandums concerning the work of the council and its subsidiary bodies, with such memorandums circulated as U.N. documents. They may also consult with the U.N. Secretariat on matters of mutual concern. General category organizations may even submit proposals for the council's agenda. For example, in 1997 NGOs dedicated to the environment, women's rights, and human rights addressed a special session of the General Assembly on the implementation of Agenda 21, the blueprint for sustainable development agreed upon at the 1992 U.N. Conference on Environment and Development (UNCED) in Rio de Janeiro (the "Earth Summit"). It was the first time in U.N. history that NGOs had addressed the General Assembly. The United Nations has also collaborated extensively with NGOs that have played an integral part in pursuing the eight Millennium Development Goals for improving human security around the globe. The prominence of NGOs' role has been highlighted by their participation in U.N. conferences and special sessions of the General Assembly.

Since 2006, the Human Rights Council, once administered under ECOSOC and called the Human Rights Commission, has been overseen by the General Assembly. Under the General Assembly, the Human Rights Council undertakes the Universal Periodic Review (UPR) to review member states' progress on human rights obligations and commitments. As part of this review, NGOs with consultative status are able to submit information on human rights, which is bundled into an "other stakeholders" report that is included in the UPR working papers. In addition, NGOs can attend the UPR's working group sessions as observers, though at these sessions they are not able to make oral or written submissions. However, NGOs are able to make statements at the Human Rights Council meetings where member states' reviews are appraised.

Nongovernmental organizations and associations exert influence on the whole range of decision functions (intelligence, promoting, prescribing, invoking, applying, terminating, and appraising). They can take stands that state officials are unable or unwilling to take, and they often represent minority interests threatened by the state. They can campaign intensely for their purposes unhampered by overall policy considerations. Some NGOs such as Amnesty International, are able to successfully employ a dual strategy, working directly with the U.N. system while maintaining an independence that allows public criticism of U.N. shortcomings and failures.[3]

In terms of the intelligence function, NGOs provide a vast global network for gathering, processing, and disseminating information on a wide range of subjects covering every value sector. This is the core function of many. They not only supplement information from governmental sources but often obtain data unavailable from governmental sources. They provide important information concerning the conditions of human rights, political participation, literacy and communications, global environment, health, hunger or disasters, economic development, developing science and technology, population and family planning, religious conflicts, and so on. In exposing governmental deprivations of human rights, nongovernmental organizations have played a vital role. They have represented their constituencies so well in exposing injustices that in some countries they function as the "ersatz opposition" and have become themselves a target of government repression.[4] Regular reports by Amnesty International on the status of torture in various countries have been instrumental in curbing governmental abuses in the treatment of prisoners of conscience. Information concerning slavery and slavery-like practices, as furnished by Anti-Slavery International, has kept alive humanity's continuing campaign to eradicate such practices. The global watch to protect and maintain a livable human environment depends in no small measure on the vigilant efforts of various environmental groups.

It is no secret that most nongovernmental organizations and associations are specialized in making recommendations and advocating policy alternatives, including intense efforts toward securing enactment of prescriptions. Thanks to modern means of communication and transportation, NGOs have developed a vast network of contacts around the globe. Aside from access to governmental officials on a personal or small-group basis, they rely increasingly on mass communication media, appealing directly to the citizens of the world. By mobilizing world public opinion they have achieved notable successes in such fields as human rights, environmental protection, economic development, peace movements, and armament control.

Although the formal prescribing function is generally within the domain of governmental officials, NGOs have occasionally played a direct role in the prescribing process, going well beyond that of promotion. The role played by the International Committee of the Red Cross (ICRC) in adopting the protocols additional to the Geneva Conventions (1949) is well known in international legal circles. The two additional protocols, enhancing the protection of victims of international armed conflicts (Protocol I) and of non-international armed conflicts (Protocol II), were adopted at the Diplomatic Conference on the Reaffirmation and Development of International Humanitarian Law Applicable in Armed Conflicts. The ICRC was the driving force in the preparatory work leading to the adoption of the two additional protocols, in response to the changing needs of the world community. Before the diplomatic conference, the ICRC organized several consultative meetings of experts to study the 1949 Geneva Conventions, making and scrutinizing proposals until the additional protocols could be drafted for adoption at the diplomatic convention.

Less well known is the special role played by the Carnegie Endowment for International Peace in securing the adoption of the Protocol Relating to the Status of Refugees (1967), which expands the scope of the applicability of the Convention Relating to the Status of Refugees (1951) and enlarges the function of the Office of United Nations High Commissioner for Refugees. By removing the temporal restriction—refugees "as a result of events occurring before January 1951," as in the convention of 1951—the protocol extends the substantive protection of the convention from refugees caused primarily by World War II and by the incipient Cold War, as originally contemplated, to refugees worldwide who had otherwise been left unprotected. The Carnegie Endowment, approached by the U.N. High Commissioner for Refugees, sponsored a meeting of legal experts (both scholars and governmental officials) to recommend alternatives for liberalizing the convention of 1951 in order to deal with the growing worldwide problem of refugees in the 1960s.[5] That colloquium's recommendation that the dateline of 1951 be removed by means of a protocol to the existing convention led in December 1966 to the U.N. General Assembly's adoption of the protocol, which entered into force on October 4, 1967. (The protocol of 1967 is often called the Bellagio Protocol.) NGOs also played a significant role in drafting the Convention on the Rights of the Child and have assumed key functions in its implementation and monitoring.[6]

The invoking function normally involves provisional characterization of certain conduct or events in terms of conformity with or deviation from existing community prescriptions. In the U.N. General Assembly, although formal invocation in the sense of placing a matter on the provisional agenda is restricted to member states, an NGO may do so indirectly by finding an acquiescent member delegation. Provisional characterization of a particular conduct or event as a deviation from community prescription often precedes the formal process of authoritative application. Access to such formal decisional arenas is still limited, but nongovernmental organizations are increasingly playing an important role in international litigation. Most of the major transnational structures for the implementation of human rights (for example, the U.N. Human Rights Council, the European Court of Human Rights, and the Inter-American Commission on Human Rights) permit NGOs to be petitioners directly or to represent individual victims (see chapters 7 and 23). Not to be ignored, however, is the role of nongovernmental organizations in informal invocation, which does not take the form of a particular legal complaint addressed to a particular tribunal. Nongovernmental organizations often find informal invocation highly useful in curbing governmental abuses or lawlessness to publicize specific violations of international norms by particular governments, especially in such fields as human rights and environmental protection.

In terms of application, some nongovernmental organizations play an extremely important role in securing compliance with prescribed norms, For example, the International Committee of the Red Cross, a major component of the International Red Cross, plays a unique role in international humanitarian law. As an independent humanitarian institution, the ICRC serves as a neutral intermediary in cases of armed conflicts and disturbances. It is entrusted with the task of protecting and assisting the victims of wars, both international and internal, under the Geneva Conventions and Protocols for the protection of war victims.

In the field of transnational air transport, the International Federation of Airline Pilots' Association (IFALPA), which consists of national associations of pilots in approximately one hundred countries, plays an important role in combating aerial hijacking. It has contributed to effective application of the antihijacking prescriptions through boycotting all air traffic to states unwilling to take effective antihijacking measures. It has also played a part in the safety regulations for transnational air transport developed and maintained by the International Civil Aviation Organization (ICAO).

The terminating function, in putting an end to the authority of existing prescriptions, is the other side of the same coin. Any new prescription involves modifying or terminating existing expectations of authority. Nongovernmental actors thus play as important a role in termination as in prescription. Given accelerating change in our time and the characteristic inertia of governmental officials and bureaucrats, initiatives to modify or terminate outmoded prescriptions often come from nongovernmental organizations and associations.

The appraising function, which is designed to assess successes and failures in terms of projected goals and policies, is highly democratic and open to all participants. Nongovernmental organizations can play an especially important role in this function, since official actors tend to be immersed in their own pressing business, moving from crisis to crisis or simply from daily routine to daily routine. The functioning of world constitutive process and the overall quality of world public order can be greatly improved by mobilizing the creativity, expertise, skills, and resources of nongovernmental organizations and associations that specialize in various fields.

Private Associations

Multinational corporations play an increasingly important role in contemporary transnational interactions. Because they are profit-oriented, multinational corporations are commonly treated as distinct from NGOs in general. Multinational corporations are corporations and associations that operate transnationally in finance, transportation, communication, technology, mining, fishing, agriculture, manufacturing, wholesaling, retailing, and other areas of economic life. They apply modern technologies to activities ranging from production and marketing to finance and management. Multinational corporations have grown in number, size, activities, and importance thanks to technological developments, new management techniques, and transnational networks of communication and transportation. Because they operate across many state boundaries, they serve as a global vehicle to transfer and disseminate capital, skill, and technology. Transnational trade policy is largely formulated, directly or indirectly, by participants in international wealth processes. The larger transnational corporations negotiate directly with nation-state representatives in a new form of diplomacy: agreements with these corporate giants may surpass treaties between states in terms of values affected and the prescribing effect engendered. They have contributed greatly to the internationalization of production, finance, and ownership, and to the growing integration of national economies into a world economy. According to the U.N. Conference on Trade and Development (UNCTAD), the world economy is more integrated than at any other time in history, and multinationals and foreign direct investment are leading the globalization of trade and finance that is reshaping business and labor markets around the world.[7]

Because they may possess more resources than most nation-states, multinational corporations have sometimes been seen as threats to nation-states. Their impact on the shaping and sharing of values, both actual and potential, has provoked increasing alarm. Profit-oriented by nature, multinational corporations have come to be perceived variously as exploiters of the labor and physical resources of the developing countries, environmental polluters, manipulators of currencies and commodities, tax dodgers, users of corrupt business practices, supporters of reactionary regimes, corrupters of the democratic process, and instruments of their national governments. They have gained particular notoriety due to the exposure of the widespread practice of bribery, corrupting and conspiring with power elites to the detriment of democratic values and the masses of the population. Concerns about such practices have led to the passage of national laws such as the United States' Foreign Corrupt Practices Act and the United Kingdom's Bribery Act of 2010. As of 2013, forty countries had become signatories to the Anti-Bribery Convention developed by the Organisation for Economic Co-operation and Development. However, despite efforts of this kind, a growing body of evidence shows that the globalization of free markets may produce devastating results in some parts of the world, ranging from community social collapse to increasing gaps between rich and poor as large numbers of the world's people are marginalized by globalization trends.[8]

Though they are labeled multinational, transnational, or international, all corporations owe their creation to national laws. Their success in operation, however, depends greatly on the transnational recognition of such national laws. Typically, a multinational corporation is incorporated under the domestic law of a nation-state, acquiring nationality of the state of incorporation. Yet as their operations expand in geographical reach and in magnitude of impact, it has become increasingly apparent that conflicting national laws are inadequate to deal with manifold problems arising from the activities of multinational corporations. Some commentators have expressed the belief that in the post–Cold War era, multinational corporations are more powerful actors than governments, and that they even behave imperially.[9] Thus, although multinational corporations have become effective actors in the global processes of wealth, power, skill, and enlightenment, they have also become the target of special concern and international regulation. The United Nations has become a center for such undertaking.

In 1972, the Economic and Social Council called together a group of eminent experts to study the role and impact of transnational corporations and to recommend measures toward international accountability. As a result, in 1974, two permanent bodies were established to deal with the problems of multinational corporations. After reorganization only one body remained and is now called the Commission on International Investment and Transnational Corporations. The locus of U.N. activities concerning international investment has shifted to the UNCTAD and the Department of Economic and Social Development in the Secretariat. (The commission was retained largely because developing countries, wary of the influence of multinationals, insisted on continuing U.N. oversight.) The commission has given special attention to ways to halt corrupt practices involving multinational corporations, making it a top priority to develop a code of conduct for the activities of transnational corporations. This was an arduous task that finally collapsed under ECOSOC auspices but still continues in interstate discussions in bilateral, regional, and plurilateral settings. Whereas some states have undertaken exclusive, unilateral programs of investment liberalization, others have demonstrated a greater readiness to join in more inclusive, plurilateral agreements concerning the rules of foreign investment.[10]

The role of multinational corporations has persisted as an issue in many fora, both inside and outside the United Nations. It must not be forgotten that transnational corporations can and do serve as important sources for the protection and fulfillment of human rights. For example, during the apartheid regime, the role of American-based multinational corporations in South Africa sparked considerable debate and provocation in many arenas. The United States responded with various governmental attempts at limiting the apparent widespread criticism of American investments there. Many American companies asserted that their presence in South Africa would help promote change and weaken the effects of apartheid by employing workers from all socioeconomic and racial groups within the country in accordance with the Sullivan principles of promoting equality.

It is certain that disinvestment in apartheid South Africa by foreign companies resulted in a major outflow of capital, and the new democratic South Africa struggled until the 2000s in rebuilding its economy and rejoining the community of nations. It cannot be overemphasized that in a global economy of ever-increasing interdependence, the common interest would require that a code of conduct and related measures not contain provisions so inimical to the interests of transnational enterprises as to cause their general withdrawal from the developing countries. At the same time, transnational corporations can have a positive impact, for example, by voluntarily complying with fair labor and environmental standards, even when they are not required to do so by relevant domestic law.

The United Nations promotes good corporate citizenship through the work of the Global Compact initiative (UNGC). Since 2000, the UNGC has encouraged corporations around the globe to adopt practices favorable to the protection of human rights, the environment, and fair labor standards while stamping out corruption. The campaign is organized around ten principles that include a commitment to human rights and a pledge to not remain complicit to human rights abuses, the elimination of forced labor and child labor, and the development of environmentally friendly technologies. Additionally, the United Nations has been able to draw attention to the issue of corporate responsibility through the work of the secretary-general's special representative on business and human rights, Professor John Ruggie. Operating under a mandate from the Human Rights Council, Ruggie has helped articulate a framework under which states and transnational corporations can work together with other stakeholders to protect and respect human rights while remedying abuses. Through a series of influential annual reports, Ruggie has been able to promote this three-part framework and enlist the global business community as a partner in the United Nations' ongoing mission.[11]

Other private associations of concern in international law are more nefarious and include international criminal syndicates involved in activities such as drug smuggling, human trafficking, terrorism, and other crimes. These groups, which possess varying levels of sophistication and resources, have attracted tremendous attention in recent decades, especially following the attacks of September 11, 2001. The U.S. Department of State currently recognizes around fifty organizations that it considers as foreign terrorist groups. A large part of U.S. foreign policy since September 11, 2001, has focused on locating and dismantling terrorist organizations around the world, notably al-Qaeda. In May 2011, U.S. forces undertook a successful clandestine mission to kill al-Qaeda's leader, Osama bin Laden, at a residential compound in Pakistan. Other members of the organization have been targeted and killed, increasingly through the use of unmanned aerial drones. However, the so-called War on Terror has also taken a deadly toll on innocent people. Civilian casualties have numbered in the tens of thousands as a result of military operations in countries including Iraq, Afghanistan, Pakistan, and Yemen since 2001.

The United Nations has taken a leading role in coordinating efforts to combat terrorism and other forms of international crime. The General Assembly adopted a comprehensive global counterterrorism strategy in 2006.[12] The plan represents the first unified strategy against terrorism ever agreed to by all U.N. member states. In 2000, the United Nations adopted the Convention against Transnational Organized Crime, also known as the Palmero Convention, which is focused on eliminating human trafficking, especially involving women and girls and migrant workers. The number of victims of human trafficking who are engaged in forced labor around the world is estimated to be around 2.5 million, while many women and girls are forced into prostitution by their traffickers.[13] Human trafficking is a problem that occurs on every continent, with more than one hundred sixty nations serving as either a source, transit point, or destination for human trafficking. Other U.N. programs include the U.N. Office on Drugs and Crime, which was established in 1997 to coordinate efforts to combat the flow of illegal drugs through research and reporting and providing technical assistance to national governments. Other international crime-fighting bodies include the International Criminal Police Organization (INTERPOL), which was established in 1923. It is the world's largest police organization with nearly one hundred ninety member nations.

Private associations, whether concerned with wealth or with other values, characteristically seek and attain effects on transnational decision making. Their efforts bear directly both on the constitutive process, in the making and application of law, and on all the features of effective power and public order that sustain the constitutive process. The wealth, enlightenment, skill, well-being, and other values under their control afford them important bases in effective power. By influencing many of the structures of interaction through which global society is established and maintained, they affect the production and distribution of all public order values, with consequent effects on the quality and direction of the constitutive process. The danger from private associations, like that from pressure groups or criminal syndicates, is that they may use their resources in ways incompatible with genuine, long-term common interest. Some are interested in long-term effects, but others seem interested in maximizing short-term outcomes because of their preoccupation with one value or a narrow range of values and their limited identifications.

Notes

1. *See* Yearbook of International Organizations, Union of Int'l Assoc., http://www.uia.be/yearbook.

2. *See* Antonio Donini, *The Bureaucracy and the Free Spirits: Stagnation and Innovation in the Relationship Between the U.N. and NGOs, in* NGOs, the UN, and Global Governance 67 (Thomas G. Weiss & Leon Gordenker eds., 1996).

3. *See* Helena Cook, *Amnesty International and the United Nations, in* The Conscience of the World: The Influence of Non-Governmental Organizations in the UN System 181 (Peter Willetts ed., 1996).

4. N.Y. Times, Oct. 30, 1996, at A11, col. 1.

5. John Goormaghtigh, *How an INGO Contributed to Broadening the Scope and Competence of an IGO, in* Unofficial Diplomats 250, 254 (M. Berman & J. Johnson eds., 1977).

6. *See* Lung-chu Chen, *Human Rights and World Public Order: Major Trends of Development, 1980–2010 and Beyond, in* Looking to the Future: Essays on International Law in Honor of W. Michael Reisman 440 (Mahnoush H. Arsanjani et al. eds., 2011).

7. Wash. Post, Sept. 8, 1994, at B11.

8. Wash. Post, Jan. 23, 1997, at A17.

9. Richard J. Barnet & John Cavanaugh, Global Dreams: Imperial Corporations and the New World Order (1993).

10. United Nations Assoc. of the United States of America, A Global Agenda: Issues Before the 50th General Assembly of the United Nations 129 (1995–1996).

11. *See, e.g.,* U.N. Special Representative of the Secretary-General, *Protect, Respect and Remedy: A Framework for Business and Human Rights: Rep. of the Special Representative of the Secretary-General on the Issue of Human Rights and Transnational Corporations and Other Business Enterprises, delivered to the Human Rights Council,* U.N. Doc. A/HRC/8/5 (Apr. 7, 2008).

12. The United Nations Global Counter-Terrorism Strategy, A/RES/60/288 (Sept. 30, 2006).

13. United Nations Office on Drugs and Crime, *Global Report on Trafficking in Persons* (Feb. 2009), *available at* http://www.unodc.org/documents/human-trafficking/Global_Report_on_TIP.pdf.

5   The Individual

INDIVIDUAL HUMAN BEINGS, acting through all the group and institutional forms already mentioned, communicate and collaborate continuously in every phase of effective and authoritative decision as well as in the shaping and sharing of all values. Individuals may act in the name of, or as representatives of, organizations and associations, or they may act simply in their own right as individuals. Whatever their multiple identifications, individuals are the ultimate actors in all social processes. In addition to their common roles in effective power, individuals increasingly are achieving recognized roles in the processes of authoritative decision and review.

One of the dominant historical myths in international law (especially in the latter nineteenth and early twentieth centuries) had been that states, not individuals or their other associations (even nations), are the only appropriate "subjects" of international law. Under this exaggerated and unrealistic expectation of the nation-state as the exclusive subject of international law, as buttressed by the inordinate emphasis on positivism and state sovereignty, there had been a tremendous reluctance to recognize other participants in world social process as active subjects of international law. Even international governmental organizations were once denied acceptance as subjects of international law; their role was obscured and their legal personality questioned. The role of nongovernmental participants—political parties, pressure groups, and private associations—was regarded as a matter of sociology rather than law. Individuals often were regarded as objects, not subjects, of international law. As "objects" of international law, individuals were for all practical purposes treated in the same breath as territory, resources, treaties, and so on.

Under the positivist doctrine of subject-object dichotomy, the individual was not deemed the bearer of rights or duties in international law. Under such a myth, an individual enjoys benefits and bears burdens under international law not directly but only indirectly, as bestowed by the nation-state. Any direct contact between the individual and international law is viewed as an exception, an aberration. An individual has no direct access to transnational tribunals for remedies and can secure transnational protection only through a nation-state protector. Thus, Emmeric de Vattel's famous dictum that an injury to an individual is an injury to the state of which he or she is a member. This fiction is closely linked to the concept and requirement of nationality and makes the security and fulfillment of the individual dependent on the willingness of the state to protect him or her (see chapter 12). Only the state of nationality is permitted to espouse claims of deprived individuals at the international level against other states. Because a state's competence to protect its nationals is regarded as independent of the interests of the individual concerned, the state has the discretion to decide whether to espouse claims on behalf of its nationals.

The positivist-oriented notion that states are the only proper subjects of international law is belied by all the contemporary facts about participation in the global processes of effective power and authoritative decision as well as the existence of private rights and duties. This notion, unknown to international law's founding fathers and deriving from certain parochial misconceptions of the late nineteenth century, lingers because it may expediently serve the power purposes of state elites, especially those who govern without authority. One significant factor in contemporary effective power is that many state elites will not tolerate their nationals complaining to other state elites or the larger community of humankind about the deprivations within their particular communities.

However clever the Vattelian fiction might have been, the fact remains that the individual is the ultimate beneficiary even of the remedy of diplomatic protection. State responsibility is incurred for failure to comply with the international standard for the treatment of aliens. The international standard protecting aliens (meaning potentially all human beings) and state responsibility for injuries to aliens constitute a vital part of customary international law, not an exception or aberration. The proscriptions of piracy, war crimes, breaches of neutrality, violence against ambassadors, and the slave trade, for example, were clearly directed to the individual. Even before the era of the United Nations, individuals were permitted a certain degree of access to transnational arenas of authority, such as the right of petition under the Mandates system (established by the League of Nations to administer the former colonial territories of Germany and Turkey toward the ultimate goal of self-government), the Central American Court, and the regime for the protection of minorities. Additionally, in many domestic settings, individuals had access to domestic courts and other decisional fora for presentation of claims based on international law, especially in the United States.

A major development after World War II was of course the trials of Nazi war criminals. The Charter of the International Military Tribunal (IMT) at Nuremberg held individual persons responsible for crimes against peace, war crimes, and crimes against humanity. At the IMTs at Nuremberg and Tokyo and in subsequent proceedings, thousands of individuals were tried and convicted, and many were executed. These trials clearly imposed direct personal responsibility on individuals and dismissed the defenses of superior orders and of obedience to state law. Moreover, they put leaders on notice that crimes against humanity would not go unpunished. "Crimes against international law," in the words of the International Tribunal, "are committed by men, not by abstract entities, and only by punishing individuals who commit such crimes can the provisions of international law be enforced."[1] In recent decades, specialized tribunals have been established to try individuals accused of violating international human rights laws amid conflicts in the former Yugoslavia, Rwanda, and Cambodia. More recently, the International Criminal Court (ICC) has been given general jurisdiction over crimes committed by individuals around the world. Individual criminal responsibility under international law will be explored further in chapter 29.

As international law expanded its concern from abstract entities of nations and states to real-life human beings, it ushered in a new era of human rights, underscoring the central place of human beings in transnational interaction and the fundamental dignity and worth of all human beings. The atrocities of the Third Reich not only led to the Nuremberg trials but also brought home the vivid message that human rights and peace are indivisible. Massive deprivations of human rights, if unchecked, would not only devastate individuals and groups but would also threaten international peace and security. Thus, the U.N. Charter recognized the precept of human dignity, enunciated the protection of human rights as a major goal of the organization, and imposed human rights obligations on member states. The Security Council today has continued to use its authority under the charter to protect the rights of individuals, creating special international tribunals to bring rights violators to trial for war crimes, genocide, and crimes against humanity.

Thanks to the contemporary human rights movement, a global bill of human rights has emerged and is developing (see chapter 12). The changes from the positivist orientation of the late nineteenth and early twentieth centuries have been noteworthy. Human rights are no longer matters of domestic jurisdiction but are of international concern. Global concern for human welfare has extended from alien rights in particular to human rights in general. International law has expanded its scope of concern for the protection of all human beings—protecting them against mistreatment not only by foreign governments but also by their own governments. The international law of human rights protects all human beings, regardless of nationality.

The intense demands of the peoples of the world for all human dignity values have been incorporated into the corpus of international human rights law. Through the adoption of the Universal Declaration of Human Rights in 1948, the entry into force of the International Covenant on Civil and Political Rights and its first optional protocol and of the International Covenant on Economic, Social, and Cultural Rights in 1976, and the workings of customary law, a comprehensive global bill of human rights is developing. This global bill of rights, which originated with the U.N. Charter and has been sustained by a multiplying host of specific human rights conventions (both global and regional), additional protocols, authoritative decisions, and expressions, represents a tremendous collective effort. It is assuming the attributes of customary international law, and several more specific rights have already obtained such a status. The human rights prescriptions, expressing the widely shared and intensely held demands and expectations of humankind, are made extremely difficult to modify or terminate.

Transnational structures of authority and procedures for application have been established and maintained to supplement long-standing domestic procedures and to secure greater compliance with the high legal standards set forth in the global bill of human rights. More important, individuals and private groups are given increased, though still limited, access to arenas of transnational authority to bring complaints about human rights deprivations against even their own governments. The capacity of individuals and private groups to invoke human rights prescriptions before appropriate transnational decision makers is so enhanced that the subject-object theory cannot explain or wish it away. Indeed, a state-centered international law is being transformed into an international law of homocentricity.

The subject-object dichotomy would appear highly superficial and confusing; even its proponents have tremendous difficulty in agreeing to what is meant by a "subject" of law. The intellectual confusion and unreality of the subject-object theory stem largely from its positivist roots of rule orientation, conceiving international law as a body of rigid, autonomous rules capable of automatic problem-solving without human choice. The inadequacies associated with the rule-oriented approach were pointed out in chapter 1. Students of international law must emancipate themselves from the trap of the subject-object dichotomy.

Viewed comprehensively and realistically, international law is a continuing process of decision and review aimed at identifying, clarifying, and securing the common interest of the members of the world community. It is a process in which various participants (actors) play various roles in making and applying international law and the related decision functions, granting the continuing dominance of nation-states in the whole process. The meaningful inquiry concerns not what persons are technically subjects and objects for a body of static rules but who actually participates in the global process of decision making and who performs what functions.

In playing varying roles in this process, different participants—states, non-state actors, and individuals—make different claims for protection. Understandably, nation-states are interested in making such claims as comprehensive and continuous control over territory, resources, international agreements, and employment of other instruments of policy; yet individuals are particularly concerned with access to particular territorial communities and with protection and enjoyment of various human rights. Although nation-states continue to play the most prominent role in the prescribing (and terminating) and applying functions, individuals and private groups play important roles in regard to other decision functions: intelligence, promotion, invocation, and appraisal. Further, as noted above, individuals (whether in the name of the state, as private groups, or on their own) are realistically the ultimate participants.

The decision functions in which individuals, as individuals, have long played a significant part transnationally include the intelligence, promoting, and appraising functions. Under the concept of "custom," which creates law through widely congruent patterns of human behavior and other communications, individuals and their private associations have always participated in the prescribing function. To invoke the authoritative application of transnational prescriptions, individuals have had and continue to have access to national courts; they are increasingly afforded access to transnational arenas of authority, notably in the field of human rights protection.

Although the dominant role of the nation-state at the international level remains a contemporary reality, it is worth noting that the "omnipotent" nation-state is but one of many structures or processes that individuals develop to protect and fulfill their interests. The nation-state is a human institution that does not realistically exist apart from individuals who enjoy the sharing of values or who are relatively oppressed. Nothing inherent in international law would preclude individuals or non-state entities from playing recognizably greater roles in the global process of decision making. In fact, they play such roles whether they or we perceive such a fact and whether such a role is merely one of deference.

Indeed, some notable individuals have wielded great influence, by virtue of their wealth, fame, or personality, that has allowed them to play an increasingly prominent role on the international stage. Philanthropists such as Bill Gates and Warren Buffet have persuaded wealthy individuals from around the world to commit funds to solving global problems in the areas of education, economic development, and public health. Their work has even influenced the actions of individual states and many nongovernmental organizations through the coordination of resources—both financial and human—to research and promote effective solutions to problems. The American media tycoon Ted Turner has played an instrumental role in the growth of the United Nations Foundation through contributions of both leadership and capital. Well-known individuals ranging from media celebrities to artists and writers have long played a role in raising awareness of global issues, especially human rights, and building support for efforts to enhance human security. Examples include the Irish musician Bono, whose efforts have helped raise awareness of challenges facing some African nations, as well as various well-known individuals who have been appointed U.N. Goodwill Ambassadors to help build awareness of important projects worldwide. Religious leaders of different faiths can play an important role as conciliators in a turbulent world of growing disorder. For example, Pope Francis has earned a reputation as global peacemaker since his papal inauguration, calling for greater interfaith dialogue, tolerance, and a lessening of disruptive economic inequality. The Dalai Lama has attained a celebrity unmatched by most rock stars and has traveled the world lecturing on the importance of human dignity over his long career. Former national leaders including Jimmy Carter, Bill Clinton, Nelson Mandela, and Mary Robinson have continued to exercise influence on the global stage well after leaving political office in their respective home countries. Former U.S. Vice President Al Gore has gone on to campaign for global action against climate change. His efforts to raise awareness earned him a Nobel Peace Prize. These examples demonstrate that individuals, even those who are not officeholders, are able to contribute directly to the development and maintenance of world order in a way that transcends their identity as a citizen of any one state.

Originally designed to shield individuals from the tyranny, exploitation, and anarchy of feudalism, the nation-state has generally been assumed to be the structure most appropriate for achieving a more fulfilling life for all. Like all other human institutions, when the nation-state fails to serve such common interest, its traditional role is subject to critical scrutiny in the light of other competing institutions. In the face of both the ever-growing pressures of global interdependencies that defy artificial and arbitrary national boundaries and the growing perception of these interdependencies, the contemporary state system can be expected to be under increasingly severe challenge.

The alternatives in world constitutive process of authoritative decision open to individuals who aspire toward a world community of human dignity need not be misconceived. The choice open to humankind is not one of simple dichotomy: either a world controlled solely by sovereign nation-states or a world government that supplants all existing nation-states. Our world is one of pluralism and diversity, a global arena in which various participants—groups (territorial and functional, governmental and nongovernmental) and individuals constantly interact under changing conditions. All group participants—nation-states, international governmental organizations, political parties, pressure groups, and private associations—are forms of associations through which individuals cooperate to fulfill their demands. In the final analysis, these group forms are highly malleable instruments created and maintained by people to clarify and secure their common interest. They offer an almost infinite spectrum of potentiality for arranging and rearranging functional and geographic structures and practices toward this end.

Note

1. International Military Tribunal (Nuremberg), Judgment and Sentences, Oct. 1, 1946, 41 A.J.I.L. 172, 221 (1947).

III Perspectives

6   Minimum World Order and Optimum World Order

THE PERSPECTIVES OF the effective elites of the world, which infuse the global processes of authoritative and controlling decision, can be described in terms of demands, identifications, and expectations amid projections of contending systems of public order. The New Haven School posits that the basic policy objectives for which the effective elites of the world ought to maintain the global constitutive process of authoritative decision are to promote the common interests of all peoples and to reject all claims of special interest. In the most comprehensive sense, the function of law in any community is to maintain uniformity in decision in clarifying and securing common interest and to minimize decisions that are made without regard to the consequences for others. The common interests that are sought to be protected fall into two broad categories: inclusive interests and exclusive interests. By inclusive interests is meant demands and expectations about activities that have a high degree of collective impact, having important consequences across community lines on a transnational or global scale. By exclusive interests is meant demands and expectations about activities whose effect extends primarily to the peoples of a single territorial community.

From a global perspective, the inclusive interests of the peoples of the world include first, maintaining minimum order in the sense of minimizing unauthorized violence and other coercion. The provisions of the U.N. Charter vividly reflect the aspirations and general expectations of the peoples of the world regarding this fundamental interest. It is the one interest indispensable to any community governed by law. Arbitrary decision by coercion is inimical to our very concept of law as uniformity of decision in accord with community expectation. Beyond minimum order, however, the peoples of the world have more extensive interests in what may be called optimum order, in the sense of the greatest production and widest distribution of all demanded values that can be attained with available resources. Taken together, minimum and optimum world order make up the concept of human security, which refers to the totality of the shaping and sharing of all widely demanded values under conditions of peace and security.

The establishment of the United Nations ushered in a new era, projecting eloquently the fundamental goals—minimum order and optimum order—for the general community of humankind. The United Nations, like its predecessor, the League of Nations, seeks to maintain minimum world order (peace and security) as a primary goal. From the Westphalian concept that tolerated and condoned the use of force as an instrument of change, through the Hague Conferences, the League of Nations, and the Kellogg-Briand Pact, there developed an ever more insistent demand for outlawing the use of force save for purposes of self-preservation and collective enforcement action. This demand was crystallized and incorporated in the U.N. Charter. The charter provisions, including Article 2(4) and other ancillary provisions, have contributed immensely to the clarification, if not consistent implementation, of this most intense demand for minimum order. It is widely recognized today that the most important purpose for which the global constitutive process of authoritative decision is established and maintained is that of achieving a basic public order both by minimizing unauthorized coercion and by protecting the expectations created by agreement and customary behavior. This reflects a shared perception that only when minimum order is secured can optimum order (in the sense of the greatest production and widest possible sharing of all values) be seriously pursued and attained.

But there is a corresponding recognition that, in a world community of growing interdependence, minimum order cannot be securely established and maintained without the supporting conditions of a viable optimum order, enabling a greater production and wider distribution of all values under conditions of security. Minimum and optimum order constantly interact: they affect and reinforce each other.

Again, the goal of optimum order has found eloquent expression in authoritative prescription, reflecting the rising common demands of the peoples of the world for a greater production and a wider sharing of all basic values: respect, power, enlightenment, well-being, wealth, skill, affection, and rectitude. These rising common demands for enhancement of the quality of life in every value sector are the demands for human rights in the most comprehensive and dynamic sense.

Beginning with the U.N. Charter, extending through the Universal Declaration of Human Rights, to the international covenants on human rights and a host of more specialized conventions and ancillary expressions about human rights, a growing body of prescriptions makes comprehensive and detailed reference to the same basic values embodied in the bills of rights of the more mature nation-states and expressed in other forms for centuries past. The U.N. Charter, in its preamble, reaffirms "faith in fundamental human rights, in the dignity and worth of the human person, in the equal rights of men and women" and pledges to "promote social progress and better standards of life in larger freedom" and to "employ international machinery for the promotion of the economic and social advancement of all peoples." Proclaiming the protection of human rights as a major goal, Article 55 of the charter emphasizes that "universal respect for, and observance of, human rights and fundamental freedoms" is indispensable to "the creation of conditions of stability and well-being which are necessary for peaceful and friendly relations among states." The Universal Declaration of Human Rights, regarded at its adoption in 1948 merely as "a common standard of achievement" without authoritative effect, has become widely accepted as a customary international law binding on all nation-states and also as an authoritative standard for interpreting human rights guaranteed under the U.N. Charter. Although the declaration is more than sixty years old, it remains as relevant today as it was in 1948. The International Covenant on Civil and Political Rights (and its optional protocols) and the International Covenant on Economic, Social, and Cultural Rights, providing further treaty-based protections, have been in effect since 1976. Together these three are widely regarded as an international bill of human rights. The demands for human dignity values, as prescribed in this international bill of human rights, find further specifications in the host of specialized human rights conventions and other ancillary expressions that seek to protect a particular category of individuals, deal with a particular value, or apply to a particular region.

Viewed from the historical evolution of international law, this twentieth-century movement for the transnational protection of human rights is remarkable, although the domestic protection of human rights has had a long, rich history that has too often gone unnoticed by international scholars. Centered on national elites, international law was long preoccupied with the interrelations of states as entities. When human rights problems were conceded to fall within the legal domain, they were often treated as matters of "domestic jurisdiction" of particular states. It was commonly assumed in the late nineteenth and early twentieth centuries that how a state treated its own nationals was beyond the realm of international law, precluding interference by other states.

Common Humanity and Diverse Identifications and Expectations

The identifications of the effective elites that establish and maintain the global constitutive process, like those of the general population, remain multiple and ambivalent, manifesting tendencies toward both expansion and contraction. In a world in which social process is characterized by increasing perceptions of comprehensive interdependencies as well as rising demands for self-determination and autonomy among groups, it can be expected that the identifications of effective and authoritative decision makers will waver between a rational concern for all humanity and less constructive parochial concerns. The best promise of the future is that a deepening understanding of the conditions of both minimum world order and optimum world order will facilitate a better balance between inclusive and exclusive identifications and interests.

One manifestation of the trend toward inclusive identification is the increasing reference to the term mankind (or humankind) in legal instruments. Examples abound: the U.N. Charter refers in its preamble to wars as the "scourge of mankind"; the Nuclear Nonproliferation Treaty admonishes the "devastation that would be visited upon all mankind by a nuclear war"; the Antarctic Treaty seeks to protect the "interests of science and mankind"; the Outer Space Treaty declares outer space to be the "province of mankind" and astronauts to be the "envoys of mankind." The concept of the "common heritage of mankind," as made popular by Ambassador Arvid Pardo of Malta, spotlights this growing inclusive identification with humanity. This concept has been expressed in the U.N. Convention on the Law of the Sea and in the Moon Agreement, respectively making the ocean floor and its resources beyond the limits of national jurisdiction, and the natural resources of the moon and other celestial bodies the "common heritage of mankind."

The expectations of peoples that affect the constitutive process would appear, under the universalizing influence of science and technology, to include an increasingly common and realistic map of world social process. Expectations have often been unrealistic in the past, when modes of communication were few, education was poor, and interchanges across national boundaries were rare. Whatever the facts of interdependence, they were not always perceived realistically. Thanks to increasing communication and literacy and wider use of science and technology, peoples everywhere are acquiring far more comprehensive, realistic maps of the world. Expectations about manifold events in world affairs are on the whole becoming more contextual and rational. Although expectations of violence and of continuing deprivations and nonfulfillments in a world of real and perceived scarcity are still widely shared, there is a growing recognition of the conditions of interdependence under which individuals and groups can fulfill their demands for values.

The end of the Cold War and the transformation of the international system have brought radical changes in conceptions of national authority.[1] International human rights programs have supplanted the older absolute notions. The increasing perception by peoples of a global interdependence has greatly contributed to fostering a more realistic recognition that a paramount goal of global constitutive process must be that of protecting the common interests of peoples while rejecting all claims of special interest.

Contending Systems of World Order

Basic ideological differences in political, social, and economic systems once led to manifested differences in the types of public order systems demanded and projected, both domestically and transnationally. However, these demands are changing, and even converging, in the post–Cold War, postcommunism world, as peoples around the globe seek the market economy and as the number of democracies increases.[2] Though the East-West ideological confrontation came to an end in the early 1990s, it has been replaced by new divisions based on emerging economic interests, as characterized by the concept of the "global North and South." Developed and developing worlds differ on a growing number of issues, especially on issues related to finance and trade and the global environment.

In their classic 1959 article, "The Identification and Appraisal of Diverse Systems of Public Order," McDougal and Lasswell pointed out that there was at that time no comprehensive universal legal order with a consensus about goals on the global scale.[3] The world was characterized by "diverse systems of public order," and thus to speak of "universal international law" would be to indulge in make-believe. Many who wished to see such a universal international legal order nevertheless spoke as though it were already a reality. In so doing, they risked drawing attention away from "the vital issues on which the diverse systems of public order that now dominate the world scene are not united." According to McDougal and Lasswell, a major detrimental result of indulging in "make believe universalism" would be the tendency to undercut the norms of international law that did enjoy a general consensus and were generally effective in bringing about a degree of world public order. It was more appropriate "to speak of international laws or multinational law, than of international law,"[4] the authors concluded by stressing that only by keeping these vital divisions out in the open would progress be made toward a more comprehensive legal order.

Until the collapse of the Soviet Union, two rival views of international law posed an enormous challenge to humankind. While the Western perspective stressed both customary law and treaty law, the communist (socialist) perspective emphasized the law of agreement (tacit or express) and distrusted the customary law developed mainly by Western powers.

The Western perspective, with long customary roots, is basically the outgrowth of three centuries of relations among the major Western European nations. Although the principle of *pacta sunt servanda* (agreements must be kept) in the realm of international agreements has been called the heart of international law, custom has brought about the lion's share of law governing international relations in the West. It has been noted that in recent decades international law has been drifting more and more toward a treaty basis; yet customary law remains vigorous in governing transnational interactions, and the realistic process of treaty law functions in a manner not unlike the dynamic process of customary law, based as they are on patterns of expectation and behavior through time.

In contrast, the communist (socialist) perspective, as led by the now-defunct Soviet Union, adopted a nineteenth-century positivist orientation that minimized the significance of customary international law, emphasizing instead the value of international agreements. In 1917, the Soviet Union entered the "world stage" perceiving itself as a radically new phenomenon and refusing to accept customary international law as binding.

It reasoned that customary law had arisen in the pre-communist era and represented a public order of which the Union of Soviet Socialist Republics (USSR) was not a part. The Soviet Union showed a tendency to choose from among principles of customary law, and even in the realm of treaty law played fast and loose with traditional law by asserting that the cardinal principle of *pacta sunt servanda* was qualified by an exception for "unequal treaties."

Above all, the Soviet Union advocated the principles of peaceful coexistence as the paramount guide of contemporary international law, at least with respect to international law between so-called socialist and nonsocialist states. Discounting variations in different versions of formulation, the core principles of peaceful coexistence (among socialist and nonsocialist states), as originally enunciated, were five: mutual respect for sovereignty and territorial integrity; mutual nonaggression; nonintervention in internal affairs; equality and mutual benefits; and peaceful coexistence.[5] The principles of peaceful coexistence, originating in the Pancha Shila principles, adopted by China and India in 1954, found various expressions in Soviet foreign policy statements and legal writings.

The West was hesitant to accept these principles at face value. A major cause of Western distrust of peaceful coexistence was the original communist doctrine of the inevitability of war between the communist and capitalist worlds and the doctrine of wars of national liberation. Although this inevitability theory had to be revised in light of the nuclear threat of mutual annihilation, its theme of continuing class struggle remained unabated. Most important, the Soviet government did not appear to practice what it preached, as witnessed in its treatment of the Balkan states, especially its military suppression of the internal changes in Hungary and in the former Czechoslovakia. Its standard answer was that the principles of peaceful coexistence were applicable only to the relations between communist and capitalist states, and did not extend to the "fraternal" relations between socialist states.

Such a double standard was of course incompatible with the goal of securing a world public order of human dignity. Furthermore, on close examination, none of the first four core principles of peaceful coexistence were really new as international norms; all had been incorporated earlier in the U.N. Charter. Only the fifth, proclaiming "peaceful coexistence" as a guiding principle of international law, was new.

The Cold War between East and West, in terms of lives affected, wealth consumed, geographical reach, and long-term environmental consequences, was one of the greatest conflicts of human history.[6] Marked by continuing high expectations of violence and continuous mobilization for war by two military antagonists whose alliances incorporated a large part of the globe, the Cold War involved more human beings than any other conflict. It "deformed" traditional international law, as the long effort to restrict unilateral action, the "hallmark of civilized political arrangements," was impeded by the veto power of the superpower security system.[7] At the height of the Cold War, two worlds existed on the planet, between which trade and other human contact were drastically reduced in many ways—there were two systems of international law and two systems of world public order, and few thought it would ever end.[8]

But end it did. On the heels of a 1980s revival of the Cold War, a rapid succession of largely peaceful revolutions spread across Eastern Europe and to Russia. The Soviet Union dissolved and its empire collapsed. The international system was transformed, as the Warsaw Pact disintegrated and the Brezhnev Doctrine was discarded. The norms governing superpower conflict and the underpinnings of the international system were completely changed.

The comparatively peaceful collapse of the Soviet Empire was a virtually unprecedented event in world history. Contrary to expectations of rule-oriented and neo-realist theories, the fall of the Soviet bloc was not the result of war, different alliance patterns, or the emergence of another superpower, nor even the outcome of a sudden gap in military capabilities.[9] One important factor was the fact that at that time, the strongest powers in the international system were, or aspired to be, liberal democracies.[10] Externally, a nonthreatening West and its support for Mikhail Gorbachev's reforms, accompanied by invitations to join multilateral institutions and offers of large-scale financial aid for economic reform, helped the transition along, encouraging reformers, swaying hard-liners, and heightening expectations. Internally, after decades of efforts by opposition groups, a "civil society" was created under which human values of existence and initiative independent of the communist state could develop.[11] Direct contacts and learning between opposition groups began to flourish and spread, first through Polish society and then across Eastern Europe and Russia. Economic modernization, increased communications across boundaries, and an improvement in optimum order created a better-educated constituency with new values and expectations, and new demands for institutional and constitutive changes.

Soviet elites began to think inclusively, demonstrating that the Soviet government was no longer willing to use the Eastern European countries as a means to the Communist Party's ends. Realist theories cannot explain why the Soviets did not instead become more aggressive in response to instability at home and throughout the bloc states, nor why the capitalist West did not behave opportunistically in response to the weakening empire.[12] Under perestroika, glasnost, and "the new thinking" in Soviet foreign policy, the Soviet state moved to join the "community of nations" and "the common European home," embracing multilateralism. Significantly, for Mikhail Gorbachev the community of nations was not simply the sum of states recognized in accordance with international law, but a collection of states participating in the multilateral institutions of the postwar era.[13]

The end of the Cold War may have meant the lessening of one particular pattern of violence, but it did not necessarily mean the beginning of peace.[14] The collapse of the Soviet Union was followed by a belated decolonization, and the result was increasing instability, the effects of which are still felt today. The resulting conflicts shattered the dream of unity that existed in the early days of the post–Cold War era. Other conflicts around the globe, which were not merely phenomena of the Cold War but existed in their own right, continue to diminish both minimum and optimum world order, and these areas may become more prone to North-South division as their former strategic value decreases. The revolutionary appeal of socialism may have subsided, but there is no shortage of ideologies to take its place for which people are willing to resort to violence. The capitalist West is "hardly impervious" to stress and instability; environmental degradation and rapid economic transformation threaten many human values around the planet.[15] It is not settled that globalization is the way to achieve optimum values and the sharing of all human values. In an increasingly interdependent world, the West, despite victory for its free-market ideology, cannot ignore processes that may disrupt hopes for the new international order.

Differing Perspectives Today

The end of the Cold War and the collapse of the Soviet Empire solidified Western influence over the development of the international system. However, this should not be taken to mean that all non-Western perspectives were stamped out or rendered ineffectual. Indeed, quite the opposite is true. Other competing systems, representing exclusive identifications and wielding effective control over a range of base values, have challenged prevailing norms with varying degrees of intensity. Representing both territorial and ideological communities, these systems, not unlike the USSR before them, sometimes manifest a desire to reform or, in some cases, to overwhelm or dismantle institutions with which they compete.

RELIGION AND WORLD ORDER

Throughout history, religion has played an important role in world affairs. A great many of the world's peoples identify themselves as members of religious groups and seek to peacefully adhere to norms corresponding with their groups' traditions. In some cases, however, such norms are at odds with the inclusive demands of others, whether they are neighbors or distant members of the world community. In today's world, which is increasingly interconnected and in which individuals interact with ever-increasing frequency, such conflicts may be inevitable. This fact was made shockingly apparent on September 11, 2001. To many, 9/11 and the events that followed, represented a clash of civilizations; one secular and globally inclusive, the other parochial and militant in its exclusivity. How are we to reconcile the two? And is it possible to integrate such perspectives into a world community in which human dignity is central?

The freedom of thought, conscience, and religion are at the heart of widely shared projections of rights and are affirmed throughout key international and regional human rights instruments. Article 18 of the International Covenant on Civil and Political

Rights affirms both theistic and nontheistic beliefs as well as the right not to belong to a religious group. These prescriptions recognize the individual's right to inquire into the nature of the universe and life on earth and to live according to his or her convictions. Indeed, the recognition and protection of religious freedom is closely related to the attainment of other fundamental values. Conditions necessary for the full realization of individuals' freedom of belief include the freedom of thought, conscience, and religion; the right to equal protection and freedom from religious discrimination; the protection of religious minorities; and the freedom from intimidation and violence having to do with one's religious beliefs.

The connection between religious beliefs and community are well known and profound. Individuals' belief systems shape and reinforce personal identities and offer a mode of living that often implies a strong affiliation with one group and a separation from others.[16] Even still, religious convictions have played their part in the recognition and promotion of human rights which transcends group identity. Every major religious tradition emphasizes a duty to society and to humanity at large. In this duty lies the potential for the promotion of civil and political, economic, social, and cultural rights for all humankind, regardless of religious affiliation.

Sadly, egregious violations of human rights may also be tainted by religious conflict, whether between or on behalf of religious groups or by oppressive states against religious adherents. The events of 9/11, and the response that followed, dramatized the role of religion as a vital factor in perpetuating divisions among peoples. The attacks, which targeted innocent citizens of every creed, were unprecedented in their scope. The perpetrators claimed to be waging a jihad (religious war) against the West that was based in Islamic principles. Their supporters, which included the former Taliban government of Afghanistan, professed ideals contrary to human dignity and freedom for all people.

Practices that deprive individuals of their fundamental rights are contrary to the ideals of human dignity and the goal of minimum world order. Yet this prohibition must also be viewed in light of competing value claims. Even a fundamental freedom such as religion must be balanced against the need to protect the common interest as well as other basic values that are essential to world order. In theory, there is a widely shared aspiration to recognize the common qualities that unite us, and to downplay those differences that divided us in the past. While the desirability of inclusive identification has been widely expressed, and at times efforts have been made toward its realization, there is also a trend toward parochialism, which emphasizes cultural relativism. Such beliefs ought not to support practices that are manifestly contrary to shared interests or that violate human rights.

Be that as it may, while popular notions of Islamic culture and its laws (sharia) emphasize characteristics seemingly inimical to Western ideals, such as the necessity of theocracy, limitations on religious freedom, and the unequal status of women, a survey of scholarship, as well as regional instruments, finds a favorable, albeit not overwhelming, trend toward greater inclusiveness and compatibility with international norms within the Islamic world.

A focal point for such an analysis can be found in the Organisation of Islamic Cooperation (OIC), whose fifty-seven member states, represent a total of approximately 1.5 billion people. The OIC's members are active participants in a range of international institutions, including the United Nations and Arab League, as well as a number of regional organizations and alliances. The OIC's charter proclaims its members' commitment "to the principles of the United Nations Charter... and International Law" in addition to "Islamic values of peace, compassion, tolerance, equality, justice and human dignity" and other values seemingly in accord with international norms, such as national sovereignty and the rule of law. The charter, which was revised in 2008, states in its preamble that its members are committed "to promote human rights and fundamental freedoms, good governance, rule of law, democracy and accountability in Member States in accordance with their constitutional and legal systems." Furthermore, Article 14 of the charter authorizes the International Islamic Court of Justice in Kuwait to serve as its principal judicial organ, while Article 15 calls for the creation of the Independent Permanent Commission on Human Rights to "promote the civil, political, social and economic rights enshrined in the organisation's covenants and declarations and in universally agreed human rights instruments, in conformity with Islamic values."

In 1990, the OIC adopted the Cairo Declaration of Human Rights in Islam, in which it affirmed its commitment to fundamental human rights in accordance with Islamic principles. Critics of the Cairo Declaration have asserted that the document is at odds with the United Nations' Universal Declaration of Human Rights because of its religious nature. To the contrary, some have argued the aspirations contained in the Cairo Declaration are largely compatible with the Universal Declaration. A 2012 report by the International Law Association entitled "Islamic Law & International Law" noted that, while proponents of sharia hold it to be superior to all man-made law, the OIC's fifty-seven member states were not uniform in their application of sharia. Indeed, the report concluded that certain precepts within sharia were consistent with international norms and offered hope for the emergence of a strong rule of law and individual protections within Islamic states.[17]

Further evidence is found in the events of the Arab Spring, in which popular movements spread throughout the Middle East and Northern Africa beginning in 2011. Though difficult to generalize, at least one common feature unites them: there is a popular demand among the people of the region for greater internal self-determination, that is to say, equal and effective participation in the political processes and a greater role in the shaping and sharing of power and other values. In countries that have overthrown long-standing authoritarian regimes, the potential exists for new power structures that are more respectful of citizens' demands for dignity and political participation. Though much uncertainty remains, there is hope that the region, which includes many OIC members, will see the emergence of more democratic institutions in line with universal projections toward human rights and dignity for all. Indeed, the outcome may be critical to the well-being of the region's peoples, for as the International Law Association's 2012 report states, "especially in the context of international peace and security, there is agreement that the concepts of the rule of law, democracy, and human rights (and increasingly others, such as development) are indivisibly linked."

CHINA AND WORLD ORDER

The rise of the People's Republic of China (PRC) as a major world power has prompted endless questions about how Chinese elites will wield the country's newfound influence both regionally and globally. Will China upend the existing world order in its pursuit of wealth and power? Or will it become a "responsible stakeholder," strengthening and enriching today's institutions, while aligning its domestic policies with the expectations of the world community? Chinese leaders are often circumspect about their long-term policy intentions. And, in any case, it is not possible to predict how human decision makers will behave in the future. Nevertheless, a consideration of past trends in decision and present conditioning factors may offer some indication about the themes that will likely inform the Chinese state's conduct in the coming years.

Historically, Chinese elites perceived their society as the "middle kingdom" at the center of the universe, with the emperor holding a quasi-divine position around which the state was organized.[18] This belief persisted for hundreds of years until the mid-nineteenth century when Western powers knocked at China's door. During this time, surrounding lands (to say nothing of distant European nations) were considered inherently inferior, and neighboring peoples were expected to make tributes to the Chinese state in exchange for the emperor's goodwill. In sharp contrast to the Westphalian concept of coequal states, the Chinese approach to international relations reinforced the unequal status of lands outside of its territorial community. This arrangement went virtually unquestioned so long as China reigned as Asia's preeminent state power. However, it would come to a sudden and violent end as Western nations increasingly sought to project their military and economic might into the region.

To many Chinese, the period from 1839 to 1949 represents "the Century of Humiliation." During these years, the country suffered a series of political, military, and cultural indignities at the hands of foreigners. Major events during the Century of Humiliation included the First Opium War (1839–42), the Taiping Rebellion (1850–64), the Second Opium War (1856–60), the Sino-French War (1884–85), the First Sino-Japanese War (1894–95), the Boxer Uprising (1898–1900), and the British invasion of Tibet (1903–04). In 1842, the First Opium War ended with the signing of the Treaty of Nanking, in which China ceded Hong Kong Island to the British in perpetuity, followed by the Kowloon Peninsula in 1860 (later in 1898, the British were granted a ninety-nine-year lease to the adjacent New Territories and would exercise authority and control over the crown colony until 1997). In the twentieth century, China was subjected to the Twenty-One Demands by Japan (1915), and suffered the Japanese invasion during the Second Sino-Japanese War (1937–45). Following the end of the Chinese Civil War in 1949, the Century of Humiliation figured heavily in the communist regime's historical narrative. For some observers, clues about China's intentions are rooted in its desire to settle scores and regain its once hegemonic status.

The contemporary Chinese perspective on international law began to take shape under the leadership of Chairman Mao Zedong following World War II. Likening states in the developing world to the international proletariat, Chinese leaders proclaimed that the "rural" nations would rise up to overtake the developed, urban nations, just as Mao Zedong's forces had overtaken the Nationalist Chinese on the mainland. The communists rejected Western institutions for the most part, preferring instead to embrace a vision of a global communist world order. Ultimately, however, the Sino-Soviet split threatened to isolate China, and the nation had to learn to tolerate the West, eventually opening itself to relations with the United States during the administration of U.S. President Richard Nixon and the establishment of formal diplomatic relations during the Jimmy Carter administration in 1979.

The thawing of relations between the United States and the People's Republic of China (PRC) was a watershed moment leading to China's integration into the global community. Soon, the intense demand for economic development had overtaken communist orthodoxy, putting the mainland on the road to rapid growth and urbanization. By 1971, the PRC was seated in the United Nations to replace the Republic of China (exiled in Taiwan), occupying China's permanent seat on the U.N. Security Council. China could no longer excuse itself from the international order. Indeed, it was benefiting tremendously from institutions put in place by Western powers after World War II, which had fostered a stable order within which to pursue trade and economic partnerships. In 1989, the year of the Tiananmen Square incident, Chinese leader Deng Xiaoping advised the Chinese people to "maintain a low profile, hide brightness, not seek leadership, but do some things." Deng's prescription appeared on its face to advocate for a gradual and nonthreatening approach to international relations, with a heavy emphasis on economic development.

At times, China has shown a commitment to participating robustly in global institutions, even taking on a type of spokesperson role for the Third World, for instance, preaching the "Five Principles of Peaceful Coexistence." Yet, at other times, Chinese elites have expressed hesitation in affirming international norms in which their country had little or no hand in shaping. Were it not for the existing international system, China's rapid advance in wealth and power may not have been possible, and therefore, the system cannot simply be rejected outright. At the same time, the Chinese state often exhibits an exaggerated notion of sovereignty, resisting calls to reform its domestic practices to achieve greater conformity with international norms, most notably in the areas of human rights and democracy. Like the Great Wall, Chinese elites have built up a conception of nation-state sovereignty that repels outside influences, often to the exclusion of other cardinal principles.

Take for example, China's insistence on "core interests." To Chinese elites, the state's core interests are those for which there is no room for negotiation with outside powers. These interests, which are noticeably territorial in nature, include not only claims to Tibet, Xinjiang, and Hong Kong but also claims to Taiwan and to ownership over the South China Sea. Within this geographic zone, China claims exclusive rights, warning others to avoid meddling in its internal affairs and threatening military assaults in response to perceived slights. In late 2013, for example, China declared an Air Defense Identification Zone (ADIZ) over the East China Sea, demanding that foreign aircraft submit flight plans before passing through the area. The move was instantly denounced by the United States and others, who considered it to be highly provocative and potentially destabilizing, given that the purported zone included airspace above the disputed Senkaku (Diaoyu) Islands, which are under Japanese control. Shortly after, the United States and Japan showed their defiance by flying aircraft through the zone. The Chinese responded by announcing that military aircraft would begin patrolling the area to monitor against foreign intrusions. The invention of the ADIZ was reminiscent of the "nine-dotted line" drawn by the PRC on maps of the South China Sea, seemingly without regard to neighboring states' territorial claims.

Such provocations, when coupled with the threat of the military instrument, are generally contrary to the principle of the nonuse of force enshrined in the U.N. Charter. In the case of Taiwan, Chinese's threats are also contrary to the principle of self-determination (for more details see the discussion in chapter 2).

An exclusionist strategy is apparent also in the Chinese state's disregard for many fundamental human rights. In spite of its newfound economic dynamism, China has yet to recognize and respect many of the human rights that are commonplace throughout the industrialized world, rights that find authoritative expression in instruments including the Universal Declaration of Human Rights and numerous treaties. Instead, China has embraced relativity, arguing that human rights ought to be considered in light of "Asian values," with an emphasis on state control and de-emphasis on individual freedoms. This approach has been termed by some as a "Beijing Consensus," wherein policies that promote economic growth are paired with political repression. Some scholars have even contrasted the Chinese model with the neoliberal "Washington Consensus," as championed by the United States, which emphasizes open markets and individual freedoms as hallmarks of development. As China pursues new markets and strategic resources, particularly in Africa, the Beijing Consensus may very well be exported to other places, with unknown consequences for human rights and other values.

China's continued development from a preindustrial society to a major world power will inevitably deepen its involvement with global institutions, shaping them and shaping China in the process. Constructive engagement between the PRC and the West could lead to a new global power configuration that, under the right conditions, could nurture both minimum and optimum world order. Meanwhile, like peoples before them, the Chinese, increasingly cosmopolitan in their outlook, are likely to demand greater participation in decision making and in the sharing of values such as wealth and enlightenment, though whether Chinese elites would encourage such an evolution remains to be seen. With this potential in mind, some commentators and Western political elites have increasingly urged China to act as a "responsible stakeholder" in world affairs. This phrase, first applied by Deputy Secretary of State Robert Zoellick, envisions a Chinese state that is an active participant in the world community, upholding fundamental principles of international law, and strengthening the global system from which it has benefited over the past half century.[19]

Indeed, it is perhaps hard to imagine an optimum world order in which China does not play a central role, given its vast quantities of both human and nonhuman resources. Therefore, it is crucial that Chinese elites do not seek to emulate ancient emperors but rather recognizes its place in a global community of human dignity in which all peoples seek to identify, clarify, and secure their common interests.

THIRD WORLD APPROACHES TO INTERNATIONAL LAW (TWAIL)

Since the period of decolonization that began after World War II, Third World nations—those nations that were aligned with neither the West nor the communist bloc during the Cold War—have played an increasingly important role in the world community. These nations have sought greater influence in authoritative decision processes, and their numeric advantage has been used to great effect to draw attention to issues facing developing countries. As discussed in chapter 2, the Group of Seventy-Seven, consisting of roughly two-thirds of the U.N. General Assembly, has wielded considerable voting strength throughout the United Nations' history. However, the Group's relatively weak effective power vis-à-vis developed nations has limited the Third World's capacity to set a global agenda that prioritizes developing nations in the formulation of policies and international law generally. Take, for example, the movement to establish a new international economic order in the years following the Cold War (as will be discussed in chapter 18). The project failed to mobilize the support of effective power holders, despite achieving considerable momentum among its Third World proponents and some First World intellectual elites.

In response to this disparity, an increasingly vocal network of global scholars representing disciplines as diverse as law, economics, history, and philosophy has sought to challenge the long-held primacy of the United States and European powers in the shaping of international law. Loosely organized under the banner of "Third World Approaches to International Law" (TWAIL), these scholars have hosted conferences and published extensively on topics concerning the place of Third World nations in world order. Although rejecting a formal orthodoxy, their works generally express skepticism of principles that ring of past colonial or imperialistic norms. Among these are practices that reinforce the latent notion of "the Other," a term denoting colonized peoples who were the targets of Europe's so-called "civilizing mission." According to a common TWAIL critique, a similar conceptualization takes place today, wherein Third World nations are frequently looked upon as corrupt, backward, imperiled, or failed and in need of Western guidance. Issues such as human rights, economics, and good governance, rather than inviting Third World perspectives, offer yet another means for imposing Western prerogatives on weaker nations, albeit more stealthily, by reference to supposed universal norms.

The TWAIL movement can generally be divided into two generations, which some scholars have conveniently labeled TWAIL I and TWAIL II. The first generation concerned itself with questions fundamental to the era of decolonization, particularly having to do with the desire for newly independent states to have equal legal status with their former colonizers. TWAIL I proponents argued for a strong conception of sovereignty, emphasizing the centrality of the state as the ultimate participant in international law and the importance of the Westphalian principle of nonintervention. In doing so, TWAIL I scholars sought to provide new countries with the legal armor needed to advance their interests globally while resisting Western powers' efforts to exert undue influence over their domestic policies. More recently, scholars who self-identify with the TWAIL II approach have shifted focus away from state actors to pay greater attention to the human beings living in the developing world. While maintaining that international law has tendencies to perpetuate colonial power structures, TWAIL II scholarship places greater emphasis on the experiences of Third World peoples and seeks to recenter international law through a consciousness raising that underscores potentials for a meaningful role for a range of Third World actors in authoritative decision making. As Professor Makau Mutua told a gathering of the American Society of International Law in 2000:

> The project of TWAIL advocates the full representivity of all voices, particularly those non-state, nongovernmental, rural and urban poor who constitute the majority in the Third World. Here, TWAIL opposes the complicity of Third World states in the international legal and economic order with a view to silencing the voices of the powerless. TWAIL calls for the full democratization of the structures of both national and international governance so that all voices can be heard. TWAIL embraces the project of subalternity, in which those who do not fit the frames of Eurocentrism and modernity can be heard and become full participants in their governance. In this regard, TWAIL has a basic interest in the internal reconstruction and genuine democratization of Third World states.[20]

Indeed, the spirit of the TWAIL movement has inspired notable successes in international law, chief among them the hastening of the end of the colonial era in the twentieth century. The themes advanced by TWAIL scholars have figured prominently in debates over the content of trade and investment laws, particularly in the areas of trade barriers and the permissibility of expropriation, although criticisms abound over U.S. and European dominance of key institutions in these fields. As described in chapter 9, the Convention on the Law of the Sea recognizes certain deep sea resources as a "common heritage of mankind," preserving them from exploitation solely by developed nations. And in the area of environmental law, negotiations for a post-Kyoto climate change agreement have included proposals for industrialized economies to compensate Third World nations for damages caused by rising sea levels, as noted in chapter 10. Such proposals would seem to accord with the values espoused by the current generation of TWAIL scholars, whose work affirms the centrality of people and human security in international law and the ever-growing roles played by a wide cast of participants, representing diverse territorial communities and distinctive patterns of demands, identifications, and expectations in a globalized world.

People and Human Security at the Center of World Order

The end of the Cold War and the transformation of the international system have brought radical changes in conceptions of national authority. International human rights programs have supplanted the older absolute notions. The increasing perception by peoples of a global interdependence has greatly contributed to fostering a more realistic recognition that a paramount goal of global constitutive process must be that of protecting the common interests of peoples while rejecting all claims of special interest.

Although it has been expressed in different terms, there has been in recent decades an increasing recognition of the interconnectedness of minimum and optimum world order. Most frequently, this recognition has been expressed in terms of the three "generations" of human rights. First-generation rights are those related to civil and political rights. Second-generation rights are those related to economic, social, and cultural rights. Third-generation rights are group rights, such as the right of self-determination, the right to a healthy environment, the right to development, and the rights to peace. That each of these three generations of rights are interconnected has become widely accepted and has come to be expressed in the evolving concept of human security.

The concepts of minimum and optimum world order are complementary. On one hand, it is only in the absence of unauthorized coercion and violence that all demanded values can be securely and optimally shaped and shared. On the other hand, given the level of global interconnectedness, it has become quite clear that international peace and security cannot be realized so long as individuals are denied the ability to participate in the shaping and sharing of all widely demanded values. The term "human security" was meant to encapsulate the conditions under which both minimum and optimum world order are realized.

The concept of human security found formal expression in the U.N. Development Programme's (UNDP) 1994 Human Development Report. The report began: "The world can never be at peace unless people have security in their daily lives." The concept of human security expressed in the report has since been embraced and echoed by officials—global, regional, and national—and nonofficials alike. Secretary-General Kofi Annan offered the following explanation of human security:

> Human security, in its broadest sense, embraces far more than the absence of violent conflict. It encompasses human rights, good governance, access to education and health care and ensuring that each individual has opportunities and choices to fulfill his or her potential. Every step in this direction is also a step towards reducing poverty, achieving economic growth and preventing conflict. Freedom from want, freedom from fear, and the freedom of future generations to inherit a healthy natural environment—these are the interrelated building blocks of human—and therefore national—security.[21]

What is most important is that the focus of inquiry with respect to security has shifted from the nation-state to the individual. That is not to say that national security is in any way irrelevant. Human security cannot exist if the state is not secure, in the sense of being free from external coercion. Likewise, the best foundation for national security is a population that is free from want and fear. National security cannot be achieved at the expense of human security; the two concepts mutually reinforce each other.

It should be clear from the preceding discussion that human security knows no national boundaries. Whether the discussion is framed in terms of minimum and optimum world order or human security and national security, the conclusion is comparable: the domestic peace and security of any given state is relative to the domestic peace and security that exists in neighboring states (broadly conceived). For this reason, efforts must be made to promote human security at all community levels—global, regional, and national. Similarly, there is an important role to be played by nongovernmental actors in the promotion and fulfillment of human security. Civil society can and must play a role in its fulfillment and protection.

This positive movement has been challenged by the global financial crisis that manifested itself in 2008. Individuals and even states have been forced to confront a changed economic reality that has threatened the existing public order and the obtainment of values essential to human security. Meanwhile, a desire for greater economic opportunities and political participation led to uprisings in early 2011 in the Middle East and North Africa (MENA). Aided by technology, and growing support from around the world, the Arab Spring challenged governments in the region to respond to the wider aspirations of their peoples.

The Arab Spring provides a dramatic example of people as the driving force in the trend toward a world order based on human security and dignity. Recent decades have witnessed frequent and intensified demands for the protection and fulfillment of values by peoples throughout the world community. With information technologies, it is now possible to look beyond national borders to see what conditions are like elsewhere. Greater awareness has inspired individuals everywhere to hope for and demand the protection of human rights.

The international political system is at the threshold of a time of hope, but the need for international law will now be more urgent than during the Cold War.[22] A new world order has emerged, made up of multilateral institutions that have provided mechanisms for building consensus and cooperation among and between the industrial democracies as well as other developing nations. This new, cooperative pattern of relations may have to coexist with the historic, conflict-prone pattern that continues to mark relations among other former communist states and among many lesser developed countries, as well as between all those states and the developed Western world.[23] Thus, the challenge to decision makers in the post–Cold War era must be to clarify the common interests that harmonize inclusive and exclusive interests in a world community that is ever changing. Decision makers and their advisors may continue to draw on historic policies—bearing in mind, of course, that the constitutive and institutional arrangements that were once devised to achieve those policies may no longer be pertinent or effective.[24]

Notes

1. Michael W. Doyle, *Liberalism and the End of the Cold War, IN* INTERNATIONAL RELATIONS THEORY AND THE END OF THE COLD WAR 85 (Lebow & Risse-Kappen eds., 1995); *see, e.g.,* BEYOND WESTPHALIA? STATE SOVEREIGNTY AND INTERNATIONAL INTERVENTION (Gene M. Lyons & Michael Mastanduno eds., 1995).

2. W. Michael Reisman, *International Law after the Cold War,* 84 A.J.I.L. 859 (1990).

3. Myres S. McDougal & Harold D. Lasswell, *The Identification and Appraisal of Diverse Systems of Public Order,* 53 A.J.I.L. 1, 3 (1959).

4. *Id.* at 10.

5. *See* Leon Lipson, *Peaceful Coexistence,* 29 LAW & CONTEMP. PROB. 871, 874 (1964).

6. *See* Reisman, *supra* note 2, at 874.

7. *Id.* at 859.

8. *Id.*

9. Rey Koslowski & Friedrich Kratochwil, *Understanding Change in International Politics: The Soviet Empire's Demise and the International System, in* Lebow & Risse-Kappen, *supra* note 1.

10. Jack Snyder, *Myths, Modernization, and the Post-Gorbachev World, in* Lebow & Risse-Kappen, *supra* note 1, at 109.

11. *Id.*

12. Koslowski & Kratochwil, *supra* note 9, at 131.

13. *Id.* at 130–31.

14. *See* Reisman, *supra* note 2, at 863.

15. *Id.* at 864.

16. *See* Myres S. McDougal, Lung-chu Chen, & Harold D. Lasswell, *The Right to Religious Freedom and World Public Order: The Emerging Norm of Nondiscrimination,* Yale Faculty Scholarship Series. Paper 2646. (1976), *available at* http://digitalcommons.law.yale.edu/fss_papers/2646.

17. International Law Association Islamic Law and International Law Committee, *The Rule of Law and the Islamic Legal System* (2012), *available at* http://www.ila-hq.org/download.cfm/docid/013429B1-1D57-43F0-88CD775684AB0694.

18. DeLisle, Jacques, *China's Approach to International Law: A Historical Perspective,* 94 AM. SOC'Y INT'L L. PROC. 267 (2000).

19. Robert B. Zoellick, Deputy Secretary of State, "Whiter China: From Membership to Responsibility?" Remarks to National Committee on U.S.-China Relations, Sept. 21, 2005.

20. *What Is TWAIL?,* 94 AM. SOC'Y INT'L L. PROC. 31 (2000).

21. Press Release, Secretary-General Salutes International Workshop on Human Security in Mongolia (May 8, 2000), U.N. Doc. SG/SM/7382, *available at* http://www.un.org/News/Press/docs/2000/20000508.sgsm7382.doc.html.

22. Reisman, *supra* note 2 at 865.

23. Lebow & Risse-Kappen, *Introduction, supra* note 1, at 16.

24. Reisman, *supra* note 2, at 865.

IV Arenas

7 Establishment of and Access to Arenas of Authority

THE STRUCTURE OF authority and other situations in which the participants in the international legal system interact have shown both a remarkable expansion and a modest movement toward organized inclusive form. A major contribution of the United Nations and other intergovernmental organizations is to provide a range of diplomatic, parliamentary-diplomatic, parliamentary, adjudicative, and executive arenas in which all the effective participants in the world power process can interact. This development has been fortified by a comparable interactive network established by burgeoning nongovernmental organizations primarily concerned with values other than power. Consequently, the interactions of the decision makers whose choices in sum shape global policy have become more timely and continuous—less episodic and more responsive to crisis.

Similarly, though certain official arenas remain closed to some effective participants, there has been a general trend toward openness in arenas and a parallel movement toward making appearance compulsory for participants whose choices affect community policy. Both openness and compulsoriness are necessitated by growing interdependence in effective power.

Establishment

The institutional structures, in which both official and unofficial interactions occur and which manifest varying degrees of organization, may be depicted in terms of five distinctive patterns of interaction.

1. Diplomatic: The diplomatic arena, characterized by interelite communications, has a long tradition. From foreign office to foreign office various matters concerning international law are handled. From recognition of a state or a government to the establishment of formal diplomatic relations, the necessity of ensuring the sanctity of diplomatic missions and premises, the inviolability of diplomatic personnel, and the confidentiality of diplomatic communications have long been sustained. Absent formal diplomatic relations, contacts are maintained in unorganized arenas.

2. Parliamentary-Diplomatic: Occasional conferences dealing with a broad range of international law concerns have grown in frequency and importance. The comprehensive, protracted Third United Nations Conference on the Law of the Sea (UNCLOS III, 1973–82) is the most important recent development. Other important conferences include the Vienna Conference on the Law of Treaties (1969), the Diplomatic Conference on the Reaffirmation and Development of International Humanitarian Law Applicable in Armed Conflicts (Geneva, 1974–77), the U.N. Conference on the Human Environment (Stockholm, 1972), the World Food Conference (Rome, 1974), the U.N. Decade for Women Conference (Nairobi, 1985), the United Nations Conference on Environment and Development (Earth Summit) (Rio de Janeiro, 1992), the World Conference on Human Rights (Vienna, 1993), the International Conference on Population and Development (Cairo, 1994), the World Summit for Social Development (Copenhagen, 1995), the World Conference on Women (Beijing, 1995), World Conference against Racism (Durban, 2001), World Summit on Sustainable Development, or Earth Summit 2002 (Johannesburg), International Conference on Financing for Development (Doha, 2008), and the United Nations Conference on Trade and Development (Midrand, 1996; Bangkok, 2000; Sao Paulo, 2004; Accra, 2008; Doha, 2012). These conferences, touching on various value sectors and subjects on a global scale, contribute in many ways to the making and application of international law. They have greatly facilitated the performance of such important functions as intelligence (gathering and exchange of information and knowledge) and planning, appraisal (evaluating past and existing inadequacies), promotion (suggesting concrete proposals and advocating future courses of action), and prescription (adopting new international agreements). Although they may exude more rhetoric than action, they are vital to generating and crystallizing expectations of the members of the world community in the manifold concerns of international law.

3. Parliamentary: Guided more or less by doctrines of majority rule and of equality in representation, parliamentary arenas are, as compared to the two previous arenas, characterized by a higher level of organization and continuity. On the global level, the foremost parliamentary arena is of course the U.N. General Assembly, as assisted by a host of subsidiary entities. Next come the Security Council, the Economic and Social Council (and its functional commissions), and the Trusteeship Council.

The emergence of institutions having the characteristics of parliamentary bodies is not confined to the United Nations. It extends to specialized agencies and regional organizations. Note, for example, the International Labor Conference of the International Labour Organization (ILO, characterized by the tripartite system of representation), the General Conference of the United Nations Educational, Scientific, and Cultural Organization (UNESCO), the World Health Assembly of the World Health Organization (WHO), the Board of Governors of the International Monetary Fund (IMF, characterized by the principle of one state, one governor, wielding unequal votes based on a system of quotas), the Board of Governors of the World Bank, the General Council of the World Trade Organization (WTO), the Consultative Assembly of the Council of Europe, the General Assembly of the Organization of American States (OAS), the General Council of the League of Arab States, the Assembly of Heads of State and Government of the African Union (AU), and the Council of Heads of State and the Council of Heads of Government of the Commonwealth of Independent States (CIS). These arenas provide forums for discussing virtually any problem relating to international law and affairs.

4. Adjudicative: Adjudicative arenas, characterized by third-party decision as well as by distinctive procedures and criteria of decision, include tribunals of all degrees of organization. Typical examples are the International Court of Justice, the International Criminal Court, the Court of Justice and the Court of First Instance of the European Communities, the European Court of Human Rights, the Inter-American Court of Human Rights, International Tribunal for the Law of the Sea, World Trade Organization Dispute Settlement Panel, and numerous arbitral tribunals, such as the International Centre for Settlement of Investment Disputes within the World Bank. The International Criminal Court is the latest addition to the world adjudicative arena, although the spirit of cooperation has been tempered by disagreement over its jurisdiction. On the national level, recourse is increasingly made to judicial tribunals for matters regarding transnational law.

5. Executive: Executive arenas include the international secretariats of both official and nonofficial participants and the executive arenas of nation-states. Among notable official international secretariats are the U.N. Secretariat, the International Labour Office of ILO, and the secretariats of UNESCO, WHO,

FAO, and so on. The office of the Secretary-General of the United Nations, given its comprehensive global responsibilities, is especially important.

In terms of geographical range, institutional structures may be universal, general, plurilateral, regional, or bilateral. The scope of participation may extend to the entire earth-space arena or to small groups of actors.

All these types of arena have historically exhibited many, not always compatible, trends: from unorganized interactions to organized structures of decision; from loose association to a high degree of institutionalization; from the elementary diplomatic and parliamentary-diplomatic arenas to the more complex parliamentary, adjudicative, and executive arenas; from ad hoc to permanent and continuous structures of authority; and from imbalance in geographic and functional structures toward balanced development of both territorial (national, regional, and global) and functional organizations.

The structuring of arenas per se does not guarantee the content and quality of international law. Nevertheless, the more pluralistic the structures, the greater the likelihood that different interests will be protected. As a wide range of structures of authority becomes available, different participants with varying bases of power may take advantage of opportunities to enhance the protection accorded many individuals and groups.

In a state-centered world, the global arena is still characterized by an absence of centralized institutions specialized to the decision functions relevant to international law. In terms of geographical diffusion, modest movement has been made toward appropriate regionalism, as exemplified by the European Union, the OAS, the AU, the CIS, the League of Arab States, the Association of Southeast Asian Nations (ASEAN), and the Pacific Islands Forum (PIF). This movement falls far short of appropriate and effective regionalism necessitated by global interdependencies. Wide gaps continue to exist between the structures of the global community and those of national communities.

Access

The established transnational arenas of authority are generally open to nation-states; many remain closed to individuals and private groups. Most notably, non-state claimants still lack access to the International Court of Justice. Article 34(1) of the statute of the court stipulates that "only States may be parties in cases before the Court." Thus, in contentious proceedings, access is denied not only to private groups and individuals but also to international governmental organizations.

Some international governmental organizations, however, are able to request advisory opinions on certain general questions. Article 96(1) of the U.N. Charter authorizes the General Assembly and the Security Council to request "the International Court of Justice to give an advisory opinion on any legal question." Article 96(2) enables other organs of the United Nations and specialized agencies to seek, with the approval of the General Assembly, advisory opinions of the court "on legal questions arising within the scope of their activities." Neither states nor individuals can make such requests.

Generally speaking, the individual still depends largely on a protecting state for access to other transnational arenas. Unless the individual's state of nationality is willing to espouse his or her claim, he or she may get little succor (see chapter 12). But individuals have always enjoyed access to municipal and national courts under varied conditions. Access by individuals and groups of persons to transnational arenas of authority has appeared recently to be increasing.

The right of individual petition was firmly established to facilitate the process of decolonization; individuals and groups in colonial territories were accorded ample access to the Trusteeship Council, the Special Committee on the Situation with regard to the Implementation of the Declaration on the Granting of Independence of Colonial Countries and Peoples (commonly known as the Special Committee of 24 or the Special Committee on Decolonization), the Council of Namibia, and so on. The Court of Justice of the European Communities, which was created to serve the projected objectives of the European Economic Community, the European Coal and Steel Community, and the European Atomic Energy Community, provided an early example in a regional context. In addition to member states of the communities, individuals, firms, and institutions of the communities were given access to the court under prescribed conditions.

The most notable development in affording individuals and private groups access to transnational arenas of authority is in the field of human rights. The trend toward greater access for the individual may be noted especially in relation to developments within the U.N. Human Rights Council, the first optional protocol to the International Covenant on Civil and Political Rights, the International Convention on the Elimination of All Forms of Racial Discrimination, the European Convention on Human Rights, the Inter-American Commission on Human Rights, the optional protocol to the Convention on the Elimination of All Forms of Discrimination Against Women, the optional protocol to the Convention on the Rights of Persons with Disabilities, the Convention on Migrant Workers, and certain parties under Article 22 of the Convention Against Torture.

The fundamental significance of this trend is underscored by A. H. Robertson:

> The real party in interest, if a violation occurs, is the individual whose rights have been denied; and the violation will in all probability have been the act of the authorities of his own government. Under the classic concept of international law the individual has no *locus standi* on the theory that his rights will be championed by his government. But how can his government be his champion, when it is *ex hypothesi* the offender? What is necessary, therefore, is to give the individual a right of appeal to an international organ which is competent to call the offending party to account.[1]

The trend toward the right of individual petition within the United Nations began with the trusteeship system. The U.N. Charter provides in Article 87(b) that the General Assembly and the Trusteeship Council may "accept petitions and examine them in consultation with the administering authority." The council prescribed detailed provisions for dealing with petitions by its rules of procedure. With the acceleration of the decolonization process, the right of individual petition was extended from the trust territories to non-self-governing territories. The Special Committee on Decolonization, the Special Committee on the Policies of Apartheid of the Government of the Republic of South Africa, and the Council of Namibia all played important roles in receiving and acting on individual petitions.

The access of individuals and private groups to the Commission on Human Rights, now the Human Rights Council, has had a more tortured path. When the commission commenced its work in 1947, it declared itself without authority to deal with specific complaints about human rights. The Economic and Social Council quickly confirmed this self-denying policy. For the next two decades, the many thousands of complaints to the United Nations, made annually by individuals and groups, were practically ignored, unless such complaints related to a colony or to South Africa. The ritualistic response of the United Nations was simply to forward the "communication" to the government concerned.

As the world community became increasingly apprehensive about apartheid, racial discrimination, and other gross human rights deprivations, repeated attempts were made to modify this self-denying rule so as to augment "the capacity of the United Nations to put a stop to violations of human rights *wherever they may occur.*"[2]

In 1970 the Economic and Social Council adopted the famous Resolution 1503, establishing procedures for the Commission and the Sub-Commission on Prevention of Discrimination and Protection of Minorities to deal with "communications relating to violations of human rights and fundamental freedoms" and authorizing the subcommission to adopt rules on the admissibility of communications.[3] Under these procedures a working group of the subcommission is authorized to make the initial examination of all communications concerning human rights, and of replies by governments, received by the United Nations, and to decide which communications are to be referred to the full subcommission. Admissible communications may originate "from a person or group of persons" who are "victims" of "a consistent pattern of gross and reliably attested violations of human rights and fundamental freedoms," from "any person or group of persons who have direct and reliable knowledge of those violations, or nongovernmental organizations acting in good faith... and having direct and reliable knowledge of such violations."[4] On receipt of the communications brought by the working group, the subcommission decides whether to refer to the Commission on Human Rights particular situations "which appear to reveal a consistent pattern of gross and reliably attested violations of human rights and fundamental freedoms within the terms of reference of the Sub-Commission."[5] It was the responsibility of the commission to review the situations referred to it by the subcommission and to decide whether a situation calls for a thorough study by the commission or an investigation, contingent on "the express consent of the state concerned" and "constant cooperation" with that state. The commission would then decide whether to make recommendations to the Economic and Social Council.

However, by 2005 the Commission on Human Rights was tainted by partiality and dubious credibility. In 2006 the United Nations Human Rights Council (UNHRC) replaced the commission and became a subsidiary body of the General Assembly. In 2007, the UNHRC adopted Resolution 5/1, which established a Complaint Procedure.[6] The communication requirements of Resolution 5/1 mirror those of Resolution 1503, but the procedure is drastically different. The UNHRC created two working groups: the Working Group on Communications (WGC) and the Working Group on Situations (WGS). The WGC consists of independent, highly qualified experts, and they undertake the initial screening of complaints. The complaints that have not been screened out are passed on to the WGS, which reviews the complaint and may dismiss or present the case to the UNHRC.

Although this access to the UNHRC by individuals and private groups is indirect and limited, it is vital. The UNHRC is for all practical purposes the only official forum potentially open to all the individuals of the world for bringing complaints about human rights violations and not confined to particular individuals and groups identified through the jurisdiction of a particular ratifying state to a particular convention.

Under the International Covenant on Civil and Political Rights, the right of individual petition is stipulated not by the covenant itself but by the first optional protocol to the covenant. Any contracting state to the covenant, in becoming a party to the optional protocol, recognizes the competence of the Human Rights Committee "to receive and consider communications from individuals, subject to its jurisdiction, who claim to be victims of a violation by that State Party of any of the rights set forth in the Covenant" (Article I). A substantial body of case law is now based on this right.

Under the International Convention on the Elimination of All Forms of Racial Discrimination, the Committee on the Elimination of Racial Discrimination is empowered to deal with complaints filed by one state party against another and with petitions by individuals under the conditions prescribed in Article 14. Unlike the state-to-state complaint procedure, the procedure of individual petitions is made subject to the option of state parties to the convention. "A State Party," under Article 14(1), "may at any time declare that it recognizes the competence of the Committee to receive and consider communications from individuals or groups of individuals within its jurisdiction claiming to be victims of a violation by that State Party of any of the rights set forth in this Convention." The same provision, however, adds that "no communication shall be received by the Committee if it concerns a State Party which has not made such a declaration." Further, the competence of the committee regarding individual petitions is operative "only when at least ten States Parties" have made the requisite declarations of acceptance, a condition that was finally fulfilled in 1982, thirteen years after the convention entered into force.

The most successful story is the system of individual petitions developed under the European Convention on Human Rights. Under Article 25 of the convention, individuals were given the ability to bring complaints before the European Commission on Human Rights—even against their own governments. Concerned that not all governments were ready for such a radical innovation in international law, the European Convention made the right of individual petition optional. Any "person, non-governmental organization or group of individuals claiming to be the victim of a violation by one of the High Contracting Parties of the rights set forth in the Convention" may file petitions to the Secretary-General of the Council of Europe. Complaints may be brought regardless of nationality or domicile of the petitioner, provided that the petitioner was within the jurisdictional domain of the respondent government when the alleged violation occurred. Today, this right is codified in Article 34 of the convention, which gives individuals the right to bring petitions before the European Court of Human Rights, which succeeded the Commission.

Originally, access to the European Court of Human Rights was accorded to states parties to the convention and to the European Commission on Human Rights, not to individuals or private groups. But this has not entirely precluded the individual applicant (who is, after all, the interested party) from having his views presented before the court. Although the individual could not require the case to go to the court, he or she became a full party once the commission brought the case. There would thus be three parties before the court: the defendant government, the plaintiff (the individual), and the commission. This was changed in November 1998, when Protocol No. 11 came into effect and the European Court of Human Rights replaced the two-tiered control system of the commission and the court, opening up direct access to individuals. However, opening up the court did not come without a price; the court's backlog amounted to over 110,000 cases in 2008 compared to about 6,000 around the time Protocol 11 came into effect. In June 2010, the member states adopted Protocol No. 14, which was designed to streamline the judicial process and limit the number of unmeritorious cases before the court.[7]

Another regional body, the Inter-American Commission on Human Rights did not enjoy authority to act on individual petitions when it came into operation in 1960. In 1965 the commission was empowered to consider individual petitions complaining of violations of certain rights contained in the American Declaration of Rights and Duties of Man of 1948. Thanks to a protocol amending the Charter of the Organization of American States, adopted in Buenos Aires in 1967 and continuing into effect in 1970, the commission has been elevated in status from "an autonomous entity" to a principal organ of the OAS, and its authority in handling individual petitions and discharging other functions has been greatly fortified.

In Africa, individuals and certain nongovernmental organizations have a limited right to petition the African Court on Human and Peoples' Rights. The court, which held its first session in 2006, is tasked with interpreting member states' compliance with the

African Union's African Charter on Human and Peoples' Rights (the Banjul Charter). The charter, which entered into force in 1986, recognizes fundamental civil and political, economic, and social and cultural rights, as well as collective rights owing to groups, including families. Individuals may bring cases involving a member state only if the state has given the court jurisdiction to hear individual cases against it under Article 34(6) of the protocol on the establishment of an African Court on Human and Peoples' Rights. As of 2013, twenty-four of the African Union's member states had ratified the protocol, while only five had made a declaration permitting individuals and nongovernmental organizations to petition the court.

Two other regional bodies, the Association of Southeast Asian Nations and the League of Arab States, while having adopted human rights charters, lack mechanisms that would allow individuals to allege violations of the charters' provisions. Rather, the ASEAN Intergovernmental Commission on Human Rights and the Arab Human Rights Committee, have been tasked with serving as consultative bodies, receiving reports, and appraising member states' compliance with their charters' provisions. Critics of both systems argue that the lack of an individual petition undermines opportunities for meaningful enforcement because individuals—as ultimate stakeholders—are denied access to forums where they might effectively invoke their rights (see chapter 23).

Turning to national arenas, individuals have always enjoyed, under various prescribed conditions, access to national and municipal courts. Domestic courts have always been the traditional forum for individuals to bring claims, and their use continues to increase. However, their treatment of international law has not always been consistent with and sometimes in disregard of international authority, despite the theoretical supremacy of international law. A series of cases depicts, in sharp contrast, the different treatment that nations have accorded individuals in this respect. The first case that gave rise to the subsequent "dialogue" between the U.S. courts and the International Court of Justice (ICJ) was the 1999 *LaGrand* case (discussed in chapter 15). The *LaGrand* case involved the conviction and execution of two German nationals by the United States despite protests from Germany over the fact that they had not been informed of their consular rights under the Vienna Convention on Consular Relations. The ICJ ultimately ordered the United States to provide effective "review and reconsideration" of criminal convictions of foreign nationals, especially cases involving capital punishment, to ensure defendants learned of their consular rights.

After the *LaGrand* decision, Mexico, whose nationals constitute the largest foreign population in U.S. prisons and on death row, filed a case in the ICJ against the United States on behalf of forty-four nationals facing execution.[8] In the *Avena* case, the ICJ once again reiterated that the United States was required to implement the "review and reconsideration" process from *LaGrand*. After the ruling, President George W. Bush issued a memorandum directing state courts to give effect to the *Avena* decision. Despite such efforts, however, the states have yet to accord full weight to the ICJ decision.

In 2007, the U.S. Supreme Court granted certiorari in *Medellín v. Texas,* in which a Mexican national was convicted and sentenced to death for rape and murder.[9] Here, the Supreme Court held that the ICJ's *Avena* decision was not directly enforceable as domestic law in state courts, and that the president's memorandum did not require states to provide review and reconsideration to foreign nationals. In August 2008, Medellín was executed, despite objections from the federal government. Mexico immediately filed another case against the United States in the ICJ.[10] For the third time, the ICJ found that the United States was in violation of ICJ orders and reaffirmed the binding obligations of the ICJ judgments.

A contrasting outcome was reached in Germany, where the German Federal Constitutional Court (the German counterpart of the U.S. Supreme Court) held in 2006 that violations of Article 36 rights were equivalent to violation of constitutional rights to a fair trial and required their lower courts to take the ICJ's decision into account.[11]

A matter of special importance in international law has to do with access by foreign states or governments to domestic courts. The key to such access is "recognition" by the forum state. Generally speaking, only a recognized state or government may bring a lawsuit as plaintiff in the domestic courts of the recognizing state. Unrecognized states or governments cannot bring lawsuits before the courts of the state refusing recognition. Thus, for example, the Soviet government was consistently denied access to both federal and state courts in the United States before it received U.S. recognition.

Compulsory Third-Party Decision Making

Closely related to the question of access by complainants is that of bringing recalcitrant respondent states into contentious proceedings. Generally speaking, there is still no way to compel or ensure the attendance of defendant states before transnational tribunals.

INTERNATIONAL COURT OF JUSTICE (ICJ)

Suits brought before the International Court of Justice depend largely on the consent of the state being charged. The court's jurisdiction to try contentious cases is based on the consent, either express or implied, of the state parties. Consent may be given ad hoc by a special agreement between the parties concerned or by prior agreement. About a quarter of the cases before the court came through such special agreements. Prior consent takes two forms: by an international agreement conferring jurisdiction on the court and by a general declaration accepting the "compulsory" jurisdiction of the court. Some 265 international agreements involving more than sixty states have conferred jurisdiction on the court regarding the interpretation and application of these agreements, which cover subjects ranging from commerce, navigation, and fisheries to consular relations.

The Iranian hostage case, for example, was brought to the court by invoking several treaties dealing with diplomatic and consular relations.[12]

The optional acceptance of "compulsory jurisdiction" of the court is based on Article 36(2) of the Statute of the International Court of Justice. This provision, commonly known as the "optional clause," reads as follows:

> The states parties to the present Statute may at any time declare that they recognize as compulsory ipso facto and without special agreement, in relation to any other state accepting the same obligation, the jurisdiction of the Court in all legal disputes concerning:
> a. the interpretation of a treaty;
> b. any question of international law;
> c. the existence of any fact which, if established, would constitute a breach of an international obligation; and
> d. the nature or extent of the reparation to be made unconditionally or on condition of reciprocity on the part of several or certain states or for a certain time.

As of 2013, only 70 of 193 eligible states had accepted the court's compulsory jurisdiction under this optional clause. The percentage today of the accepting states in relation to the total membership of the court is much lower than during the era of the Permanent Court of International Justice (in 1940, 32 of 52 states). Of the five permanent members of the Security Council, only the United Kingdom has continued to accept it. Neither the Soviet Union nor any other state of the Soviet bloc ever accepted the court's compulsory jurisdiction; the Russian Federation, successor state to the former Union of Soviet Socialist Republics (USSR), has not accepted compulsory jurisdiction either, although some former bloc states have.

For states that have accepted the compulsory jurisdiction of the court, reservations attached to their acceptances are so many as to greatly diminish the scope of its jurisdiction. The so-called Connolly Reservation exemplifies such limitation. In subscribing to the optional clause in 1946, the United States made a reservation to exclude from the court's compulsory jurisdiction "disputes with regard to matters which are essentially within the domestic jurisdiction of the United States of America *as determined by the United States of America*" (emphasis added).[13] When a state continues to act as the judge of whether a particular matter falls within its domestic jurisdiction, it becomes obvious that what the right hand grants is, by one and the same stroke, taken away by the left hand. This bad example has been followed by many other countries. In the same vein, the United Kingdom, in its adherence to the optional clause, retains the competence to reject the court's jurisdiction in any dispute at any time before a case is actually filed.[14]

The difficulty caused by reservations is further exacerbated by the fact that the optional clause operates on the basis of reciprocity: each state accepts compulsory jurisdiction vis-à-vis another state only to the extent that the obligations undertaken in their respective declarations mutually correspond. Consequently, the court can acquire compulsory jurisdiction over a particular dispute only when both plaintiff and defendant states made declarations that bring that dispute within the court's domain.

In November 1984 the court was uncharacteristically bold in asserting its jurisdictional authority, over the strong objections of the United States, to hear a case brought by Nicaragua against the United States, *Case Concerning Military and Paramilitary Activities in and against Nicaragua*. The court's decision on the issue of jurisdiction followed its prior issuance of provisional measures in May 1984, ordering the United States to cease any attempts to blockade or mine Nicaraguan ports and to refrain from threatening the territorial integrity and political independence of Nicaragua by any military or paramilitary activities.[15] The United States claimed that the court lacked jurisdiction partly on the ground that Nicaragua had never validly accepted the court's compulsory jurisdiction because it had failed to deposit the requisite ratification of the Protocol of Signature of the Statute of the Permanent Court of International Justice (the predecessor of the incumbent court), which contained the optional clause of compulsory jurisdiction. The court rejected this claim, finding that Nicaragua's 1929 declaration—as distinguished from "ratification"—accepting the compulsory jurisdiction of the permanent court unconditionally was "valid from the moment it was received" and remained so "at the moment when Nicaragua became a party to the Statute of the new Court." The court stressed the "constant acquiescence" on the part of Nicaragua, noting especially that for nearly forty years international organizations authorized to handle "such declarations" had consistently included Nicaragua in the lists of states accepting the compulsory jurisdiction of the court.[16] The court stated that when Nicaragua, as an original member participating in the San Francisco Conference, signed and ratified the U.N. Charter, thereby accepting the statute of the new court, it consented to transfer its 1929 declaration (which was valid for an unlimited period) to the International Court of Justice.

Another ground of U.S. opposition to the court's jurisdiction related to the principle of reciprocity involving temporal factors. When the United States subscribed to the optional clause in 1946, it stated that "this declaration shall remain in force for a period of five years and thereafter until the expiration of six months after notice may be given to terminate this declaration."[17] On April 6, 1984—three days before Nicaragua formally filed suit against the United States in the ICJ—the United States sought to modify its 1946 declarations by stating that

[t]he aforesaid [1946] declarations shall not apply to disputes with any Central American state arising out of or related to events in Central America, any of which disputes shall be settled in such a manner as the parties to them may agree. Notwithstanding the terms of the aforesaid declaration, this proviso shall take effect immediately and shall remain in force for two years.[18]

The court was thus faced with the question whether the United States was free to disregard the six months' notice requirement contained in its 1946 declaration before a competent state had filed a claim. The United States contended that it was free to do so because Nicaragua was not similarly bound by such a temporal restriction in its 1929 declaration and could withdraw without six months' notice. The United States and Nicaragua were not, in the United States' view, "accepting the same obligation," as stipulated in Article 36(2) of the court statute. The court again rejected the U.S. contention, declaring that "reciprocity cannot be invoked in order to excuse departure from the terms of a State's own declaration, whatever its scope, limitations or conditions."[19] The court stated that the principle of reciprocity applies only to the scope and substance of commitments, not to the formal conditions of their duration.

Additionally, the court based its jurisdiction in part on the dispute settlement clause embodied in the 1956 Treaty of Friendship, Commerce, and Navigation between the United States and Nicaragua despite that treaty's exception for national security. The court also rejected the U.S. contention that the case was inadmissible or nonjustifiable because it involved issues of national security and self-defense and that matters of peace and security fall within the domain of the Security Council and are unsuitable for adjudication by the court.

In protest of the court's November 1984 decision on jurisdiction, the United States, on January 18, 1985, formally withdrew from "the proceedings initiated by Nicaragua in the International Court of Justice."[20] It reiterated that the proceedings "are a misuse of the Court for political purposes" and that "the Court lacks jurisdiction and competence over such a case."[21] Characterizing the court's decision as "a marked departure from its past, cautious approach to jurisdictional questions,"[22] the United States stressed that the decision "is erroneous as a matter of law and is based on a misreading and distortion of the evidence and precedent."[23] On October 7, 1985, the United States took a further step by terminating its acceptance of the compulsory jurisdiction of the court. It was a severe blow to the prospects of compulsory third-party decision making. Yet, despite withdrawing its acceptance of the court's compulsory jurisdiction, the United States has subsequently been a party to several cases before the court.[24]

On a more encouraging note, the International Court of Justice found itself busier than ever when its fiftieth anniversary arrived. In 1999, the court had the largest number of cases in its history, which included several important cases such as the aerial incident of August 10, 1999—*Pakistan v. India*; the armed activities in the territory of the Congo; and the legality of the use of force in Kosovo. In addition, the United Nations has set up a special fund to assist developing states in litigating before the International Court of Justice.

Furthermore, a number of human rights conventions do confer jurisdiction on the International Court of Justice over disputes concerning interpretation and application of such conventions. The list includes the Convention on the Prevention and Punishment of the Crime of Genocide, 1948 (Article 9); the Supplementary Convention on the

Abolition of Slavery, the Slave Trade, and Institutions and Practices Similar to Slavery, 1956 (Article 10); the Convention on the Political Rights of Women, 1953 (Article 9); the Convention Relating to the Status of Refugees, 1951 (Article 38); and the Convention on the Reduction of Statelessness, 1961 (Article 14). Typically, the relevant provision reads as follows: "Any dispute which may arise between any two or more Contracting States concerning the interpretation or application of this Convention, which is not settled by negotiation, shall at the request of anyone of the parties to the dispute be referred to the International Court of Justice for decision, unless they agree to another mode of settlement."

The movement toward compulsory third-party decision received reinforcement in the Vienna Convention on Diplomatic Relations of 1961 and the Vienna Convention on Consular Relations of 1963. There was an optional protocol concerning the compulsory settlement of disputes in relation to each of the two conventions. Article 1 of each of the optional protocols, in identical words, stipulates: "Disputes arising out of the interpretation or application of the Convention shall lie within the compulsory jurisdiction of the International Court of Justice and may accordingly be brought before the Court by an application made by any party to the dispute being a party to the present Protocol."

The next important development came with the Vienna Convention on the Law of Treaties of 1969. The shared concern for compulsory third-party decision finds expression in Article 66 of the convention and the annex to the convention, which were adopted after painstaking efforts. According to Article 66, any party to a dispute arising under the *jus cogens* articles of the convention may submit the dispute to the International Court of Justice for adjudication when the procedures in Article 33 of the U.N. Charter have failed to reach a solution within twelve months, provided the parties have made no agreement to refer the dispute to arbitration. A party to a dispute concerning "the application or the interpretation of any of the other articles in Part V" of the convention may set in motion certain conciliation procedures embodied in the annex to the convention through a request to the Secretary-General of the United Nations.

Incidentally, it may be worth nothing that there has been a gradual movement toward compulsory third-party decision in matters relating to human rights. Unlike the right of individual petition that is provided for on an optional basis under the existing human rights conventions (global and regional), the state-to-state complaint system is made compulsory under both the International Convention on the Elimination of All Forms of Racial Discrimination and the European Convention on Human Rights. The Convention on the Elimination of All Forms of Racial Discrimination stipulates in Article 11(1) that "if a State Party considers that another State party is not giving effect to the provisions of this Convention, it may bring the matter to the attention of the Committee [on the Elimination of Racial Discrimination]. The Committee shall then transmit the communication to the State Party concerned." The detailed procedures for dealing with such a state-to-state complaint are specified in the remainder of Article 11 and in Articles 12 and 13. Similarly, the European Convention on Human Rights provides for a compulsory state-to-state system in Article 33: "Any High Contracting Party may refer to the Court any alleged breach of the provisions of the Convention and the protocols thereto by another High Contracting Party." (The American Convention on Human Rights makes it optional.) In a decentralized world in which reciprocity operates, states are understandably reluctant to resort to such complaint procedures against other states for human rights violations, as attested by the experiences under these two conventions. Nevertheless, the availability of these compulsory state-to-state complaint procedures does contribute significantly to the international protection of human rights, thanks to the abiding impact of prevention and deterrence.

AD HOC ARBITRAL TRIBUNALS

The settlement of disputes by ad hoc arbitral tribunals depends as much on state consent as on judicial settlement. Occasionally, states may even refuse to participate in arbitral proceedings to which they have given prior consent. Though arbitration was highly popular in medieval times as a means of settling international disputes, its use greatly diminished with the rise of the modern state system, which overemphasized the sovereign quality of states. Thanks largely to the series of Jay Treaties concluded by the United States with Great Britain and other nations and to the Alabama Arbitration (1871) between the United States and Great Britain, arbitration was revived as a method of third-party decision in the nineteenth century. This revival culminated in the establishment of the Permanent Court of Arbitration under the Hague Convention for the Pacific Settlement of International Disputes, concluded in 1899, amended in 1907, and still in effect. The name Permanent Court, however, appears to be a misnomer. The entity consists of little more than a permanent panel from which arbitrators can be chosen, and the court itself must be constituted from case to case on an ad hoc basis. There is no machinery whatsoever for compulsory jurisdiction; few states are willing to make unequivocal prior commitment to arbitrate potential disputes.

An apt example of how even a prior commitment to compulsory arbitration may be frustrated is the case of *Interpretation of Peace Treaties with Bulgaria, Hungary, and Romania* (1950).[25] The peace treaties, concluded by the Allies with Bulgaria, Hungary, and Romania, coming into effect in September 1947, contained certain provisions for observance of human rights. They also provided, on the insistence of the Soviet Union, that disputes arising under the treaties be referred to arbitral tribunals ("conciliation commissions") rather than to the International Court of Justice. In 1949 the United States and the United Kingdom brought complaints before the U.N. General Assembly, accusing the governments of Bulgaria, Hungary, and Romania of having violated the human rights obligations of the peace treaties. Having duly followed and exhausted the treaty procedure for the settlement of the disputes, the United States and the United Kingdom requested in August 1949 that Bulgaria, Hungary, and Romania join in forming the conciliation commissions contemplated in the treaties. But Bulgaria, Hungary, and Romania refused to appoint an arbitrator on their behalf and hence were able to frustrate the arbitration of these disputes. The International Court of Justice, responding to a request of the U.N. General Assembly, declared in its advisory opinion that, unless and until both parties to the dispute had appointed their arbitrators, the Secretary-General of the United Nations was not empowered to appoint a third arbitrator.

Fortunately, in recognition of the vital importance of compulsory third-party decision for settling disputes in a decentralized world, a slow trend has continued toward the establishment of such decision.

After the United Nations came into being, the International Law Commission undertook the first major effort to formulate a comprehensive draft convention on arbitral procedure. At its first session in 1949, the commission selected arbitral procedure regarding international disputes as one of the topics for codification. Convinced that every phase of arbitral procedure should reflect some degree of compulsoriness, the commission prepared a draft convention and presented it to the General Assembly in 1953. According to the draft, an undertaking to arbitrate would entail the consequence of empowering the International Court of Justice to decide the arbitrability of the dispute, thereby preventing one of the parties from evading arbitration by claiming the dispute to be outside the scope of the agreement. The court would further be authorized to maintain the immutability of the tribunal, once constituted, even if one of the parties chose to withdraw its arbitrator.

The draft was unfavorably reviewed by the General Assembly, which especially criticized the "quasi-compulsory jurisdictional procedure" and the proposal for concluding a convention on arbitral procedure. In 1955 the assembly decided to return the draft to the commission for further consideration, in light of the comments of governments and the discussion in its Sixth Committee. In 1957, the commission, instead of undertaking a thorough revision of the draft, decided to keep the substance of the draft intact and to submit it to the General Assembly as a set of draft articles that could serve as model rules for states in particular arbitrations. "[No] longer presented in the form of a potential general treaty of arbitration,"[26] the Model Rules on Arbitral Procedure prepared by the commission were submitted to the General Assembly in 1958. The assembly voted to bring these model rules to "the attention of Member States for their consideration and use, in such cases and to such extent as they consider appropriate, in drawing up treaties of arbitration or *compromis*."[27]

DISPUTE SETTLEMENT UNDER THE CONVENTION ON THE LAW
OF THE SEA

Another significant attempt toward establishing compulsory third-party decision occurred at the U.N. Conference on the Law of the Sea in 1958. In addition to the four conventions (dealing with the territorial sea and the contiguous zone, the high seas, fisheries, and the continental shelf), the conference adopted an optional protocol of signature concerning the compulsory settlement of disputes (entering into force on September 30, 1962). The optional protocol, forerunner to the present compulsory third-party dispute resolution system, which entered into force with the 1982 Convention on the Law of the Sea, and provided for the compulsory jurisdiction of the International Court of Justice regarding "disputes arising out of the interpretation or application of any Convention on the Law of the Sea" (except that on fisheries). Any party to the optional protocol could bring a dispute before the court, or, if the parties so chose, submit the dispute to conciliation or arbitration.

The regime of dispute settlements under the Convention on the Law of the Sea (the LOS Convention) of 1982 became a reality when the convention went into effect in 1994. This convention, recognizing the imperative of compulsory third-party decision making, contains elaborate provisions for the settlement of disputes, stipulated in more than two dozen articles and several annexes. Such imperative is particularly compelling for its comprehensive and complex treaty. Though the ratification process of the 1982 convention represents extraordinary compromise between many competing interests and demands, some formulas of generality and deliberate ambiguities bound to generate controversy in its interpretation and application remain.

The regime for settling disputes under the convention is characterized by simplicity, flexibility, and complexity, containing elements of both choice and compulsoriness. The convention mandates that contracting parties settle by peaceful means their disputes relating to the convention's interpretation and application. It enunciates an overriding policy of honoring freedom of choice of contracting parties, respecting above all the agreement dispute parties make regarding which mode of dispute settlement they will use. Disputing parties can not only bypass the procedures set forth in the convention by prior agreement and use some other mode of dispute settlement (bilateral, regional, or general) but also can agree at any time to settle their dispute by a different method even after they have submitted themselves to a procedure provided for in the convention. When they cannot agree on the means of settlement, they are obligated to submit most types of dispute to a compulsory procedure entailing decisions binding on all parties concerned. Here again flexibility prevails. Instead of providing a unitary system of dispute settlement, the convention offers states a number of options: the Tribunal for the Law of the Sea under the convention, the International Court of Justice, an international arbitral tribunal, or a special technical arbitral tribunal. Certain types of dispute are placed under the conciliation procedure, a procedure whose outcome is not binding on the parties. The provisions for exceptions to the compulsory judicial settlement or arbitration, embodied notably in Articles 297, 298, and 186–191 of the convention, are where the real complexities lie. In a nutshell, the three major exceptions relate to (1) disputes relating to the exercise by a coastal state of its sovereign rights or jurisdiction in the Exclusive Economic Zone; (2) disputes concerning sea boundary delineation, military or law enforcement activities, or disputes brought before the Security Council of the United Nations; and (3) disputes relating to seabed mining.

DISPUTE SETTLEMENT IN THE WORLD TRADE ORGANIZATION (WTO)

The most recent and important development in this area relates to the dispute settlement occurs in the World Trade Organization (WTO). The creation and development of the WTO was a direct response to the vastly expanding global economy and trade. By the early 1990s member states of the original General Agreement on Tariffs and Trade (GATT) (1947) became aware that the GATT was antiquated for the modern global market. Furthermore, the GATT dispute settlement procedure was proven to be inefficient and harmed the market economy because negotiations were easily dragged out, while the process often favored politically and economically stronger nations. Thus, the WTO placed great emphasis on developing an impartial and efficient dispute settlement procedure. According to the WTO: "[d]ispute settlement is the central pillar of the multilateral trading system, and the WTO's unique contribution to the stability of the global economy.... The WTO's procedure underscores the rule of law and makes the trading system more secure and predictable. The system is based on clearly-defined rules, with timetables for completing a case."[28]

The WTO greatly emphasized efficiency and expediency through setting up a "soft" timeline, with a targeted time of one year, absent an appeal, and an extra three months for an appeal. In addition, the WTO created the Dispute Settlement Body, which has the sole authority to establish panels, accept or reject panel rulings and appeals, and further the authority to retaliate against members that do not comply with a ruling.

The WTO's dispute settlement process begins with a consultation period during which the parties are encouraged to reach an amicable resolution through negotiation. During this time, the parties may negotiate among themselves, as well as request mediation or other assistance from the WTO Director-General. All parties reserve the right to settle disputes at any time. If the consultation is unsuccessful, the parties may request the appointment of a panel consisting of three or five experts. A panel hearing may last up to six months and generally consist of two sessions: (1) written and oral arguments, and (2) written and oral rebuttals. After the hearings, the panel issues a first draft outlining the facts and arguments of both sides for review by the parties before issuing a final report that may include suggestions or recommendations in the case where a panel finds any violations. The final report is distributed to all WTO members.

The parties in a WTO case may appeal the findings of the panel on questions of law. However, once the WTO's Dispute Settlement Body accepts the panel's final report, the parties are obligated to comply with its recommendations within a set amount of time.

Since its establishment, the WTO has had over four hundred cases. Approximately 50 percent of the cases settled through consultation, and approximately 75 percent of panel rulings were appealed. The United States and the European Union have been the predominant parties, with the United States appearing in approximately two hundred cases and the European Union in about one hundred fifty.[29] Generally, the WTO's dispute settlement system is considered to be successful, and compliance has not been a major issue. Notable examples of cases resolved through the WTO process include *United States–Shrimp-Turtle* (Asian countries successfully challenged the United States' discriminatory import practices),[30] *European Communities–Hormones* (the United States and Canada came to an interim settlement with the European Community regarding beef trade sanctions),[31] and *Mexico–Tax Measures on Soft Drinks and Other Beverages* (the United States successfully challenged Mexico's violation of the North American Free Trade Agreement (NAFTA) by restricting imports of artificial sweeteners and sugar substitutes).[32] However, at least one issue has been met with noncompliance by the United States, which has refused to change the way it calculates margins for "anti-dumping" purposes. This issue, known as zeroing, has spurred roughly one dozen reports from the Appellate Body.

INVESTOR-STATE DISPUTE RESOLUTION

Under traditional international law, nation-states were held to be immune from claims by private parties. However, increasingly, states are abandoning the concept of total state immunity, permitting certain claims against them by private parties in both domestic courts and a variety of international arbitral forums. A striking example of this trend is found in the area of investor-state dispute resolution, wherein states have consented to claims brought by foreign investors who allege mistreatment within the host state's territory. Often, the motive for giving this consent is the desire to attract foreign investors, who demand certainty that their economic resources will be safeguarded from hostile actions by the host government. Such conditions have led to increased development globally in sectors included energy, mining, infrastructure, and other areas, where developing countries seek transfers of capital, knowledge, or technological resources from foreign partners.

Declarations of consent are usually provided in the form of a bilateral investment treaty (BIT) between two or more states. Since the first BIT was signed by Germany and Pakistan in 1959, more than 2,500 such treaties had been listed with the U.N. Conference on Trade and Development (UNCTAD). Other examples of treaties authorizing investor-state arbitration include the global Energy Charter Treaty, as well as free trade agreements such as the NAFTA. Dispute resolution may also be authorized by agreements between an entity and the host state as a condition of an investment.

Though the investor-state arbitral system provides historically significant protections, investors are nevertheless limited in the types of claims they may bring against a host state. The types of claims permitted under bilateral investment treaties include unfair treatment vis-à-vis domestic competitors, direct or indirect expropriation (nationalization) of property without compensation, and arbitrary or unjust treatment by an instrumentality of the host state. In addition to securing such grounds for investors, BITs may require certain actions of contracting states designed to encourage free trade or to promote other policy objectives. For example, a model BIT adopted by the U.S. government in 2012 includes provisions regarding environmental and labor standards, in addition to measures to encourage regulatory transparency within adopting states.

Aggrieved investors may bring claims in forums such as the popular International Centre for Settlement of Investment Disputes (ICSID) headquartered in Washington, D.C. Other common forums include the U.N. Commission on International Trade Law (UNCITRAL), Stockholm Chamber of Commerce, and International Chamber of Commerce. Importantly, although the designated forum will provide the rules and institutional framework governing a particular arbitration, the proceedings may take place nearly anywhere in the world. The ICSID, which operates under the auspices of the World Bank, was created in 1966 following the adoption of the Convention on the Settlement of Investment Disputes between States and Nationals of Other States (also known as the Washington Convention, or ICSID Convention). As of 2013, nearly one hundred fifty states had ratified the convention. In addition to assenting to the ICSID's jurisdiction, the convention's contracting parties make their domestic judicial mechanisms available to foreign disputants who wish to enforce an arbitral decision within a member state's territory.

Since its inception, the ICSID has hosted nearly four hundred arbitrations, the vast majority of which have taken place within the past decade. A significant number of claims brought before the ICSID are settled between the disputants. However, a majority of the cases are presented before a tribunal, which renders its decisions in accord with the ICSID rules. Once a decision has been made, the parties may seek an annulment of the decision before an ad hoc committee. However, the grounds for such an appeal are limited. Article 52 of the ICSID Convention provides just five conditions under which the ad hoc committee may annul a tribunal's award:

a. that the Tribunal was not properly constituted;
b. that the Tribunal has manifestly exceeded its powers;
c. that there was corruption on the part of a member of the Tribunal;
d. that there has been a serious departure from a fundamental rule of procedure; or
e. that the award has failed to state the reasons on which it is based.

In practice, few investor-state arbitral awards have been annulled under the ICSID system, although an increasing number of cases have been appealed under Article 52 over the past decade.[33] The small number of annulments may speak to the quality and finality of ICSID tribunals for the settlement of disputes. However, concerns have arisen about prevailing parties' ability to collect on judgments, as evidenced by Argentina's refusal to pay awards owed as the result of disputes arising from its economic crisis. While such difficulties are to be expected, particularly among states, which have historically enjoyed immunity from such claims, reliable enforcement of arbitral awards will be critical to maintaining expectations of authoritative decision and control essential to international legal arrangements.

Nevertheless, such institutionalized mechanisms for dispute resolution between investors and states or between state parties offer an overall flexibility and choice on the part of disputants. Furthermore, the role of national courts in the enforcement of their decisions further illustrates the interconnections of authoritative processes horizontally and vertically. As such forums proliferate, parties, including individuals and private entities, are likely to strengthen demands for access to these arenas for the purposes of adjudicating disputes and safeguarding rights under international agreements. Their availability may encourage their use and thus add to the growing body of international jurisprudence and comprehensive decision making.

Notes

1. A. H. ROBERTSON, HUMAN RIGHTS IN THE WORLD 72–73 (1972).

2. G.A. Res. 2144 A, 21 U.N. GAOR Supp. (No. 16) at 46, U.N. Doc. A/6316 (Oct. 26, 1966) (italics added).

3. E.S.C. Res. 1503, 48 U.N. ESCOR Supp. (No. 1A) at 8, U.N. Doc. E/4832/Add. 1 (May 27, 1970).

4. Res. 1 (XXIV) of the Sub-Commission on Prevention of Discrimination and Protection of Minorities, August 13, 1971, *Report of the Twenty-Fourth Session of the Sub-Commission on Prevention of Discrimination and Protection of Minorities to the Commission on Human Rights, New York, 2–20 August 1971*, at 50–52, U.N. Doc. E/CN.4/1070 (E/CN.4/Sub.2/323) (1971).

5. E.S.C. Res. 1503, *supra* note 3.

6. Human Rights Council Res. 5/1, Rep. of the Human Rights Council, 5th Sess., June 11–18, 2007, U.N. GAOR, 62d Sess., Supp. No. 53, A/62/53 (June 18, 2007).

7. *See* Protocol No. 11 to the Convention for the Protection of Human Rights and Fundamental Freedoms, E.T.S. No. 155, (May 11, 1994), *available at* http://conventions.coe.int/Treaty/en/Treaties/html/155.htm; Protocol No. 14 to the Convention for the Protection of Human Rights and Fundamental Freedoms, CETS 194 (May 13, 2004), *available at* http://conventions.coe.int/Treaty/en/Treaties/html/194.htm.

8. Avena and Other Mexican Nationals (Mex. v. U.S.), 2003 I.C.J. 77 (Feb. 5).

9. Medellín v. Texas, 552 U.S. 491 (2008).

10. Avena and Other Mexican Nationals (Mex. v. U.S.), Interpretation of the Judgment of 31 March 2004, 2009 I.C.J. 3 (Jan. 19).

11. Bundesverfassungsgericht (BVerfG—Federal Constitutional Court), 2 BvR 2115/01, (Sept. 19, 2006), *available at* http://www.bundesverfassungsgericht.de/entscheidungen/rk20060919_2bvr211501.html.

12. Case Concerning United States Diplomatic and Consular Staff in Iran (U.S. v. Iran), Judgment, 1980 I.C.J. 3 (May 24).

13. United Nations, Multilateral Treaties Deposited with the Secretary-General, Status as at 31 December 1984, U.N. Doc. ST/LEG/SER.E/3, at 24 (1985) [hereinafter Multilateral Treaties].

14. *Id.*

15. Military and Paramilitary Activities in and Against Nicaragua (Nicar. v. U.S.), Order on Provisional Measures, 1984 I.C.J. 169 (May 10).

16. *See, e.g.*, Multilateral Treaties, *supra* note 13, at 25.

17. *Id.* at 24.

18. *Id.* at 25.

19. Military and Paramilitary Activities in and Against Nicaragua (Nicar. v. U.S.), Judgment, 1984 I.C.J. 392, 419 (Nov. 26).

20. Statement on the United States Withdrawal from the Proceedings Initiated by Nicaragua in the International Court of Justice, *reprinted in* 24 I.L.M. 246 (1985).

21. *Id.*

22. *Id.* at 248.

23. *Id.* at 247.

24. *See, e.g.,* Case Concerning Oil Platforms (Iran v. U.S.), Application, 1992 I.C.J. 2 (Nov. 2); Questions of Interpretation and Application of the 1971 Montreal Convention Arising from the Aerial Incident at Lockerbie (Libya v. U.S.), Application, 1992 I.C.J. 2 (Mar. 3); Aerial Incident of 3 July 1998 (Iran v. U.S.), 1992 I.C.J. 225 (June 5); Electronica Sicula S.p.A. (ELSI) (U.S. v. Italy), 1989 I.C.J. REP. 15 (July 20). *See generally* Robert Jennings, *The UN at Fifty: The International Court of Justice after Fifty Years*, 89 A.J.I.L. 493 (1995).

25. Interpretation of Peace Treaties with Bulgaria, Hungary and Romania, Advisory Opinions, 1950 I.C.J. 221 (Mar. 30, July 18).

26. UNITED NATIONS, OFFICE OF PUBLIC INFORMATION, THE WORLD OF THE INTERNATIONAL LAW COMMISSION 37 (1967).

27. G.A. Res. 1262, 13 U.N. GAOR Supp. (No. 18) at 53, U.N. Doc. A/4090 (1958).

28. *Understanding the WTO: Settling Disputes*, WORLD TRADE ORGANIZATION, http://www.wto.org/english/thewto_e/whatis_e/tif_e/disp1_e.htm.

29. Press Release, World Trade Organization, WTO Disputes Reach 400 Mark (Nov. 6, 2009), *available at* http://www.wto.org/english/news_e/pres09_e/pr578_e/htm.

30. Appellate Body Report, United States—Import Prohibition of Certain Shrimp and Shrimp Products, WT/DS58/AB/R (Oct. 12, 1998).

31. Appellate Body Report, *Hormones: European Communities—Measures Affecting Meat and Meat Products*, WT/DS26/AB/R, WT/DS48/AB/R (Jan. 16, 1998).

32. Appellate Body Report, *Mexico—Tax Measures on Soft Drinks and Other Beverages*, WT/DS308/AB/R (Mar. 6, 2006).

33. International Centre for Settlement of Investment Disputes, *Background Paper on Annulment for the Administrative Council of ICSID* (Aug. 10, 2012), *available at* https://icsid.worldbank.org/ICSID/FrontServlet?requestType=ICSIDNewsLettersRH&actionVal=Show Document&DocId=DCEVENTS11.

V   Bases of Power

THE AGGREGATE BASES of power of nation-states are not a static quantum but are in constant flux. They represent an ongoing community process in which the decision makers of nation-states manage resources and people through a variety of institutional practices and arrangements to pursue their goals in the world arena. Though dynamic in nature, these bases of power can be conveniently described in terms of resources, people, and authority. To participate in the global power process, nation-state elites seek to control resources and people and to exert authority in decision making.

Nation-states claim and employ many resources, including not only land masses but also rivers, oceans, airspace, outer space, ships, aircraft, and so forth. These resources exhibit varying degrees of exclusivity and shareability. Though some, notably land masses and closely proximate waters and air space, permit only some shared use and competence, others, such as international rivers, the oceans, airspace over the oceans, and outer space, are highly shareable. Claims by nation-states to these resources differ in comprehensiveness of authority and in scope and duration of control.

People are important assets for nation-states, but people differ from other bases of power in that they are rational beings with inherent dignity—the ultimate actors in any social interaction. Although elites seek to control people, people demand protection and fulfillment; they demand human rights in a comprehensive and dynamic sense. A human rights dimension is present in every social interaction and in every authoritative decision.

Authority is an important source of power. Authority builds on authority. Its essence is the freedom to make decisions, the freedom to create and maintain institutions and practices. In the contemporary world, allocation of authority to nation-states is effected both vertically and horizontally: vertically between the general community and the nation-states, and horizontally between and among nation-states in relation to particular events.

8 Control over Territory

THE CONTEMPORARY STATE system, building on a key notion that a nation-state occupies a definite part of the surface of the earth, embodies territorial organization with a high degree of exclusivity. Unlike other resources, land masses are generally perceived to tolerate, only in the most modest degree, shared use by states and shared competence in administration of such use.

Under the traditional notion of "territorial sovereignty," a nation-state normally exercises, subject to the limitations imposed by international law, the competence to prescribe and apply law to persons, things, and events within its territorial domain to the exclusion of other states. In principle, the boundaries of a state's territory define the reach of its authority based on territoriality.

Territorial authority ("territorial sovereignty") of a state extends to all rivers and lakes within its territory and to its internal waters and territorial sea. The state's authority over such waters is as plenary as the authority it exercises over land masses. Territorial sovereignty extends further to the airspace superjacent to its territory and to the airspace above all waters of its territorial reach.

National control over territory historically bears a striking resemblance to private ownership of land. Early international law relied heavily on the Roman law of property in developing principles to govern the acquisition of territory.

The customary international law governing the acquisition of territory developed when the European powers were the dominant participants in the world arena. Acquiring territory was part of the "empire-building" processes of the competing colonial powers. In acquiring vast overseas territories, resources, and markets, the rival powers proudly proclaimed themselves to be carrying the "white man's burden" on a "civilizing mission" around the world.

These empires, sharing the heritage of Christianity and a strong sense of national unity, acquired substantial military strength due to the dynamic growth of science, technology, and industry. Immediate targets of expansion were uninhabited regions or regions inhabited by "savages or semi-civilized peoples." Areas suitable for migration, such as the land masses of North and South America, Australia, New Zealand, and parts of Africa, were occupied through full settlement. The next target was Asia. In the populous areas of Asia, European migration for permanent settlement was not especially important. The paramount pursuits were physical resources and markets, linked in various ways to expansion in religion, culture, education, health, and other sectors. In one form or another, weak territorial communities of the Asian continent became the prey of European colonial powers. The next major targets were the remaining areas of the African continent, which, though not fully suitable for permanent settlement, were valuable as a resource base and as a potential market. The polar areas and rather isolated islands, finally, though practically uninhabitable or with scarce resources, were sought primarily for their potential significance in modern strategy.

In the course of expansion all instruments of policy, especially military force, were mobilized. Among the colonial powers there were early settlers and latecomers, and relative power positions fluctuated in the world balancing of power. Within loose restrictions the use of military force, even to acquire territory, was permitted as an instrument of change. The damaging repercussions of the use of force were, understandably, not as far-reaching as in today's world, given the low interdependence and rudimentary technology of weaponry at that time. Further, the concept of the survival of the fittest was at its height in both international and domestic arenas in the nineteenth century. Since the expansionist powers identified their role as a civilizing mission, concern for the aspirations of the local inhabitants of a newly acquired territory received little weight in developing customary international law regarding the acquisition of territory. The overriding concern of the decision makers, the major powers at that stage of history, was how, in a power-balancing world, to stabilize community expectations in favor of consolidating the fruits of expansion.

As they eventually developed, the modalities of acquiring territory under traditional international law have been generally classified into five categories: accretion, occupation, prescription, conquest (or subjugation), and cession.

Accretion results from the natural (slow) or artificial formation of land. It presents little problem. In contrast, avulsion—the sudden, unnatural shift in boundary matters—does not change ownership.

Occupation applies only to "unappropriated territory"—that is, *terra nullius*. Occupation has a private law analogy. According to Roman law property not owned by any person (*res nullius*) is subject to appropriation by occupation, which required both the intent to assert ownership (*animus*) and manifestation of physical control (*factum*). By analogy this private law rule was extended to cover the acquisition by a state of title over uninhabited territory. During the era of colonial expansion, a vital question was whether this principle could apply to territory inhabited by relatively uncivilized native tribes.

Prescription is technically defined as "the acquisition of sovereignty over a territory through continuous and undisturbed exercise of sovereignty over it during such a period as is necessary to create under the influence of historical development the general conviction that the present condition of things is in conformity with international order."[1] Thus conceived, the definition of this technical term differs significantly from that of the prescribing function referred to elsewhere in this book. Jennings sums up the distinction between occupation and prescription in these words:

> Occupation can only apply to territory that is *res nullius*; it is in all cases lawful in origin, and the mere passage of time has no place in it, provided only that the apprehension of the territorial sovereignty be effective. Prescription, on the other hand, is a portmanteau concept that comprehends both a possession of which the origin is unclear or disputed, and an adverse possession which is in origin demonstrably unlawful. For prescription, therefore, the possession must be long continued, undisturbed, and it must be unambiguously attributable to a claim to act as sovereign. It depends as much on the quiescence of the former sovereignty as on the consolidation through time of the new.[2]

One element common to all acquisition of territories is "effective control," irrespective of modalities. This has been clearly demonstrated by such famous cases as the *Island of Palmas* case (United States v. Netherlands, 1928),[3] *Sovereignty over Clipperton Island* (France v. Mexico, 1931),[4] and the *Legal Status of Eastern Greenland* (Denmark v. Norway, 1933).[5] Claims based on discovery, or symbolic acts, are generally insufficient to acquire title. Unlike bare discovery, in the sense of first sighting, claims based on symbolic or ceremonial acts of possession (such as flag raising or making a proclamation) have been given considerably greater weight in practice. In almost every territorial dispute, the contesting states have generally sought to establish, by proof of symbolic acts of possession, the earliest possible connection with the disputed area. Though claims based on such symbolic acts were once regarded as sufficient to establish title, the necessity of limiting such claims soon became apparent with their proliferation. Hence, the recognition of claims based on discovery and symbolic acts of possession was transformed into the requirement of actual occupation or possession. In other words, effective control is required, despite the abundance of the literature debating what constitutes effective control. The kind of effective control historically required to acquire title to the larger land masses of the earth involves not only some single act of assertion of naked power but a continuous and comprehensive process in use and enjoyment. This process has been observed to require

> an identifiable participant taking effective control of the resource, as effectiveness may be determined by the varying characteristics of the resource and context, giving notice to the world through appropriate ceremonials or otherwise of its intent to acquire, asserting authority over the resource in its management as a continuing base of power, and employing the resource in strategies appropriate to its characteristics in the production of values.[6]

Evidently, the underlying policy consideration is to maximize resource use, because an effective occupant is in the best position to exploit resources fully.

The profound changes since World War II are vividly reflected in the flow of decisions dealing with former colonies. Because of the tremendous proliferation of new nation-states, the older European powers no longer take the initiatives that lead to territorial change. Instead, the ex-colonies-turned-new-states have become the dynamic participants in redrawing the map of the world. The chief objective in acquiring territory is no longer proclaimed to be a "civilizing mission" or part of building empires. New objectives enter the political process and stimulate new justifications for permissible alterations of territory. Foremost among these innovations is an intense demand that the boundaries of bodies politic conform to popular aspirations so as to protect human rights and enhance world public order.

The bases of power among nation-states continue to show patent discrepancies. The patterns of disputes over territory, however, have changed markedly. In the colonial era the dominant controversies were either between great powers and small powers or among great powers. High expectations of violence accompanied these confrontations; lesser powers formerly were quickly policed by a major power or their cause escalated into conflict between great powers. Then, during the Cold War, territorial clashes between small powers generated a threatening climate, punctuated by overt acts of violence. Today, in the post–Cold War era, the greatest threat to public order and human rights is the proliferation of ethnic-based violence, as ethnic hatreds long suppressed or ignored have unleashed "centrifugal forces," pulling states apart from Africa to Europe to South and Central Asia.[7]

The territorial problems that have arisen from the demise of colonial empires, the fall of the Soviet Union, and the emergence of new states are far too different and complex to be met adequately by the customary rules of the past. As unappropriated land masses on the planet have vanished, the traditional law originally designed to deal with territorial changes involving such land masses has diminished in relevance. (It may, however, experience a resurgence in an age of astropolitics, although the 1967 Space Treaty prohibits nation-state acquisition of ownership of celestial bodies.) Furthermore, constitutive changes in the international order, relating to human rights, have led to the recognition that self-determination is no longer limited to decolonization but includes internal and external self-determination as well. New norms in international law are needed to account for these changes.[8]

Though all instruments of policy continue to be employed by claimant states to support territorial claims, the use of military force as a means of change, particularly of territorial change, is explicitly prohibited by the Charter of the United Nations. Before the establishment of the United Nations, the use of military force to acquire territories or other valued assets was not regarded as impermissible—even in the form of large-scale "war." The "subjugation" (or "conquest") of a territory and its people as a result of armed attack was an acceptable mode of affecting transfers of a territory from one nation-state to another. Though the Covenant of the League of Nations made "resort to war" unlawful under certain circumstances, it fell short of outlawing "war" altogether. In the nineteenth and early twentieth centuries, there was, understandably, less common interest in restraining violence. The prevailing policy then sought to localize coercion by giving community approval to quick settlement of disputes through superior strength.

Because territorial expansion and acquisition often disrupted world order, there were, even during that period, some initiatives to deny the fruits of expansion to aggressors through collective nonrecognition. The Stimson doctrine, named after Secretary of State Henry L. Stimson under U.S. President Herbert Hoover for his advocacy of refusing to recognize as legally valid any changes resulting from Japan's seizure of Manchuria in 1931 in violation of treaty obligations, typified this line of effort. The traditional international law regarding conquest, however, has been most profoundly affected by the new expectations incorporated in the U.N. Charter. The charter projects both a negative policy of minimizing the deliberate use of coercion as a means of value change and a positive policy of promoting the shaping and shaping of values by persuasion. In its negative formulation, the principle seeks to ban any unilateral use of coercion by one state against another as an instrument of value change. Article 2(4) of the charter states, "All Members shall refrain in their international relations from the threat or use of force against the territorial integrity or political independence of any state, or in any other manner inconsistent with the Purposes of the United Nations." In its positive formulation, it seeks to foster the stability in the expectation of freedom from unauthorized coercion that is indispensable to the optimum production and distribution of values. Article 2(3) stipulates, "All Members shall settle their international disputes by peaceful means in such a manner that international peace and security, and justice, are not endangered." Taking the charter as a whole, it would appear that the threat or use of force is generally prohibited except for self-defense and community enforcement action. Although a minority dissents, it is increasingly conceded that contemporary international law has no place for the acquisition of territory through conquest or subjugation.

It has been asserted that the acquisition of territory resulting from self-defense against an aggressor state is still permissible, since self-defense remains permissible. That argument, however, misconceives the scope of self-defense. Under contemporary international law, self-defense is regarded as permissible insofar as it is necessary and proportionate to repel aggression (see chapter 19). As soon as aggression is repelled, the state acting in self-defense must cease its defensive operations lest it become an aggressor. It is not necessary to acquire title over the aggressor's territory in order to exert the "necessary and proportionate" degree of self-defense required to repel aggression. To draw a fine distinction between the acquisition of territory by permissible coercion and by impermissible coercion would most assuredly open a Pandora's box, highly destructive of the fundamental policy of maintaining world order. A clear and ever-present danger is posed by licensing "acquisition by permissible coercion" in this decentralized world, where the maintenance of minimum public order depends so heavily on the reciprocity and mutual restraint of nation-states in their interaction. In this vein, the Declaration of Principles of International Law concerning Friendly Relations and Cooperation among States in accordance with the Charter of the United Nations (1970) provides that "the territory of a State shall not be the object of acquisition by another State resulting from the threat or use of force. No territorial acquisition resulting from the threat or use of force shall be recognized as legal."[9] This provision has been interpreted to mean that no acquisition of territory is permitted by the use of force, even if it is a lawful exercise of self-defense in accord with the U.N. Charter. The Security Council's denunciation under Resolution 242 of Israel's occupation of territory taken during the 1967 war is a reflection of this community policy.[10] Another was the series of Security Council resolutions that began in August 1990 with Resolution 660[11] in which the Security Council condemned Iraq's invasion of neighboring Kuwait and demanded the immediate and unconditional withdrawal of Iraqi forces. The series of resolutions culminated with Resolution 678[12] in November 1990, which authorized "all necessary means" to force Iraq to remove its troops from Kuwait after it failed to abide by the previous resolutions.

Cession involves the transfer of territory by treaty from one nation-state to another; its counterpart in private law is transfer of property in land. Traditionally, there have been two types of cession: noncoercive and coercive. Cession made free from coercion, as in the U.S. purchase of Alaska, leaves little ground for objection if the necessary internal processes of decision conform to appropriate standards. But cessions resulting from coercion require a critical reappraisal in the light of contemporary community policies. Since the U.N. Charter makes it impermissible to acquire territory by conquest, a cession designed to formalize the fruit of unlawful coercion evidently cannot be accepted. The issue of cession was raised most recently in regard to Crimea, which was annexed by Russia following the signing of an accession treaty in March 2014. Only days before, Crimea declared itself the Republic of Crimea after a public referendum in favor of independence from Ukraine. To many, the hastily organized referendum and the speedy integration into Russia that followed (with Russian soldiers close at hand) were impermissible under international law due to the appearance of coercion by Crimea's larger neighbor.

When considering the impermissibility of coercion, note the operation of intertemporal law—that is, this fundamental change in community policy cannot be applied retroactively to the acquisition of territory by conquest or coercive cession in the past; otherwise, established usages would suddenly dissolve, and the world order would become ever more insecure.

The world community today faces a number of territorial problems either inadequately settled or left unsettled after World War II. Affecting cession after a large-scale armed conflict via a peace treaty is a time-honored practice. A peace treaty is commonly regarded as an authoritative expression of the shared expectations of both victorious and defeated powers following the formal termination of a state of "hostility." Even when conquest was fully permissible, traditional international law deferred to peace treaties as superseding provisional arrangements made during hostilities. The underlying policy consideration is profound. Expectations expressed amid hostility are generally dictated by military expediency and necessity for victory. Other relevant policy considerations tend to disappear or to receive scant attention. The commitments made under the emergency conditions of wartime offer, at best, a precarious foundation for future order; they are most likely to lead to the disruption of public order sooner or later. Hence the imperative and practice of a cooling-off period for noncoercive negotiation after hostilities cease. Only in an atmosphere of relative nonviolence and nonemergency can both sides be expected to consider all the relevant interests at stake in shaping a more durable policy. This explains the importance attached to the role of the "peace treaty" under traditional international law. A primary function of such an instrument is to ascertain unequivocally the shared expectations of the parties, especially the defeated powers, concerning any change of territory. Territorial clauses are particularly well drafted in order to prevent subsequent claims of ambiguity; any transfer of territory is prescribed in no uncertain terms.

The establishment of the United Nations has not altered the significance of peace treaties as an authoritative expression of the shared policy of both victorious and defeated states at the close of hostilities. But its charter does inject a new community policy into the situation involving territorial changes: the principle of self-determination. Even in the nineteenth century, efforts were made to mitigate deprivations imposed on inhabitants in cases of cession by mandating a plebiscite, which enabled the populations most concerned to express their preferences and make their choices. Several treaties concluded during that period stipulated that cession could not take effect without the genuine consent of the inhabitants, as expressed through a plebiscite. President Wilson's championing of the principle of self-determination did reach grandly throughout the globe but achieved limited success in the territorial settlements after World War I. It was in the establishment of the United Nations that a great multilateral treaty proclaimed the principle of self-determination to be a fundamental policy of the world community. The practice of the United Nations to date has made it clear that respect for the genuine aspirations of the people concerned is the ultimate guide for effecting territorial change.

The principle of self-determination, as elaborated in chapter 2, assumes particular significance in the context of territorial transfer.

This principle was most eloquently reaffirmed in the famous opinion on Western Sahara rendered by the International Court of Justice in 1975.[13] Western Sahara, administered as Spanish Sahara until 1976, borders Morocco, Mauritania, and Algeria. Although Spain expressed its willingness to decolonize the territory in accord with the relevant U.N. resolutions calling for self-determination, Morocco and Mauritania pressed their respective territorial claims to the territory. In December 1974 the U.N. General Assembly requested the International Court of Justice to render an advisory opinion on the following two questions:

1. Was Western Sahara … at the time of colonization by Spain a territory belonging to no one (*terra nullius*)?

If the answer to this question is in the negative,

2. What were the legal ties between this territory and the Kingdom of Morocco and the Mauritanian entity?[14]

In its opinion of October 16, 1975, the court answered the first question in the negative. In response to the second question, the court found that certain legal ties existed between the territory and Morocco and the Mauritanian entity but that these were not ties of "territorial sovereignty." The court concluded that it "has not found legal ties of such a nature as might affect the application of resolution 1514 (XV) in the decolonization of Western Sahara and, in particular, of the principle of self-determination through the free and genuine expression of the will of the peoples of the Territory."[15]

Since the court opinion the following have occurred: the purported division ("annexation"), in defiance of the court opinion, of Western Sahara upon Spain's withdrawal from the territory in February 1976; the proclamation of the establishment of the Sahara Arab Democratic Republic (SADR) by the POLISARIO Front on February 28, 1976; the subsequent Moroccan occupation of the Mauritanian zone in 1979; recognition of the POLISARIO Front as the legitimate representative of the Saharan people by the U.N. General Assembly on November 21, 1979; admission of SADR as the fifty-first member of the Organization of African Unity (OAU) on February 22, 1982, despite Morocco's strong opposition; Morocco's withdrawal from the OAU on November 12, 1984, in protest over the seating of the POLISARIO delegation; and the continuing desert war between Moroccan forces and POLISARIO Front guerrillas. Despite a ceasefire declared in 1991, and the presence of U.N. peacekeeping forces to implement a referendum on self-determination, the Western Sahara issue remains at an impasse. Notable efforts by James Baker, personal envoy for the U.N. Secretary-General for Western Sahara, failed to overcome the stalemate. Baker formulated two plans (known as Baker

I and II) in 2000 and 2003 that laid out a proposal for an independence referendum for Western Sahara. Morocco, however, rejected the plans, insisting instead that Western Sahara could become a semi-autonomous region within Morocco. Baker resigned his post soon after. These events confirm again the contemporary importance of respecting the paramount principle of self-determination in the case of territorial transfer.

Many of the important points made in this chapter—especially the prohibition of the use of force in the acquisition of territory—were vividly illustrated by the dispute between Argentina and the United Kingdom over the Falkland Islands. On April 2, 1982, the armed forces of Argentina invaded the Falkland Islands of the South Atlantic over the sovereignty of these islands (called Islas Malvinas by the Argentinians), inhabited by fewer than two thousand people. Its title had been disputed intermittently by Argentina since 1833, when the British seized and occupied the islands. During seventeen years of negotiations preceding the invasion, the United Kingdom and Argentina failed to resolve the dispute. The Argentine forces overran a small British garrison and quickly captured the islands. One day later, April 3, the U.N. Security Council adopted Resolution 502, which determined the existence of "a breach of the peace," demanded "an immediate cessation of hostilities" and "an immediate withdrawal of all Argentine forces from the Falkland Islands," and called on Argentina and the United Kingdom to seek a diplomatic solution to the dispute.[16] Following failed mediation by the United States and the U.N. Secretary-General, the United Kingdom succeeded in retaking the islands by force of arms as a matter of self-defense. Argentina surrendered on June 14, and the seventy-four-day war came to an end. On November 4, 1982, the General Assembly passed a resolution urging the United Kingdom and Argentina to negotiate their dispute over title to the Falkland Islands.[17]

In support of their respective claims for title to the islands, both Argentina and the United Kingdom have invoked such traditional modalities for the acquisition of territory as discovery, occupation, and prescription and raised the issue of self-determination, but they have emphasized different sets of relevant facts and temporal features. Argentina has stressed its succession to Spain's early title to the islands upon its independence from Spain in 1816 and the factor of contiguity. The United Kingdom has insisted that its title to the Falkland Islands has long been perfected and hence cannot be disturbed by mere protest or claim to contiguity, because the United Kingdom has exercised effective, unbroken, open, and peaceful control and administration over the islands since 1833, aside from the fact that all the inhabitants there today are British and wish to remain under British rule.

As the matter stands, a negotiated solution appears remote. So does an authoritative determination by an international tribunal. But the Falkland Islands conflict has underscored the utmost importance of a fundamental community policy governing territorial disputes under contemporary international law stressing nonuse of force. This bedrock principle of the United Nations was also at the heart of the world community's response to Iraq's invasion of Kuwait in 1990. In 1922, Britain set the modern-day state boundaries for Iraq, Kuwait, and Saudi Arabia. Since that time, Iraq had occasionally claimed part or all of Kuwait as its territory. This came to a head in 1990 when Iraq invaded

Kuwait, overthrew its government, and, aside from violently terrorizing the Kuwaiti people, claimed Kuwait as its nineteenth province. The world community condemned Iraq's actions and the U.N. Security Council, through Resolutions 661 and 662, quickly imposed economic sanctions on Iraq[18] and called on member states to refrain from recognizing Kuwait as Iraqi territory.[19] Global condemnation resulted in the Security Council passing Resolution 678, which explicitly authorized "Member States.... to use all means necessary to uphold and implement ... relevant resolutions and to restore international peace and security in the area."[20] In January 1991, the United States, acting under the authority of Resolution 678, led a coalition of forces into Kuwait to push the Iraqi army out. By February, the U.S.-led forces had succeeded in liberating Kuwait.

In any event, today it is keenly perceived that much more than acreage is involved in changing the status of a territory; human beings simply cannot be disposed of as if they were sand and rocks. In the celebrated dictum of Judge Hardy C. Dillard in *Western Sahara*, "It is for the people to determine the destiny of the territory and not the territory the destiny of the people."[21] When a territorial transfer occurs, it involves more than territory in the abstract—indeed, the entire community process of authority and control over people, resources, and institutions is at stake. Changes extend to the external as well as the internal process of a given domain. If territorial changes are to occasion the least peril to world public order, any settlement must be in accord with two interdependent policies: minimization of unauthorized coercion and self-determination. Any territorial change imposed against these basic community policies carries the seeds of its own destruction and resembles a time bomb that threatens world security.

In addition to the rules governing title to territory, international law has developed a distinct and extensive body of principles dealing with the delimitation of boundaries. Although state boundaries are usually established by treaty or custom in general terms, the precise delimitation of a particular boundary can encounter enormous difficulties. Delimitation problems not only arise between new states with ill-defined boundary lines but may also involve particular areas for delimitation within states having long-standing uncontested boundaries. A preferred state practice is to form commissions, which are mandated to implement the guidelines agreed on by the parties involved in a particular boundary dispute.

Several important decisions of the International Court of Justice (ICJ) have shed light in this area. Notable examples include the ICJ's 1962 award of the centuries-old Preah Vihear Temple to Cambodia despite claims of ownership by Thailand;[22] a 2001 settlement of a dispute between Qatar and Bahrain over the Hawar Islands;[23] a 2002 decision to hand over control of the peninsula of Bakassi to Cameroon following a years-long dispute with Nigeria;[24] and the 2008 resolution of a disagreement between Singapore and Malaysia over the status of island formations, including Pedra Branca, located in a waterway between the two nations.[25] The role and importance of the ICJ in the resolution of disputes in the process of authoritative decision and the maintenance of public world order has been explored in chapter 7.

Another important concept in delimitating borders between nation-states is *uti possidetis*, which refers to the practice of granting new nations the same borders as those that existed during its occupation by another power, particularly during the colonial era. Under this principle, a new nation is presumed to inherit its colonial boundaries unless otherwise decided. This practice has had a tremendous impact on the decolonization process in Africa, South America, and elsewhere, including the former Soviet Union. Many nations in these regions continue to exist according to administrative boundaries that were developed in past eras without an expectation that they would someday become international borders.

While *uti possidetis* provides a useful and convenient tool for locating the borders of a new nation, it may also perpetuate divisions imposed by a colonial power that are not in the interest of the new state. For example, previous borders may have cut across population groups in ways that disturbed social patterns. In the absence of a stabilizing power, such as a former colonizer, these divisions may lead to the outbreak of violence based on issues such as religion or ethnicity. For these reasons, some scholars have argued that the process of drawing borders around new nations should look to other principles, such as self-determination, for a more rational method of demarcation that emphasizes human security. At the same time, it seems the importance of international borders is diminishing as people become increasingly interconnected and interact more frequently across nation-state lines.

Notes

1. LASSA OPPENHEIM, INTERNATIONAL LAW 576 (H. Lauterpacht ed., 8th ed. 1955).

2. ROBERT JENNINGS, THE ACQUISITION OF TERRITORY IN INTERNATIONAL LAW 23 (1963).

3. 2 Rep. Int'l Arb. Awards 829 (1948).

4. *Award Rendered at Rome*, Jan. 28, 1931, 26 A.J.I.L. 390 (1932).

5. 1933 P.C.I.J. (ser. A/B), No. 53.

6. Myres S. McDougal, Harold D. Lasswell, Ivan A. Vlasic, & Joseph C. Smith, *The Enjoyment and Acquisition of Resources in Outer Space*, 111 U. PA. L. REV. 523, 559 (1963).

7. Steven R. Ratner, *Drawing a Better Line: Uti Possidetis and the Borders of New States*, 90 A.J.I.L. 590 (1996).

8. W. Michael Reisman, *Sovereignty and Human Rights in Contemporary International Law*, 84 A.J.I.L. 866, 873 (1990). *See also, e.g.*, Makau wa Mutua, *Why Redraw the Map of Africa? A Moral and Legal Inquiry*, 16 MICH. J. INT'L L. 1113 (1995); Charles William Maynes, *The New Pessimism*, FOREIGN POLICY (1995).

9. G.A. Res. 2625, 25 U.N. GAOR Supp. (No. 28) at 121, 123, U.N. Doc. A/8028 (1970).

10. S.C. Res. 242, U.N. SCOR, 22d Sess., 1382d mtg.

11. S.C. Res. 660, 45 U.N. SCOR at 19 (Aug. 2, 1990).

12. S.C. Res. 678, 45 U.N. SCOR at 27 (Nov. 29, 1990).

13. Western Sahara, Advisory Opinion, 1975 I.C.J. 12 (Oct. 16).

14. *Id.* at 14.

15. *Id.* at 68.

16. S.C. Res. 502, U.N. SCOR, 37th Sess., 2350th mtg. at 15 (Apr. 3, 1982).

17. G.A. Res. 37/9, 37 U.N. GAOR Supp. (No. 51) at 18, U.N. Doc. A/37/51 (Nov. 4, 1982).

18. S.C. Res. 661, ¶ 3, U.N. Doc. S/RES/661 (Aug. 6, 1990).

19. S.C. Res. 662, ¶ 2, U.N. Doc. S/RES/662 (Aug. 9, 1990).

20. S.C. Res. 678, ¶ 2, U.N. Doc. S/RES/678 (Nov. 29, 1990).

21. Western Sahara, Advisory Opinion, 1975 I.C.J. 12, 122 (Oct. 16) (Separate Opinion of Judge Dillard).

22. Temple of Preah Vihear (Cambodia v. Thailand), Judgment on Merits, 1962 I.C.J. 6 (June 15).

23. Maritime Delimitation and Territorial Questions between Qatar and Bahrain, Judgment on Merits, 2001 I.C.J. 40 (Mar. 16).

24. Case Concerning the Land and Maritime Boundary Between Cameroon and Nigeria, Judgment, 2002 I.C.J. 303 (Oct. 10).

25. Case Concerning Sovereignty Over Pedra Branca/Pulau Batu Puteh, Middle Rocks, and South Ledge (Malay./Sing.), Judgment, 2008 I.C.J. 12 (May 23).

9   Control and Use of the Sea

ANY REALISTIC CONSIDERATION of the international law of the sea must begin with the peculiarities of the social process by which the seas are exploited and enjoyed. This process has many salient features. The sea, well known for its spatial-extension resources, can accommodate manifold needs for navigation and transit. Unlike the land masses, the sea is a relatively shareable resource; it is vast and its expanses are great. Its known resources comprise both renewable, flow resources and nonrenewable, stock resources. Tremendous numbers of people have the technologies to exploit these resources. Many objectives can be satisfied from using and exploiting the seas, notably transportation, communication, the production of food, and the exploitation of minerals. The use of the oceans may affect every value people cherish, and scientific knowledge and developing technologies may yet disclose new uses. The strategy employed may be cooperative and noncompetitive: what one gets, others may also get. The cooperative use and enjoyment of the oceans over the past three centuries has resulted in a tremendous production of goods and services for distribution to all humankind.

It has been traditionally assumed that the ocean space and its resources were inexhaustible; hence each participant has been accorded a high degree of freedom on the high seas to engage in accepted activities without undue interference.

Contemporary realities have rendered this earlier assumption invalid, with the growing realization that the extent to which the resources of the sea can be exploited is limited. Certain species of fish have been overexploited. Problems of economic recoverability greatly affect the availability of nonliving resources from the sea. Growing competition among states over the exploitation of finite fossil fuel resources has sparked controversy as actors strive to establish control over the materials that fuel national economies. Problems of marine pollution associated with oil and waste disposal, moreover, require attention in the community effort to protect the ocean ecosystem. The threat of non-state actors presents a new challenge in the age of global interdependence in assuring the safety and navigability of the high seas for the benefit of all.

Broadly conceived, three types of claims on the sea can be identified. The first are claims to access—the use and enjoyment of the ocean. The second are claims to competence (jurisdiction) in making and applying law regarding activities on the oceans. The third are claims to resources.

These three types of claims may be made with regard to any of the waters of the globe—to areas technically described as internal waters, the territorial sea, the contiguous zone, continental shelf, and the exclusive economic zone. They are, of course, always made in relation to the high seas. Some caution is in order in using the aforementioned terms. These technical terms, normative-ambiguous, refer both to facts and to legal consequences and purport both to describe and to state preferences. At this point it is better to keep clear their factual reference in terms of the geographical distribution of these types of claims to global waters. Too often the labels are used merely to express justifications behind different decisions or choices among competing claims.

Basic Community Policy

The paramount function of the international law of the sea is to protect and secure the common interests, inclusive and exclusive, of the peoples of the world and to reject all claims of special interest. Consisting of a flow of decisions that emanate from the larger constitutive processes of the world community, it is designed to establish an ordered, economic, effective way for the peoples of the world to most fully exploit the sea in their common interest.

The common interests to be protected fall into two broad categories: inclusive and exclusive. By inclusive interests is meant demands and expectations about activities that have a degree of collective impact, generating significant transnational or global consequences. By exclusive interests is meant demands and expectations about activities whose impact extends primarily to the peoples of a territorial community. The common interests are secured through the proper harmonization of both inclusive and exclusive interests.

Perceived comprehensively, the inclusive interests of the peoples of the world include maintaining minimum order, in the sense of minimizing unauthorized coercion and violence, and pursuing optimum order, in the sense of the greatest production and widest distribution of all demanded values that are attainable with available resources. For centuries the public order of the oceans has sought to achieve both minimum order and optimum order. Keeping the oceans of the world open for the shared use of all those having the necessary capacities and skills has contributed mightily to the greater aggregate production and distribution of goods and services to benefit all humankind.

An exclusive interest, as an essential component of the common interest, refers to interests regarding which community members have a shared concern because of the distinct impacts of the activities involved, though not exactly in the same manner and degree. For instance, an important interest of every state of the world is to protect the community processes on its land masses from dangers and threats from the oceans. Hence, every state has an interest in the waters proximate to it, which will permit it to preserve the security and integrity of its community processes and to pursue the greatest productivity and fairness in distribution. No two states of the world, however, have the same interest in proximate waters. Canada and Mexico, respectively, have different interests in the waters immediately off their coasts from those the United States has in the waters off its coasts. Given the length of its coastlines, the United States has the most extensive interests of this kind; many other states, meanwhile, have comparable interests, though in different degrees. Because of this comparability in interest it has long been perceived to be in the common interest of all states that every state be accorded some degree of control over proximate waters.

By a special interest is meant a claim that is destructive in its impact on others and bears no rational relation to a genuine exclusive interest that can be shared with others. For example, the extravagant claims once made by some countries (such as Chile, Peru, and Ecuador) for two-hundred-mile territorial seas are claims of special interest, made without regard for their impact on others and with destructive consequences for the total production and distribution of goods and services. Such claims cannot be made with promises of reciprocity and do not represent genuine exclusive interests. Should other states follow suit and make comparable claims, the common interest would disintegrate completely, with some countries losing out in the end.

Special interests are by definition inimical to common interests. When states depart from the yardstick of common interest, the only alternative is naked power. If a state makes a claim that it cannot make with a promise of reciprocity to other states, it invites coercive response and violent retaliation. What is meant, then, by special interests are those interests that are asserted against the community without regard to their impact. A major purpose for which the global constitutive process is maintained is to reject claims of special interest and to secure a public order based on common interest.

For every state of the world, exclusive interests increase the closer one is to shore, and the farther one moves from the shore, the more inclusive interests predominate. It would appear, in light of several centuries of successful cooperative enjoyment of the oceans, that a strong presumption is given in favor of the inclusive interest. Where many people are able and willing to engage in production, where the resource is highly shareable, and where the utmost production can be achieved by sharing, a presumption exists in favor of sharing. This does not mean that exclusive interests should be disregarded. What is required for rational decision is a way of accommodating the exclusive interests of the coastal states in proximate waters with the inclusive interests of all states in the utmost enjoyment of all waters in the light of differences in context.

The perception of what constitutes inclusive interest and exclusive interest has evolved over time, reflecting the changing demands and expectations of the peoples of the world under ever-changing conditions, especially the advancement in science-based technology. The task of attaining the common interest by harmonizing both inclusive and exclusive interests and by rejecting special interests is a complex and dynamic process. The tension inherent in this delicate task has been manifested in the trends in decision and development.

Trends in Decision and Conditioning Factors

Since 1609, when Hugo Grotius propounded the doctrine of the freedom of the seas, the bulk of the international law of the sea has developed through custom. This body of customary law sustained a public order of the sea for more than three centuries. Customary law, as policed by reciprocity, retaliation, and self-restraint, gives some assurance of rationality and stability.

Historically, as underscored by the early debate between Grotius and John Selden— open sea versus closed sea—tension between the freedom of the seas for inclusive use and the appropriation of the seas for exclusive use has been perennial. The regime of the territorial sea represented exclusive use and that of the high seas, inclusive use. Within the narrow confine of territorial seas, inclusive use for the general community was circumscribed to accommodate the exclusive interest of the coastal state: though noncoastal states enjoyed the right of innocent passage, they had no right to its resources. In contrast, beyond the territorial sea was the regime of the high seas, providing inclusive use to all states, allowing them to navigate freely and to use its resources.

The international law of the sea is not a mere static body of rules but a whole decision-making process. It is a process of uninterrupted interaction, of continuous demand and response, in which the decision makers of particular nation-states unilaterally put forward diverse claims to use the world's seas, and other decision makers, both national and transnational, respond by either accepting or rejecting them. This process, grounded in the practices and sanctioning expectations of nation-state officials, is always changing and developing, as the demands and expectations of peoples are modified by the exigencies of new interests and technology and by other evolving conditions in the world arena.

Although the customary law of the sea offered considerable rationality and stability for more than three hundred years, the slow evolutionary process tended to fall behind the changing pace of the world. Despite the emergence of international cooperation during the era of the League of Nations, attempts toward codification made at the Hague Conference in 1930 were without success.

After the creation of the United Nations, the first major undertaking for codification was the First United Nations Conference on the Law of the Sea (UNCLOS I) in 1958, in which more than eighty states participated. Four conventions were adopted, dealing, respectively, with the territorial sea and the contiguous zone, the high seas, the continental shelf, and fishing and conservation of the living resources of the high seas. With the exception of the convention on the continental shelf, the other three conventions reflected essentially the long-acknowledged customary law.

The failure to agree on the breadth of the territorial sea at the Second United Nations Conference on the Law of the Sea (UNCLOS II) in 1960 was a significant omen of the collapse of an old order of the sea and an accelerating search for a new order to govern the use, exploitation, and enjoyment of the oceans.

The advancement of technology has led not only to new uses of the ocean, especially the exploitation of oil and gas on the continental shelf and the future harvesting of rare-earth elements from the deep seabed, but also to intensified demands for access to the ocean resources. The rush by coastal states to grab the resources of the seas through extravagant claims for the expansion of maritime zones, the growing concern about overfishing and marine pollution, and the insistent demands of developing states have become highly pronounced. The imperative search for the common interest in a world of complex interdependencies and of proliferating nation-states of diverse backgrounds, amid conflicting national claims and the rapid development of science-based technologies, has led to a sustained, collective effort in formulating a comprehensive convention on the law of the sea.

The Third United Nations Conference on the Law of the Sea (UNCLOS III) was an ambitious and comprehensive undertaking. It dealt not just with particular problems but with the entire spectrum of issues in the contemporary law of the sea. From its first organizational session in December 1973 to the adoption of the final act in December 1982 (with 149 delegations participating), the third conference took eleven formal sessions, holding altogether some ninety-four weeks of meetings. The conference proceeded by a consensus approach without formal vote-taking, seeking to accommodate, in dealing with a wide range of issues, competing and conflicting demands and interests of participants—notably, between the major maritime powers and the coastal states; between coastal states and landlocked and geographically disadvantaged states; between food supply through optimum yield and conservation of living resources; between coastal fishing and distant-water fishing; between states with broad continental shelves and states with narrow continental shelves; between developed and developing nations; between exploitation of mineral resources and environmental concerns; and between marine research and national security.

When the Convention on the Law of the Sea (the LOS Convention) came up for formal adoption on April 30, 1982, member states adopted it by a vote of 130 to 4, with 17 abstentions. The convention contains 320 articles and nine annexes. Its seventeen parts deal with the following: (1) use of terms and scope (Article 1); (2) territorial sea and contiguous zone (Articles 2–33); (3) straits used for international navigation (Articles 34–45); (4) archipelagic states (Articles 46–54); (5) exclusive economic zone (Articles 55–75); (6) continental shelf (Articles 76–85); (7) high seas (Articles 86–120); (8) regime of islands (Article 121); (9) enclosed or semi-enclosed seas (Articles 122–123); (10) right of access of landlocked states to and from the sea and freedom of transit (Articles 124–132); (11) the Area (international seabed area beyond the continental shelf of a state) (Articles 133–191); (12) protection and preservation of the marine environment (Articles 192–237); (13) marine scientific research (Articles 238–265); (14) development and transfer of marine technology (Articles 266–278); (15) settlement of disputes (Articles 279–299); (16) general provisions (Articles 300–304); and (17) final provisions (Articles 305–320).

The nine annexes are: (1) highly migratory species; (2) Commission on the Limits of the Continental Shelf (containing nine articles); (3) basic conditions of prospecting, exploration, and exploitation (twenty-two articles); (4) statute of the enterprise (thirteen articles); (5) conciliation (fourteen articles); (6) statute of the International Tribunal for the Law of the Sea (forty-one articles), (7) arbitration (thirteen articles); (8) special arbitration (five articles); and (9) participation by international organizations (four articles).

Finally, postconvention accompanying agreements have added to the convention's scope. These include: the Agreement Relating to Part XI of the Convention; the 1995 United Nations Fish Stocks Agreement; and Agreement for the Implementation of the Provisions of the Convention relating to the Conservation and Management of Straddling Fish Stocks and Highly Migratory Fish Stocks.

Part XI of the 1982 convention originally called for a highly interventionist administration of deep seabed resources, reflecting the demands of a then socialist-leaning Third World to an extent unacceptable to "pioneer investors" and to the United States (under the Reagan administration) and other developed nations. Because of strong objections by these parties to Part XI, ratification of the LOS Convention was held up for ten years. However, in response to significant political and economic changes, as well as an approaching ratification deadline, consultations that started in 1990 brought all nations together to form the agreement, a compromise that allowed the implementation of the entirety of the LOS Convention in 1994. The LOS Convention (and the accompanying agreements) builds on the prevailing practice of participating states, reflects the evolution of international law in response to the changing globe, and charts a new course in some areas, notably in its ratification procedures and its compulsory third-party dispute settlement system. Many nations, including nonratifying nations such as the United States, generally regard the LOS Convention as the authoritative expression of the law of the sea.

The discussion of the LOS Convention that follows will examine the core of its framework, highlighting areas of interest and concern in order to address its fundamental importance in managing the shared use of the world's oceans. Examination of the convention's maritime zones begin with the exclusive interests found in its internal waters and territorial sea, then moves to the conflict between exclusive interests and inclusive interests in the exclusive economic zone and continental shelf, and lastly onto the high seas and the deep abyss to examine the predominant inclusive interests in open waters.

INTERNAL WATERS

Article 8 of the LOS Convention refers to internal waters as the waters on the landward side of the baseline by which the territorial sea is measured. These waters include lakes, rivers, canals, ports, bays, and historic bays (Articles 9–14). International law authorizes states to make law for their internal waters—to regulate the use of these waters and to decide who can come in, who has to keep out, and what they may do while there.

A coastal state has complete authority over its internal waters, because internal waters adjoin the land territory of a state. This authority is nearly as comprehensive as sovereignty over the land masses, and it extends to authority over the resources of its internal waters with a preference of exclusive national exploitation.

A state has complete authority to control access of vessels, both private and governmental, to internal waters. In this zone of waters, no right of innocent passage for foreign vessels exists. Under customary international law, foreign ships do not enjoy a general right of access to a state's ports. The Convention and Statute on the International Regime of Maritime Ports of 1923 enunciated the policy of freedom of access to ports by foreign merchant ships on the basis of reciprocity. Although it has not been widely ratified, such access is generally and widely executed through bilateral treaties on the condition of reciprocity.

Once foreign ships enter ports or other internal waters, they are subject to the territorial sovereignty of the coastal state. The coastal state may prescribe and apply its laws against foreign ships and those on board, with such exceptions as operations of sovereign and diplomatic immunities, matters of the captain's discipline over the crew, and matters of "internal economy" of foreign ships. Every foreign ship (including warships) in internal waters must comply with the laws governing navigation, health, safety, and port administration of the coastal state.

THE TERRITORIAL SEA

The territorial sea, also known as territorial waters, refers to the belt of sea adjoining the coast over which a coastal state asserts sovereign authority. The sovereignty of the coastal state extends to the airspace over the territorial sea and its seabed and subsoil. The territorial sea is measured seaward from the baselines delimiting internal waters.

Before the LOS Convention, wide disagreement existed about the most basic issue concerning the law of the seas: the breadth of the territorial sea. The three-mile territorial sea, which originated in the cannon-shot rule, was strongly challenged in the 1960s and the 1970s. In the early 1980s, of the 137 independent coastal states, only a small minority (24) followed the three-mile rule, a few claimed six miles, the overwhelming majority (79) claimed twelve miles, and others (26) claimed a territorial sea of more than twelve miles (some reaching as far as two hundred miles). The first U.N. conference in 1958 failed to agree on the width of the territorial waters, and the second U.N. conference in 1960 failed by one vote to adopt the proposal to extend the territorial sea to six miles. The LOS Convention settles this long-contested issue, providing under Article 3 that the outer limits of the territorial sea are not to exceed twelve nautical miles from the baseline.

Although the United States is not a party to the LOS Convention, it believes that unchallenged territorial sea claims may become valid over time through acquiescence. In 1979, the United States established the Freedom of Navigation Program (FON) to protest excessive territorial sea claims. The program recognizes not only the vital national interest of the United States to ensure that its maritime rights are protected, but also the interest to protect the freedoms agreed to by the international community. FON operates on a "triple track" that involves not only diplomatic negotiations and "operational assertions" by American naval patrols, but also bilateral and multilateral consultations with other governments. Importantly, this effort highlights the ongoing effort to promote harmonization of the inclusive and exclusive interests by policing the obligation of all states to adhere to the customary rules and practices reflected in the LOS Convention.

The normal baseline from which the width of the territorial sea is measured is the low-water mark. But because of peculiar geographical configurations or other considerations, some states have departed from this practice by drawing straight baselines across bays and areas of the coast indented by fjords and islands. This delimitation method was approved by the International Court of Justice (ICJ) in 1951 in the *Anglo-Norwegian Fisheries* case.[1] The court held that the Norwegian scheme of baseline delimitation, employing a series of straight lines of varying lengths to link a number of points most of which were not on the mainland, was permissible in international law. This method, incorporated in the Geneva Convention on the Territorial Sea of 1958, is reaffirmed by the LOS Convention in Article 7.

The territorial sea is functionally regarded as the seaward extension of a coastal state's territory over which it exercises sovereignty, limited only by the corresponding exercise of the right of other states to "innocent passage." This right affords ships of all states the right to navigate through the territorial sea, for the purpose of traversing it without entering internal waters, or of proceeding to or from internal waters, provided the passage is innocent. Passage is innocent if it does not prejudice the peace, good order, or security of the coastal state. Under the LOS Convention, Article 19(2) specifies a list of acts that are "prejudicial to the peace, good order or security of the coastal state" in order to secure greater stability and to minimize potential conflicts of arbitrary unilateral determinations and retaliations. It also prohibits discrimination based on the flag or destination of a ship.

The right of innocent passage is applicable to all ships, including warships. Notably, the LOS Convention deliberately does not distinguish between merchant ships and warships. The right of innocent passage, however, does not extend to aircraft or submerged submarines. Aircraft are not permitted to pass over territorial waters without the coastal state's consent, and submarines must navigate on the surface and show their flags pursuant to Article 20.

INTERNATIONAL STRAITS

With the expansion of the territorial sea from three to twelve miles, the high seas corridors of some 116 straits used for international navigation whose widths are between six and twenty-four miles, would be lost. For instance, the closure of the Straits of Gibraltar, Hormuz, and Malacca would have significant transnational consequences to the global supply chain if commercial shipping were forced to navigate without these "short-cuts" of the sea. What would the consequences be to the long-established freedom of navigation of international straits, a freedom clearly affirmed by the ICJ in the *Corfu Channel* case of 1949?[2]

From the outset of UNCLOS III, the major maritime powers were acutely concerned with this problem. They predicated their acceptance of a twelve-mile territorial sea on a guarantee of unimpeded passage, for warships as well as merchant ships, through the straits thus affected.

In response, Article 37 of the LOS Convention prescribes a regime of transit passage, applicable to straits "used for international navigation between one part of the high seas or an exclusive economic zone and another part of the high seas or an exclusive economic zone." It is designed to secure the common interest by providing freedom of navigation through, over, and under these straits, as well as safeguarding the safety and environmental interests of straits states. It seeks to redress a deficiency of the pre-UNCLOS III framework that failed to make a meaningful distinction between passage through the territorial sea and the transit of straits.

The right of transit passage is to be distinguished from the right of innocent passage: the former applies to straits used for international navigation, whereas the latter applies to passage through all other territorial seas not located within such straits. Transit passage involves freedom of navigation and overflight for the sole purpose of continuous and expeditious transit of the strait. Transit passage extends to aircraft and embraces the right of submerged transit by submarines through such straits. In addition, states bordering straits are not permitted to hamper or suspend transit passage.

The importance of the international strait is not only limited to today's needs but also the needs of tomorrow. Take for example the Northwest Passage. For hundreds of years seafarers have sought a sea passage along the North American frontier to link the Atlantic Ocean to Pacific Ocean. Although some have successfully navigated the Northwest Passage, most attempts to operate large commercial vessels have been stymied due to the presence of impenetrable polar ice. Today, rising sea temperatures resulting from global climate change is thinning the polar ice and will soon make such a northerly shipping route commercially feasible.

Although the predictions of the thinning of the polar ice caps vary within the scientific community, the general consensus is that the Northwest Passage will become navigable to large merchant vessels within the next twenty-five years. The Northwest Passage represents an attractive and valuable commercial shipping route to maritime powers because of its proximity to the rich oil and natural gas resources located within the Arctic Circle. Significantly, this future passage has the potential to shorten the journey from both Northwest Asia and the Arctic Circle to Europe by as much as 40 percent.

Controversy over international legal status of the Northwest Passage first arose as an issue between Canada and the United States in 1969 when oil was discovered at Prudhoe Bay, Alaska. Shortly thereafter, an American oil company successfully navigated a crude oil tanker through the passage. The Canadians were angered by what they considered a breach to their territorial sovereignty. In an effort to assert its jurisdictional competence, Canada passed national legislation to regulate foreign ships navigating in what they considered to be their territorial waters.

The controversy over the Northwest Passage encompasses claims of access, jurisdiction, and, most important, resources. Specifically, there is much debate over who actually controls the waters in which the Northwest Passage lies.[3] The United States, the European Union, and other maritime powers have asserted their inclusive interests, arguing the passage is an international strait subject to the right of passage. Limiting the freedom to navigate the Northwest Passage would generate significant transnational consequences; the transport of natural resources from the Arctic would be subject to absolute Canadian regulation or transporters would be forced to navigate around Canadian waters. If such a result would materialize, shipping expenses for commodities transiting the passage would most likely negate any commercial value of this route. In defense of its territorial sovereignty, Canada has asserted that the Northwest Passage lies within its historic internal waters and therefore falls within Canada's jurisdictional competence.

Facially, the Northwest Passage controversy seems tense. However, good relations between the parties on a number of other matters have allowed the dispute to be managed diplomatically. In 1988, Canada and the United States entered into the Arctic Cooperation Agreement to manage transit through the Northwest Passage. Although the Arctic Cooperation Agreement eased tensions over the Northwest Passage, nothing in the agreement changed the respective legal positions of the parties. Notably, in 2007, the Canadian prime minster reasserted Canada's claim to these waters, reasoning that "as oil, gas and minerals of the Arctic become more valuable, northern-resource development will grow ever more critical. The need to assert our sovereignty and protect our territorial integrity in the Arctic on our terms has never been more urgent."[4] Although diplomacy has eased tensions, Canada has invested significant resources to assert its jurisdictional control over what it alleges is Canadian territory.

As climate change continues to wreak havoc on the polar ice caps and the international community continues to rely on fossil fuels as the primary source of energy, the importance of the Northwest Passage and the right of transit passage through the Arctic will only intensify.

ARCHIPELAGOS

A number of states (such as Indonesia, the Philippines, and Fiji) whose territories consist of groups of islands lying near one another have made claims to have the waters between their islands recognized as internal waters so as to achieve national unity, integrity, and security. The potential impact on the freedom of navigation is enormous.

The LOS Convention endows archipelagic states with sovereign authority over all waters within the archipelagos but in Article 53 subjects such authority to a right of "archipelagic sea lanes passage" through archipelagic waters. This right, similar to transit passage, extends to all aircraft and ships, including submerged submarines. The LOS Convention prescribes specific guidelines for delimiting archipelagic sea zones.

Archipelagic states retain sovereignty over airspace above their waters and to the seabed below and may designate sea lanes and air routes for the purpose of transit passage. These courses should follow the normal traditional passage routes to afford foreign ships and aircraft an unobstructed right of passage. Archipelagic sea lane passage is thus essentially equivalent to the right of transit passage through straits.

THE CONTIGUOUS ZONE

Beyond the territorial sea, all coastal states are accorded under Article 33 of the LOS Convention a contiguous zone, an area not extending more than twenty-four nautical miles from the baselines from which the territorial sea is measured. In this belt, a coastal state may exercise its authority to prevent or punish violations of its regulations concerning customs, immigration, fiscal, and sanitary matters committed or intended to be committed within its territory or territorial sea.

When the coastal state has good reason to believe that a ship has violated its laws and regulations, it may undertake "hot pursuit" of a foreign ship in order to apprehend it pursuant to Article 111. The chase must be commenced when the foreign ship is in the pursuing state's territorial sea or contiguous zone and must cease when the pursued ship enters the territorial sea of its own state or of a third state. A coastal state's exercise of criminal jurisdiction on board a foreign ship is proper only when such ship is passing through the territorial sea and is limited to prosecution for acts that would have deleterious effects in the coastal state's territory.

THE EXCLUSIVE ECONOMIC ZONE

One of the most radical and far-reaching transformations in the law of the sea under the LOS Convention is the authority given to coastal states over an enormous ocean area, designated as the exclusive economic zone (EEZ). The EEZ is a belt of ocean two hundred nautical miles wide in which coastal states have sovereign rights to explore and exploit natural resources of the superjacent waters and seabed. Collectively, coastal states' EEZs constitute about one-third of the world's oceans. Importantly, the establishment of the EEZ within the UNCLOS III framework recognized that contemporary realities of a coastal state's exclusive interests begin to merge with the inclusive interests of all other states in a hinterland-like zone between the high seas and territorial sea.

Importantly, an EEZ tends to be especially rich in fisheries resources, with some estimates finding that about 99 percent of the world's fisheries lying within the EEZs of all nations. The Convention on Fishing and Conservation of Living Resources of the High Seas of 1958 recognized the particular interest a coastal state has in maintaining the productivity of the living resources in any area of the high sea adjacent to its territorial sea. Many states simply went ahead to claim a two-hundred-mile territorial sea to protect fisheries.

The trend toward a two-hundred-mile EEZ began with the claims for exclusive fishery areas off the shores of Latin American states and was fortified by whaling industries eager to protect their rights of access. In the EEZ, coastal states enjoy sovereign rights not for comprehensive purposes but for particular purposes, especially the management of natural resources. All other states of the world community may share in the use of and access to any state's EEZ. Article 56 under the LOS Convention grants sovereign rights to coastal states over natural resources, certain economic activities, and certain types of authority over scientific research and environmental protection. A state's sovereign rights to explore, exploit, conserve, and manage extend not only to all living resources in the zone but also to nonliving resources of the seabed, its subsoil, and superjacent waters and other related activities, such as the production of energy from the water, currents, and winds.

The LOS Convention stresses the importance of reciprocity between coastal states and all other states. Although the coastal state must give due regard to the rights and duties of other states in the EEZ, all other states must regard the rights and duties of the coastal state and comply with its laws. Significantly, landlocked and geographically disadvantaged states (especially those in the region surrounding a coastal state) are accorded the right to participate in exploiting part of the zone's fisheries when the coastal state cannot harvest them all itself (Articles 69 and 70).

The nature of the EEZ has been disputed. Many maritime nations regard it as essentially part of the high seas that is subject to special economic rights for the coastal states. Some others regard it as a further extension of the territorial sea within which foreign states may exercise certain high seas rights.

All other states enjoy the high seas freedoms prescribed under Article 58. In the framework of the LOS Convention, the EEZ creates an intriguing legal construct when interpreted in light of the high seas freedoms of Article 58. While the coastal state has the right to regulate some activities, other states retain much of their high seas freedoms contained in Articles 88–115—namely freedom of navigation and overflight and a variety of permissible uses relating to these freedoms, including certain naval operations and meteorology studies. However, the indeterminacy of regulating military activities in the EEZ has sparked a debate whether such coastal state action is permissible. It seems as though the majority of state parties—and nonratifying nations such as the United States—interpret the rights of the coastal state much more narrowly, espousing to the traditional freedoms of the high seas. Nevertheless, China, Bangladesh, Brazil, India, Malaysia, Pakistan, and Uruguay have each made statements asserting significantly broader rights of the coastal state to regulate the military operations of other states operating within their respective EEZs.

Although the underlying basis for the EEZ emanates from a state's desire to protect its fishing industries, coastal states have used the LOS Convention to expand their authority over the EEZ for other uses such as oil and natural gas exploration. The quest for asserting greater control over vast areas of the sea that were originally considered the high seas creates a rich breeding ground for controversy. One such dispute is observed in the competing claims over the control and use of the South China Sea.

The South China Sea dispute is perhaps one of the most dangerous points of conflict in Asia. Competing claims of control and jurisdiction have been asserted by China, Taiwan, Vietnam, Indonesia, Malaysia, Cambodia, Thailand, Singapore, and the Philippines. Although most of the controversy involves issues arising from overlapping EEZ claims, China and Taiwan's competing claims do not involve disputes over overlapping EEZs, but rather assertions that most, if not the entirety, of the South China Sea lies within its jurisdictional competence.

The dispute arises from a number of factors. Notably, much of the dispute is over who controls the oil and natural gas fields located beneath the seabed of the South China Sea. Discovery of energy deposits is a significant factor for not only the region but also the international community because of the need to exploit the earth's natural resources to power national economies. The dispute also involves claims to fishing bounties and control over shipping lanes vital to international commerce.

Some commentators have suggested that the dispute over the South China Sea will likely be resolved through multilateral agreements rather than through the more formal adjudicatory dispute settlement procedures of the LOS Convention. Significantly, no party to the South China Sea dispute has initiated a legal proceeding before either the ICJ or the International Tribunal for the Law of the Sea for fear that the outcome cannot be controlled. A number of feasible alternatives have been proposed, namely a joint development authority that will manage the exploitation of the oil and natural gas resources of the South China Sea.[5] The private sector—which has much to gain from the resource exploitation of the South China Sea—may even assist in encouraging competing states to reach a consensus.

Whichever dispute resolution mechanism is deployed, it must contend with China's unilateral policy toward the South China Sea that runs counter to the common interest. China regards its claims in the South China Sea as a "core" national interest similar to its claims to Taiwan. Like many global powers, China would like to assert control over the fossil fuel resources of the South China Sea in order to exploit them. Moreover, China has begun to invest heavily in its sea power and has told the United States to keep out of the dispute. China's growth as a world power creates a significant power imbalance among the parties concerned and, therefore, may dampen the chance of an equitable resolution. However, recently the United States has urged China to legitimize its claims to parts of the South China Sea by providing evidence of its claims in keeping with standards of international law.

THE CONTINENTAL SHELF

Geographically speaking, the continental shelf constitutes the area of the seabed that is the natural prolongation of the coastal land beneath the sea to the point where the seabed begins its precipitous descent into the ocean abyss. The continental shelves contain virtually all of the oceans' known nonliving organic resources, including oil and natural gas.

Contemporary international law on the continental shelf is said to have begun with President Truman's proclamation of 1945 claiming the natural resources of the subsoil and seabed of the continental shelf adjacent to the United States. This act was quickly emulated by the United States' regional neighbors (Mexico, Argentina, and so on) and other countries across the globe.

By the convening of the First United Nations Conference on the Law of the Sea in 1958, the question of the continental shelf had become a major subject of common concern, leading to the conclusion of the Convention on the Continental Shelf. The convention, in Article I, recognized the sovereign rights of coastal states to explore the continental shelf and to exploit its natural resources, extending "to a depth of 200 meters or, beyond that limit, to where the depth of the superjacent waters admits of the exploitation of the natural resources." The second of the two criteria—known as the exploitability test—was less than precise and soon became a major source of controversy because of the changing technology of resource exploitation.

In the protracted process of negotiation under UNCLOS III, the task of defining the continental shelf was enormous, because the competing interests of the coastal states with extensive continental shelves, the two superpowers, the Arab states (none of which has a continental shelf exceeding two hundred miles), and the landlocked and geographically disadvantaged states were to be given balanced and judicious considerations. A complex formula of delimiting the continental shelf was thus adopted.

Under Article 76 of the LOS Convention, the continental shelf of the coastal state extends to the edge of the continental margin, where the seabed drops off into the deep ocean, or to a distance of two hundred miles where the continental margin does not extend that far. When the outer edge of the continental margin extends beyond two hundred miles from the coastal state's baselines, the limit of the continental shelf shall lie where the thickness of sedimentary rocks is at least 1 percent of the shortest distance from such point to the nearest point on the continental slope, as long as this distance is no more than sixty miles from the continental slope. In no case shall the limit of the shelf lie more than three hundred fifty miles from the coastal state's baselines or more than one hundred miles beyond the 2,500-meter depth line (isobath), whichever is greater. Thus, in effect, the continental shelf has four possible outer limits: two hundred nautical miles; the outer edge of the continental margin; three hundred fifty nautical miles; and one hundred miles from the 2,500-meter isobath.

The coastal state has sole sovereign rights to the natural resources of its continental shelf. But this does not affect the status of the waters above it. The two are legally independent. The rights of the coastal state must not, therefore, in their exercise, cause any "unjustifiable interference" with any rights of other states that may inhere in these superjacent waters. The status of a seabed area as continental shelf likewise does not affect the rights of other states to lay submarine cables or pipelines across it.

The LOS Convention imposes three duties on the coastal state in reference to its continental shelf: (1) the state must set up environmental standards as to resource exploitation on its entire continental shelf; (2) the state must pay a percentage of all revenue derived from exploitation of the shelf, beyond a two-hundred-mile distance, into a special international fund for the benefit of developing countries to a fund administered by the International Seabed Authority; and (3) the coastal state may not prohibit marine scientific research on the shelf beyond a two-hundred-mile distance outside specified development areas.

States with opposite or adjacent shorelines must decide on a boundary between their continental shelves in accordance with Article 83. The overriding guidance is to reach an "equitable solution." One interesting example of such delimitation is set forth in the *Gulf of Maine* case, decided by the ICJ under its chambers procedure in October 1984.[6] In drawing a single maritime boundary dividing both the continental shelves and the exclusive fisheries zones of Canada and the United States in the Georges Bank area, centering around the Gulf of Maine, the court interestingly steered clear of all sociological or scientific arguments and instead based its decision on more clearly apparent geographical factors.

Due to the rich, untapped natural resources beyond the two-hundred-mile demarcation, state parties to the LOS Convention have scrambled to assert their jurisdictional competence over yet unclaimed portions of the continental shelf. Article 81 grants coastal states the exclusive right to authorize and regulate drilling on the continental shelf for all purposes. Coastal states that intend to establish, in accordance with Article 76, the outer limits of the continental shelf beyond two hundred miles must submit supporting scientific data to the Commission on the Limits of the Continental Shelf (CLCS) within ten years of entry into force of the LOS Convention for that state. An international cadre of scientific experts from the fields of geology, geophysics, and hydrography reviews the coastal state's documentation and recommends a boundary on the basis of equitable geographic representation. The limits of the shelf established by a coastal state on the basis of the CLCS's recommendations are final and binding and may be appealed pursuant to the dispute settlement mechanisms under the convention.

Claims to the continental shelves under the sea have varied and most likely will add controversy to an area of the sea that was once off limits to claims of state control. Interestingly, some nations, including France, Ireland, Spain, and the United Kingdom have made joint claims to the continental shelf in the Celtic Sea and the Bay of Biscay, while Malaysia and Vietnam have made claims in the South China Sea. Nevertheless, other nations—such as China—have asserted controversial claims of their own. Roughly half of the Arctic Ocean's seabed is classified as a continental shelf and is up for grabs. Overlapping claims to jurisdictional competence among the nations who border the Arctic Ocean—the United States, Canada, Denmark, Norway, and Russia—are inevitable because of the potential for the exploitation of natural resources in this vast, unclaimed region.

HIGH SEAS

Although Grotius formulated the doctrine of freedom of the seas in the sixteenth century, the concept did not gain acceptance until the mid-nineteenth century. During the early nineteenth century, England had become the supreme power on the high seas and used its navy to open the way for merchant ships to carry commerce without interruption. England, along with the fledging United States, combated special interests, namely piracy, to ensure the international lanes of commerce remained open.

Both nations realized that if large tracts of the seas were to be the sovereign territory of one state, international commerce could be restricted to the detriment of all. Therefore, the view was accepted that the sea should remain free for all nations. Over time, more and more states acknowledged the necessity of the freedom of the seas. This consensus has been embraced in the LOS Convention under Article 87: "The high seas are open to all States." On the high seas, every state has the competence to sail ships under its flag, while merchant ships, warships, and state-owned or state-operated ships enjoy complete immunity from the jurisdiction of any state other than their flag states while on the high seas.

In a time of greater globalization, the doctrine of the freedom of the seas is just as salient as it was two centuries ago. The seas remain a vital mode of transportation in the global supply chain that permits the interconnected economies of the world to thrive. Remarkably, this doctrine has permitted roughly 70 percent of the earth's surface to remain a shared, community resource for the benefit of all humankind. In addition to the traditional freedom of navigation, the freedoms under Article 87 include overflight, the laying submarine cables and pipelines, construction of artificial islands and other installations, fishing, and scientific research.

With the inclusion of the EEZ, the LOS Convention does not define the high seas but simply applies its provisions on the high seas to all parts of the seas beyond the EEZs. Moreover, the convention makes most of the provisions on the high seas applicable within the EEZ insofar as they are not incompatible with the prescriptions governing the EEZ.

Ships on the high seas are required, as a matter of common interest, to comply with regulations governing the safety of navigation, the protection of life at sea, and the minimization of marine pollution, as prescribed by the flag state and treaty obligations for participating state parties under the International Maritime Organization (IMO).

Unless otherwise permitted by treaty, passage of a foreign vessel on the high seas may be interfered with only in certain circumstances. On the high seas, any state's warship may also board a ship suspected of engaging in the slave trade or one that is a "stateless vessel." Under the LOS Convention, it is also permissible under certain circumstances for a state's ship to board a foreign ship that is engaged in unauthorized broadcasting on the high seas.

Another significant exception is when a vessel is engaged in acts of piracy. A pirate ship is defined as one used by private individuals for private acts of violence or detention, or any act of depredation committed for private ends against another ship, its passengers, or their property while outside the jurisdictional domain of any state.

In light of the indiscriminate violent nature of piracy, Article 105 grants the right to every state "[o]n the high seas, or in any other place outside the jurisdiction of any State" to seize a pirate ship or a ship taken by piracy and under control of pirates and arrest the persons on board. Although piracy was believed to be something of a bygone era, the ancient criminal trade has proliferated in hot spots around the globe from the Malacca Strait to the Gulf of Aden. These regions are in close proximity to both shipping lanes vital to international trade and coastal states that are challenged by issues of insecurity.

The most striking contemporary acts of piracy have occurred off the coast of Somalia. Following years of civil war, poverty, and instability, Somalia devolved into a failed state, with limited governance capacity and virtually no rule of law. The lack of law enforcement and judicial mechanisms helped to incubate a criminal trade that was in direct conflict with the inclusive interest of the freedom to navigate the high seas. Although the proliferation of Somali piracy has some roots in efforts by Somali fisherman to protect Somalia's abundant fisheries in both its territorial waters and EEZ from foreign predation, it evolved into a lucrative criminal enterprise creating an unprecedented, indiscriminate menace to all ships navigating in the Gulf of Aden and Indian Ocean. Both ships and crews have been captured and ransomed for large sums. The piratical acts of Somali nationals have threatened the safety of innocent seafarers as well as key lanes of international commerce.

By 2008, the Somali piracy controversy became so acute that the international community took collective action to mitigate the destructive and destabilizing effects of piracy on commerce in the region. The U.N. Security Council granted state naval patrols the authority to use force against ships suspected of engaging in piratical acts. Soon thereafter, a multilateral naval force was dispatched to the Gulf of Aden and the Indian Ocean for a maritime security action designed to combat and deter piracy and apprehend suspected pirates.

The Somali piracy crisis grew out of many complex domestic issues in the chaos of a failed state and threatens the inclusive interests of the international community. Hence, the complexity of the controversy requires a response tailored not only to relieve the high seas of piratical violence but also to mitigate human insecurity on land. The appropriate international response must consider the needs of both the world community and the Somali people in order to ensure that peace and security are attained. Under no circumstances should piracy be condoned.

So far, the international response has addressed both needs to varying degrees. Pirates have been captured, tried, and convicted in domestic courts in the United States, the Seychelles, and Kenya. In some cases, lethal force has been used when lives were in immediate danger. There have also been efforts to alleviate Somali insecurity; however, because of the complexities involved in such a nation-building project, feasible alternatives to alleviate the land-based factors fueling piracy have been less forthcoming.

THE AREA

A novel development in the LOS Convention is the inclusion of a comprehensive legal regime to explore and exploit the bottom of the deep ocean in areas beyond the continental shelf of any state. "The Area," as the international seabed area has come to be known, comprises the seabed and subsoil beyond the limits of national jurisdiction. In 1967, the U.N. General Assembly established the Seabed Committee to consider the question of the deep seabed lying beyond the limits of national jurisdiction. The impetus for the international seabed arose from Arvid Pardo, Malta's then-ambassador to the United Nations, who first called world attention to the immense resources of the seabed and ocean floor beyond the limits of national jurisdiction and proposed that such resources be kept as the "common heritage of mankind."[7] Following these early efforts and negotiations during UNCLOS III, the Area was incorporated in the LOS Convention.

In making the mineral resources of the Area a "common heritage of mankind," the LOS Convention does not permit any state to claim, exercise sovereign authority over, or appropriate any part of the deep seabed or its resources. Instead, the convention established the International Seabed Authority (ISA) to govern the deep seabed under a "parallel system" of exploration and exploitation. An enterprise will be responsible for directing activities in the Area and for the transporting, processing, and marketing of minerals recovered from the Area. However, the enterprise has yet to be tested since no mining operations are currently being undertaken in the Area.

The ISA, having the standard structure of an international governmental organization, consists of an assembly, a council, and a secretariat. The assembly, composed of all states parties to the convention, is the supreme organ of the ISA and is responsible for prescribing general policies. Matters of substance are decided by a two-thirds majority.

The council, consisting of thirty-six members, is endowed with the important authority to prescribe mining regulations and procedures, restrictive environmental orders, and so on. The formula for representation on the council, a result of intense negotiations, is complex, seeking to accommodate the demands and expectations of the important producers of certain minerals with those of the most important consumers and to balance the needs of various communities in terms of technology and actual production.

Interest in the mining of the sea floor since implementation of the LOS Convention has steadily grown. Much of the growth has been attributed to rising prices for so-called rare-earth elements and China's present monopoly over much of the world's supply. Two elements that can be harvested from the Area are of particular interest to miners of the seabed: polymetallic nodules (nodules) and polymetallic sulfides (sulphides).

So far, much of the ISA's work has focused on the management of nodules. These potato-shaped lumps are rich in the rare-earth elements including manganese, cobalt, copper, and nickel and are found mainly in the Clarion-Clipperton Zone in the Pacific Ocean. These elements are essential for hundreds of commercial applications and are likely to be used in an ever-expanding array of high-tech products. Moreover, the dwindling supply of terrestrial copper, which is used in wires, pipes, and numerous other products, has also raised an interest in seabed mining. Although mining of these nodules is currently limited to territorial waters, the ISA is beginning to explore the seabed beneath the high seas. As of 2014, the ISA has contracted with more than a dozen governmental or quasi-governmental entities from countries including Russia, China, France, Japan, India, Germany, and the Republic of Korea and with an Eastern European consortium to explore for nodules. However, before any mining operations commence, the ISA must formulate environmental plans to prepare and mitigate for any adverse environmental consequences resulting from the mining of the deep seabed. In addition to nodules, sulphides have sparked greater interest in the deep seabed. Like nodules, sulphides contain high concentrations of copper, gold, zinc, and silver. However, unlike nodules, sulphides are gigantic, sometimes stretching for two hundred meters, containing several million tons of ore.

Environmental consequences are likely to ensue from the mining of the deep sea-bed. Already, critics argue that the mining of sulphides will have repercussions for the fragile ecology of the deep seabed, particularly around sea-floor vents that are rich in biodiversity. Advocates of mining the sea floor have argued environmental protections can be accommodated. Whatever the case may be, the future of deep-sea mining will hinge on balancing the needs of resource exploitation and the necessity of proper protection and management of an otherwise alien ecosystem in the grand abyss of our oceans.

Besides the environmental considerations, the cost of mining the seabed is prohibitively expensive. Nevertheless, as technology progresses and is transferred from other industries—namely offshore drilling—mining of the Area will become commercially feasible.

The impact of the ISA on the mining of the seabed has yet to be seen. Market conditions and the increasing need for rare-earth elements will most likely increase interest in mining the seabed. Although the ISA has yet to finish a comprehensive set of rules or regulations for exploiting the resources of the seabed, it has issued mining regulations pertaining to both nodules and sulphides.

THE 1994 AGREEMENT

The LOS Convention took nearly twelve years to ratify, owing to the developed nations' perception that ISA provisions and representation on the council did not correspond to their interest and investment in deep seabed mining operations. However, by 1994, factors including the fall of the Soviet Union, increased international cooperation following the end of the Cold War, a strong shift toward market-oriented economies, and a weakened Group of Seventy-Seven, all contributed to the signing of the Agreement Relating to Part XI of the Convention (1994 Agreement).[8] Moreover, by this time, many developing nations were now, for all practical purposes, "developed" nations, more appreciative of the need to reach an agreement on the exploitation of the deep sea bed.

As the ISA's power to impose production limitations was eliminated, and the enterprise was streamlined, some of its advantages over private mining companies were taken away. In addition, objectionable provisions requiring an annual fee of $1 million from each mining company, transfers of technology, and sharing the surplus wealth with less developed nations were completely eliminated. The 1994 Agreement ensures that market approaches will dominate, with industrialized countries guaranteed an influence commensurate with their interests and investments. Importantly, the United States is guaranteed a seat on the council if it ever decides to ratify the treaty.

Thus, key provisions to redistribute global wealth—in decision making, production limitation, financing, and amendment procedures—were revised in the 1994 Agreement to reflect a preference for emphasizing interests, not merely numbers, in international decision making.

Article 4(2) of the 1994 Agreement states that "no state or entity may establish its consent to be bound by the Agreement unless it has previously established or establishes at the same time its consent to be bound by the Convention." The agreement is to be applied as a single document with the LOS Convention. All future ratifications or accessions to the convention imply consent to the agreement, and no state may consent to the agreement without consent to the LOS Convention. This linkage is essential, because in reality Part XI was not the most important subject under negotiation at UNCLOS III. The deep seabed negotiations concerned a use that had not yet taken place, whereas other parts of the convention address contemporary activities with direct benefits for the international community. With this linkage, widespread adherence to the entire convention will protect many important interests in the oceans.

The procedures devised for ratification of the 1994 Agreement were quite flexible, allowing, for example, consent either directly or by implication and allowing provisional application under certain conditions. Notably, the Seabed Council granted provisional membership to the United States until November 1998. This flexibility, in contrast to formalistic procedures from the nineteenth century, is due to the increased role in international law played today by international institutions and multipartite diplomacy since the time of the League of Nations.

Dispute Settlement under the 1982 Convention

As discussed in chapter 7, the regime for settling disputes under the convention is elaborate and contains elements of both choice and compulsoriness. Part XV of the LOS Convention establishes the dispute settlement procedure regarding the interpretation and application of its provisions. Its approach was designed to encourage all participants to accept compulsory and binding dispute settlement, and it reflects the growing trend in international law for the acceptability of such third-party dispute resolution.

Parties are encouraged to settle disputes by the means of their mutual choice, including negotiation and conciliation. If these fail the compulsory binding dispute settlement system becomes operative. All participants, upon signing, ratifying, or acceding to the convention, are allowed to choose one or more of three forums: (1) the Tribunal for the Law of the Sea; (2) the International Court of Justice; and (3) arbitration. Disputes involving marine fisheries, the marine environment, and marine scientific research and navigation are assigned a fourth forum. Disputes regarding the Area are referred to the Seabed Disputes Chamber of the International Tribunal of the Sea. Where disputing parties have not agreed to the same forum or have chosen none at all, arbitration becomes the compulsory mechanism. If the disputing parties prefer the same forum, that forum has jurisdiction beginning upon the unilateral application of either disputant.

Part XV, the world's first compulsory dispute settlement system, is designed to encourage all participants to accept compulsory, binding settlement of disputes as a key part of the LOS Convention. Because it provides a variety of options, the convention encourages the peaceful settlement of disputes, which is, after all the most important objective of international law.[9]

Disputes arising or relating to the LOS Convention have been successfully resolved under its dispute settlement procedure. Although the convention contains its own unique judicial review under the International Tribunal for the Law of the Sea, parties continue to avail themselves of the ICJ for resolution of their conflicts and disputes. Since implementation of the LOS Convention in 1994, the ICJ has dealt with a number of cases concerning disputes encompassing issues such as delimitation of maritime boundary disputes and whaling in the Antarctic.

In 1997, the tribunal issued its first judgment in the *M/V Saiga* case helping to resolve a dispute involving the apprehension of a ship alleged to be engaged in smuggling activities.[10] Since this case, the tribunal has heard many other cases, generally involving disputes surrounding captured vessels and crews, fisheries, and outliers such as disputes involving pollution, land reclamation, and delimitation of maritime boundaries. In addition, the Seabed Disputes Chamber has been activated once to render an advisory opinion for the ISA.

Outside of the traditional judicial review of cases and controversies, state parties have chosen to have their disputes resolved by arbitration under the Annex VII of the LOS Convention. So far, six disputes have been brought to arbitration. In five of those cases, the Permanent Court of Arbitration (PCA) has acted as the registry overseeing disputes such as delimitation of the EEZ and continental shelf in *Barbados v. Trinidad and Tobago (2006)*[11] and assisted in the resolution of a pollution controversy involving nuclear material in *Ireland v. United Kingdom (2003)*.[12]

LAW OF THE SEA CLAIMS

To recapitulate the substantive law of the sea in terms of functional claims rather than maritime zones:

1. Claims for access (navigation, passage): A state has complete authority to control access of vessels to internal waters; there is no right of innocent passage for foreign vessels. Within the territorial sea, all states enjoy the right of innocent passage. The right of transit passage applies to international straits. The archipelagic sea lane passage, a functional equivalent of transit passage, applies to archipelagic waters. The freedom of navigation and overflight applies to exclusive economic zones as well as the high seas.

2. Jurisdictional authority (competence to make and apply law): Within internal waters and the territorial sea, the coastal state has exclusive competence to make and apply law to any activities occurring therein. Within the contiguous zone,

the coastal state may assert a competence to make and apply law in control of activities relating to customs, fiscal matters, immigration, and sanitation. On the high seas, each state makes and applies law to its own ships, and no state can apply its unilateral competence to the ships of other states except for violations of certain norms of international law, absent other agreements between individual states.

3. Resources: The control of resources within internal waters and the territorial sea is in the hands of the coastal state. The coastal state's control of the resources of its continental shelf is exclusive in that the nonuse of all or part of them does not give any other state the right to exploit them. In contrast, the coastal state's control of the resources within its exclusive economic zone is qualified by the right of other states to harvest surplus resources under prescribed conditions. The living resources of the high seas are open to all. But the mineral resources in the deep seabed area are internationalized under the rubric of "the common heritage of mankind."

Appraisal

Rather than relying on formulaic rules found only in precedent and archives, the law of the sea derives from a multiplicity of perspectives and agreements brought together through a dynamic process of patient negotiation, quiet consultation, and public debate.[13] Hailed as "the Constitution of the Oceans," the LOS Convention is a comprehensive legal system under the auspices of the United Nations, reflecting vast advances in the making of international law during the twentieth century. Now, as we progress through the new millennium, the LOS Convention will be tested to determine whether it can adapt to the changing needs of the future.

The LOS Convention is a success in the field of international law because it has united more than 160 state parties into a convention designed to ensure the cooperative use and enjoyment of the sea. The principles of the LOS Convention benefit all members of the international community, giving each state a seat at the table to not only ensure that respective interests are met but also by assuring collaborative governance of the legal regime for control and use of the sea. The LOS Convention has gone far toward fulfilling Professor McDougal's vision for a world public order through a framework that is perhaps the most comprehensive multilateral agreement in existence after the U.N. Charter, not to mention one of the most widely accepted global treaties.[14] Significantly, an overwhelming majority in the international community recognizes the convention as the legitimate legal authority for the world's oceans.

The LOS Convention will undoubtedly continue as a powerful force in international law in the years to come. Nevertheless, significant challenges lie ahead for the convention if the vision of its drafters is to be realized. Chief among these challenges is bringing the United States into the convention. Upon the initiation of the UNCLOS III in 1974, the United States sent the largest delegation by far of any nation to the opening session. But eight years later, when the convention was adopted and opened for signature on December 10, 1982, the United States was absent. Owing largely to its opposition to the deep seabed mining provisions, the United States refused to sign the convention and, further, refused to participate as an observer at the preparatory commission.

Shortly thereafter in 1983, President Reagan issued the Statement on United States Ocean Policy announcing three decisions to promote and protect the oceans interests of the United States in a manner consistent with the LOS Convention and international law. Under Reagan's sea policy, the United States would: act in accordance with the balance of interests relating to traditional uses of the oceans; exercise and assert its navigational and overflight rights and freedoms on a worldwide basis in a manner that is consistent with the balance of interests reflected in the LOS Convention; and establish an EEZ that reflected in essence the relevant prescriptions embodied in the convention.[15] Although the 1994 Agreement embodied changes in Part XI seeking to assure that the United States, along with other industrialized states, would be given a voice commensurate with their interests, these remedial measures have so far failed to bring the United States into the LOS Convention.

Despite bipartisan support in Congress and from the Clinton, George H. W. Bush, and Obama administrations, the LOS Convention has stalled in the U.S. Senate. A small, yet significant caucus of senators known as the "Sovereignty Caucus" believes that membership in the LOS Convention is contrary to the best interests of the United States. The Sovereignty Caucus and other opponents to the LOS Convention argue that it is unneeded given the strength of U.S. sea power, the lack of incentives for adopting the convention, and the belief that U.S. sovereignty would be undermined by incurring additional treaty obligations. Proponents of accession argue that the principles embodied in the treaty are consistent with U.S. naval strategy, create the rule of law for prosecuting pirates and other threatening non-state actors, and hold economic importance by promoting a variety of commercial uses for the world's oceans, including offshore oil and natural gas drilling and mining in the Area. Most important, proponents assert that the United States should enter into a treaty in which it fundamentally participated, shaped, and endorsed. Although previous administrations have attempted to push the LOS Convention through the Senate ratification process, such attempts have proven futile in the face of entrenched opposition and the difficulty of attaining the two-thirds majority required to ratify the treaty. Nevertheless, in 2010, President Barack Obama issued an executive order establishing a comprehensive national oceans policy, with the understanding that the stewardship of the oceans is "intrinsically linked to environmental sustainability, human health and well-being, national prosperity, adaptation to climate, and other environmental changes, social justice, international diplomacy, and national and homeland security."[16] The policy is tied to both national and international goals. The shift in ocean policy represents the necessities of a reality in which American policy must reflect an interdependent world in which national and international interests are interwoven. Is this shift in sea policy a prelude to accession to the LOS Convention? It may be; nevertheless, proponents still have many political hurdles to overcome.

Beyond the accession of the United States, another compelling challenge for the LOS Convention is China's emergence as a global sea power. Such a shift will inevitably influence the distribution of authority across the sea. Whereas China once limited its naval strategy to its littoral territory, today its focus lies on a grander scale of supporting its economic aspirations not only in the South China Sea but also beyond, such as in Libya, the Persian Gulf, the Straits of Malacca, Africa, and Central America. China is fully aware that the expansion of its economic interests requires a stronger navy to better protect the country's transportation routes and the safety of its major sea lanes. With the projection of China's power into areas of American economic interests, comes overlap in spheres of influence and inevitable disputes. Will the law of the sea assure the seas remain peaceful and minimum world order is achieved? So far, disputes between these nations have been resolved peacefully (and will most likely continue as such in the future). Nevertheless, the dispute over jurisdiction and resources in the South China Sea could eventually become considerably troublesome. So far, the LOS Convention has influenced the debate on all sides of the conflict, but beyond the rhetoric, will the dispute settlement procedure play a role in extinguishing tense relations among neighboring states? Only time will tell.

Beyond the questions raised by the redistribution of global power lie important shared challenges related to the environmental protection of the sea. Critics point to an inconsistent regime of excessive environmental regulations by coastal states that drive up the operational costs of the global supply chain; limited protection of the sensitive marine environment from land-based sources of pollution; and the failure to address the impact of global climate change. UNCLOS III contributed to ensuring environmental stewardship; however, the changing times call for remedial measures to mitigate humankind's destructive impact on the environment. Today, the public order goals of the LOS Convention must also include protection for the sensitive marine ecosystems, restoration of ocean health, promotion of sustainable use and access to the sea, and help to remedy the ill effects of climate change while simultaneously striving to ensure that international lanes of commerce remain open to trade.

The scope of the LOS Convention will most likely require some of the criticisms to be addressed through amendments or additional postimplementation agreements to achieve a functional, yet flexible framework striving toward achieving world optimum order. However, due to the breadth of the convention and the number of state parties to it, change will arrive slowly and will require patience and strong leadership to better realize how the convention in action can harmonize the exclusive interests of individual states and the inclusive interests of the world community.

Aside from situational-based criticisms, the LOS Convention will require further interpretation to mature as a legal order. The need for judicial interpretation is great because precedent is necessary to manage future disputes and lessen indeterminacies that are inevitably present in such a comprehensive and complex global treaty. So far, the ICJ and the Tribunal for the Law of the Sea have had a limited effect on the interpretation of the convention. These authoritative bodies require the opportunity to develop precedent so that future disputes may be settled more expeditiously and questions surrounding certain provisions of the convention may be resolved.

Although challenges lie ahead, the LOS Convention remains a monumental achievement in international law and will continue as the preeminent global legal framework that has achieved an ordered, economic, and efficient public order for the sea. All participants have been able to adapt and compromise in a world transformed by deep social, political, economic, and technological changes amid a growing recognition of our ecosystem's fragility and exhaustibility and the need to protect it. Whatever the critics may assert, one thing is certain: the U.N. Convention on the Law of the Sea has implemented a successful framework for the shared use of the sea.

Notes

1. Fisheries Case (U.K. v. Nor.), Judgment, 1951 I.C.J. 116 (Dec. 18).

2. Corfu Channel Case (U.K. v. Alb.), Judgment on Merits, 1949 I.C.J. 4 (Apr. 9).

3. *See* CANADIAN PARLIAMENTARY INFORMATION AND RESEARCH SERVICE. CANADIAN ARCTIC SOVEREIGNTY (Library of Parliament 2006).

4. Prime Minister of Canada Stephen Harper, Prime Minister Stephen Harper Announces New Arctic Offshore Patrol Ships (July 9, 2007), *available at* http://www.pm.gc.ca/eng/news/2007/07/09/prime-minister-stephen-harper-announces-new-arctic-offshore-patrol-ships.

5. Wendy N. Duong, *Following the Path of Oil: The Law of the Sea or Realpolitik—What Good Does Law Do in the South China Sea?*, 30 FORDHAM INT'L L.J. 1098, 1136 (2007).

6. Delimitation of the Maritime Boundary in the Gulf of Maine Area (Can./U.S.), Judgment,1984 I.C.J. 246 (Oct. 12).

7. 22 U.N. GAOR C.1 (1516th mtg.) at 1–3, U.N. Doc. A/C.1PV.1516 (1967).

8. Agreement Relating to the Implementation of Part XI of the United Nations convention on the Law of the Sea of 10 December 1982, *reprinted in* 33 I.L.M. 1309 (1994).

9. Jonathan Charney, *The Implications of Expanding International Dispute Settlement Systems: The 1982 Convention on the Law of the Sea*, 90 A.J.I.L. 69 (1996).

10. M/V Saiga (No. 1) (St. Vincent v. Guinea), Case No. 1, Order of Jan. 20, 1998, 2 ITFLOS Rep. 4–5.

11. Barbados v. Trinidad & Tobago (Perm. Ct. Arb. Apr. 11, 2006).

12. OSPAR Arbitration (Ir. v. U.K.) (Perm. Ct. Arb. July 2, 2003).

13. L. B. Sohn, *International Implications of the 1994 Agreement*, 88 A.J.I.L. 696 (1994).

14. James Kraska, *The Law of the Sea Convention: A National Security Success—Global Strategic Mobility Through the Rule of Law*, 39 GEO. WASH. INT'L L. REV. 543, 544 (2007).

15. Proclamation by President Ronald Reagan, Mar. 10, 1983; Proclamation No. 5030, 48 Fed. Reg. 10605 (1983).

16. Exec. Order No. 13547 of July 19, 2010. 75 Fed. Reg. 43023 (2010) (Stewardship of the Ocean, Our Coasts, and the Great Lakes).

10 Control and Use of Other Resources

IN THE PRECEDING two chapters, we examined claims by states to acquire territory and resources for their exclusive use. We now turn to certain resources that, except airspace over national territorial domain, are not subject to exclusive appropriation by states. These resources, which permit a high degree of shared use by appropriate accommodation, are shareable resources, also known as strategic resources. The common interest in achieving the optimum production of goods and services to benefit all humankind depends on shared use and an inclusive competence in defense of such use.

Among the important shareable resources are international rivers, airspace (over the oceans), outer space, the polar regions, and the global environment. We examine them in succession.

International Rivers

International rivers, lying in part within the borders of two or more states or forming the boundary between two or more states, affect, geographically and economically, the territories of two or more states. Contiguous rivers serve as state boundaries, and successive rivers traverse two or more states.

International rivers offer multiple uses, both navigational and nonnavigational. The interest in navigation has long historical roots. Before the modern industrial era, the flow of water in most international rivers met the needs of all participants, and the unilateral diversion of water, if it occurred at all, caused few hardships for different riparian communities. The coming of the industrial age, with the proliferation of large urban centers and highly developed irrigation and other technologies, has radically changed that: the flow of water in many rivers has appeared insufficient to meet the requirements of all claimants, especially in the absence of appropriate river basin development and management. Increasingly, communities make claims to use the waters for irrigation, hydroelectricity generation, industrial uses, domestic consumption for drinking and sanitation purposes, "municipal use" for whole communities, fishing, and recreational use. States that share watercourse systems are hypersensitive to any diversion of waters, pollution by fertilizers and pesticides, or other interference with enjoyment. The pattern of claim and counterclaim and the factors affecting decision about particular river systems have thus become much more complex.

How to accommodate competing claims for multiple uses of riparian states within one international river system? Although navigational use was once considered paramount, this need not be so. The traditional concern for freedom of navigation has been increasingly overshadowed by growing demands for equitable use. Indeed, navigational use needs to be accommodated with competing demands for other uses.

Inherent in the demands and potential for multiple use of international rivers are certain unities or interdependencies within particular drainage basins. Because of a physical unity or interdependence, activities carried out upstream may affect downstream uses, and vice versa. Hydroelectric power generation, for example, may divert a significant quantity of water from an international river at the expense of downstream users. Irrigation by an upper riparian state may substantially diminish the amount of water available to downstream users and may pollute an international river with fertilizers and pesticides. Pollution and heavy consumption by industrial users may curtail water available for domestic and recreational use. In contrast, the unilateral appropriation of water for irrigation by an upstream state may be frustrated by the threat of the downstream state to close the river for navigational purposes. A lower riparian state may refuse to receive a natural flow of water by erecting a dam for hydroelectric power purposes and cause that water to flood valuable land in a neighboring state.

In sum, the very unities or interdependencies within any particular drainage basin make international rivers an important shareable resource suitable for inclusive competence and shared enjoyment. It requires comprehensive, integrated regional planning to achieve the common interest in the optimum production and equitable distribution of values for all participants.

Because of divergent configurations of factors and different participants involved in differing international river systems, this overriding policy of shareability has found expression neither in general customary law nor in general multilateral treaties. Instead, it has been expressed in a large number of specific agreements entered into by only the riparian states. Notable among such treaty arrangements are those relating to the Danube, the Rhine, the Oder, the Elbe, and the Columbia.

In terms of navigation, there appears to be no customary right concerning freedom of navigation in international waterways, despite a contrary assertion going back to Hugo Grotius. The efforts to establish such freedom through treaty, beginning with the Treaty of Paris of 1814 and the Congress of Vienna of 1815, led to the conclusion of the Barcelona Convention on the Regime of Navigable Waterways of International Concern of 1921. Under the Barcelona Convention the contracting states mutually agree that their vessels shall navigate freely on defined navigable waterways of international concern, and riparian states are authorized to regulate navigation and take police and customs measures in a nondiscriminatory manner. The Barcelona Convention, however, is of more theoretical than practical importance because of the small number of ratifications. The practical enjoyment of freedom of navigation in international rivers, in Europe and in other continents, depends in large part on specific treaty arrangements (for which international river commissions were thus established) for particular river systems.

Turning to nonnavigational uses, two principles governing inclusive use appear to be emerging: a riparian state may not act unilaterally so as to harm the interests of other riparian states, and the priority of uses of waters should be guided by the test of reasonableness, despite the divergences of variables involved in different river systems.

Riparian states generally have equal rights to use an international river, so that the waters and their benefits are equitably apportioned, taking into account such factors as prior use practices, historic rights, beneficial (nonwasteful) use, and relative need. Transnational decisions in the area reflect the concern to accommodate the respective interests of riparian states. The needs of upper and lower riparian states, for instance, are typically regulated with the requirement of advance notice and consultation regarding particular uses. Some problems may arise without such procedures in large-scale irrigation cases, as where waters are drastically diverted to benefit one state only or where waters flowing to the lower riparian are contaminated. One prominent example concerned the United States' use of the Colorado River for irrigation, which caused a great increase in the salinity of the river. Tremendous areas of Mexican farming land were devastated when contaminated waters reached them.

In order to protect these rights to equitable use, states have widely accepted the Helsinki Rules on the Uses of the Waters of International Rivers.[1] Adopted in 1966 by the International Law Association, the Helsinki Rules are regarded as reflecting then-existing international law. The Helsinki Rules provide in Article 4 that "each basin State is entitled, within its territory, to a reasonable and equitable share in the beneficial uses of waters of an international drainage basin." A "reasonable and equitable share" is to be determined in the light of all the relevant factors in a particular context. Such factors, as illustrated in Article 5(2) of the rules, include the geography of the basin, the hydrology of the basin, the climate affecting the basin, past practice in using the waters of the basin, the relative economic and social needs and population dependencies of each basin state, the comparative costs of alternative uses available, and so on. Such a contextual approach is essential in the pragmatic search for the common interests of all participants.

The International Law Commission began to include the nonnavigational uses of international watercourses in its agenda of work in 1973, and the U.N. General Assembly adopted the Convention on the Law of the Nonnavigational Uses of International Watercourses in May 1997. Whereas the Helsinki Rules employed the concept of an "international drainage basin," in the sense of "a geographical area extending over two or more States determined by the watershed limits of the system of waters, including surface and underground waters, flowing into a common terminus,"[2] the International Law Commission has employed a more comprehensive term, "international watercourse." This distinct shift extends the concern of the commission not only to international river basins but to all other transnational waterways, including lakes, canals, dams, reservoirs, and other surface and subsurface waters. Article 5(2) of the convention provides that "watercourse States shall participate in the use, development and protection of an international watercourse in an equitable and reasonable manner. Such participation includes both the right to utilize the watercourse and the duty to cooperate in the protection and development thereof, as provided in the present Convention." In addition, each system state is entitled to "a reasonable and equitable participation" (within its territory) in this shared resource.[3] It has been noted that the choice of the word *participation* suggests the concomitant duty of states to contribute constructively to the management and conservation of watercourse systems. The pledge to independently and jointly preserve the ecosystems of international watercourses, embodied in Article 20, reflects a commitment to sustainable development and inclusive behavior. The convention employs a dispute settlement system providing for a series of stages beginning with consultation and negotiation and moving to impartial fact-finding, mediation, conciliation, and arbitration or judicial settlement. As of 2013, there were thirty-one parties to the convention, and sixteen signatories.

Airspace

The advent of aircraft at the turn of the twentieth century raised new problems in international law: who has authority to control access to the superjacent airspace of nation-states and of the high seas and to regulate aviation activities by aircraft, both commercial and military?

Territorial communities have important interests in activities in the airspace superjacent to their territories. The most important interests include the security of the state's territorial base, enhancement of wealth through transportation of people, goods, and mail by air, and safety for persons and property on land. The security of a state may be threatened from the superjacent airspace in many ways: manned or unmanned aerial intelligence, observation, and attacks; unauthorized penetration into airspace; parachuting agents into territory; dropping supplies to agents and local insurgents; disseminating propaganda material hostile to the subjacent state; and so on.

Because of these critical factors, states have shown a remarkable uniformity in claiming comprehensive, exclusive authority over territorial airspace. By this claim they seek to control access to and use of the airspace above their land masses and territorial waters and to prescribe and apply authority over all activities taking place within such airspace. Any theoretical desirability for inclusive, shared use of the domain of airspace is simply overwhelmed by the general preoccupation with national security in a divided world marked by continued expectations of violence.

International law, through both customary practice and explicit agreement, has accorded nation-states a high degree of exclusive authority, at once comprehensive and continuing, over the airspace above their territories. Every state enjoys "complete and exclusive sovereignty" over the airspace above its territory, including its territorial sea.

The view in support of extending the historic doctrine of "freedom of navigation" to airspace, as advanced in the early days of air flight, was quickly relegated to oblivion when World War I vividly demonstrated the monstrous threats posed by aerial warfare and activities.

The overriding policy of airspace sovereignty found expression in the Paris Convention on the Regulation of Aerial Navigation of 1919 and in subsequent multilateral treaties. It is unequivocally reaffirmed in the Chicago Convention on International Civil Aviation of 1944, commonly regarded as the Constitution of Air Law. Article 1 of the Chicago Convention states: "The contracting States recognize that every State has complete and exclusive sovereignty over the airspace above its territory."

Airspace is now commonly accepted as an appurtenance of the subjacent territory. Under the comprehensive, continuing, exclusive authority thus established, access to such airspace depends on the explicit permission of the subjacent state, at its pure discretion.

Efforts to secure through a multilateral treaty some measure of shared access to territorial airspace for regular international air services have been less than successful. Though high hopes were expressed at the Chicago conference in 1944, participants on the whole insisted too heavily on exclusive control to concede any inclusive use of territorial airspace. The Chicago Convention itself failed to incorporate any of what came to be known as the "five freedoms." Instead, two supplementary agreements were formulated: the International Air Services Transit Agreement and the International Air Transport Agreement. The former contains the first two freedoms:

1. The privilege of free passage without landing;
2. The privilege of flying across with noncommercial, technical landing only (for instance, refueling, repairs, emergencies).

The latter contains the other three freedoms:

3. The privilege of commercial discharge from the home state of the aircraft or airline;
4. The privilege of commercial embarkation to the home state of the aircraft or airline;
5. The privilege of conveying passengers, cargo, and mail between any two contracting States.

The first two, also known as transit rights, are widely accepted. The latter three, also known as traffic rights, which relate to commercial conveyance of passengers, cargo, and mail, have not gained much acceptance. The fifth freedom in particular has become the focal point of bargaining among states in the exchange of traffic rights.

Whatever concessions to the inclusive use of territorial airspace of states that have been granted have resulted largely from bilateral agreement. In practice, an extensive network, of thousands of such agreements covers every state of the world. The trend has been accentuated by the proliferation of newly independent states. This reflects the need for states to participate in the flow of world air commerce in an interdependent world of growing mobility and the jealous promotion of national wealth processes, including special protection of domestic aviation industry. It is of course also a matter of prestige.

In spite of the many treaty exceptions to the principle of exclusivity in territorial airspace, nation-states have shown readiness to prevent or repel, by force if necessary, any unauthorized intrusions into their aerial domain. On occasion, certain states have gone so far, in defense of the inviolability of their aerial domain, to use brute force in reacting to the intrusions by an unarmed civilian aircraft either in distress or unintentionally off course. The incident of Korean Air Lines 007, involving the shooting down of a strayed South Korean civilian aircraft over Soviet airspace in September 1983, is a notable example.

The exclusive authority of states extends only to the airspace above state territory, including the territorial waters. Beyond its territorial domain, no state has comprehensive, continuing authority over airspace; that is, the airspace over the high seas is a domain for inclusive use. States are permitted to exercise, as regards ships on the water, an occasional, limited exclusive competence for particular purposes in airspace over the high seas.

Outer Space

The launching of Sputnik I in 1957 ushered in the space age. Two fundamental concepts that have affected humankind—space and time—have thus undergone radical changes, moving from an earth-oriented concept of space and distance to one that encompasses the galaxies. Distance and the time required to traverse it have likewise been altered. No longer is space an immense void, gazed at by humans from their earthly environment; it is now part of their experience, a place to walk or float untethered, to cover miles in seconds. Thanks to these spectacular developments, humankind today is capable of leaving the earth and exploring and using outer space. Space law has emerged as a distinct branch of international law.

Though a vast frontier has opened up for exploration and use, the people conducting activities in space are the same people who have been acting on earth. The relevant actors, group and individual, pursue the precise objectives they have sought on earth: power, wealth, enlightenment, skill, and so on. Space is potentially a great shareable resource for humankind: it provides new vistas and challenges. The possibilities to produce greater goods and services through new modes of communication, transportation, and weather control and through newly discovered resources are enormous. At the same time, access to space has endowed humankind a new capability to destroy itself. As space activities generate great collective impact on all peoples of the world, the interdependencies in the shaping and sharing of values that have characterized the earth arena of our time can only intensify with the accelerating conquest of space.

Many important issues of international space law have engaged the attention of experts, scholars, and decision makers. The issues, both existing and potential, relate to access and competence in the domain of space; maintaining both minimum order and optimum order in space; the nationality of spacecraft; jurisdiction over space activities and spacecraft; the enjoyment and acquisition of resources; the establishment of enterprisory activities; and theoretical interactions with advanced forms of non-earth life. This inventory of major specific issues suggests the relevance of human experience on earth to the emerging legal problems in space.

An impressive corpus of space law has developed within a remarkably short time, thanks to the heritage of customary law and the codification efforts of international governmental organizations, notably the United Nations and the International Telecommunication Union. The U.N. Committee on the Peaceful Uses of Outer Space (UNCOPUOS), created in 1959, has figured prominently in this endeavor. Thanks to its draftsmanship, five major international agreements concerning space have come into being:

1. Treaty on Principles Governing the Activities of States in the Exploration and Use of Outer Space, Including the Moon and Other Celestial Bodies, 1967 (hereafter Outer Space Treaty of 1967) (effective October 10, 1967);

2. Agreement on the Rescue of Astronauts, the Return of Astronauts, and the Return of Objects Launched into Outer Space, 1968 (effective December 3, 1968);

3. Convention on International Liability for Damage Caused by Space Objects, 1972 (effective October 9, 1973);

4. Convention on Registration of Objects Launched into Outer Space, 1975 (effective September 15, 1976); and
5. Agreement Governing the Activities of States on the Moon and Other Celestial Bodies, 1979 (effective July 1984) (hereafter Moon Agreement).

The boundless and inexhaustible vastness of space makes it highly suitable for shared use by multiple participants at a minimum cost in mutual interference. The cumulative experience of humankind in the productive shaping and sharing of values through the inclusive enjoyment of the oceans, the airspace above the oceans, international rivers, and the polar regions clearly points to the high desirability of comparable inclusive use of space—opening up the vast domain of space to free and equal access of all peoples who can attain the necessary capabilities.

Fortunately, the United Nations enunciated this policy early on. In its famous Resolution 1721 on International Cooperation in the Peaceful Uses of Outer Space, the General Assembly in 1961 proclaimed the following guiding principles:

1. International law, including the Charter of the United Nations, applies to outer space and celestial bodies;
2. Outer space and celestial bodies are free for exploration and use by all States in conformity with international law and are not subject to national appropriation.[4]

It was clear from the outset that outer space would not be subject to the same restrictions as airspace—where each state has exclusive sovereignty over its airspace. This policy has been reaffirmed by the Outer Space Treaty of 1967, sometimes dubbed the Magna Carta of space law. Article I states in part:

The exploration and use of outer space, including the moon and other celestial bodies, shall be carried out for the benefit and in the interests of all countries, irrespective of their degree of economic or scientific development, and shall be the province of all mankind. Outer space, including the moon and other celestial bodies, shall be free for exploration and use by all States without discrimination of any kind, on a basis of equality and in accordance with international law, and there shall be free access to all areas of celestial bodies.

Article II bans national appropriation: "Outer space, including the moon and other celestial bodies, is not subject to national appropriation by claim of sovereignty, by means of use or occupation or by any other means." Other provisions deal with other aspects relating to space activities.

A comparable regime of freedoms and obligations was set forth in the Moon Agreement of 1979. Included in these freedoms are those for scientific investigation, exploration, and use without discrimination and for establishment of manned and unmanned stations.

Article II makes the moon and its natural resources "the common heritage of mankind" and forbids national appropriation of any portion of the moon. The Moon Agreement is the first treaty to effectuate the concept of the "common heritage of mankind." Going beyond the vague notion of the "province of mankind," it mandates that an international regime be established to govern the exploitation of the natural resources of the moon and other celestial bodies as soon as such exploitation is feasible.

From the inception of the space age, one persistent question has been the upward extent of sovereign authority of territorial communities. A state enjoys "complete and exclusive" sovereignty in the airspace above its territory, and, theoretically, outer space begins where airspace ends. But, where does airspace end? In other words, where and how to demarcate the line between airspace and outer space? The issue defies an easy solution.

Three major contending approaches exist: the "spacial" (geographical), the functional, and the pragmatic. The spacial approach favors an agreement on an easily determinable boundary at a certain altitude above sea level (say, 70 or 100–110 kilometers). The functional approach, rejecting any arbitrary boundary, focuses on the nature of space activities and asserts that airspace cannot exceed the lowest point at which free orbit of satellites may efficiently occur. The pragmatic approach maintains that a delimitation between airspace and outer space would serve no practical purpose and could unwittingly stifle future space activities and the growth of space law.

The delimitation issue, though regarded as academic by some, was dramatized in 1976 when eight equatorial countries joined in issuing the Bogota Declaration to claim sovereignty over segments of the geostationary orbit lying above their national territories. The geostationary orbit, essential for many broadcasting activities, is that position directly above the equator in which a satellite orbits with the same rotation and speed as the earth. In asserting exclusive authority over what is deemed to be a finite resource in a unique part of space, the declaration states that "the geostationary synchronous orbit is a physical fact linked to the reality of our planet and its existence depends exclusively on its relation to gravitational phenomena generated by the earth, and that is why it must not be considered part of outer space."[5] This view clearly contradicts the widely shared expectation that the geostationary orbit is a shared resource not subject to national appropriation.

Though the demarcation issue remains an open question, space activities have moved forward and are expanding. It has become part of customary law that artificial satellites orbiting the earth operate in the domain of outer space, beyond the territorial sovereignty of the underlying state. And a state enjoys complete and exclusive authority over its space vehicles, laboratories, or stations in free space.

The claim for exclusive authority and control over geostationary orbit, though unacceptable to the world community at large, is another manifestation of the general demand of the developing nations for transfers of technology and sharing of resources, moving from the earth to the space arena. As space activities expand, new problems arise. The increasing commercialization of space has led to problems ranging from "space debris" pollution to the possibility of advertising from outer space. The problems relating to the space shuttle and to the "Star Wars" proposal have engaged particular attention.

The overall success of the use of space shuttles has opened the door for developing a routine distinct transportation system and eventually for establishing large colonies in space. A highly versatile aerospace vehicle, the space shuttle ascends into space with the aid of rockets and returns to earth landing on a runway much like a conventional aircraft. Unlike traditional expendable launch vehicles, the space shuttle is practically reusable and is capable of placing satellites in orbit much more economically than could expendable launch vehicles. The advent of the space shuttle raises the question whether the space shuttle is to be regarded as "aircraft" or "spacecraft" and whether, during its ascent and descent, its flights should be regulated by conventional air law and related traffic regulations or governed by the treaties relating to outer space activities. The retirement of the U.S. Space Shuttle Program in 2011 and the increasing use of commercial space vehicles for governmental and civilian purposes in the twenty-first century will raise new questions about who is permitted to travel into space and for what purposes.

The question of minimum order in space—peaceful use of outer space—has been a matter of continuing concern since the dawn of the space age. Although the overriding goal of "peaceful use" has been affirmed and reaffirmed, views have diverged about what is meant by peaceful use, especially when the military instrument is somehow involved. The issue was sharpened thanks to President Reagan's proposal for research in the Strategic Defense Initiative, popularly known as Star Wars. Research on anti-satellite weapons and lasers continues to consume staggering amounts of resources, and the proliferation of spy satellites, many of them commercial, threatens to unleash an arms race in space, plaguing hopes for space's peaceful and nonmilitary use.

From man orbiting the earth, walking in space, and setting foot on the moon, to the advent of a reusable winged space shuttle, the International Space Station, and unmanned research vehicles sent to Mars and beyond, humankind has indeed come a long way in its half-century endeavor to conquer space. But the concern for peace in space is in the final analysis earthbound. Minimum order in space and minimum order on earth are inseparable.

Polar Regions

Because of their location and climate, the polar regions—the Arctic and the Antarctic—present unique problems in international law. As knowledge concerning the polar regions has increased and the technology necessary to exploit them has developed, legal problems have likewise increased.

The Arctic and Antarctic regions are commonly conceived of as more or less similar in nature. This is true only to a limited extent. Whereas the Arctic consists of an ocean nearly surrounded by land and covered by shifting masses of ice, the Antarctic is a vast ice-covered continent encircled by a frozen sea. The Antarctic is appreciably colder and more prone to intense storms than the Arctic. In terms of human habitation, the Antarctic is also more remote. Both regions are rich in living resources; but the extent of mineral resources is yet to be determined.

Territorial claims over the polar regions involve complex issues, due largely to their extreme and uninhabitable conditions. In general, the norms governing the acquisition of territory by states, especially the requirements of effective occupation, have been relaxed in the polar regions because of these characteristics.

In the Arctic, despite the lack of any truly effective occupation, the claims of surrounding states have now achieved the level of a legal status quo. Territorial sovereignty in the Arctic is no longer questioned, though the legal bases for the various territorial claims of the five Arctic powers—Russia, Denmark, Norway, Canada, and the United States—are not identical. The validity of these claims extends only to the various Arctic islands and their attendant territorial seas, not to the Arctic Ocean proper.

The Soviet Union, however, claimed that several extensive Arctic seas on its coast constituted so-called historic seas and as such were Soviet internal waters, and Russia in its place continues to assert the same. Claims to sovereignty over the Arctic Ocean have been advanced in terms of the "sector theory." The sector theory involves delimiting Arctic claims according to boundaries created by the extension of the longitudinal meridians from the existing boundary between states northward to the North Pole. It is designed, in part, to ensure sovereignty over islands within the sector, whether or not discovered. As such, it would dispense with the minimal requirement to establish valid claims to new territory under customary international law. The Soviet Union was the most strident supporter of the sector theory. To a lesser degree Canada has also relied on it for claims of Arctic sovereignty. Both the United States and Norway have expressly rejected its validity.

United States sovereignty in the Arctic extends to Alaska and certain specified adjacent islands under a treaty of transfer with Russia of 1867. Canadian sovereignty over the Arctic archipelago to its north, though once claimed under the sector theory, is definitely achieved by various expeditions. Denmark's sovereignty over all of Greenland was recognized in 1933 by the Permanent Court of International Justice in the famous case of *Legal Status of Eastern Greenland*.[6] Norwegian sovereignty over Spitsbergen and Bear Islands was recognized in the Treaty of Paris in 1920. Under the terms of the treaty, however, mining rights are reserved to the forty other parties to the agreement. Besides Norway, only the Soviet Union, today the Russian Federation, has taken advantage of these rights. Although the Soviet Union insisted that its sovereignty over the islands to its north is satisfied under the sector theory, its long-undisputed possession and control of these islands was said to give it title beyond doubt. Russia continues to enjoy this status.

Another unsettled issue is the Soviet, now Russian, claim to sovereignty over the Northeast Passage. This route passes through several large seas that indent the northern coast of the former Soviet Union. The Russians consider these seas "historic" and, as such, internal waters in which no right of innocent passage by foreign ships exists. In opposition to the Russian position, it has been argued that the term "historic seas" is unknown under international law and that "historic bays" are inconceivable without headlands between which a baseline can be drawn. As to the contention that passage through these waters requires the assistance of Russian icebreakers, the counterargument is simply that a nation using the passage could supply its own icebreakers. (In any event, such reasoning is at least inapplicable to air navigation.) If this route were to become an internationally used passage, then the straits between the Russian mainland and its islands should also be opened to foreign use as transit straits under the Convention on the Territorial Sea and Contiguous Zone of 1958.

The situation concerning claims of territorial sovereignty in the Antarctic is not as well settled as in the Arctic. A principal reason has been the lack of any generally agreed-on criteria by which valid claims can be established. Thus, while one nation will proclaim an area to be its sovereign territory, another nation, based on the same facts, will deny that claim. In one region, three nations have simultaneously claimed sovereignty.

Thus far seven states have made claims to portions of Antarctica: United Kingdom (1908); New Zealand (1923); France (1924); Australia (1933); Norway (1939); Chile (1940); and Argentina (1942). These claims consist of pie-shaped sections that extend, except in one instance, from latitude 60° south to the South Pole. The British sector extends further north to include the Falkland Island Dependencies.

Two legal bases are set forth for the territorial claims in Antarctica. The Northern Hemisphere claimants have invoked discovery, whereas the Southern Hemisphere claimants have relied on the theory of contiguity (similar to the sector theory), under which Antarctic territory within the same approximate meridians of latitude as the claiming state are held subject to sovereignty.

The United States, though having made no claims of sovereignty in Antarctica, has expressly reserved the right to put forth such a claim in the future. In the meantime, neither the United States nor Russia recognizes any claims of sovereignty on the continent.

Interest in the Antarctic was heightened by the commemoration of the International Geophysical Year (IGY), 1957–58. The IGY began a period of cooperative scientific investigation precipitating the building of numerous Antarctic state research bases. This development, coupled with attempts to assert exclusive control, posed a threat of cold war and militarization; hence, interested states were prompted to enter into the Antarctic Treaty of 1959. The treaty was concluded by all seven claimant states, United States, the Soviet Union (now Russia), and other states with substantial Antarctic interests (including Belgium, Japan, and South Africa). The treaty represents an important step in international cooperation.

The primary objectives of the treaty are twofold: the peaceful use of Antarctica and the promotion of free scientific investigation and cooperation. The application of the treaty is limited to the area south of 60° south latitude. Article 1(1) stipulates that military measures are prohibited, including "the establishment of military bases and fortifications, the carrying out of military maneuvers as well as the testing of any weapons." The driving force behind the original signing of the treaty was the interest in guaranteeing that state activities in the region would not affect existing claims to territorial sovereignty. Article 6 incorporates this guarantee, freezing all claims of territorial rights in the continent and precluding new territorial claims during the life of the treaty. The treaty also seeks to control the actions of nonsignatories as far as they relate to the Antarctic. The treaty does not attempt to keep nonsignatories out of Antarctic affairs but encourages the participation of all states in Antarctic research carried out in conformity with the treaty provisions.

The treaty creates a mechanism to work out future disputes regarding such issues as resource exploitation, which is not specifically addressed otherwise. Article 9 provides that the original contracting parties or those that conduct substantial scientific research shall participate in periodic consultative meetings to consider and recommend "measures in furtherance of the principles and objectives of the Treaty." Whereas the United States, in keeping with its policy of nonrecognition of Antarctic claims, would allow free access, claimant states would deny such access to their claimed sectors. Hence, management of the system has an administrative problem.

Though the treaty is open to accession by other states, only those judged to have undertaken "substantial scientific research activities" are to become "consultative parties" and to participate in managing the system. As of 2013, thirty-eight states had joined the original twelve as voting, consultative parties, in addition to twenty nonvoting, nonconsultative parties.

When the treaty was concluded, the primary focus was on scientific investigation and cooperation. With recent reports of Antarctica's resource potential, both living and mineral, world attention has increasingly shifted to exploring and exploiting the potential mineral resources of Antarctica. Several developing nations, led by Malaysia, have charged that the treaty is unfair and demanded that the United Nations declare the resources of Antarctica a "common heritage of mankind" and establish a committee on Antarctica; some treaty powers feared that any revision might jeopardize the treaty. In 1991, however, the Protocol on Environmental Protection to the Antarctic Treaty was finally signed in Madrid, banning mineral and oil exploration outright in the continent for at least fifty years. The protocol, setting forth a comprehensive, legally binding system of environmental regulations for wildlife protection, waste disposal, marine pollution, and continued monitoring of Antarctica, reaffirms the status of Antarctica as an area reserved for peaceful purposes.

Although there was disagreement over whether Antarctica should be governed by the present treaty or by the United Nations, the General Assembly has been able to reach consensus on "the question of Antarctica," recognizing the treaty and its associated instruments "as furthering the purposes and principles of the U.N. Charter." Agencies of the United Nations are regularly invited to participate as expert organizations in Antarctica Treaty meetings.[7]

The Global Environment

In talking about the global environment, there is a tendency to associate it narrowly with the questions of pollution of all kinds—water, air, river, marine, industrial, oil spill, waste, and so on. The questions of pollution have undoubtedly done much to sensitize the environmental concern of our time. But pollution does not exhaust the range of problems concerning the global environment.

In a comprehensive sense, the global environment relates to the entire earth-space arena. All of the respective resources discussed above are but components of the larger global environment. The plants, Homo sapiens and other animals, and microorganisms that inhabit the planet are united with one another and with their nonliving surroundings by a network of complex and interdependent components, both natural and cultural, which constitute a planetary ecosystem. But, in the opinions of many competent experts, this delicate ecological unity is in grave jeopardy. In the words of McDougal and Schneider:

> It is the more specific ecological unities or interdependences—physical, engineering and utilization—of this comprehensive ecosystem which make our whole earth-space environment a single shareable, and necessarily shared resource. What is true about the shareability of the oceans, the atmosphere, the airspace and the enfolding outer space, and the land masses when considered separately, is no less true of the indivisible whole which they comprise.[8]

State activities having potentially harmful transnational effects are wide ranging and include exploitation of resources, uses of international rivers, nuclear testing, weather modification, industrial waste disposal, oil transport, and exploration of the oceans and outer space. The devastating potential of nuclear weapons testing has been widely recognized. Efforts to change weather by cloud seeding or diversion of hurricanes or tornadoes may have devastating consequences for other communities. Concentrated industrial activities may cause acid rain, increased acidity levels in precipitation (sulfur dioxide), which can harm structures, as well as crops, fish, and other organisms across national boundaries. The failure by both developed and developing countries to reduce emissions of "greenhouse gases" such as carbon dioxide is predicted to contribute to ever-increasing global warming and devastating climactic change. Nuclear accidents, such as the 1984 explosion at the Chernobyl atomic power plant near Kiev, can result in increased levels of deadly radiation around the globe. (Eleven days after Chernobyl, increased levels of radiation were detected as far away as Japan.) In 2011, a massive earthquake and tsunami crippled a nuclear power plant in Fukushima Prefecture, Japan, releasing significant amounts of radiation into the surrounding region. It may take years for the aftereffects of this disaster to become apparent. However, some nations, such as Germany, have reconsidered their use of nuclear power following the events in Fukushima. This shift increases the danger that these nations may return to the use of heavily polluting fossil fuels to meet their energy needs.

Pollution knows no boundary. In keeping the earth-space arena a healthy, livable environment for future as well as present generations, it is crucial that a high degree of inclusivity be maintained in dealing with manifold problems associated with the global environment. Professor Edith Brown Weiss referred to this abundant shared environment as humankind's "intergenerational equity."[9] Current generations have a responsibility of stewardship that includes caring for and protecting the earth's resources for the continued benefit of future generations, both in the near and distant future. Historically, serious transnational pollution was tackled by invoking and applying international law relating to the responsibility of states, territorial sovereignty, and the freedom of the sea. A customary expectation is that states are obliged not to use or permit the use of their territories so as to cause substantial transnational environmental harm. Three transnational decisions—the *Corfu Channel* case,[10] the *Trail Smelter* case,[11] and the *Lake Lanoux* case[12]—have been especially influential in this regard.

In *Corfu Channel*, Albania's knowing failure to warn a British warship passing through its territorial waters of the existence of a minefield in those waters obliged Albania to compensate Britain for injury to its ship and crew. The International Court of Justice held that a state has an "obligation not to allow knowingly its territory to be used for acts contrary to the rights of other States."[13] In the *Trail Smelter* arbitration, it was ruled that a privately owned Canadian smelter that emitted sulfur dioxide fumes causing substantial damage to privately owned farmland in the state of Washington should be subject to strict emission controls to prevent future damage. Like *Corfu Channel*, this decision signifies that a state may not act to permit serious transnational injury. This has obvious implication for activities generating transfrontier pollution. In the *Lake Lanoux* arbitration, Spain disputed France's right to divert waters from the lake (which is situated in France but empties into a stream that crosses into Spain) in order to generate hydroelectric power. The tribunal decided in favor of France because the activity was determined not to adversely affect Spain—there would be no diminution in water quality or harm to agriculture or other human needs.

The contemporary environmental concern entered a new era with the convening in 1972 of the U.N. Conference on the Human Environment in Stockholm. The conference adopted the Declaration on the Human Environment,[14] commonly known as the Stockholm Declaration, calling on "the Governments and peoples to exert common efforts for the preservation and improvement of the human environment, for the benefit of all the people and for their posterity," and an action plan spotlighting a global monitoring system. The declaration contains a set of principles that deal with the protection of the natural environment, the preservation and protection of flora and fauna, the use of renewable resources, restrictions on the discharge of toxic substances, the prevention of marine pollution, and the relation between environmental protection and economic development. A key provision seeks to accommodate the sovereign right of states to exclusive enjoyment of their resources with the need for environmental protection.

Two decades after Stockholm, in the largest gathering of its kind in human history, world leaders met at Rio de Janeiro to discuss common environmental challenges in what became familiarly known as the "Earth Summit," the U.N. Conference on Environment and Development (UNCED, 1992). Several important documents were approved, including a U.N. Framework Convention on Climate Change. Most important, as part of the Rio Declaration, an agreement was signed on a comprehensive plan of action. Called "Agenda 21," the plan serves as a blueprint for fighting pollution and poverty, advancing toward better use of world resources into the twenty-first century and charting a new course of global partnership for sustainable development.[15]

A key topic at Rio was the debate over "sustainable development." The relation between economic growth and environmental degradation has become an increasingly contentious issue: as many poorer countries focus on economic growth to meet needs of growing populations, they are concerned that the industrialized North will use environmental considerations to curb developing countries' growth, in a sort of "green" colonialism consigning those countries to permanent economic inequality.[16] Environmentalists, on the other hand, fear that developing countries will not sufficiently recognize the severity of threats to the global environment as they pursue economic growth. So it has been, unfortunately, that political disputes, economic disparities, and an overemphasis on exclusive interests have hampered progress and dampened the spirit of Rio. Environmental trends have not improved; atmospheric concentration of greenhouse gases continues to grow, species are being extinguished at an unprecedented rate, and deforestation continues.

The shared concern for a healthy environment was amply manifested by the acute concern for marine pollution in the course of negotiating and formulating the U.N. Convention on the Law of the Sea (LOS Convention), which was discussed at length in chapter 9. Several marine environmental disasters beginning in the 1960s, especially the 1967 Torrey Canyon disaster, underscored the urgent need to preserve and protect the marine environment and its creatures. Unfortunately, the Torrey Canyon disaster has since been overshadowed by oil spills such as the Exxon Valdez disaster, which spewed nearly eleven million gallons of oil onto the Alaskan coast in 1994, and the Deep Water Horizon disaster that spilled millions of gallons of oil into the Gulf of Mexico in 2010. These events were the direct cause of severe damage and suffering to birdlife, sea mammals, and fisheries in the regions, not to mention the damage done to the regions' natural beauty.

The LOS Convention contains a rather elaborate chapter (Part XII, Articles 192–237) designed to protect and preserve the marine environment. Article 192 stipulates the general obligation of states to protect and preserve the marine environment. To fulfill this obligation, states are required under Article 194 to take, individually or jointly, all measures "necessary to prevent, reduce and control pollution of the marine environment from any source"; using "the best practicable means at their disposal and in accordance with their capabilities." The convention identifies the sources of marine pollution: land-based sources; pollution due to seabed activities within national jurisdiction; pollution due to seabed activities outside national jurisdiction; marine dumping; pollution from ships; and pollution from and through the atmosphere.

Several of these provisions constitute entirely new prescriptions. In the area of land-based pollution, no new international law is created by the convention, and each state is left to control such sources within its national jurisdiction. However, some provisions dealing with pollution due to seabed activity within national jurisdiction are new law. No problem should arise as to pollution resulting from the exploitation of the deep seabed, since all such activities will be carried out under the supervision of the International Seabed Authority in accordance with international standards. Pollution from ships is a major issue, since it is by this means that pollution moves most easily from one jurisdiction to another or to the high seas. The newly created "port state jurisdiction" is a particularly innovative feature (see Articles 218–220). A compromise was struck between the coastal states, which supported the competence to adopt supplementary legislation concerning pollution control in the exclusive economic zone, and the flag state bloc, which opposed such proposals. According to the compromise formula: (1) states should accept the universal jurisdiction of port states to punish discharge violations of international rules and standards; (2) ships are to be bound only by the national laws and regulations of the flag state and by the applicable international rules and standards; and (3) coastal states will have, within their exclusive economic zones, the right to enforce international rules and standards applicable to foreign ships. This balance allows coastal states to protect their interests while preventing unilateral actions by them and ensures uniformity of regulations applicable to all ships.

Although pollution of the oceans has significant transboundary implications, the international community has been slow to collectively develop standards to mitigate environmental degradation stemming from oil exploitation from the sea. Beyond the broad LOS provisions discussed in chapter 9, the International Convention on Oil Pollution, Preparedness, Response and Cooperation of 1990 stands as the sole international legal mechanism to mitigate environmental catastrophes caused by the exploitation of oil.

The need for greater international regulation became apparent on April 20, 2010, when an explosion rocked the British Petroleum (BP) Deepwater Horizon oil platform located within the U.S. exclusive economic zone (EEZ) in the Gulf of Mexico. At the time of the explosion, an exploratory well was being drilled at an extreme water depth of 5,000 feet. The explosion spewed millions of gallons of oil into the Gulf of Mexico and caused a leak that ran unchecked for three months until it was finally capped on July 25, 2010. Although the leak was contained at last, residual oil from the spill washed ashore for some time after.

The Deepwater Horizon spill is distinguishable from previous oil spills not only due to its immense size but also in its impact to both the surface and subsurface environments. Oil that rose to the surface created a slick that expanded to cover hundreds of miles and threatened the sensitive marine environment and coastal wetlands. Oil that made it to shore killed off wetland grass and threatened the habitats of birdlife and fisheries that were important to the Gulf Coast economy. In addition, the oil that reached the coast sped up coastal erosion placing certain areas of the Gulf Coast of the United States in greater peril from the effects of powerful hurricanes. Below the surface, submerged plumes of oil stretching for miles were identified at varying depths causing an unknown impact on the gulf's ecosystem. Aside from the pollution caused directly by the spill was the damage caused by a chemical dispersant used to break down the oil. Although U.S. authorities indicated the dispersant degraded to nontoxic levels, the exact long-term impact on the gulf's ecosystem remains unknown. Due to the unprecedented impact of the Deepwater Horizon oil spill, BP agreed to provide U.S. federal and state authorities with funds for remediation projects in the Gulf of Mexico to clean up the environmental damage caused by the spill.

Beyond the catastrophic environmental consequences came the economic impact to industries important to the Gulf Coast economy. Fishing and shrimp harvesting were prohibited until the oil was cleaned up. Beaches that normally saw thousands of tourists were empty. The severe environmental and economic consequences of the Deepwater Horizon oil spill caused the United States to place a six-month moratorium on offshore drilling below a depth of five hundred feet within its EEZ and continental shelf. Although the United States needed to critically reassess its policy on deepwater drilling to ensure any further harm to the environment was mitigated, U.S. energy policy was (and still is) being formulated in a continuing quest for energy independence through continued domestic hydrocarbon exploitation. However, such events emphasize that there is no room for complacency in efforts to protect the long-term health of the global environment.

Toward Global Cooperation on Climate Change

In the twenty-first century, climate change has emerged as the most prominent environmental concern facing the international community. Global warming indicators such as receding polar ice caps, extreme weather events, and changing agricultural yields, have led most in the scientific community to conclude that the planet has already begun its slide down the slippery slope of environmental disaster. Climate change is believed to be at least partly the result of emissions released by the burning of fossil fuels and the razing of vast tropical forests. Such activity creates a concentration of carbon dioxide and other heat-trapping greenhouse gases in the atmosphere. Recent research has shown that methane, which flows from landfills, livestock, and oil and gas facilities, also has an enormous negative impact on the earth's atmosphere. Some fluctuations in the planet's temperature are inevitable, regardless of human activity (the natural result of ocean and solar cycles, for example). But it is believed the rate and extent of global warming brought about by human activities far exceeds that which would result from earth's natural patterns. The projected consequences of humankind's unfettered abuse of resources include substantial disruption in water supplies, agriculture, ecosystems and coastal communities; the impairment of human health; and the extinction of plant and animal species.

In 2000, the General Assembly of the United Nations adopted a resolution to actively address the global community's most vital environmental concerns.[17] The resulting Millennium Declaration includes provisions for the "Protection of the Common Environment." Article IV of the declaration states: "We must spare no effort to free all of humanity, and above all our children and grandchildren, from the threat of living on a planet irredeemably spoilt by human activities, and whose resources would no longer be sufficient for their needs." Thus, care for the environment was once again openly acknowledged as the collective responsibility of all the nations of the world.

As discussed previously, in 1992, following years of lobbying by environmentalists on the potential danger of global warming, the U.N. Framework Convention on Climate Change (UNFCCC) was established to work toward reducing the global mean temperature. In 1997, the UNFCCC adopted the landmark treaty, the Kyoto Protocol (entered into force in 2005), with the stated objective of stabilizing greenhouse gas concentrations in the atmosphere at a level that would prevent dangerous anthropogenic interference with the climate system. The Kyoto Protocol set binding targets for thirty-seven industrialized countries and the European Union for reducing greenhouse gas emissions. These targets amounted to a reduction of 5 percent on average below 1990 levels over the five-year period between 2008 and 2012. Recognizing that developed countries are principally responsible for the current high levels of greenhouse gas emissions in the atmosphere (as a result of more than one hundred fifty years of industrial activity), the Kyoto Protocol placed a heavier burden on developed nations under the principle of "common but differentiated responsibilities."

Under the Kyoto Protocol, countries must meet their emissions targets primarily through domestic measures. However, the treaty offers additional means of meeting targets by way of three market-based mechanisms:

1. Emissions Trading. Commonly referred to as "cap and trade," emissions trading is a system by which parties to the Kyoto Protocol accept certain "caps" on their emissions production (measured in units). If a party produces less than its allowable emissions, it can then sell (or "trade") its excess units to a country that is over its limit. "Cap and trade" has created a new commodity in the form of emission reductions or removals: carbon is now tracked and traded like any other commodity. This is known as the "carbon market."

2. Clean Development. The Clean Development Mechanism (CDM) allows a party to the Kyoto Protocol to implement an emission-reduction project in a

developing country in exchange for saleable certified emission reduction (CER) credits, which can be counted toward its own Kyoto targets. This mechanism stimulates sustainable development and emission reductions, while giving industrialized countries some flexibility as to how they meet emission reduction targets.

3. Joint Implementation. Joint implementation allows one party to the Kyoto Protocol to earn emission reduction units (ERUs) through participation in an emission-reduction or emission removal project in another. Joint implementation offers parties a flexible and cost-efficient means of fulfilling a part of their Kyoto commitments, while the host party benefits from foreign investment and technology transfer.

As of 2013, 191 countries and one regional economic organization (the European Union) had become parties to the Kyoto Protocol. The most notable nonratifying party was the United States, which objected to the fact that the treaty required no steps by China or other fast-growing developing countries. Despite the lack of participation on the part of the United States, however, the United Nations continued to emphasize the importance of implementing the Kyoto Protocol in the twenty-first century as a "first step" toward achieving a notable reduction in emissions of carbon and other greenhouse gases.

In 2007, climate change again took center stage when the United Nations' scientific committee, the Intergovernmental Panel on Climate Change (IPCC), and former American Vice President Al Gore were awarded with the Nobel Peace Prize "for their efforts to build up and disseminate greater knowledge about man-made climate change, and to lay the foundations for the measures that are needed to counteract such change." Following this much-hyped, worldwide recognition of the urgent need to address climate change, the U.N. General Assembly convened in Bali in December 2007 to determine the next stage in climate change objectives. The resulting "Bali Road Map" set out a two-year process to culminate in a binding agreement in Copenhagen (2009).

With the issue of climate change gaining momentum, and the Kyoto Protocol due to expire in 2012, hopes were high that the 2009 Copenhagen Climate Summit would at last yield a tangible international commitment to environmental legislation. However, there were significant differences of opinion going into the summit with regard to the impact and responsibilities of developing nations versus those of already industrialized countries. In the end, the 192 nations in attendance agreed to little more than continuing their negotiations at a follow-up meeting in Cancun, Mexico, in December 2010.

At the heart of the international debate is the struggle between rich and poor countries over who has the obligation to take the first steps toward environmental protection and who should shoulder the burden of financing such measures. Fast-growing, emerging economic powerhouses, led by China and India, still oppose taking on mandatory obligations to curb their emissions, as they claim these obligations will stymie their economic growth. The world's poorest countries, on the other hand, are seeking payments to help make them less vulnerable to the impacts of climate change (longer summers, drought, and more severe storms, for example). These countries maintain that the buildup in climate-warming gases so far has come mainly from richer nations, who ought to be accountable. Such aid has been promised since the 1992 summit, and a fund was set up under the Kyoto Protocol. But while tens of billions of dollars are said to be needed, only millions have flowed so far.

In many ways, the debate over global climate policy is a result of a global "climate divide." Emissions of carbon dioxide per person range from less than two tons per year in India, where four hundred million people lack access to electricity, to more than twenty tons in the United States. The richest countries are also best able to use wealth and technology to insulate themselves from climate hazards, while the poorest, which have done the least to cause the problem, are the most exposed.

In preparation for the U.N. Framework Convention on Climate Change, slated for December 2010 in Cancun, Mexico, representatives of various nations met in China in October 2010 to lay groundwork. There, environmental protection was discussed in terms of political balance, technology cooperation, capacity-building, and long-term financing. The Cancun talks resulted in an agreement for the establishment of a multibillion dollar fund to assist developing nations meet their obligations and cope with the effects of climate change. It also called on developed nations to continue efforts to reduce their own greenhouse gas emissions. Although the nations in attendance in Cancun failed to come up with a plan for a treaty to succeed the Kyoto Protocol, negotiators expressed hope that progress would be made at a follow-up conference scheduled to take place in Durban, South Africa, in December 2011. The Durban conference resulted in several important successes as nations agreed to extend their commitments under the Kyoto Protocol and adopted an enhanced system for the reporting of reductions in carbon emissions. Participants also moved forward with plans to establish a $100 billion fund to assist developing nations in reducing their carbon emissions. Most important, participants agreed to work together to adopt a global legal framework on climate change by 2015. These international efforts to combat climate change must, and will, continue.

Notes

1. INT'L LAW ASSOC., REPORT OF THE FIFTY-SECOND CONFERENCE HELD AT HELSINKI, AUGUST 14TH TO AUGUST 20TH, 1966, at 477–533 (1966).

2. *Id.* at 484–85 (Article 2).

3. Convention on the Law of the Non-Navigational Uses of International Watercourses, art. 5(2), *reprinted in* 36 I.L.M. 700, 705 (1997).

4. G.A. Res. 1721, 16 U.N. GAOR Supp. (No. 17) at 6, U.N. Doc. A/5026 (1961).

5. *Declaration of the First Meeting of Equatorial Countries (1976), reprinted in* 2 MANUAL ON SPACE LAW 383 (N. Jasentuliyana & R. Lee eds., 1979).

6. Legal Status of Eastern Greenland (Den. v. Nor.), Judgment, 1933 P.C.I.J. (ser. A/B) No. 53 (Apr. 5).

7. U.N. Doc. A/37/P.V. 10 (1982). For a discussion of the General Assembly's relationship with the Madrid Protocol, *see, e.g.,* INTERNATIONAL ENVIRONMENTAL LAW FOR ANTARCTICA (Francesco Francioni ed., 1992); Douglas M. Zang., *Frozen in Time: The Antarctic Mineral Resources Convention,* 76 CORNELL L. REV. 722 (1991).

8. Myres S. McDougal & Jan Schneider, *The Protection of the Environment and World Public Order; Some Recent Developments,* 45 MISS. L.J. 1085, 1086 (1974).

9. *See* Edith Brown Weiss, *The Planetary Trust: Conservation and Intergenerational Equity,* 11 ECOLOGY L.Q. 495 (1984); Edith Brown Weiss, *Intergenerational Equity in International Law,* 81 AM. SOC'Y INT'L L. PROC. 126 (1987); Edith Brown Weiss, *Our Rights and Obligations to Future Generations for the Environment,* 84 A.J.I.L. 198 (1990).

10. Corfu Channel Case (U.K. v. Alb.), Judgment, 1949 I.C.J. 4 (Apr. 9).

11. Trail Smelter Case, 3 Rep. Int'l Arb. Awards 1905 (1949).

12. The Lake Lanoux Case, France, Spain, Arbitrated Decision of Nov. 16, 1957, [1957] INT'L L. REP. 101; 53 A.J.I.L. 156 (1959).

13. Corfu Channel Case, *supra* note 10, at 22.

14. Declaration of the United Nations Conference on the Human Environment, U.N. Doc. A/CONF. 48/14 (1972); *reprinted in* 1972 Y.B.U.N. 319; 11 I.L.M. 1416 (1972).

15. Rio Declaration on Environment and Development (in Agenda 21) Adopted June 14, 1992, at the United Nations Conference on Environment and Development, Rio de Janeiro, U.N. Doc. A/CONF. 151/5/Rev. 1, *reprinted in* 31 I.L.M. 874 (1992).

16. *See* A GLOBAL AGENDA: ISSUES BEFORE THE 50TH GENERAL ASSEMBLY OF THE UNITED NATIONS 34 (1995).

17. United Nations Millennium Declaration, A/RES/55/2 (Sept. 8, 2000).

11 Control of People: Nationality and Movement

PEOPLE ARE THE most important element of statehood; without people territory, resources, and institutions are meaningless. The viability of a territorial community depends on people sufficient in numbers, capabilities, skills, and loyalties.

Nation-state elites naturally seek to exert comprehensive and continuing control of people to protect and consolidate their value positions within the state and to control state power. The basic way they do this, in the contemporary world of the nation-state system, is through nationality. Bearing in mind all the normative ambiguities associated with the concept of nationality. Nationality is a tie, a link, the membership, to a nation-state. Through it state elites acquire, exercise, and terminate control over people. Nationality determines who the members of a national political community are and is employed by state elites to assert continuing control over certain people for comprehensive and manifold purposes.

A related device is to regulate the movement of people across state lines. This is the question of who is to be admitted (for what purposes, why, and how long) and excluded by states and who is allowed to stay and who is to be expelled (deported) or extradited. In an age of nation-states, state boundaries represent boundaries of movement. By controlling transnational movement of people, state elites control who may gain and maintain physical access to territorial communities and resources. Physical access is of course the key to full participation and enjoyment in the value processes of a territorial community.

Nationality is relevant not only in the context of movement across borders but in a variety of legally regulated human endeavors: political rights and duties, diplomatic protection, access to resources, conflicts over states' competencies to prescribe and apply law, and so on, as will be discussed further in chapters 12 and 14.

In seeking to control people in terms of both membership and movement, state elites are dealing with human beings. Human beings, unlike nonhuman resources, are not mere objects of manipulation by power elites. They pledge allegiance and obey commands, but they also demand protection and fulfillment.

Thus, although state elites characteristically claim a comprehensive and continuing competence to control and regulate people by conferring and withdrawing nationality and transnational movement, individual human beings have become increasingly assertive in demanding human rights protection concerning nationality and freedom of movement, both internally and transnationally. They demand the freedom to acquire and change membership affiliation with a political community; they demand the freedom to enter, to stay in, and to leave a particular territorial community to maximize pursuit of different values.

Inherent in the question of membership affiliation and movement of people are two distinct dimensions: power and human rights. The tension between the two is clear. How then can the clashing demands be harmonized to serve the common interest of all?

Basic Community Policy

In the face of the increasing assertiveness of the individual in the name of human dignity and human rights, nation-state elites generally strive to maintain and exercise their traditional competence to control and regulate the national membership and flow of people, in addition to controlling the flow of capital, goods, and services. The primary concern of state elites is, all too commonly, to control people in relation to resources as a base of national power. The underlying question is how to harmonize the individual's freedom of affiliation and movement with the need of the nation-state to regulate and control people because of its security, development, quality of life, capacity to absorb newcomers, or other considerations, with due regard to the value consequences beyond the claimants immediately involved.

The established decision makers of the international community historically have honored, in varying degrees, two complementary policies in allocating competence over people. The first, greatly favored when expectations of large-scale violence are low, promotes human rights and encourages freedom in the movement of people and easy changes in group membership, much the same as it fosters the free flow of goods, services, capital, and ideas. The other, gaining prominence under conditions of continuing expectations of imminent violence, puts a premium on the interests of states to consolidate their bases of power through rigorous controls over people, including restrictions on change of national membership and on freedom of transnational movement.

From a long-term perspective, the first policy would progress toward a nonsegregated world of human dignity in which people, resources, and ideas can move freely to achieve optimum shaping and sharing of all values and in which the present disparities in the distribution of people in relation to the earth's resources could eventually be redressed equitably around the globe. Its support for the general freedom of group membership and movement would foster the utmost freedom for the individual in choosing a place to live, work, and enjoy.

Yet policies, like legal doctrines, operate in pairs of complementarity. From a short-term perspective, given the present structure of the world arena, states do share some interests that may in varying contexts require limiting this preferred policy of the utmost individual freedom. Despite contemporary technological developments, people remain an important base of power for each territorial community in the world. Both the security, in the minimum sense of freedom from external violence and coercion, and the quality of society, in terms of the greater production and wider sharing of all values, that a community can achieve depend intimately on the numbers and characteristics of its members. Furthermore, territorial communities share important interests in maintaining harmonious relationships among themselves and in avoiding situations of potential conflict in their claims to ascribe national membership and to regulate the flow of people. Different communities have a common interest in a certain economy in expending resources in their practices to allocate members and provide regulation and protection in transnational processes of authoritative decision.

The cardinal task in search of the common interest is that of achieving an accommodation in particular instances between the complementary policies reflected in the demands of states and the demands of individuals, an accommodation that will, in the long run, best promote the largest net, aggregate achievement of human dignity values. The strong presumption for freedom of movement needs to be balanced by other genuine public order considerations, such as the maintenance of security, health, food, livelihood, development, morals, and so on for the particular community, taking into account also the impact on neighboring states, the regional community, and the world community.

Trends in Decision and Conditioning Factors

Regarding trends in decision, we shall deal first with the claims relating to control of community members via nationality and then with the claims relating to control of movement of people. The overall trends in decision were shaped in the past by the paramount interests of state elites in the control of people as important bases of power and are increasingly influenced by human rights considerations. The interplay of the power dimension and the human rights dimension is discernable.

CONTROL OF COMMUNITY MEMBERSHIP VIA NATIONALITY

We shall deal in sequence with (1) conferment of nationality; (2) withdrawal of nationality, voluntary and involuntary; (3) statelessness; and (4) multiple nationality.

Conferment of Nationality

Nation-states enjoy a high degree of discretion in conferring nationality under international law. The limitations on this discretionary competence remain far from clear. The Hague Convention on Nationality of 1930 contains, not without ambivalence, both a grant of competence and a limitation. Articles 1 and 2 state that it is "for each State to determine under its own law who are its nationals" and that any question "whether a person possesses the nationality of a particular State shall be determined in accordance with the laws of that State." But the nationality law of each state "shall be recognized by other States in so far as it is consistent with international conventions, international custom, and principles of law generally recognized with regard to nationality." The convention fails to specify the criteria of conferment that are recognized or required by international law.

Thus, criteria for limiting states' competence to confer nationality are to be inferred from customary expectations and practice. For conferment of nationality at birth, states have commonly employed either one or both of two principles: *jus sanguinis* (conferment of nationality by blood relation) and *jus soli* (conferment of nationality based on place of birth). The principle of *jus sanguinis*, at least as old as Roman law, is favored by the civil law countries. The principle of *jus soli*, an outgrowth of the feudal system, is preferred by the common law countries. The general trend is toward a mixed system, employing both principles in varying combinations. The uniformity in exclusive reliance on these two principles has been such that some commentators consider it a customary rule that no other grounds are permissible.

As a reflection of the traditional power concern of state elites, these two principles of conferment of nationality at birth disregard human volition. An individual cannot choose his or her parents or place of birth. The bulk of humankind have their nationality thrust upon them, with little effective prospect of change.

Concerning grounds subsequent to birth, states have sought to confer nationality on the basis of consent or a variety of factors, including marriage, recognition by affiliation, legitimation, adoption, paternity, residence or domicile, land ownership, and holding a public post.

Conferment of nationality on the basis of consent is in keeping with a policy of human dignity. The essence of naturalization is to foster a person's voluntary choice of a particular nationality.

In contrast, imposing nationality on individuals against their will, individually or collectively, is incompatible with the generally accepted principles of international law. Compulsory naturalization on such bases as land ownership or residence is impermissible. In the nineteenth century, for example, when certain Latin American countries (such as Mexico and Peru) undertook to impose nationality on aliens who owned real property in the country, such a practice of "expropriating" people was vigorously protested by other states and declared inimical to international law by international tribunals.

Similarly, compulsory naturalization simply on the ground of residence is impermissible. In 1889, for example, the Provisional Government of Brazil proclaimed that all aliens residing in Brazil on November 15, 1889, would automatically become Brazilian nationals unless they should express a contrary intention before appropriate Brazilian officials within six months. This decree provoked severe condemnation and protests of nonrecognition by other states, including France, Great Britain, Italy, Portugal, Spain, and the United States. Another notorious example is the mass imposition of German nationality on nationals of German ethnicity of the territories occupied by Nazi Germany during World War II.

Consent to naturalization need not be explicit but may be inferred. Thus, in conferring nationality on such grounds as marriage, adoption, legitimation, and recognition by affiliation, decision makers commonly infer or assume an element of volition on the part of the individual concerned or those representing him or her.

The effect of marriage on nationality differs widely in national laws. Thanks to the influence of two competing principles—the traditional principle for the unity of the family and the new principle honoring the freedom of a married woman to choose her own nationality—national laws exhibit three basic patterns: (1) the nationality of the wife follows automatically that of the husband; (2) marriage to a man of a different nationality affects the nationality of the wife, but provisions are made to minimize the wife's statelessness or double nationality; and (3) the woman has the right to choose her own nationality, and marriage will not affect her nationality.

From a human rights perspective, marriage should have no automatic effect on the nationality of either spouse. In marrying a national, an alien woman does not necessarily signify her intention to identify with the state of which her husband is a national or to sever her ties with the state of her nationality. As the demand for the equality of the sexes intensifies, the trend is toward the principle honoring the freedom of choice of nationality for a married woman. The Convention on the Nationality of Married Women of 1957 emphatically affirms this trend in Article I: "Each Contracting State agrees that neither the celebration nor the dissolution of marriage between one of its nationals and an alien, nor the change of nationality by the husband during marriage, shall automatically affect the nationality of the wife."

With regard to minor children, the considerations of family unity sustain the general practice that the child follows the father's nationality in the case of legitimation and adoption and that minor children are included in the naturalization process of their parents. Because the element of volition on the part of minors is absent, it has increasingly been urged that minors be accorded the option to resume their original nationality on attainment of adulthood.

Compulsory naturalization has tended to occur in the case of territorial transfer. In the past, when one state ceded a territory to another, the ceding state was generally considered competent to transfer the allegiance of the inhabitants, and the acquiring state was expected to confer its nationality on those inhabitants. These harsh results are often mitigated by human rights considerations, however. Sometimes a plebiscite is conducted to ascertain whether a transfer of territory accords with the wishes of the majority of its inhabitants. Frequently, as stipulated in many treaties of cession or of peace, state practice offers individual inhabitants of the ceded territory an option on nationality, including retaining their original nationality.

In contrast to compulsory naturalization, state elites seek to control membership in a territorial community by denying naturalization to people who actively seek it. A long-established doctrine states that naturalization is a privilege within the discretion of the state, not a right of the applicant.

States differ widely in the scope and severity of limitations attached to voluntary naturalization. Limitations placed on the applicant may relate to residence, age, race, moral character, political belief, health, wealth, and skill. When these preconditions are coupled with onerous administrative requirements, applicants are often effectively denied naturalization.

Events following September 11, 2001 have complicated these questions for many states. In the United States, for example, the events of 9/11 were a complicating factor that exacerbated a long-term controversy over illegal immigration. Laws enacted by the U.S. Congress since 2001 exemplify how a state can flex its sovereign power over the movement of people. The United States has adopted policies aimed at restricting the movement of people across its borders, including the implementation of more entry and residency restrictions along with stricter enforcement of harsh immigration penalties.

In the decade after 9/11, harsher penalties for immigration violations have erected a barrier to naturalization for many potential U.S. citizens. The Illegal Immigration Reform and Immigrant Responsibility Act of 1996 placed certain time bars on noncitizens for reentering the United States after receiving a conviction for certain crimes.[1] The successful passage of stricter immigration laws following 9/11 has extended some of these restrictions indefinitely and applied them to a wider range of violations. Even people who have lived in the country for decades may face new burdens for themselves and their families as a result of new policies.

The requirement of residence, as the most important index of a person's factual attachment to a territorial community, is a common precondition for naturalization. Fulfilling the residence requirement depends on access to territory, with appropriate immigrant status. Yet, such access is itself subject to difficult and often arbitrary conditions. Residence requirements, moreover, vary from state to state in terms of the necessity of physical presence and the length of stay and range from two to ten years. (In special cases, such as sports celebrities needed for the Olympics, top scholars, or scientists, the required length of stay could be eliminated.)

Some states require that an applicant for naturalization be of good moral character at the time of filing a petition. The United States insists that the applicant demonstrate good moral character throughout the requisite probationary period of residence. The requirement of good moral character, elusive and highly susceptible to arbitrary application, has been the major source of litigation concerning naturalization in the United States. The requirement of good moral character was introduced in 1790, but the term received no statutory definition until 1952. In that year Congress sought to clarify the law by enumerating specific grounds that would preclude a finding of good moral character, including adultery, polygamy, prostitution, drunkenness, and gambling. The good moral character test nevertheless remains a source of uncertainty and inhibition for persons seeking naturalization; both the Immigration and Naturalization Service and the courts continue to exert wide discretion in its application. The arbitrary and inconsistent application of the requirement is evidenced by the decisions concerning the sexual behavior of unmarried aliens and the suitability of homosexuals for citizenship. The courts, moreover, are permitted to find in their discretion that, although an applicant for naturalization has committed none of the statutorily proscribed acts, he or she is for "other reasons" a person not of good moral character.

It appears that conferment of nationality at birth is far from an individual act of volition. Although consent receives greater emphasis in connection with conferment of nationality after birth, involuntary naturalization is not a thing of the past, and efforts toward voluntary acquisition of nationality often fail. The power concern of state elites tends to overshadow the concern for individual human rights.

Withdrawal of Nationality

Nationality may be withdrawn or lost at the initiative of the individual or of the state conferring nationality, with or without the consent of the individual. An individual who takes the initiative to terminate his or her nationality is engaged in voluntary expatriation. The withdrawal of nationality based on the genuine consent of the individual does not cause alarm. The real difficulty is to draw the fine line between genuine consent and involuntary withdrawal. We treat in sequence the three traditional categories: (1) voluntary expatriation; (2) withdrawal upon consent, genuine or constructive; and (3) involuntary withdrawal.

Voluntary expatriation. The right to change one's nationality is gaining recognition as a fundamental human right. Such a right affords individuals opportunity to escape the bondage of the effective elites of any community. Voluntary expatriation—the right to renounce nationality—is at the heart of the right to change it. Just as access to a territorial community is crucial to any realistic right to acquire nationality, so is the right of egress to any effective right of voluntary expatriation.

State practice in this area appears to be quite restrictive and harsh toward the individual. Many states still do not recognize the right of unconditional voluntary withdrawal of nationality. Where the right receives nominal recognition, the conditions commonly imposed are so many and onerous as to practically vitiate the right. State elites are understandably reluctant to yield their control over people as important bases of power.

Notable among the barriers to voluntary expatriation are the following:

1. Fulfillment of exacting procedures is required for renunciation of nationality. A U.S. national, when in a foreign country, for example, is required to make a statement of renunciation before a U.S. diplomatic or consular officer in the form prescribed by the secretary of state, although this serves the purpose of assuring requisite intent.

2. A person is not allowed to expatriate him- or herself while in the territory of the expatriating state. Foreign naturalization often results in the automatic loss of initial nationality, and expatriation is expected to occur abroad. Obviously, an effective right of voluntary expatriation depends on an effective right of emigration.

3. A person is barred from expatriating him- or herself while the expatriating state is at war. For instance, Great Britain and many other Commonwealth nations prohibit expatriation in a "foreign" (non-Commonwealth) state in time of war to prevent nationals from evading military service. Naturalization in an enemy state may be regarded as an act of treason, a political offense against the state.

4. Expatriation may be contingent on the grant of official permission by the expatriating state. Most states will not grant such permission unless and until the individual has fulfilled certain obligations, especially military service and tax payments. The "conditional expatriation" under the former Soviet Union and its fraternal states was particularly harsh and inimical to human dignity because the required conditions were not publicly disclosed.

5. Voluntary expatriation is commonly contingent on acquisition of another nationality. The purported purpose is to minimize statelessness.

It would appear that state elites show little disposition of loosening control of people as bases of power, although there is increasing community support of the individual's right to voluntary expatriation. Both the Universal Declaration of Human Rights and the American Convention on Human Rights provide that no one shall be "arbitrarily" denied the right to change his or her nationality.

Withdrawal upon genuine or constructive consent. In contrast to the withdrawal of nationality based on the genuine consent of the individual, states may, in the interest of promoting harmonious relations with other countries, withdraw nationality on the basis of the "voluntary" performance of particular acts. The inquiry then becomes: Are the potentially severe consequences for individuals justified by a sufficient common interest in the avoidance of conflict among nations?

Nation-states have traditionally imposed the loss of nationality as the consequence of particular acts, ranging from the most explicit form of voluntary renunciation of nationality to instances in which consent is either absent, contrived, or fictitious. Acts evidencing consent may include execution of formal instruments of renunciation, deliberate acquisition of the nationality of another state, taking an oath of allegiance to another state, protracted residence abroad, military service in foreign armed forces, voting in foreign political elections, employment by foreign governments, marrying an alien man, and the naturalization of parents by another government.

Regarding some of these acts, the withdrawal of nationality occurs under conditions that clearly approximate genuine consent. Transnational recognition of withdrawal in such circumstances may indeed be necessary to afford effective protection to the expatriate. This applies to executing formal instruments of renunciation, deliberately acquiring the nationality of another state, and taking an oath of allegiance to another state. Executing a formal instrument of renunciation is explicitly designed for voluntary expatriation. The element of voluntariness is present in the case of foreign naturalization that is based on deliberate choice rather than compulsion. An individual's oath or other formal declaration of allegiance to a foreign state implies that he or she is dividing allegiance between that foreign state and the state of nationality; the individual concerned is thus placed in the position where his or her services might be claimed by more than one state, rendering it virtually impossible for the state of nationality to provide him or her protection vis-à-vis that foreign state. Many states make military service in a foreign country a ground for withdrawal of nationality under the assumption that such service is incompatible with loyalty to the state of nationality. Voting in a foreign political election as a ground for loss of nationality may be unique to the United States. It is reasoned that participation in the public affairs of another country implies such a political attachment to the foreign country as to be incompatible with continued allegiance to the United States. The constitutionality of this particular imposition was first sustained in *Perez v. Brownell* (1958)[2] and later rejected in *Afroyim v. Rusk* (1967)[3] by the U.S. Supreme Court, with attention to human rights precepts.

Nationality is sometimes withdrawn if a national has resided abroad continuously over an extended period, normally ranging from two to ten years. This reflects policy considerations inherent in the requirement of a genuine link as the basis of nationality. Although this policy is generally directed to naturalized nationals, it is extended to nationals by birth in some countries.

The effect of marriage on a wife's nationality varies in national laws. Just as a woman may automatically or by certain action acquire the nationality of her foreign husband on marriage, so may she automatically or by certain action lose her original nationality by marrying an alien. Historically, under the twin doctrines of family unity and of implied consent, a woman automatically lost her original nationality and acquired her husband's nationality on marrying a foreign national in most states. The recent trend is distinctly moving away from the fiction of implied consent and toward the equality of the sexes—marriage to a foreign national will entail no automatic loss or acquisition of nationality for the wife.

With respect to minor children, nationality laws are again far from uniform.

In converse to the acquisition of nationality, a minor's nationality may be withdrawn upon the foreign naturalization of the father or widowed mother. This practice, though promoting the unity of family allegiance, does not reflect genuine consent on the minor's part. Hence, the trend is moving toward retaining the minor's nationality after the foreign naturalization of his or her parents, even if this means possessing multiple nationality. However, if the minor must automatically lose his or her original nationality upon the foreign naturalization of the parents, it is increasingly urged that the minor be given an option to choose his or her nationality upon reaching majority.

Withdrawal without consent as punishment. Assertions are sometimes made that the state has the unlimited competence to withdraw nationality. In practice, states act only on certain relatively restricted grounds. Questions have been raised about the permissibility of such withdrawal. Within the United States it is urged with increasing vigor that the withdrawal of nationality as a sanction for misconduct having no bearing on the common interest in the management of people may constitute cruel and unusual punishment in violation of the U.S. Constitution. An analogous inquiry would be applicable in the realm of international law.

States may currently seek to impose loss of nationality as a sanction in response to crimes against the state, including evasion of military service or desertion from the armed forces in time of war; hostile political affiliations and activities; and possession of certain racial, ethnic, or religious characteristics.

States often impose loss of nationality for conviction of crimes regarded as serious attacks on the state. The range of such conduct typically includes treason, desertion from the armed forces, and evasion of military service. The Soviet Union at an early date employed the sanction of denationalization and expulsion against individuals convicted of being "enemies of the toiling masses."

In the United States, the question whether deprivation of nationality is a permissible sanction for desertion or evasion of military service has been litigated. In *Trop v. Dulles* (1958),[4] the U.S. Supreme Court declared that denationalization because of a court-martial conviction for desertion in time of war was "cruel and unusual punishment" in violation of the Eighth Amendment to the Constitution. Characterizing denationalization as "the total destruction of the individual's status in organized society," the court emphasized that "it is a form of punishment more primitive than torture, for it destroys for the individual the political existence that was centuries in the development."[5] Similarly, the Court, in *Kennedy v. Mendoza-Martinez* (1963),[6] declared unconstitutional a statute purporting to denationalize individuals who left or remained outside the United States to evade military service, again on the ground that such measures constituted cruel and unusual punishment.

Denationalization for hostile political affiliations and activities is peculiar to the twentieth century. Although the ancient world was not unfamiliar with banishment for certain hostile political activities and affiliations, deprivation of nationality for such conduct was rare before World War I. After that war denationalization was frequently resorted to as a sanction against "disloyalty or disaffection, acts prejudicial to the State or its interests, collaboration with the enemy," or "advocacy of subversive activities."[7]

Perhaps the most pervasive denationalization measures of this kind occurred in Russia in the wake of the Bolshevik Revolution. In 1921 the Bolshevik government issued a decree that in substance provided that all persons who remained outside the confines of Russia and who had either been absent for four years without official permission, served in hostile foreign armies, or participated in counterrevolutionary organizations would be deprived of Russian citizenship. These denationalization measures were aimed at Russian nationals who had opposed the Bolshevik regime; the upshot was an unprecedented mass denationalization of some two million people, ushering in a tragic era of political refugees.

Other states, including Italy, Turkey, and Germany, subsequently employed denationalization widely and expanded its sanctioning power to cover various types of undesirable conduct. Following World War II, for instance, several Eastern European nations mandated that any national who committed "any act prejudicial to the national and state interests" would be denationalized.[8] Similarly, the United States, during the Cold War, enacted the Expatriation Act of 1954, which purported to denationalize persons who advocated the overthrow of the government under the doctrines of the Communist Party.

The final category in which denationalization has occurred—on racial, ethnic, religious, or other related grounds—is particularly notorious because of its association with Nazi and fascist atrocities. In 1933 the newly ascendant Nazi regime used the artifice of denationalization to help institute and secure its policy of "racial purity." In that year Hitler's government denaturalized thousands of naturalized citizens (primarily Jews) and in 1941 denationalized all German Jews residing abroad. Confiscation of property accompanied deprivation of nationality. A mass exodus of Jews followed these anti-Semitic measures. Denationalization was applied both to persons who had emigrated from Germany during the Third Reich and to Jews of German nationality who had never set foot in Germany. The Jewish wives and children of all such nonresident Germans were also denationalized. Several satellite states of the Axis undertook similar measures against Jews.

After World War II, in reaction to the Holocaust, Czechoslovakia imposed losses of nationality en masse on persons of the German and Hungarian "races." Poland and Yugoslavia similarly denationalized persons of the German "race."

In spite of past assertions by such distinguished authors as Manley Hudson and Paul Weis that international law sets no limit on the competence of states to deprive individuals of nationality, general community expectations today would appear to be moving toward curtailing such allegedly "unlimited" competence. The views of Hudson and Weis, reminiscent of the traditional emphasis on the elite control of people as a basis of national power, may reflect the expectations of the past, but they do not represent community expectations of the present and the probable future.

International law has historically established restraints on this competence: a state cannot deprive individual persons of nationality and then expel them to other states. And as the contemporary global concern for human rights intensifies, additional restraints on such competence are evolving. The fundamental community policy of minimizing statelessness has had general and growing support. The peremptory norm (*jus cogens*) of nondiscrimination, outlawing differentiations based on such invidious grounds as race, sex, and religion, will make unlawful many types of denationalization. Indeed the whole network of more fundamental policies for the protection of human rights, as incorporated in the U.N. Charter, the Universal Declaration of Human Rights, the International Covenants on Human Rights, and other human rights instruments, global and regional, may be properly construed to prohibit use of denationalization as a form of human indignity and of "cruel, inhuman and degrading treatment or punishment,"[9] much in the same manner as the interpretation by the U.S. Supreme Court.

Statelessness

The status of statelessness—a person without formal membership in any body politic—entails a dramatic deprivation of the power and other values of an individual. Just as nationality is the "right to have rights" within the state, so nationality is the right to have protection in rights by a state on the transnational level. Treated as an international outcast—an "unprotected person"—the stateless person may be subjected to severe and all-encompassing deprivations far beyond those common to aliens. He or she has little or no access to authoritative decision, on either national or international levels. The stateless person has no state to protect him or her and lacks even the freedom of movement to find a state that will protect him or her. In a world based on nation-states, statelessness means "the loss of a community willing and able to guarantee any rights whatsoever."[10]

The powerlessness of the stateless person is most pronounced in the limitation on freedom of movement—to enter, to stay in, and to leave a particular territorial community. Because of widespread rigorous requirements for travel documents, notably a valid passport and an entry visa, a stateless person, lacking necessary documents, usually encounters great difficulty in locating a state willing to receive him or her. Unable to enter the territory of a state lawfully, the individual is often compelled to do so clandestinely. Such illegal entry haunts the stateless person.

The important causes of statelessness derive from the formulation and application of the nationality laws of states without adequate regard to human rights. The diversity of nationality laws, as exacerbated by the inherited myth of viewing nationality regulation as a matter of domestic jurisdiction, has created many gaps in the conferment of nationality both at and after birth.

Statelessness at birth generally arises from the inadequacy and diversity of nationality laws, which usually employ the principles of *jus soli* and *jus sanguinis*, but not always *jus soli* and varying forms of *jus sanguinis*. A notable example is a child born in a *jus sanguinis* country of parents of a strict *jus soli* country. Statelessness subsequent to birth arises when a person loses nationality or nationalities without acquiring another.

In a succession of efforts since World War I, the international community has sought to eliminate or to reduce statelessness and to improve the position and treatment of stateless persons through mitigation of attendant hardships. During the era of the League of Nations, the landmark development was the Hague Conference for the Codification of International Law of 1930, which adopted the Convention on Certain Questions Relating to the Conflict of Nationality Laws and the Protocol Relating to a Certain Case of Statelessness. The renewed efforts after the creation of the United Nations have been represented in general human rights protection and specific conventions relating to stateless persons.

To minimize statelessness at birth, the fundamental policy is that a person is presumed to have acquired the nationality of the state of birthplace where no other nationality is acquired at birth. This policy has found authoritative expression in both general and specific formulation of various conventions. The Universal Declaration of Human Rights provides most generally, in Article 15(1), that "everyone has the right to nationality." The International Covenant on Civil and Political Rights, though lacking a nationality provision applicable to everyone, stipulates in Article 24(3) that "every child has the right to acquire a nationality." Article 20(2) of the American Convention on Human Rights is most to the point: "Every person has the right to the nationality of the state in whose territory he was born if he does not have the right to any other nationality." The Convention on the Reduction of Statelessness of 1961 deals more specifically with contingencies of statelessness. It requires, for example, a contracting state to grant its nationality to a person born in its territory who would otherwise be stateless. And a foundling present in the territory of a contracting state is presumed to have been born within the territory and of parents possessing the nationality of that state. Birth on a ship or in an aircraft will be deemed as having occurred in the territory of the state whose flag the ship flies or in the territory of the state in which the aircraft is registered.

To minimize statelessness subsequent to birth, a parallel policy is to make loss of nationality contingent upon acquiring another nationality. This policy has been reflected in prescriptions governing the consequences of voluntary renunciation of nationality. The Hague Convention provides, in Article 7, for example, that an expatriation permit issued by a state "shall not entail loss of the nationality of the State which issues it unless the person to whom it is issued possesses another nationality or, unless and until he acquires another nationality." Similarly, Article 7 of the Convention on the Reduction of Statelessness reads in part: "If the law of a Contracting State entails loss or renunciation of nationality, such renunciation shall not result in loss of nationality unless the person concerned possesses or acquires another nationality."

The policy of minimizing statelessness, however, may on occasion operate to tie a person involuntarily to a political community with which he or she has lost all sense of identification and loyalty and from which he or she cannot expect genuine protection. To obviate such an outcome, the Convention on the Reduction of Statelessness underscores that implementation of the policy of minimizing statelessness should neither interfere with the freedom of movement, including ingress and egress, nor with the right of asylum, as projected in the Universal Declaration of Human Rights.

To make "the right to a nationality" meaningful, the liberalization of states' requirements for naturalization is crucial. Facilitation of naturalization by removing burdensome requirements is widely perceived as the key to reducing existing statelessness. But states are notoriously reluctant, for various real or imagined reasons, to undertake the necessary humanitarian measures. A modest step forward is reflected in Article 32 of the Convention Relating to the Status of Stateless Persons of 1954: "The Contracting State shall as far as possible facilitate the assimilation and naturalization of stateless persons. They shall in particular make every effort to expedite naturalization proceedings and to reduce as far as possible the charges and costs of such proceedings." A comparable provision is found in Article 34 of the Convention Relating to the Status of Refugees.

The general policy of making the loss of one nationality contingent upon acquisition of another applies to situations in which withdrawal of nationality is based on the individual's consent, real or constructive. As described above, consent is normally inferred from a wide range of acts, including deliberate acquisition of the nationality of another state, pledging an oath of allegiance to another state, protracted residence abroad, marriage to an alien man, naturalization of parents by another government, legitimation, and adoption.

Thus the Convention on the Reduction of Statelessness provides, in Article 7(2), that a national seeking "naturalization in a foreign country shall not lose his nationality unless he acquires or has been accorded assurance of acquiring the nationality of that foreign country." And, with limited exceptions, a national shall not be made stateless because of "departure, residence abroad, failure to register or on any similar ground." Concerning the effect of marriage on the nationality of women, the trend has moved not only away from the woman's automatic loss of her nationality on marriage to an alien but toward the equality of the sexes. Thus the Convention on the Nationality of Married Women of 1957 declares, in Article 1, that "neither the celebration nor the dissolution of marriage between one of its nationals and an alien, nor the change of nationality by the husband during marriage, shall automatically affect the nationality of the wife." It adds in Article 2 that "neither the voluntary acquisition of the nationality of another State nor the renunciation of its nationality by one of its nationals shall prevent the retention of its nationality by the wife of such national."

Efforts to mitigate or improve the treatment of stateless persons, contrasted with efforts to minimize statelessness, are commonly considered in conjunction with the treatment of refugees. Technically speaking, the concept of statelessness (having no nationality) and the concept of being a refugee (fleeing one's country in fear) differ. Just as refugees may or may not be stateless, so stateless persons may or may not be refugees. Refugees who have a nationality, nominally, may not be any better off than stateless persons in terms of governmental protection. Refugees who have a nominal nationality but enjoy no protection from their home government are known as *de facto* stateless refugees—as distinguished from *de jure* stateless refugees. The majority of refugees in the contemporary world belong to the *de facto* stateless category. Such refugees and stateless persons share one fate—they are left unprotected. This intimate, though not identical, relationship between stateless persons and refugees finds concrete expression in the substantially identical provisions of two parallel conventions: the Convention Relating to the Status of Stateless Persons of 1954, and the Convention Relating to the Status of Refugees of 1951 and its protocol.

Patterned after the Refugee Convention of 1951, the Convention Relating to the Status of Stateless Persons adopts five broad, somewhat overlapping categories of treatment to be accorded stateless persons: (1) general protection (regarding rights granted apart from the convention, access to courts, administrative assistance, identity papers, travel documents, nonexpulsion, naturalization, nondiscrimination, transfer of assets, and personal status); (2) national treatment (regarding access to courts, elementary education, rationing, artistic rights and industrial property, public relief, labor legislation and social security, and religion); (3) favorable alien treatment (regarding right of non-political association, nonelementary education, housing, movable and immovable property, wage-earning employment, self-employment, and liberal professions); (4) treatment accorded to nationals of the country of habitual residence (regarding access to courts, artistic rights, and industrial property); and (5) alien treatment (regarding general provision and freedom of movement).

Multiple Nationality

Individuals with multiple nationality, in contrast with stateless persons, are claimed by more than one state and may sometimes enjoy the advantages of greater protection in terms of multiple protecting states and permanent physical access to more than one state. They may, however, find themselves subjected to greater responsibilities and burdens. They may be in multiple jeopardy in terms of military service, taxation, and subjection to jurisdiction.

Multiple nationality, like statelessness, results from the diversity of state laws in conferring and withdrawing nationality. Dual nationality, occurring at birth, is most commonly the product of the simultaneous application of the principles of *jus soli* and *jus sanguinis*. A person becomes a dual national, for example, when born in a *jus soli* country of parents with the nationality of a *jus sanguinis* country. Multiple nationality occurs after birth when a person acquires another nationality through application or events such as marriage and adoption without losing his or her original nationality.

International efforts to regulate multiple nationality, as with statelessness, have been twofold: minimizing the occurrence of multiple nationality and ameliorating the deprivations imposed on people of multiple nationality.

The Hague Conference for the Codification of International Law of 1930 remains the most important effort to deal with the problem. Theoretically, multiple nationality at birth could be eliminated by an outright universal adoption of a single principle for conferment. Such an approach, however, was found unacceptable as intruding on sovereign legislative power. Attention centered on minimizing the number of cases of multiple nationality.

Although the desire for minimizing dual nationality found unanimous expression in the final act of the conference, adopted solutions to the question of multiple nationality were limited in scope. The Hague Convention, in Article 6, provides:

> Without prejudice to the liberty of a State to accord wider rights to renounce its nationality, a person possessing two nationalities acquired without any voluntary act on his part may renounce one of them with the authorization of the State whose nationality he desires to surrender.
>
> The authorization may not be refused in the case of a person who has his habitual and principal residence abroad, if the conditions laid down in the law of the State whose nationality he desires to surrender are satisfied.

The most profound hardships imposed on persons of multiple nationality are those that result from the traditional restrictive doctrine of protection, as expressed in Article 4 of the Hague Convention: "A State may not afford diplomatic protection to one of its nationals against the State whose nationality such person also possesses." An international tribunal will thus ordinarily decline jurisdiction where the claimant is alleged to be a national of both the claimant state and the respondent state.

The harsh effects of this doctrine have been ameliorated by applying the principle of effective nationality, also known as active or dominant nationality. The Hague Convention provides that under the doctrine of effective nationality an individual is ascribed the nationality of either the country in which he or she is habitually and principally resident or that of the country to which, under the circumstances, he or she appears to be most closely connected.

The International Court of Justice eloquently expounded the principle of effective nationality in the *Nottebohm* case (1955),[11] notwithstanding the unfortunate outcome based on the inappropriate application of the genuine link theory in the absence of a multiple nationality issue. The court, building on the analogy of dual nationality, stated:

> International arbitrators have decided in the same way numerous cases of dual nationality, where the question arose with regard to the exercise of protection. They

have given their preference to the real and effective nationality, that which accorded with the facts, that based on stronger factual ties between the person concerned and one of the States whose nationality is involved. Different factors are taken into consideration, and their importance will vary from one case to the next: the habitual residence of the individual concerned is an important factor, but there are other factors such as the center of his interests, his family ties, his participation in public life, attachment shown by him for a given country and inculcated in his children, etc.[12]

Similarly, the Italian–United States Conciliation Commission, in the *Mergé* case (1955), stated:

> The principle, based on the sovereign equality of States, which excludes diplomatic protection in the case of dual nationality, must yield before the principle of effective nationality whenever such nationality is that of the claiming State. But it must not yield when such predominance is not proved, because the first of these two principles is generally recognized and may constitute a criterion of practical application for the elimination of any possible uncertainty.[13]

The most dramatic deprivation for a person of multiple nationality relates to the burdens of military service. Intense demands for military service appear to be the principal source of friction between states in their competing claims to control individuals having multiple nationality. Thus the 1930 Hague Conference adopted the Protocol Relating to Military Obligations in Certain Cases of Double Nationality. Under Article I of the protocol, a person having multiple nationality "who habitually resides in one of the countries whose nationality he possesses, and who is in fact most closely connected with that country, shall be exempt from all military obligations in the other country or countries." Elaborate provisions governing military obligations are found in the European Convention on Reduction of Cases of Multiple Nationality and Military Obligations in Cases of Multiple Nationality of 1963.

CONTROL OF MOVEMENT OF PEOPLE

We deal in sequence with the following: (1) state competence to admit, to exclude, and to expel versus individual demands to enter, to stay, and to leave; (2) asylum; and (3) extradition.

Competence to Admit, Exclude, and Expel vs. Individual Demands to
Enter, Stay, and Leave

In earlier times, when national boundaries were relatively open, transnational interaction was less frequent, and means of transportation and communication were relatively underdeveloped, freedom of transnational movement was a minor question. Furthermore, as international law was regarded as concerned "exclusively" with nation-states, it was often indifferent to the fate of the individual. The whole problem of movement for people was approached not from the perspective of protecting individual human rights but from the paramount consideration of protecting and consolidating the bases of power of states, control over people being a principal source of power bases. Hence customary international law recognized the exclusive competence of the nation-state to control and regulate people for entry into, sojourn within, and departure from, its territory, a manifestation of what was said to be "sovereignty" of the state.

The growing contemporary concern for the protection of human beings, as symbolized by global and regional human rights programs, is challenging the traditional exclusive competence of the nation-state to regiment people and to regulate their movement. As state power is deemphasized, people's power is stressed. Concern for the right to enter, to stay, and to leave is an expression of the increasing general concern for the protection and fulfillment of human rights. Specific new prescriptions have developed in regard to the freedom of transnational movement.

The Universal Declaration of Human Rights, in Article 13, proclaims:

1. Everyone has the right to freedom of movement and residence within the borders of each State.
2. Everyone has the right to leave any country, including his own, and to return to his country.

Comparable freedom of movement is provided in Articles 12 and 13 of the International Covenant on Civil and Political Rights, with greater detail. Article 12 reads:

1. Everyone lawfully within the territory of a State shall, within that territory, have the right to liberty of movement and freedom to choose his residence.
2. Everyone shall be free to leave any country, including his own.
3. The above-mentioned rights shall not be subject to any restrictions except those which are provided by law, are necessary to protect national security, public order (*ordre public*), public health or morals or the rights and freedoms of others, and are consistent with the other rights recognized in the present Covenant.
4. No one shall be arbitrarily deprived of the right to enter his own country.

Article 13 deals with the expulsion of aliens:

Any alien lawfully in the territory of a State party to the present Covenant may be expelled therefrom only in pursuance of a decision reached in accordance with law and shall, except where compelling reasons of national security otherwise require, be allowed to submit the reasons against his expulsion and to have his case reviewed by, and be represented for the purpose before, the competent authority or a person or persons especially designated by the competent authority.

These provisions, although phrased in general terms, unequivocally affirm community expectations about the right to enter (return) for nationals, the right to leave for both nationals and nonnationals, and the right to stay (including not only freedom of internal movement and residence but also freedom from arbitrary expulsion). Comparable prescriptions in the regional human rights conventions, European and American, have reinforced these expectations.

Under customary international law it is generally accepted that a nation-state is competent to limit the admission of aliens to its territory, for either temporary or permanent purposes. The authority of a state to regulate matters of immigration is deemed plenary and "inalienable." The actual exercise of this competence is restrained by treaty, domestic laws, comity, and the practical need of intercourse with people of other communities. This continues to be the prevailing practice today, as evidenced by the omission of any stipulation of the right of access of nonnationals to a territorial community in any of the human rights conventions mentioned above. The prime exception is to allow long-term residents (nonnationals) to return to the land of domicile, which is sometimes justified on the theory of "acquired rights." But it is equally well established that nationals shall not be denied the right of entry into their own country, as seen in customary international law and recent human rights prescriptions.

The general right of nationals to return to their own country is hampered and frustrated by various practical limitations and pretexts:

1. Claimants are subjected to onerous burdens in proving their nationality;
2. Some nation-states use decrees of denationalization to deny the right of entry of their own nationals;
3. Cumbersome requirements for obtaining passports or reentry permits are made applicable to nationals;
4. Excessive fees for return are imposed;
5. Certain people are classified as a special category of nationals whose right to entry is curtailed;
6. Persecution or the threat of persecution is used to prevent or deter refugees from returning to their land of origin.

In the matter of sojourn, the focus is commonly on aliens. An alien resident—lawfully admitted—does enjoy a measure of protection against arbitrary expulsion. In exercising its authority to control people, a state may in general deport (expel) an alien for violating its laws and, under special circumstances, order the alien expelled on reasonable grounds of public policy, provided due process requirements are met. But a government is not permitted to engage in the collective expulsion of a group of people for discriminatory reasons. President Idi Amin Dada's mass expulsions of some forty thousand naturalized citizens of Indian origin from Uganda in 1972 was clearly a gross violation of international law. In January 1983 Nigeria ordered approximately two million foreign workers to be expelled and deported; about half of those were Ghanaian nationals. Ghana's prompt reception of its returning nationals averted an international crisis. Some European nations, such as Germany and France, have come under criticism in recent years for the proposed expulsion of ethnic Romani (also referred to as gypsies).

The right to leave a territorial community in theory applies to nationals as well as aliens. But in practice this right is greatly constrained in many communities, especially for nationals, because of rigorous requirements of travel documents (passport or its equivalents) and other practical barriers. The right to leave, or the right to travel, may be for temporary purposes or for permanent emigration. Temporary or otherwise, the right to leave is contingent on obtaining a passport or its equivalent. The passport serves not only as a certificate of identity but as some sort of guarantee of "returnability"—the receiving state is assured that the passport holder can return to another country.

Some governments refuse to issue passports on grounds of national interest (security, foreign relations, brain drain, and so on) or on various spurious, arbitrary grounds; some offer no explanation. Sometimes strings are attached, such as area restrictions, keeping certain countries off limit. Other barriers to the exercise of the right to leave include: (1) requiring renunciation of nationality as a condition to leave the country; (2) suspiciously viewing the exercising of the right to leave as a crime; (3) imposing exorbitant fees or exit taxes; (4) making reprisals, sanctions, and harassments against an applicant and family. The question of emigration of Soviet Jews attracted particular attention in the 1970s.

The desire of nation-states to control the movement of individuals is made more difficult by the existence of activities such as human smuggling and human trafficking. Human smuggling occurs when an individual pays another person to arrange for safe passage—most often in secret—between one nation and another. Human trafficking involves the forced movement of individuals, many of whom are women and girls, either within a nation or across national boundaries. Victims are often coerced into activities including prostitution and indentured servitude, sometimes with little recourse available to them on the part of national governments.

In 2001, the United Nations adopted the Convention against Transnational Organized Crime, also known as the Palermo Convention,[14] whose aims include eliminating human trafficking and smuggling, especially involving women and girls and migrants. The convention is supplemented by two protocols. The first is the Protocol against the Smuggling of Migrants by Land, Sea and Air. The second is the Protocol to Prevent, Suppress and Punish Trafficking in Persons, Especially Women and Children. It defines human trafficking:

> [T]he recruitment, transportation, transfer, harbouring or receipt of persons, by means of the threat or use of force or other forms of coercion, of abduction, of

fraud, of deception, of the abuse of power or of a position of vulnerability or of the giving or receiving of payments or benefits to achieve the consent of a person having control over another person, for the purpose of exploitation. Exploitation shall include, at a minimum, the exploitation of the prostitution of others or other forms of sexual exploitation, forced labour or services, slavery or practices similar to slavery, servitude or the removal of organs.[15]

Human trafficking is a problem that occurs on every continent, with more than 160 nations serving as either a source, transit point, or destination for human trafficking. The number of victims of human trafficking who are engaged in forced labor around the world is estimated to be around 2.5 million. Many of the victims are women and girls who are subjected to forced labor, including prostitution.

Asylum

Asylum, in contemporary international law usage, has become a term of art, referring to admission of a special category of aliens—refugees—people who flee their land of origin because they genuinely fear persecution for political, racial, or religious reasons. This fear of persecution distinguishes refugees from ordinary immigrants.

The twentieth century has been called the century of homeless people. Together with stateless persons, refugees are unprotected people. Increasingly the world community is witnessing a new type of people "in orbit," not astronauts but "refugees in orbit." A typical refugee in orbit wanders from country to country in quest of some one country that will let him or her in to stay. During the protracted period of quest, the refugee is shuffled from airplane to airplane and confined in airports. Compelled to leave the country of residence and lacking proper identity and travel documents, many people cannot disembark legally anywhere. In earlier times one could always jump ship. But today, under the closed national boundary system policed by more sophisticated entry and exit control, such unfortunate persons are condemned to a nightmarish cycle of enforced airplane journeys and periods of practical imprisonment in airport waiting rooms. In addition to refugees in orbit, the plight of "boat people," cast adrift and at the mercy of predators, including undocumented Haitian and Central American refugees, and people fleeing strife in Libya, Syria, and other areas in the Middle East and North Africa, have also dramatized the plight of refugees in our time.

Continuous transnational effort has been made, beginning under the League of Nations and extending through the U.N. system under the aegis of the Office of the United Nations High Commissioner for Refugees, to improve the status and treatment of those who flee their country in fear of persecution because of political, religious, or other reasons. The Convention Relating to the International Status of Refugees of 1933 and the Convention Relating to the Status of Refugees of 1951—whose scope of application has been greatly expanded by the adoption of the Protocol Relating to the Status of Refugees in 1967—contain elaborate provisions for the treatment of refugees. But they have side-stepped the prior question of whether refugees are to be accorded a right of asylum under international law. The reluctance to confront the issue of asylum reflects significant deference to the sensitivity of state elites in relation to political dissenters and other refugees.

The first important attempt to remedy this basic inadequacy in prescription came in 1948 with the adoption of the Universal Declaration of Human Rights. Article 14 of the declaration provides that "everyone has the right to seek and to enjoy in other countries asylum from persecution." Though the critical wording, "enjoy" instead of "be granted," is not as strong as it should be, this prescription does signify a deep community concern to transform the matter of asylum from the domain of "state discretion" to that of international humanitarian concern. Regrettably, the International Covenant on Civil and Political Rights fails to include a comparable, much less a stronger, provision.

This deficiency has been partially remedied by the adoption of the Declaration on Territorial Asylum by the U.N. General Assembly in December 1967, in clear recognition of the growing importance of according asylum to the politically or otherwise persecuted.[16] This declaration, in Article 1(1), provides that "asylum granted by a State, in the exercise of its sovereignty, to persons entitled to invoke Article 14 of the Universal Declaration of Human Rights, including persons struggling against colonialism, shall be respected by all other States." The declaration emphasizes that an act of asylum is not an unfriendly act toward other states but a humanitarian act. An individual thus protected shall not be, in the words of Article 3(1), "subjected to measures such as rejection at the frontier or, if he has already entered the territory in which he seeks asylum, expulsion or compulsory return to any State where he may be subjected to persecution." The follow-up effort to give the declaration more body and substance in the form of a convention, though slow and protracted, is expected to be completed in due course.

No rejection at the frontier, no expulsion or compulsory return to a state—these are the essential ingredients of what has come to be known as the principle of nonrefoulement, a principle related to the responsibility of the state not to become an accomplice in foreseeable deprivations of human rights. This principle has become well established in international law. According to the convention of 1951 and the Protocol Relating to the Status of Refugees of 1967 and other related instruments, refugees shall not be returned against their will to the land of origin where they are in danger of persecution on political, racial, religious, or other grounds. Meanwhile, efforts have been made to establish the right of voluntary repatriation for refugees, as symbolized by Article 5 of the Organization of African Unity Convention Governing the Specific Aspects of Refugee Problems in Africa of 1969. This article reads in part as follows:

1. The essentially voluntary character of repatriation shall be respected in all cases and no refugee shall be repatriated against his will.
2. The country of asylum, in collaboration with the country of origin, shall make adequate arrangements for the safe return of refugees who request repatriation.

3. The country of origin, on receiving back refugees, shall facilitate their resettlement and grant them the full rights and privileges of nationals of the country, and subject them to the same obligations.

4. Refugees who voluntarily return to their country shall in no way be penalized for having left it for any of the reasons giving rise to refugee situations.

Extradition

Extradition involves the formal surrender by one state to another, at the latter's request, of an individual reasonably accused or convicted of a crime. A newer form involves the rendering of an accused to an international criminal tribunal. The alleged offense has ordinarily been committed within the territory of the requesting state or aboard a ship or aircraft flying its flag, and the alleged offender has taken refuge within the territory of the surrendering state. Requests for extradition are generally handled through the diplomatic channel.

Extradition and asylum are closely related, inasmuch as refusal of extradition may in effect constitute the granting of asylum and extradition the denial of asylum. But they are neither identical nor merely two sides of the same coin. The institutional practices of extradition and asylum have developed side by side, with distinct purposes and functions. Extradition is designed to secure criminal justice and to minimize crime by denying criminal fugitives a safe haven and by having them brought to justice through orderly procedures of transnational cooperation. Asylum, by contrast, is peculiarly humanitarian, designed to provide a safe haven for individuals fleeing their land of origin to escape political, religious, or racial persecution. (In practice, asylum may be extended to alleged criminal offenders, especially political offenders who have not engaged in acts of international crime.)

Increasing mobility of people across national borders means that it also becomes easier for criminal fugitives to move from country to country. Transnational cooperation is required to facilitate crime detection and criminal justice. Such cooperation may take various forms: police cooperation is one, extradition another.

In our contemporary world where nation-states remain jealous of their "territorial sovereignty," state boundaries are, legally at least, barriers to transnational judicial cooperation. Customary international law does not mandate such cooperation. International law does not require states to extradite criminals in the absence of treaty arrangements. The United States will not formally extradite without a treaty but will receive individuals without a relevant treaty.

As a matter of practical necessity and common interest, nation-states have established an extensive network of extradition treaties (both bilateral and multilateral), as supplemented by national laws, to secure judicial cooperation on the basis of reciprocity. These treaties are mostly bilateral, but the number of multilateral treaties, such as various regional conventions on extradition in Latin America and the European Convention on Extradition of 1957, is growing.

Although provisions for extradition vary from treaty to treaty, they exhibit certain common features: (1) the principle of dual or double criminality, also known as the principle of double extraditability; (2) the principle of specialty or specificity of crimes; (3) the principle of nonextradition of nationals; and (4) the principle of nonextradition of political offenders.

Under the principle of double criminality, an act is extraditable only when it constitutes a crime according to the laws of both the requesting state and the requested state or, of course, international law. The treaty may enumerate extraditable offenses or may refer to extraditable offenses generally as any acts that, under the laws of both parties, are criminal offenses and punishable by a certain minimum penalty. Rooted in the considerations of reciprocity, it is designed to ensure that a person will not suffer punishment for offenses not recognized as criminal by the requested state. How to determine whether the requirement of dual criminality is met—by the name of crimes listed or by substantive facts adduced in support of the request for extradition—can sometimes be a taxing question.

In this connection, is the requesting state required to present evidence of guilt before the requested state as a precondition for granting a request for extradition? As a general practice, the United States and the United Kingdom consider it essential to make out a prima facie case of guilt against an alleged fugitive criminal. Many other countries consider it sufficient when the warrant has been duly issued, and identity established, and the procedural and substantive stipulations of the extradition treaty are met.

Under the principle of specialty, the extradited person may be tried in the requesting state only for the offenses for which extradition was granted. Normally, the consent of the extraditing state can be obtained post hoc by waiver.

According to the principle of nonextradition of nationals, a state is under no obligation to extradite an alleged criminal who is one of its own nationals. This is traditionally justified on the grounds that a person should not be withdrawn from his or her natural judge and that a state owes to its nationals the protection of its laws. In general, civil law countries seek to exempt nationals in bilateral treaties, whereas common law countries do not. The United States, for example, will surrender its own nationals, unless the relevant treaty provides otherwise, and does not consider exemption of nationals to be customary.

The principle of nonextradition of political offenders, though well known, is fairly recent in origin. In ancient times and in the Middle Ages, extradition arrangements were designed primarily to secure the surrender of political offenders, rather than common criminals, as a means of wiping out political enemies. The trend to limit the surrender of political offenders gained influence in the wake of the French Revolution. In the turbulent arena for brute power struggle, where winners take all and losers not only lose power but may well become targets of persecution or liquidation, such a humanitarian exception is vital, especially for power elites, present and potential.

This notable exception for crimes of a political character, though laudable in theory, has sometimes generated considerable difficulty in application. How to determine what constitutes political offenses? By the motive, act, character, or effect involved? Theories diverge, although there are two basic types: (1) the pure political offense (for example, crimes against the state such as subversion or espionage), and (2) the mixed or relative political offense. The problem is exacerbated when the elements of a common crime and a political offense are intertwined (that is, in the case of a so-called relative political offense)—an act of killing, for example, that fits the schedule of such extraditable offenses as murder but was committed with a political motive or to flee political or other persecution. In spite of the vast literature in this area, political motive seems essential, although a workable test is yet to be formulated.

States may also use the extradition process as an opportunity to express disapproval with certain practices. This was demonstrated most clearly in the case of *Soering v. United Kingdom.*[17] The case involves the United Kingdom's efforts to extradite a German citizen, Jens Soering, who was accused of committing two murders before fleeing to the United Kingdom. In keeping with the 1972 Extradition Treaty between the United States and the United Kingdom, British authorities sought assurances that Soering would not face the death penalty in Virginia, where the murders occurred. Following proceedings in the United Kingdom, an order for Soering's extradition was signed in 1988. Soering then requested a review of the decision by the European Commission of Human Rights under the European Convention on Human Rights and Fundamental Freedoms.

Soering based his appeal to the commission on Article 3 of the convention, which outlawed the use of "inhuman or degrading treatment or punishment." While the convention permitted the death penalty itself under some circumstances, Soering argued that he would face treatment in prison that was tantamount to inhuman and degrading treatment.

The commission rejected Soering's claim after considering whether a state could be held responsible under the convention for a defendant's inhuman or degrading treatment following extradition. The commission held that the extraditing state could be held responsible in cases where a defendant faces a "serious risk" of such treatment, but that Soering had failed to show such a risk.[18] Soering appealed the decision to the European Court for Human Rights, which reversed the commission's holding and found that his extradition would violate Article 3. Eventually, the U.K. government received additional assurances from Virginia, and he was extradited to Virginia, where he was found guilty in 1990 and sentenced to two life terms in prison.

Examples such as this demonstrate how nations can influence one another through the extradition process in order to secure greater recognition of values including human rights. However, this may also cause friction where the need for extradition is related to a nation's national security or in cases of terrorism. Take for example the conflict between the United States and Russia over the extradition of Edward Snowden, a government contractor who released classified information about U.S. electronic surveillance programs. Snowden fled the United States and eventually arrived in Moscow, where he was given refuge. Russian officials refused to extradite Snowden, citing the lack of an extradition treaty with the United States. Snowden remained in Russia as of 2014. Other examples, such as "extraordinary rendition," where a nation takes clandestine steps to remove individuals from another nation, suggest that some states may seek to circumvent international norms in order to prosecute individuals who are accused of certain crimes.

TERRORISM

It has been clearly established that certain acts are per se excluded from the purview of political offenses. These include such violations of international law as war crimes, genocide and other crimes against humanity, hijacking, and other impermissible terrorist acts, which are especially abhorrent and widely condemned.

Terrorism in all its forms has aroused worldwide concern in our time. There has been a deepening shared perception that terrorism threatens all members of the world community: the taking of hostages or the killing of innocent civilians, for whatever reasons, violates fundamental human rights and is no more justifiable in a struggle for national liberation than it is in international warfare. In 1985, the United Nations resolutely condemned as criminal all forms of terrorism, and in 1990 the International Law Commission adopted a provision expressly condemning such conduct in the framework of a Draft Code Against the Peace and Security of Mankind. The common interest, or "enlightened self-interest," in conventional wisdom requires transnational cooperation to combat transnational terrorism. International efforts continue to be directed against aircraft hijacking and sabotage, hostage taking, and bombing attacks against civilian targets.

One effective way to deal with offenders of acts of terrorism—hijacking, kidnapping, and so on—is to deny them refuge. Refusal of asylum, via extradition in particular, is crucial in efforts to combat transnational terrorism. This policy is incorporated in important conventions designed to combat terrorism: (1) the Hague Convention for the Suppression of Unlawful Seizure of Aircraft, 1970; (2) the Montreal Convention for the Suppression of Unlawful Acts Against the Safety of Civil Aviation, 1971; (3) the Convention on the Prevention and Punishment of Crimes Against Internationally Protected Persons, including Diplomatic Agents, 1973; and (4) the International Convention Against the Taking of Hostages, 1979. Common to these antiterrorist conventions is the requirement that states "extradite or submit to prosecution" persons reasonably accused of the proscribed offenses. A contracting state enjoys universal jurisdiction by treaty over an offender, and the plea of political reasons is greatly curtailed under these conventions. In 2006, the United Nations adopted its Global Counter-Terrorism Strategy, which, in part, calls on member nations:

1. To cooperate fully in the fight against terrorism, in accordance with our obligations under international law, in order to find, deny safe haven and bring to justice, on the basis of the principle to extradite or prosecute, any person who

supports, facilitates, participates or attempts to participate in the financing, planning, preparation or perpetration of terrorist acts or provides safe havens.

2. To ensure the apprehension and prosecution or extradition of perpetrators of terrorist acts, in accordance with the relevant provisions of national and international law, in particular human rights law, refugee law and international humanitarian law. [Nations] will endeavour to conclude and implement to that effect mutual judicial assistance and extradition agreements, and to strengthen cooperation between law enforcement agencies.[19]

Despite these and other efforts, the international community has yet to adopt a comprehensive definition of terrorism. Nevertheless, certain U.N. resolutions do refer to actions considered terroristic and inimical to community values. Resolution 1566 (2004) urges member nations to condemn all

criminal acts, including against civilians, committed with the intent to cause death or serious bodily injury, or taking of hostages, with the purpose to provoke a state of terror in the general public or in a group of persons or particular persons, intimidate a population or compel a government or an international organization to do or to abstain from doing any act, which constitute offences within the scope of and as defined in the international conventions and protocols relating to terrorism, are under no circumstances justifiable by considerations of a political, philosophical, ideological, racial, ethnic, religious or other similar nature.[20]

Appraisal

Under the interplay of the power dimension and the human rights dimension, the present state of practice governing nationality and transnational movement for the individual leaves much to be desired, despite considerable progress toward humanitarianism. The traditional state competence to control and regulate territorial membership of people and their movement and activities is matched, and challenged, by intensifying demands for freedom in membership affiliation and in transnational movement.

Central to the contemporary state system is the concept of nationality. The question of nationality is closely linked to the freedom of transnational movement. The degree to which the right to enter, to stay, and to leave a territorial community is protected depends largely on whether a person is a national, an alien, or a refugee. The traditional emphasis on "sovereign rights" in the conferment and withdrawal of nationality and in exclusion and expulsion, if left unchecked, would not only threaten the human rights of the individual but jeopardize friendly relations among states and even world minimum public order.

Nationality is a concept created in the past to foster a minimum organization of the world under past conditions. The reference and function of the concept cannot and must not remain static. It must be dynamic and responsive to the demands, expectations, and identifications of peoples under changing conditions of the global and national constitutive processes.

In an ideal world, all individuals would enjoy optimum freedom of movement, irrespective of nationality or state affiliation. However, the reality is that states continue to flex their sovereign power to control the movement of people within their borders. Take for example recent legislation in U.S. states such as Arizona and Alabama that have sparked controversy for what some perceive as overzealous efforts to stem the tide of illegal immigration at the expense of individual rights.[21] Policies in the future ought to focus comprehensively on balancing the rights of people with states' legitimate need to safeguard their borders, especially as the threat of terrorism grows increasingly transnational in scope.

As human beings seek greater protection and fulfillment of all values, through ever-growing transnational interactions and movement, in an interdependent world of universalizing science and technology, nationality must be made to serve the development and happiness of human beings. Nationality must not be used to perpetuate human bondage by anchoring people, against their will, in a particular territorial community or alternatively casting them adrift when it is withdrawn. The time has come to make the international law of nationality and transnational movement defend and fulfill the rights of the individual. When freedom of membership affiliation and freedom of movement become a reality, when people are free to identify and change community membership and to choose the place to live, work, and enjoy, we may bid farewell to "the century of homeless people" and help usher in a new era of human dignity.

Notes

1. Illegal Immigration Reform and Immigrant Responsibility Act of 1996, Pub. L. No. 104–208, 110 Stat. 3009 (codified as amended in scattered sections of 8 U.S.C.).

2. Perez v. Brownell, 356 U.S. 44 (1958).

3. Afroyim v. Rusk, 387 U.S. 253 (1967).

4. Trop v. Dulles, 356 U.S. 86 (1958).

5. *Id.* at 101.

6. Kennedy v. Mendoza-Martinez, 372 U.S. 144 (1963).

7. PAUL WEIS, NATIONALITY AND STATELESSNESS IN INTERNATIONAL LAW 119 (2d ed. 1956).

8. *E.g.*, Albania, Nationality Act No. 377 of 16 December 1946, Art. 14, *in* LAWS CONCERNING NATIONALITY, U.N. Doc. ST/LEG/SER. B/4, at 4, 6 (U.N. Legislative Series 1954); Poland, Nationality Act of 8 January 1951, Art. 12(b), *id.* at 386, 388.

9. Universal Declaration of Human Rights, art. 5, G.A. Res. 217 (III) A, U.N. Doc. A/RES/217(III) (Dec. 10, 1948); International Covenant on Civil and Political Rights, art. 7, G.A. Res. 2200 (XXI), U.N. Doc. A/RES/2200(XXI) (Dec. 16, 1966).

10. HANNAH ARENDT, THE ORIGINS OF TOTALITARIANISM 297 (new ed. 1973).

11. Nottebohm Case (Liech. v. Guat.), Second Phase, 1955 I.C.J. 4 (Apr. 6).

12. *Id.* at 22.

13. Mergé Claim (U.S. v. Italy), 14 R.I.A.A. 236, 247 (1955).

14. United Nations Convention against Transnational Organized Crime, G.A. Res. 55/25, U.N. Doc. A/RES/55/25 (Jan. 8, 2001).

15. Protocol to Prevent, Suppress and Punish Trafficking in Persons, Especially Women and Children, G.A. Res. 55/25, U.N. Doc. A/RES/55/25, at 32 (Jan. 8, 2001) (supplementing the U.N. Convention against Transnational Organized Crime).

16. G.A. Res. 2312 (XXII), U.N. GAOR, 22nd Sess., Supp. No. 16, U.N. Doc. A/6716, at 81 (Dec. 14, 1967).

17. Soering v. United Kingdom, 11 Eur. Ct. H.R. (ser. A) 439 (1989).

18. *Id.* at 83.

19. United Nations Global Counter-Terrorism Strategy, G.A. Res. 60/288, U.N. Doc. A/RES/60/288, at Annex § II(3) (Sept. 20, 2006).

20. S.C. Res. 1566, § 3, U.N. SCOR, U.N. Doc. S/RES/1566 (Oct. 8, 2004).

21. *See* ARIZ. REV. STAT. ANN. § 13-2929 (2010) (Arizona's illegal immigration law); 2011 Ala. Acts 2011-535 (Alabama's illegal immigration law).

12 Protection of People: From Alien Rights to Human Rights

EVEN THE POSITIVIST theory of international law, which regarded the nation-state as the only subject of international law, recognized that customary law had developed to protect individual aliens outside of the state of their nationality. Aliens visiting a host community are "nationals abroad" from the perspective of the state of their nationality. Statehood, in the long tradition of international law, consists of three essential elements: territory, people, and institutions. Since people are an important base of power for nation-states, the practice of proper treatment of aliens quickly spread through reciprocal understanding: if you respect and protect our nationals abroad, we will respect and protect your nationals within our borders. Such reciprocal deference benefits not only individuals but also the friendly relations of states.

The Remedy of Diplomatic Protection

Customary law for the protection of aliens is well developed. Though the host state where aliens reside regards them as aliens, the state of their origin (nationality) simply regards them as nationals abroad. The host state sees it as a question of treatment of aliens. The state of nationality sees it as a question of protecting nationals abroad. These are two sides of the same coin. Since nationals abroad are regarded as important assets for the state of nationality, any deprivations imposed on nationals abroad are considered an offense against the state of nationality.

The diplomatic instrument historically has played an important part in protecting nationals abroad. This diplomatic remedy, commonly known as "diplomatic protection," developed in response to state responsibility incurred for failing to conform to the international standard for the treatment of aliens and was greatly colored by the state-centered perspective of the nineteenth century. Though long established, this remedy is often cumbersome in application.

If individuals are excluded as subjects of international law, the individual in principle must turn to the state of nationality for protection against external entities when the domestic remedies of the depriving state are of no avail. This remedy requires the nationality link and permits the state of nationality, and only the state of nationality, to protect injured persons, to espouse their claims against other states.

Influenced by Emmeric de Vattel's theory that an injury to a national abroad is an injury to the state of nationality, traditional international law regards a state's competence to protect its nationals as independent of the individual's interest. The state thus enjoys discretion whether to espouse claims on behalf of its nationals at the international level. Because of their overriding concern for national interests of all sorts (such as minimizing friction with a friendly nation), state elites tend to give short shrift to individual deprivees, placing them largely at the mercy of state officials.

Under the requirement of the continuity of nationality, an individual claimant must possess the nationality of the espousing state from the instant of deprivation, through the presentation of the claim, and normally until final settlement. An individual claimant who loses or changes nationality after having sustained a deprivation may find him- or herself unable to secure remedy. Although the state of nationality at the time of deprivation is precluded from espousing the claim because the individual is no longer its national, the new state of nationality is disqualified because the individual was not its national at the time of deprivation. Such technical limitation has led arbitral tribunals to reject innumerable claims.

The concept of nationality itself may sometimes be questioned or distorted so as to deny protection to individual persons. As discussed in chapter 11, states enjoy a broad competence in conferring nationality on individuals and commonly defer to one another's conferments. But individuals occasionally find themselves devoid of a protecting state and denied a hearing on the merits of their claims because ambiguous and spurious conceptions of nationality are invoked, or tests over and beyond any customary conception are imposed. Several famous cases, such as *Nottebohm*,[1] *Flegenheimer*,[2] and *Barcelona Traction*[3] dramatically illustrate such miscarriages of justice.

In *Nottebohm*, Friedrich Nottebohm, born a German national in 1881, moved to Guatemala in 1905 to reside and do business there, without ever applying for Guatemalan citizenship. He lived there until 1943, when he was arrested and sent to the United States for internment as an enemy alien. In between these dates, Nottebohm had made trips from Guatemala to Liechtenstein to visit his brother and to Germany. In October 1939 he went to Liechtenstein and was granted naturalization on an exemption from the three-year residence requirements. He took an oath of allegiance to Liechtenstein and consequently forfeited his German nationality under the nationality law of Liechtenstein. He returned to Guatemala early in 1940 and registered his change in nationality in the Guatemala Register of Aliens.

Following his release from prison in the United States in 1946, he applied for readmission to Guatemala but was rejected; hence, he took up residence in Liechtenstein. In the meantime, the Guatemalan government, having classified him as an enemy alien, expropriated his extensive properties without compensation.

Liechtenstein thus brought an action against Guatemala in the International Court of Justice, charging that Guatemala had violated international law "in arresting, detaining, expelling and refusing to readmit Mr. Nottebohm and in seizing and retaining his property."[4] Guatemala contended that Liechtenstein's claim on behalf of Nottebohm was inadmissible in light of the nature and circumstances of his naturalization.

In denying Liechtenstein's competence to protect Nottebohm and declaring the case inadmissible, the court relied on a "genuine link" theory of "real and effective nationality."[5] Under this theory certain "factual ties" or "genuine connections" between the naturalized person and the naturalizing state must exist. These ties might include habitual residence, center of interests, family ties, participation in public life, or other attachments. Since such genuine connection was found missing here, the court concluded that Guatemala was not obligated to recognize Nottebohm's naturalization.

The application of the genuine link theory, borrowed from the very different context of dual nationality problems, deprives an individual of a hearing on the merits and the protection by a state willing to espouse his or her claim in the transnational arena. The net effect is an immense loss of protection of individual human rights.

In *Flegenheimer*, one Albert Flegenheimer, on the basis of his U.S. citizenship, claimed that he was protected against prior property seizures by the government of Italy under the terms of the Treaty of Peace with Italy of 1947. The property seizures took place during World War II. Flegenheimer's father had been a naturalized U.S. citizen who in 1874 had returned to his native land, Germany (Kingdom of Wurttemberg). Flegenheimer was born there in 1890, but since his father was a U.S. citizen, the United States recognized his U.S. citizenship in 1942, after Flegenheimer had fled to Canada to escape Nazi persecution. Flegenheimer was granted a U.S. passport in 1946 and a certificate of nationality in 1952.

A claim brought on Flegenheimer's behalf by the United States was rejected by the Italian-American Conciliation Commission. According to the terms of the relevant treaty provision, only "United Nations nationals" could be parties to such claims. In concluding that Flegenheimer was not a U.S. national (thus not a U.N. national), the commission substituted its own criterion for that of the conferring state. The commission even took upon itself the act of looking to a treaty of 1868 between the United States and Wurttemberg, even though the United States obviously considered Flegenheimer a full U.S. citizen. The case has been criticized as a usurpation of the claimant state's right to appraise the facts on which it has based its decision to confer nationality. The result, as in *Nottebohm*, is that the claimant is denied a forum in which to present international claims and have them judged on their merits.

A somewhat different situation existed in *Barcelona Traction*. Instead of denial of a nation's right to represent an individual to whom it has granted citizenship, in this case the state that could have successfully brought a claim on behalf of the injured party, a corporation, declined to do so. The case involved a corporation formed in Canada to supply the city of Barcelona, Spain, with lighting and electricity. In 1948 Spain declared the corporation bankrupt and seized its assets. For reasons not made public, Canada refused to follow through on an international claim against Spain. Belgium, a large number of whose nationals owned stock in the Barcelona Traction Company, thus filed suit with the International Court of Justice. As part of its opposition to jurisdiction, Spain claimed that Belgium lacked standing to bring a claim on behalf of shareholders in a foreign corporation. The court accepted this contention, and again the case was dismissed without judgment on its merits.

The court reasoned that, although the shareholders really suffered the financial harm resulting from Spain's actions against Barcelona Traction, so long as the corporation survived as a legal entity and was not dismantled, only it was capable of raising claims based on misdeeds against it. Since this could be accomplished only through Canadian intervention, and since Canada had sole discretion to decide whether such a claim should be pressed, its decision was final, and the shareholders lacked international recourse.

In the contemporary world, diplomatic remedies to protect individuals are further subject to limitations inherent in decentralized lawmaking and application. Dominated by considerations of reciprocity and effective power, a state's decision to act as a protector does not guarantee that the individual national will receive effective protection. Vacillation, trade-offs, and compromises among state elites are not uncommon.

Standard for the Treatment of Aliens

Closely linked to the question of diplomatic protection is when a particular state responsibility occurs for failing to treat aliens properly. In other words, what is the commonly accepted standard for the treatment of aliens?

In ancient times the alien was commonly looked on as an enemy, outside one's "tribe," and hence was treated as an outlaw; parochial community expectations kept him powerless and unprotected. As the Roman Empire expanded, aliens were gradually accorded protection under the *jus gentium*, a law made applicable to foreigners as well as citizens, as distinguished from the *jus civile*, which applied exclusively to Roman citizens. The earlier harsh treatment of aliens was, theoretically at least, further ameliorated with the spread of Christian and other religious ideas of the unity of mankind. In the feudal period of the early Middle Ages in Europe, international commerce was sufficiently local-ized so that the few persons living abroad for commercial purposes had only minimal property rights. With the expansion of international commerce and the development of more powerful centralized governments, the rights of aliens increased correspondingly.

With the coming of the modern nation-state system, a more humanitarian attitude toward aliens began to develop. The founding fathers of contemporary international law asserted that all persons, alien or other, were entitled to certain natural rights, or inalienable rights of mankind. Francisco de Vitoria was among the first to emphasize fair treatment of aliens and subjugated people. Taking for granted the right of free access to territorial communities, Hugo Grotius stressed the idea that as far as possible states must accord the alien a status equal to that of its nationals. It was Vattel, however, who first expounded a coherent and influential doctrine for the protection of aliens. Writing more than a century after Grotius, as mercantilism was becoming modern capitalism and as a vast European expansion overseas was beginning, Vattel created the theoretical basis for much subse-quent decision. Viewing the state as an entity composed of the sovereign and his citizens, Vattel stressed that the state had a right to protect its citizens, wherever they might be. An injury to an individual alien was asserted to be an injury to the state of nationality.

Ever since Vattel, and following the spread of the industrialization and of European culture throughout the world, a unique customary international law for the special pro-tection of aliens has developed. This body of law is constituted by decisions from foreign office to foreign office, as well as by decisions of international and national tribunals (often in terms of the "denial of justice"); it is fortified by the opinions of publicists and a vast network of relatively uniform treaties of "friendship, commerce, and navigation." The competence of states to protect their members from injuries abroad in this relatively unorganized world serves in many contexts to protect the interest of a state in an impor-tant base of power (its nationals), as well as the basic human rights of the alien individual.

Within the broad, historic development of this law, two standards about the responsibil-ity of states, both of which purport to include a norm prohibiting discrimination against aliens, have competed for general community acceptance. One is described as the doctrine of "national treatment," or "equality of treatment," and provides that aliens should receive equal, and only equal, treatment with nationals. The second is described as a "minimum international standard" and specifies that, however poorly a state may treat its nationals, certain minimums in humane treatment cannot be violated in relation to aliens. A review of the flow of decision and communication in the development of the customary law about aliens, especially the recent, more general prescriptions about human rights, indicates that the second of these standards has become the widely shared community expectation.

Because it is generally assumed that states may differentiate between nationals and aliens in a manner that reasonably reflects the varying obligations and loyalties of the two groups, states reciprocally honor the lawfulness of a variety of such differentiations: in, for instance, permissible access to territory, participation in government, and ownership or control of important natural resources. But it is almost universally accepted that with respect to aliens' participation in many important social processes, states may discriminate only when such discrimination is substantially related to differential obligations and loyalties, not merely on the basis of national origin.

The principle of "national treatment," whereby a state will autonomously invoke its own subjective interpretation of the required standard of treatment, would effectively leave aliens at the mercy of their host state. In a world in which many states are tyrannical, totalitarian, or otherwise oppressive, such an outcome is not desired and cannot be accepted. States ought not to be permitted to escape accountability for violating the rights of aliens vis-à-vis the artifice of the "national treatment" principle.

The doctrine of a "minimum international standard," in sharp contradiction to the doctrine of "national treatment," insists that a state cannot escape responsibility for the inhumane treatment of aliens by alleging that it treats its own nationals inhumanely. This widespread, long-accepted doctrine prescribes a minimum common standard in relation to many important sectors in the social process that states must observe in treating aliens, irrespective of how they treat their own nationals: the established standards of justice and civilization, recognized as part of universal international law. The standard was refined through a synthesis of a series of decisions, including those from international conferences, the Permanent Court of International Justice, various domestic and international or regional tribunals, and treaties, especially those concerning friendship, navigation, and commerce.

The minimum international standard for treatment of aliens, like all prescriptions that must be related to the many features of differing contexts, is necessarily abstract. The distinction between lawful differentiation of the status between nationals and aliens on a reasonable basis and arbitrary and unlawful discrimination against the alien must depend not only on the values that are primarily at stake but also on varying features of the institutional practices by which such values are sought and shaped. The minimum international standard has, despite this fundamental difficulty (shared by most important prescriptions), been frequently and widely applied to protect aliens in many value and institutional contexts. The protection typically extends to the alien's legal capacity and access to domestic courts; respect for the alien's physical safety and religious freedom; equity of commercial treatment as to other aliens, especially in regard to property expropriation; and respect for the alien's substantive and procedural legal rights, including the right to adequate remedy.

The Contemporary Global Human Rights Movement

In the latter part of the nineteenth century focus was placed primarily on the category of aliens. Broadly speaking, any individual is a potential alien and may thus enjoy the special protection of international law at some time. However, this recognition carries with it the interrelated notion that states may treat their own nationals as they choose. Hence the irony that aliens sometimes enjoyed more protection than nationals, at least at the international level.

How to resolve this irony? Take away customary protection accorded to aliens? No. That would be a step back toward a public order of human indignity.

The lessons of World War II, more particularly the atrocities of the Third Reich, brought home that large-scale deprivations of human rights not only decimate individuals or groups but endanger peace and security. Hence the U.N. Charter underscored the close link between human rights and peace and security, the intimate interplay between minimum world order and optimum world order. The promotion and protection of human rights was made a prime objective of the United Nations, along with those of maintaining peace and security and promoting self-determination.

This new perception inspired what would become the contemporary human rights movement. The aim was not to take away the customary protection accorded nationals abroad (only when abroad) or to ignore the corpus of human rights that developed in the eighteenth century and found greater protection domestically, but to upgrade the standard of protection for all human beings—nationals and nonnationals. It has increasingly become apparent that nation-states (or those who control them) are often the most significant deprivers of human rights. Human beings—even those tied to a particular territorial community through the link of nationality—must not be treated merely as resources or objects to be manipulated by state elites. They are individual human beings entitled to human dignity and as such must be accorded decent protection and treatment. Hence the growing demands for human rights for every human being.

The atrocities of the Nazis also brought home that individual decision makers must not be allowed to hide behind the abstract entity of the state to escape personal responsibility. Crimes and atrocities against humanity must not escape persecution merely because perpetrators were acting in the name of the state. The trials of war criminals at Nuremberg and Tokyo imposed direct responsibility on individuals and dismissed the defense of superior orders, acts of state, and related claims to immunity.

This signified the clear and universal recognition that the individual is the ultimate actor—the ultimate beneficiary and the ultimate victim—in any interaction or decision, whether national or transnational. Such recognitions, combined with precedents from previous centuries, provide the driving force behind the contemporary global human rights movement. The movement is heir to other great historic movements for human dignity, freedom, and equality. It expresses the enduring elements in most of the world's great religions and philosophies. It builds on the findings of modern science about the close link between respect for human dignity and all other values and between human rights and peace.

A Developing Global Bill of Human Rights

The peoples of the world, whatever their differences in cultural traditions and institutional practices, today demand most intensely all the basic rights conveniently summarized in terms of the greater production and wider sharing of values of human dignity. This heightening intensity in demand and expectation is observable in every feature of the global process of effective power. This intensity can be seen in the official and nonofficial participants making the demands, the spectrum of values demanded, the global reach of these demands, enormous resources and manpower committed, all modalities of communication employed, and the range of functions and activities undertaken.

This intensity of demand for the better effectuation of human rights infuses every constituent community, national and regional, of the larger global community. The history of the establishment of bills of rights within many of the more mature nation-states (as, for example, within the United Kingdom, the United States, and France) is well known. Most newly independent states have clearly expressed comparable aspirations by incorporating, or making reference to, the provisions of the Universal Declaration of Human Rights in their formal constitutions. And regional communities have established or sought to establish on a broader geographic basis effective bills of rights in light of their peculiar cultural attitudes and institutional practices.

In a comparable fashion, a comprehensive global bill of human rights has emerged and is developing. A bill of rights, as an expression of widely shared and intensely demanded values, is sometimes given a variety of technical names, such as fundamental law, higher law, *jus cogens*, or peremptory norms. In a dynamic sense, a bill of rights in action manifests the following features:

Prescription: The bill of rights seeks to protect the most intensely demanded values of human dignity. The fundamental freedoms and rights of the individual are so widely shared, intensely demanded, and highly cherished that they are given special protection by formal prescriptions.

Invocation: Special provision is made to enable individuals who allege that their human rights have been violated to challenge putative deprivations and to secure remedies before authoritative decision makers. Provision is made for specialized invocation by representatives of the community.

Application: Provision is made for applying intensely demanded individual rights prescriptions to all decision makers and community members, whether official or nonofficial. Officials at all levels of government are required to observe and promote these rights. Prescriptions designed to protect human rights are buttressed by specialized institutions of application.

Termination: Such intensely demanded prescriptions can be changed only with extraordinary difficulty or in the same way in which they were created. Special difficulties are placed in the way of formally amending or terminating intensely demanded prescriptions about human rights. Commonly, such prescriptions can be changed only in the ways that they are created.

We turn first to prescription—the projection of authoritative community policies.

Prescriptions about human rights range from the most deliberate form (agreement) to what can be the least deliberate form (customary development), with the United Nations increasingly playing a paramount role.

The common rising demands of all peoples for all basic values—respect, power, enlightenment, well-being, wealth, skill, affection, and rectitude—have received authoritative expression in a host of human rights prescriptions, from the U.N. Charter to the Universal Declaration of Human Rights, the two international covenants on human rights, and a host of ancillary instruments, both global and regional.

The deliberate efforts to create an international bill of human rights began even before the formal establishment of the United Nations. Although the delegates were not prepared to include an international bill of human rights in the U.N. Charter itself, the charter, as finally adopted, did contain several important human rights provisions.

When the Commission on Human Rights was created in February 1946, atop its agenda was "an international bill of rights." It was soon decided that the contemplated international bill of human rights would consist of a declaration, a convention (covenant), and "measures of implementation." The first part of this international bill—the Universal Declaration of Human Rights—was adopted unanimously on December 10, 1948, by the General Assembly as a resolution. Ideological divisions after its adoption led to the General Assembly's decision in 1952 to create two covenants—one on civil and political rights and the other on economic, social, and cultural rights—each containing its own "measures of implementation." The two international covenants, plus the first optional protocol to the Covenant on Civil and Political Rights, were adopted in 1966 and became operative in 1976. Thus, in familiar form, the International Bill of Human Rights, as contemplated at the founding of the United Nations, has been projected.

More than the familiar form, this developing International Bill of Human Rights has been greatly strengthened in substance by various ancillary instruments dealing with particular categories of participants (women, refugees, stateless persons, aliens, youths, children, the elderly, mentally disabled persons, and so on) or with particular values or subjects (genocide, apartheid, discrimination, racial discrimination, sex-based discrimination, slavery, forced labor, war crimes, crimes against humanity, torture, nationality, political participation, employment, education, environment, marriage, and so on), by decisions and recommendations of international governmental organizations (especially by U.N. organs and entities), and by customary developments in the transnational arena. Signifying a new era, the United Nations has projected in no uncertain terms a new commitment toward world order, seeking to secure not only a minimum order (in the sense of minimizing unauthorized coercion) but also a maximum order (in the sense of the greater production and wider distribution of all values). The U.N. Charter contains multiple provisions—notably Articles 1(3), 55, and 56—that suggest that the protection of human rights is a coequal, even indistinguishable, goal in relation to the maintenance of peace and security. Article 1(3) specifies a primary purpose of the United Nations: "To achieve international cooperation in solving international problems of an economic, social, cultural, or humanitarian character, and in promoting and encouraging respect for human rights and for fundamental freedoms for all without distinction as to race, sex, language, or religion." Article 55 states:

> With a view to the creation of conditions of stability and well-being which are necessary for peaceful and friendly relations among nations based on respect for the principle of equal rights and self-determination of peoples, the United Nations shall promote:
>   a. higher standards of living, full employment, and conditions of economic and social progress and development;
>   b. solutions of international economic, social, health, and related problems; and international cultural and educational cooperation; and
>   c. universal respect for, and observance of, human rights and fundamental freedoms for all without distinction as to race, sex, language, or religion.

"All Members pledge themselves," under Article 56, "to take joint and separate action in cooperation with the Organization for the achievement of the purposes set forth in Article 55."

In spite of lingering dissent, the human rights provisions of the charter appear to be accepted (at least since the 1970s) as law in the sense of imposing definite legal obligations on member states and others. This position was authoritatively confirmed by the International Court of Justice in the advisory opinion concerning Namibia of 1971.[6]

The general human rights prescriptions of the U.N. Charter were given somewhat more detailed specification in the Universal Declaration of Human Rights, which celebrated its sixtieth anniversary in 2008. This declaration has acquired the attributes of authority in two ways. First, it is widely accepted as an authoritative identification and specification of the content of the human rights provisions of the U.N. Charter. Second, its frequent invocation and application by officials, at all levels of government and in many communities around the world, have conferred on its content those expectations characteristic of customary law (see chapter 22).

The two international covenants on human rights and the optional protocols to the Covenant on Civil and Political Rights are naturally binding for all states (and their nationals) that have ratified or acceded to them. In addition, like the Universal Declaration, they constitute not only authoritative interpretations of the charter provisions on human rights but also vital components in the flow of communication that creates and shapes the expectations comprising customary international law. By further specifying the content of internationally protected human rights and providing structures and procedures (albeit with inadequacies) to remedy deprivations, they help stabilize authoritative expectations about the defense and fulfillment of human rights. In the same vein, a growing body of more particular conventions dealing with certain types of deprivations or people to be protected has also fostered the enrichment and growth of the core content of the human rights prescriptions projected in the U.N. Charter.

Together these important human rights instruments extend to all basic values widely cherished:

- *Respect*:
  - right to recognition as a person before the law;
  - right to individual dignity and worth;
  - freedom from slavery or servitude;
  - freedom from forced labor;
  - freedom from discrimination on such invidious grounds as race, sex, religion, language, opinion, and birth status;
  - right to equal protection of the law;
  - right to privacy;
  - right to personal honor and reputation.
- *Power*:
  - right of self-determination;
  - right of participation in the political process;
  - right to an authoritative government based on the will of the people;
  - right to vote;
  - right to hold office, elective and appointive;
  - right to nationality;
  - freedom from deprivation of nationality;
  - right to change nationality;
  - freedom of movement and residence;
  - right to leave any country;
  - right to return to one's own country;
  - right to seek asylum from persecution;
  - right of access to appropriate tribunals for remedies and to effective remedies;
  - right to a fair and public hearing by an impartial tribunal;
  - protection of minorities.
- *Enlightenment*:
  - freedom of opinion and expression;
  - freedom of peaceful assembly and association;
  - right to education;
  - right to take part in cultural life;
  - right to enjoy the benefits of science and technology.
- *Well-being*:
  - right to life;
  - freedom from genocide;
  - right to liberty and security of person;

- freedom from arbitrary arrest, detention, or exile;
- freedom from imprisonment for inability to fulfill a contractual obligation;
- freedom from torture;
- freedom from cruel, inhuman, or degrading treatment or punishment;
- right to a high standard of physical and mental health.
- *Wealth*:
  - right to own property;
  - right to share public resources;
  - freedom from arbitrary deprivation of property;
  - right to work;
  - right to free choice of employment;
  - right to just and favorable conditions of work;
  - right to equal pay for equal work;
  - right to an adequate standard of living;
  - right to social security for unemployment, disability, old age, and so on;
  - right to special protection and assistance.
- *Skill*:
  - right to form and to join trade unions;
  - right to vocational education and skill training;
  - right to protection of intellectual property.
- *Affection*:
  - right to marry and to found a family;
  - freedom of association;
  - right to special protection of motherhood and childhood;
  - parental rights regarding children's education.
- *Rectitude*:
  - freedom of thought, conscience, and religion;
  - right to presumption of innocence;
  - freedom from ex post facto law.

Some commentators have observed the remarkable development of contemporary human rights in terms of first-generation rights (civil and political rights), second-generation rights (economic, social, and cultural rights), and third-generation rights ("solidarity" or group rights). The solidarity rights, with their emphasis on the aggregate, are said to include the right to self-determination, the right to enjoy other group processes or institutions, the right to development, the right to participate in and benefit from "the common heritage of mankind," the right to peace, the right to a healthy environment, and the right to humanitarian disaster relief.[7] Human rights are also at stake with respect to international crimes.

In any event, the authoritativeness of the charter provisions on human rights, and of the specification of these rights in the Universal Declaration and related instruments, has received tremendous fortification by the practice of international governmental organizations, especially the organs of the United Nations, and by regional and related domestic efforts. The successful model of the European Convention of Human Rights is widely admitted and has been emulated. Within the framework of the Organization of American States (OAS), the commitment to a regional bill of rights is enunciated in the OAS Charter, the American Declaration of the Rights and Duties of Man, and the American Convention on Human Rights adopted in 1969. The Organization of African Unity, in fulfilling its aspirations for a bill of rights for Africa, adopted in 1981 the African Charter on Human and Peoples' Rights, also known as the Banjul Charter on Human and Peoples' Rights. (Note the inclusion of "Peoples" in the title.) In 1990, the Organisation of the Islamic Conference adopted the Cairo Declaration of Human Rights in Islam as a regional response to the Universal Declaration of Human Rights. The Association of Southeast Asian Nations established its Intergovernmental Commission on Human Rights in 2009.

Another important body of practice contributing to the establishment and maintenance of a global bill of rights is the customary international law of the responsibility of states concerning the treatment of aliens. This vital inheritance continues to serve common interest. In fact, the customary international law of state responsibility, in constant interaction with and as an integral part of the contemporary human rights movement, has contributed mightily to the sum total of the human rights protection, helping to lift the level of transnational protection of nationals as well as of aliens.

The upshot of this comprehensive and continuing prescription, ranging in modality from the most deliberate to the least deliberate, would appear to be that the core content of the various communications has been prescribed as a global bill of human rights. This bill is in both form and policy content much like the bills of rights created and maintained in some national communities. Its core content expresses the intensely demanded values of human beings about the world. Some call it a global bill of human rights, some talk in terms of *jus cogens*, some speak of customary law. The point is that there are crystallized expectations for the defense and fulfillment of human rights that are widely shared and articulated, even though the degree of deprivation and fulfillment differs from community to community, the degree of achievement varies widely, and institutional practices diverge.

Turning to *invocation*, the central question is: When human rights deprivations occur, can victims or others bring complaints to appropriate transnational (as well as domestic) decision makers for remedies?

The provision by global constitutive process for the invocation of human rights prescriptions is progressing in directions appropriate to a genuine bill of rights. The most notable improvement is in the increasing opportunity accorded to the individual to challenge in appropriate transnational structures of authority the lawfulness of deprivations imposed on him or her. The change in authoritative interpretation permitting individuals and private groups to petition the U.N. Human Rights Council regarding certain gross violations of human rights now seems fairly established. The right of individual petition is provided in the first optional protocol to the International Covenant on Civil and Political Rights and in the International Convention on the Elimination of All Forms of Racial Discrimination, the Convention on the Protection of All Persons from Being Subjected to Torture and Other Cruel, Inhuman or Degrading Treatment or Punishment, and the Convention on the Rights of Migrant Workers. The continuing importance of individual petition is amply demonstrated by cumulative experience under the European Convention on Human Rights. Indeed, the great bulk of the complaints brought before the former European Commission on Human Rights originated from either individuals or private groups.

A further improvement in invocation comes from expansion of the historic modality of state complaint. Because of the realities of effective power (especially the enormous discrepancy between the power of the state and that of the individual), proposals continue to be made for more effective invocation through representatives of the general community. It is often too formidable a task for the deprived individual successfully to confront, even before an authoritative decision maker, the depriving state. Demands for the improvement of international constitutive process prevailed, over the opposition of many states, when the Vienna Declaration (1993) proposed that the General Assembly establish a U.N. High Commissioner for Human Rights. The high commissioner's mandate is to advance cooperation, comprehensive approaches, and the participation of all actors in accounting for the protection of human rights at international, national, and local levels.

The *application* of prescriptions in particular instances is, of course, crucial to human rights. This and the enjoyment of rights are the outcomes sought in all human rights policies. As important as it is to challenge unlawful deprivations, it is equally urgent to secure applications that both put basic community policies into controlling practice and mobilize a continuing consensus, in support of prescription, toward the greater future protection and fulfillment of human rights. Human rights committees, such as the Committee on the Rights of the Child (established under the Convention on the Rights of the Child), have worked to fight human rights abuses worldwide.

The contemporary transnational prescription for the protection of human rights would appear to project the same broad compass in applicability characteristic of the bills of rights in some national communities. These prescriptions apply to the United Nations and its organs and other international governmental organizations, to nation-states and all their officials, and to all the nongovernmental groups and individuals active in world social process.

The U.N. Charter is commonly expected to be the most fundamental law of the global community binding all participants. For member states this is explicitly stipulated in Article 103, the charter's supremacy clause: "In the event of a conflict between the obligations of the Members of the United Nations under the present Charter and their obligations under any other international agreement, their obligations under the present Charter shall prevail." Member states and their global audience were not to understand by these words that the members were creating an organization or agencies competent to transgress the obligations, regarding security and human rights, that they themselves were assuming. In light of the charter as a whole and the broader flow of community expectation, it appears incontrovertible that any exercises of authority by the organization or its subsidiary organs must, if they are to be lawful, accord with the basic human rights prescriptions of the charter, as supplemented by the Universal Declaration of Human Rights and other legally relevant instruments.

With regard to nation-states and their officials, these human rights prescriptions apply to all state acts, whether unilateral acts or bilateral or multilateral agreements. The applicability of the human rights prescriptions to the unilateral acts of particular states is inherent in the nature of international law as supreme over national law and the law on which legitimate sovereignty is based. The doctrine of the supremacy of international law has been affirmed and reaffirmed. This doctrine makes contemporary international law for the protection of human rights paramount over all incompatible state practice. It is well established, for example, that a state cannot evade its international responsibility arising from injuries to aliens by invoking its internal decision processes, constitutive or otherwise.

It seems axiomatic that what states may not lawfully do by their unilateral acts in contravention of human rights prescriptions they may not lawfully do in concert or combination through agreement, whether bilateral or multilateral. The contemporary human rights prescriptions apply to all activities of nation-states and their officials. This has been clearly fortified not only by Article 103 of the charter but also by the emerging doctrine of *jus cogens* and the increasing recognition of the lack of claimed immunities for violations and the reach of international law.

The newly emphasized notion of *jus cogens* had its origin in various national legal systems, as expressed in such technical terms as public policy and public order. In the modern law of nations the concept of a *jus cogens*, so fundamental that it cannot be changed by agreement, begins with the great founders of the system. The more recent developments in the formulation of the doctrine are traceable to the International Law Commission in its work on the law of treaties.

The consensus favoring some doctrine of *jus cogens* gained authoritative expression in the Vienna Convention on the Law of Treaties of 1969, which for the first time offered some identification in empirical terms of what prescriptions might be *jus cogens*. The Vienna Convention, in dealing with "treaties conflicting with a peremptory norm of general international law (*jus cogens*)," stipulates in Article 53: "A treaty is void if, at the time of its conclusion, it conflicts with a peremptory norm of general international law. For the purposes of the present Convention, a peremptory norm of general international law is a norm accepted and recognized by the international community of States as a whole as a norm from which no derogation is permitted and which can be modified only by a subsequent norm of general international law having the same character." Article 64 of the convention adds: "If a new peremptory norm of general international law emerges, any existing treaty which is in conflict with that norm becomes void and terminates."

It should not be surprising that the great bulk of the contemporary human rights prescriptions, so insistently demanded by so many peoples around the world, and projecting (along with peace and security) the basic purposes for which the contemporary global constitutive process is maintained, should be widely regarded today as among the principles clearly identifiable as *jus cogens*. Thus, particular states, whether or not members of the United Nations, will not be protected today by global constitutive process in the making (with or without reservations) and performance of agreements, any more than in the performance of unilateral acts, that contravene the basic policies of contemporary human rights prescriptions.

The contemporary human rights prescriptions would appear to apply equally to individuals and private groups—that is, to all nongovernmental actors, and to states and international governmental organizations and their officials. Indeed, most of the prescriptions are documented in terms of the right of persons and not in terms of participation in or protection from the state. They are, in the words of the International Court of Justice, *obligatio erga omnes* (owing by and to all humankind). This applicability to individuals and private groups is achieved sometimes through the international prescriptions being made part of the international law of particular states either directly or indirectly and sometimes through a more direct subjection of individuals and groups to the international prescriptions. Whether the human rights prescriptions are expressed through customary expectation or multilateral agreement or both, states have no real difficulty in making such prescriptions internal law through their constitutive processes.

The appropriate specialized institutions at the international level to ensure the application of the human rights prescriptions are still being established. The bulk of the application of such prescriptions occurs in the foreign-office-to-foreign-office diplomacy of nation-states. Whatever transnational redress most private parties can secure for deprivations of their rights has to do with this traditional remedy, although the domestic arena has been and still is the primary arena for effective invocation, application, and enjoyment of human rights. There are, however, some initiatives toward more inclusive and more effective institutions and procedures. The United Nations' then-Human Rights Commission, as assisted by the Sub-Commission on Prevention of Discrimination and Protection of Minorities, had removed its self-imposed shackles in order to deal with complaints not only from states but also from private groups and individuals. In spite of its somewhat cautious attitude, today the Human Rights Council apparently constitutes a worldwide forum with authority, both existing and potential, in general community expectation to apply the basic prescriptions to systematic, gross deprivations of human rights wherever they may occur. The Human Rights Committee, established under the International Covenant on Civil and Political Rights and its optional protocols, is charged with applying the important policies of the covenant to a significant segment of the world's population. The Committee on the

Elimination of Racial Discrimination, established under the International Convention on the Elimination of All Forms of Racial Discrimination, has dealt with many issues involving racial discrimination and is quickly becoming a major institution to combat racial discrimination in all its manifestations. Experts serving on the Committee on the Elimination of Discrimination Against Women are tasked with appraising the implementation of the provisions of the Convention on the Elimination of All Forms of Discrimination Against Women.

On the regional level, an excellent model for the application of human rights prescriptions is, as is well known, the system established by the European Convention on Human Rights. The application of the European convention is effected by a complex of specialized institutions, consisting of the then-European Commission on Human Rights, the European Court of Human Rights, the Committee of Ministers of the Council of Europe, and the recently established European Union Agency for Fundamental Rights. The U.N. High Commissioner for Human Rights has also recently established a regional office to address international human rights in Europe. Within the framework of the Organization of American States, the Inter-American Commission on Human Rights, with its expanding authority, and the Inter-American Court of Human Rights are making serious efforts toward application. In Africa, the recently established African Court on Human and Peoples' Rights has authority to interpret member states' obligations under the African Charter on Human and Peoples' Rights. Notably, the African Charter includes protections for third-generation group rights, including the rights to equality, self-determination, development, security, and control over wealth and resources, as well as the right to a good environment.

In addition to transnational institutions (global and regional) established to secure compliance with the high standards set forth in the global bill of human rights, transnational prescriptions of human rights are increasingly invoked and applied in domestic courts. Recently, prosecutors in Spain invoked universal jurisdiction to initiate criminal actions under Spanish law against former Argentinean military officers, based on the disappearances, detentions, and torture of Spanish nationals during Argentina's "dirty war" against dissidents in the 1970s. In the famous decision of *Filartiga v. Pena-Irala*, the U.S. Court of Appeals for the Second Circuit in 1980 applied international human rights law to establish that freedom from torture is protected under customary international law, which forms a part of the supreme law of the land in the United States.[8] Therefore, the alleged act of torture committed in Paraguay by a local police chief, Pena-Irala, against a Paraguayan national became an actionable tort before U.S. courts under the Alien Torts Claim Act. In 2006, in *Hamdan v. Rumsfeld*, the U.S. Supreme Court held that detainees at Guantanamo Bay, Cuba were entitled to protections under the Geneva Conventions because the Conventions had been incorporated into the U.S. military's Uniform Code of Military Justice." The Court ruled that the president could not use military commissions to try detainees that did not offer the minimal protections established by Common Article 3 of the Conventions.

In addition, some European countries, invoking international human rights instruments that prohibit capital punishment, have refused extradition of their nationals to the United States and other countries in death penalty cases.[10] This concept was discussed in chapter 11 in relation to the case of *Soering v. United Kingdom*.

We turn finally to *termination*, which means ending an existing prescription. Since the human rights prescriptions are so widely and intensely demanded and so highly cherished, modification or termination of such prescriptions has been made extremely difficult. The difficulties that the global constitutive process presents to terminating or modifying contemporary human rights prescriptions appear comparable to those presented by some national constitutive processes to changing basic, most intensely demanded policies. Under prevailing customary international law these prescriptions can be changed only by modalities in prescription comparable to those in which they were created. For the human rights prescriptions properly regarded as *jus cogens*, which, as indicated above, include the bulk of such prescriptions, this consequence is made explicit by Article 53 of the Vienna Convention on the Law of Treaties. This article, in its somewhat tautological definition, describes a "peremptory norm of general international law" as one that permits "no derogation" and "can be modified only by a subsequent norm of general international law having the same character."

As has been observed, the contemporary human rights prescriptions have been created through a comprehensive, complex process of continuing communication that embraces both the deliberate and formal modalities of multilateral agreement and parliamentary procedures and the less deliberate and mostly informal modalities of customary behavior and expectation. The cumulative and mutually reinforcing effect of these modalities of communication establishes the core content of the human rights prescriptions as authoritative and controlling within the expectations of most of humankind. Termination or modification of these expectations must require a process of communication no less comprehensive and complex, employing the same modalities. The special difficulties that the global constitutive process places in the way of employing each of these modalities for purposes of change may be noted.

Insofar as the human rights prescriptions are grounded in the U.N. Charter, any formal change in these prescriptions must conform to the procedures established to change the charter. Because of the obvious difficulty associated with the built-in veto in the amending procedure contained in Article 108 of the charter, formal amendment of the charter has been extremely modest, reflecting only the numerical changes in the composition and voting procedures of key organs as a consequence of the vast expansion of U.N. membership. Any proposal to terminate or drastically alter the human rights prescriptions would not be immune from this difficulty.

When the human rights prescriptions are incorporated in other multilateral agreements, any proposals for change must encounter the characteristic difficulties in changing agreements between many parties. The two pillars—the International Covenant on Civil and Political Rights (and its optional protocols) and the International Covenant on Economic, Social, and Cultural Rights—contain no provision for denunciation; the commitments undertaken under the covenants are so fundamental and intensely demanded that they are not expected to be modified, certainly not by unilateral action. Even in human rights conventions containing provisions for denunciation, such provisions are so hedged that they cannot easily be made effective.

Insofar as the human rights prescriptions are based on the uniformities that create customary law, any termination or modification of their content requires the development of new customary expectation and behavior. The difficulty in this mode of terminating the human rights prescriptions is obvious in the requirement of the subjectivities of "rightness" or "oughtness" that must attend the behavior from which customary expectations are inferred. Given the intensities with which the basic content of the human rights prescriptions is presently demanded by the peoples of the world, it is difficult to foresee a context in which opposite content could be demanded with the requisite subjectivities of "rightness," as attested by the failure of those who have attempted to undermine the universality of the Declaration of Human Rights. This is in no way intended to suggest that the existing human rights prescriptions cannot be changed, refined, and improved. What is being suggested is that, so long as the peoples of the world continue to exhibit the same widespread and high intensities in demand for the basic human rights expressed in the existing prescriptions, any changes in the fundamental content of such prescriptions must encounter enormous difficulties and be effected through the same modalities by which the prescriptions were created.

Conjunction of Human Rights and State Responsibility

The new epoch in the international protection of human rights ushered in by the United Nations has, paradoxically, been attended by unnecessary confusion about the continued protection of aliens. The rapid multiplication of newly independent states (arising from the emancipation of colonial peoples and, in recent years, the breakup of existing states), differing conceptions about authority and self-determination in various social contexts, and the ideological rifts about the world have brought intense challenges to many customary norms, including those concerning the responsibility of states. The principle of the minimum international standard for the protection of aliens has been attacked especially severely.

The objections to such a universal standard, voiced by Latin American states as well as newly independent states, stress that these rules were fashioned without their participation and that the minimum standard reflects and perpetuates the imbalance of power between the industrialized world and themselves. They further claim that the customary law of responsibility of states for aliens in general should not be considered an authoritative, universal norm of international law. The minimum standard constitutes an infringement on state sovereignty by requiring states, without their consent, to provide special protection to the alien's person and property. It is contended that this practice, whereby a state affords such protection to aliens but not its own nationals, destroys transnational interaction by institutionalizing disparate treatment between aliens and nationals.

This line of argument ignores the role of the international standard in maintaining a world economy and society, underestimates the interests of any particular state in achieving such an outcome, minimizes the importance of the international protection of the human rights of a state's own nationals, undercuts the vast flow across states' lines of prescriptive communication about the protection of both nationals and aliens, and aggrandizes the technical concepts of sovereignty and of territorial jurisdiction.

In the context of such confusion it is understandable that the International Law Commission had made little headway in the early years of its protracted effort to clarify and codify the law of state responsibility. The first special rapporteur of the commission, Francisco V. Garcia-Amador, essayed a noble "synthesis" of the newer emerging law of human rights and the older law designed to protect aliens in proposing both that the newer human rights prescriptions be employed to give more precise content to the inherited minimum international standard for aliens and that the newer remedies being established for the protection of human rights generally be made to supersede certain aspects of the hallowed state interposition on behalf of its injured nationals. His basic proposal was for equality of nationals and aliens, with both a minimum and a maximum in internationally recognized "fundamental human rights."[11]

This imaginative proposal by Garcia-Amador had failed to obtain wide support. Whereas some thought his proposal went too far, some thought it might weaken an important traditional remedy to protect aliens before any effective new remedy was established in replacement. (Subsequently, as the International Law Commission scrapped Garcia-Amador's efforts and shifted its focus away from state responsibility for injuries to aliens to state responsibility in general, the task of codifying international law governing the treatment of aliens fell to the Sub-Commission on Prevention of Discrimination and Protection of Minorities in 1972, with Baroness Elles of Great Britain as its driving force. The effort culminated in the adoption of the Declaration on the Human Rights of Individuals Who Are Not Nationals of the Country in Which They Live by the General Assembly in December 1985).[12]

The newly emerged contemporary human rights prescriptions, including both the U.N. Charter and ancillary expressions, would appear to have importantly increased the transnational protection that the world constitutive process affords aliens. Although nowhere in the charter or other nondiscrimination prescriptions is alienage specifically included as such among the impermissible grounds of differentiation, clearly in the future differentiation of treatment because of alienage will be much more strictly confined, and unlawful discrimination, regarding many values, may be much more readily found. Moreover, Article 2 of the Universal Declaration contains the interrelated prohibition of discrimination per se on the basis of national origin, a prohibition mirrored in other human rights instruments.

Although the U.N. Charter enumerates only four grounds of impermissible differentiation—race, sex, language, and religion—these are intended to be illustrative and not exhaustive. The more detailed formulation in the Universal Declaration of Human Rights makes this abundantly clear. The standard formula employed by the universal declaration is: "Everyone has the right to...." Negatively, the formula is: "No one shall be...." "Everyone" certainly refers to all human beings, national and alien alike. Only in Article 21 does the declaration reserve a specified right exclusively to nationals:

1. Everyone has the right to take part in the government of his country, directly or through freely chosen representatives.
2. Everyone has the right of equal access to public service.

This provision reflects only the long-shared community expectation that differentiation on the basis of alienage is permissible in regard to participation in the making of local community decisions—namely, voting and holding office. The concern in the declaration that human rights be protected for every human being, regardless of nationality, is further manifested in the latter half of Article 2: "Furthermore, no distinction shall be made on the basis of the political, jurisdictional or international status of the country or territory to which a person belongs, whether it be independent, trust, non-self-governing or under any other limitation of sovereignty."

The same concern for the protection of all human beings, based on the same prescriptive formulas, is equally evident in both international covenants on civil and political rights and on economic, social, and cultural rights. Even human rights conventions with a more restrictive focus are, again, formulated generally in terms of each human being.

Similarly, the European and American conventions are cast in broad language designed to protect aliens as well as nationals. The European convention, in Article 1, provides: "The High Contracting Parties shall secure to everyone within their jurisdiction the rights and freedoms defined in Section I of this Convention." Thus, the European Commission on Human Rights had over the years received innumerable individual petitions ("applications") brought by nonnationals resident in the member states of the Council of Europe. Contrary to the traditional practice, nationality is not prerequisite to the protection of individuals. Significantly, the American convention contains, in its preamble, the unique proclamation that "the essential rights of man are not derived from one's being a national of a certain state, but are based upon attributes of the human personality." The convention proceeds to specify in Article 1:

1. The States Parties to this Convention undertake to respect the rights and freedoms recognized herein and to ensure to all persons subject to their jurisdiction the free and full exercise of those rights and freedoms, without any

discrimination for reasons of race, color, sex, language, religion, political or other opinion, national or social origin, economic status, birth, or any other social condition.

2. For the purposes of this Convention, "person" means every human being.

In short, the principal thrust of the contemporary human rights movement is to accord nationals the same protection formerly accorded only to aliens while at the same time raising the standard of protection for all human beings, nationals as well as aliens, far beyond the minimum international standard developed under earlier customary law. When the new human rights prescriptions are considered en masse, they extend to all the basic human dignity values the peoples of the world today demand, and the more detailed standards specified with regard to each of these values exhibit all the precision that rational application either permits or requires. This makes the continuing debate about the doctrines of the minimum international standard and equality of treatment highly artificial, because an international standard is now authoritatively prescribed for all human beings. It does not follow, however, that these new developments in substantive prescription about human rights have rendered obsolete the protection of individuals through the traditional procedures developed by the customary law of the responsibility of states for injuries to aliens.

The notion, popularized by Vattel, that an injury to an alien is an injury also to the state of nationality served to justify the protection of the interests both of the state and of an important category of individuals in a later epoch when the nation-state was often regarded as "the exclusive and sole subject" of international law. Even when more catholic conceptions of the subjects of international law prevail and individuals are being given more direct access to authoritative arenas for their self-protection, however, the historic remedy of state claims to protect the individual would not appear to have ceased to serve common interest. Rather, the transnational channels of protection through a state, together with the newly developed procedures under the contemporary human rights program of claim by individuals, would appear to achieve a cumulative beneficent impact, each reinforcing the other, in the defense and fulfillment of individual human rights. Individuals have recently gained, for remedy of deprivations, either direct or derivative access to transnational arenas of authoritative decision, both global and regional. Notable among them are the U.N. Human Rights Council, Human Rights Committee, the Committee on the Elimination of Racial Discrimination, the European Court of Human Rights, the Committee Against Torture, and the Inter-American Commission on Human Rights. Yet the prospect of further direct access by individuals to authoritative transnational arenas, though encouraging, remains far from adequate. As long as states remain the most important and effective participants in transnational processes of decision, espousal of claims by states for deprivations suffered by individuals would appear indispensable to full protection. Remedy through claim by a protecting state and through individual petition need not be mutually incompatible (they are not mutually exclusive); they can be made to reinforce each other for the better defense and fulfillment of the human rights of the individual. And traditional remedies at the domestic level, of course, must continue to be nurtured and enhanced.

Universality of Human Rights vs. Cultural Relativism

Along with the emergence of the human rights movement and the global bill of human rights, has come an important debate concerning whether human rights standards should be applied universally or whether considerations of cultural relativism should permit deviations from international norms. On one side of the debate stand advocates of the universality of human rights. According to the universalists, the standards for the treatment of human beings set forth in the major human rights instruments (the Universal Declaration of Human Rights, the International Covenant on Civil and Political Rights, the International Covenant on Economic, Social, and Cultural Rights) express absolute minimum requirements and do not allow for deviation. On the other side of the debate stand relativists, who argue that at least some human rights standards must be viewed within the context of the society where they are to be applied. According to this view, human rights standards must have some flexibility to accommodate the dictates of various cultures.

The difficulty with treating certain human rights standards as universal arises when two seemingly absolute standards conflict. The debate is especially salient when it comes to women's rights, perceptions of which can vary significantly from region to region. Is the requirement that a woman cover herself in a veil or other garment a matter of custom or a symbol of oppression? What about the subordination of women in some traditional cultures and societies? The right of girls to receive an education? To what extent should other nations make demands for change and with what level of urgency? To what extent should opponents of the practice of female circumcision acquiesce to cultural tradition? Should we assume that such practices will fade over time as similar ones have elsewhere?

What is the best way to resolve these difficult issues? To the universalist, a practice such as female circumcision (also termed genital mutilation) violates minimum human rights standards and must yield to those requirements. To the cultural relativist, and especially to those members of a society who tolerate such practices, Western prescriptions suggest cultural and religious "imperialism."

The difficulty of resolving these tensions in no way diminishes the importance of doing so. As discussed previously, many fundamental human rights have attained the status of *jus cogens* and should be seen as constituting an emerging global bill of human rights. As Professor Rosalyn Higgins (later president of the International Court of Justice) has stated:

> Human rights are rights held simply by virtue of being a human person. They are part and parcel of the integrity and dignity of the human being. They are thus

rights that cannot be given or withdrawn at will by any domestic legal system.... I believe, profoundly, in the universality of the human spirit. Individuals everywhere want the same essential things: to have sufficient food and shelter; to be able to speak freely; to practise their own religion or to abstain from religious belief; to feel that their person is not threatened by the state; to know that they will not be tortured or detained without charge, and that, if charged, they will have a fair trial. I believe there is nothing in these aspirations that is dependent upon culture, or religion, or stage of development. They are as keenly felt by the African tribesman as by the European city-dweller, by the inhabitant of a Latin American shantytown as by the resident of a Manhattan apartment. [13]

The Evolving Notion of Popular Sovereignty: From State Sovereignty to the Responsibility to Protect

As the preceding discussion of state treatment of aliens and the emerging global bill of rights makes clear, the notion of sovereignty is in the process of an important and fundamental transformation. The traditional notion that a state is responsible for ensuring minimum standards of protection for the nationals of other states who are within its boundaries is rooted in concern for the protection of state interests, not those of individuals. By contrast, the developing global bill of human rights, which seeks to protect the interests of all individuals, not just aliens, is rooted in concern for individual rights, not those of states. In fact, the emerging "responsibility to protect" doctrine goes further, asserting that where a state fails to protect the basic human rights of the people within its boundaries (nationals and aliens alike), that state has in effect surrendered its sovereign right to be free from external coercion and the international community may intervene, even at the expense of the offending state's territorial integrity. The responsibility to protect doctrine represents a radical shift in traditional notions of state sovereignty and the traditional focus on protection of aliens.

Traditionally, the concept of sovereignty distinguished between two polar concepts: domestic jurisdiction and international concern (see chapter 13 for further exploration). According to this traditional view, areas of international concern were largely restricted to breaches of the peace and the treatment of a state's nationals while they were in another state's jurisdiction. By contrast, the internal affairs of a sovereign state were a matter of domestic jurisdiction, and hence beyond the pale of international concern. This distinction between areas of domestic jurisdiction and areas of international concern was closely linked to the notion of territorial integrity, that is, the right of a sovereign to be free from external coercion within his or her sphere of exclusive domain. According to this traditional concept of sovereignty, human rights were regarded as a matter of domestic jurisdiction, permitting no outside interference.

Sovereignty in today's world means "popular" sovereignty—people are at the heart of a state. This notion of popular sovereignty reflects the fact that a government derives its legitimacy from the consent and support of its people, as stipulated in Article 21(3) of the Universal Declaration of Human Rights. When ruling elites abuse and oppress their people, rather than protect them, they can no longer claim immunity in the name of defending "sovereignty," as has been done so many times in the past.

The traditional notion of sovereignty began to shift in response to South Africa's apartheid government. The large-scale human rights deprivations of that government squarely confronted the international community with the tension between the traditional concern for protection of sovereignty at all costs and the more recent concern for protecting individual human rights. This tension was raised in bold relief in the post–Cold War period, which saw an alarming rise in largely intrastate ethnic and religious armed conflicts, characterized by shocking large-scale human rights abuses, including those in the former Yugoslavia and Rwanda.

The responsibility to protect doctrine emerged in response to the growing tension between state sovereignty and the protection of individual human rights. The doctrine has its formal origins in a 2001 report by the International Commission on Intervention and State Sovereignty (ICISS), which had been convened by the Canadian government to examine the changing nature of sovereignty in light of the modern human rights movement. The report reflects a drastic departure from the traditional notion that a state's treatment of its own people was purely a matter of domestic jurisdiction left to the sovereign state's discretion, stating in its synopsis:

> State sovereignty implies responsibility, and the primary responsibility for the protection of its people lies with the state itself.
>
> Where a population is suffering serious harm, as a result of internal war, insurgency, repression or state failure, and the state in question is unwilling or unable to halt or prevent it, the principle of non-intervention yields to the international responsibility to protect.[14]

The report goes on to embrace three elements of the responsibility to protect: (1) the responsibility to prevent internal conflicts and other man-made humanitarian crises; (2) the responsibility to react to "situations of compelling human need," including by the use of military force where necessary; and (3) the responsibility to rebuild, especially in the wake of military intervention and including efforts at reconciliation and efforts to address the causes of the harm. While the responsibility to protect doctrine has won support from many international legal scholars, others question its compatibility with existing international law standards, most importantly the U.N. Charter's prohibition on the nondefensive use of force. Critics of humanitarian intervention in the name of the responsibility to protect point to the potential for abuse of such a right, for example, by states using the responsibility to protect as a mere pretext for an unlawful intervention.

Critics also cite the difficulties inherent in enumerating criteria by which to evaluate the need for humanitarian intervention.

These are difficult issues, but, given their urgency, ones that cannot be avoided. It is clear that the traditional, formalistic concern for state sovereignty must give way to the need to protect individual human beings. Sovereignty exists, after all, only to the extent that the sovereign state enjoys the consent and support of its people. To the extent that an entity claiming sovereignty fails to protect its people from mass human rights abuses, or, even worse, is directly responsible for those abuses, that entity cannot legitimately claim sovereignty or seek the protection of the doctrines of nonintervention and territorial integrity. In some cases, humanitarian intervention by the international community will be required.

Rather than whether humanitarian intervention is justified, the more important question now for international lawyers is under what circumstances humanitarian intervention is justified. Although, as further elaborated in chapter 19, the issue continues to be debated among those who support the recognition under international law of the legality of humanitarian intervention, some widely agreed upon fundamental principles have emerged:

- The use of military force as a humanitarian intervention must be a last resort that is turned to only after all peaceful remedies have been exhausted.
- The use of military force is only appropriate as a response to especially grave and widespread violations of human rights.
- Collective action is far preferable to unilateral action, although most proponents of the responsibility to protect maintain that unilateral action may be justified where grave violations persist in the face of a failure to respond collectively.
- Humanitarian intervention must comply with the law of war, including the principle of proportionality, but there is also debate as to whether a higher standard of care should be imposed in the case of humanitarian interventions.

The Security Council has a critically important role to play in the authorization of force for the purpose of humanitarian intervention. In light of the atrocities committed in Bosnia, Kosovo, Rwanda, and Darfur, and more recently in other states such as Libya and Syria, the Security Council must take its responsibility especially seriously, given the profound effect that gross human rights violations have on the maintenance of international peace and security.

Notes

1. Nottebohm Case (Liech. v. Guat.), 1955 I.C.J. 4 (Apr. 6).

2. Flegenheimer Claim, 25 I.L.R. 91 (Italian–United States Conciliation Commission 1963).

3. Barcelona Traction, Light, & Power Co., Ltd. (Belg. v. Spain), Judgment on Second Phase, 1970 I.C.J. 3 (Feb. 5).

4. Nottebohm Case, *supra* note 1, at 6–7.

5. *Id.* at 23.

6. Legal Consequences for States of the Continued Presence of South Africa in Namibia (South West Africa) Notwithstanding Security Council Resolution 276 (1970), Advisory Opinion, 1971 I.C.J. 16 (June 21).

7. *See, e.g.,* Stephen P. Marks, *Emerging Human Rights: A New Generation for the 1980s?,* 33 RUTGERS L. REV. 435 (1981).

8. Filartiga v. Pena-Irala, 630 F.2d 876 (2d Cir. 1980).

9. 548 U.S. 557 (2006).

10. *See, e.g.,* Soering v. United Kingdom, 161 Eur. Ct. H.R. (ser. A) (1989).

11. *International Responsibility: Second Report,* [1957] 2 Y.B. INT'L L. COMM'N 104, 112–13, U.N. Doc. A/CN.4/106 (1957).

12. G.A. Res. 40/144, 40 U.N. GAOR Supp. (No. 53) at 252, U.N. Doc. A/40/53 (1985).

13. ROSALYN HIGGINS, PROBLEMS AND PROCESS: INTERNATIONAL LAW AND HOW WE USE IT 96–97 (1994).

14. ICISS, THE RESPONSIBILITY TO PROTECT, at XI (2001).

13 Vertical Allocation of Authority

AUTHORITY, CONCEIVED AS the expectations of community members about who will decide what and how, has always been an important base of power. As Lord Acton and others have long observed, authority in this sense builds on itself and constitutes a most effective base of power for any decision maker. A conception of authority, with its concomitant role in decision making, is apparent, in various equivalent forms, in the notions of customary law prevalent in primitive societies, ancient China, India, classical Greece, ancient Rome, Western Europe, and the Americas. This conception represents the insistent historic demands made by many peoples through the centuries and up to the contemporary democratic politics that authority rightfully comes from the whole people. It is reflected, further, in Article 21(3) of the Universal Declaration of Human Rights and also finds expression in the interrelated principle of self-determination. The importance of such a conception in international law is easily demonstrable.

In the world arena, allocation of authority takes two basic forms: the vertical allocation of authority between the general community and particular states, and the horizontal allocation of authority between and among states. We deal with the former here and the latter in the next chapter.

In the vertical allocation of authority between the general community and particular states, the most conspicuous development is the continuing expansion of the concept of "international concern," along with the concomitant erosion of the concept of "domestic jurisdiction." As transnational interaction accelerates and the interdependencies of peoples everywhere are better perceived, the authority of the organized community has grown steadily.

Domestic Jurisdiction vs. International Concern

The dichotomy between matters of international concern and those of domestic jurisdiction inheres in the very concept of international law, even in a world rationally organized on a geographic basis. It signifies the necessity of a continuing allocation and balancing of competence between the general community and its component territorial communities, states, or regions, in ways best designed to serve the common interest. The technical terms international concern and domestic jurisdiction and their equivalents represent two polar concepts, like the blades of scissors, designed to maintain a proper balance between inclusive and exclusive competence. Neither is absolute. Hence, by international concern is meant that certain matters, including events occurring within the territorial boundaries of particular states, are relatively important to a general, transnational community so that such a community can make and apply law to such matters in defense of the common interests of peoples affected by those matters. An important function of international law is to permit external decision makers to intercede in matters that would otherwise be regarded as essentially internal to a particular state.

In contrast, domestic jurisdiction refers to certain matters that are regarded as of predominant importance only to a particular state. Ever since the rise of the modern state system, built on the notion of sovereign equality of all states, particular states have enjoyed, and continued to insist on, a large domain of exclusive competence. This insistent demand has been made and protected under such technical concepts as equality of states, sovereignty, independence, and nonintervention. The cumulative effect of these concepts is to insulate internal elites from external regulation.

Sovereignty, as made popular by Jean Bodin in the sixteenth century with the emergence of the modern state system, referred to the alleged supreme authority and power wielded by the absolute monarch. Whereas the concept of sovereignty in Bodin's sense was somewhat fitting in an era of absolute monarchs, it is not at all apt in describing the authority enjoyed by the individual nation-state in the contemporary epoch of popular sovereignty (authority in the people) and growing interdependences. The persisting assertion and use of sovereignty, with its sixteenth-century absolutist connotation, thus appear out of place in today's world of interdependence. Indeed, sovereignty was never so absolute as to prevent community intervention and sanctions. As discussed in chapter 12, the concept of sovereignty is increasingly giving way to one of state responsibility to protect the rights of citizens. States can no longer insulate themselves behind the concept of sovereignty while violating human rights.

The use of the technical term "domestic jurisdiction" to protect the exclusive competence of internal elites is relatively recent in origin. It made its first, formal appearance in the Covenant of the League of Nations. Article 15(8) of the covenant stated: "If the dispute between the parties is claimed by one of them, and is found by the Council, to arise out of a matter which by international law is solely within the domestic jurisdiction of that party the Council shall so report, and shall make no recommendation as to its settlement." The Charter of the United Nations has adopted this formula with slight modification. Article 2(7) of the charter reads: "Nothing contained in the present Charter shall authorize the United Nations to intervene in matters which are essentially within the domestic jurisdiction of any state or shall require the Members to submit such matters to settlement under the present Charter; but this principle shall not prejudice the application of enforcement measures under Chapter VII." Consequently, the label "domestic jurisdiction" has largely superseded its many historic equivalents for claiming exclusive competence.

Although some commentators have read great significance into the difference in wording—the substitution of "essentially" for "solely" and the omission of specific reference to "international law" in the new formulation—the real significance of Article 2(7) can be meaningfully ascertained only by reference to its application.

Time and again competing claimants have invoked the legislative history of Article 2(7). Yet the records of the San Francisco Conference offer no conclusive answer. The framers of the charter neither saw fit to deprive the United Nations of the authoritative competence essential to the effective performance of its tasks, or curtail that competence, nor wanted the organization to pry into matters generally regarded to be within the exclusive domain of individual states. The line to draw between what is essentially of domestic jurisdiction or of international concern is far from obvious.

Concepts in international law are definite to the extent that they are uniformly understood in content and procedure. Expectations about content are necessarily vague, since the contingent circumstances to which they refer are alluded to in general terms. Hence the importance of procedure—of who is authorized to act and how to apply the content to concrete situations.

Whenever a dispute comes to the notice of the United Nations, Article 2(7) necessarily receives initial attention, save in certain clear-cut cases. Claims and counterclaims concerning U.N. authority are generally juxtaposed. No one state has a monopoly on invoking the plea of domestic jurisdiction. It has been claimed by many states large and small, new and old, authoritarian and nonauthoritarian.

Though it may appear simple to ascertain the immediate objective sought by competing claimants who repudiate or accept U.N. authority in a particular dispute, it is by no means easy to detect and demonstrate the real policy considerations that underlie their claims. Even the attitudes of a single state are far from consistent. Its position is more often than not dictated by the degree of involvement and interest perceived in a particular dispute, and it often appears to fluctuate independent of the level of crisis at a given time.

In particular controversies, the critical question confronting decision makers, representing the larger community of humankind, is how best to relate options in allocating inclusive and exclusive competence to the more fundamental policies of the larger community. Fortunately, the intellectual task involved in making a rational choice among options in the allocation of those competences was clearly recognized as requiring careful, contextual scrutiny. This view found authoritative expression from the Permanent Court of International Justice in the *Tunis-Morocco* case of 1923.[1] In that case, the issue was whether the dispute between France and Great Britain over the applicability to British subjects of certain French nationality decrees, proclaimed in 1921 in Tunis and the French zone of Morocco (both under French protection), fell within the domain of Article 15(8) and thus lay outside the competence of the League Council. In rejecting the French claim, the court held that in principle questions of nationality are within a state's "reserved domain" but that certain treaties concerning Tunis and Morocco to which France and Great Britain were respectively parties made the instant dispute over the nationality decrees an international dispute. The court added that the question of treaty obligation "does not, according to international law, fall solely within the domestic jurisdiction of a single state." The court further proclaimed, in words that have since become well worn: "The question whether a certain matter is or is not solely within the domestic jurisdiction of a State is an essentially relative question; it depends upon the development of international relations."[2] Determining whether a matter is of "international concern" or essentially within "domestic jurisdiction" thus depends not only on facts but on changing facts in light of the context of world conditions and relevant legal policies; this permits a continuing readjustment of inclusive and exclusive competences as conditions might require.

Expanding International Concern in a Globalized World

The trend in authoritative decision within the United Nations toward expansion of international concern can be seen by the scope of subjects handled by various U.N. organs. In spite of the familiar, understandable invocations of the plea of domestic jurisdiction in resisting inclusive authority, especially in the early years of the organization, the United Nations has exercised its authority to deal with a wide range of matters extending to every value sector of community life.

The long and comprehensive list includes matters of peace and security (including peacekeeping operations, matters of disarmament, and arms control); matters of decolonization and self-determination (including trust territories, non-self-governing territories, and others); territorial disputes; humanitarian emergencies; questions concerning the form of government of a state; international cooperation in economic, social, and cultural fields; human rights matters; codification and development of international law; and so on. The list can be greatly multiplied by reference to the ongoing activities carried out by various U.N. specialized agencies and other international governmental organizations. It will inevitably grow as the international community responds to the challenges of an increasingly globalized and interdependent world.

The trend toward inclusive authority through expansion of international concern has been further facilitated by clarifying the meaning of "intervention" contained in Article 2(7) of the charter. The following definition offered by Hersch Lauterpacht has gained wide acceptance: "Intervention is a technical term of, on the whole, unequivocal connotation. It signifies dictatorial interference in the sense of action amounting to a denial of the independence of the State. It implies a demand which, if not complied with, involves a threat of or recourse to compulsion, though not necessarily physical compulsion, in some form."[3] Thus conceived, it would appear that a vast difference exists between the unilateral interference by one state in the internal affairs of another state and the general community's inclusive making and application of law to protect the common interest of all (and, thus, the affairs of all). One is prohibited by law; the other is in defense of law.

The Security Council continues to give broad scope to expanding the definition of "threat to" and "breaches of the international peace," authorizing increasingly multifunctional actions in intrastate conflicts, such as missions to Somalia, Kurdish regions in Iraq, Darfur and South Sudan, and in Libya.[4] In March 2011, the U.N. Security Council passed Resolution 1973, authorizing "all necessary measures" to protect Libyan civilians from assaults by forces loyal to Muammar Gaddafi. The resolution invoked Article 7 of the U.N. Charter by declaring that hostilities in Libya constituted "a threat to international peace and security."[5] In doing so, the council demonstrated that the international community would step in to protect human rights in extraordinary circumstances. This concept is explored further in chapter 19 regarding the use of the military instrument.

The expansion of international concern in U.N. practice is manifested in all decision functions. In terms of the intelligence function (that is, the gathering, processing, and dissemination of information), Article 2(7) is no bar to inscription in the agenda of, and debate on, any issue having an "undeniable international impact, even if there is no consensus over the degree to which international law does or should regulate the matter."[6] The United Nations is fully competent "to talk about a situation, to discuss it, to debate, to persuade, to negotiate,"[7] without doing violence to the mandate of Article 2(7). In terms of the promoting function (advocacy and recommendations), the organs and agencies of the United Nations, as amply shown in countless resolutions, have not been deterred from making recommendations on subject matters claimed to be beyond their competence. With regard to the prescribing function (that is, the projection and communication of authoritative policies), no limit has been easily identifiable; it encompasses practically every aspect of human life, every value sector. The Security Council was at one point becoming so active in enforcing collective security that some commentators suggested the possibility that the World Court might soon have to "judicially review" the legality of certain Security Council resolutions.[8] But it appears that there has been a "diminishing willingness to insulate internationally important activity from international legal control by deference to the dogma of domestic jurisdiction"[9] or the equally circular notion of "intervention" into the affairs of a state versus the affairs of the community.

The exercise of the invoking function (that is, the provisional characterization of concrete circumstances in terms of authoritative prescriptions) has found little impediment in Article 2(7); this is most vividly illustrated by the remedies of state complaint and individual petition against human rights violations and by the statements of states to monitor, even in political arenas, human rights compliance by other states, as this is no longer a matter of domestic jurisdiction. In terms of the applying function (that is, authoritative characterizations of particular events in terms of prescriptions), the U.N. organs have overruled the plea of domestic jurisdiction in numerous cases relating to threats to peace and security, to self-determination, to human rights, and to numerous other situations. As to the terminating function (the ending of prescription and other arrangements) and the appraising function (the evaluation of decision process), it is generally assumed that the general community has the same broad inclusive competence, free of domestic jurisdiction barriers, that it has in relation to the intelligence and prescribing functions.

Note that it is the general community, the global constitutive process, that ultimately determines what matters are within international concern and what within domestic jurisdiction. As the dynamics of interdependence accelerate and peoples' perceptions of their interdependence deepen and become more realistic in a globalized world, the established processes of authoritative decision can be expected to encounter less difficulty in bringing matters having transnational ramifications within the compass of inclusive competence. Events occurring inside the boundaries of one state with appreciable effects on others have always been subject to claim, decision, and review on the international plane. Individual states rarely succeed, even by invoking the plea of domestic jurisdiction, in precluding effective accommodations in keeping with inclusive interest when transnational impacts are clearly generated. Domestic jurisdiction means little more than a concession by the general community to particular states of a primary, though not exclusive, competence over matters arising within the boundaries and predominantly affecting the internal public order of such states. When particular events engender significant inclusive impacts, the general community can be expected to internationalize jurisdiction and to authorize appropriate inclusive decision and action.

Limits on Domestic Jurisdiction

There is an overwhelming trend toward the expansion of international concern. Notwithstanding this trend, nation-states are prone to invoke, and often abuse, the plea of "domestic jurisdiction" in order to insulate abusive conduct from international scrutiny.

An example of this tendency was seen in Sudan during its civil war, prior to the formation of the nation of South Sudan in 2011, as well as in its western region Darfur.

Sudanese leaders invoked the principle of sovereignty to shield the state from international scrutiny as a result of human rights abuses committed against ethnic groups. Despite these protests, the Security Council acted to intervene, establishing peacekeeping missions in the regions and supporting the peoples of South Sudan in their efforts to establish an independent state.[10] Events such as these are more likely to fall under the scope of international concern when there is a question of self-determination, as discussed in chapter 2.

Another example is China's unceasing threat toward Taiwan in the name of domestic jurisdiction, which exemplifies such an abuse of the concept of domestic jurisdiction. The threat of the People's Republic of China (PRC) to use missiles and other types of force against Taiwan constitutes a lawless act in violation of the U.N. Charter, but the PRC has sought to justify it by claiming that Taiwan is "part of China" and that the issue is "an internal affair of China."

In light of the discussions in this chapter and in chapter 2, it would appear that Taiwan's present and future status are not internal affairs of China but are matters of international concern. To elaborate:

1. As stated in chapter 2, Taiwan is a sovereign, independent state, not part of China. For more than sixty years since its founding in 1949, the PRC never exerted "effective control" over Taiwan for a single day.
2. Controversies over Taiwan's sovereignty and international legal status involve an interpretation of international agreements (such as the San Francisco Peace Treaty with Japan) and hence fall within the scope of international concern.
3. The PRC's introduction of extraterritorial laws on anti-secession designed to harass and intimidate the people of Taiwan and its acts of unceasing military threat, including the targeting of missiles, and state terrorism against Taiwan endanger peace and security in the Asia-Pacific region and in the world and constitute "threats and breaches of the peace" in violation of the U.N. Charter.
4. Taiwan's past, present, and future involve the principle of self-determination under international law.
5. Taiwan's present and future status will affect the fundamental human rights of its 23 million inhabitants and hence fall within the scope of international concern.

Given these facts, it would be wrong to concede that Chinese military threats toward Taiwan are simply a matter of domestic jurisdiction as asserted. China's actions encroach upon the right of the Taiwanese people for democratic self-governance free from outside intervention. Moreover, such actions are at odds with Taiwanese statehood. The unauthorized coercion of one state toward another has no place in contemporary international law as it is contrary to the principle of self-determination and the conditions necessary for minimum world order.

Notes

1. Tunis-Morocco Nationality Decrees, Advisory Opinion, 1923 P.C.I.J. (ser. B) No. 4 (Feb. 7).

2. *Id.* at 24.

3. HERSCH LAUTERPACHT, INTERNATIONAL LAW AND HUMAN RIGHTS 167 (1950).

4. S.C. Res. 814, U.N. SCOR, U.N. Doc. S/RES/814 (May 26, 1993) (Somalia); S.C. Res. 688, U.N. SCOR, U.N. Doc. S/RES/688 (Apr. 5, 1991) (Iraq); S.C. Res. 1769, U.N. SCOR, U.N. Doc. S/RES/1769 (July 31, 2007) (Sudan); S.C. Res. 1973, U.N. SCOR, U.N. Doc. S/RES/1973 (Mar. 17, 2011) (Libya).

5. S.C. Res. 1973, U.N. SCOR, U.N. Doc. S/RES/1973 (Mar. 17, 2011).

6. HENRY J. STEINER & DETLEV F. VAGTS, TRANSNATIONAL LEGAL PROBLEMS: MATERIALS AND TEXT 324 (2d ed. 1976).

7. UNITED NATIONS, *Article 2(7)*, 1 REPERTORY OF PRACTICE OF UNITED NATIONS ORGANS 109 (Supp. 3 1972).

8. *See* Jose E. Alvarez, *Judging the Security Council*, 90 AM. J. INT'L L. 1 (1996); W. Michael Reisman, *The Constitutional Crisis in the United Nations*, 87 AM. J. INT'L L. 83 (1993).

9. Richard A. Falk, *On the Quasi-Legislative Competence of the General Assembly*, 60 AM. J. INT'L L. 782, 785 (1966).

10. S.C. Res. 1769, U.N. SCOR, U.N. Doc. S/RES/1769 (July 31, 2007).

14 Horizontal Allocation of Authority

THE HORIZONTAL ALLOCATION of competence between and among states remains vital in the contemporary state-centered world, where most authority over particular events is still exercised at the national level. In the preceding chapter, we dealt with the vertical allocation of authority—the allocation between the general community and the territorial communities. Here we are concerned with horizontal allocation—allocation of authority among different territorial communities regarded as equal.

The central concern of this chapter differs from the claims for comprehensive, continuing control over territory, resources, and people as described in chapters 8 through 12. The concern here is with a state's assertion of competence to make and apply law to particular events, persons, and property. The emphasis is on "particular events" rather than "comprehensive and continuing control." This, in the conventional usage, is the question of jurisdiction. Jurisdiction as a term of art has been given a wide range of references.

Some have used the term so broadly as to embrace all the subjects covered in chapters 8 through 12 and in this chapter. Others take an extremely restrictive view, confining it to what is called "judicial jurisdiction," or "jurisdiction to adjudicate." For those who adhere strictly to the artificial distinction between "public" and "private" international law (popularly known as conflict of laws in the United States), they tend to refer to cases in which states are parties as public international law and to cases in which individuals and private associations are parties as private international law.

In an interdependent and globalized world in which transnational interaction has grown enormously, and in which non-state and state actors are in constant interplay under changing, complex conditions, generating value outcomes of varying magnitudes across state boundaries, it is highly artificial to delineate between public and private international law. As Judge (then Professor) Philip C. Jessup pointed out, the term "transnational law" would be a more fitting description and more in tune with the realities of contemporary international life.[1]

The factual situations that would give rise to claims to prescribe and apply law to particular events range over every value and phase of interaction of a particular value process, as seen in these examples:

- Three U.S. GIs stationed in Okinawa kidnap and rape a Japanese schoolgirl and are then tried and sentenced by a Japanese court.
- Fighting their own "war on drugs," Mexican police detain and kill U.S. citizens in Mexico allegedly involved in the marijuana trade. Some claim the murders are part of a cover-up to hide Mexican police involvement in the drug trade.
- The U.S. Coast Guard boards an American-owned vessel twelve miles from land in the Bahamas, finding half a ton of marijuana and arresting the crew, including Jamaican and Bahamian nationals.
- Gas leaks at a pesticide plant of a multinational chemical corporation, headquartered in the United States, causing thousands of deaths and injuries in Bhopal, India.
- Two Shiite Muslim gunmen commandeer Trans World Airlines Flight 847, with 153 aboard (104 of them American), forcing it to fly from Athens to Beirut, to Algiers, and back to Beirut. Negotiators arrange for all the hostages to be freed in stages, but one American marine is killed.
- A Pakistani terrorist, wanted for the deaths of two CIA agents, is extradited and flown from Pakistan to the United States on an American military plane with no formal hearing in his home country.
- Four Palestinian terrorists hijack the Italian cruise ship *Achille Lauro* on the high seas as it approaches Port Said, Egypt. After killing an American passenger, the hijackers surrender to the Egyptian government in return for a promise of safe passage. Four U.S. fighter planes intercept an Egyptian aircraft carrying the hijackers to freedom and force it to land at the NATO airbase at Comiso, Sicily. The Italian authorities take custody of hijackers but allow the person believed to be the mastermind of the hijacking to leave Rome for Belgrade aboard a Yugoslavian airline (later, however, trying and convicting him in absentia).
- A Georgian diplomat is tried and convicted in the United States, despite claiming diplomatic immunity, for a drunken driving incident that resulted in the death of a young girl. The Georgian government agrees to withdraw his diplomatic immunity so that he may be tried by a U.S. court.

- Holocaust survivors and their families, now U.S. citizens, claim millions of dollars in gold and assets that Swiss banks allegedly seized and hid in collaboration with the Nazis during World War II.

- The British government refuses to extradite a German national wanted for homicide in the United States, claiming that waiting on death row in the United States will be "cruel and unusual punishment" under international human rights law.

- The U.S. Congress passes a law enabling domestic courts to seize the assets of non-U.S. companies that buy Cuban properties expropriated from owners who now live in the United States, punishing such companies for activities they have conducted completely outside of U.S. territory.

- United States courts in Florida decide to return Elian Gonzalez, a child who was found in the ocean after his mother and stepfather died while trying to escape from Cuba to the United States, to his father in Cuba, even though his Miami relatives objected.

- An Indian airplane is hijacked for eight days on Christmas Eve, 1999. Many blame Pakistani terrorists, but Pakistan rejects India's accusations concerning the hijacking. India launches a plan to place armed commandos ("sky marshals") aboard flights on a random basis.

- The U.S. Drug Enforcement Agency (DEA) used Mexican nationals to abduct another Mexican national from Mexico to stand trial in the United States for the torture and murder of a DEA agent.

- A former Somali prime minister used his power to enable torture, rape, and extrajudicial murders. He currently resides in the United States. Former victims, now also residing in the United States, bring suit against the general in U.S. federal courts. On appeal, the U.S. Supreme Court holds that he was not entitled to immunity as a former government official.

Which state or states have authority to make and apply law to such events? What are the limits on laws that may be chosen for application? When more than one state asserts competence to make and apply law to a particular event or to prosecute the same person, how should competing claims for jurisdiction be resolved? What factors are to be taken into account?

From a transnational perspective, jurisdiction as used here is confined neither to criminal or civil jurisdiction nor to judicial jurisdiction. Jurisdiction (horizontal allocation of authority) is concerned here with the competence of a state to make and apply law to particular events, which may or may not occur within the borders of a state and which may or may not involve nationals of the state. It extends to all activities having to do with making and applying law and involves not only the judicial branch of government but the legislative and executive branches (including the latter's administrative agencies). In this sense, it certainly encompasses what have been characterized, by the American Law

Institute in its work of revision on "Restatement (Third) of the Foreign Relations Law of the United States," as the three key components of jurisdiction: jurisdiction to prescribe, jurisdiction to adjudicate, and jurisdiction to enforce.[2]

We speak in terms of the state's competence to make and apply law to particular events. The competence to apply law includes the competence to adjudicate and enforce law. Although it is convenient to approach the field in terms of competence to prescribe, to adjudicate, and to enforce because of the familiar tripartite system of government—the legislative, the judicial, and the executive—this distinction is more formal or structural than functional. It is closely tied to the traditional notion of the separation of powers under such a tripartite form of government. From a functional perspective, the twofold distinction between the competence to prescribe and the competence to apply would suffice.

In an inherited, horizontal legal order, the authority of states is, initially, allocated under certain reciprocally honored principles of jurisdiction—namely, the principle of territoriality, the principle of nationality, the principle of impact territoriality (also known as the protective principle), the principle of passive personality (also known as the victim theory), and the principle of universality. The passive personality principle is highly controversial.

The principle of territoriality empowers states to prescribe and apply law to all events occurring within their boundaries, regardless of whether such events involve nationals or nonnationals. The nationality principle authorizes states to make and apply law to their own nationals, wherever they may be. Under the principle of impact territoriality, a state may take measures against direct attacks on its security and against activities having substantial impact on its other important values, though the events occur outside its territory. The principle of passive personality authorizes states to make and apply law to people who injure their nationals, wherever the events may occur. The principle of universality, rooted in the perception that certain events (such as those involving piracy, slave trading, war crimes, and genocide) are great threats to common interests of all humanity, authorizes any state having effective control over the offenders to apply certain inclusive civil or criminal prescriptions on behalf of the international community. Together these principles confer on any state the competence to make and apply law regarding all events having significant effect on it.

The competences over particular events achieved by states under most of these primary principles of jurisdiction are complemented by certain secondary allocations of competence under doctrines such as "act of state" and "sovereign immunity." In a world social process in which people and goods constantly move across state lines, the primary principles of jurisdiction cannot achieve their appropriate ordering purpose if states do not substantially honor one another's exercises of authority. Hence, states that have effective control over persons and resources are often required, under the doctrine of the act of state, to forgo the exercise of their own authority in deference to the prior legislative, executive, and judicial acts completed within another state. Or they may be required to do so because of immunities accorded heads of state, diplomats, public ships, public corporations, and state agencies, under the doctrine of sovereign immunity.

The five principles of jurisdiction relate to both the competence to make law for particular events and the competence to apply law. In the case of competence to apply law in the restrictive sense of "judicial jurisdiction," it further requires considerations of fairness and convenience by taking into account such factors as the presence of persons and assets, domicile of the parties, the place of business, and intent or foreseeability and consent (express or implied) of the parties to adjudication.

International law accords nation-states broad grants of competence in making and applying law to particular events through the five familiar principles of jurisdiction.

The Principle of Territoriality

Under the principle of territoriality, states are authorized to make law and apply law to all events occurring within their borders, regardless of whether such events involve nationals or nonnationals. It reflects the overriding importance of territoriality in the present-day state system. Under this principle the authority of the state extends to the limits of its territory. This territorial domain of the state, as described in chapters 8, 9, and 10, includes not only land masses but also internal waters, territorial waters, and the airspace above its territorial lands and waters. Within this domain the state exerts comprehensive and continuing authority.

The state's competence to make law to regulate actors and activities within its territorial domain and to apply law to events, persons, and property within its borders are both manifestations of such authority.

The Principle of Nationality

Under the principle of nationality, a state is empowered to make law with respect to its nationals, wherever they may be, and to apply such law within its territory, outside the territory of other states, or in another state with permission. A state can thus exercise jurisdiction over the conduct of its nationals in foreign states and outside the jurisdiction of any state. This follows from a state's claim to control its own people as a base of power.

Examples of application of the nationality principle are the exercise of jurisdiction over U.S. nationals violating trademark laws overseas (*Steele v. Bulova Watch Co., Inc.*, 1952)[3], the taxing of income derived from foreign property by a foreign-domiciled U.S. citizen (*Cook v. Tait*, 1924)[4], and the regulation of U.S. military service personnel (*United States v. Calley*, 1973).[5] The War Crimes Act of 1996 extended U.S. jurisdiction to cover "grave breaches" of the Geneva Conventions where the perpetrator or victim was a U.S. national. It fails to apply universal jurisdiction.

The issues of nationality relate not only to natural persons (human beings), as discussed in chapter 11, but also to juristic persons, including corporations, ships, aircraft, and spacecraft. Many treaty provisions define nationals to include corporations for various purposes, and many contain provisions ascribing a national character to corporations and other associations, based on the place of their incorporation or of their principal office of business.

The competence of nation-states to ascribe national character to vessels has long been recognized, although such competence is most often related to the fiction of territoriality. This policy has historically made enormous contributions to the maintenance of the public order of the oceans.

The nationality of aircraft, as provided by the Chicago Convention of 1944, is governed by the state of registration. The Tokyo Convention on Offenses and Certain Other Acts Committed on Board Aircraft of 1963 stipulates that the state of registration has exclusive competence to make and apply law to offenses and acts committed on board. The general practice is to sustain freedom in conferring national status by registration.

The Outer Space Treaty of 1967 refrains from employing the concept of nationality in relation to objects launched into outer space. Under Article VIII of the treaty, the state of registration "shall retain jurisdiction and control over such object, and over any personnel thereof, while in outer space or on a celestial body." The launching state is required to maintain a registration of space objects under the Convention on Registration of Objects Launched into Outer Space of 1974.

The Principle of Impact Territoriality

The principle of impact territoriality, once called the protective principle, authorizes a state to take measures against direct attacks on its security or against activities that have substantial impacts on its important value processes, even though the activities may occur outside its territorial limits. The principle of impact territoriality is sometimes strictly distinguished from the protective principle. The former allows for jurisdiction, for example, when there is an intent to produce effects (or such is foreseeable), and the events to be controlled are not within state territory but their detrimental effects do occur there, whereas the latter seeks to prevent value deprivations within the state before they occur. It is not necessary to draw too fine a line, since the potential events encompassed often constitute a continuum.

In an interdependent world, acts committed partly or wholly outside the territory of a state not infrequently generate effects within the state's territory. Under a strict application of the territorial principle, such acts would not fall within the jurisdiction of the affected state. Thus has developed the doctrine of impact territoriality, whereby a state may exercise jurisdiction over such extraterritorial acts when there is an intent to produce effects (or such is foreseeable) and their adverse effects, actual or potential, are felt within the state's territory. Examples would be extraterritorial acts of drug smugglers, of those involved in stock fraud, and of people fraudulently fabricating, selling, or obtaining visas to enter a state.

This principle has been slowly accepted by U.S. courts, due to the generally accepted requirement that some nexus be demonstrated between the extraterritorial acts and actual, intended, or potential in-state effects. As early as 1804, however, the U.S. Supreme Court recognized the applicability of the principle by a foreign state in *Church v. Hubbart*,[6] which involved a suit by the owner of a ship seized by the Portuguese off the coast of Brazil against its insurers. The court found that the law of nations allowed Portugal to seize the vessel beyond the limits of its territorial domain in order to "secure itself from injury."[7]

The efforts by the United States to prescribe and apply its antitrust law on the basis of impact territoriality has been especially controversial, causing friction with other countries.[8] Such attempts at extraterritorial application by a state of its economic regulatory laws are regarded as especially intrusive and intolerable when the challenged conduct was lawful where it took place.

In an interdependent world, states, by their exercises of competence to make and apply law to particular activities, will have substantial impacts on the internal value processes of other states. The only relevant question is whether a state can reasonably exercise its competence with respect to extraterritorial events and how appropriate accommodation can be reached in the common interest.

The Principle of Passive Personality

The principle of passive personality allows a state to exercise jurisdiction over a party based on the effects of that party's conduct on the state's nationals. Recent attempts on the part of the United States to secure and prosecute perpetrators of acts of international terrorism, from the Lockerbie bombing to the attacks of September 11, 2001, are based in part on this principle, although they rest on universal jurisdiction by treaty. Champions of the U.S. Helms-Burton Act, which fortified the U.S. trade embargo against Cuba, have invoked the principle of passive personality as well, although with less success. This is partly because many of those affected were not U.S. citizens at the time of the nationalizations, and because the targets of the legislation are private firms rather than the Cuban government itself, the source of the injury.[9]

Perhaps the most notable assertion of the passive personality principle was in the dictum in the case of the S.S. Lotus, argued before the Permanent Court of International Justice in 1927.[10] The central issue was whether Turkey had the competence to apply its criminal laws to the conduct of a French officer, whose faulty navigation caused a collision on the high seas between his vessel and a Turkish vessel, resulting in the sinking of the Turkish vessel and the death of a number of Turkish nationals. Although the majority decision was based largely on the principle of impact territoriality and expressly refused to decide the issue whether passive personality was acceptable, several judges expressed willingness to accept Turkish justifications in terms of the principle of passive personality.

Some commentators consider this principle redundant, reasoning that the principle of universality, aided by the doctrines of state responsibility, is sufficient to cover the situations in which it has been applied. For example, in the *Eichmann* case (1961),[11] which involved the chief organizer of Hitler's "final solution," the District Court of Jerusalem upheld Israeli jurisdiction on the universality principle but further justified its jurisdiction on the ground that Jews were the principal victims of the defendant's war crimes.

The Principle of Universality

Under the principle of universality, a state is authorized to punish certain offenses that pose threats to the common interests of humankind wherever the offenses may occur and whoever may be the perpetrators or victims. Community prescriptions identifying customary international crimes are regarded as so vital to the world community that any state which apprehends or secures effective control over an offender is deemed authorized to apply such prescriptions. Any state that possesses an accused violator of specified prescriptions is authorized to try and, if appropriate, to punish an offender without the need to consider links of territoriality with the offense or of nationality with the offender or the victim. The trend in recent practice, for example, is to invoke universality in jurisdictional claims relating to individual terrorist activities.[12]

The number of offenses subject to universal jurisdiction has historically been relatively few, notably war crimes, piracy, breaches of neutrality, attacks on diplomatic personnel, slave trading, and a few others.

As discussed in chapter 9, piracy has long been considered "an offense against the law of nations." In the absence (until recently) of an international criminal court, criminal and civil sanctions for piracy have been left to the state that seized the offender and to private suits with domestic fora. Building on the Convention on the High Seas of 1958, the Law of the Sea Convention of 1982 deals with piracy in Articles 101 through 107. "Piracy," as defined by Article 101, "consists of any of the following acts":

(a) any illegal acts of violence or detention, or any act of depredation, committed for private ends by the crew or the passengers of a private ship or a private aircraft, and directed:
  (i) on the high seas, against another ship or aircraft, or against persons or property on board such ship or aircraft;
  (ii) against a ship, aircraft, persons or property in a place outside the jurisdiction of any State;

(b) any act of voluntary participation in the operation of a ship or of an aircraft with knowledge of facts making it a pirate ship or aircraft;

(c) any act of inciting or of intentionally facilitating an act described in subparagraph (a) or (b).

In recent decades, thanks to a keen sense of human dignity and solidarity under global conditions of intimate interdependence, the list of offenses covered by universal jurisdiction has expanded considerably to include genocide, apartheid, and hijacking of aircraft. According to the Rome Statute of the International Criminal Court, which entered into force in 2002, the International Criminal Court has jurisdiction over (1) the crime of genocide; (2) crimes against humanity; (3) war crimes; and, in the future, (4) the crime of aggression.[13]

The concept of war crimes was expanded and genocide became a subject of universal jurisdiction after World War II. The principles of the Nuremberg Charter and Judgment, punishing crimes against peace, war crimes, and crimes against humanity, received unanimous approval by the U.N. General Assembly in 1946.[14] "Crimes against peace" include the "planning, preparation, initiation or waging of a war of aggression, or a war in violation of international treaties, agreements or assurances."[15] "War crimes" involve "violations of the laws or customs of war."[16] "Crimes against Humanity" include "murder, extermination, enslavement, deportation, and other inhumane acts committed against any civilian population, before or during the war; or persecutions on political, racial or religious grounds."[17]

The Charter of the Nuremberg Tribunal sought to introduce "crimes against peace" and "crimes against humanity" into the same commonly abhorred categorization as war crimes but fell short of total success. Indeed, the failure of the International Military Tribunal at Nuremberg to accept jurisdiction over "crimes against humanity" in times of peace precipitated the formulation and acceptance of the Genocide Conventions, designed to apply international law directly to offending individuals and groups.

To mobilize the conscience of humanity in the wake of the Nazi atrocities and the war crimes trials, the General Assembly in 1948 adopted the Convention on the Prevention and Punishment of the Crime of Genocide, imposing international proscriptions against the intentional destruction, in whole or in part, of racial, ethnic, national, and religious groups. The convention forbids not only acts of "genocide" but also conspiracy, incitement and attempt to commit genocide, and "complicity in genocide." All persons, "whether they are constitutionally responsible rulers, public officials or private individuals," who commit genocide or any of the other prohibited acts are subject to punishment. The contracting states are obligated to "enact, in accordance with their respective Constitutions, the necessary legislation to give effect" to the convention and to provide "effective penalties." Trial is expressly appropriate in "a competent tribunal of the State in the territory of which the act was committed" or "such international penal tribunal as may have jurisdiction with respect to those Contracting Parties which shall have accepted its jurisdiction." The convention has been widely adhered to, although universal jurisdiction to punish genocide has been established as a matter of customary law. International tribunals for the former Yugoslavia and Rwanda, established under the Security Council's Chapter VII authority, are now in full operation to try individuals for war crimes, genocide, and crimes against humanity. The International Criminal Court, which has been in operation since 2002, provides yet another forum for bringing to justice the perpetrators of these crimes.

The Genocide Convention has also served as a model for the prohibition of other activities regarded as serious threats to the common interest. This is exemplified by the International Convention on the Suppression and Punishment of the Crime of Apartheid (Apartheid Convention) adopted by the General Assembly in 1973. Building on the Genocide Convention, the Apartheid Convention makes apartheid a "crime against humanity" subject to universal jurisdiction. Article 5 spells out universal jurisdiction in these words:

Persons charged with the acts [of apartheid] of the present Convention may be tried by a competent tribunal of any State Party to the Convention which may acquire jurisdiction over the person of the accused or by an international penal tribunal having jurisdiction with respect to those States Parties which shall have accepted its jurisdiction.

Terrorism, as an international crime, presumably is subject to universal jurisdiction. On December 9, 1985, the General Assembly unanimously adopted a landmark resolution condemning as criminal "all acts, methods and practices of terrorism wherever and by whomever committed."[18] In addition, the International Law Commission has included terrorist acts in its Draft Code of Crimes against the Peace and Security of Mankind. As discussed in chapter 11, the United Nations adopted its Global Counter-Terrorism Strategy in 2006, which encourages member nations to take steps collectively to combat the threat of terrorism around the globe.

In August 1992, the United States urged the creation of a war-crimes tribunal to try those indicted on the basis of evidence collected by the Balkans War Crimes Commission of war crimes and crimes against humanity in the former Yugoslavia. The alleged crimes against humanity included murders of men, women, and children, mass executions and rapes, torture, and forced expulsion of civilians from their villages, most carried out under the banner of "ethnic cleansing." In 1993, the Security Council adopted a resolution (15–0) establishing an eleven-judge court for the trial of the accused individuals.

It is sometimes debated whether the community prescriptions being applied partake of the "true nature" of national or of international law. If the fundamental policies in the protection of common interest incorporated within the prescriptions are applied, the issue of labeling would appear a matter of Tweedledum and Tweedledee. Indeed, universality has always operated as a domestic competence to impose or allow criminal or civil sanctions with respect to what is proscribed under international law.

The need to apply such inclusive community prescriptions by domestic courts was recognized in the United States in the Judiciary Act of 1789, which granted federal district courts original jurisdiction over cases arising from a tort committed "in violation of the law of nations."[19] The famous decision of *Filartiga v. Pena-Irala*,[20] as rendered in 1980 by the U.S. Court of Appeals for the Second Circuit, inspired keen interest in this area. In *Filartiga*, Judge Irving R. Kaufman applied international human rights law in finding that freedom from torture is protected under customary international law, which forms a part of the law of the land in the United States. The alleged act of torture committed in Paraguay by a local police chief, Pena-Irala, against a Paraguay national thus became an actionable tort before U.S. courts under the Alien Torts Claim Act. The dead victim's family was able to bring suit against Pena-Irala, held in custody pending deportation for illegally overstaying his visa in the United States. In 2004, the U.S. Supreme Court confirmed *Filartiga*'s central holding, that the U.S. federal courts have jurisdiction over claims of violations of international norms, generally accepted by other nations and defined with specificity comparable to recognized paradigms.[21] Similarly, prosecutors in Spain, claiming universal jurisdiction, recently brought actions under Spanish criminal law against former Argentinean military officials. The charges are based on the detention, torture, and disappearance of Spanish nationals and their families during Argentina's "dirty war" in the 1970s. This line of actions was dramatized by Pinochet's case in November 1998, when the Law Lords of the House of Lords, Britain's highest court, ruled that General Augusto Pinochet, the former Chilean dictator, did not have sovereign immunity from arrest under British law and that such crimes as hostage-taking and torture could not be considered part of public functions of a head of state. In sum, cases such as these show the universal principle in action.

Though the *Filartiga* precedent initially received less than uniform support, its continuing impact has been enormous, especially in bridging the traditional gap between international human rights activists and domestic civil liberties practitioners. It has contributed to a growing awareness of the dynamic interplay between transnational and national processes of decision in the defense and fulfillment of human rights and has stimulated continuing efforts in the United States to use domestic courts to defend and enforce international human rights.

Sovereign Immunity

That a nation-state generally cannot be sued without its consent has long been established under both international law and the law of most states. This immunity from suit, commonly known as sovereign immunity, finds its historical roots in the eighteenth century. In a famous decision, *The Schooner Exchange v. M'Fadden* (1812),[22] in which plaintiffs were denied a hearing for the recovery of their ship, seized on the high seas and condemned without due process by France, Chief Justice John Marshall declared (in words that have since lost some validity):

> This full and absolute territorial jurisdiction being alike the attribute of every sovereign, and being incapable of conferring extraterritorial power, would not seem to contemplate foreign sovereigns nor their sovereign rights as its objects. One sovereign being in no respect amenable to another; and being bound by obligations of the highest character not to degrade the dignity of his nation, by placing himself or its sovereign rights within the jurisdiction of another, can be supposed to enter a foreign territory only under an express license, or in the confidence that the immunities belonging to his independent sovereign station, though not expressly stipulated, are reserved by implication, and will be extended to him.
>
> This perfect equality and absolute independence of sovereigns, and this common interest impelling them to mutual intercourse, and an interchange of good offices with each other, have given rise to a class of cases in which every sovereign is understood to waive the exercise of part of that complete exclusive territorial jurisdiction, which has been stated to be the attribute of every nation.[23]

This is often thought to reflect an absolute theory of sovereign immunity, but the U.S. Supreme Court recognized that U.S. territorial jurisdiction was absolved and that foreign immunity was basically a matter of discretion. Ten years later, dictum in *The Santissima Trinidad* recognized an exception to immunity for acts in violation of international law. When nation-states confined themselves essentially to traditional functions of states, the absolute theory was widely accepted.

After World War I, with the establishment of communist and socialist regimes, the pattern of international commerce began to change radically, and nation-states increased their participation in the process. This trend accelerated greatly after World War II. No longer are commercial activities the monopoly of the private sector. More and more states embark on the path of state trading, though they differ in the degree of state participation.

When sovereign immunity was made applicable to disputes arising from business transactions involving states, non-state trading parties suffered. This upset the stability of expectations so essential to an effective global economy and to other transnational interactions. Although sovereign immunity continues to play a useful role in interstate transactions, a shift with respect to commercial transactions—that is, from the so-called absolute theory to the restrictive theory of sovereign immunity—has been visible.

Unlike the absolute theory, which would treat all governmental activities as "governmental," "public," and "sovereign," the restrictive theory extends sovereign immunity only to truly governmental functions. Hence the distinction between public acts (*jure imperii*) and private acts (*jure gestiones*). This is designed to secure the stability of expectations necessary to promote the free flow of goods and services across national boundaries and the wide shaping and sharing of values.

In the United States, the restrictive theory was enunciated in the famous Tate Letter of 1952,[24] which espoused the idea that immunity from suit be granted only to *jure imperii*. In practice, the State Department thereafter assumed an important responsibility in deciding whether a particular dispute fell within the sphere of *jure imperii*. When a foreign state thus became a defendant in U.S. courts, it generally turned to the State Department for an indication of immunity in its plea of defense. The State Department instituted an informal hearing procedure permitting litigants to argue the issue before its legal adviser, who would decide whether the defendant was sovereign and whether immunity should be granted. The department's nonreviewable determination for or against immunity shaped the response of the courts, which generally followed the department's suggestions almost to the point of subserviency. In the absence of application to the State Department, the courts felt free to apply their own standards—usually those embodied in the Tate Letter.

What began as a prudent attempt to minimize potential friction and foster good relations with other states gradually became an onerous burden that ill served the best interests of the United States and those of private parties dealing with foreign governments. Hence, the enactment of the Foreign Sovereign Immunities Act (FSIA) of 1976.[25] The FSIA relieves the State Department of the burden of deciding pleas of sovereign immunity and shifts this responsibility to the judicial branch.

Cases heard under the FSIA include *Samantar v. Yousuf* (2010), in which the U.S. Supreme Court considered whether a foreign official qualified as a "foreign state" within the meaning of the FSIA.[26] In this case, Somalian citizens brought an action against former vice president and minister of defense General Samantar seeking damages for acts of torture and human rights violations committed against them by government agents. General Samantar, who was residing in the United States, claimed that he was immune under the FSIA, because the alleged acts were committed while he held office in Somalia. Here, the Supreme Court held that the text and legislative history of the FSIA defines "foreign state" to include its subdivisions, agencies, and instrumentalities, but not individual officials.

The FSIA enunciates the general principle of sovereign immunity but excludes commercial acts, *jure gestiones*, of a foreign state from the purview of immunity. What is meant by commercial activity is to be determined by reference not to the purpose but to "the nature of the course of conduct or particular transaction or act."[27] This is not an easy task. The U.S. Supreme Court defined "commercial activity" in *Republic of Argentina v. Weltover, Inc.* (1992).[28] Argentina and its central bank, in danger of defaulting on its government bonds, unilaterally issued substitute instruments to bondholders, which essentially delayed its payments. Bondholders brought a breach-of-contract action in the United States under the commercial activities exception of the FSIA. Here, the court looked at the "nature of the course of conduct or particular transaction or act" as directed by the FSIA.[29] However, it noticed that this definition failed to identify which conduct, transaction or act constituted a "commercial activity." Here, the court held that bonds were a common debt-instrument, and therefore, the commercial activities exception was appropriate.

Other exceptions exist to sovereign immunity, and the treatment defers greatly through jurisdictions. In *Sosa v. Alvarez-Machain* (2004), the Supreme Court addressed the non-commercial tort exception enacted under the Federal Tort Claims Act (FTCA).[30] In *Sosa*, U.S. Drug Enforcement Agency (DEA) agents used Mexican nationals to abduct Alvarez-Machain, also a Mexican national, from Mexico to stand trial in the United States for the torture and murder of another agent. After the acquittal, Alvarez-Machain sued the United States under the FTCA, which waives sovereign immunity "for… personal injury… caused by… wrongful act… of any [Government] employee while acting within the scope of his office or employment."[31] While the court acknowledged the tort exception, it ultimately held that the exception enacted under the FTCA did not waive sovereign immunity for actions that occurred on foreign territory.

A new development questions whether there should be a *jus cogens* exception to sovereign immunity. Recently, Italian and Greek courts have rendered judgments against Germany for its atrocities against persons during World War II. In 2008, Germany instituted proceedings against Italy in the International Court of Justice, alleging that Italy failed to respect its sovereign immunity. In 2012, the court ruled that Italy "violated its obligation to respect the immunity which the Federal Republic of Germany enjoys under international law" by allowing civil suits to proceed against the German state and by enforcing awards rendered in Greece.[32]

In other countries, comparable prescription exists. The United Kingdom, for instance, enacted the State Immunity Act of 1978,[33] incorporating essentially the provisions contained in the European Convention on State Immunity of 1972. The general support for restrictive sovereign immunity reflects a common interest of nation-states in bestowing reciprocal immunity from suit so as to facilitate harmonious interstate relations.

The problem of diplomatic immunity raises different policy considerations from those of sovereign immunity and will be dealt with in the next chapter.

The Act of State Doctrine

The act of state doctrine is closely linked to and supplements that of sovereign immunity. When a controversy involves private parties and the foreign state is not a direct defendant, the act of state doctrine is frequently invoked.

The act of state doctrine requires that the courts of one state honor, rather than sit in judgment on, the lawfulness of the public acts of another state taken and completed within their jurisdiction and in accord with relevant substantive international law. These state acts include acts of different branches of government—legislative, executive, and judicial.

Like the policy of reciprocal honoring of sovereign immunity, the act of state doctrine is designed both to secure friendly relations among nation-states through minimizing interference in legitimate acts of others and to achieve the stability of expectations essential to the optimum production and distribution of goods, services, and other values in the world economy and other transnational interactions.

In the United States, the controversy concerning the act of state generated by *Banco Nacional de Cuba v. Sabbatino* (1964)[34] has continued to reverberate. In this case, involving a confiscation of sugar by the Cuban government, the U.S. Supreme Court held that "the Judicial Branch will not examine the validity of a taking of property within its own territory by a foreign sovereign government [subject to certain possible limitations]."[35] This decision was built on a famous passage contained in *Underhill v. Hernandez* (1897): "Every sovereign State is bound to respect the independence of every other sovereign State, and the courts of one country will not sit in judgment on the acts of the government of another done within its own territory. Redress of grievances by reason of such acts must be obtained through the means open to be availed of by sovereign powers as between themselves."[36]

In the view of the court in *Sabbatino*, the act of state doctrine is mandated neither by international law nor by the U.S. Constitution but does have "constitutional underpinnings,"[37] meaning presumably separation of powers considerations.

Though the lawfulness of the Cuban expropriation measure was under severe attack, the court was not swayed. Deeming the content of customary international law governing expropriation uncertain and unclear, Justice John M. Harlan, speaking for the majority, defended the applicability of the act of state doctrine. In his words:

> [R]ather than laying down or reaffirming an inflexible and all-encompassing rule in this case, we decide only that the Judicial Branch will not examine the validity of a taking of property within its own territory by a foreign sovereign government, extant and recognized by this country at the time of suit, in the absence of a treaty or other unambiguous agreement regarding controlling legal principles, even if the complaint alleges that the taking violates customary international law.[38]

The property involved in this case was taken by the government of a recognized state within its own territory, and the legal challenge to the act of taking was grounded in claims concerning customary international law rather than a specific international agreement, but the Court was unpersuaded that the content of custom was clear.

The critical response to the *Sabbatino* decision was immediate and overwhelming, leading Congress to pass the Second Hickenlooper Amendment to the Foreign Assistance Act of 1963.[39] The amendment declared that no court shall decline to adjudicate a case on the merits dealing with any claim of title traced through a foreign expropriation measure that violated international law. The amendment was expressly made inapplicable in cases where the expropriation is lawful under international law or where the president determines that the act of state doctrine should be applied. The presumption relied on by the *Sabbatino* Court, that foreign acts of state should not be questioned by the courts absent an indication from the executive branch, was thus reversed.

In subsequent decisions, the Supreme Court has sought to contain the harm caused by the *Sabbatino* decision but has not seen fit to overrule it. In *First National City Bank v. Banco Nacional de Cuba* (1972),[40] for example, the National Bank of Cuba brought suit to recover deposits and excess of collateral held by Citibank of New York. Having sold the property of the Cuban bank to pay off a loan, with the proceeds of the sale exceeding the outstanding balance on the loan, Citibank sought to set off this balance against its claims stemming from nationalization of Citibank's branches in Cuba. The issue was whether the act of state doctrine prevented Citibank from litigating its counterclaim on the merits. The Supreme Court said no. A majority of the Court held that the act of state doctrine was no bar to a counterclaim.

The Court did not give an opinion. Three justices (William Rehnquist, Warren Burger, and Byron White) reached the result by recognizing what is known as the Bernstein exception to the act of state doctrine. They recognized the position taken by the State Department that "the act of state doctrine should not be applied to bar consideration of a defendant's counterclaim or setoff against the Government of Cuba in this or like cases." Justice William Douglas invoked the *Republic of China*[41] case, rather than the doctrine of act of state, to support the setoff. Justice Lewis Powell, who had joined the court after *Sabbatino*, concurred in the judgment because he doubted the soundness of the *Sabbatino* decision. The four dissenting justices (William Brennan, Potter Stewart, Thurgood Marshall, and Harry Blackmun) rejected the Bernstein exception, mandating the Court to follow direction by the executive branch, and considered *Sabbatino* applicable.

In *Alfred Dunhill of London, Inc. v. Republic of Cuba* (1976),[42] U.S. importers of Cuban cigars made payment to interveners appointed by the Cuban government following the nationalization by the Cuban government of the assets of cigar manufacturers. Payment was made not only for postnationalization shipments but, mistakenly, also for prenationalization shipments. When the importers demanded the return of the monies mistakenly paid, the Cuban interveners refused and invoked the defense of an act of state in the ensuing litigation. The Supreme Court rejected the act of state claim on the ground that the interveners possessed no sovereign authority. Four justices took the position that repudiation by a foreign government of a commercial debt does not constitute an act of state. This has become known as the "commercial exception" to the act of state doctrine, despite that only four justices joined this part of the opinion and that four other justices wrote against carving out a commercial exception. Such ambiguity has led to different interpretations in the lower courts. A fifth justice maintained that a mere statement by counsel in court was not an act of state.

In another case, *W.S. Kirkpatrick & Co., Inc. v. Environmental Tectonics Corp., Int'l* (1990), Kirkpatrick obtained a construction and equipment contract with Nigeria through offering bribes to Nigerian officials.[43] Environmental, an unsuccessful bidder, learned of the transaction and informed Nigerian and U.S. authorities, which brought charges under the Foreign Corrupt Practices Act. All parties pleaded guilty. Environmental then brought a civil suit and the defendants invoked the defense of an act of state. More specifically, they claimed that the underlying policies, including the avoidance of embarrassment, are implicated in this case. The Supreme Court recognized that the act of state doctrine is a valid defense for acts of foreign sovereigns taken within their own jurisdictions, but rejected the defendants' claim, stating that the underlying policies are not a doctrine unto themselves. Here, the Court held that the act of state doctrine did not apply because the action in question was not of a foreign sovereign.

In its work on revising the restatement on foreign relations law of the United States, the American Law Institute has tendered this formulation: "In the absence of a treaty or other unambiguous agreement regarding controlling legal principles, courts in the United States will generally refrain from examining the validity of a taking by a foreign state of property within its own territory, or from sitting in judgment on other acts of a governmental character done by a foreign state within its own territory and applicable there."[44] Some feared this formulation to be a resurrection of *Sabbatino*, but the Helms-Burton Act specifically prohibited any U.S. court's use of the act of state doctrine to decline making a determination on the merits in any action brought under the law against a foreign company who "traffics" in confiscated Cuban property.

Some view the *Sabbatino* doctrine as requiring the honoring of acts of state even when such acts are contrary to international law, but others disagree. In *Sosa v. Alvarez*, Justice Souter noted that, while *Sabbatino* "did not directly apply international law," it also did not "question the application of [international] law in appropriate cases, and it further endorsed the reasoning" that the federal courts' continued application of international law should not be precluded. The genuine doctrine is built on a strong policy in common interest. The genuine doctrine of act of state, very different from *Sabbatino*, has a clear place in international law. This doctrine is a functional equivalent of the U.S. Constitution's Full Faith and Credit Clause in the world arena.[45] In a global arena in which people, goods, and services move across state lines constantly and rapidly, it would be inimical to both minimum order and optimum order if prior prescriptions and applications of one state were subject to perpetual challenge by others. All participants have a common interest in ensuring that the necessary stability of expectations be maintained by affording reciprocal deference to official acts of other states, provided those acts conform with international law. The emphasis is on lawful acts. Unlawful acts—acts that fail to conform to international law—are beyond the authority of the state and do not, and should not enjoy such respect, for a nation-state cannot be expected to be an accessory to an act of lawlessness. In their dual role, both as claimants and decision makers, state officials are expected to defend, not subvert, international law. And national courts should be encouraged to play a more active part in applying and developing international law under a decentralized international legal system where transnational judicial tribunals, lacking compulsory jurisdiction, have played only a modest role.

In short, the genuine act of state must be distinguished from a spurious one. The act of state doctrine, as a protector of genuine acts of state, has an important part to play in international law, but it must not be subverted into a device to compel domestic (national) courts to enforce lawless acts of foreign states.

Toward a Test of Reasonableness

In an interdependent and decentralized world where everything affects everything else and the assertions of sovereign equality remain strong, states are apt to stretch their jurisdictional arms as far as they can. The broad grants of competence to prescribe and apply law in terms of the five principles often lead to overlapping and conflicting claims, subjecting the same events to many competences. Hence the existence of frequent clashes arising from assertions of competing, concurrent jurisdiction—on the same or different bases—over the same events. Finding ways to resolve such controversies so as to serve the common interest is crucial in a decentralized, horizontal legal order.

Although no hierarchy has been set among the four distinctive principles of jurisdiction other than universality, the principle of territoriality has been widely applied simply because the state system is the cornerstone of our contemporary international legal order. Similarly, the principle of nationality has gained wide acceptance. When it comes to the principle of impact territoriality or the principle of passive personality, the matter grows more tangled. The discussion of extraterritorial application of a state's law is interlocked with these principles. For instance, when the United States seeks to extend its competence to reach events abroad having adverse antitrust impact, other states may simply invoke the principle of territoriality or that of nationality in response. What then? The United States should not press its competence to make and apply law to events occurring within the borders of some other states without considering possible effects on others. For some, the crucial test is whether a particular exercise of competence, as ascertained by reference to the degree of value impact on the claimant state and other communities, and other relevant factors involved in a particular context, is reasonable. Others note that these tests are insufficiently concerned with individual and community interests in effective remedies for value deprivation. The overall test of reasonableness seems to have gained growing support both in theory and in practice.

At the secondary level, although the act of state and sovereign immunity should be kept distinct both in theory and in practice, there is a tendency to blur the distinction. Each in its own way may achieve the outcome of deference to legitimate acts of foreign states that are not violative of international law: sovereign immunity, by refusing to entertain a lawsuit against a foreign state, and act of state, by honoring substantively the public acts completed within its territory by a foreign state. But the policy for the restrictive theory of sovereign immunity may be subverted by virtue of applying a so-called absolute act of state doctrine that fails to distinguish properly "genuine" from "spurious" acts of state.

The operation of these doctrines of secondary competence may result in immunizing state officials from responsibility for deprivational acts and thus compound and exacerbate the original wrong. These principles, designed primarily to protect the interests of state elites in controlling people and resources as bases of power, must be tempered by considerations of the rights of private parties and overall interests of the community reflected in international legal standards.

Notes

1. *See, e.g.*, PHILIP JESSUP, TRANSNATIONAL LAW (1956).

2. RESTATEMENT (THIRD) OF THE FOREIGN RELATIONS LAW OF THE UNITED STATES § 401 (1987).

3. Steele v. Bulova Watch Co., Inc., 344 U.S. 280 (1952).

4. Cook v. Tait, 265 U.S. 47 (1924).

5. United States v. Calley, 46 C.M.R. 1131 (A.C.M.R. 1973), *aff'd*, 22 C.M.A. 534 (C.M.A. 1973), *petition for writ of habeas corpus granted*, Calley v. Calloway, 382 F. Supp. 650 (M.D. Ga. 1974), *rev'd*, 519 F.2d 184 (5th Cir. 1975), *cert. denied*, 425 U.S. 911 (1976).

6. Church v. Hubbart, 6 U.S. (2 Cranch) 187 (1804).

7. *Id.* at 234.

8. *See, e.g.*, United States v. Nippon Paper Industries Co., 109 F.3d 1 (1st Cir. 1997).

9. *See* Andrew F. Lowenfeld, *Agora: The Cuban Liberty and Democratic Solidarity (LIBERTAD) Act*, 90 AM. J. INT'L L. 419 (1996).

10. S.S. Lotus (Fr. v. Turk.), 1927 P.C.I.J. (ser. A) No. 10 (Sept. 7).

11. DC (Jer) 40/61 Attorney Gen. Gov't of Isr. v. Eichmann, IsrDC 45(3) (1961) (Isr.); *reprinted in* 56 AM. J. INT'L L. 805 (1962).

12. *See, e.g.*, United States v. Yunis, 924 F.2d 1086 (D.C. Cir. 1991).

13. Rome Statute of the International Criminal Court art. 5–8, July 17, 1998, 2187 U.N.T.S. 90.

14. G.A. Res. 95 (I), at 188, U.N. Doc. A/236 (Dec. 11, 1946).

15. International Military Tribunal (Nuremberg), Judgment and Sentences, Oct. 1, 1946, *reprinted in* 41 A.J.I.L. 172, 174 (1947).

16. *Id.*

17. *Id.* at 175.

18. G.A. Res. 40/61, at 302, U.N. Doc. A/40/53 (Dec. 9, 1985).

19. 28 U.S.C. §1350 (1948).

20. Filartiga v. Pena-Irala, 630 F.2d 876 (2d Cir. 1980).

21. *See* Sosa v. Alvarez-Machain, 542 U.S. 692 (2004).

22. The Schooner Exchange v. M'Fadden, 11 U.S. (7 Cranch) 116 (1812).

23. *Id.* at 137.

24. Letter from Acting Legal Adviser Jack B. Tate to Acting Attorney General Philip B. Perlman (May 19, 1952), *reprinted in* 26 DEP'T STATE BULL. 984 (1952).

25. Foreign Sovereign Immunities Act, 28 U.S.C. §§1330, 1602–11 (1976).

26. Samantar v. Yousuf, 130 S. Ct. 2278 (2010); *see also* 28 U.S.C. §1603(a) (defining foreign state within FSIA).

27. 28 U.S.C. §1603(d).

28. Rep. of Argentina v. Weltover, Inc., 504 U.S. 607 (1992).

29. *Id.* at 612; 28 U.S.C. §1603(d).

30. Sosa v. Alvarez-Machain, 542 U.S. 692 (2004).

31. *Id.* at 698; 28 U.S.C. §1346(b)(1).

32. Jurisdictional Immunities of the State (Germany v. Italy: Greece intervening) Judgment, I.C.J. Reports 2012, p. 99.

33. State Immunity Act, 1978, c. 33, *reprinted in* 17 I.L.M. 1123 (1978).

34. Banco Nacional de Cuba v. Sabbatino, 376 U.S. 398 (1964).

35. *Id.* at 428.

36. Underhill v. Hernandez, 168 U.S. 250, 252 (1897).

37. Banco Nacional de Cuba, 376 U.S. at 423.

38. *Id.* at 428.

39. 22 U.S.C. §2370(e)(2).

40. First Nat'l City Bank v. Banco Nacional de Cuba, 406 U.S. 759 (1972).

41. Nat'l City Bank of N.Y. v. Rep. of China, 348 U.S. 356 (1955).

42. Alfred Dunhill of London, Inc. v. Rep. of Cuba, 425 U.S. 682 (1976).

43. W.S. Kirkpatrick & Co., Inc. v. Environmental Tectonics Corp., Int'l, 493 U.S. 400 (1990).

44. RESTATEMENT (THIRD) OF THE FOREIGN RELATIONS LAW OF THE UNITED STATES §443 (1987).

45. U.S. CONST. art. IV, §1.

VI Strategies

THE STRATEGIES EMPLOYED in global constitutive process can be conveniently examined by reference to the basic instruments of policy: diplomatic, ideological, economic, and military. These instruments, or strategies, involve the management of two critical components: communications (symbols) and resources. The diplomatic instrument refers to communications from elite to elite, and the ideological instrument involves communications directed to general audiences. The economic instrument relates to the management of goods and services, whereas the military instrument involves resources specialized to violence. All may be employed singly or in varying combinations.

15 The Diplomatic Instrument

THE DIPLOMATIC INSTRUMENT is concerned with certain communications between elites of nation-states. The most common policy instrument, it is the one by which other measures are often transmitted. Elite-centered and from foreign office to foreign office, diplomatic communication can be carried out either by signs (verbal and written) or by deeds, openly or secretly.

The diplomatic instrument is ordinarily employed for constructive purposes in the framework of order. In the course of diplomatic communication, a nation-state transmits its position on a controversy to another nation-state and receives the other's response. Its directness of communication, its relatively noncoercive nature, and its subtlety and flexibility have enabled it to resolve differences between nation-states through the continuous process of adjustment and accommodation. Although nation-states may intensify their differences through various measures, they can also settle differences by extensive use of the diplomatic instrument, provided all participants are willing to negotiate. As modern means of transportation and communication have greatly diminished the importance of distance and boundaries, communications from official elites to elites will continue to loom large in interstate relations.

The diplomatic instrument is indispensable to effectuating international agreements between nation-states and peaceful accommodation of conflicts. The making of international agreements is so paramount that the next chapter is devoted to this subject.

Establishment of diplomatic relations between the recognizing state and the recognized state generally follows "recognition" (see chapter 2); but it is not necessarily so. Recognition and the establishment of diplomatic relations, though linked, are distinct steps. Even before recognition, nation-states may need to communicate with one another, to negotiate outstanding issues, and thus find ways to communicate with one another without being deterred by lack of a formal ritual of recognition or of formal diplomatic relations. In the 1950s and 1960s, for example, the United States withheld recognition from the People's Republic of China, but both countries did send their diplomatic representatives to engage in bilateral negotiations on a range of issues.

Diplomatic and Consular Privileges and Immunities

Once diplomatic relations are established, with official elite-to-elite communications, especially exchange of diplomatic missions, it is in the common interest that such relations be kept harmonious and effective. Essential to maintaining such effective and harmonious diplomatic relations is the reciprocal bestowal of diplomatic and consular privileges and immunities.

Although the granting of diplomatic privileges and immunities was theorized in terms of extraterritoriality (viewing the premises of a diplomatic mission as an extension of the territory of the sending state) or governmental representation in the past, the dominant view today is that of functional necessity. For diplomats to perform effectively in the host country, it is vital that they enjoy protection from interference so that they may operate within an environment of security and confidentiality.

In an interactive world of reciprocity, almost every state plays the dual role—both as a sending state and as a receiving state of diplomatic missions. Just as a state wishes to have its own diplomats, embassies, and diplomatic communications protected, so it must reciprocate, in hosting the diplomatic missions of other countries, by providing such protection. The interests of the sending state and those of the receiving state require proper accommodation.

The shared perception of such common interest has long been manifested. In fact, international law for the protection of diplomats and legations is one of the oldest areas of customary law, perhaps as old as diplomacy itself, having its roots in the relations of the city-states of ancient Greece. As Hugo Grotius stated in 1625, "Now there are two rights of ambassadors which we see are everywhere referred to the law of nations: The first is that they be admitted; the second, that they be free from violence."[1]

In our time, the centuries-old customary law in this area has found concrete codification in the Vienna Convention on Diplomatic Relations of 1961 and the Vienna Convention on Consular Relations of 1963. (In the United States, the Diplomatic Relations Act was enacted in 1978 to give effect to these conventions.)[2]

The Vienna Convention on Diplomatic Relations protects the performance of the diplomatic function by forbidding local interference and by requiring positive protection by the receiving state. Special protection, phrased in terms of "inviolability," is extended to personnel, premises, and communications. Diplomatic immunities and privileges are accorded the diplomatic staff (people having diplomatic rank), the administrative and technical staff (such as administrative officers, secretary-typists, mail and file clerks), the service staff (for example, chauffeurs, butlers, gardeners, cooks, and maids), and the members of a diplomatic agent's family (including private servants). Diplomatic immunities include immunity from ordinary criminal, civil, and administrative jurisdiction of the receiving state. Diplomatic missions enjoy exemption from local taxes and customs duties. Diplomatic agents and their families are exempt from social security provisions, all taxes, personal services, military obligations, customs duties, and baggage inspection. Individual immunities and privileges run from the moment of entry into the receiving state, are good while in transit through third states, and cease on departure from the receiving state or on lapse of a reasonable period for departure.

The convention protects the premises of a diplomatic mission from external interference. Article 22 states:

1. The premises of the mission shall be inviolable. The agents of the receiving State may not enter them, except with the consent of the head of the mission.
2. The receiving State is under a special duty to take all appropriate steps to protect the premises of the mission against any intrusion or damage and to prevent any disturbance of the peace of the mission or impairment of its dignity.
3. The premises of the mission, their furnishings and other property thereon and the means of transport of the mission shall be immune from search, requisition, attachment or execution.

This inviolability extends to the private residence of a diplomatic agent, including his or her papers, correspondence, and property.

The inviolability of communications covers official correspondence, diplomatic papers and archives, diplomatic bags, and diplomatic couriers and messages in code or cipher.

The institution of the consul is traceable to medieval Italy. Though the consular function was historically concerned with commercial and trade matters, the line between commercial and diplomatic activity is becoming ever more difficult to draw. Just as diplomatic negotiation and trade promotion go hand in hand, diplomatic and consular services tend to merge in practice. The major consular functions, as noted in the Vienna Convention on Consular Relations of 1963, are promotion of commerce, supervision of shipping, protection of nationals, and representational functions. Like diplomatic functions, consular functions require immunity from local jurisdiction. Thus the Vienna Convention on Consular Relations incorporates most of the protections and assistance embodied in the Convention on Diplomatic Relations. There is a basic difference. In theory, consuls are not diplomatic agents. Hence they enjoy immunity from local jurisdiction only in respect of acts performed in the exercise of consular functions, and not in respect of private acts, unless otherwise provided by bilateral agreement.

The degree of compliance is high in this area because the perception of common interest is widely shared, as policed by reciprocity and retaliation. Gross violations do occur, however. Vivid in memory is, of course, the Iranian hostage case.

On November 4, 1979, several hundred militant Iranian students stormed the U.S. embassy in Tehran, seizing as hostages ninety diplomatic personnel present on the premises, including sixty-six Americans. The Iranian students demanded that the United States extradite the former Shah of Iran, Muhammad Reza Pahlavi, who, having been overthrown in a revolution late in 1978, was then in the United States for medical treatment. Though the Iranian government had not expressly called for the embassy takeover, it soon became apparent that it backed the militants.

On November 9, the United States asked the U.N. Security Council to take measures to effectuate the release of the hostages, and on the same day both the president of the Security Council and the president of the General Assembly made declarations appealing to Ayatollah Ruhollah Khomeini, the head of Iran's government, to release them. In defiance, Khomeini publicly threatened on November 18 to try some of the embassy personnel as spies.

In response, President Jimmy Carter froze all Iranian assets in U.S. banks, cut off oil imports from Iran, severed diplomatic relations with Iran, and called for the collective deportation of Iranian students illegally in the United States.

Meanwhile, the United States continued its efforts to appeal to the world community to take steps against Iran. On November 29, 1979, the United States filed an application and a request for interim measures of protection in proceeding against Iran. The United States requested the International Court of Justice both to adjudge and declare that Iran had violated its legal obligations under both customary and treaty law by failing to ensure the inviolability of diplomatic and consular officials and premises, and to order Iran to ensure the release and safe departure of the hostages, to pay reparations to the United States, and to prosecute those responsible for the illegal seizure of the embassy and the hostages.

Although Iran neither argued before the court nor submitted formal written arguments (except two letters), the court proceeded to render, on December 15, 1979, a unanimous interim order granting provisional measures in favor of the United States,[3] and on May 24, 1980, its final judgment against Iran.[4] The court based its jurisdiction on the fact that both the United States and Iran were parties to the Vienna Convention on Diplomatic Relations (1961) and the Vienna Convention on Consular Relations (1963) and to the optional protocols thereto affording the court compulsory jurisdiction in "disputes arising out of the interpretation or application of each convention."

In issuing interim measures of protection, the court emphasized:

[T]here is no more fundamental prerequisite for the conduct of relations between States than the inviolability of diplomatic envoys and embassies, so that throughout history nations of all creeds and cultures have observed reciprocal obligations for that purpose; and... the obligations thus assumed, notably those for assuring the personal safety of diplomats and their freedom from prosecution, are essential, unqualified, and inherent in their representative character and their diplomatic function....

[T]he institution of diplomacy, with its concomitant privileges and immunities, has withstood the test of centuries and proved to be an instrument essential for effective cooperation in the international community, and for enabling States, irrespective of their differing constitutional and social systems, to achieve mutual understanding and to resolve their differences by peaceful means.[5]

In its final judgment, the court, after dismissing "the alleged criminal activities of the United States in Iran," concluded that "Iran, by committing successive and continuing breaches of the obligations laid upon it by the Vienna Conventions of 1961 and 1963 on Diplomatic and Consular Relations, the Treaty of Amity, Economic Relations, and Consular Rights of 1955, and the applicable rules of general international law, has incurred responsibility towards the United States. As to the consequences of this finding, it clearly entails an obligation on the part of the Iranian State to make reparation."[6] By unanimous vote, the court ordered the immediate release of the diplomatic and consular staff and other nationals of the United States and the restoration of the embassy to U.S. control (including the premises, property, archives, and documents) and enjoined Iran from subjecting the hostages to Iranian judicial proceedings in any form.

Another example involved the case of former Chilean dictator General Augusto Pinochet Ugarte, who was arrested in London on October 16, 1998. A Spanish judge presented Britain with an extradition warrant to bring Pinochet to trial in Spain for human rights abuses. Although the High Court did accept that he had a prima facie case to answer, it also accepted the main defense presented by Pinochet's lawyers that since he was Chile's head of state at the time of the crimes, international law granted him sovereign immunity from prosecution. Furthermore, since the Chilean government protested the arrest, refusing to exercise its power to waive Pinochet's immunity, the High Court ruled that it had no legal right to begin extradition proceedings against him. The crimes allegedly committed by General Pinochet, however, are crimes that cannot be considered as normal acts of a head of state. Thus, in November 1998, the House of Lords overturned the High Court, and on October 8, 1999, a British magistrate cleared the way for General Pinochet's extradition to Spain. However, in a turn of events, British Home Secretary Jack Straw blocked the extradition in 2000, citing Pinochet's declining health. Pinochet returned to Chile, where he died in 2006, without ever having faced charges. Despite this outcome, the fact that Pinochet's extradition was approved was a landmark moment in the development of international law's ability to hold state officials accountable for their wrong actions. The case is also an example of the overlap of the concepts of sovereign immunity and diplomatic privileges and immunities. Perhaps unsurprisingly,

Pinochet appealed to both concepts in his efforts to resist extradition and responsibility for his actions as a head of state.

In less dramatic fashion, the world community is increasingly witnessing abuses of such immunities and privileges. In 1984 a British policewoman was murdered by shots fired from the Libyan embassy during a protest demonstration outside the embassy (the Libyan People's Bureau, as Libya called it) in London. The embassy was not stormed, and after diplomatic relations were broken by the United Kingdom, the gunman, a Libyan national, was given safe passage out of the country, on account of diplomatic immunity, and his diplomatic bags (which certainly contained the weapons) were not seized. In 1983 two women were raped in New York City allegedly by the son of a Ghanaian attaché. The man was arrested, then released and sent back to Ghana. In 1982, a bouncer was shot at a bar in Washington, D.C. Charged with shooting was the eighteen-year-old son of a Brazilian diplomat. But the youth was allowed to leave the United States without detention or prosecution—again, on account of diplomatic immunity. In addition, certain diplomatic missions are known to have used diplomatic bags to import firearms calculated to intimidate and harass the dissident elements of their expatriate community in the host country.

The problem of abuse has become more serious today partly because of a vast increase of diplomatic missions and personnel, thanks to a rapid growth of new states with less diplomatic experience. Such abuses have generated outcry by local residents and prompted calls for change, as witnessed by a past uproar over diplomatic parking "privileges" in New York City.

The outcry of local residents, demanding an end to such abuses, is understandable. But the problem it reflects cannot be fixed quickly. Remedies to deal with violations in this area depend in large measure on sanctions of reciprocity and retaliation. The right of agreation and the power to demand recall, though not fully effective, are important safeguards against abuse in a decentralized system.

Diplomatic Asylum

The degree of immunity, inviolability, and protection accorded the diplomatic premises of accredited states makes those premises a potential refuge for local fugitives wanted by their governments. Should diplomatic premises be used as an instrument to defend human rights at the risk of endangering the normal diplomatic function? In other words, how does international law deal with claims for diplomatic asylum?

Unlike territorial asylum, which, as discussed in chapter 11, occurs within the granting state's territory, diplomatic asylum is granted by the granting state in its embassies or legations. Diplomatic asylum is thus extraterritorial in nature and meets more objection.

International law does not recognize a state's competence to grant diplomatic asylum. In the *Asylum* case (1950) brought before the International Court of Justice by Colombia against Peru, Colombia, having granted asylum to a Peruvian national (Haya de la Torre) at its embassy in Lima, requested that the Peruvian government guarantee his safe passage from Peru.[7] Peru refused to offer such a guarantee and challenged the legal effect of the Colombian grant of asylum. The court rejected Colombia's claim that a custom existed for granting diplomatic asylum. Given "so much uncertainty and contradiction" and "so much fluctuation and discrepancy" in state practice and views, the court was unable to find "any constant and uniform usage, accepted as law" regarding diplomatic asylum.[8] Thus the court held that there is no general right to grant diplomatic asylum and that it can be granted, on a temporary basis, only in cases where the individual seeking asylum is in imminent danger or where a treaty or local custom recognizes it.

The Vienna Convention on Diplomatic Relations deliberately does not include any provision on diplomatic asylum. Presumably, the reference to "special agreements" in its Article 41 would allow recognition of such right by virtue of a specific agreement.

The practice of diplomatic asylum is fragmented and uneven. It is a challenging task to determine how to secure the common interest by using diplomatic premises to shelter fugitives from political persecution and augment human rights protection in ways that would not unduly interfere with the diplomatic function of interelite communication.

Another aspect of diplomacy is its constructive function to protect nationals vis-à-vis external entities. This refers to the customary remedy of diplomatic protection, discussed in chapter 12. In recent times, as the transnational impact of human rights deprivations has been more realistically perceived, states have been somewhat willing to use the diplomatic instrument to protect not only their own nationals but also nonnationals. The diplomatic instrument readily lends itself to inquiries about alleged violations, to expressions of general and particular concern, to suggestions about the termination of certain practices, to recommendations of measures of amelioration, and to subtle messages of possible consequences of continuing practices of deprivation. This is the essence of what is called "quiet diplomacy," which should not be allowed to degenerate into a diplomacy of timidity and inaction. For instance, in securing "people power" in the Philippines in February 1986 and in achieving "the political miracle" in South Korea in the summer of 1987, the U.S. diplomatic role was by no means trivial.

Coercive Use of the Diplomatic Instrument

Although the diplomatic instrument is normally used for constructive purposes, it may occasionally be used for coercive purposes, especially measures designed to block a target state's access to the transnational arenas of formal authority. Charges of unlawfulness tend to arise in connection with what is regarded as premature recognition or deliberate nonrecognition, as mentioned in chapter 2.

An additional charge often relates to severance of diplomatic relations. This type of coercion includes withdrawing or requiring the target state to withdraw heads of diplomatic missions, trade agencies, and consular officials. The severance of diplomatic relations may be partial or complete. It may be carried out gradually by first withdrawing heads of diplomatic missions only. It may be taken as an expression of disapproval of a target state's conduct or as a deliberate means of coercion. At times it serves as a preliminary warning to a target state of more drastic coercion. Often it is used as a form of sanction against a prior, unlawful act.

Diplomatic Sanctions

In an interactive world of decentralization, because the attitudes and concomitant behavior of other participants bear critically on the establishment or stabilization of any situation, the organized community of nations has increasingly resorted to a collective policy of nonrecognition as a sanctioning measure against situations considered to violate fundamental international policy. This policy had its origin in the Stimson Doctrine, which called for nonrecognition of any situation, treaty, or agreement brought about unlawfully, in response to the Japanese invasion and occupation of Manchuria in 1931. The League of Nations soon reinforced this policy, in dealing with any situation, treaty, or agreement brought about by means contrary to its covenant or to the Pact of Paris of 1928 (the Kellogg-Briand Pact, which denounced war as an instrument of national policy).

Within the framework of the United Nations, the policy of nonrecognition played a prominent role in dealing with the Southern Rhodesian and Namibian situations. When the Ian Smith regime declared unilateral independence of Southern Rhodesia in November 1965, the Security Council characterized the Smith regime as illegal and called on all member states not to recognize it.

In the case of Namibia, the United Nations called on member states to adopt a policy of nonrecognition toward the continued illegal occupation of the territory by apartheid South Africa after the U.N. decision to terminate the mandate in 1966. In its famous Namibia opinion of 1971, the International Court of Justice expressed an array of views by individual judges on the question of how third states should behave regarding South Africa's continued illegal presence in Namibia.[9]

Namibia, known as South West Africa until renamed in 1968 by the General Assembly, is the only one of seven African territories once under the mandate system of the League of Nations that was not placed under the trusteeship system of the United Nations after World War II. Over the years South Africa, purporting to act as mandatory, intensified its control over the territory in defiance of the resolutions of U.N. bodies and decisions of the International Court of Justice.

In 1950, in Advisory Opinion on International Status of South-West Africa, the International Court of Justice declared that South Africa, lacking unilateral "competence to modify the international status of the territory," remained subject to, despite the demise of the league, the terms and obligations prescribed in the covenant and the mandate, and that the supervisory function of the league was to be assumed by the United Nations.[10] This opinion laid the legal framework for subsequent U.N. action regarding Namibia.

After the 1950 opinion, South Africa continued its course of defiance, refusing to submit its administration of the territory to U.N. supervision. Hence, in 1966, the General Assembly adopted Resolution 2145, terminating the mandate of South Africa over South West Africa (Namibia) and assuming direct responsibility for the territory until its independence.[11] The Security Council reiterated this resolution in 1969 and 1970, declaring that "the continued presence of the South African authorities in Namibia is illegal and that consequently all acts taken by the Government of South Africa on behalf of or concerning Namibia after the termination of the Mandate are illegal and invalid."[12]

Confronted with the continued defiance of the South African government, the Security Council turned to the International Court of Justice for an advisory opinion on the following question: "What are the legal consequences for States of the continued presence of South Africa in Namibia, notwithstanding Security Council resolution 276 (1970)?"[13] The court held that "the continued presence of South Africa in Namibia being illegal, South Africa is under obligation to withdraw its administration from Namibia immediately and thus put an end to its occupation of the Territory"[14] and that "States Members of the United Nations are under obligation to recognize the illegality of South Africa's presence in Namibia and the invalidity of its acts on behalf of or concerning Namibia, and to refrain from any acts and in particular any dealings with the Government of South Africa implying recognition of the legality of, or lending support or assistance to such presence and administration."[15]

In accord with the duty of nonrecognition imposed by Security Council Resolution 276 (1970), U.N. member states were obliged, among other things, "to abstain from sending diplomatic or special missions to South Africa including in their jurisdiction the Territory of Namibia, to abstain from sending consular agents to Namibia, and to withdraw any such agents already there."[16] The court emphasized that "no State which enters into relations with South Africa concerning Namibia may expect United Nations or its members to recognize the validity of such relationship, or of the consequences thereof."[17] The court also added that "it is incumbent upon States which are not Members of the United Nation to give assistance,... in the action which has been taken by the United Nations with regard to Namibia."[18]

The U.N. Charter and numerous General Assembly resolutions, several International Court of Justice opinions, and a host of international human rights treaties provided the basis for a new international legal norm of racial equality. This new legal norm in turn inspired the response of the international community, in support of Namibia and in the form of diplomatic sanctions. The force of diplomatic sanctions played a great role in dismantling apartheid in South Africa and allowing Namibia to proclaim its independence. The success of both Namibia and South Africa in finding self-determination and independence illustrates the potential impact of diplomatic sanctions in a world where the force of international law is respected by all parties.

Consular Protection of Nationals Abroad and the Intersection of Domestic and International Law

Another aspect of diplomacy is its function to protect nationals vis-à-vis external entities. This refers to the customary remedy of diplomatic protection, discussed in chapter 12. Traditionally, when an alien abroad was the subject of internationally wrongful conduct by the host state, the only available recourse was the remedy of diplomatic protection, which was available only to the state of nationality, not to the wronged individual. This practice reflected the now-outdated notion that only states, not individuals, were the appropriate subjects of international law. Fortunately, this notion has begun to erode and continues to lose credibility. Nonetheless, the remedy of diplomatic protection, whereby a state asserts the rights of its nationals abroad, continues to be an important function of the diplomatic instrument.

A particularly important subset of diplomatic protection is consular protection, the right of a state to assist its nationals who are arrested or detained in a foreign state. Article 36 of the Vienna Convention on Consular Relations provides the relevant standard under international law concerning consular protection of a state's nationals who are arrested or detained while abroad. Article 36(1)(b) provides:

> [I]f he so requests, the competent authorities of the receiving State shall, without delay, inform the consular post of the sending State if, within its consular district, a national of that State is arrested or committed to prison or to custody pending trial or is detained in any other manner. Any communication addressed to the consular post by the person arrested, in prison, custody or detention shall be forwarded by the said authorities without delay. The said authorities shall inform the person involved without delay of his rights under this subparagraph....

Article 36 requires that when a foreign national is arrested or detained while abroad, the arresting State has an obligation to inform the arrested individual of his or her right to contact his State's consular post. The purpose of the right of consular notification is set forth in subsection c of paragraph 1:

> [C]onsular officers shall have a right to visit a national of the sending State who is in prison, custody or detention, to converse and correspond with him and to arrange for his legal representation.

It is central to the concept of diplomatic protection that a state has the right to assist its nationals who are arrested abroad with legal representation. This right was traditionally viewed as belonging to the state and was primarily conceived of as the right of states to protect their nationals, not as a right of individuals to receive such protection.

The failure of the United States to satisfy the requirements of Article 36 formed the basis for a pair of cases in the International Court of Justice: the *LaGrand* case (Germany v. United States of America) in 2001[19] and the *Case Concerning Avena and Other Mexican Nationals* (Mexico v. United States of America) in 2004.[20] Article 36 was also prominent in a recent decision by the U.S. Supreme Court, *Medellín v. Texas*, decided in 2008.[21]

The *LaGrand, Avena*, and *Medellín* decisions all presented their respective courts with difficult questions concerning the implementation of international law by U.S. federal and state courts. (The reader should be mindful in this section of the difference between nation-states and states in the U.S. federal system.) More specifically, these cases concerned the application by U.S. state courts of state procedural rules to deny giving effect to international treaties and court decisions. The state procedural rule at issue in these cases was the procedural default rule, which operates to prevent a claim from being raised on appeal or in an application for habeas corpus if that claim had not been brought during the initial proceedings.

In each of these cases, criminal defendants in the United States, who were nationals of other states, were arrested, tried, and convicted without having been informed of their rights under Article 36. That the United States had violated its obligations under the convention was never in doubt; the difficult issue in these cases was that of the appropriate remedy for its violation, which was complicated by concerns for federalism and by the need for domestic courts to give effect to international law.

The *LaGrand* case arose out of an attempted bank robbery by two brothers, Karl and Walter LaGrand, in Marana, Arizona, in January 1982. In the course of the robbery attempt, the bank manager was murdered and a teller was stabbed multiple times. The LaGrand brothers were arrested and each charged with first-degree murder, attempted first-degree murder, attempted armed robbery, and two counts of kidnapping. Both were found guilty and sentenced to death. The LaGrands did not become aware of their rights under Article 36 until some eight years after their convictions and death sentences were handed down. Upon learning of the violation, the LaGrands raised the issue for the first time in a petition for a writ of habeas corpus brought in U.S. federal court in Arizona. The district court, however, denied their habeas petition on the ground that their Vienna Convention claim was barred by the procedural default rule.[22] The Supreme Court ultimately declined to review the case.[23]

Karl LaGrand was executed on February 24, 1999, following the failure of German diplomatic intervention and the rejection of last-minute appeals. On March 2, 1999, the day before Walter LaGrand's execution, Germany instituted proceedings against the United States before the International Court of Justice (ICJ). Included in its application to the ICJ was a request for provisional measures requiring the U.S. federal government "to take all measures at its disposal to ensure that Walter LaGrand is not executed pending the final decision in these proceedings," which was granted.[24] Walter LaGrand was nonetheless executed on March 3, 1999.

The case required the court to decide, for the first time, whether Article 36 created individual rights in nationals arrested or detained abroad. To resolve this question, the court looked to the language of Article 36, which provides that "[t]he said authorities shall inform the person concerned without delay of his rights under this subparagraph." The court also pointed to language in subparagraph c, which provides that the arrested or detained person may choose not to receive the benefit of consular assistance. The court found that the United States had violated both the right of Germany to provide its nationals with diplomatic protection and the rights of the LaGrands to receive that diplomatic protection. The court also found that, as applied, the procedural default rule violated the obligation of the United States to give full effect, through its domestic laws and regulations, to the purposes of Article 36. Moreover, the court held that in future cases of this type:

> [I]t would be incumbent upon the United States to allow the review and reconsideration of the conviction and sentence by taking account of the violation of the rights set forth in the Convention. This obligation can be carried out in various ways. The choice of means must be left to the United States.[25]

In the *Case Concerning Avena and Other Mexican Nationals* (Mexico v. United States of America), the ICJ was confronted with issues that were largely similar to those presented in *LaGrand*. In *Avena*, Mexico brought suit against the United States for alleged violations of the Vienna Convention with respect to fifty-two Mexican nationals being held on various death rows in the United States.[26] Mexico argued that the United States had violated the rights of both Mexico and of the individuals concerned under Article 36(1) of the Vienna Convention.

Of the fifty-two cases before it, the court found that the United States had violated its obligation to notify defendants of their consular rights in all but one of those cases. The court also found that the United States had violated its obligation to inform Mexico of the arrest of its nationals in all but two of the cases. Moreover, the United States had infringed on Mexico's right of free communication with arrested or detained nationals, the right of access to arrested or detained nationals, and the right to provide legal assistance to arrested or detained nationals in the majority of the cases. As with the right of consular notification under Article 36(1)(b), these rights belong both to the state and to the individual. The court also held that the United States had violated its obligations under Article 36 in many of the cases by applying the procedural default rule as it had done in the *LaGrand* case. The court's final judgment was that the violations of Article 36 required the effective review and reconsideration, through the judicial process, of the subsequent convictions and sentences, taking consideration of the effect of such violations on those convictions and sentences.

Despite the unambiguous holdings of the ICJ in *LaGrand* and *Avena*, U.S. courts, at both the state and federal levels, have continued to apply the procedural default rule to prevent defendants from raising claims of Article 36 violations. This practice is an ongoing illustration of the tension that often exists between international and domestic law and the reality that, although international law is theoretically supreme to domestic law, given its dependence upon domestic law institutions for enforcement, international law often yields to domestic law. Likewise, the refusal of U.S. state courts to implement the ICJ's judgments in *LaGrand* and *Avena* further illustrates the unique problems posed by the federalist system of government in the United States.

The U.S. Supreme Court confronted this issue in the case of *Medellín v. Texas* in 2008.[27] Ultimately, the Court concluded that the ICJ decisions did not create binding domestic law to which state courts were obligated to give effect.

Medellín was one of the Mexican nationals named by Mexico in the *Avena* case. He had been convicted and sentenced to death in Texas state court for the rape and murder of two teenage girls. Following the unsuccessful appeal of his conviction, Medellín petitioned the Texas state courts for habeas relief. It was in his state habeas petition that Medellín first raised the denial of his right of consular notification and protection. Like almost every other U.S. court faced with such a challenge, the Texas state courts concluded that, in spite of *LaGrand* and *Avena*, Medellín's claim was barred by the procedural default rule.

In response to the *Avena* decision, President George W. Bush issued a memo, stating that, "the U.S. will discharge its international obligations under [*Avena*], by having state courts give effect to the decision in accordance with general principles of comity...."[28] When Medellín's application for a certificate of appealability for his federal habeas petitions was denied by the Fifth Circuit, Medellín next brought a second petition for state habeas relief, this time relying upon the Bush memo.

The Supreme Court's holding as to the legal effect of the *Avena* decision on U.S. courts was based on the distinction between a self-executing treaty and a non-self-executing treaty (see chapter 16). As the Court explained, while all treaties create international commitments upon ratification, treaties do not become domestic law unless "the treaty itself conveys an intention that it be 'self-executing' and is ratified on these terms" or, in the absence of such an explicit intent, Congress has enacted an implementing statute. The question before the Court was whether the treaties that bound the United States to give effect to decisions of the ICJ were self-executing or non-self-executing.

The Court went on to examine three relevant treaties that Medellín argued were self-executing, and thus made the *Avena* decision automatically binding domestic law: the Optional Protocol [to the Vienna Convention] Concerning the Compulsory Settlement of Disputes, the U.N. Charter, and the ICJ Statute. The majority concluded that each of these treaties was non-self-executing and was thus not binding upon domestic courts in the absence of a congressionally-enacted implementing statute. Having concluded that the relevant treaties were non-self-executing, and that Congress had not enacted statutes implementing any of them, the Court concluded that while there was an international obligation to comply with the ICJ's judgment in *Avena*, that decision did not of itself have any domestic legal effect. In sum, in the absence of some further congressional action, state and federal courts were free to disregard the ICJ's decision in *Avena*.

Notes

1. Hugo Grotius, The Law of War and Peace 440 (Francis Kelsey trans., 1925).

2. 22 U.S.C. §254a (1978).

3. United States Diplomatic and Consular Staff in Tehran (U.S. v. Iran), Provisional Measures Order, 1979 I.C.J. 7 (Dec. 15) [hereinafter Iran Provisional Measures].

4. United States Diplomatic and Consular Staff in Iran (U.S. v. Iran), Judgment, 1980 I.C.J. 3 (May 24) [hereinafter Iran Judgment].

5. Iran Provisional Measures, *supra* note 3, at 19.

6. Iran Judgment, *supra* note 4, at 42–43.

7. Asylum Case (Colom./Peru), Judgment, 1950 I.C.J. 266 (Nov. 20).

8. *Id.* at 277.

9. Legal Consequences for States of the Continued Presence of South Africa in Namibia (South West Africa) Notwithstanding Security Council Resolution 276 (1970), Advisory Opinion, 1971 I.C.J. 16 (June 21) [hereinafter Namibia Advisory Opinion].

10. International Status of South West Africa, Advisory Opinion, 1950 I.C.J. 128, 144 (July 11).

11. G.A. Res. 2145 (XXI), U.N. Doc. A/6316 (Oct. 27, 1966).

12. S.C. Res. 276, ¶ 2, U.N. Doc. S/RES/276 (Jan. 28, 1970); S.C. Res. 264, U.N. Doc. S/RES/264 (Mar. 20, 1969).

13. S.C. Res. 284, ¶ 1, U.N. Doc. S/RES/284 (July 29, 1970).

14. Namibia Advisory Opinion, *supra* note 9, at 58.

15. *Id.*

16. *Id.* at 55.

17. *Id.* at 56.

18. *Id.* at 58.

19. LaGrand Case (Ger. v. U.S.), 2001 I.C.J. 104 (June 27).

20. Avena and Other Mexican Nationals (Mex. v. U.S.), 2004 I.C.J. 128 (Mar. 31).

21. Medellín v. Texas, 552 U.S. 491 (2008).

22. LaGrand v. Lewis, 883 F.Supp.469 (1995).

23. LaGrand v. Stewart, 525 U.S. 971 (1998).

24. LaGrand Case, *supra* note 19, at 498.

25. *Id.* at 514.

26. Although Mexico had originally brought its claim on behalf of fifty-four Mexican nationals, it subsequently withdrew its claim with respect to two of the individuals, on the ground that on was a dual-national of the United States and Mexico and that one had been informed of his Article 36 rights.

27. Medellín v. Texas, 552 U.S. 491 (2008).

28. *Id.* at 503.

16 International Agreements

THE INTERNATIONAL AGREEMENT, in all its many manifestations, represents the most deliberate form of prescription in which governments cooperate with one another in explicitly formulating and undertaking commitments. International agreements perform a critical lawmaking function in the contemporary world. The making of international agreements is an important strategy by which nation-states choose to commit themselves to particular policies. The shared commitment results from the process of persuasion in search of the common interest of the participants.

In a world community lacking centralized legislative institutions, international agreements offer a convenient avenue through which to project shared expectations of future policy. The making of an international agreement, as a most deliberate form of prescription, is somewhat comparable to the act of legislation in national arenas. It is through agreement making that states project their policies into all areas of the international legal system. The amazing growth of the network of international agreements testifies vividly that the mechanism of agreement making is crucial in the pursuit of world public order. With the ever-increasing volume and tempo of transnational interaction, the number of international agreements has increased remarkably. Since the establishment of the United Nations, nearly 50,000 international agreements (with varying designations) have been registered or filed and recorded with the U.N. Secretariat. Agreement making will undoubtedly accelerate as transnational interaction increases.

International agreement instead of treaty is chosen as a generic term of reference here. A variety of labels have been used to designate international agreements, including act, agreement, articles of agreement, charter, concordat, convention, covenant, declaration, exchange of notes, *modus vivendi*, pact, protocol, statute, and treaty. Though the labels are not legally significant, some may be used more frequently to design agreements on a particular subject or those of an especially solemn nature. (For instance, convention has been used most frequently in connection with specific categories of human rights, and treaty is the common designation for agreements of friendship, commerce, and naviga-tion.) The lack of uniform terminology is due partly to the survival of diplomatic tradi-tions and partly to a reluctance on the part of nation-states to standardize treaty usage.

Under Article 2 of the U.S. Constitution, the term treaty refers specifically to an international agreement made by the president with the advice and consent of the Senate by a two-thirds vote. Other international agreements, not concluded in accordance with the procedure of Article 2, are generally known as executive agree-ments. Unlike a treaty, an executive agreement does not require Senate approval. Technically speaking, executive agreements can be further divided into three types: (1) congressional-executive agreements, which are concluded with prior authorization or subsequent approval by Congress; (2) treaty-executive agreements, which are autho-rized by treaty; and (3) sole executive agreements or presidential agreements, which are concluded under the authority of the president acting as the chief executive and spokesperson of the United States in dealing with other countries. In terms of external effect, executive agreements are functional equivalents of treaties. The commitments assumed under executive agreements must be performed in good faith. In terms of internal effect, there are nuances of difference. Perhaps the most well-known and con-troversial executive agreement is the Yalta Agreement, concluded by President Franklin D. Roosevelt on February 11, 1945.

International agreements exhibit significant differences in terms of number of par-ticipants sharing commitment, the subject and content of policies projected, and the expectations concerning the degree of permanence engendered. Building on the func-tional categories developed by Lord McNair in 1930,[1] international agreements can be grouped as follows:

1. *Constitutive* (organic) agreements, which establish basic feature of the com-prehensive process of authoritative decision, such as the Charter of the United Nations.
2. *Lawmaking* (legislative) agreements, which prescribe particular policies concerning particular events or values, such as the Vienna Convention on Diplomatic Relations and the International Convention on the Elimination of All Forms of Racial Discrimination.
3. *Contractual* agreements, which create shared expectations of commitment between two or more states for policies of differing scope and importance, and

generate expectations of general community prescription, such as trade agreements of all kinds.

4. *Dispositive* agreements in the nature of conveyances, which involve exchange in relatively consummated transactions, with minimal projection of future policy, such as treaties of lease or cession and boundary treaties.

It is sometimes debated what agreements between nation-states are lawmaking and what are not. But this quest is futile, since all agreements between nation-states project policies into the future. The number of participants affected by such projections is a matter not for dogmatic assertion about the nature of agreement but for empirical, rational inquiry in light of all the values at stake. Making, performing, and terminating international agreements involves more than just words on paper. An international agreement is a process of communication through which shared policies toward the future are formulated and reformulated.

The process of agreement, like the prescribing process generally, can realistically be understood only by reference to the participants and their perspectives, situations of interaction, base values, modalities in communicating commitment, outcomes in shared expectations, and effects on value processes. The relevant participants are state officials and the other parties with whom they interact. Their demands, identifications, and expectations are shaped largely by nuances in culture, class, interest, personality, and crisis. The general objective of parties in making an international agreement is to project a community policy toward a future distribution of values. The more detailed objectives of the parties may relate to any value (security, power, respect, enlightenment, well-being, wealth, skill, affection, and rectitude) or to any feature of a value process (participation, situations, base values, strategies, and outcomes). The range of values sought to be secured by international agreements may be illustrated by reference to some of the more important types of international agreement made by states: treaties of alliance and mutual defense (security, power); conventions for the protection of human rights (respect); agreements relating to communications and cultural exchange (enlightenment); agreements concerning narcotic control and environmental protection (well-being); treaties of friendship, commerce, and navigation (wealth); agreements for the transfer of technology and the exchange of technical personnel (skill); agreements for facilitating family reunion (affection); and treaties guaranteeing freedom of religion (rectitude).

The situations in which international agreements are negotiated and performed vary in features relevant to the communication of demands and expectations about commitment. Such differences relate to temporal and geographical features, degree of institutionalization, and intensities in exposure to crisis. All values potentially serve as base values in processes of negotiation, and the relative positions of the parties in control over particular base values significantly affect both the degree and content of their commitment. The sequence of negotiations and other activities by which the parties mediate their subjectivities to achieve outcomes in shared commitment may be direct and explicit or indirect and implicit, expressed in both words and deeds. International agreements differ in many ways: the number of parties sharing commitment, the scope and content of policies projected, and the expectations of permanence or impermanence attending commitment.

In the most comprehensive and dynamic sense, the process of agreement can be divided further into a complex of component subprocesses: the making of a commitment, the performance or nonperformance of commitments, and the modification or termination of commitment. An exposition of the law of international agreements would require examination of each of these subprocesses by reference to the familiar institutional categories of participants, perspectives, situations, base values, strategies, and outcomes. Here only some of the more important features of each subprocess can be highlighted.

Basic Community Policy

Three fundamental policies pervade the field of the law of treaties. First, the policy of freedom of choice, which encourages and fosters persuasion and voluntary cooperation in transnational interaction. Treaty commitments must be freely expressed and voluntarily assumed. Second, the sanctity of treaty commitments, or *pacta sunt servanda*. Once treaty commitments are voluntarily assumed, they must be carried out in good faith. Once shared expectations are created, the stability of expectations must be honored and maintained. Without this policy, the basic stability of transnational interaction cannot be secured. Indeed, when the fundamental policy of *pacta sunt servanda* is flouted, the very foundation of international law will crumble. Third, the policy of recognizing the necessity of change. International agreements do not operate in a vacuum. They do not exist merely as pieces of paper. The working expectations must be sustained through time. As social process is in perpetual flux, so is the context of conditions. In the realm of treaty law, as in other areas, room must be made to allow such change to accommodate the changing demands and expectations of the parties in the light of changing conditions.

To strike a proper balance between stability of expectations and the necessity of change is a delicate, yet vital task. These policies are substantially reflected in the development of the law of international agreements.

Trends in Decision and Conditioning Factors

The development of treaty law long depended largely on customary law. A milestone in the development and codification concerning international agreements is the Vienna Convention on the Law of Treaties, concluded in 1969. Known as "the treaty of treaties," the Vienna Convention represents an extremely useful formulation of contemporary treaty law. It came into effect on January 27, 1980, on ratification by the requisite thirty-five states. Even before its entry into force, the convention had been widely recognized as "the authoritative guide to current treaty law and practice."[2] It sets forth community prescriptions governing the various phases and aspects in the processes of commitment, performance, and termination (modification). It has struck a remarkable balance between demands for stability and demands for change. The principle of *pacta sunt servanda* and the impartial procedures for settlement of disputes are matched by the doctrines of *jus cogens* and *rebus sic stantibus*.

The traditional literature concerning international agreements is generally concerned only with agreements to which nation-states are parties. This follows from the traditional doctrine that only states are subjects of international law. By the time the Vienna Convention on the Law of Treaties was signed, there existed mutual recognition of the need to address international agreements involving international governmental organizations. In an attempt to address this issue, the International Law Commission (ILC) drafted the Vienna Convention on the Law of Treaties between States and International Organizations or between International Organizations (hereinafter the IGO Treaty Convention), which the U.N. Conference adopted in 1986.

The most significant development of the IGO Treaty Convention is that it formally recognizes that international organizations possess the capacity to conclude treaties. The convention's proponents believe the codification enhances the legal order in international relations and serves the purposes of the United Nations. This convention is closely tied to and includes all the terms of the Vienna Convention on the Law of Treaties of 1969, with supplemental terms applicable to international organizations. The IGO Treaty Convention included a new Article 73 to specify its relationship to the 1969 convention, and additionally bestowed upon international organizations "full powers," which the ILC had originally meant to limit to nation states. Currently, the IGO Treaty Convention has been signed by ten international organizations, including the United Nations, and twenty-six states have deposited instruments of ratification, accession or succession. The convention is to enter into force thirty days after thirty-five states deposit instruments of ratification, accession, or succession, and is still open for signatures.

For present purposes, the usage adopted in Article 2(1)(a) of the Vienna Convention of 1969 is followed: "Treaty means an international agreement concluded between states in written form and governed by international law, whether embodied in a single instrument or in two or more related instruments and whatever its particular designation." The trends in decision and development are highlighted by reference to the three subprocesses of agreement.

THE PROCESS OF COMMITMENT

This is the process by which contracting parties obtain rights and assume obligations. It involves not one act but various steps toward reaching shared commitment. Among the issues of primary concern are whether the contracting parties have made any commitment, and, if so, what is its substantive content.

The process of commitment is complex; officials of all participating states perform a number of distinct yet related functions:

1. Formulating national policies to govern the conduct of negotiations with other states: a nation-state begins by formulating national policies as guidelines for negotiations with other states;
2. Conducting negotiations with the representatives of other nation-states: after the decision to commence negotiations with others, the first step is to appoint representatives with appropriate powers and credentials, to conduct negotiations with the representatives of other nation-states;
3. Approving an agreement for internal application;
4. Approving an agreement to signify the external commitment of the state; and
5. Communicating the external commitment of the state to other states, through final utterance of the agreement and a complex of other events.

Competence

Within individual nation-states, the constitutional allocation of competence to perform these functions varies widely but also exhibits, with exceptions, a remarkably similar pattern.

In relation to the process of commitment, the Vienna Convention begins by affirming, in Article 6, that "[e]very state possesses capacity to conclude treaties." Assuming the capacity of a nation-state to conclude an international agreement, the question immediately arises as to who is authorized to represent a state to conduct negotiations and other acts leading to the conclusion of an agreement. Such authority is generally determined by a formal document known as "full powers," which designates a person or persons to represent the state to negotiate and conclude an agreement. The representative of a state is generally expected to produce appropriate full powers unless, as stated in Article 7(1), "it appears from the practice of the States concerned or from other circumstances that their intention was to consider that person as representing the State for such purposes and to dispense with full powers."

The concept of full powers historically assumed much greater significance than it does today. During the era of absolute monarchy, an international agreement was regarded as an expression of the sovereign's will, and the full powers was designed to clothe the personal agent of the sovereign with authority to bind his principal, provided that he acted within his authority. Hence, the authority of the sovereign representative was, as a rule, defined with precision in advance of the negotiation so as to minimize subsequent refusal to ratify on the ground that the agent acted in excess of his authority.

Since the demise of this era, the importance attached to full powers has greatly diminished. As a measure of democratic control over foreign policy gradually took hold, in the wake of the American and French revolutions, "ratification" became discretionary in state practice, even if the representative who had negotiated the agreement acted entirely within the limits of the authority embodied in the full powers. The ever-increasing ease of communications, as accentuated by the development of telecommunications and other technologies, has made it possible to ensure that negotiators do not exceed the limits of their authority.

In addition, nation-states have shown a tendency to conclude agreements in simplified form, such as by exchanging notes or letters, thereby dispensing with full powers. Such an informal approach is necessitated by the increasing complexity and frequency of transnational interaction, calling for a growing network of treaty arrangements to deal with all kinds of subjects and to cope with manifold complex relationships accentuated by the proliferation of new states.

Adoption and Authentication of the Text

Successful negotiations will result in the adoption of the text. For a bilateral agreement this will require unanimity. The unanimity rule will also apply to a multilateral agreement with limited participation (for example, a treaty between riparian states concerning the development of a river basin). For a multilateral agreement, designed for and opened to wide participation, and generally concluded through an international conference, the unanimity rule obviously will not be practicable. Hence, the Vienna Convention, in Article 9(2), prescribes that "the adoption of text of a treaty at an international conference takes place by the vote of two-thirds of the States present and voting unless by the same majority they shall decide to apply a different rule." This is commonly effected through a final act, which also serves to authenticate the text of the treaty.

Consent to Be Bound

"The consent of a State to be bound by a treaty," as stipulated in Article 11 of the Vienna Convention, "may be expressed by signature, exchange of instruments constituting a treaty, ratification, acceptance, approval or accession, or by any other means if so agreed." It admits considerable flexibility in the modality of expressing consent, giving particular deference to the choice of the contracting parties.

Ratification, however, remains the most common form. Where required, ratification is the final and formal act by which a state becomes bound by an international agreement. It is an unequivocal expression of consent to be bound; it signifies the external commitment of the ratifying state. Because of the vast proliferation of international agreements in the contemporary world, the cumbersome process of ratification is applied to more solemn types of agreement. Ratification is not retroactive in effect. Even after an agreement is signed by a state's delegate, the signatory is in theory under no legal obligation to ratify it. In practice, however, good faith is expected. Contracting parties may also agree to apply a treaty provisionally pending ratification.

The ratification procedure is maintained for several reasons. Additional time after signing affords a state the chance to scrutinize closely the provisions of a complicated agreement. This is especially so for nations that are relatively inexperienced in making international agreements. Occasionally an agreement requires changes in a state's domestic law before becoming operative, and ratification allows for an interim period of preparation. In some states, the treaty-making power is vested in a body that can neither directly negotiate nor delegate its power to the actual negotiators. In democratic politics, ratification affords the opportunity of public exposure and approval through consultation with elected legislative representatives.

Reservation

A state interested in establishing a treaty relationship will naturally seek to shape the terms of the agreement to its advantage in the process of negotiation. If it fails to fully convince its negotiating partner or partners but still wishes to be a party to the agreement, it may resort to the device of reservation as a safeguard.

A reservation, as defined by Article 2 of the Vienna Convention, is "a unilateral statement, however phrased or named, made by a State, when signing, ratifying, acceding to, accepting or approving a treaty, whereby it purports to exclude or to vary the legal effect of certain provisions of the treaty in their application to that State." For bilateral agreements, a reservation constitutes in effect a counteroffer by the reserving state, to be accepted or rejected by the other state. If rejected, there will be no agreement; if accepted, there is an agreement on the terms of the counteroffer.

In the case of multilateral agreements, reservations tendered by one or more parties present more complex and troublesome problems. Though in principle reservations should not be valid without the consent of all parties to an international agreement, this principle is not adhered to in practice. The use of reservations is so common and objections to them so infrequent that a requirement of consent of all parties is far too cumbersome to work adequately. Therefore, two alternate methods of determining the status of a state's reservations in the face of objections by other ratifying states have been available in international law.

The Pan-American formula is to allow the agreement to operate in its original form between the states that accept it without reservation and to operate between the reserving state and any other states willing to accept the reservations made. Under this scheme, objecting states will likely have no treaty relationship with reserving states but a third state may establish treaty relations with both. This system operates to augment the number of participants to multilateral agreements but tends to fragment large multilateral agreements into a number of small bilateral treaty regimes.

The International Court of Justice, in the famous case *Reservation to the Genocide Convention*,[3] employed a different test, permitting reservations to be effective on all parties (objecting or not), provided the reservations are "compatible with the object and purpose" of the agreements.[4] Articles 19–23 of the Vienna Convention reflect the compatibility test. The major difficulty with this test is that, in the absence of compulsory third-party decision making, the determination of what is compatible is left to the subjective autointerpretation of the individual states. The danger of potential misinterpretation is obvious.

The potentially catastrophic difficulties involved with reservations in theory rarely occur in practice. The element of surprise is minimized through careful draftsmanship in expressing genuinely shared commitments. Also, as an anticipatory measure, most formal agreements contain specific reservation clauses to stipulate guidelines for dealing with particular reservations and to specify provisions not susceptible to reservations.

Registration

Upon the ratification (or its equivalent) of an international agreement, the written documents that evidence consent to be bound are deposited or exchanged. In the case of multilateral agreements, the ratifications are placed in the care of a depositary. The depositary may be the foreign office of one or more states or an international organization such as the United Nations. International agreements ordinarily contain a provision as to how the deposit will be handled. According to Article 77 of the Vienna Convention, the functions of a depositary generally include custody of the text of the agreement and all documents relevant to its ratification, providing information as to the time of its effective operation, and registering the treaty.

Registration of international agreements is provided by the U.N. Charter. Article 102(1) of the charter requires that "[e]very treaty and every international agreement entered into by any Member of the United Nations after the present Charter comes into force shall as soon as possible be registered with the Secretariat and published by it." The central purpose is to discourage secret diplomacy and to make public the texts of international agreements so as to elicit public concern. The act of registration in no way implies that a determination has been made by the United Nations as to the nature or validity of the documents. Failure to comply with Article 102(1) will not affect the validity of an agreement, though it may not be invoked before any organ of the United Nations, including the International Court of Justice. In October 1984, this question was dramatized in connection with the military operations in Grenada conducted by the United States and certain Caribbean nations. The military operations were in part justified by reference to the terms of the collective security treaty among these Caribbean nations—the Treaty Establishing the Organization of Eastern Caribbean States, concluded on June 18, 1981 (Treaty of Basseterre)—as a collective self-defense measure authorized by the treaty. However, the treaty was not registered with the United Nations until November 1983.

Lack of Genuine Commitment (Grounds for Invalidity)

Central to the process of commitment is concern over whether genuine commitments are shared by the contracting parties. Defects in the original commitment may bear on the genuineness of such commitments and preclude the parties from being bound by the agreement. Such defects may thus give rise to claims to invalidate the agreement.

Such defects include violation of internal law, error, fraud, representative's corruption, coercion of a state or its representative, conflict with a peremptory norm of general international law (*jus cogens*), and conclusion of "unequal treaties."

Although it is sometimes asserted that national constitutional limitations determine the validity of a treaty on the international plane, it has long been established that a state is bound regardless of internal limitations (constitutional or otherwise) if consent has been given by a properly authorized agent under international law. This is an aspect of the supremacy of international law. Thus, the Vienna Convention, in Article 46(1), stipulates that "[a] State may not invoke the fact that its consent to be bound by a treaty has been expressed in violation of a provision of its internal law regarding competence to conclude treaties as invalidating its consent unless that violation was manifest and concerned a rule of its internal law of fundamental importance." A violation is deemed "manifest," as stated in Article 46(2), "if it would be objectively evident to any State conducting itself in the manner in accordance with normal practice and in good faith." Article 47 deals with the separate but related issue of consent granted by a state's representative in violation of an executive or administrative restriction on his authority. Such a violation may not be put forth as a ground for invalidity "unless the restriction was notified to the other negotiating States prior to [the representative's] expressing such consent."

The related issue of error and fraud as grounds for invalidity, though sometimes treated as one and the same, is distinct and addressed in the Vienna Convention in Articles 48 and 49. Article 48, dealing with error, places several restrictions on invoking error as a ground for invalidity. The error must relate to a fact or situation assumed by the invoking party to exist when the treaty was concluded, and this supposed fact or situation must have been an "essential basis" of the state's "consent to be bound by the treaty." Furthermore, the error will not be deemed sufficient if the state "contributed by its own conduct to the error or if the circumstances were such as to put that State on notice of a possible error."

For the purposes of Article 48, no distinction is made between unilateral or mutual mistake, as is the case under some domestic legal systems. Purely textual mistakes, agreed to be such by all parties, are handled under a separate article.

"Fraudulent misrepresentation of a material fact inducing an essential error" is also covered by Article 48. Attempts were made to deal with other forms of fraud in a separate article. Due to the difficulty in reconciling the various domestic concepts of "fraud," however, the Vienna Convention left its precise formulation in the treaty context to be worked out in practice. The effect of Article 49 is not to make a treaty void *ab initio* but only "voidable at the option of the injured party."

Although it was argued that a state representative's corruption in negotiating a treaty would be adequately covered by a general provision regarding fraud as a basis for invalidity, the Vienna Convention, following the International Law Commission's report, incorporated a separate article to deal with such a situation. Article 50 allows the state whose representative was corrupted by other negotiating parties to claim corruption as the basis for the treaty's invalidity. "Corruption," as it is used in the article, includes "only acts calculated to exercise a substantial influence on the disposition of the representative to conclude the treaty."

On the matter of coercion, the Vienna Convention adopted two articles: Article 51 deals with the coercion of a representative in his or her personal capacity, and Article 52 deals with coercion by the threat or use of force against a state itself. Article 51 includes threats of violence, both physical and psychological, and moral pressure regarding the representative's private acts of indiscretion, a disclosure of which might be devastating. "A treaty is void," according to Article 52, "if its conclusion has been procured by the threat or use of force in violation of the principles of international law embodied in the Charter of the United Nations." Although a condemnation of "economic or political pressure" appears in the conference's final act, the suggestion that such conduct be prohibited within Article 52 was rejected, in part as being too vague.

The notion of peremptory norms (*jus cogens*) was incorporated in the Vienna Convention, though not without controversy. In the treaty context, it means that there are certain agreements into which states may not enter in the interest of maintaining world public order. It limits the freedom of states to make agreements, comparable to limits on the freedom of contract that exist in virtually all national legal systems. Article 53 of the convention defines "a peremptory norm of general international law" in terms of "a norm accepted and recognized by the international community of states as a whole as a norm from which no derogation is permitted and which can be modified only by a subsequent norm of general international law having the same character." It requires general, rather than universal, acceptance by the members of the world community. The specific norms of international law that fall within this category of *jus cogens* were not spelled out in the Vienna Convention due to a lack of consensus. Further, it was thought better to leave such specification to the developing patterns of state practice and decisions of international tribunals. Nevertheless, some of the intensely demanded prescriptions, such as those relating to the principle of nonuse of force, the principle of self-determination, and the core content of international human rights, are widely regarded as within the domain of contemporary *jus cogens*. If an international agreement conflicts with a peremptory norm at the time of its conclusion, it is void. Further, under Article 64, when a new peremptory norm emerges, any existing agreement which conflicts with that norm becomes void and terminates.

Claims for invalidation based on the concept of "unequal treaties" are highly controversial.[5] The concept itself is ill-defined, and its utility is seriously questioned. For those who espouse this concept, a treaty is said to be unequal when it contravenes the basic principle of sovereign equality of states, as measured by the relative bases of power of the contracting parties, the objects of the treaty, the degree of coercion involved in the strategies employed, and the outcomes of treaty performance. First espoused by communist states, the concept of unequal treaties has been echoed by newly independent states. Western jurists generally reject the concept as vague and elusive. The Vienna Convention did not incorporate this concept, though such elements as coercion are treated elsewhere in the convention.

THE PROCESS OF PERFORMANCE

The process of performance involves implementation of the agreed-upon commitment. From the fundamental principle of good faith, through the task of interpretation, to actual performance by the contracting parties and effects on third parties, a paramount concern is that performance approximates as closely as possible the shared commitment.

Pacta Sunt Servanda

Central to the law of treaties is the doctrine of *pacta sunt servanda*, the sanctity of treaties. This doctrine has roots in Greco-Roman-Christian tradition and in other religious and cultural traditions. Article 26 of the Vienna Convention phrases it as: "Every treaty in force is binding upon the parties to it and must be performed by them in good faith." *Pacta sunt servanda* is indispensable to the common interest in establishing and maintaining the stability of expectations for all parties concerned. Stable international relations depend on the ability of states to put faith in one another's expressed intent to fulfill treaty commitments.

In dealing with the doctrine of *pacta sunt servanda*, the Vienna Convention was faced with the task of defining its limits. The doctrine is deemed *jus cogens*, since it admits such exceptions as *clausula rebus sic stantibus*, the doctrine of fundamental change in circumstances. A link has further been suggested between Article 2(2) of the U.N. Charter and *pacta sunt servanda*. The choice of words, "treaty in force," in Article 26, is understood to refer only to "valid treaty"—one based on "the consent of the parties and having a lawful purpose."

The Task of Interpretation

Once an international agreement comes into effect, the question of interpretation occurs sooner or later. Indeed, the bulk of the cases coming before the International Court of Justice and its predecessor have involved disputed interpretations of international agreements. In view of the relevant features involved in the processes of agreement, claim, and decision, some interpretation obviously is always necessary in applying agreements to particular circumstances. Since the words used in an agreement rarely have exact and entirely unambiguous meanings, and since all possible contexts that may arise under it cannot be fully foreseen and explicitly provided for by the parties in the process of reaching the agreement, the necessity of interpretation occurs.

Two polar positions are taken. One extreme holds that the text of an international agreement speaks for itself, and the task of interpretation is simply to give it a "plain and ordinary" meaning. The opposite extreme maintains that the task of interpretation is so enormously complicated as to render it an exercise in futility.

The reality would appear to fall between these two extremes. The words of an international agreement cannot be regarded as timeless absolutes. They have meaning only in light of all the relevant contexts in which they are employed. It is hardly possible to impose a literal, plain, or natural meaning on any legal language, particularly on that of a constitutive document such as the U.N. Charter, whose admittedly broad language is designed to meet the changing conditions of an undefined future. But the posture of impossibility and futility is highly destructive, in that it is an attempt to escape the realities of complex international relations. To accept it will result in the failure to mobilize all available intellectual skills toward problem solving. The end result would likely be stagnation or anarchy.

Efforts toward treaty interpretation have thus traditionally taken the form of formulating particular canons of construction or principles of interpretation. Notable among these are the principle of plain and ordinary meaning, the principle of effectiveness, the principle of major purposes, and the principle of restrictive interpretation. These canons of construction, presented without a coherent, contextual framework, tend to contradict or overlap one another in application.

True to their policy-oriented approach, McDougal and Lasswell, in collaboration with James C. Miller, offer a contextual alternative in *The Interpretation of Agreements and World Public Order: Principles of Content and Procedure*,[6] building on the insights of contemporary communication theories. The goals of interpretation, as they postulate, are threefold: (1) ascertaining the genuinely shared expectations of the particular parties to an agreement; (2) supplementing such shared expectations by reference to community policies when gaps, contradictions, or ambiguities exist in the parties' communication; and (3) integrating or policing, in the sense of the appraisal and possible rejection of the parties' expectations, however explicit or implicit they may be, so as to ensure their conformity with fundamental community policies.[7] To further these goals, they recommend the systematic employment of a comprehensive set of principles of content and procedure, grounded in the full contextuality of the processes of agreement, claim, and decision.

The interpreter of an international agreement should thus consider all relevant signs and deeds taking place at any time before, during, or after the agreement is concluded. The interpreter should consider the whole process of agreement and its context of conditions, the process of claim and decision, and possible impact on expectations of the current decision process. It is essential to inquire: Who says what to whom for what objectives, how, under what conditions and with what effects. The interpreter should not allow any detail to dominate his or her judgment before all has been considered. Above all, he or she should give preference both to interpretations that have been considered in the context of factors affecting the processes of agreement and claim and all the community policies at stake, and to interpretations that "harmonize most fully with public order prescriptions" and "will probably do most to influence future agreements toward harmony with public order goals."[8]

A considerable degree of contextuality is reflected in the guidelines for interpretation in the Vienna Convention on the Law of Treaties. The two key provisions are Articles 31 and 32. Article 31, setting forth the "general rule of interpretation," provides:

1. A treaty shall be interpreted in good faith in accordance with the ordinary meaning to be given to the terms of the treaty in their context and in the light of its object and purpose.

2. The context for the purpose of the interpretation of a treaty shall comprise, in addition to the text, including its preamble and annexes:

   (a) any agreement relating to the treaty which was made between the parties in connection with the conclusion of the treaty;

   (b) any instrument which was made by one or more parties in connection with the conclusion of the treaty and accepted by other parties as an instrument related to the treaty.

3. There shall be taken into account, together with the context:

   (a) any subsequent agreement between the parties regarding interpretation of the treaty or the application of its provisions;

   (b) any subsequent practice in the application of the treaty which establishes the agreement of the parties regarding its interpretation;

   (c) any relevant rules of international law applicable in the relations between the parties.

4. A special meaning shall be given to a term if it is established that the parties so intended.

Article 32, dealing with "supplementary means of interpretation," stipulates:

Recourse may be had to supplementary means of interpretation, including the preparatory work of the treaty and the circumstances of its conclusion, in order to confirm the meaning resulting from the application of Article 31, or to determine the meaning when the interpretation according to Article 31

   (a) leaves the meaning ambiguous or obscure; or

   (b) leads to a result which is manifestly absurd or unreasonable.

Another provision, Article 33, is concerned with "interpretation of treaties authenticated in two or more languages."

The formulation of the Vienna Convention, as embodied in Articles 31, 32, and 33, has raised the question whether it represents a textualist or a contextual approach. It is neither; it represents an eclectic approach, combining the essential elements of both. Fidelity to the text of the treaty, to be sure, is the starting point, but the convention avoids the trap of a rigid, simplistic version of "plain and ordinary" meaning. The ordinary meaning will be given to the terms of the treaty "in their context and in the light of its object and purpose." The principle of major purposes (effectiveness) is thus incorporated. So is the principle of contextuality. Though the relevant contextual factors specified here are not as comprehensive and open-ended as those urged by McDougal and Lasswell, they do embrace the preamble, annexes, and related instruments made by the contracting parties, the whole flow of subsequent agreements and practice, "any relevant rules of international law applicable," and "the preparatory work of the treaty and the circumstances of its conclusion" as well as other supplementary means. Such a framework of interpretation, when appropriately employed, could contribute significantly to the necessary task of treaty interpretation.

Interparty Application

The concern here relates to the geographical and temporal aspects of treaty performance.

Depending on the subject of an international agreement, the territorial scope of its applicability may or may not be expressly stated. Sometimes the territorial applicability need not be delimited, as in treaties of extradition, under which the territorial scope is deemed the entire territory over which a state exerts formal authority and control. In other treaties, a territorial scope less than that of the state's entire territory may be specified. The Vienna Convention, in Article 29, stipulates that "[u]nless a different intention appears from the treaty or is otherwise established, a treaty is binding upon each party in respect of its entire territory." Special difficulties may arise when federal-state clauses are involved.

An international agreement operates prospectively rather than retroactively, unless the agreement itself indicates otherwise. This is inscribed in Article 28 of the Vienna Convention, which also allows for proof of a retroactive effect based on circumstances outside of the parties' intent as that appears in the agreement.

International law requires that negotiating states to an agreement do nothing to frustrate the objectives of the agreement already negotiated but not yet ratified. This "provisional application" was included in Article 25 of the Vienna Convention, which also allows a state to terminate the provisional applicability of the treaty as to itself by notifying negotiating states of its intention not to become a party.

Questions may arise concerning which agreement's provisions apply when two successive agreements deal with the same subject or in some other way interrelate or conflict. The Vienna Convention covers this issue in Article 30, under which an agreement may specify that it is subject to the provisions of an earlier or later agreement. When the parties to a previous agreement are all parties to a later one, the provisions of the first are applicable insofar as they are compatible with those of the second, in the absence of express arrangements to the contrary. When all the parties to an earlier agreement are not parties to a later agreement, as between states that are parties to both, the provisions of the earlier agreement apply to the extent they are compatible with the later; and, as between a state-party to both agreements and a party to only one, the provisions of the agreement in common apply.

Effects on Third Parties

That international agreements apply only to the contracting parties is expressed in the maxim *pacta tertiis nec nocent nec prosunt*, meaning that agreements neither impose obligations nor confer rights on third parties. This reflects the policy of volition in treaty commitments in independent states. A controversial issue has been whether this principle allows for exceptions under international law. According to Article 35 of the Vienna Convention, two conditions must be met in order for a nonparty to be bound by a treaty provision: (1) the parties to the treaty must have intended it, and (2) the nonparty must agree to be so bound. Its acceptance of the obligation must be express and in writing.

Even more controversial than the means by which obligations may be imposed on third-party states is the question of when rights so conferred on third states become "perfect and enforceable" by them. There are two different views. One holds that a third state may so benefit only if it assents to a conferring of the rights, expressly or implicitly. Another maintains that what is determinative is not assent by the third state but the intent of the contracting parties to confer the right. Article 36 of the Vienna Convention took a middle course, requiring the third state's assent and simultaneously presuming such assent in the absence of contrary expression. A failure to exercise the rights thus conferred may be considered evidence of nonassent.

A major exception to the prescription that obligations may not be placed on third states without their consent exists in the U.N. Charter. According to Article 2(6), states not members of the United Nations are required to act in accordance with the charter principles to the extent necessary to ensure the "maintenance of international peace and security." Even though the Vienna Convention made no reference to this provision, the U.N. Charter has become the fundamental and supreme law of the world community, endowed with unique, overall responsibilities to maintain world public order.

THE PROCESS OF CHANGE AND TERMINATION

An international agreement involves the shared expectations of the contracting parties. From the process of commitment to the process of performance, such shared expectations may change for various reasons, especially a fundamental change in circumstances. Such a change may affect the common interest in varying degrees.

In a decentralized world, lacking appropriate centralized institutions with compulsory authority to monitor and respond to the flow of facts and demands for change, heavy reliance continues to be placed on individual states to deal with claims relating to change in treaty relationships. How demands for change are to be accommodated with the stability of expectations is a delicate, yet extremely important, task.

In response to different kinds of change demanded, the Vienna Convention has adopted a number of distinct yet related terms: amendment, modification, withdrawal, denunciation, suspension, and termination. Whereas amendment means revision of the commitment of all original parties, modification involves revision of the commitment between certain of the parties only. A withdrawal is effected by a party's declaration that it is no longer a party to a multilateral treaty, and in a denunciation, a party simply declares that it regards a multilateral treaty as terminated. Whereas suspension involves the postponement of performance for a definite or indefinite time till the particular conditions alleged to have been changed are restored to normalcy, termination entails ending a commitment.

Amendment and Modification

Amendment and modification, though related, involve distinct aspects and extents of applicability. Amendment of a treaty changes its provisions, affecting all the parties to the treaty. Modification of a treaty, in contrast, involves an *inter se* agreement entered by particular parties to a treaty, designed to vary some of the treaty provisions as between or among themselves only.

A treaty may of course be amended by the unanimous consent of all the parties concerned. For a bilateral treaty, this presents little problem. For a multilateral treaty, however, the unanimity requirement would mean frustration of any demand for change. Hence many multilateral treaties set forth specific conditions for amendment.

For example, Article 108 of the U.N. Charter adopts the two-thirds rule instead of the unanimity rule: "Amendments to the present Charter shall come into force for all Members of the United Nations when they have been adopted by a vote of two thirds of the members of the General Assembly and ratified in accordance with their respective constitutional processes by two thirds of the Members of the United Nations, including all the permanent members of the Security Council." Note, however, the formidable requirement of unanimity among the five permanent members of the Security Council.

The Vienna Convention contains a catch-all provision in Article 40 to deal with amending problems for multilateral treaties that lack provisions for amendment.

Modification, under Article 41 of the convention, may be effected by two or more parties to a particular treaty when the treaty expressly allows it. In the absence of such an explicit authorization, modification is permissible only if it has not been prohibited by the treaty, does not affect the rights or obligations of the other parties, and is not inimical to "the effective execution of the object and purpose of the treaty as a whole."

Withdrawal, Denunciation, Suspension, and Termination

The means of bringing a treaty to a temporary or permanent end include withdrawal, denunciation, suspension, and termination. Such occurrences may be provided for in the treaty itself, for example, after a specified period has passed, on the occurrence of a certain event, or on the fulfillment of certain conditions. Such occurrences may also result from the consent of all the contracting parties.

In the absence of explicit treaty provision or of mutual consent, does an implied right of denunciation or withdrawal exist? While one school of thought denies such an implied right, another affirms its existence under customary international law. Article 56 of the Vienna Convention cautiously incorporates the latter view, requiring that at least a year's advance notice be given. In determining whether such a right is implied in a treaty, the intent of the parties is crucial; absent a clear intent, the nature of the treaty itself must be considered. For example, it would not be correct to imply a right of denunciation for a peace treaty, but the same cannot be said of a treaty of alliance. In addition, as will be elaborated in chapter 25, it would be inappropriate to infer a right of denunciation regarding human rights conventions.

Suspending or terminating the operation of a treaty may be accomplished either in accordance with the terms of the treaty or by the unanimous consent of the parties. The Vienna Convention, in Article 58, enables parties to a multilateral treaty to suspend the operation of some or all of its provisions as between themselves alone, much in the manner of modification. Termination or suspension may also result by implication when the same contracting parties conclude a new treaty, as prescribed in Article 59.

The most troublesome area in the process of change relates to termination or suspension in the absence of mutual consent. This raises the issues of breach of a treaty (nonperformance of treaty obligations), a fundamental change in circumstances, and impossibility of performance.

A breach of a treaty generates certain legal consequences: A breach not only constitutes an internationally wrongful act that gives rise to state responsibility but also makes it lawful for certain unilateral responses that would otherwise be impermissible. Among such unilateral responses is the option for the aggrieved party to suspend or terminate the treaty. But the breach that gives rise to such an option must meet certain standards of materiality and cannot be trivial. The Vienna Convention distinguishes a material breach from all other breaches. Article 60(3) defines "a material breach of a treaty" in terms of either "a repudiation of the treaty not sanctioned by the present Convention" or "the violation of a provision essential to the accomplishment of the object or purpose of the treaty." To ascertain what constitutes a material breach is not an easy task, as was exemplified by the U.S.-USSR exchange of charges of noncompliance with the Treaty on the Limitation of Anti-Ballistic Missile Systems of 1972, popularly known as the ABM treaty. It would require not a mechanism of automation but a contextual scrutiny by reference to relevant features involved in the processes of commitment and performance.

When a material breach occurs in a bilateral treaty, the aggrieved party has the option of "terminating the treaty or suspending its operation in whole or in part." When a material breach occurs in a multilateral treaty, action may be taken by individual states or by all parties in concert. If the former method is employed, the party may repudiate its obligations under the treaty only as to the breaching party and must not jeopardize the interests of other, nonbreaching parties.

Customary international law allows a party to a treaty to unilaterally repudiate its obligations under the treaty when there is a fundamental change in circumstances. This is the controversial doctrine of *rebus sic stantibus*, involving a basic incongruence between the original expectations of the parties and the changed conditions. It exemplifies the tension between the policy for stability of expectations and the policy for responsive change. The Vienna Convention, in Article 62, affirms this customary doctrine but places rigorous restrictions on invoking it as "a ground for terminating or withdrawing from the treaty." The changed circumstance involved must be "fundamental," one that relates to circumstances "existing at the time of the conclusion of a treaty" and "was not foreseen by the parties." In addition, "the existence of those circumstances" must have "constituted an essential basis of the consent of the parties to be bound by the treaty," the "effect of the change" must be "radically to transform the extent of obligations still to be performed under the treaty," and the change must not be "the result of a breach by the party invoking it either of an obligation under the treaty or of any other international obligation owed to any other party to the treaty." Article 62 further stipulates that the doctrine of changed circumstances is inapplicable to boundary treaties. Incidentally, the grounds that enable a state party to withdraw from a treaty or terminate it can be invoked for the purpose of suspension.

Rebus sic stantibus is to be distinguished from a closely related doctrine of "supervening impossibility of performance." The former applies to circumstances that existed when a treaty came into force, whereas the latter comes into play as a result of the temporary or permanent "disappearance or destruction of an object indispensable for the execution of the treaty" (Article 61). Examples of the latter would include situations in which the submergence of an island or the drying-up of a river makes it impossible to perform the treaty. Article 61 of the Vienna Convention makes impossibility of performance a ground for termination or suspension (in the case of temporary impossibility). The article is expressly limited to loss of an "object" necessary for performance, and such situations as the severance of diplomatic relations may not be invoked as a case of impossibility of performance. (Article 63 separately deals with the consequences of severing diplomatic relations.)

A party invoking any of the foregoing grounds for "terminating a treaty, withdrawing from it, or suspending its operation" is required under Articles 65–67 to give notice of its claim and reasons to the other parties and to comply with other procedural requirements set forth in these provisions. The outcome of withdrawal, termination, or suspension will not be automatic but is contingent on compliance with the procedural requirements.

Finally, note that a treaty is deemed terminated as the result of the emergence, after the entry into force of the treaty, of a new and contradictory peremptory norm (*jus cogens*) of international law. Such a situation will have no retroactive effect.

The Relation between International Agreements and U.S. Constitutional Law

In a world of global communications, an increasingly interdependent economy, transboundary environmental impacts, and modern weapons and techniques of war, people from opposite sides of the globe have a real and dramatic effect on each other. Decisions made locally can have inclusive effects, with impacts reaching the national, regional, and international levels. Consequently, just as decision processes within the United States have effects on the international community, decision processes in other nations and in international organizations impact and affect conditions, and ultimately the law, in the United States.

The dynamics of this interpenetrating process of decision mean that, at times, there will be conflicts between national and international law. When such conflicts arise, it is imperative that international law should prevail. The supremacy of international law is essential to the maintenance of world order and ensures that the inclusive policies of the world community are put into effective practice. The conflict has become more pronounced in modern history due to an expanding notion of foreign affairs in general. As the international community becomes increasingly interdependent in economic, social, environmental, human rights, and other areas, the line between international and domestic affairs has blurred. On one hand, aspects of governance that were traditionally considered domestic in nature now have international ramifications. On the other hand, regional and global efforts are often required to solve domestic problems, such as in the areas of trade and economy.

The constitutional process of the United States operates in the context of a world community of ever-growing interdependence. The supremacy of international law is generally recognized within the constitutional system of the United States. The U.S. Constitution itself provides that treaties are the supreme law of the land.[9] Through practice and judicial interpretation, other types of international agreements have been held to have the same status as treaties. International customary law, although not supreme law in the sense of treaties and other international agreements, is considered to be part of the federal common law, applicable by both state and federal judges. Through each of these modalities, the inclusive policies and world order goals of the international community become effective law in the United States, binding on the nation itself as a member of the community of nations, and sometimes upon individuals within the United States.

The Supremacy Clause of the U.S. Constitution provides: "This Constitution, and the Laws of the United States... and all Treaties made..., under the Authority of the

United States, shall be the supreme Law of the Land," and the states are bound to observe that law.[10] Based on the exclusive authority of the federal government in the foreign affairs area, the courts have held that not only treaties but other international agreements and customary law are also part of the supreme law of the United States and are therefore binding on the states.

Nothing in the U.S. Constitution expressly provides for the exclusive federal foreign affairs power. Nevertheless, it is generally accepted that the foreign affairs powers are exclusively federal, either expressly, as in the treaty power, or inherently, as in the power to declare war. States generally lack competence to act in the arena of foreign relations. While the foreign affairs power is not expressly granted in the Constitution, various aspects of this power are. For example, the Constitution provides that Congress shall have the power to regulate commerce with foreign nations, to establish uniform rules of naturalization, to define and punish offenses against the law of nations, and to declare war.

In the U.S. constitutional system of government, the president serves as both the head of state and the head of government. The president is generally considered to have the paramount power to represent the United States in relations with other nations. The Constitution expressly empowers the president "by and with the Advise and Consent of the Senate, to make treaties provided two thirds of the Senators present concur."[11] While the Constitution on its face authorizes only the president to enter into treaties with foreign nations, three different modalities of agreement making are supported by practice and affirmed by the courts: treaties, congressional-executive agreements, and sole executive agreements. In addition, the president, as the sole representative of the United States in foreign affairs, has a role in the progressive development of customary international law.

As the sole representative of the United States in foreign affairs, and through the exercise of the treaty power, the president appoints and supervises the individuals who negotiate agreements with a foreign power. The president then transmits the concluded treaty to the Senate for approval. If the Senate approves the treaty by a two-thirds vote, the president then ratifies it, and the treaty becomes binding on the United States. The constitutional consequences of concluding treaties through the Article II process are numerous: The Constitution expressly provides that treaties concluded in this manner are the supreme law of the land, binding not only on the federal government but on the states as well. In addition, the judicial branch of the federal government has the express power to review cases and controversies that arise under treaties so concluded, and Congress can implement and enforce treaty obligations through the passage of "necessary and proper" domestic legislation.

Under separation of powers principles, Congress is normally the sole legislative organ, with the president's role limited to recommending legislation, and signing or vetoing laws passed by Congress. Regarding international relations, however, the Constitution gives the president primary lawmaking authority. The president was provided with this primary authority for a variety of reasons. First, political theory and the example of British constitutional practice at the time of the Constitution's drafting suggested that the power to bind the nation as a whole normally rested in the chief executive power, such as the British crown. Moreover, problems under the Articles of Confederation, where Congress had the sole responsibility for negotiating and ratifying treaties, and the need for "secrecy and dispatch" in diplomatic activities demonstrated the need for creating an executive agent vested with the treaty-making power.

Congress has both an express and implied role in the making of international agreements. The degree and modality of congressional participation in international lawmaking depends on what type of agreement is being considered: a treaty, a congressional-executive agreement, or a sole executive agreement. The Constitution gives the Senate an express role in the treaty adoption process. It specifically provides that the president makes a treaty by ratifying or acceding to it only after the two-thirds of the Senate gives its consent. While Senate consent is required before the president can ratify a treaty, the president is under no obligation to ratify once the Senate has given its consent. In addition, the president retains complete discretion over the decision to "make" treaties.

The Senate cannot amend or make reservations to a treaty negotiated by the president. It can, however, condition its consent on modifications or reservations, or on a certain interpretation of the treaty's meaning. The president can ignore such conditions, but cannot proceed to ratify the treaty until such conditions are met. The Constitution does provide that the president may make treaties with the "advice and consent" of the Senate. It has been acknowledged, however, that Senate "advice," as distinguished from its "consent," is not a necessary component of treaty negotiation. At the time the Constitution was drafted, the drafters probably envisioned a Senate role whereby the Senate, which at that time would only be twenty-six Senators, would serve as a type of advisory council, consulting with the president as a treaty was negotiated. No president ever used the Senate in this role, and the Senate since acquiesced, particularly when the number of senators began to grow as the nation expanded.

Congressional-executive agreements may be struck by Congress or the president. Congress may authorize the president in advance to make an agreement, or the president may seek approval from the House of Representatives and the Senate for an agreement already made. In the latter case, the Senate does not have to adopt the agreement by a two-thirds majority, as it must when consenting to a treaty. However, the agreement must receive majority support in both houses of Congress. Sole executive agreements, based on the president's plenary foreign affairs powers, by their nature do not need congressional authorization before they become binding, and therefore there is theoretically no congressional role.

This allocation of authority is not without controversy. Questions of whether the president can make an agreement inconsistent with an act of Congress, or whether Congress can adopt legislation regulating sole executive agreements have not been authoritatively settled. This ambiguity has given rise to fears of an "imperial presidency" in which the executive wields undue influence in the shaping and adoption of foreign policy and international law. As a result, Congress has required the executive branch to report periodically on its activities so that lawmakers can stay abreast of the president's activities in the international arena. However, in practice, executive agreements are adopted much more frequently than treaties and are comparable as to their internal and external effects. As a report to the Senate Foreign Relations Committee noted: "By virtue of actual practice and judicial edification... it is now well-settled that the treaty mode is not an exclusive means of agreement-making for the United States and that executive agreements may validly co-exist with treaties under the Constitution."[12]

While the U.S. Constitution vests the bulk of foreign affairs powers in the executive and legislative branches of the federal government, it also provides for a significant and important role for the judicial branch. The constitutional grant of jurisdiction to the federal courts includes the power over cases arising under treaties, cases affecting ambassadors, cases to which the United States is a party, and cases between U.S. citizens and foreign states. These provisions have served as the basis for the Supreme Court's exercise of jurisdiction over cases involving foreign nations, suits by U.S. citizens against foreign nationals and diplomats, and cases involving the interpretation and application of treaty provisions. In addition, the Court's power to review cases arising under the laws of the United States provides a basis for reviewing domestic legislation implementing treaty obligations.

The treaty-making power is the only method of concluding international agreements expressly recognized under the U.S. Constitution. Because the treaty-making power is an inherent aspect of nationhood and sovereignty, the subject of a treaty may properly include any aspect of that sovereign power, subject only to constitutional limitations. The Constitution itself does not limit the subject of treaties to "matters of international concern," and assertions to this effect have long been rejected.

International agreements duly concluded by the federal government are capable of application in U.S. courts and can be the source of individual rights and remedies in individual cases. The Supremacy Clause of the Constitution provides that treaties are the supreme law of the land. In theory, treaties negotiated by the president, consented to by two-thirds of the Senate, and subsequently ratified by the president are equivalent to other federal laws and are capable of direct application by federal and state courts without any further congressional action. The Supreme Court has determined, however, that neither all treaties, nor all treaty provisions, automatically have legally binding authority. The Court makes a distinction between self-executing treaties and treaty provisions, which are automatically capable of application in the courts, and non-self-executing treaties and treaty provisions, which require an additional act of Congress before they can be enforced in the courts.

U.S. courts have held a variety of international agreements to be self-executing. The most common self-executing treaties include treaties of friendship, commerce, and navigation, and agreements conferring rights on foreign nationals, such as treaties protecting foreign creditors from cancellations of their debts, treaties ensuring inheritance rights, and extradition treaties. In contrast, some international agreements in the human rights area have been held to be non-self-executing. The U.S. Court of Appeals for the Seventh Circuit, for example, held that the human rights provisions of the Helsinki Accords are not self-executing because the provisions of the treaty "contemplate further action by the participating states" to carry them out.[13] Similarly, the 1967 U.N. Protocol Relating to the Status of Refugees is considered non-self-executing. The human rights provisions of the U.N. Charter have also been declared non-self-executing, although the charter provisions requiring compliance with U.N. Security Council resolutions have been held to be self-executing.

With the proliferation of intergovernmental organizations (IGOs) throughout the twentieth century, another layer of complexity has been added to the vertical allocation of powers between the federal and state governments. Intergovernmental organizations—whether global, as in the case of the United Nations; regional, as in the case of the Organization of American States; or issue-specific, as in the case of the General Agreement on Tariffs and Trade (GATT)—often include intergovernmental decision-making bodies and third-party dispute resolution mechanisms that, at least theoretically, have power to set policy, resolve disputes, and establish law for their members. The existence of IGOs raises a variety of questions under U.S. constitutional law: To what extent do decisions of IGO decision-making bodies create binding obligations within the United States? Does participation in IGOs alter the basic outline of shared powers within each level of government or between the federal and state levels?

In general, whether a resolution by a decision-making body of an IGO imposes binding obligations on the United States depends on the authority conferred upon such organizations in the constitutive agreements that create them. For example, the International Monetary Fund (IMF) may prescribe rules regarding exchange rates and currency depreciation. The International Civil Aviation Organization may set binding standards applicable to the civil aviation industry. The U.N. Security Council may authorize the use of force to maintain international peace and security.

Thus far, however, there is no IGO to which the United States has ceded sufficient sovereignty paralleling the arrangement between the states and the federal government in the U.S. Constitution, and there is no international "Supremacy Clause" that would make an IGO's resolution the "law of the land" in the United States in the same sense that federal law may supersede the laws of the states. As a result, the international obligations of the United States are subject to normal constitutional processes before they become binding.

Organically, the U.S. Constitution recognizes three branches of government as the decision-making organs of the federal government. In reality, individuals are involved in all seven decision functions that characterize the process of authoritative decision making in the foreign affairs arena: intelligence, promoting, prescribing, invoking, applying, terminating, and appraising. The most direct impact a citizen has on U.S. foreign policy is through the electoral process. Individuals, working individually, in political parties, and through nongovernmental organizations (NGOs) devoted to specific issues areas, work to get candidates on the ballot, support their campaigns with time and money, and ultimately go to the polls to vote. Exercising the right to vote, citizens have the most direct influence on who their senators, representatives, presidents, and vice presidents will be, and hence, what kinds of international policies will be pursued by the government.

But citizen input into U.S. foreign policy is not limited only to elections. Another significant modality for influencing U.S. foreign policy is through the power of public opinion. Elected representatives, even if not immediately facing an upcoming election, are nevertheless sensitive to the demands and expectations of the general citizenry. Publicity and public pressure on any given issue will influence the decision makers responsible for developing and implementing U.S. foreign policy. The experience during the Vietnam War provides a classic example of this process: growing discontent and protest over the conduct of what became an unpopular war was one of the factors that eventually forced the government to withdraw from the conflict. The general lesson of the war was that when the government in a democracy loses the support of the people, it will be very difficult to conduct successful foreign policy. Indeed, similar forces are at play today in respect to U.S. engagements in Iraq, Afghanistan, and other regions throughout the world.

Notes

1. Duncan McNair, *The Functions and Differing Legal Character of Treaties*, 11 BRIT. Y.B. INT'L L. 100 (1930); *see also* MYERS S. MCDOUGAL & W. MICHAEL REISMAN, INTERNATIONAL LAW IN CONTEMPORARY PERSPECTIVE 1119–20 (1981).

2. Richard D. Kearney & Robert E. Dalton, *The Treaty of Treaties*, 64 A.J.I.L. 495 (1970).

3. Reservations to the Convention on the Prevention and Punishment of the Crime of Genocide, Advisory Opinion, 1951 I.C.J. 15 (May 28).

4. *Id.* at 29.

5. *See* LUNG-FONG CHEN, STATE SUCCESSION RELATING TO UNEQUAL TREATIES (1974).

6. MYERS S. MCDOUGAL, HAROLD D. LASSWELL, & JAMES C. MILLER, THE INTERPRETATION OF AGREEMENTS AND WORLD PUBLIC ORDER: PRINCIPLES OF CONTENT AND PROCEDURE (1967).

7. *Id.* at 39–45.

8. *Id.* at 48.

9. U.S. CONST. art. VI, § 2.

10. *Id.*

11. U.S. CONST. art. II, § 2, cl. 2.

12. CONGRESSIONAL RESEARCH SERVICE, TREATIES AND OTHER INTERNATIONAL AGREEMENTS: THE ROLE OF THE UNITED STATES SENATE: A STUDY PREPARED FOR THE COMMITTEE ON FOREIGN RELATIONS UNITED STATES SENATE 77 (2001).

13. Frolova v. Union of Soviet Socialist Republics, 761 F.2d 370, 376 (7th Cir. 1985).

17 The Ideological Instrument

THE IDEOLOGICAL INSTRUMENT, unlike the elite-to-elite communication of the diplomatic instrument, is directly communicated to a wide audience. Concerned with reaching a wide audience, it possesses tremendous potential to mobilize world public opinion to protect the common interest of all humankind. It involves the mobilization both of enlightenment and of transnational identifications and loyalties as bases of power.

Constructive Use

The potential to manage world public opinion in the enhanced protection of common interests, though yet to be realized, has started to find expression, as vividly illustrated by the movement toward "nuclear freeze" and effective arms control, and the increasing demands for democracy around the world.

The potential to communicate instantaneously around the globe to mass audiences beyond elite groups promises both to generate increased participation in the global constitutive process and to affect many policy functions, especially promoting, prescribing, and applying. The ideological instrument is particularly important to international governmental organizations in performing their functions. Because of limited resources, international governmental organizations have tended to stress the use of symbols to publicize and focus world attention on matters of common concern and to enlighten and stimulate members of the public as vanguards in protection. It is the ideological instrument, stressing contemporary communication technology and skills that enable these organizations to use bases of power that would otherwise be unavailable to them. As the late Secretary-General of the United Nations U Thant put it, "a purposeful and universal programme of public information is, in fact, a programme of implementation—an essential counterpart of the substantive activities of the Organization."[1]

The major weapon the United Nations relied on to combat apartheid in South Africa, for example, was sustained use of the ideological instrument. A protracted world war of publicity was waged to enlighten public opinion on the evils of apartheid and to overcome the vehement resistance of the South African government. The achievements in consciousness-raising against apartheid cannot be overemphasized. The use of publicity has been extended from the antiapartheid crusade to other human rights matters. With its global constituency, the United Nations has employed a strategy of selective attention through publicity by commemorating a particular day, year, or decade to bring awareness to a particular matter of vital shared concern such as Human Rights Day (December 10 of each year, in commemoration of the adoption of the Universal Declaration of Human Rights); International Day for the Elimination of Racial Discrimination (March 21 of each year, the anniversary of the Sharpeville incident in South Africa); International Year of the Child (1979); the United Nations Decade for Women: Equality, Development, and Peace (1975–85); the United Nations Decade of the World's Indigenous Peoples (1994–2003); the United Nations Decade for Human Rights Education (1995–2004); and the United Nations Decade for the Eradication of Poverty (1997–2006).

Private groups and individuals are able, through the availability of the ideological instrument, to mobilize a wide range of effective participants in both the private and public sectors to awaken, educate, engage, and even enrage public opinion. In the race to win the hearts and minds of the world's population, private groups and individuals are formidable, despite limited resources and government regulations. The nongovernmental sector can offer more inclusive identifications to humanity and is less inhibited by such parochial notions as sovereignty and domestic jurisdiction. It is freer to tell the truth as it is. With appropriate skill, the ideological instrument can be mobilized to reach a worldwide audience and to build a global constituency in support of both minimum world order and optimum world order.

Rhetoric is far from cheap. Increased rhetoric in articulation and support of the common interest can help to generate, cultivate, sustain, and fortify the expectations of the peoples around the globe in the direction of a world order of human dignity.

Coercive Use

Although the ideological instrument is commonly identified with its constructive use for enlightenment, it may also be put to coercive use. This is nothing new; it has been used sporadically on a small scale since time immemorial. It was not recognized as an influential instrument and largely ignored, however, until about the time of the French Revolution. World War I was the first total war in human history, not only because of its mobilization of industrial and human resources but also in the systematic use of the ideological instrument, the "propaganda warfare." People came to realize that total war could be won only by attacking people's minds as well as their bodies, and the ideological instrument was resorted to on a larger scale.

All the techniques of the ideological instrument used in World War I were repeated in World War II, but their effectiveness was greatly enhanced by vaster and more efficient governmental machinery and the spectacular development of radio broadcasting.

Since World War II, the use of the ideological instrument has been greatly amplified and systematically organized. The Cold War era was one of great tension. With little or no apparent restraint, charges of coercive use of the ideological instrument were made almost daily, becoming routine. Even after the end of the Cold War, the ideological instrument continues to be used as a means of coercion, employed singly or in combination with the military, economic, or diplomatic instruments—take, for example, the use of terrorist tactics engaged in by governments or others as part of an effort "to send a message."

Certain types of coercive use of the ideological instrument have caused particular concern, including: (1) communications designed to deprive respect (libelous communications against heads of state or other government officials and race-mongering propaganda); (2) communications likely to cause significant deprivations of power (such as those calculated to foment civil strife, popularly known as subversive propaganda); and (3) communications calculated to incite major coercion (war-mongering propaganda, incitement of war). Charges are generally matched by countercharges.

A significant example is the Radio Marti incident. When the United States inaugurated its official Radio Marti broadcast to Cuba on May 20, 1985, the Cuban government immediately condemned the new broadcasting service as "an aggressive act" against Cuba and an insult in usurping the name of a Cuban independence hero, Jose Marti. Cuba responded sharply by taking retaliatory measures, including suspending implementation of a major immigration agreement with the United States, which contemplated the return to Cuba of 2,746 "undesirable" Cubans languishing in U.S. prisons and mental health facilities and the release of 3,000 political prisoners by Cuba, and the admission of up to 20,000 Cuban immigrants to the United States annually; and imposing a ban on visits to Cuba by Cubans living in the United States.[2]

Radio Free Asia (RFA) offers another example. Radio Free Asia, which began broadcasting on March 12, 1996, is a private, nonprofit corporation that broadcasts news to listeners in China and other Asian countries where full and accurate news reports are unavailable. RFA broadcasts in nine different Asian languages. The content of RFA's news reports focus on events affecting the country to which it broadcasts. In 2004, RFA extended its influence via the Internet, launching websites in nine Asian languages.

To facilitate the operation of RFA, the U.S. Congress adopted the International Broadcasting Act in 1994.[3] The act established the Broadcasting Board of Governors (BBG), an independent federal agency whose mission is to promote freedom and democracy through the communication of accurate news and information about America and the world to audiences overseas. The BBG serves as RFA's board of directors, authorizing annual grants for the purpose of carrying out radio broadcasting to China, Burma, Cambodia, Laos, North Korea, Tibet, and Vietnam.

In the East, however, RFA has not been widely accepted. The countries targeted by RFA broadcasts view the whole operation as a propagandistic tool used by the West to interfere in their internal affairs and create confusion through the news media. China in particular has openly objected to RFA, accusing the United States of trampling upon diplomatic norms. Since 1996, the Chinese government has jammed RFA broadcasting signals and blocked Internet websites. In response, RFA created websites with instructions on how to create anti-jamming antennas as a way to cut down on interference.

Despite efforts to promote the free flow of information from countries abroad, tough new regulations aimed at monitoring Internet usage have been implemented in some nations, including China. For example, Internet cafes in China are tightly controlled and routinely monitored by officials. In 2010, China released the White Paper, the first ever government policy paper on Internet usage. The White Paper emphasizes the importance of the "safe" flow of information online and forbids any content that "endangers state security," "divulges state secrets," or "subverts state power."[4] The new government regulations have already affected Internet users in China. China's powerful Internet filter, "The Great Firewall," now blocks searches about forbidden topics, including Radio Free Asia.

It appears that without greater pressure from external sources, countries like China will continue to undermine the objectives set forth in Article 19 of the Universal Declaration of Human Rights, limiting the potential for humans to move forward into a new Information Age based on the free and open flow of information and communication.

The central issue raised is: To what extent does international law regulate the use of the ideological instrument? In other words, when is the use of the ideological instrument impermissible? How to draw the line between impermissible propaganda as a means of coercion and permissible use of the ideological instrument as a means of persuasion?

Basic Community Policy

At the heart of these issues is the paramount policy that would promote the free flow of information across state lines to foster enlightenment, to facilitate transnational interaction by persuasion. The complementary policy is to ensure that activities designed to secure enlightenment through the free flow of information would not unduly disrupt minimum public order and destroy other states' values, especially security, power, and respect.

Simply put, the basic community policy is to encourage enlightenment and persuasion and to discourage regimentation and coercion. But the line between permissible and impermissible use of the ideological instrument is extremely delicate to draw.

Trends in Decision and Conditioning Factors

The world community long tolerated any use of ideological strategy (propaganda) at a time when major use of coercion and violence was permitted in interstate relations. With the rise of radio and its massive use and impact, as dramatized during World War I, transnational propaganda through radio became a topic of concern and regulation.

The problem of radio broadcasting first came before the League of Nations in 1926, and in 1936 the Convention Concerning the Use of Broadcasting in the Cause of Peace was enacted. The contracting states undertook, under Article 1 of the convention, to prohibit radio broadcasting within their territories of any transmission calculated to disturb international understanding or to "incite the population of any territory to acts incompatible with the internal order or the security" of a contracting party. It may be noted that this proscription covers precisely the activities in which the major contending powers in the Cold War engaged after the end of World War II. The convention further forbade the use of false or distorted statements or news and required the contracting states to provide correct information and news over their broadcasting stations. The convention, still in force today, is regarded as applicable to television broadcast.

The Nuremberg trials represented an important development in this area. A major charge of the indictment that led to the trials was that the defendants had committed "crimes against peace" by "the planning, preparation, initiation and waging of wars of aggression."[5] Preparation included psychological and educational dimensions. The indictment referred specifically to the participation or promotion of the "educational" and "psychological preparations of war"—acts calculated to reshape the German educational system and cultural activities and to disseminate the Nazi ideology to secure citizens' support of an overall aggressive plan.[6]

In the United Nations' efforts to define aggression through the International Law Commission and the Special Committee on the Question of Defining Aggression, suggestions were made that "ideological aggression," in the sense of war propaganda, subversive propaganda against another state, or incitement of civil strife by propaganda, be included in the concept of aggression.[7] Though the proposals were rejected as vague and unworkable, they reflected contemporary apprehension about the coercive use of the ideological instrument. Article 20 of the International Covenant on Civil and Political Rights, moreover, prohibits any "propaganda for war" and any "advocacy of national, racial or religious hatred that constitutes incitement to discrimination, hostility or violence."

In this connection, the International Convention on the Elimination of All Forms of Racial Discrimination (1965) has given rise to a comparable controversy concerning race-mongering propaganda. Article 4 of the convention condemns "all propaganda and all organizations" preaching the "superiority" of one race and promoting "racial hatred and discrimination" and seeks the elimination of "all incitement to, or acts of," racial discrimination. Toward this end, the article mandates state parties to "declare an offence punishable by law all dissemination of ideas based on racial superiority or hatred, incitement to racial discrimination, as well as all acts of violence or incitement to such acts against any race or group of persons of another color or ethnic origin, and also the provision of any assistance to racist activities, including the financing thereof," and, further, to "declare illegal and prohibit organizations, and also organized and all other propaganda activities, which promote and incite racial discrimination, and [to] recognize participation in such organizations or activities as an offence punishable by law." Although Article 4 also states that "due regard" be given to "the principles embodied in the Universal Declaration of Human Rights and the rights expressly set forth in article 5 of this Convention"—ostensibly with special reference to the rights of "freedom of opinion and expression" and "freedom of peaceful assembly and asso-ciation"—it has not allayed a shared sense of anxiety about its far-reaching ramifica-tions. In the United States, for example, this article is widely regarded as incompatible with the First Amendment freedom of expression and association protected by the U.S. Constitution.

Similarly, in 2010, the Review Conference of the Rome Statute met in Kampala, Uganda, and adopted a resolution that amended the statute to include the crime of aggression as defined by General Assembly Resolution 3314 (1974) and the con-ditions under which the International Criminal Court could exercise jurisdiction with respect to the crime. The actual exercise of jurisdiction is conditioned upon the ratification of the amendment by at least two-thirds of the state parties after January 1, 2017.

The conference defined the individual "crime of aggression" as the planning, prepa-ration, initiation, or execution by a person in a leadership position of an act of aggres-sion against another state. Moreover, it includes the threshold requirement that the act of aggression must amount to a violation of the Charter of the United Nations, which would include acts taken without the justification of self-defense or authori-zation by the Security Council. Both definitions are based on language set forth in General Assembly Resolution 3314. Examples of aggression include invading or bomb-ing another state, blockading ports, using mercenaries against another state, or pro-viding support to a third-party that commits acts of aggression against another state. The conference's use of terms referred to in the Nuremberg trials, such as "planning, preparation, and initiation" reflected its ongoing concern about the coercive use of the ideological instrument.

The Drive toward a New World Information and Communication Order

For centuries proponents of freedom of information and proponents of rigid state control have struggled to control the ideological instrument. Recently this struggle has been accentuated on a global scale by the intense demands for and debates concerning a new world information and communication order.

Human history has been accelerated by communication technology. From sole reliance on oral communication to the invention of writing and printing, from movable type to a penny press, from the visual dimension of camera and film through the audio dimension of radio and telephone to the complete audiovisual mass communication symbolized by television and new computer and mobile networks, humankind is entering a new epoch of information-rich civilization.

Modern technology has enabled almost instantaneous transmission of messages around the globe; it has overcome the natural barriers of time and space. Recent developments, such as broadcasting satellites, computers, data processing, and telephonetics, have had a revolutionary impact on the concept of communication and on the breadth of the flow of information. The rapid development and merger of computer and telecommunications technology have led to what has come to be known as the "information society," a society in which information is a predominant factor in economic, social, political, and other important sectors of life. The size and pace of information flow are staggering. The contributions, both existing and potential, that modern communications can make to enhance people's perceptions of the intimate interdependencies of humanity and the world community are enormous. Modern communications have the tremendous potential to bind the peoples of the world and make a global village a reality. The Internet has afforded many people access to information that they normally would not have. For example, many nongovernmental organizations advocating the rights of indigenous and oppressed peoples have helped to bring greater awareness to the international community of the claims of these peoples throughout the world, in particular, their claims for self-determination. The Internet and mobile phones were instrumental in organizing and publicizing the events of the Arab Spring and helping to build worldwide public support for demonstrators by providing an outlet for unfiltered information about events directly to a worldwide audience.

Although electronic communications and information technologies have created and promised tremendous benefits, they also raise increasingly complex questions. Advances in communications and information technologies and services open up new frontiers: outer space, terrestrial, and undersea communications, with the practical global linkage of information flows and the potential for extraterrestrial communications.

As modern technologies overcome the barriers of time and space in communication, the problem of the flow of information across national boundaries grows more pressing.

More barriers to the free flow of information (both transnationally and internally) are being erected by an increasing number of countries. A wide range of governmental measures based on varying degrees of formal or effective power are employed to interfere with the flow of information, operating directly on the content of communication itself, on the reporters of information, or through imposition of undue economic burdens.

Such unilateral national measures of restrictions are increasingly justified in terms of national sovereignty, national security, national interest, cultural heritage, internal order, development need, privacy interest, and so on.

The trend toward assertions of greater national controls over the transfrontier flow of information occurs at a time when nation-states, both developed and developing, are becoming more sensitive and manifesting divergent perspectives about the nature and role of communication and information in the global process of decision and in the nation-building processes. The imbalances in the transnational flow of information (one-way rather than two-way flow) and the great disparities in the distributions of communication technologies and resources are keenly perceived and felt. Moreover, information can be threatening to power elites seeking to maintain their value position in less-than-democratic countries. Hence, in addition to unilateral national measures, some developing nations united in the decade after the Cold War in demanding the establishment of a "new world information and communication order."

Although the precise demands made in the name of the new world information order remained somewhat elusive and uncertain, the thrust of these was propagated with intensity. Notable among this constellation were demands for:

Freedom from distorted communications;
Freedom from external domination and monopoly of the media of communication;
Effective participation in the transnational process of communication;
An aggregate, balanced flow of information;
Access to communication technology and resources;
Special assistance in acquiring and developing communication capacities to over-
  come handicaps;
National control of the flow of information;
Responsible journalism; and
Freedom to initiate and constitute institutions specialized in the gathering, pro-
  cessing, and dissemination of information at all community levels.

In a fundamental sense, the demand for a new world information and communication order involved more than just information and communication and entailed an attempt to modify significantly the functioning of the global constitutive process of authoritative decision and to achieve reallocation of power, wealth, skill, and other values. The demand for a new world information order injected a new dimension in the evaluation of the right to information. The predominant demand for the new order shifted the traditional concern for individual freedom in the gathering, processing, and dissemination of information to the concern of particular states or official elites about the overall flow and content of information across national boundaries. Claims were made in the name not of the individual but of the nation-state as a participant in the global process of communication and decision.

Easing the flow of information across community boundaries in ways to promote the common interest must be a paramount concern of a genuine new world information order. How can communication between people and groups be freed from the fetters that inhibit rational decisions in relation to value processes?

The fundamental policy in defense of the freedom to acquire, use, and communicate information and knowledge has been eloquently projected in both the Universal Declaration of Human Rights and the International Covenant on Civil and Political Rights and in other documents. The Universal Declaration, today widely accepted as part of customary international law, and the civil and political covenant are two key components of the developing global bill of human rights.

The Universal Declaration, in Article 19, provides that "[e]veryone has the right to freedom of opinion and expression; this right includes freedom to hold opinions without interference and to seek, receive and impart information and ideas through any media and regardless of frontiers." This generic right to transnational and domestic freedom of expression is necessarily broad; its formulation is as profound as it is simple. It includes freedom to seek, receive, and impart information and ideas through any media regardless of frontiers. This freedom of information, as prescribed, encompasses all activities relating to the gathering, processing, and dissemination of information. It embraces not only the passive reception of information but also the active role in seeking and disseminating information—it protects activities relevant to the communicator-communicatee relationship. Its concern extends to the process as well as the content of communication. It protects communication activities through any media and extends to both internal and transnational communications. In its broadest reach, the freedom is indeed a functional equivalent of the "right to communicate," as reflected in recent proposals.

Similarly, the International Covenant on Civil and Political Rights, in Article 19(1) and (2), stipulates:

> Everyone shall have the right to hold opinions without interference.
>
> Everyone shall have the right to freedom of expression; this right shall include freedom to seek, receive and impart information and ideas of all kinds, regardless of frontiers, either orally, in writing or in print, in the form of art, or through any other media of his choice.

The addition of "either orally, in writing or in print, in the form of art, or through any other media of his choice" is meant to be all-inclusive, making more explicit what is meant by "through any media" in the Universal Declaration. The third paragraph of Article 19 adds:

> The exercise of the rights provided for in paragraph 2 of this Article carries with it special duties and responsibilities. It may therefore be subject to certain restrictions, but these shall only be such as are provided by law and are necessary:
>   (a) For respect of the rights and reputations of others;
>   (b) For the protection of national security or of public order (*ordre public*), or of public health or morals.

In relation to the Universal Declaration, a comparable general limitation clause is found in Article 29(2):

> In the exercise of his rights and freedoms, everyone shall be subject only to such limitations as are determined by law solely for the purpose of securing due recognition and respect for the rights and freedoms of others and of meeting the just requirements of morality, public order and the general welfare in a democratic society.

These provisions reflect clear recognition that a person's freedoms and rights must be accommodated with the comparable rights and freedoms of others and with the aggregate common interest. The built-in safeguards also suggest that states may not impair the individual's right to full participation in the enlightenment process merely on a pretext or to stay in power, especially in view of the requirement of a "democratic society." Application of these prescriptions to concrete cases requires a disciplined, contextual scrutiny. Comparable provisions can also be found in European and American regional human rights conventions.

Whereas the projection of the fundamental freedom of information, both globally and regionally, has received widespread early support, U.N. efforts to prescribe more detailed content to this fundamental freedom and related measures of implementation have encountered tremendous difficulty.

The General Assembly, at its first session in 1946, characterized freedom of information as "a fundamental human right" and "the touchstone of all the freedoms to which the United Nations is consecrated."[8] Subsequently, the U.N. organs concerned have experienced considerable difficulty in formulating a more detailed content to freedom of information and related measures of implementation. Although the Convention on the International Right of Correction of 1952 entered into force in 1962, the General Assembly has continued to postpone consideration of its agenda item on "Draft Convention on Freedom of Information" from year to year.

The United Nations' failure to give substance to what was once proclaimed "a fundamental human right" and the "touchstone" of all the other rights reflects vividly the changing dynamics of global politics within the United Nations as a result of the massive influx of the newly independent states, the new patterns of bloc politics and voting coalition, and the divergent perspectives representing different cultures, communities, and systems. For many years now the issue of freedom of information has been put on the back burner in the agenda of the General Assembly.

The U.N. Educational, Scientific, and Cultural Organization (UNESCO) emerged in past decades to fill this vacuum as the focal organization of action in the field of transnational information and communication. The constitution of UNESCO, in Article I, mandates the organization to "collaborate in the work of advancing the mutual knowledge and understanding of peoples, through all means of mass communication and to that end recommend such international agreements as may be necessary to promote the free flow of ideas by word and image." As the specialized agency responsible for promoting the free flow of ideas and knowledge through the use of the mass media, UNESCO has undertaken a wide range of activities in the field of communication throughout its history.

UNESCO sought to meet the challenge of the vastly increased volume of international communication and flow of information and to develop the means and structures to gather, process, and disseminate information and knowledge in all countries. Its approach was premised on the idea that a truly free flow of information must be balanced and free.

From emphasizing technical assistance to fostering communication infrastructures in the developing world in the 1950s and 1960s, UNESCO shifted its focus in the 1970s to the content of news and the role of the media in society. Among its notable achievements were the adoption of the Mass Media Declaration of 1978 (Declaration on Fundamental Principles Concerning the Contribution of the Mass Media to Strengthening Peace and International Understanding, the Promotion of Human Rights and to Countering Racialism, Apartheid and Incitement to War),[9] the work of the International Commission for the Study of Communication Problems (the MacBride Commission), and the establishment of a formal International Program for the Development of Communication (IPDC). Thanks to these efforts, the complex problems involved in communication and information have been seriously studied from a comprehensive global context.

Included in this agenda were two matters of special concern to the International Telecommunication Union (ITU) worthy of notice. The first was the global allocation of the radio spectrum. Radio frequencies had historically been allocated on a first-come-first-served basis through the World Administrative Radio Conference (WARC) under ITU sponsorship. This policy naturally favored the developed nations that already possessed substantial communications capacities (it is estimated that at present some 10 percent of the world's population controls 90 percent of the spectrum). This patent disparity and inequity, together with the growing demands for telecommunications services, has made the use of the radio spectrum a highly complex issue—how this limited resource can be equitably shared among different communities and different users in ways that would maximize the potential uses of the spectrum and minimize interference. The developing nations have demanded that the first-come-first-served policy be replaced by a priori planning so that an adequate number of frequencies and orbital slots will be available to them when they achieve advanced communications technologies. But the developed nations have generally maintained that improvements in technology will ease expanded use of the spectrum when the developing nations need it and that the policy of a prior allocation could stifle technological developments.

The second was the use of satellites for direct television broadcasting. Direct broadcast satellites (DBS) have been in use since 1963, when the first trans-Atlantic color television pictures were sent via satellite. Although many benefits can be gained from direct broadcast satellites, particularly in education, many countries fear that their nascent telecommunications industries would be obliterated by these transmissions. And many countries, developed and developing, fear that even greater cultural homogenization would result, with concomitant loss of national identity. Others fear loss of control over political content. The problem related to DBS can be reduced to two issues: whether the state undertaking such broadcasting is required to obtain the prior consent of the receiving states, and whether the receiving state may exercise any control over the signals being transmitted.

In any event, endeavors revolving around the intense demands for a new world information and communication order (NWICO) led to many strong reaffirmations of the crucial importance of the freedom of information in the world community. But they also generated controversies, including the proper role of UNESCO. States in which the free press prevails, in particular, tended to view this demand with skepticism and reservation; for some, a new world information and communication order would be nothing but a code word for state elite control of the press. Indeed, charges of "politicization" and mismanagement culminated in the formal withdrawal of the United States from UNESCO, effective as of January 1, 1985. The United Kingdom took similar steps and withdrew from organization on December 31, 1985. Both countries, however, subsequently rejoined UNESCO; the United Kingdom in 1997, and the United States in 2003 (the United States withdrew funding again in 2011 after UNESCO voted to admit Palestine as a member).

The withdrawal of the United States and the United Kingdom had a damaging impact on UNESCO's budget and the organization in general. The 1989 General Conference marked the end of the NWICO vision. The conference's focus on obtaining new principles for information and communication in the world was replaced by a new communication policy, with its stress on development and practical measures. Thus, the issue of an NWICO became history, an international ideological debate, or an "expression of the spirit of the times."[10]

Toward a Global Information Society in the New Era of Globalization

Beginning in the 1990s and continuing today, the world has entered a new era of globalization. Prompted by rapid advances and diffusion in information and communication technology (ICT), a new global information society has evolved. Today, the Internet and new communication technologies allow people to seek, receive, and impart information and ideas quickly and efficiently like never before. These technological advances have "penetrated deeply into the production process of a wide range of industries and transformed the global economy."[11] Inventions such as mobile phones, on-demand television, and computers have provided people with the capability to communicate at the click of a button. E-mail and social media websites such as Facebook and Twitter have given people new ways to forge connections and share information instantaneously and cheaply. Reactions to this new technological era have made it increasingly necessary for law reformers and policy makers to take account of the effects of technology as it relates to societies' economic, social, and cultural rights in conjunction with their civil and political rights.[12] This new information society reflects the ability of technology to level the field for all humanity so that the world may work together in the shaping and sharing of human values.

However, not everyone has the means or ability to participate in this digital revolution. Many communities, particularly those found in developing countries, lack the basic infrastructure, education, and resources to benefit from these digital opportunities. As a result, the ability to control these technological advancements and their benefits continues to lie in the hands of an elite group of nations. The phrase "digital divide" has become a common term in referring to the worldwide gap between those who have access to the essential tools of the information society and those who do not. Those left on the unfortunate side of this divide miss out on the benefits available in today's society and, as a result, they are left at a disadvantage. For instance, in 2006, over half the world's population lived more than three miles from a telephone line—never mind an Internet connection.[13] Furthermore, the European Commission released a report in early 2006 that found Africa had a continent-wide broadband connection of 0.1 percent, compared with 27.7 percent broadband connection for Europe.[14]

Although there has been an increase in Internet access in many developed countries, the same cannot be said for developing states. As of 2002, developed countries represented more than 80 percent of the world market for information technology. Although developing countries increased their share of mobile phone subscribers to 70 percent by 2007, some countries such as Burundi, Central African Republic, Eritrea, Ethiopia, and Papua New Guinea had fewer than five mobile phone subscribers per one hundred people.[15]

Furthermore, the average price for access to the Internet in Sub-Saharan Africa continues to be well above the world average. According to the World Development Indicators published by the World Bank, in 2006 the Internet tariff for Sub-Saharan Africa was 62 percent of average monthly per capita income.[16] Broadband connectivity (effective rate of data transfer), which lowers cost and raises productivity, continues to increase faster in developed countries than in developing countries. Thus, rural villages in isolated parts of the world remain virtually unconnected even with new advances in communication technology.

Both developed and developing nations must harmonize their interests in an effort to enhance both minimum and optimum world order. The free flow of information and the spread of fundamental freedoms would allow humans to use technology as a tool of empowerment and not deprivation. Article 19 of the Universal Declaration of Human Rights provides: "Everyone has the right to freedom of opinion and expression; this right includes freedom to hold opinions without interference or to seek, receive and impart information and ideas through any media regardless of frontiers."[17] Thus, the key goal for bridging the digital divide should be "not to eradicate absolute equalities of access to all information via all networks at all time, but to ensure that each person has meaningful access to the Internet and new communications technologies,"[18] such that they may seek, receive, and impart information and ideas regardless of frontiers.

Equal opportunity and participation in the information society benefits all people on all levels. By bridging the digital divide, common interests such as education, wealth, empowerment, and freedom can be spread and shared by all. The flow of information in both directions would allow all nations to make more informed decisions as well as publicize human rights' violations on an international stage. Also, the free flow of information would help countries acquire the concept of "soft power," or the ability for countries to accomplish goals through persuasion rather than coercion.

In an effort to overcome digital inequality, the United Nations established the World Summit on the Information Society (WSIS).[19] WSIS was held in two phases. The first phase was hosted by the Swiss government in Geneva in 2003, and the second phase was hosted by the Tunisian government in Tunis in 2005. In conjunction with WSIS, the U.N. General Assembly set forth its Millennium Development Goals to end poverty by 2015. The General Assembly recognized that the free flow of information and equal access to communication technologies plays an important role in overcoming poverty.

The second phase of the WSIS marked the creation of the Tunis Agenda, which took the first step in transforming ideas into action. Focused primarily on Internet governance, the Tunis Agenda requested the U.N. Secretary-General, in an open and inclusive process, to convene, by 2006, a meeting of the new forum for multi-stakeholder policy dialogue—called the Internet Governance Forum (IGF). Paragraph 72 of the Tunis Agenda set out the mandate for the IGF, outlining the objectives of the organization, stating in relevant part:

> Discuss public policy issues related to key elements of Internet governance in order to foster the sustainability, robustness, security, stability and development of the Internet.
>
> Facilitate discourse between bodies dealing with different cross-cutting international public policies regarding the Internet.
>
> Promote and assess, on an ongoing basis, the embodiment of WSIS principles in Internet governance processes.[20]

The first IGF was held in Athens, Greece, in 2006 and has since met three other times, including most recently in Sharm El Sheikh, Egypt, in 2009. However, it is still too early to tell what type of success the IGF will have in bridging the digital divide. Although the IGF has not been outright rejected, many nations, including the United States, India, and China, have half-heartedly accepted these trends of development as mere guidelines. As a result, the effectiveness of the United Nations and the IGF is conditioned upon government participation and stability, geography, education, and affordability.

Looking ahead, the most promising future prospect for bridging the digital divide is the rapid spread of mobile technology. Mobile technology is especially important for developing countries and rural, isolated communities that lack the money and infrastructure to be connected by land-based infrastructure. Mobile technology, used by almost four billion people worldwide, has been successful over the past decade for several reasons. First, the mobile system is easier to use than the traditional Internet system. Since mobile technology can be operated by voice only, it has the ability to overcome language barriers and literacy problems. Mobile phone service had become available to 90 percent of the world's population by 2010, according to ITU. Second, a wireless connection does not require a fixed landline, making it a favorable form of communication for isolated, rural locations. Also, wireless service requires less upfront investment in physical infrastructure, allowing for lower prices and stronger customer demand. Finally, mobile technology presents developing countries with the opportunity to "leapfrog" the technology gap. Wireless connectivity can bring communications to whole communities that previously had little or no access to fixed landlines, allowing them to advance more quickly without building the infrastructure necessary for the earlier technology.[21]

Appraisal

Amid the continuing debate about the shape of order to come in the field of world information and communication, the fundamental community policy of protecting the freedom of information—the freedom to acquire, use, and communicate information and knowledge—must be sustained and fortified. The increasing concern for the interests of particular states must not be at the expense of the classic concern for individual freedom. The individual should remain the cornerstone concern of any communication system.

The way to foster a more efficient and equitable world order of information and communication is not to erode, dilute, or hamper this fundamental policy. The key, rather, is positive facilitation by making pertinent technology, knowledge, and resources available to all and by increasing the capacity for communication at every community level. More channels of communication and more voices is the answer.

Genuine freedom and enlightenment for all human beings will be possible only when necessary conditions are created and maintained to enable them to be effective, active, and equal participants in the communication processes at different community levels and in different social settings. Individuals need not be the mere passive recipients of messages dictated by the top elite but must be able to think and speak for themselves. In the most profound sense, this is the essence of a free and balanced flow of information, an interactive, horizontal pattern of communication. A new order must move toward making the individual a communicating being who can think, choose, and express: think freely, with adequate access to the total stock of human knowledge and information; choose freely and intelligently; and express opinions and ideas freely. This is the essence of the emerging right of communication, with all its emphases on participation and access at every community level.

Wisely applied in a spirit of cooperation for the common interest, the new technologies can generate an unprecedented abundance of communication channels, more diversified message flows, and greater citizen participation in a pluralistic world of globalization and interdependence. Concerted community efforts at positive facilitation, within a framework fostering the free and balanced flow of information, would contribute mightily to the aggregate enlightenment and ultimately toward a world community of human dignity. A genuine new world information and communication order, if established, should be a new order of human dignity in which persuasion prevails over coercion and the wide shaping and sharing of enlightenment and all other values are secured. It should be a world order that contributes to the maintenance of minimum public order, in the sense minimizing unauthorized coercion, and to the achievement of optimum public order, in the sense of the widest possible shaping and sharing of all values.

Notes

1. Introduction to the Annual Report of the Secretary-General on the Work of the Organization, 16 June 1965–15 June 1966, 21 U.N. GAOR, Supp. No. 1A, at 2, U.N. Doc. A/6301/Add.1 (1966).

2. Joseph B. Treaster, *Radio Marti Goes On Air and Cuba Retaliates by Ending Pact*, N.Y. TIMES, May 21, 1985, at A12.

3. 22 U.S.C. 6208.

4. *China Expands Internet Controls*, RADIO FREE ASIA (June 25, 2010), http://www.rfa.org/english/news/china/controls-06252010122203.html.

5. International Military Tribunal (Nuremberg), Judgment and Sentences, Oct. 1, 1946, *reprinted in* 41 A.J.I.L. 172, 174 (1947).

6. *Id.*; UNITED STATES DEPT. OF STATE & ROBERT H. JACKSON, TRIAL OF WAR CRIMINALS 25, 39 (1945); Quincy Wright, *The Crime of War-Mongering*, 42 A.J.I.L. 128, 129–30 (1948).

7. *See* B. S. MURTY, PROPAGANDA AND WORLD PUBLIC ORDER: THE LEGAL REGULATION OF THE IDEOLOGICAL INSTRUMENT OF COERCION 160–65 (1968).

8. G.A. Res. 59 (I), U.N. Doc. A/RES/1/59 (Dec. 14, 1946).

9. U.N.E.S.C., Declaration on Fundamental Principles Concerning the Contribution of the Mass Media to Strengthening Peace and International Understanding, the Promotion of Human Rights and to Countering Racialism, Apartheid and Incitement to War (Nov. 28, 1979), *available at* http://portal.unesco.org/en/ev.php-URL_ID=13176&URL_DO=DO_TOPIC&URL_SECTION=201.html.

10. Ulla Carlsson, *The Rise and Fall of NWICO—and Then?: From a Vision of International Regulation to a Reality of Multilevel Governance* (May 2003), *available at* http://www.bfsf.it/wsis/cosa%20dietro%20al%20nuovo%20ordine.pdf.

11. Mark N. Cooper, *Inequality in the Digital Society: Why the Digital Divide Deserves All the Attention It Gets*, 20 CARDOZO ARTS & ENT. L.J. 73 (2002).

12. Roy Balleste, *The Internet Governance Forum & Technology: A Matter of Human Development*, 7 LOY. L. & TECH. ANN. 37, 39 (2006).

13. *See* Dave Tansley, *Mind the Gap: 2006 Will Witness the Deepening of the Digital Divide*, FIN. TIMES, Feb. 13, 2006, http://www.ft.com/cms/s/0/a4022b12-9c35-11da-8baa-0000779e2340.html.

14. EUR. COMM'N, TOWARDS A GLOBAL PARTNERSHIP IN THE INFORMATION SOCIETY: FOLLOW-UP ON THE TUNIS PHASE OF THE WORLD SUMMIT ON INFORMATION SOCIETY (WSIS) (2006), *available at* http://eur-lex.europa.eu/LexUriServ/LexUriServ.do?uri=COM:2006:0181:FIN:EN:HTML.

15. *See* WORLD BANK, WORLD DEVELOPMENT INDICATORS 2009, at 266 (2009).

16. *Id.*

17. Universal Declaration of Human Rights, G.A. Res. 217 (III), art. 19, U.N. Doc. A/RES/217(III) (Dec. 10, 1948).

18. Peter K. Yu, *Bridging the Digital Divide: Equality in the Information Age*, 20 CARDOZO ARTS & ENT. L.J. 1, 32 (2002).

19. G.A. Res. 56/183, U.N. Doc. A/RES/56/183 (Jan. 31, 2002). The first stage of the WSIS was held in Geneva in 2003 and the second was held in Tunisia in November 2005.

20. WSIS, TUNIS AGENDA FOR THE INFORMATION SOCIETY, at ¶ 72 (Nov. 15, 2005), *available at* http://ec.europa.eu/information_society/activities/internationalrel/docs/wsis/tunis_agenda.pdf.

21. Abdul Paliwala, *Digital Divide: Globalization and Legal Regulation*, 6 U. TECH. SYDNEY L. REV. 24 (2004).

18 The Economic Instrument

THE ECONOMIC INSTRUMENT involves activities and facilities to manage a flow of capital, goods, and services across nation-state lines. Its employment affects not only all phases of wealth processes—production, conservation, distribution, and consumption—but also other value processes. The economic instrument can be used by the general community of states, through a growing network of international governmental organizations, and by individual states to promote aggregate interests. Positively, it can facilitate fulfillment of wealth and other values. Negatively, it can serve as a sanctioning measure against violations of international law. Given the enormous importance of wealth (control of and access to capital, goods, and services) as a base for all other values, the economic instrument is obviously important for multiple purposes.

The positive use of the economic instrument by the general community has greatly expanded, thanks to a global network of organizations consisting of the United Nations, its subsidiary organs and programs, and many specialized agencies. This expanding network of agencies has employed the economic instrument to foster development in its manifold dimensions and to maximize the production and distribution of all important values. The basic goal, as projected in the preamble of the U.N. Charter, is to "promote social progress and better standards of life in larger freedom" and to "employ international machinery for the promotion of the economic and social advancement of all peoples." This growing network encompasses the Economic and Social Council (including its four regional economic commissions and a number of functional commissions), the U.N. Conference on Trade and Development (UNCTAD), the U.N. Development Programme (UNDP), the World Bank Group (the International Bank for Reconstruction and Development, the International Finance Corporation, and the International Development Association), the International Monetary Fund (IMF), and the World Trade Organization (WTO). Together they deal with international investment, monetary policy, human power, health, education, food and agriculture, and transportation and communication of all kinds.

Economic Coercion

Although the economic instrument is commonly used for productive and constructive purposes, it can also be manipulated as a means of coercion. A host of measures ranging from boycott and trade embargo to freezing of assets and withholding of economic aid can generate coercive effect in varying circumstances.

The Arab boycott of pro-Israeli enterprises and the oil embargo of 1973–74 in particular dramatized the impact of economic coercion and generated a continuing debate about the lawfulness of economic coercion under contemporary international law. Most recently the debate has continued over embargoes against Iran, Cuba, and North Korea and the impact of such sanctions on ordinary citizens in those countries as opposed to elites.

When military force was a permissible form of value change, economic coercion naturally did not receive serious attention. Today, with the U.N. Charter ban of the threat or use of force and the ostensibly disruptive impact of economic coercion under an interdependent world economy, the lawfulness of economic coercion has become a matter of continuing debate. The debate has centered on the interpretation of Article 2(4) of the charter, which stipulates: "All Members shall refrain in their international relations from the threat or use of force against the territorial integrity or political independence of any state, or in any other manner inconsistent with the Purposes of the United Nations." What does "force" mean? Does it refer only to military force? Or does it include nonmilitary coercion (economic, ideological, and diplomatic) as well?

One view takes the position that since coercion generated by economic and other nonmilitary measures may conceivably be more coercive and produce equally or more devastating outcomes than that generated by military force, economic coercion is included in the proscription of Article 2(4). The coercive effect created in a particular context and the consequences of such coercion, not the modality of instrument employed, are said to be determinative.[1] Further, the word "force" in Article 2(4) is not limited by the word "armed," which framers of the charter used in Article 51. The opposing view, which appears to prevail, maintains that the Article 2(4) ban does not extend to economic coercion. Its conclusion is based largely on argument concerning the ordinary meaning attached to the word force and the intent of the framers of the charter.[2]

In the real world, though any instrument can be used singly, it is most often used in various combinations with other instruments of policy. A particular use of a non-military instrument can conceivably be highly coercive under rare circumstances; yet when the military instrument becomes involved, the question of lawfulness of a particular coercion tends to become more serious. To what extent does Article 2(4) forbid the threat or use of military force? This question, controversial as it is, continues to receive a priority consideration in the international law literature (see chapter 19).

Economic Sanctions

Just as the economic instrument can be used to coerce, it can also be used as a means of sanction in response to a prior violation of international law. Economic sanctions may be undertaken unilaterally or collectively and by any effective participants in the world social process. A unilateral undertaking of economic sanctions is more apt to raise the question of its lawfulness, quite apart from its effectiveness.

Unilateral or collective use of the economic instrument as a measure of sanction against violations of international law brings formidable difficulties. The difficulties are accentuated in cases of sanctions taken unilaterally.

Employed as a means of sanction, the economic instrument may isolate the violator state from the flow of outside resources and services, upset its economic influence in third states, and impair its efficient use of internal resources. The most notable economic measures designed to sanction the violator state are commodity and financial controls. Commodity controls seek to regulate or cut off the trade relations of both the sanctioning states and third-party states with the violator state. They may involve imposing an embargo on direct exports from the sanctioning states to the violator state and on direct imports by the sanctioning states from the violator, and preventing re-exportation or transshipment from third states of goods from the sanctioning states to the violator state or vice versa. An embargo on exports, total or selective, is designed to weaken the violator state by denying its access to strategic and other critical supplies; and an embargo on imports (boycott) is calculated to deprive the violator state of the foreign exchange needed to finance its purchases from abroad. Embargoes may be enforced and supplemented by ancillary controls on communications and transportation (land, sea, and air) lines and facilities and by such other measures as blacklisting.

Financial controls may involve halting the flow of capital to the violator state by such measures as the denial or withholding of grants (aid), loans investments, and credits, and the suspension of payments. Other measures include blocking or freezing assets of the violator state and its nationals. Like the import embargo (boycott), the measures of financial control are designed to minimize the violator's purchasing power abroad.

The effectiveness of economic sanctioning strategies depends on many variables relevant to a particular context. Among the important factors are the vulnerability of the violator state to economic sanctions, the costs of such sanctions, capabilities for bearing costs, the extent of coordination, and time factors. The relative vulnerability of the violator state to the impact of economic sanction is affected by the degree of its industrial development and of its dependence on foreign trade. A highly industrialized state that relies heavily on foreign trade for markets or energy and other raw materials, or both, may be particularly vulnerable to embargoes. A state with a larger agrarian sector may not be significantly affected by an embargo on food or raw materials (food especially is likely to affect the masses first and foremost), but its capabilities to maintain internal order by coercion may be greatly weakened by being denied access to arms and strategic materials. Conversely, an arms embargo may be ineffective against a highly industrialized state. The violator state, moreover, may be able to offset the adverse effect of economic sanctions through its network of established or potential trading partners and through a host of remedial measures including stockpiling, substituting, and rationing commodities and reallocating resources.

Note that economic measures of sanction are not without cost to the sanctioning states that employ them. The damage done to the violator state may in measure be matched by a corresponding loss spilled over into the economies of the sanctioning states. The costs may thus become prohibitive to the sanctioning states, unless the burden is widely shared and sanctions are collectively applied. Similarly, the efficacy of economic sanctions imposed for a protracted period against states capable of economic endurance tends to diminish as time passes. Sanctioning states gradually tend to defect unless economic sanctions are well coordinated and effectively applied in conjunction with other strategies.

The upshot is that, because of the continuing domination of the world's wealth by individual nation-states, the general community cannot expect to employ the economic instrument effectively as a sanction against violations of international law without the cooperation of many nation-states. Since any use of the economic instrument is so closely interlocked with the welfare of particular states, it appears extremely difficult to persuade states to undertake and coordinate economic sanctions to defend the common interest. During the tenure of the League of Nations, for example, collective economic sanctions against Italy for its invasion of Ethiopia were less than successful.

Under the regime of the United Nations, the experiences of economic sanctions against Southern Rhodesia and against South Africa are illuminating. In response to the unilateral declaration of independence of Southern Rhodesia by the minority regime of Ian Smith on November 11, 1965, the Security Council, acting under Chapter VII of the U.N. Charter, took the unprecedented action of imposing mandatory, though selective, sanctions against Southern Rhodesia under Resolution 232 of December 16, 1966. The Security Council, in urging "all States to do their utmost to break off economic relations with Southern Rhodesia," mandated that all U.N. members impose import and export embargoes against Southern Rhodesia and refuse financial or other economic aid to the Smith regime.[3] Although the record of compliance was for the most part dismal, the collective sanctions were in part responsible for the ultimate solution leading toward majority rule in the new state of Zimbabwe.

In the case of South Africa's policies and practices of apartheid and its "illegal occupation" of Namibia, both the General Assembly and the Security Council passed numerous resolutions urging U.N. members to undertake, among other things, embargoes on arms and other goods (both export and import) and measures of financial control. A point of particular emphasis was to "dissuade the main trading partners of South Africa and economic and financial interests from collaborating with the Government of South Africa and companies registered in South Africa."[4] For many years, collective action against apartheid remained far from effective. As Michael Reisman sharply observed: "In a world of fragmented and selfish loyalties... one of the sad ironies of the struggle for freedom in Africa has been that a number of African states, vociferous in their condemnation of racism, have slipped under the economic dam which they themselves erected against white minority regimes in southern Africa."[5]

In July 1985, the South African government, faced with heightening racial violence and tension, declared a state of emergency in thirty-six cities and towns, empowering police to impose curfews, make arrests without warrants, and detain people indefinitely. These illegal acts spurred the world community into renewed action. The Security Council in July 1985 urged member states to adopt sanctioning measures against the Republic of South Africa, including suspension of all new investment in South Africa; prohibition of the importation or sale of Krugerrands; restrictions on sports relations; suspension of guaranteed export loans; prohibition of all new contracts in the nuclear field; and a ban on all sales of computer equipment that could be used by the South African army and police.[6]

States with economic ties to South Africa responded, individually and collectively. The European Parliament urged that the European Community sever all economic, financial, cultural, and military ties with South Africa. The member states of the European Community agreed on such measures as a ban on arms trade, a sports boycott, an end to all oil exports, and cessation of exports of sensitive equipment destined for the police and armed forces of South Africa.[7] The Canadian government took a firm stand, undertaking such measures as fortifying the voluntary "Code of Conduct Concerning the Employment Practices of Canadian Companies Operating in South Africa"; abrogating the Canada–South Africa double taxation agreements; banning exports of such sensitive equipment as computers for use by the police and the armed forces; placing an embargo on the importation of arms from South Africa; discontinuing the program designed to assist Canadian exporters with market development in South Africa; placing an embargo on both cargo and passenger air flights to or from South Africa; and recommending a voluntary refusal to buy Krugerrands, a voluntary ban on loans to the government of South Africa and all its agencies, and a voluntary ban on the sale of the crude oil and refined petroleum products to South Africa.[8]

Within the United States, the subject of economic sanctions against South Africa became a topic of serious concern not only for the public sector—federal, state, and local governments—but also for the private sector. Consciousness raising—most notably through arrests courted by peaceful demonstrations in front of the South African Embassy in Washington, D.C. (a forbidden zone) by celebrities and noncelebrities alike—was accompanied by specific measures. Under mounting congressional and popular pressures, President Reagan preempted imminent legislation on economic sanctions by issuing an executive order of limited economic sanctions on September 9, 1985.[9] The order banned all computer exports to agencies involved in enforcing apartheid and to security forces exports of nuclear goods and technology to South Africa, loans to the South African government, and imports of arms from South Africa. The ineffectiveness of these executive measures led Congress to impose, overriding a presidential veto, tougher economic sanctions on South Africa in October 1986. The congressional act prohibited new U.S. investments in South African businesses, banned the importation of such products as steel, coal, uranium, and textiles from South Africa, and canceled South African airlines' landing rights in the United States.[10]

The issue of divestment of stock in corporations doing business in South Africa became a *cause célèbre* around university campuses and for pension funds. Closely related was the effort to secure wide adherence to the "Sullivan principles," named after Reverend Leon Sullivan who served on the board of directors of General Motors, a company that employed many blacks at its plants in South Africa and was integral to the divestment efforts in South Africa. The Sullivan principles were designed to promote racial equality in employment practices for U.S. firms operating in South Africa toward ending apartheid. The Sullivan principles, as initially formulated in 1977 and subsequently amplified, are as follows:

1. Non-segregation of the races in all eating, comfort, and work facilities;
2. Equal and fair employment practices for all employees;
3. Equal pay for all employees doing equal or comparable work for the same period of time;
4. Initiation of and development of training programs that will prepare, in substantial numbers, Blacks and other nonwhites for supervisory, administrative, clerical and technical jobs;
5. Increasing the number of Blacks and other nonwhites in management and supervisory positions; and
6. Improving the quality of employees' lives outside the work environment in such areas as housing, transportation, school, recreation, and health facilities.[11]

Throughout 1985, protest raged and pressures—internal as well as external, private as well as public—mounted as the antiapartheid momentum grew. When U.S. and other foreign banks curbed their lending to South Africa by refusing to extend deadlines for the repayment of debts, the impact was swift and dramatic. Effects included the sharp plunging of South Africa's currency, the temporary closing of the stock and currency markets in South Africa, and a four-month moratorium imposed by the Botha government on repayments of principal on South Africa's debt.

The gathering momentum was slowed when the South African government imposed sweeping news curbs to seal South Africa's black townships from outside scrutiny. Vivid television images of protest and violent suppression that had previously galvanized U.S. opposition to the apartheid regime of South Africa were removed.

Frustrated by the slow pace of reform toward dismantling the apartheid system, Reverend Sullivan, after a decade of crusading with the Sullivan principles as a weapon to end apartheid, adopted a new position in June 1987. He called on all U.S. corporations to withdraw from South Africa within nine months and to end all commercial ties with South Africa. In addition, he urged the United States to impose a total trade embargo on South Africa and to sever diplomatic relations with South Africa. The United Nations stepped up its international campaign, which eventually extended across the globe, increasingly isolating South Africa. The United Nations persisted with embargoes and boycotts of arms, oil, sports, and cultural events, attracting support from virtually every nation, including South Africa's main trading partners. The process was undeniably slow but eventually led to the downfall of apartheid and the democratic election of Nelson Mandela as president of the Republic of South Africa in April 1994.

Thus, the general difficulties with mobilizing effective economic sanctions do not mean that the economic instrument is under all circumstances ineffective as a sanctioning measure against violations of international law. Given a wide range of potential sanctioning states and other entities and the intricate division of labor in the contemporary world, skillful management can exploit selective vulnerabilities. For instance, in the field of human rights, the U.S. Congress has made it the policy of the United States to refuse "security assistance" (both military and economic) to "any country the government of which engages in a consistent pattern of gross violations of internationally recognized human rights."[12] Although a blanket application of this policy may not produce desired results in the short run, its long-term beneficial effect on the protection of human rights cannot be doubted. Comparable observations could be made in regard to attempts by multilateral lending agencies, such as the World Bank, to withhold international loans from states that grossly violate human rights. Freezing Iranian assets in the United States in response to the 1979 Iran hostage crisis was instrumental in achieving a final settlement.

Other attempts at economic sanctions, as initiated by the United States, include the following:

1. In response to the Soviet invasion of Afghanistan, the United States, in January 1980, imposed an embargo on wheat exports ("the grain embargo"), fishing privileges, and export of high-technology equipment to the Soviet Union.

A boycott of the 1980 Summer Olympics in Moscow by the United States and other countries soon followed. Four years later, the Soviet Union and most of its allies retaliated by boycotting the 1984 Summer Olympics in Los Angeles.

2. In May 1985, the United States imposed an embargo on U.S.-Nicaragua trade to punish the Sandinista government for its "aggressive activities" in Central America and for its threat to U.S. national security. Nicaraguan aircraft and ships were also banned from the United States.

3. The United States in January 1986 imposed a ban on importation of Libyan oil and froze all Libyan government assets in the United States and in U.S. bank branches overseas in response to Libya's purported role in support of international terrorism. In 1996, Congress passed the Iran-Libya Sanctions Act, allowing Washington to impose sanctions on foreign companies doing business with Libya.

4. In March 1988, the United States suspended scheduled U.S. payments to Panama and froze the flow of funds to Panamanian banks to hasten the passing of the "illegitimate" regime of General Manuel Antonio Noriega, amid the mounting crisis precipitated by the grand jury indictments in Miami, Florida, of Noriega for his involvement in narcotic trafficking and by his usurpation of power in Panama. The sanctioning measures largely backfired.

5. In 1996, the Helms-Burton Act codified many existing sanctions against Cuba and added new, innovative sanctions against foreign companies doing business with Cuba. Under Title III, foreign companies who "traffic" in property confiscated by the Cuban government from U.S. nationals (who may have been Cuban nationals at the time of the confiscation) are liable for damages of up to three times the value of the property and may have their assets on U.S. soil seized.

6. On August 19, 1997, as a result of Iran's alleged sponsorship of international terrorism and pursuit of weapons of mass destruction (WMD), the United States tightened existing economic sanctions against Iran, confirming that virtually all trade and investment activities with Iran by U.S. persons, wherever located, were prohibited.

7. In 2004, the United States introduced sanctions against Syrian elites concerning that regime's support of terrorist groups and involvement in other activities that threatened stability in the Middle East. U.S. sanctions against Syria intensified in response to violence committed by the Syrian government against its people beginning in 2011.

8. In June 2008, the United States tightened economic sanctions against North Korea out of concern for the threat of terrorism, communism, and the proliferation of weapons of mass destruction. The sanctions, among other things, prohibited goods of North Korean origin from being imported into the United States without prior notification to and approval of the Treasury Department's Office of Foreign Assets Control.

9. In February 2011, the United States joined the other Security Council members in voting 15–0 for a resolution to freeze assets belonging to Libyan leader Muammar Qaddafi and others and to restrict arms sales to the country in an effort to halt a violent crackdown against civilians there.

In these instances, U.S. appeals to its allies for support elicited lukewarm response or mere lip service for many reasons. Those allied countries had their own perceptions of the situations involved and their own calculations of potential gains and losses. The mutual defense responsibilities of alliance members are not always perceived to extend automatically to the peacetime trade of commercial goods. In addition, there has been real concern as to how far certain states can jointly apply trade sanctions under international law when their proposal to do so has failed in the United Nations. Furthermore, it often raises a range of complex jurisdictional issues. In response to the Helms-Burton Act mentioned above, for instance, some European countries challenged the U.S. assertion that it could extend its jurisdiction over foreign companies beyond its own borders and "pass laws on a global scale."[13]

The Struggle toward a New International Economic Order

Although direct control over resources and the management of wealth processes are still largely within the exclusive competence of nation-states, the international community is acquiring more experience in promoting economic development and in managing credit and monetary policies. The increasing realization on the part of the elites of nation-states that their own prosperity depends on the prosperity of all communities, especially those less developed, has injected a critical dimension in the global program of development.

The widening gap between the developed and the developing nations in an interdependent and globalized world has caused the international community to pay special attention to the developing areas. Economic strategies to enhance the development of less developed communities include programs to pool and make available technological and managerial skills and provision for a continuing and expanded flow of international capital into developing communities. Other important components include environmentally sustainable development, the achievement of high and stable levels of employment, the integration of production potential into the global economy, the avoidance of widespread depressions, the coordination of the increasing number of national and transnational agencies concerned with economic assistance and financing programs, and, in the decade since the collapse of communism, privatization and commitment to a market ideology.

Frustrated by the slow pace of development and the persistence of glaring gaps, Third World countries continued to demand the establishment of a "new international economic order." Their demands first found formal expression in the Declaration and

Programme of Action on the Establishment of a New International Economic Order (General Assembly Resolution 3201) and in the Charter of Economic Rights and Duties of States (General Assembly Resolution 3281), both adopted by the General Assembly in 1974.[14] These resolutions were adopted during a period marked by a series of crises that threatened the stability of the world economy. The international monetary system instituted in 1944, popularly known as the Bretton-Woods system, had collapsed in 1971. The global energy crisis of skyrocketing oil prices, as precipitated by the Organization of Petroleum Exporting Countries (OPEC) in the wake of the outbreak of hostilities in the Middle East in October 1973, captured headlines day after day. Other signs of instability included rising prices of other commodities and manufactured goods; shortages of food; depletion of reserves; trade imbalances; growing burdens of debt; and spiraling inflation.

It is highly significant that the famed Agenda for Peace issued by Boutros Boutros-Ghali in 1992 was followed by a twin Agenda for Development in 1994.[15] The Agenda for Development proclaimed economic development to be a "fundamental human right" and "the most secure basis for peace," affirmed the Bretton-Woods institutions as an integral source of policy advice and assistance, and called for increased long-term international cooperation in economic matters. Together these resolutions have all addressed a wide range of different yet interrelated economic matters, including production and prices of raw materials and primary commodities; international trade; international monetary and financial matters; sharing of resources; foreign aid; transfer of technology; private foreign investment; regulation of transnational corporations; participation in the global decision-making process affecting wealth; and North-South or East-West economic relations. Among other things, they have called for nonreciprocal, preferential access to the markets of developed countries for manufactured goods of developing countries; equality between developed and developing nations in decision making within multilateral monetary institutions concerning financial and monetary matters instead of the present weighted voting based on the amount of each state's subscribed capital; allowing formation of interstate "producer associations" and price fixing; indexing the export prices of Third World goods according to the cost of exported manufactured goods and capital from the developed nations; the right of developing countries to financial assistance for industrialization from developed countries; special measures to alleviate the burden of external debt contracted by developing countries on hard terms; and the formulation of an international code of conduct for transnational corporations to facilitate the transfer of technologies.

In the decade following the end of the Cold War, representatives of organizations from the Group of Seventy-Seven and former Eastern bloc nations pledged to move toward development policies that emphasize "individual initiative." The new approach was conciliatory, reflecting Western approaches to development and turning away from socialist doctrines. Although there are no longer the radical appeals for redistribution of the world's wealth as made in the 1970s, leaders from developing states continue to call for more aid from developed states.

With the end of the Cold War, there was an increased rivalry between the southern hemisphere and Eastern Europe. At the 1992 Earth Summit in Rio, it became clear that the developing countries, for the first time, had in environmentalism new leverage to get much-needed funds. Those countries demanded increasing aid and transfer of technology in exchange for compliance with the tougher environmental measures necessary to the new "sustainable development."

Wealth deprivation, commonly known as expropriation or nationalization—the taking by a state of foreign property located within its territory—remains a very controversial subject. Article 2(2)(c) of the Charter of Economic Rights and Duties of States (Assembly Resolution 3281) declares that each state has the right to

> nationalize, expropriate or transfer ownership of foreign property, in which case appropriate compensation should be paid by the State adopting such measures, taking into account its relevant laws and regulations and all circumstances that the State considers pertinent. In any case where the question of compensation gives rise to a controversy, it shall be settled under the domestic law of the nationalizing State and by its tribunals, unless it is freely and mutually agreed by all States concerned that other peaceful means be sought on the basis of the sovereign equality of States and in accordance with the principle of free choice of means.

This is a radical departure from the customary international law in the field, under which a taking of foreign property is lawful, provided three conditions are met: (1) the taking is for a public purpose; (2) it is not discriminatory; and (3) prompt, adequate, and just compensation is made.

The subject of expropriation has been one of the most controversial areas in contemporary international law. Beginning with the nationalization measures taken by the Soviet and Mexican revolutionary governments following World War I, differences of opinion developed over what constitutes a lawful taking under international law. The debate intensified with the rapid multiplication of newly independent states after World War II. Although the "nondiscrimination" and "public purpose" criteria are generally accepted, controversy has raged over the issue of compensation.

Most of the old communist states contended, at least in theory, that no compensation was required, in keeping with the general Soviet rejection of the binding nature of customary international law. In practice, however, communist states did not act on this theory; in the years following World War II, at least seventy-two relevant agreements entered into with communist states never repudiated the compensation requirement.

Capital-exporting states have generally followed the customary law mentioned above and have insisted that a taking of property be accompanied by compensation. They may differ about what precisely the standard of compensation entails—"prompt, adequate, and just" compensation or simply "just" or "appropriate" compensation. Just compensation ordinarily refers to fair market value.

Conversely, capital-importing states have increasingly asserted that whether compensation is granted and how much, if any, depends on the circumstances. The backbone of this contention is the assertion that all states exercise "permanent sovereignty" over their natural resources. The relevant factors are said to include the entire historical relations between the foreign enterprise and the host state; the ability of the taking state to pay compensation; the degree of unjust enrichment, if any, on the part of the taking state; the extent of prior exploitation by the foreign enterprise; and the extent of undue advantage enjoyed by the foreign property owner before expropriation.[16]

The formulation of Article 2(2)(c), as noted above, expresses largely the demand of the capital-importing countries and ostensibly seeks to substitute the standard of "appropriate" compensation for that of "prompt, adequate, and just" compensation. More fundamentally, it represents an attempt to remove the matter entirely from the realm of international law and to place it within the domain of national law. It is obviously unacceptable to the capital-exporting states, and it might in the long run be self-defeating for the capital-importing states. It is at odds with the prevailing state practice and in clear contradiction to General Assembly Resolution 1803, "Permanent Sovereignty over Natural Resources," adopted in 1962. This resolution, in paragraph 4, declares:

Nationalization, expropriation or requisitioning shall be based on grounds or reasons of public utility, security or the national interest which are recognized as overriding purely individual or private interests, both domestic and foreign. In such cases the owner shall be paid appropriate compensation, in accordance with the rules in force in the State taking such measures in the exercise of its sovereignty and in accordance with international law. In any case where the question of compensation gives rise to a controversy, the national jurisdiction of the State taking such measures shall be exhausted. However, upon agreement by sovereign States and other parties concerned, settlement of the dispute should be made through arbitration or international adjudication.[17]

The authoritative effect of the above-mentioned resolutions, particularly the Charter of Economic Rights and Duties of States and the Resolution on Permanent Sovereignty over Natural Resources—as law, "law in the making," or pious aspirations—remains a subject of continuing controversy. This point will be further discussed in chapter 22 on the prescribing (lawmaking) function.

Controversy notwithstanding, continuing adoption of these resolutions, though changing somewhat, represents what is called a "normative strategy" on the part of the Third World countries. The fact of their adoption serves to illustrate and underscore the essence of how international law is made and remade—search for the common interest amid competing claims and claimants, in response to the changing demands and expectations of participants under ever-changing conditions. The expectations of the members of the world community do not remain static but are in constant flux. Although any claim of wholesale repudiation of customary international law cannot be taken seriously, demands to modify particular international norms in light of changing demands, expectations, and conditions cannot be lightly dismissed.

The new international economic order called for would have represented a conspicuous power shift to the Third World. Although it failed to get the gains demanded in the 1970s, efforts have continued, although emphasis has shifted away from socialism. The new order continues seeking to generate basic changes in world economic relations and especially to remedy past deprivations and injustices through a new world trade pattern and economic arrangements favorable to the developing nations.

Toward Human Development in the New Era of Globalization

International law is a continuing process, constantly being adjusted in an attempt to balance competing interests under changing conditions. Now, as the world enters a new era of globalization, the international community carries forward its call for a new economic order. Unilateral demands, predicated on the size of nations and their number of votes, have proven to be unsuccessful in this sense. A new economic order requires that common interests be identified and the world as a whole commit itself to achieving these interests for the benefit of all.

There has been a shift of focus to policies that emphasize the right to development. Development in the sense of human development is, by its very nature, multidimensional. Yes, economic development is important, but it must be addressed in its broadest sense, that is, human development on all levels, in order to achieve optimum world order. This concept has been given concrete expression, in part, at the Millennium Summit in September 2000, where world leaders adopted the Millennium Development Goals (MDGs), a set of development targets aimed at reducing poverty and improving the lives of people around the world, especially those in developing countries, by the year 2015. The eight MDGs embrace poverty, hunger, education, rights of women, child mortality, maternal health, combating pandemic disease, ensuring environmental sustainability, and developing a global partnership for development. The MDGs provide a framework for accountability—a global commitment by both developed and developing countries "to create an environment—at national and global levels alike—which is conducive to development and the elimination of poverty."[18]

More important, the MDGs impart a sense of urgency and provide the world community with a timetable against which to measure its efforts. Economic growth is essential to improving lives; however, sustainability requires an aggregate approach with development in many areas over a certain period of time. Thus, the MDGs themselves give the concept of sustainable development a concrete expression—"a multidimensional vision that integrates political factors such as civil rights and democratic representation, social factors such as education and health, and economic factors such as growth and employment."[19] This vision is supported by the work of U.N. programs, in partnership with governments and NGOs, including the World Bank, the World Food Programme (WFP), the World Trade Organization (WTO), the U.N. Environment Programme (UNEP), the U.N. Conference on Trade and Development (UNCTD), and the U.N. Children's Fund (UNICEF).

Goal eight—creating a global partnership for development—is particularly important for achieving sustainable economic growth and leveling the playing field between developed and developing countries. Goal eight addresses the needs of the least developed countries to further develop an open, rule-based, predictable, nondiscriminatory trading and financial system. In doing so, developing countries gain greater access to the markets of developed countries and enjoy benefits such as tariff reductions. Also, as the demand grows for information and communication technology, the MDG program, in conjunction with the private sector, hopes to make available benefits of new technology, especially information and communications. Thus, commitment to partnerships between the public and private sectors as well as between developed and developing countries continues to be a key instrument for human development.

Applying these principles, a collective effort toward achieving the MDGs has created significant economic growth in developing regions and has put the world on track to achieve at least some of the goals. According to the 2010 U.N. Millennium Development Report, the developing world as a whole is on track to reach the poverty reduction target by 2015. To this end, major advances have been made in the poorest countries to educate children, slow the rate of deforestation, to improve the availability of clean water in rural areas, and to introduce key health interventions that have cut childhood deaths from 12.5 million in 1990 to 8.8 million in 2008.[20]

While recent reports indicate significant progress, they also illustrate common barriers. The U.N. Development Programme revealed in its 2010 MDG Synthesis Report that the lack of capacity and financing along with inadequate resources has delayed economic growth and the delivery of basic services. Poor infrastructure exacerbates the economic gap between urban and rural areas. Poor data and monitoring mechanisms continue to be a problem, especially on a national level. Likewise, there is little pressure on developed countries to report their progress in the areas of access to trade, aid, and debt relief, weakening accountability and transparency. Conflicts and natural disasters also pose a serious challenge to human development and can hinder job opportunities and the delivery of social services, while increasing the risk of crises.

Moreover, as the economic crisis of 2008 showed, the stability of the global economic system is precarious, and problems in one part of the world can quickly spread to others. Even developed and wealthy nations were vulnerable to the global recession that followed, and decision makers were forced to reconsider many fundamental economic policies in an effort to contain the damage and restore normal patterns of growth. Although the long-term consequences of the crisis are yet unknown, it appears that the global economy and the relationships between developed and developing nations will be forever altered.

Despite these challenges, the MDGs continue to be within reach. The international community can achieve its agenda if it continues to find long-term solutions and implement them through partnerships in both the public and private sector. Accountability and responsibility must be maintained at local, national, and international levels. Commitment to the right programs together with the appropriate resources can break down these barriers and put the world on the path to obtaining optimum world order; however, as a matter of priority, this requires effort from all people in both developed and developing nations.

Appraisal

Notwithstanding the effort toward achieving the MDGs, there are still far-reaching implications involved that would engender the reshaping not only of world economic relations but, ultimately, the entire global constitutive process of authoritative decision. These demands for a new international economic order based on development, at best, represent demands to better employ the economic instrument to facilitate greater fulfillment worldwide of wealth and other values, especially for the vast and increasing segment of the world's population that remain deprived and underfulfilled; at worst, they are said to be demands for aggrandizement of local elites at the expense of multitudes. In any event, the legitimate aspirations of the peoples in the developing world can be ignored only at the peril of the common interest.

The capital-importing countries cannot go it alone in meeting their long-term agenda of development. They need the cooperation of the capital-exporting countries. Numbers in voting strength are no substitute for effective control of wealth, resources, skills, and technology. The inflow of outside capital cannot be expected without adequate assurance of safety, return, and clean growth. The painstaking and persevering effort to identify and secure the common interest is the key to such cooperation between the developed and developing nations. Law, after all, is a continuing process of clarifying and securing the common interest of interacting participants under changing conditions.

Common interests require a cooperative approach. The positive use of the economic instrument can facilitate an integrated solution to the global problems of sustainable development, enhancing aggregate production and fulfillment of wealth and other values. The expansion of this constructive role, built on rich experience, could greatly augment the potential of the economic instrument to promote a desired world order of human dignity, provided the imperative of common interest is taken seriously and given effective expression.

Notes

1. *See* Jordan P. Paust & Albert P. Blaustein, *The Arab Oil Weapon—A Threat to International Peace*, 68 A.J.I.L. 410 (1974); *The Use of Nonviolent Coercion: A Study in Legality Under Article 2(4) of the Charter of the United Nations*, 122 U. PA. L. REV. 983, 997–1011 (1974).

2. *See* Hartmut Brosche, *The Arab Oil Embargo and United States Pressure Against Chile: Economic and Political Coercion and the Charter of the United Nations*, 7 CASE W. RES. J. INT'L L. 3, 16–35 (1974).

3. S.C. Res. 232, U.N. Doc. S/RES/232 (Dec. 16, 1966).

4. G.A. Res. 2506 (XXIV), ¶ 5, U.N. Doc. A/RES/2506 (XXIV) (Dec. 10, 1969).

5. W. Michael Reisman, *Polaroid Power: Taxing Business for Human Rights*, 4 FOREIGN POLICY 101, 103–04 (1971).

6. S.C. Res 569, U.N. Doc. S/RES/569 (July 26, 1985).

7. European Community News, No. 24/1985 (Aug. 8, 1985) and No. 26/1985 (Sept. 11, 1985); *reprinted in* 24 I.L.M. 1474 (1985).

8. Code of Conduct Concerning the Employment Practices of Canadian Companies Operating in South Africa, 24 I.L.M. 1464 (1985).

9. Exec. Order No. 12532, 50 Fed. Reg. 36861 (1985).

10. Comprehensive Anti-Apartheid Act of 1986, Pub. L. No. 99-440, 100 Stat. 1086 (1986); *see* Raymond Paretsky, *The United States Arms Embargo Against South Africa: An Analysis of the Laws, Regulations, and Loopholes*, 12 YALE J. INT'L L. 133 (1987).

11. The Sullivan principles were drafted by Rev. Leon Sullivan, a Baptist minister and member of the General Motors Corporation Board of Directors. As initially formulated, they are reprinted in Editor's Note, *Perspectives*, 15 LAW & POL. INT'L BUS. 445, 445–46 (1983), *reprinted in* 24 I.L.M. 1496 (1985).

12. Foreign Assistance Act of 1974, Pub. L. No. 93-559, 88 Stat. 1795, at § 502(B) (1974); Foreign Assistance Act of 1976, Pub. L. No. 94-330, 90 Stat. 771 (1976); *see* John Salzberg, *Human Rights and U.S. Foreign Policy Under Carter: A Congressional Perspective*, 8 DEN. J. INT'L L. & POL. 525, 526 (1979).

13. Roger Cohen, *Frances Scoffs at U.S. Protest over Iran Deal*, N.Y. TIMES, Sept. 30, 1997, at A12.

14. Declaration on the Establishment of a New International Economic Order, G.A. Res. 3201 (S-VI), U.N. Doc. A/RES/S-6/3201 (May 1, 1974); Charter of Economic Rights and Duties of States, G.A. Res. 3281 (XXIX), U.N. Doc. A/RES/3281(XXIX) (Dec. 12, 1974).

15. U.N. Secretary-General, *An Agenda for Development*, U.N. Doc. A/48/935 (May 6, 1994).

16. *See* Eduardo Jiménez de Arechaga, *State Responsibility for the Nationalization of Foreign-Owned Property*, 11 N.Y.U. J. INT'L L. & POL. 179, 185 (1978).

17. G.A. Res. 1803 (XVII), art. 1, § 4, U.N. Doc. A/RES/1803(XVII) (Dec. 14, 1962).

18. United Nations Millennium Summit, *The Millennium Development Goals* (2000), *available at* http://www.oecd.org/dac/ictcd/docs/otherdocs/OtherDAC_MDGs.pdf.

19. Sakiko Fukuda-Parr, *Millennium Development Goals: Why They Matter*, *in* 10 GLOBAL GOVERNANCE: A REVIEW OF MULTILATERALISM & INTERNATIONAL ORGANIZATIONS No. 4, 395–402 (Tom Farer & Timothy D. Sisk eds., 2004).

20. United Nations, *The Millennium Development Goals Report* (2010), *available at* http://www.un.org/millenniumgoals/pdf/MDG%20Report%202010%20En%20r15%20-low%20res%2020100615%20-.pdf.

19 The Military Instrument

THE MILITARY INSTRUMENT, involving implements of destruction, is commonly associated with coercion and the destruction of values. But, constructively employed for collective security, either by the organized general community or by individual states, this instrument is vital to the maintenance of minimum world order. And minimum world order is indispensable to achieve the optimum shaping and sharing of all values.

The employment of violence and other intense coercion against human beings is inimical to human dignity. A general community aspiring toward human dignity values must seek to minimize the employment of such violence and coercion as an instrument of change in the shaping and sharing of values. Violence and coercion in authoritative sanctioning measures can only be used as a last resort.

The employment of the military instrument for the purpose of maintaining minimum world order (peace and security) has not been very effective. This remains a critical problem in the contemporary international legal system. Individual nation-states continue to control the implements of military strategy. Efforts to transfer to the general community the sole privilege of permissible employment of force have not been successful. The original plan to establish a permanent U.N. military force to maintain world order was stillborn.

Basic Community Policy of Peaceful Change

International law governing the use of the military instrument by nation-states has undergone profound changes since the establishment of the U.N. Charter. Although the charter avoids the difficulties created by the term *war*, by no means has it removed the controversy about the permissibility of the exercise of certain coercions.

Before the conditional prohibition of major coercion, as established by the Covenant of the League of Nations, international law did not prohibit resort to war, conceived as the most intense and comprehensive form of violence. In the nineteenth century, there was understandably less of a common interest in restraining violence because the effects of an instance of violence were less than they would be today. Private coercion and violence were then accepted as permissible not only for self-help and self-vindication of rights but also for effecting changes in the distribution of values among nation-states.

Despite the permissibility of major coercion, certain concepts about the responsibility of states governed minor coercion. A few prescriptions purported to regulate noncomprehensive and less intense uses of coercion, the so-called measures short of war. The permissible application of minor coercion was restricted to cases in which a previous unlawful act, or a failure to carry out international obligations, was imputable to the state against which coercion was applied. Conceptually, it may be likened to "a municipal enactment that punished petty thieving while condoning armed robbery."[1] This apparent paradox illustrates the manner in which international law has developed over the centuries in a world of sovereign states. The resort to major coercion was difficult to control because nation-states in modern times employed major coercion only when a conviction of some vital interests to be served seemed to provide justification, at least in their own eyes. If the interest involved was not sufficiently great to justify, internally or externally, a resort to major coercion, it was a degree of magnitude susceptible to legal regulation.

As shown by past practices, measures short of war were generally taken only by a stronger state against weaker ones. A nation-state, in resorting to those measures, frequently invoked such concepts as intervention and reprisal to communicate its allegedly limited objectives to nonparticipants, thus hoping to allay their fears and prevent their possible involvement prompted by balance of power considerations. The initiating state could at any time characterize its operations as war and thus escape the application of the above-mentioned prescriptions. In fact, the methods employed in the instances of measures short of war were more often than not indistinguishable from those used in undertakings to which the label "war" was attached. In sum, it reflected the general nineteenth-century policy of international law, which sought to localize coercion by giving community approval to a quick settlement of disputes through superior strength.

There is a certain unreality in attempting to formulate prescriptions regarding the exercise of minor coercion while admitting that a state might resort to major coercion without breaching the law. The Covenant of the League of Nations represented the first significant break with traditional doctrine. "Resort to war" was made unlawful under certain circumstances, and an attempt was made to distinguish permissible from impermissible resort to coercion (Articles 12–16). But the continued availability of various labels to justify the use of coercion became the focus of considerable concern. "Resort to war," as proscribed in the covenant, gave rise to confused contention with respect to the continuing legality of force and violence if participants used some labels other than "war," such as "reprisal" or "intervention" or other "measures short of war."

The General Treaty for the Renunciation of War of 1928, also known as the Pact of Paris or the Kellogg-Briand Pact, sought to close these gaps. Condemning "recourse to war for the solution of international controversies," the Pact of Paris denounced "war as an instrument of national policy" and sought to resolve "all disputes or conflicts, of whatever nature or whatever origin they may be" exclusively by "pacific means" (Articles 1 and 2). But by keeping the term "war," the pact failed to eliminate the continued debate regarding the permissibility of armed force that participants might verbally designate a "measure short of war."

The establishment of the U.N. Charter has fundamentally changed the traditional community prescriptions about the exercises of coercion between nation-states. Discarding the confused term "war," the charter has prohibited the deliberate use of coercion in terms of "threat or use of force," "threat to the peace," "breach of the peace," and "act of aggression" (Articles 2[4] and 39–51). These references, taken as a whole, cover not only war, understood as comprehensive and highly intensive use of the military instrument, but also those applications of force or threats of force of a lesser intensity and magnitude that in the past had been labeled short of war.

Article 2(4), which is the cornerstone of the charter system, states: "All Members shall refrain in their international relations from the threat or use of force against the territorial integrity or political independence of any state, or in any other manner inconsistent with the Purposes of the United Nations." This provision is not explicit with respect to whether the nature of "force" to be prohibited was limited to military force. It was generally thought that it was not intended to cover coercive measures of an economic, ideological, or political nature, but there is a split of opinion on the issue.

Although the charter avoids the difficulties created by the legalistic invocation of the term "war," the fundamental distinction it provides between permissible and impermissible coercion has by no means eliminated the controversy regarding the permissibility of the exercises of certain coercion. The issue of whether the use of military force for purposes other than self-defense and community police action is still permissible under Article 2 of the charter has continued to arouse debate among decision makers and international lawyers.

Self-Defense

That self-defense, individual or collective, in case of an armed attack, remains permissible is beyond doubt. The fundamental community policies in defense of minimum world order, as projected in customary international law and in the U.N. Charter, are complementary. In a world arena in which authoritative and effective power remains largely unorganized and decentralized, various lesser communities can hardly be expected to achieve even minimum security, much less optimal fulfillment of all values, if they are denied appropriate capabilities and measures of response. The authoritative prescriptions of customary international law and the U.N. Charter thus make a rational distinction between impermissible coercion (acts of aggression, threats to the peace, breach of the peace, intervention, and so on) and permissible coercion (self-defense, collective self-defense, enforcement action, and so on).

Central to the maintenance of minimum world order is to distinguish impermissible coercion from permissible coercion. The general proscription of the threat or use of force in the U.N. Charter is accompanied by preservation of the inherent right of self-defense. Article 51 of the charter states clearly:

> Nothing in the present Charter shall impair the inherent right of individual or collective self-defense if an armed attack occurs against a Member of the United Nations, until the Security Council has taken measures necessary to maintain international peace and security. Measures taken by Members in the exercise of this right of self-defense shall be immediately reported to the Security Council and shall not in any way affect the authority and responsibility of the Security Council under the present Charter to take at any time such action as it deems necessary in order to maintain or restore international peace and security.

What is meant by aggression? What is self-defense? Through special committees and other bodies, the United Nations was engaged in formulating a definition of aggression for more than two decades. The protracted effort resulted in the General Assembly's adoption in December 1974 of the Definition of Aggression, containing eight articles, as drafted by the Special Committee on the Question of Defining Aggression.[2] "Aggression" is defined in Article I as "the use of armed force by a State against the sovereignty, territorial integrity or political independence of another State, or in any other manner inconsistent with the Charter of the United Nations." This is almost identical to Article 2(4) of the U.N. Charter, except it is limited explicitly to "armed force." Indeed, Article 6 of the definition makes it clear that "[n]othing in this Definition shall be construed as in any way enlarging or diminishing the scope of the Charter, including its provisions concerning cases in which the use of force is lawful." Article 2 of the definition makes the first use of armed force by a state as prima facie evidence of an act of aggression, and Article 3 enumerates certain acts as acts of aggression, such as invading or bombing another state, blockading ports, using mercenaries against another state, or providing support to a third party that commits acts of aggression against another state.

Defining aggression remains a problem even today. Take for example the Rome Statute, which established the International Criminal Court (ICC). While the statute refers to the crime of aggression, treaty makers were unable to agree on a definition for such a crime, leaving the issue open for future resolution. Therefore, Article 5(2) of the final statute, adopted in 1998, acknowledged that the international community had not yet agreed on a clear definition of aggression, hence none was given in the statute. In 2010, a Review Conference adopted amendments to the Rome Statute that included a definition of the crime of aggression that was based on the General Assembly's 1974 resolution. However, the proposed changes would not take effect until after 2017, leaving the ICC without jurisdiction over crimes of aggression for the present moment.

Such definitional exercise is hardly adequate to deal with the dynamics of military coercion. In a decentralized world arena where nation-states constantly make initial and important decisions, response must be prompt in an exigent situation of major coercion. The employment of military coercion is a process, producing coercion of varying degrees of intensity and magnitude. A contextual framework of analysis, such as the one recommended by McDougal and Feliciano, which offers operational indices in distinguishing impermissible from permissible coercion, would appear to offer a more useful way of dealing with the troublesome question of aggression and self-defense.[3] According to this contextual framework, many features in the developing process of coercion must be taken into account in distinguishing impermissible from permissible coercion. In the process of transnational coercion, participants pursue various objectives by applying to one another coercion of varying degrees of intensity, by all available instruments of policy, under all the constantly changing conditions in the world arena. In a developing process of coercion there may be a culminating point that creates reasonable expectations on the part of a target state that an immediate military response is indispensable (that is, necessary) to the protection of its own existence—to safeguard its important bases of power from destruction. Because of the imminent danger of destruction, the common interest in authorizing self-defense in the form of a proportionate military response has long been recognized. Law cannot reasonably ask and expect a target state to wait like a sitting duck to see its own destruction in the face of such danger. Whether reasonable expectations about imminent destruction are created can be ascertained by taking into account every feature of the process of coercion—namely, through use of the familiar social process category of participants, objectives, situations, base values, strategies, and outcomes.

Self-defense involves employing the military instrument against an alleged attacker to protect territorial integrity and political independence. The classic formulation by Secretary of State Daniel Webster, in the *Caroline* incident of 1837 (which involved the destruction by a British force of a private U.S. steamer, used in support of the Canadian rebellion, while anchored at the U.S. side of the Niagara River, and resulted in the deaths of U.S. citizens), specified the element of necessity for permissible self-defense in terms of being "instant, overwhelming, leaving no choice of means and no moment for deliberation."[4] The test for lawfulness commonly applied is that the target state is permitted to use the military instrument when it reasonably decides, as third-party observers may appraise reasonableness, that the threat to its territorial integrity or political independence is so imminent that it must respond immediately by the military instrument in order to protect itself. This test involves two important elements. First, the attacker must not only possess the subjectivity to attack the territorial integrity or the political independence of the target state but must also engage in operations that are sufficiently consequential to create in the target state reasonable apprehension of imminent destruction. Second, the responding force must be necessary and proportionate in relation to the provocation. Whether the requirements of necessity and proportionality are met must be subject to a disciplined, contextual scrutiny by reference to each feature surrounding the provocative acts and the responding measures. In addition, Article 51 of the U.N. Charter mandates that the provisional measures of response by individual states be subject to the inclusive community review process. Member states of the United Nations must report immediately to the Security Council the self-defense measures they have taken; and the Security Council, of course, is empowered with the authority and responsibility to maintain international peace and security.

A focal point of contention in applying Article 51 of the charter relates to the wording, "an armed attack." Does it mean that self-defense must always wait for an actual armed attack? Or do certain circumstances warrant what is known as "anticipatory" self-defense? The question is not a matter for mere academic exercise but a practical matter of grave concern, one of common interest and human survival in the nuclear age. The U.S. quarantine of Cuba during the missile crisis of October 1962, Israel's destruction of an Iraqi nuclear reactor in 1981, and the United States' invasion of Afghanistan and Iraq following the terrorist attacks of September 11, 2001, all raised this vital question.

Two divergent views exist. The first takes a textualist view in stressing that "armed attack" means "only if armed attack," and unless and until there is an actual armed attack or process of attack, the target state cannot respond militarily in self-defense even in the face of "imminent danger." The second view holds that the U.N. Charter is not a suicide pact and that the target state cannot be expected to be a sitting duck awaiting its own destruction in this nuclear age even if a process of attack has not begun. It adds that Article 51 was designed to reaffirm, not to curtail, the customary right of self-defense. Recent state practice would appear to support the latter view, although many disagree.

The Cuban quarantine case provides an apt example. The United States imposed a quarantine (blockade) against Cuba in October 1962 in response to Cuba's importation of offensive nuclear weapons from the Soviet Union. Although the U.S. government justified its quarantine action largely in terms of authorization by the Organization of American States (OAS), a form of regional collective self-defense, the international legal community showed keen interest in the issue of anticipatory self-defense involved. Many observers have had little difficulty in finding that the requirements of both necessity and proportionality were met by the U.S. response.

A rigorous contextual analysis at its best, made by Myres S. McDougal in the July 1963 issue of the *American Journal of International Law*, has been especially influential.[5] Appraising the Soviet threat and the U.S. response, respectively, in terms of the salient features (participants, objectives, situations, bases of power, strategies, and outcomes) of the larger context, McDougal concluded that the quarantine measure was lawful. The threat in this instance came not from Cuba but from the Soviet Union, a superpower then as powerful as the United States. The Soviet objective was expansionist rather than conservatory. The Soviet Union was moving into an area traditionally regarded as of special importance to the United States, as symbolized for many decades by the Monroe Doctrine. The Soviet Union had never before asserted a military presence of such magnitude in this area. It was moving with offensive weapons that would cut U.S. reaction time from six or seven minutes to some three minutes. The provocative operations and subjectivities of the Soviet Union thus created reasonable apprehension of imminent danger to the territorial integrity and political independence of the United States. The U.S. military response, in concert with that of other members of the OAS, was defensive, seeking only the elimination of nuclear weapons from Cuba. It was made as limited as it could possibly have been under the circumstances. The use of the military instrument to interdict certain types of weapons on the high seas entailed the least possible interference and destruction of the bases of power of other states. The United States immediately reported its undertaking to the Security Council and sought appropriate action from that body. The quarantine, reversible in nature, was a highly measured response, entailing force only to the extent necessary to removal of the provocation. In sum, the U.S. response was a lawful exercise of self-defense in accord with customary expectations about the requirements of necessity and proportionality.

In a complaint brought before the International Court of Justice in 1984, Nicaragua charged the United States with unlawful use of force and intervention in violation of the U.N. Charter, the OAS Charter, and general principles of customary law. The United States justified its position largely in terms of collective self-defense, maintaining that because Nicaragua had carried out armed attacks on El Salvador by providing Salvadoran insurgents with arms, technical support, and military guidance, it was permissible for the United States to take necessary and proportionate measures in and against Nicaragua to help El Salvador repel the attacks. Although the United States did not participate in the proceedings at the stage of the merits, as noted in chapter 7, the court rendered its judgment on the merits on June 27, 1986, rejecting the U.S. claim of collective self-defense and declaring that there is no right to use force in self-defense except in cases of "armed attack" under "customary international law," as distinguished from "multilateral treaty law." Emphasizing that "an armed attack" is the *sine qua non* for the exercise of collective self-defense, the court concluded that this condition was not met, as the flows of arms from Nicaraguan territory to opposition forces in El Salvador in early 1981 did not constitute an armed attack. Such an interpretation is indeed a far cry from the contextual approach discussed above.[6]

More recently, the justifiability of the defensive use of force has been pushed further by the emergence of the so-called "Bush Doctrine." The term was used during the George W. Bush administration to describe the notion that the use of force could be justified in the context of preemptive self-defense. Military action was seen by some as an appropriate measure if employed to combat terrorism and the spread of weapons of mass destruction, even in the absence of an imminent threat. Under the doctrine, a threat need not be imminent before the threatened state may resort to defensive force—a potential threat is sufficient. This argument played a role in the United States' efforts to justify military action against Iraq in 2003 amid an expanded effort to target threats around the world in the years after 9/11.

It is important to note that the United States, in utilizing the military instrument, has not acted alone or ignored the international community. Prior to invading Iraq in 2003, the United States sought to justify its actions by arguing that Iraq had failed to meet its obligations under previous Security Council resolutions.[7] Moreover, the United States' intervention in Afghanistan in 2001 was undertaken as part of a coalition of nations acting with authorization from the United Nations. Notably, one of the major players in the intervention in Afghanistan was NATO, whose members were called to action as a matter of collective self-defense. In 2012, NATO convened a summit hosted by U.S. President Barack Obama to consider the international community's role in shaping the future of Afghanistan following the war.[8]

Expanding the criteria by which states may legitimately invoke the use of the military instrument is not something to be taken lightly. As has been mentioned in other contexts, the U.N. Charter is not a "suicide pact," and states must be allowed to defend themselves against legitimate threats. It is crucially important that the international community chart a course that recognizes and seeks to balance these competing interests while discouraging unauthorized acts of violence and coercion for the purpose of attaining minimum world order.

Self-Help

Although there is a clear consensus on the inherent right of self-defense by recourse to the military instrument, serious debate continues about the permissibility of using the military instrument as a form of self-help for lesser transgressions. Though self-help has a number of equivalent synonyms (retortions, retaliations, reprisals, intervention, minor coercion, measures short of war), self-help is perhaps the generic term that is most useful in the present context. Self-help is broader in reference than self-defense; indeed, self-defense is the most dramatic example of self-help. Both self-help and self-defense depend for their legal characterization on the prior fact that somebody else has acted unlawfully. Self-help, even that involving the use of military force, was long regarded as vital in providing some measure of enforceability in the decentralized international system. Allowing the victim state to take enforcement into its own hands, if inclusive procedure of remedy is realistically unavailable, is an essential element in a decentralized legal order.

One view takes the position that self-help, beyond self-defense, is now impermissible. The arguments for this view may be summarized as follows: (1) Article 2(3) and 2(4) of the charter project the fundamental community policies of promoting peaceful change and of minimizing coercion; (2) Article 2(4), read in conjunction with Article 51 and the rest of the provisions contained in Chapter VII of the charter, dealing with "action with respect to threats to the peace, breaches of the peace, and acts of aggression," shows clearly that the U.N. Charter as a whole prohibits the use of military force save for self-defense and collective enforcement action (community police action); (3) the blanket prohibition of the use of force embodied in Article 2(4) suggests that self-help is inconsistent with the purposes of the United Nations and hence impermissible, a point affirmed in part by the International Court of Justice in the *Corfu Channel* case of 1949;[9] (4) highly susceptible to abuse, self-help is an instrument of aggrandizement by the powerful against the weak; and (5) in the nuclear age, when humanity lives under the shadow of nuclear holocaust, forcible self-help could readily escalate beyond management. This view, highly influential in the early years of the United Nations, has come under increasing pressure because of the contemporary realities of state practice in the use of military force.

A contrary view maintains that Article 2(4) is not a blanket prohibition of all uses of military force and expressly prohibits only threats or uses of force directed "against the territorial integrity or political independence of any state, or in any other manner inconsistent with the Purposes of the United Nations." When it seeks neither a territorial change nor a challenge to the political independence of the state concerned, an act of self-help taken in response to a prior unlawful act in order to secure compliance with international law is to help secure "justice," as enunciated in Article 2(3) of the charter, and is not inconsistent with the purposes of the organization, which are generally listed in Article 1 and the preamble to the charter. Hence, Article 2(4) is no necessary bar to an otherwise permissible act of self-help.

Although some evidence suggests that the framers of the charter intended to permit use of force only for self-defense and collective enforcement action, this is far from conclusive. Neither is the pronouncement of the International Court of Justice in the *Corfu Channel* case that force has no place in the contemporary international law.[10] Although the court held that it was unlawful for the United Kingdom to undertake minesweeping operations in the channel, it did not impose much of a penalty on the United Kingdom. In fact, the court held that it was lawful for the United Kingdom to assert its rights by force in sending its warships through the straits, with guns mounted and ready for action if necessary, in response to the prior unlawful act of Albania.

In interpreting Article 2(4), it is important to consult *travaux preparatoires*, but it is even more important, as shown in chapter 16, to interpret it in light of the entire context of the U.N. Charter, especially the major purposes of the organization and the subsequent practice. In addition to the words of the charter and preliminary negotiations, the whole subsequent flow of words and interpretation by conduct are relevant to the interpretation of what the law is today.

A critical component of the shared expectations of the framers of the charter was that the United Nations would become the effective global institution of community police action, endowed with adequate formal authority and sufficient effective power and guided by the big-power unanimity in the making of important decisions. Under this shared assumption, the charter included both Article 2(4) and Article 51, contemplating that collective machinery of law enforcement would replace self-help and there would be no need and no place for unilateral use of military force except for the inherent right of self-defense.

Unhappily, as shown by the practice and reality of the more than six decades since the founding of the United Nations, this fundamental shared expectation that was to be the keystone of the entire U.N. system, in its pursuit of both minimum and optimum world order, has been ruthlessly shattered. Individual nation-states continue to control the implements of military strategy, and efforts to bestow on the general community the sole privilege of permissible employment of force have been unsuccessful. Although there has been a renewal of hope for a more active Security Council after the end of the Cold War, the United Nations has been unable, with rare exceptions, to take effective action to deal with conflicts that threaten world peace and security and gross violations of international law. This continues to be due largely to the paralysis of the Security Council that results from the veto power. Many states have resorted to military force in situations short of the requirements of self-defense to protect national interests.

Accordingly, in the absence of effective collective machinery to protect against lawlessness and deprivation, the remedy of self-help cannot be ruled out. The charter's general proscription of the use of force was predicated on the establishment within the United Nations of effective centralized decision and enforcement. So long as this projected condition remains unfulfilled, the general community cannot afford a paralysis that invites lawlessness and deprivation by particular states with impunity. In circumstances in which the organized general community—through an authoritative organ of the United Nations or a relevant regional organization—cannot act or cannot act with adequate dispatch, the self-help of particular states may offer the only alternative to defend the common interest in securing compliance with international law. It would otherwise be tantamount to honoring lawlessness to hold that a state can violate international law with impunity, causing deprivation to other states or the international community, with no fear of response. Therefore, insofar as a self-help measure is precipitated by a prior lawless act and deprivation and conforms strictly to the international legal regulations governing the use of force—notably the principles of necessity and proportionality—such a measure constitutes a vindication and functional enforcement of international law.

Although the remedy of self-help may continue to have a place under contemporary international law, one should recognize that, in a decentralized world in which the effective power of state actors is patently discrepant, this remedy is highly susceptible to abuse and misuse. Hence, assertions of necessity and proportionality must be subjected to the most searching community scrutiny lest self-help become an impermissible weapon of the powerful against the weak. Any state engages in self-help at its own peril. The characterization of particular activities as requiring self-help partakes of the nature of a provisional determination in precisely the same way as a claim of self-defense and remains subject to both the contemporaneous appraisal of other states and to any subsequent review the organized community may eventually exercise.

No easy and dogmatic intellectual procedures distinguish genuine from spurious acts of self-help. Serious review requires contextual scrutiny. Lawfulness and unlawfulness must depend on the answers to many questions about each feature of the context, with the significance of anyone feature depending on the total configuration. Some of the more important questions about relevant features may be highlighted:

Participants: Who initiates the measure of self-help? Against whom? Is the measure of self-help by or against a legitimate government or by or against segments of a community only? Is the action prompted by a prior unlawful act? If so, what unlawful act?

Perspectives: Is the action taken to secure a remedy or to put an end to a prior or continuing lawless act? Are both manifest and genuine objectives related to securing compliance with international law?

Situations: How intense are expectations of imminent irreparable loss in the absence of the recourse to the military instrument? Are the violations of international norms systematic and of long duration or sporadic and occasional?

Base values: What are the disparities in relative strength of the responding state and the target state or entity? Do patent discrepancies in strength suggest coercion or overreaction?

Strategies: What instruments of policy could have been used? Have the diplomatic, ideological, and economic instruments been mobilized and employed before the recourse to the military instrument? Have bilateral negotiations, with or without the assistance of a third party, been conducted? Have the parties involved been willing to subject themselves to an impartial fact-finding process? Has recourse to available remedies through organized collective action been exhausted or futile?

Outcomes: With what intensity and destruction has the military instrument been used? What values were conserved and what values were destroyed? Was the use of the military instrument in proportion to the magnitude of actual deprivations or the threats of deprivation? Was the military action ended as soon as its manifest objectives were accomplished?

Note that the condition of necessity cannot be met until a prior lawless act and deprivation have been established and the inability to secure a remedy after having exhausted all available noncoercive means has been demonstrated. Unlike the case of self-defense, a situation calling for self-help rarely entails dangers of imminent destruction of the responding state, but certainly could entail a similar danger for its nationals or those of other states. In principle, the victim state is not authorized to take immediate, unilateral response. Good faith effort to obtain a remedy through exhaustion of all available, noncoercive means is imperative. Furthermore, a strong presumption is that, save in extremely rare circumstances, self-help in the form of military force in response to a prior nonmilitary coercion or action will fail the test of proportionality.

In a better-organized world, humankind might be able to dispense with a doctrine of self-help that permits a state unilaterally to employ even the military instrument where reasonably necessary against another state or entity, in response to a prior unlawful act for which a remedy is unavailable after all noncoercive procedures have been exhausted, including recourse to inclusive community machinery. Until that better organization is more nearly achieved, the task of those who are genuinely committed to human dignity values is, however, to clarify and apply a concept of self-help that will best serve the common interest in achieving at least the conditions of minimum order.

It may be noted that those who take the position of the blanket prohibition of the use of force except for self-defense and for community enforcement action tend to invoke the label of self-defense to justify any use of force that may be more properly characterized as self-help. Different doctrines may be invoked to justify the same recourse to force, and the same label may be used to mean quite different things. For instance, the U.S. bombing of Libya in April 1986, in retaliation for Libya's prior acts of terrorism, has been supported by some as a permissible self-defense and by others as a permissible self-help.

Humanitarian Intervention

Humanitarian intervention can be regarded as a special kind of self-help. Historically, states that have resorted to military force to protect human rights in other states, have depicted their actions in terms of the doctrine of humanitarian intervention. (There is a close connection between the doctrine of humanitarian intervention and states' responsibility to protect discussed in chapter 12.) Reflecting natural law traditions and more secular perceptions of humanitarian responsibilities that transcend community boundaries, this doctrine symbolizes a basic human solidarity to defend the sanctity of human life and dignity. Such protection has traditionally been extended, first, to nationals abroad in order to secure compliance with the minimum standard for the treatment of aliens under customary international law and, second, to nonnationals in order to deter and end atrocious deprivations of human rights by a state against its own nationals or the nationals of third states. Sometimes the label "humanitarian intervention" is used restrictively to refer only to the latter situation. According to this doctrine, where egregious human rights violations occur within a state whose government will not or cannot stop them, the general community, or in exigent circumstances a single state, may enter the territory of the defaulting state to secure an end to the outrage and compliance with minimum international standards of human rights.

The practice of humanitarian intervention gained prominence and acceptance during the nineteenth century and the early twentieth century, especially for the protection of religious minorities. Notable examples include the intervention in 1860–61 by Austria, France, Great Britain, Prussia, and Russia on behalf of the persecuted Christian population in Syria; the intervention in 1866–68 on behalf of the oppressed Christian population in Crete; the intervention in 1903–08 by Austria, France, Great Britain, Italy, and Russia against Turkey for its misrule of Macedonia; and the humanitarian intercession in 1904–16 on behalf of Armenians by the United States and other states against Turkey.

Along with the dramatic rise in intrastate conflicts in the years since the end of the Cold War, and the massive human rights deprivations that have accompanied these conflicts, there has been a corresponding increase in the need for humanitarian intervention. With the operation of the U.N. Charter, the general proscription of military force embodied in its Article 2(4) has generated continuing controversy not only about the permissibility of self-help but also about the permissibility of humanitarian intervention under contemporary international law. With the recent increase in the use of peacekeeping forces for humanitarian intervention, this controversy has grown especially acute.

As with self-help, again, two diametrically opposing views have been presented. The arguments in support and in rejection of humanitarian intervention follow essentially the lines of arguments and counterarguments concerning self-help.

Since we have concluded that self-help, as disciplined by strict requirements of necessity and proportionality, remains permissible, it is even easier to defend the permissibility of humanitarian intervention, again as policed by rigorous requirements of necessity and proportionality.

This is so because of the paramount policy to protect and promote human rights that pervades the U.N. Charter and a host of related human rights instruments. As expounded in chapter 12, the paramount policy of human rights has been made amply clear in the charter and in the emergence of a global bill of human rights. The protection of human rights is one of the two central purposes of the United Nations. The overriding commitment to protect and fulfill human rights, coequal with the goal to maintain peace and security, finds expression throughout the charter. Under Article 56, all member states commit themselves to "take joint and separate action in co-operation with the Organization" to achieve "universal respect for, and observance of, human rights and fundamental freedoms for all without distinction as to race, sex, language, or religion." This paramount commitment has been fortified by the vast flow of ancillary prescriptions, including the Universal Declaration of Human Rights, the International Covenant on Civil and Political Rights (and its protocols), the International Covenant on Economic, Social, and Cultural Rights, and a multitude of related documents. Given this overriding commitment to human rights, as well as the reality and widespread perception that human rights and peace and security are closely linked, the use of military force to defend human rights may emphatically serve the common interest as an aid to the maintenance of minimum world order.

Closely related to the justification for humanitarian intervention based on respect for human rights is a corresponding change in the understanding of the nature of sovereignty as discussed at length in chapter 12. According to the traditional view of sovereignty, events occurring within the territory of a sovereign nation were generally considered to be matters of domestic jurisdiction and, therefore, outside the appropriate scope of concern of the international community. A sovereign's treatment of his or her own people, however repugnant, was a prototypical example of a matter of domestic jurisdiction with which the international community was not to concern itself.

This notion of sovereignty has eroded over time, largely corresponding to the increased recognition of and respect for the universality of human rights; and a more functional model has emerged. According to this emerging view, the rights of a sovereign state, such as the right of territorial integrity, are not absolute. Rather, such rights are conditional and can and will yield to more fundamental principles, such as the responsibility to protect human rights. Thus, in cases in which a sovereign state is either unwilling or unable to protect the human rights of its people, it may be considered to have forfeited the absolute right to territorial integrity.

Accordingly the use of military force for purposes of genuine humanitarian necessity not only does no violence to the charter but contributes in important ways to several of the paramount goals of the United Nations, including human rights. A genuine act of humanitarian intervention, threatening neither the territorial integrity nor the political independence of the target state, is not inconsistent with the purposes of the United Nations. In conformity with the major purposes and norms of the charter, the remedy of humanitarian intervention not only remains permissible but appears to have been fortified under contemporary international law.

The continued availability in general community expectation of the remedy of humanitarian intervention would appear confirmed by recent practice. In the aftermath of the Cold War the United Nations and some nation-states have intervened forcibly in Liberia (1990), northern Iraq (1991), southern Iraq (1992), Somalia (1992), Rwanda (1994), Haiti (1993–94), Bosnia (1995), Kosovo (1999), East Timor (1999), and Libya (2011). Post–Cold War crises have seen blatant and gruesome disregard for human rights, bringing the international community to intervene increasingly in affairs of nations whose citizens are subject to widespread human rights deprivations. The Bosnia-Herzegovina mission of 1992, however, may not be considered by all to be a true example of humanitarian intervention because the conflict was international in character, and the intervention was authorized by the Security Council.

NATO's 2011 operations in Libya offer a contemporary example of the use of the military instrument for humanitarian purposes. By February 2011, the Arab Spring had made its way to Tripoli. This wave of opposition movements that began in North Africa and the Middle East in late 2010 had toppled the regimes of Tunisian President Zine El-Abidine Ben Ali and Egyptian President Hosni Mubarak. In Libya, street protests held throughout the country called for an end to the four-decade-old regime of Colonel

Muammar Gaddafi. Gaddafi's regime responded violently to the protests, and international news outlets reported that state forces had tried to crush street protests using military aircraft and other weapons, fueling urgent calls for humanitarian intervention by the international community.

What began as street protests soon became a full-fledged armed opposition seeking to forcibly remove Gaddafi from power. By March, opposition forces had established a provisional government, the National Transitional Council, with a makeshift-capital at Benghazi. The Security Council took its first official action on February 26, unanimously adopting Security Council Resolution 1970 (2011), which called upon member states to freeze Gaddafi's assets and those of members of his inner circle and referred the situation to the International Criminal Court for further investigation.[11] On March 17, the Security Council unanimously adopted Resolution 1973 (2011), which authorized the imposition of a no-fly zone for the purpose of protecting Libyan civilians and described the situation as a "threat to international peace and security."[12]

The humanitarian military intervention in Libya began on March 19, 2011. Initially, a coalition of ten states, led by France, the United Kingdom, and the United States and including Qatar, took responsibility for implementing the no-fly zone. This coalition soon expanded to seventeen states, and on March 31, operational command was handed over to NATO.

Proponents of the intervention argued that it accomplished its mission and saved potentially thousands of innocent lives by thwarting a military attack against rebels in Benghazi. Critics argued, however, that the international community had interjected itself into a civil war. Despite these and other criticisms, it does seem clear that the intervention helped prevent a large-scale attack on population centers, and in this regard, the intervention was lawful from a humanitarian perspective and largely successful.

Contrast Libya with the case of Syria, another country roiled by internal conflicts, which has sparked intense debate over the limits of humanitarian intervention. What began with street protests against the regime of President Bashar al-Assad in early 2011 quickly grew into a full-fledged civil war, which claimed as many as 100,000 lives by late 2013, with scores more displaced by the violence.[13] Opposition forces, which include several militias supported by the United States and some European nations, are currently locked in battle against al-Assad's army, whose most strident allies include Russia and Iran. International efforts to resolve the conflict have so far failed, as Russia and China have refused to support proposals that would lead the Security Council to take actions including imposing sanctions or authorizing military force against the al-Assad regime.[14]

On its face, the situation in Syria appears little different from that in Libya two years before. If that is so, why hasn't the international community taken similar steps to resolve the humanitarian crisis? One explanation can be found in the power politics taking place among individual states within the United Nations. Although many aspects and principles of international law are well defined, international law does not operate automatically, and no two crises are ever alike. One must always consider the role of human decision makers and the context of effective power processes in the resolution of international legal issues. It may be that the crisis in Libya would have been resolved differently had Colonel Gaddafi cultivated stronger alliances.

Nevertheless, on certain issues, it appears that most, if not all, nations can agree. Take for example, the use of chemical weapons by al-Assad's army against opposition forces and civilians. In September 2013, a special U.N. mission reported that it had found clear and convincing evidence that al-Assad had used chemical weapons near Damascus in August that year.[15] The report sparked immediate and widespread condemnation, and arguments in favor of intervention intensified. Soon after, al-Assad, in coordination with the United States and Russia, negotiated to declare and surrender his stockpiles of chemical weapons, which were to be destroyed under international supervision. It appears that some international norms—such as the banning of highly destructive and inhumane weaponry in civil strife—are beyond question.

Although the U.N. Charter does not expressly recognize the lawfulness of using military force to protect a people from their own government in the face of genocide, starvation, disease, and violence, it is increasingly clear that humanitarian intervention is an established norm in international law, which is necessary for both minimum and optimum world order. Moreover, there is a strong presumption of lawfulness when humanitarian intervention is undertaken collectively by a coalition of states—*a fortiori* by a regional or global governmental organization.

Like self-help, the remedy of humanitarian intervention is a weapon for the powerful and is highly susceptible to abuse and misuse. The onerous strings attached to permissible self-help are thus equally applicable in the context of humanitarian intervention. Although the remedy cannot be precluded in a world that lacks centralized, effective enforcement, its use should be subject to vigorous contextual review by the general community for its strict conformity to the requirements of necessity and proportionality.

From the Law of War to International Humanitarian Law

Traditional international law made a conceptually rigid distinction between peace and war. Different sets of law were developed and made applicable—the law of peace, the law of war, and the law of neutrality—by reference to the existence or nonexistence of a technical state of "war" or "belligerency." The law of war, for example, deals with the commencement of war, the conduct and methods of war, certain protections for the victims of war, and the termination of war. The general dissatisfaction with this traditional approach has been resounding.

The U.N. Charter, as mentioned, discarded the use of "war" employing instead the phrases "the threat or use of force" and "threats to the peace, breaches of the peace, and acts of aggression" to designate a wide continuum of coercion. The war-peace dichotomy squares neither with the modern nature of "total" war nor with the contemporary reality of no-war, no-peace conditions. It has thus been suggested that "state of intermediacy" or "a third status intermediate between war and peace" would more aptly characterize the present state of world affairs.[16]

Although the U.N. Charter does away with the technical term "war," the world has not been spared the tragedies and scourges of armed conflicts of various scales— undeclared wars perhaps, but coercion, violence, armed conflicts nevertheless. Armed conflicts, internal and transnational, remain a fact of contemporary international life.

Hence, in spite of growing dissatisfaction with the peace-war dichotomy, the traditional law of war regulating the conduct of armed conflict has not altogether lost relevance and vitality. Fundamentally speaking, two complementary policies underlie the traditional laws of war: the policy of military necessity and the policy of humanity. The policy of military necessity permits the exercise of that violence necessary to achieve legitimate belligerent objectives through conduct not otherwise proscribed, as disciplined by the requirements of relevancy and proportionality. The policy of humanity seeks to minimize unnecessary infliction of death, injury, suffering, and other destruction of values even in times of hostility, distinguishing noncombatants from combatants and directing military operations to legitimate military targets. Although it is at times extremely difficult to strike a proper balance between the two policies, attempts have been especially pronounced in two areas: the prohibition of certain types of weapons in warfare and the humanization of the conduct of warfare—humane treatment of combatants as well as noncombatants.

First, the community efforts to proscribe certain types of weapons in warfare. Beginning with the 1863 Lieber Code, which recognized a prohibition of poison, and the St. Petersburg Declaration of 1868,[17] which prohibited explosive projectiles and incendiaries under four hundred grams, a series of treaties prohibited the employment of particular weapons in warfare. All arms, projectiles, or materials of a nature to cause unnecessary death, injury, or suffering were outlawed. The Geneva Protocol of Gas Warfare of 1925 banned the use of asphyxiating, poisonous, or other gases and of bacteriological warfare. Efforts continue to fortify the prohibitions against biological and chemical warfare, as exemplified by the Convention on the Prohibition of the Development, Production, and Stockpiling of Bacteriological (Biological) and Toxin Weapons and on Their Destruction of 1972. The advent of the atomic bomb has brought notable efforts to prohibit the use, manufacture, and testing of nuclear weapons.

A second major effort was made in the humanization of the conduct of armed conflicts. This corpus of law, both customary and conventional, has received renewed attention in recent years. Increasingly, this branch of international law has been approached in terms of "international humanitarian law in armed conflicts" or even "human rights in times of armed conflict" instead of laws and regulations of warfare. It is part of the contemporary global human rights movement, the distinct emphasis of which is on the human rights dimension. Armed conflicts may be unavoidable, but humanity, not barbarism, must be made to prevail even amid a hopelessly brutal situation.

At the core of international humanitarian law are the four Geneva Conventions of 1949 and Additional Protocols I and II to these conventions, concluded in 1977. The Geneva Conventions were built on the Hague Conventions of 1899 and 1907.

The four Geneva Conventions are the Geneva Convention for the Amelioration of the Condition of the Wounded and Sick in Armed Forces in the Field; the Geneva Convention for the Amelioration of the Condition of the Wounded, Sick, and Shipwrecked Members of Armed Forces at Sea; the Geneva Convention Relative to the Treatment of Prisoners of War; and the Geneva Convention Relative to the Protection of Civilian Persons in Time of War. In force since 1950, these conventions have received wide adherence by more than one hundred eighty states and are considered to reflect customary international law.

As their titles clearly indicate, these conventions set forth detailed prescriptions for humane treatment of wounded and disabled members of the armed forces (on land or at sea), prisoners of war, and civilian populations. They make a fundamental distinction between international armed conflicts (armed conflicts between two or more states or "belligerents" in the case of a traditional civil war) and internal armed conflicts ("armed conflict not of an international character occurring in the territory of one of the High Contracting Parties," or insurgencies that are localized). The bulk of the provisions are directed to international armed conflicts. Only one provision in the 1949 conventions—generally known as common Article 3 (and Protocol II)—prescribes rules for application to internal armed conflicts.

Article 3 requires "each Party to the conflict" (notably the government, the insurgent group) to accord humane treatment to all "persons taking no active part in the hostilities, including members of armed forces who have laid down their arms and those placed *hors de combat* by sickness, wounds, detention, or any other cause" without invidious distinction on such grounds as race, religion, sex, and wealth. The article categorically prohibits certain acts, including "violence to life and person," "taking of hostages," "outrages upon personal dignity," and arbitrary sentencing and execution. It requires that the wounded and sick be "collected and cared for" and grants a special role for the International Committee of the Red Cross in offering "its services to the Parties to the conflict." Common Article 3 is now considered to be customary law and to provide a minimum set of rights and duties even during an international armed conflict.

Protocols I and II, entering into force in 1978, were designed to supplement and reinforce the four Geneva Conventions. Protocol I in general relates to international armed conflicts, and Protocol II relates to internal armed conflicts. The line between the two is becoming increasingly difficult to draw in today's world.

Of foremost concern, as humankind lives under the constant threat of nuclear holocaust, is the question of lawfulness of nuclear weapons under contemporary international law. Some people think it an exercise in futility to attempt to answer this question because "vital national interests" would be involved in any use of nuclear weapons and these weapons do not lend themselves to effective regulation. In the 1980s, however, the growing worldwide demands for effective control of nuclear weapons (no-first-strike pledge, nuclear freeze, nuclear-free zones, and so on) renewed serious interest in this question on the part of the international legal community.

The issue of the lawfulness of nuclear weapons under contemporary international law can be examined in terms of nuclear weapons possession and use. Community efforts have resulted in modest successes in banning nuclear tests in the atmosphere, space, and water, but it appears that possession of nuclear weapons per se cannot be realistically banned. The post–Cold War era is still a nuclear age, and nuclear weapons continue to reflect the realities of effective world power and to serve as weapons of deterrence and defense. Barring a genuine, comprehensive disarmament, based on effective verification and mutual trust, humankind cannot realistically expect to completely dismantle existing nuclear arsenals. The Intermediate-Range Nuclear Forces (INF) Treaty between the United States and the former Soviet Union, which has continued in effect under successor states, has been a promising first step. With developing countries such as India and Pakistan insistent upon developing their nuclear might, however, there is still a long way to go.

The debate has thus centered on the lawfulness of the use of nuclear weapons. Opinions diverge greatly. One view holds that the use of nuclear weapons is per se unlawful. The opposite view maintains that the use of nuclear weapons is lawful. A third view takes the position that the lawfulness of the use of nuclear weapons depends on the context involved and even the type of nuclear projectile.

In 1996, the International Court of Justice, at the request of the World Health Organization and the General Assembly, handed down an advisory opinion on the legality of the threat or use of nuclear weapons.[18] The decision was essentially a "non-decision," because the court, while concluding that the threat or use of nuclear force is "generally contrary" to international law, was unable to conclude definitively either way; the opinion allows the use of nuclear weapons in "extreme circumstances of self-defense."[19] Such an opinion illustrates the limitations of a United Nations still dominated by the national sovereignty mindset and the shortcomings of the rule-oriented, positivist approach.

To reach a decision, the court first decided that the relevant applicable law was that of the rules of armed conflict, as provided in various international agreements including Article 51 of the U.N. Charter, which provides for the legitimacy of self-defense. The court decided that the requirements of proportionality and necessity did not necessarily exclude nuclear force where a nation's ultimate sovereignty was threatened.

The various international agreements prohibiting poisonous, chemical, and biological weapons were also examined, but because such treaties were concluded without literal reference to nuclear weapons, the court found them inapplicable.

Nor would the International Court of Justice accept the existence of an emerging peremptory norm based on efforts to restrain the nuclear camp. Rather, the court was swayed more by the reasoning of the states that argued that the acceptance of nuclear agreements by non-nuclear states (such as the Nuclear Non-Proliferation Treaty of 1968) demonstrated international consent to the policy of deterrence rather than any emerging norm of prohibition. Also, the court agreed with the nuclear weapon states that these partial agreements only confirmed the fact that there exists no total prohibition on the use of these weapons. Trapped by a positivist approach, the court was bound by precedent without regard to the effects of its decision on the values and goals of the law examined.

Taking note of customary law that consists of the principles of neutrality and humanitarian law applicable in armed conflict, *jus in bello*, the court stated that the use of nuclear weapons was not necessarily at variance with these principles. The claimants also argued that the numerous General Assembly resolutions proclaiming the illegality of nuclear weapons use should have normative value, even if not binding. The court, however, stressed that such resolutions had been adopted with substantial numbers of negative votes and abstentions—it is generally accepted that U.N. resolutions may acquire the force of law only with overwhelming support of the member states.

The opinion appears to reflect three widely diverging views. The first view holds that use of nuclear weapons would be unlawful because it would be contrary to the twin policies of military necessity and humanity that infuse the entire law of war, customary and conventional. Thus, many dissenters relied on the Martens Clause[20] as a peremptory norm that rules out altogether any threat or use of such weapons; community proscriptions of destructive and lethal weapons would extend by analogy to nuclear weapons. Because the use of nuclear weapons would obliterate the traditional distinction between civilian populations and military targets, their threat or use is illegal.

To buttress their position, supporters of this view have drawn on diverse sources, ranging from customary law, to treaty law, to national judicial decisions (for example, the notable *Shimoda* case decided by the District Court of Tokyo in 1963).[21] They have attached a particular weight to Resolution 1653, Declaration on the Prohibition of the Use of Nuclear and Thermo-Nuclear Weapons, adopted by the General Assembly in 1961.[22] This declaration, in pronouncing the unlawfulness of the use of nuclear weapons, aptly sums up the thrust of the familiar argument:

(a) The use of nuclear and thermo-nuclear weapons is contrary to the spirit, letter and aims of the United Nations and, as such, a direct violation of the Charter of the United Nations; (b) The use of nuclear and thermo-nuclear weapons would exceed the scope of war and cause indiscriminate suffering and destruction to mankind and civilization and, as such, is contrary to the rule of international law and to the laws of humanity; (c) The use of nuclear and thermo-nuclear weapons is a war directed not against an enemy or enemies alone but also against mankind in general, since the peoples of the world not involved in such a war will be subjected to all the evils generated by the use of such weapons; (d) Any State using nuclear and thermo-nuclear weapons is to be considered as violating the Charter of the United Nations, as acting contrary to the laws of humanity and as committing a crime against mankind and civilization.

Those who flatly assert that the use of nuclear weapons is lawful rely more or less on a traditional maxim in international law, attributable to the *S.S. Lotus* decision,[23] that states are permitted to do that which is not expressly prohibited. This second view was held by Judge Schwebel, who, quoting the British attorney general with approval, stated that prohibition "would be an aggressor's charter."[24] In addition, this camp refuses to view nuclear weapons contextually in terms of their fundamental differences from ordinary weapons and asserts that analogies drawn from the laws of wars past are inapposite. It would indeed be the height of absurdity to assert that a state is free to risk the destruction of the world on the ground that nowhere is that competence expressly denied, but this was the reasoning put forth. It is clear, however, that the destruction of humankind would deprive the sovereignty of all states of all meaning.

The third view, more contextual in its approach, calls special attention to the realistic role of deterrence played by nuclear strategies in the maintenance of contemporary world public order and to the critical need of approximate conjunction between expectations of authority and control. This appears to be the view relied upon by Judge Fleischauer, who balanced the principles of humanitarian law, neutrality, and self-defense. Although all have equal ranking, self-defense trumps the others. Thus was permission granted in the noted paragraph 2E of the decision to allow the use of nuclear arms in an emergency and to accept the policy of deterrence. This view eschews a per se rule but stresses a particular context. Some nuclear projectiles, in fact, are "tactical" in nature, posing minimal risk outside legitimate military targets.

The dissenters, including Judge Weennantry and Judge Shababuddeen, pointed out some contemporary developments that should be brought to bear on legal thought. Article 2[4] of the U.N. Charter has significantly restricted the right of nation states to resort to force. The world has become interdependent, with a movement away from state sovereignty and toward a universal international community.

Because nuclear weapons have the potential to destroy civilization, the law of war must be reoriented to face the new reality. The rules must be examined not in a vacuum but contextually, in view of the purpose and relevance to the shaping and sharing of values. In dealing with the military instrument, the basic community policy must be oriented toward the principle of peaceful change and noncoercion in international affairs.

Notes

1. Myers S. McDougal & Florentino P. Feliciano, The International Law of War: Transnational Coercion and World Public Order 137 (1961).

2. G.A. Res. 3314 (XXIX), U.N. Doc. A/9631 (Dec. 14, 1974).

3. See McDougal & Feliciano, supra note 1, at 121–260.

4. Letter from Mr. Webster to Mr. Fox (April 24, 1841), in 29 British and Foreign State Papers, 1840–1841, at 1129, 1138 (1857).

5. Myers S. McDougal, The Soviet-Cuban Quarantine and Self-Defense, 57 A.J.I.L. 597 (1963).

6. Military and Paramilitary Activities in and Against Nicaragua (Nicar. v. U.S.), Judgment on Merits, 1986 I.C.J. 14 (June 27).

7. Steven R. Weisman, Threats and Responses: Security Council; Powell, in U.N. Speech, Presents Case to Show Iraq Has Not Disarmed, N.Y. Times, Feb. 6, 2003, available at http://www.nytimes.com/2003/02/06/world/threats-responses-security-council-powell-un-speech-presents-case-show-iraq-has.html?pagewanted=all&src=pm.

8. Helene Cooper and Matthew Rosenberg, NATO Agrees on Afghan Security Transition in 2013, N.Y. Times, May 21, 2012, available at http://www.nytimes.com/2012/05/22/world/nato-formally-agrees-to-transition-on-afghan-security.html.

9. Corfu Channel (U.K. v. Alb.), Judgment on Merits, 1949 I.C.J. 4 (Apr. 9).

10. Id. at 35.

11. S.C. Res. 1970, U.N. Doc. S/RES/1970 (Feb. 26, 2011).

12. S.C. Res. 1973, at 2, U.N. Doc. S/RES/1973 (Mar. 17, 2011).

13. Alan Cowell, War Deaths in Syria Said to Top 100,000, N.Y. Times, June 26, 2013, available at http://www.nytimes.com/2013/06/27/world/middleeast/syria.html.

14. Rick Gladstone, Friction at the U.N. as Russia and China Veto Another Resolution on Syria Sanctions, N.Y. Times, July 19, 2013, available at http://www.nytimes.com/2012/07/20/world/middleeast/russia-and-china-veto-un-sanctions-against-syria.html.

15. United Nations Mission to Investigate Allegations of the Use of Chemical Weapons in the Syrian Arab Republic, Report on the Alleged Use of Chemical Weapons in the Ghouta Area of Damascus on 21 August 2013 (Sept. 13, 2013), available at http://www.un.org/disarmament/content/slideshow/Secretary_General_Report_of_CW_Investigation.pdf.

16. Philip C. Jessup, Should International Law Recognize an Intermediate Status Between Peace and War?, 48 A.J.I.L. 98 (1954).

17. Text of the Declaration of St. Petersburg, in Thomas Erskine Holland, The Law of War on Land 77 (1908).

18. Legality of the Threat or Use of Nuclear Weapons, Advisory Opinion, 1996 I.C.J. 95 (July 8); see also Michael J. Matheson, The Opinions of the International Court of Justice on the Threat or Use of Nuclear Weapons, 91 A.J.I.L. 417 (1997).

19. Legality of the Threat or Use of Nuclear Weapons, supra note 18, at 266.

20. The Martens Clause originated from Fyoder F. Martens, the Russian delegate to the Hague Conferences of 1899. At his insistence, the following clause was included in the preamble to the 1899 Hague Convention concerning the Laws and Customs of War on Land: "Until a more complete code of the laws of war is issued, the High Contracting Parties think it right to declare that in cases not included in the Regulations adopted by them, populations and

belligerents remain under the protection and empire of the principles of international law, as they result from the usages established between civilized nations, from the laws of humanity and the requirements of the public conscience."

21. Shimoda Case [Tokyo Dist. Ct.], Dec. 7, 1963, *translated into English and reprinted in full in* 8 JAP. ANN. INT'L L. 212 (1964).

22. G.A. Res. 1653 (XVI), U.N. Doc. A/5100 (Nov. 24, 1961).

23. S.S. Lotus (Fr./Turk.), 1927 P.C.I.J. (ser. A), No. 10 (Sept. 7).

24. Legality of the Threat or Use of Nuclear Weapons, *supra* note 18, at 839 (separate opinion of Judge Schwebel).

VII Outcomes

THE OUTCOMES OF the comprehensive world constitutive process of authoritative decision are the various decisions taken when making and applying law to manifold problems. These decisions may be conveniently classified into seven functions: intelligence (information), promotion, prescription, invocation, application, termination, and appraisal. The effectiveness and the economy with which these functions are performed directly affect the quality of protection afforded by international law. Thanks to continuous improvement of every feature of the constitutive process, the performance of each function has improved. The relevant decisions exhibit increasing comprehensiveness in embracing all necessary policy functions; more inclusive in the extension of participants and interactions affecting common interests; more rational in the degree of conformity to the basic public order demands and expectations of the world's peoples; and more integrative by molding the potentially divisive claims of peoples into the perception and fact of common interest.

These decision functions, though distinctive, are closely interrelated. Each contributes to, and is affected by, the performance of every other function.

20 The Intelligence Function

THE INTELLIGENCE (INFORMATION) function entails gathering, processing, and disseminating information essential to making decisions. Facts must be explored in order to perform each decision function. The intelligence process directly affects this performance. The availability of a continuing flow of dependable, comprehensive, and relevant information is essential to recommend concrete proposals in pursuit of the common interest, to generate rational prescriptions, to initiate timely invocation against a violation of international law, to secure effective application of norms with minimal coercion, to foster a timely end to obsolete prescriptions, and to undertake a critical yet constructive appraisal. In a decentralized, state-centered world in which mobilization of world public opinion plays a crucial role in articulating and defending the common interest, effective and continuing exposure to the facts of compliance or noncompliance of norms is vital to maintain world order.

Most intelligence gathering is traditionally done by the officials of nation-states. This is one of the oldest activities that governments undertake. Some of these activities have been legal and some illegal. Though governmental agencies, such as the Central Intelligence Agency (CIA) of the United States and the defunct Committee for State Security (KGB) of Russia, are well known for their intelligence task, other officials and governmental agencies do gather, process, and disseminate information in the broadest sense.

The role of diplomatic officials merits some consideration. An important task of diplomats is to gather intelligence of all kinds to facilitate diplomatic and other strategies of influence. Most information is gathered from public sources, but information gathered by covert agents often supplements it. States generally maintain secrecy regarding matters of a vital or sensitive nature, and secrecy breeds curiosity, suspicion, and anxiety. Thus, great efforts are often made to penetrate the veil of secrecy, including breaking communication codes, wiretapping telephones, and planting electronic devices in diplomatic missions. The diplomatic missions themselves may employ electronic surveillance devices to intercept telephone, radio, and other communications in the host country. Are such activities compatible with the policy of affording diplomatic privileges and immunities? In spite of a tendency toward routinization and mutual tolerance, excesses and abuses in this area on occasion exacerbate difficulties in interstate relations. In 1893, for example, the French government was compelled to recall virtually the entire staff of its legation at Copenhagen because of the abortive French attempt to secure, through an intermediary, information concerning Anglo-Russian relations. Contrast this with the following incident: In September 1985, the United Kingdom ordered the ouster of twenty-five Soviet officials after a Soviet defector, the chief of the British branch of the KGB, identified them as spies. The Soviet Union retaliated by ordering the expulsion of twenty-five Britons, including diplomats, embassy staff members, journalists, and business people. The expulsion of six more Russians by the United Kingdom was further matched by the Soviet ouster of six more Britons. More recently, revelations that the U.S. National Security Agency (NSA) listened in on world leaders' cellular phone conversations sparked diplomatic tensions. In 2013, German Chancellor Angela Merkel personally expressed her displeasure to President Barack Obama after learning that the NSA had listened to her personal phone conversations. According to reports, Merkel was among dozens of leaders, including many close U.S. allies, who were targeted for surveillance in recent years.[1]

The advent of the Internet has further heightened the tension between individuals' right to receive and conceal information and states' desire to control access to information. Officials regularly seek to withhold information from the public's view, often by appealing to the need to protect a vital interest such as national security. However, the ease of sharing electronic data has frustrated efforts to suppress such knowledge. Computer hackers regularly infiltrate the computer systems of government entities and private firms in search of sensitive data. These individuals may work for personal gain or under the direction of other governments for purposes including espionage. Others seek access to classified sources in order to uncover information that may be of interest to the public. This is one of the primary functions of journalists in democratic societies where the dissemination of information is necessary to hold officials accountable for their actions. In recent years, WikiLeaks, and similar organizations, have helped shed light on the workings of governments around the world by putting secret documents into the public domain, sometimes revealing evidence of corruption and wrongdoing. In 2013, a government contractor named Edward Snowden released a trove of classified information detailing the United States' efforts to monitor electronic communications, including the private e-mails and telephone calls of U.S. citizens and individuals abroad. A dramatic worldwide manhunt ensued, and Snowden ultimately found refuge in Russia. His story, and the resulting public backlash, demonstrate the sensitivity individuals feel toward perceived violations of expectations of privacy, as well as the lengths states will go to in order to veil such activities.

States have long used the guise of domestic jurisdiction (noninterference in internal affairs) to insulate events within their borders from outside scrutiny. The press blackout imposed in the autumn of 1985 on the national and international news media by the Botha government of South Africa and the restrictions placed on the media by governments in the Middle East and North Africa during the Arab Spring protests in 2011 illustrate how power elites seek to frustrate the intelligence function. In South Africa, authorities attempted to minimize the effects of information gathering by antiapartheid governments, organizations, and individuals by restricting media coverage of violence, military rule in certain nonwhite districts, and even funeral processions. Likewise, during the Arab Spring, governments in the Middle East and North Africa attempted to impose blackouts on the media, including restrictions on Internet use by individuals. However, the ubiquity of digital media made it impossible to stem the tide of information from the region, which continued to reach audiences around the globe via advanced mobile communications and other technologies.

International governmental organizations are increasingly engaged in gathering information, making studies, and dispatching fact-finding missions, in spite of state reluctance to cooperate. Similarly, the role of private associations in such activities has grown, operating both within states and beyond their borders.

In recent times demands have increased for better information about the conduct of states and world conditions. Many voices are being raised in international organizations and private associations, and the geographic range of demands is extending to remote areas of the globe. People are agitating for fuller information about the conditions that affect security, development, the environment, human rights, and so on. Many intelligence activities perforce must go beyond the boundaries of any state. The process of disseminating information is made easier by a global network of mass communications. Consequently, there has been an immense flow of information about the shaping and sharing of values around the globe and about the conditions under which security, development, human rights, and so on can be secured.

International governmental organizations increasingly play a vital role in information gathering, processing, and dissemination through the bureaucratic structures. Specific authority is conferred on various U.N. structures and other international governmental entities. The General Assembly is empowered to initiate studies to promote international cooperation in the economic, social, cultural, educational, and health fields and to foster better protection and fulfillment of human rights. The Economic and Social Council is authorized to make or initiate studies and reports concerning international economic, social, cultural, educational, health, and related matters. The council is further authorized to take proper steps to obtain regular reports from the specialized agencies and to request member states and the specialized agencies to provide information pertaining to matters that fall within its competence.

In performance, informational activities vary and include seminars, fellowship programs, advisory services of experts, special studies, exchanges of information and documentation, technical assistance, press and information services, the reporting system, fact-finding missions, and on-the-spot observation and investigation. The U.N. Secretariat provides formally within its cellular bureaucracy for gathering, processing, and disseminating information about various problems.

A continuing flow of information reaches the U.N. Secretariat from a variety of sources, including speeches made in the general debate of the General Assembly and in other U.N. bodies, written reports from other international governmental organizations, oral and written communications between U.N. officials and national delegates, information centers, field missions, and observations and findings of visiting missions, and a host of U.N. committees, studies, and researches. The Economic and Social Council and its network of regional economic commissions, UNCTAD, WTO, and UNDP collect, process, and spread information regarding transnational wealth processes. The World Bank group and the International Monetary Fund are particularly concerned with data about the fluctuations of national economies and transnational monetary trends. UNESCO engages in informational activities relating to trends in enlightenment and skills. The concern of the International Labour Organization (ILO) extends to sectors of wealth, skill, and well-being. The World Health Organization gathers and disseminates information about health and safety conditions around the globe, and the Food and Agriculture Organization assembles and spreads information concerning the world's food resources and supplies. The U.N. Environment Programme (UNEP) collects and spreads information about the world environment. The U.N. High Commissioner for Refugees (UNHCR) is an important center for gathering and disseminating information about the plight of the world's refugees. This comprehensive flow of information, as further supplemented and fortified by various regional organizations, extends to every value sector.

International governmental organizations rely heavily on the cooperation of nation-states in performing the intelligence function. Since states remain the primary gatherers and disseminators of information, the world constitutive process must rely extensively on government reports in many matters. The League of Nations instituted the government reporting system in relation to mandated territories and the international regime of minority protection. Under the U.N. system, governmental reports on trust territories and non-self-governing territories are required by its charter. The Economic and Social Council, under Article 64(1) of the charter, may arrange with U.N. member states to "obtain reports on the steps taken to give effect to its own recommendations and to recommendations on matters falling within its competence made by the General Assembly."

The International Atomic Energy Agency (IAEA) is an example of an organization that plays a significant role in efforts to promote the safe use of nuclear energy through information gathering. The IAEA is an independent organization, but it coordinates its efforts closely with the U.N. General Assembly and the Security Council. One of the primary functions of the IAEA is to gather information regarding nations' use of nuclear technologies to ensure they are used only for peaceful purposes, such as energy production, and not for the creation of weapons of mass destruction. The IAEA accomplishes its mission through routine inspections and reporting to member nations and the United Nations. Additionally, the IAEA serves as a forum for the dissemination of knowledge useful for making nuclear technology safer and more secure.

Following the nuclear disaster in Chernobyl, Ukraine, in 1986, members of the IAEA agreed on two conventions that encourage nations to self-report in the event of nuclear accidents that pose a risk beyond their borders: the Convention on Early Notification of a Nuclear Accident and the Convention on Assistance in the Case of a Nuclear Accident or Radiological Emergency. The agreements impose on member nations a duty to report that is intended to facilitate a quick response to nuclear incidents in order to protect individuals and property and to coordinate emergency measures through the exchange of information. The importance of such a duty was made clear again following the earthquake and tsunami in Japan in 2011, which resulted in significant damage to the Fukushima nuclear power plant. Some alleged that Japanese authorities were slow to reveal information about the magnitude of the event and the danger posed by nuclear material released into the air and sea around the plant.[2]

In human rights, the reporting system has become an important channel for obtaining information about conditions of human rights in various communities. This system is maintained under the Human Rights Council and in most of the transnational human rights instruments, especially the two international covenants on human rights, the International Convention on the Elimination of All Forms of Racial Discrimination, and the Convention on the Elimination of All Forms of Discrimination Against Women. The creation of the post of high commissioner speaks to the system's increasing importance to the global monitoring of human rights violations. Though many states may be delinquent in filing required reports or self-serving in their submitted reports, this system has become an important institutional feature by which to obtain pertinent information, especially when it is coupled with the opportunity to examine, in situ or in open session, the country concerned. Even self-serving reports can affect a domestic legal process, making an impact on attitudes and behavior.

An important method of obtaining dependable information is on-the-spot investigations in the form of fact-finding commissions. This practice antedates the emergence of contemporary international organizations and has long been employed by nation-states, both bilaterally and multilaterally. It gained wide acceptance especially at the Hague Convention of 1899. International governmental organizations have since adopted this technique and used it in a wide range of contexts. The General Assembly has established commissions of inquiry and directed them into the field to collect information relating to various questions. The International Labour Organization uses this technique in the form of its Committee of Experts. The committee solicits information from local employer and worker organizations and receives the formal national reports submitted to the ILO. This fact-finding method has proved highly effective.

Nation-states are notorious in their resistance to on-the-spot investigations of human rights or other matters, in the name of "sovereignty" or "domestic jurisdiction." In U.N. history, the General Assembly's dispatch of a human rights mission in 1963 to investigate the oppression of Buddhists in South Vietnam was a notable exception, thanks to a unique combination of factors. In such other areas as southern and central Africa, the Israeli-occupied territories, and Iraq, efforts at on-the-spot-investigations have been frustrated.

A prime example is the establishment of the U.N. Fact Finding Mission on the Gaza Conflict in 2009. The mission was tasked by the U.N. Human Rights Council to investigate accusations of human rights abuses by the Israel Defence Force and Palestinian militants during the three-week Gaza War that took place from December 2008 to January 2009. The mission's four-person team was headed by Richard Goldstone, a former South African judge and war crimes prosecutor for the tribunals for Rwanda and Yugoslavia. The Israeli government refused to cooperate with the investigation or to give the mission access to military witnesses, arguing that several aspects of the investigation were biased against the country.[3]

The mission released its findings, known as the Goldstone Report, in September 2009.[4] The report detailed a series of potential war crimes and crimes against humanity committed by both sides during the conflict. It included accusations of the intentional killing of civilians, the use of human shields, and the deployment of chemical munitions in heavily populated areas. The report's findings were considered controversial at the time of its release and both the Israelis and the Palestinian group Hamas rejected aspects of it that were critical of their own sides. Eventually, the report was endorsed by the Human Rights Council and two subsequent resolutions from the General Assembly urged both sides to conduct internal investigations into the accusations of war crimes during the conflict.

The tendency of nation-states toward insulation has been remedied somewhat by the increasing role played by non-state actors in the world arena. Channels of information are open to many other actors—not only international governmental organizations but also pressure groups and private associations.

The growing role of pressure groups and private associations in the world constitutive process has made them an indispensable source of information about economic development, the environment, human rights, and so on. Because these nongovernmental organizations (NGOs) tend to focus attention on the particular value process in which they specialize, they often possess a wealth of information in their areas. An increasing number of NGOs have sought and attained consultative status in relation to the

Economic and Social Council of the United Nations and from this position disseminate to the world at large information about the value sectors of their concern. Other NGOs, national and transnational, assemble and spread information through unofficial communication channels that eventually reach both transnational and national decision makers. These organizations, representing every value sector, afford a vital dimension in the intelligence function, supplying and disseminating information that is often otherwise unavailable. Although these organizations are diverse and may present conflicting information, the aggregate flow of information generated and disseminated by them likely ensures the sifting of fact from falsehood or fantasy. The very diversity of NGOs may also aid in policing special interests in light of the common interest of a more inclusive community.

The recent proliferation of international governmental organizations and the expanded participation of political parties, pressure groups, and private associations in the constitutive process have enormously increased facilities to gather, process, and disseminate globally the information essential to rational decision. The developing technology of observation and communication through various instruments promises to augment this potential, especially with cooperation on a scale larger than ever before.

Diplomats continue to play their traditional role in gathering information, but new techniques of information gathering, especially electronic surveillance against and from foreign legations, raise new problems. In addition to electronic developments, other modern intelligence-gathering "devices," such as chemical tracers, or "spy dust," are of more questionable legality. In 1985, before the Soviet Union fell, the United States claimed that the KGB was using a potentially harmful invisible chemical agent, applied indirectly to embassy personnel and other Americans in the Soviet Union to track their movements and contacts, presumably by spreading it on doorknobs and steering wheels they would be likely to touch. The Soviet government denied these allegations, but such accusations regarding covert intelligence-gathering often pass between nation-states engaged in "high-tech" intelligence methods.[5]

Another sensitive area relates to the lawfulness of collecting information about coastal states by electronic means from the high seas. The seizure of the *USS Pueblo* by North Korea on January 23, 1968, created considerable controversy about such electronic reconnaissance from the high seas. There was some disagreement on the questions of fact. The North Korean government accused the ship of the deliberate intrusion into their territorial sea (twelve miles, as they and most states so claimed), but the United States denied this allegation. The North Korean government did not claim the authority to seize a ship engaged in intelligence missions on the high seas but asserted that the ship had deliberately intruded into its territorial waters and was engaged in non-innocent passage. It would appear that international law in principle does not ban electronic reconnaissance from the high seas (or, it may be noted, from outer space) and that the coastal state cannot interfere with foreign warships or aircraft engaged in such electronic reconnaissance unless they enter territorial waters.

A similar incident occurred when a U.S. reconnaissance plane collided with a Chinese jet over the South China Sea in 2001. The U.S. aircraft made an emergency landing on the Chinese island of Hainan, where the crew was interrogated before being released to U.S. authorities. The incident raised questions about the legality of conducting military surveillance over an exclusive economic zone of another nation. Despite Chinese protests, the United States maintained that its actions were legal under the provisions of the U.N. Convention on the Law of the Sea, which allows for unrestricted navigation by air. These issues are discussed more thoroughly in chapter 9.

Outer space provides a vast new arena for various activities involving the collection of important information, as exemplified by the use of reconnaissance satellites for strategic purposes, commercial espionage, and remote sensing of information about vital resources on the earth. The Outer Space Treaty, in Article 4, provides that the moon and other celestial bodies be used "exclusively for peaceful purposes." Article 4, however, does not contain the same blanket mandate with regard to spacecraft in earth orbit—it provides instead that nuclear weapons and other weapons of mass destruction shall not be placed in orbit around the earth. The difference in formulation is significant, having to do especially with the permissibility of using spacecraft in earth orbit for reconnaissance. More generally, Article 3 requires that activities be conducted "in the interest of maintaining international peace and security," but such a requirement does not prohibit reconnaissance serving peace and security in the common interest (that is, "in the interests of all countries" as with the meaning of Article 1). In the course of negotiating the Outer Space Treaty, the former Soviet Union, as a "closed society," contended that the use of satellites for reconnaissance purposes was unlawful and should be banned by the treaty. The United States emphatically disagreed. The use of reconnaissance satellites would prove critical in verifying compliance with disarmament agreements. This was in keeping with President Eisenhower's call during the Cold War for "open skies," on the belief that only by candidly revealing to each other the state of their military establishments could the Soviet Union and the United States ensure peace. Eisenhower called for each nation to engage in continual overflights of the other so that any attempts at large-scale attack would be impossible to conceal. Intelligence-gathering activities were thus seen as vital to maintain peace in a divided world, especially in the absence of open societies. The open skies policy was thought to be a way of bringing intelligence gathering out in the open, to prevent some of the problems and dangers associated with covert efforts, which had been highlighted during the U-2 spy plane incident of 1960 when the Soviet Union shot down a U.S. plane that was on a reconnaissance mission.

In regard to remote sensing of the earth's resources, developing nations increasingly demand that their resources not be examined or analyzed without their prior consent and that they be able to gain access to, and exercise some control over, the data collected by remote sensing satellites. In the contemporary information society, information, of course, is an important base not only for enlightenment but also for wealth, power, and other values. The legal issues stemming from remote sensing involve conflicting facts. Although the earth's resources are without doubt subject to the sovereignty of the state in which they are located, this does not preclude activities outside the state's territorial domain that have no immediate instate impact. Problems will arise when an attempt is made to use the information in the sensed state. It has been argued that there is no need to control space sensing because control of the resources remains in the state's hands. This ignores the role of information in the marketplace. The state's supreme authority could be abridged by such a use of information gathered by remote sensing, and so controls of some kind have been called for.

In spite of the great potentials of technology, it remains difficult to obtain a continuing flow of dependable and comprehensive information relevant to rational decision making for security, development, human rights, and other matters. Even where information has been gathered and processed, access to that information is much more than a question of referral to appropriate sources. Required also is the ability to comprehend and use the knowledge gained. For example, when information vital to global or individual national environmental management is only or most readily obtainable within a particular country or region, political or other barriers may interfere with its transfer. The United States and the former Soviet Union recognized that the exchange of environmental information could transcend political differences and were able to come to a bilateral Agreement on Cooperation in the Field of Environmental Protection.

In the post–Cold War world, it was hoped that new threats to global security, such as ozone depletion and global warming, could be better met through the use of U.S. spy satellite photographs from the 1960s. The declassification of these photos in 1995 marked the beginning of a new spirit of cooperation and the decline of Cold War–era secrecy. The photographs held great meaning for scientists, scholars, and environmentalists studying environmental change. More recently, advances in technology have broken through Cold War–era secrecy by virtue of its sophistication and accessibility. In the post–Cold War world, there is simply more information available and it is widely disseminated and accessible to the public. Take, for example, WikiLeaks, which was instrumental in bringing classified government information into the public forum by providing a platform that allows for anonymous posting. In 2010, WikiLeaks leaked thousands of classified documents detailing the U.S. military engagements in Iraq and Afghanistan. Though condemned by some governmental officials around the world, WikiLeaks continued to operate; albeit under greater scrutiny than before.

It is a commonplace that the nation-state remains unwilling to subject itself to effective external scrutiny. A greater difficulty is the effective processing and use of available information. Considerable interstate controversy still surrounds the subject of prior consultation concerning proposed activities. Such information is vital to project the impact on the environment or resources of bordering states. The duty to provide official and public knowledge of technical data relating to probable environmental consequences of proposed activities and the overall obligation of information and prior consultation have been accepted in General Assembly Resolution 3129, but the content and means of such notification have to be agreed on and institutionalized.

Fact-finding has its utility but also its limitations. Our data-rich civilization has no dearth of facts but, rather, suffers from an information explosion. Information is out there waiting to be tapped. It is critical that it be collected, processed, and disseminated to meet effectively and in a timely manner the ongoing, and often pressing, needs of rational decision making. A notable shortcoming is the lack of a comprehensive conception of the goals and ramifications in gathering, processing, and disseminating information. Another is the absence of a centralized clearinghouse procedure capable of absorbing and consolidating the many fragmented items of information into a coherent, contextual, and comprehensive whole. For instance, the 9/11 Commission Report dramatized the state of noncoordination between U.S. intelligence agencies before the terrorist attacks of September 11, 2001.[6] Only with such a comprehensive frame of reference can intelligence efforts yield significant, cumulative impact on the making of timely and rational decisions.

Notes

1. Alison Smale, *Anger Growing Among Allies on U.S. Spying*, N.Y. TIMES, Oct. 23, 2013, *available at* http://www.nytimes.com/2013/10/24/world/europe/united-states-disputes-reports-of-wiretapping-in-Europe.html.

2. Hiroko Tabuchi, *Delay in Disclosing Leaks at Fukushima Is Criticized*, N.Y. TIMES, July 26, 2013, *available at* http://www.nytimes.com/2013/07/27/world/asia/operator-of-fukushima-plant-criticized-for-delaying-disclosures-on-leaks.html.

3. ISRAEL MINISTRY OF FOREIGN AFFAIRS, INITIAL RESPONSE TO REPORT OF THE FACT FINDING MISSION ON GAZA ESTABLISHED PURSUANT TO RESOLUTION S-9/1 OF THE HUMAN RIGHTS COUNCIL (Sept. 24, 2009), *available at* http://mfa.gov.il/MFA_Graphics/MFA%20Gallery/Documents/GoldstoneReportInitialResponse240909.pdf.

4. HUMAN RIGHTS IN PALESTINE AND OTHER OCCUPIED ARAB TERRITORIES: REPORT OF THE UNITED NATIONS FACT-FINDING MISSION ON THE GAZA CONFLICT, A/HRC/12/48 (Sept. 25, 2009), *available at* http://www2.ohchr.org/english/bodies/hrcouncil/docs/12session/A-HRC-12-48.pdf.

5. Shirley Christian, *Soviets Said to Use Chemical to Trace Americans' Moves*, N.Y. TIMES, Aug. 22, 1985, at A1.

6. *See* FINAL REPORT OF THE NATIONAL COMMISSION ON TERRORIST ATTACKS UPON THE UNITED STATES (THE 9/11 COMMISSION REPORT) (2004), *available at* http://www.911commission.gov/report/911Report.pdf.

21 The Promoting Function

THE PROMOTING FUNCTION refers to the advocacy of policy alternatives, including taking initiatives to attain the enactment of prescriptions and mobilizing opinion toward particular policies. It adds the intensity of demand to expectation. Three sequences are often involved: the exploration of facts; the formulation of demands; and the propagation of demands by mobilizing people and resources to secure necessary commitments. In this function, effective power brings its influence distinctively to bear on authoritative community policy.

Of primary importance is the promotion of common rather than special interests. An integrated policy should be encouraged through channels of promotion open to all participants engaged in effective means of persuasion.

The promoting function has historically been performed by all groups and individuals holding or participating in processes of effective power. These promoters are sometimes governmental officials but are often active members of political parties, pressure groups, and private associations. A principal function of political parties is to organize and promote explicit programs. Pressure groups are concerned with both general and particular policy purposes. Private associations, dedicated to values other than power, seek to shape and share their specialized values. These groups and individuals operate through a variety of organizational techniques and a range of mass communication media. Promotional messages are directed not only to official and effective elites but also to general audiences. Promoters create and maintain an ever-expanding network of organizations and contacts about the world. Besides small-group bargaining, they engender a massive flow of propaganda and agitation. Their ongoing activities are crucial in managing and mobilizing world public opinion and in transforming policy alternatives into authoritative prescription and application.

The increasing democratization of participation in world processes of effective power, the availability and openness of the new structures of authority, and the modern means of communication have brought a new comprehensiveness and intensity to the active advocacy of competing policy alternatives before authoritative decision makers. The essence of promotional strategies is effective and provocative communication. As such, promotion often involves elements of intense demands, verging at times on coercion, characterized by the agitations of elite groups in order to provoke the formulation of authoritative prescriptions. Coercive strategies, however, have no place in the promotional process of a public order of human dignity.

The nation-state, with its dominant control of effective power, traditionally played a leading role in transnational promotional activities. For such activities nation-state officials do not require any particular authorization; indeed, much of the framework of international law is their charter.

The importance attached to the promotional role of international governmental organizations testifies to the imperative need for transnational cooperation. The General Assembly, for example, is authorized by the U.N. Charter to recommend international cooperation in the economic, social, cultural, educational, and health fields and to help protect and fulfill human rights. A similar mandate is extended to the Economic and Social Council. The General Assembly, the Economic and Social Council, and specialized agencies have made innumerable recommendations concerning multiple values and problems. Many of the recommendations have further matured into either multilateral treaties or customary international law.

Increasingly evident, as discussed in chapter 4, is the prominent role played by nongovernmental organizations (pressure groups and private associations) in fostering the achievement of both minimum and optimum world order. Many nongovernmental organizations have acquired consultative status with the Economic and Social Council and with other international governmental organizations (such as ILO, UNESCO, WHO, FAO, and ITU). Depending on their recognized status, such organizations may be permitted to be present at the council's deliberations or even suggest items for inclusion in the provisional agenda. Many U.N. recommendations and decisions in various fields have resulted, directly or indirectly, from the initiatives and efforts of nongovernmental organizations and associations.

To pool their resources and coordinate their activities, to minimize duplication and maximize the use of resources, and to extend their reach and influence, NGOs have increasingly formed larger networks within umbrella organizations. Notable examples include the Union of International Associations, the Conference of Non-Governmental Organizations, the International Coalition for Development Action, the International

Confederation for Disarmament and Peace, the International Council of Scientific Unions, the Non-Governmental Organization Committee on Human Rights, the Non-Governmental Organizations Forum to the Advancement of Women, and the International Baby Food Action Network.

A strategy employed with increasing frequency and effectiveness by NGOs in promotional activities is to organize parallel forums to complement and support international conferences convened by the United Nations or other international governmental organizations. Notable among these special conferences are the Conference on the Human Environment (Stockholm, 1972); Habitat: United Nations Conference on Human Settlements (Vancouver, 1976); the World Conference of the U.N. Decade for Women (Copenhagen, 1980); the World Conference to Review and Appraise the Achievements of the Decade for Women (Nairobi, 1985); the U.N. Conference on Environment and Development (Rio de Janeiro, 1992); the World Conference on Human Rights (Vienna, 1993); the Beijing Women's Conference (1995); the U.N. Millennium Forum (New York, 2000); the World Conference Against Racism (Durban, 2001); the Earth Summit (2002); the Climate Conference in Copenhagen (2009); the World Summit on Food Security (Rome, 2009); and the U.N. Conference on Sustainable Development (Rio de Janeiro, 2012). Through such parallel activities, NGOs are able to channel world attention to matters of global concern and to enhance their collective influence on governmental decision-making processes. For example, while the Seventh Special Session of the General Assembly on Development and International Cooperation was in session in September 1975, the NGO Forum on the World Economic Order was simultaneously held at U.N. headquarters in New York to both support and parallel the official proceedings, with 500 representatives from 165 organizations in attendance. By 1995, the Beijing Conference attracted so many NGOs that the parallel forum was the largest gathering of NGOs in U.N. history: approximately 35,000 people from more than one hundred countries attended the forum, compared to just 8,000 people who attended the NGO Forum at Copenhagen in 1985.[1] The 2009 Climate Conference in Copenhagen brought approximately 27,000 people together as participants, observers, and members of the media. In addition to official U.N. meetings, over two hundred side events were organized as part of the conference.[2]

Nongovernmental organizations and associations have been extremely active in such fields as human rights, advancement and equality for women, environmental protection, economic development, promoting peace, and disarmament.

In human rights, many NGOs have taken an extremely active role in specialized seminars, established and maintained close contacts with governmental delegates, and occasionally supplied the initiative to prepare draft conventions. At the U.N. conference in San Francisco in 1945, the campaign waged by a number of NGOs was instrumental in the ultimate incorporation of the comprehensive human rights provisions in the charter. Since the creation of the Commission on Human Rights, nongovernmental organizations have actively promoted the formulation and enactment of an

International Bill of Human Rights (including the Universal Declaration of Human Rights and the two covenants) and various other human rights instruments designed to protect particular categories of people or dealing with particular subjects. In the early years when the commission was preoccupied with formulating human rights standards and norms, for example, the International League for Human Rights spent an enormous amount of time and resources on extensive research and reporting for the Economic and Social Council, the Commission, and its Subcommission on Prevention of Discrimination and Protection of Minorities. The adoption in 1966 of the Optional Protocol to the International Covenant on Civil and Political Rights, affording the remedy of individual petitions for the rights protected in the covenant, was largely due to the intense and sustained effort of NGOs. The campaign to abolish torture, waged by Amnesty International and joined by the International Commission of Jurists and others, led the General Assembly to adopt the Declaration Against Torture in 1975 and the Convention Against Torture and Other Cruel, Inhuman or Degrading Treatment or Punishment in 1984. A grassroots campaign waged by the International Campaign to Ban Landmines led to the adoption of the Mine Ban Treaty (officially the Convention on the Prohibition of the Use, Stockpiling, Production, and Transfer of Anti-Personnel Mines and on their Destruction) in Ottawa in 1997. A grand coalition of NGOs lent their support to the adoption of the Rome Statute in 1998 and the establishment of the International Criminal Court.

Nongovernmental organizations have been no less active in the drive toward equality of the sexes and the advancement of the status of women. They have taken various initiatives and have greatly affected the agendas of the Commission on the Status of Women, culminating in the adoption of both the Declaration (1967)[3] and the Convention on the Elimination All Forms of Discrimination Against Women (1979) and other special conventions to protect women. From the International Women's Year (1975) to the Beijing Women's Conference (1995), women's groups have accelerated their efforts toward equality, development, and peace, and pressed on in the twenty-first century. The importance of NGOs to the cause of women is such that the General Assembly, in Resolution 40/108, "Implementation of the Nairobi Forward-Looking Strategies for the Advancement of Women," adopted in December 1985, specifically acknowledged the constructive contribution made by NGOs in general and the Non-Governmental Organizations Forum to the Advancement of Women in particular and invited their continued participation in implementing the strategies formulated at the Nairobi Conference.[4] Ten years later, the Chinese Organizing Committee for the Beijing Conference slyly moved the location of the NGO Forum to a remote site thirty-five miles away, indicating the considerable impact these groups are now recognized as having on the promotion of human rights.

Nongovernmental organizations have been vital in the global effort toward environmental protection. The Stockholm Conference on the Environment in 1972 heralded a new era of humankind's concern for global environment when the conference secretary-general, Maurice Strong, reached out to numerous nongovernmental organizations, including those not in formal consultative status with the United Nations. As a result, more than 550 NGOs attended the Stockholm Conference, and draft proposals written by one prominent NGO were considered and adopted.

In 1972 the United Nations established a new agency, the U.N. Environment Programme (UNEP), providing a built-in structural relationship between environmental NGOs and the United Nations. The wide participation on the part of nongovernmental organizations has contributed mightily to the continuing vigor of the global environmental movement. One of the largest U.N. conferences in history was the 1992 Earth Summit at Rio (UNCED), the first global gathering of heads of state on environment and development. The Earth Summit drew some 9,000 NGOs as well as delegates from 175 nations and representatives from numerous IGOs and U.N. agencies. In 1997, for the first time ever, NGOs addressed a special session of the General Assembly on implementation of Agenda 21, the program of action adopted at Rio. Thousands of representatives from NGOs participated in the subsequent Copenhagen Summit on climate change in 2009 and the U.N. Conference on Sustainable Development in Rio de Janeiro, Brazil, in 2012.

Additionally, nongovernmental organizations played a vital role in developing the commercial whaling ban of 1986, instituted by the International Whaling Commission, by lobbying governments and organizing boycotts of fish and other products from whaling countries. These environmental groups continue to oppose efforts by some countries to ease the ban for "scientific" purposes.

Development issues in the North-South context have attracted increasing attention and interest from NGOs. This is exemplified by the wide participation in the NGO Forum on the World Economic Order, as described above, and at the Earth Summit, where "sustainable development" emerged as the dominant theme. The formation of the International Coalition for Development Action represents an important attempt by many national NGOs to extend their collective influence in the development area, while the Overseas Development Council, created in 1969, has raised consciousness about North-South issues and global interdependence in the developed countries, especially the United States. The World Trade Organization (WTO), established as successor to the General Agreement on Tariffs and Trade (GATT), has provided for consultative relations with nongovernmental organizations, in the interest of promoting environmentally responsible free trade. Article V (2) of the WTO Charter reads as follows: "The General Council may make appropriate arrangements for consultation and cooperation with nongovernmental organizations concerned with matters related to those of the World Trade Organization." Nongovernmental organizations are indeed invaluable in reconciling the conflicting demands for trade, environment, and green growth.[5]

In the related area of food and hunger, the role of NGOs is no less important, as exemplified by their extensive involvement in the committee and other inner workings of the U.N.-sponsored World Food Conference held in Rome in 1974. Some NGOs, such as Church World Service and the World Conference on Religion and Peace, were even made members of drafting committees at the conference.

Oxfam, based in Great Britain, has been involved in rendering humanitarian assistance and in a wide range of other activities. Although its initial efforts focused on postwar European relief, over time the organization has expanded its scope from short-term to long-term solutions to the hunger problems in Africa. Believing that helping the Third World countries to develop and improve living conditions is essential for world peace, Oxfam works at the grassroots level and the governmental level in developing countries and has fostered a spirit of partnership and brotherhood. It has an extensive network of field specialists who guide and train local people in agricultural and medical areas.

To promote peace and disarmament, numerous peace research institutions around the world have engaged in research and made recommendations to their national governments and to relevant transnational entities. Nuclear issues have attracted an array of NGOs to the field, including the Campaign for Nuclear Disarmament, the European Nuclear Disarmament Movement, the International Confederation for Disarmament and Peace, the NGO Disarmament Committee, International Physicians for Prevention of Nuclear War (IPPNW), the Pugwash Movement, the Union of Concerned Scientists, the World Council of Churches, and the National Conference of Bishops. International Physicians for Prevention of Nuclear War was the recipient of the Nobel Peace Prize for 1985 for its dedicated work toward combating the nuclear threat by disseminating reliable information and by heightening humankind's awareness of the catastrophes of nuclear warfare. With a membership numbering in the hundreds of thousands, IPPNW has been able to transcend ideological and cultural barriers and has greatly facilitated effective communications among the world's physicians. The 1997 Nobel Peace Prize was bestowed on the International Campaign to Ban Landmines and its coordinator, Jody Williams, an American woman who organized at the grassroots level to promote a network of community coalitions that has achieved change on a global level. An international treaty outlawing landmines—the Ottawa Treaty—was adopted in 1997 and has gained more than 160 state parties as of 2013.

The promise of the promoting function resides in the ease with which private groups and individuals who entertain strong demands for values today can organize proper groups to take initiative, to agitate, and to propose alternatives. A crucial task is to find and forge sufficiently inclusive symbols to attract, manage, and mobilize world public opinion in pursuit of the common interest. In an interdependent, dynamically changing world, effective power groups are increasingly mobile and changing. More than ever it is possible to assemble the resources and to organize the activities necessary to change peoples' perceptions of common interest. The increasing effectiveness of networking and forging strategic alliances has further fortified the importance and effectiveness of this important function. This is evidenced by the recent examples of strategic alliances of nongovernmental actors that have successfully promoted policies that were eventually taken up and prescribed at the state level.

The less promising aspect of promotion is that promotional activities are still too often carried forward from parochial and fragmented, rather than inclusive, perspectives. A frequent limitation on adequate performance of the promoting function comes from the all too common domination of public channels of communication by agents (official or unofficial) of special interests. Once having degenerated into propaganda for special interests, promotional activities all too often have been perceived in terms of interbloc warfare—East against West in the past, today North against South, and so on—keeping effective elites in effective power. Problems arise, for example, when ideological polemics (such as "unilateral nuclear freeze") become a substitute for serious negotiation toward effective reduction and control of strategic and conventional armaments, or when global warming measures are opposed in the name of development and free trade. "Nonnegotiable" polemics and strategies are anything but genuine expressions of common interests.

Notes

1. *See* Valerie Oosterveld, *Reports of the ASIL Programs: U.N. Fourth World Conference on Women*, A.S.I.L. NEWSLETTER (American Society of International Law, Washington, D.C.), Nov. 1995.

2. *See Copenhagen Climate Change Conference—December 2009*, UNITED NATIONS FRAMEWORK CONVENTION ON CLIMATE CHANGE, http://unfccc.int/meetings/copenhagen_dec_2009/meeting/6295.php.

3. Declaration on the Elimination of Discrimination Against Women, G.A. Res. 2263 (XXII), U.N. Doc. A/6716 (Nov. 7, 1967).

4. G.A. Res. 40/108, U.N. Doc. A/RES/40/180 (Dec. 17, 1985).

5. William M. Reichert, *Resolving the Trade and Environment Conflict: The WTO and NGO Consultative Relations*, 5 MINN. J. GLOBAL TRADE 219 (1996).

22 The Prescribing (Lawmaking) Function

A CENTRAL YET difficult task confronting international lawyers and scholars is to explain how international law is made. Scholars and practitioners seasoned in domestic legal contexts often find their knowledge and experience inadequate for the complexities of international affairs and sometimes simply come away frustrated with the false notion that there is no international law. But international law exists—as we have seen, numerous effective international norms make possible stable, ongoing interactions across national borders in a world of ever-increasing interdependence and transnational exchange. An understanding of how international law is made and, perhaps, of how to participate in making it, is tremendously important and challenging. In any community, national or transnational, how law is made greatly affects the shaping and sharing of all values.

Inquiry about prescription (the lawmaking function) has commonly gone forward in terms of quests for "bases of obligation" or the "binding nature" of law, or of efforts to identify mysterious "sources" of international law. These sources are located variously in transempirical absolutes, in national group expectations, in the express consent of the sovereign state, or in the expectations of elites. Many ambiguities are further involved in using the term sources with these shifting references.

These inherited confusions have their roots in Article 38 of the Statute of the International Court of Justice, which provides:

1. The Court, whose function is to decide in accordance with international law such disputes as are submitted to it, shall apply:
    a. international conventions, whether general or particular, establishing rules expressly recognized by the contesting states;
    b. international custom, as evidence of a general practice accepted as law;
    c. the general principles of law recognized by civilized nations;
    d. subject to the provisions of Article 59, judicial decisions and the teachings of the most highly qualified publicists of the various nations, as subsidiary means for the determination of rules of law.
2. This provision shall not prejudice the power of the Court to decide a case *ex aequo et bono*, if the parties agree thereto.

Much of the continuing debate has centered on the comprehensiveness and priorities of these itemized "sources" and "evidences," the "formal" or "material" nature of these sources, the precise wording and meaning of each item, and the potential significance of each item in concrete application.

The Process of Prescription

What has been strikingly absent is the ability to grasp the very nature of the prescribing function, the process by which international legal norms are made. From a general community perspective, the items in Article 38 are merely components of the ongoing flow of communication and collaboration; their significance is to indicate broader community expectations as generated and reflected in a dynamic process of communication and practice. Only when the prescribing function is explicitly related to the ongoing, larger processes of communication and decision can the dynamics inherent in lawmaking be realistically and fully brought to the fore.

Thus conceived, prescription refers to the projection of an authoritative policy about the shaping and sharing of values. It results from a process of communication that proceeds on three levels: the designation of the content of a policy (factual contingencies, a norm about the future); the creation of expectations about the authority of the policy so designated; and the creation of expectations that this policy will be put into controlling practice (the potential sanction). In the world community, as in its lesser component communities, processes of communication by which prescriptions are shaped range from the most deliberate form of expression—formal agreement—through many gradations to the least deliberate form—the vast flow of expectations derived from uniformities in decision and behavior.

When prescriptive processes are most deliberate, formal, and organized, four sequential phases can be observed: initiation of the process; exploration of relevant facts and potential policies; formulation of policy to be projected as authoritative for the community; and communication of the prescriptive content and expectations about authority and control to the target audience. Even when a prescribing process is highly informal and unorganized, some rough approximation to, or functional equivalence of, these sequential phases may be observed.

The diversity and abundance of the processes of communication by which legal norms are made in the contemporary world are staggering. The peoples of the world communicate to one another expectations about policy, authority, and control through reciprocal claims and mutual tolerances in all interactions as well as through state or intergovernmental entities. The participants (communicators and communicatees) in relevant processes of communication exhibit a wide range of specialization to the prescribing function, from the most to the least specialized. Included are not only the officials of states and intergovernmental organizations but also the representatives of political parties, pressure groups, and private associations and individual human beings with all their manifold identifications. The perspectives of participants, from the most to the least deliberate, display demands, identifications, and expectations with varying degrees of compatibility or incompatibility with common interests and fundamental general community policies.

The situations of communicative interaction are both official and unofficial, direct and indirect, organized and unorganized. The organized situations include the familiar arenas (that is, diplomatic, parliamentary-diplomatic, parliamentary, adjudicative, and executive), and all situations may be described in terms of geographic reach, temporal features, degrees of institutionalization, and expectations of crisis. Many base values (including authority and effective control) are brought to bear on particular interactions by the participants. The strategies participants employ to manage their base values manifest varying degrees of explicitness and implicitness in relation to prescription and a wide continuum of persuasion and coercion. They encompass the modalities suggested in Article 38 of the Statute of the International Court of Justice (ICJ), the whole complex of procedures used in different arenas, and all the strategies characteristic of the value processes.

The culmination of this communication, as expressed in a continuing flow of words or other signs of behavior, ranges widely both in facts about shared perspectives regarding policy, authority, and control and in the evidences of such perspectives in the form of explicit formulations and unarticulated assumptions. The dynamic outcome in shared expectation, in whatever degree it approaches prescription and however it may be evidenced, is a function of the total configuration of variables that affect and produce it in ongoing social processes. In sum, the prescribing process encompasses all the historic modes of international lawmaking—including explicit formulations in agreements and official declarations and implicit communications through uniformities in behavior.

International Agreement

The most deliberate form of prescription, by which governments cooperate with one another in their interaction, is the international agreement in all its manifestations and labels. Because of its overriding importance, an entire chapter—chapter 16—has been devoted to this subject. The Vienna Convention on the Law of Treaties, in Article 2(1)(a), defines treaty as "an international agreement concluded between States in written form and governed by international law, whether embodied in a single instrument or in two or more related instruments and whatever its particular designation." In the absence of centralized legislative institutions in the world, international agreements offer the closest approach to the considered and deliberate prescription of future policies, which is characteristic of legislative institutions in national arenas. The occasional debate about what agreements between nation-states are "lawmaking" and what are not is more futile than rewarding. It would appear that all agreements between nation-states project policies into the future, and the number of participants thus affected is a matter for empirical inquiry in light of all the values at stake rather than dogmatic conclusion based on implicit assumptions about the nature of law or agreement.

The process of agreement, as described in chapter 16, can be realistically understood only by reference to the participants, their perspectives (demands, expectations, and identifications), situations of interaction, base values, modalities in expression of commitment, outcomes in shared expectations, and effects on different value processes. In projecting shared commitments and community policies through international agreements, state officials and other participants, operating under changing situations, undertake negotiations and other activities by using available base values. Agreements between states differ in various ways: the number of parties sharing commitment, the scope and content of policies projected, and the expectations of permanence or impermanence attending commitment.

In cumulative impact, agreements between states play a crucial role in the development of customary international law. Because state officials in the world arena function both as claimants and as decision makers, agreements may not only express the demands or claims of certain states against the general community but also establish the expectation of uniformities in behavior, which adds up to lawfulness. That many uniform agreements have been made and tolerated, without protest, over time is often adduced as strong evidence of customary law.

Customary International Law

The least deliberate form of prescription—customary law—builds on expectations about policies, authority, and control, as generated by official and unofficial attitudes and cooperation. The perspectives of peoples, especially of decision makers, may so crystallize that certain past uniformities in behavior are expected to continue in the future. *Restatement (Third) of the Foreign Relations Law of the United States*, in section 102(2), states: "Customary international law results from a general and consistent practice of states followed by them from a sense of legal obligation."[1] As noted, the focus on "states" is unrealistic, but the identification of two primary components of customary law is appropriate.

As stated in chapter 16, customary international law is authoritative even within the U.S. constitutional framework. Federal courts faced with questions of an international nature may draw upon customary norms that are thought to form a universal common law applicable to all nations. This principle, that customary international law is a part of the "supreme Law of the Land," has been well recognized since the early days of the United States. It found its most salient expression in the Supreme Court's decision in *Paquete Habana* in 1900, in which the court held that customary international law forbade the U.S. navy from seizing Cuban fishing vessels during wartime.[2] In the Court's words:

> By an ancient usage among civilized nations, beginning centuries ago, and gradually ripening into a rule of international law, coast fishing vessels, pursuing their vocation of catching and bringing in fresh fish, have been recognized as exempt, with their cargoes and crews, from capture as prize of war.

The Court found clear evidence for this rule beginning with proclamations made by King Henry IV of England in 1403 and 1406, by which he ordered his navy to permit safe passage to French fishing vessels pursuant to agreements between the two countries. Indeed, numerous examples of this practice were documented since the fifteenth century, showing an unmistakable expectation that persisted to the day, the Court wrote.

Most important, the Court's decision showed that the United States could be bound by customary international norms. This rule is as true in the twentieth-first century as it was in the year 1900, perhaps even more so today. Yet vigorous debates continue about the limits of customary international law in shaping U.S. conduct, particularly in the use of the military instrument and the treatment of enemy combatants. To what extent may U.S. judges and other decision makers look to customary international law for guidance? The *Paquete* court stated eloquently:

> International law is part of our law, and must be ascertained and administered by the courts of justice of appropriate jurisdiction as often as questions of right depending upon it are duly presented for their determination. For this purpose, where there is no treaty and no controlling executive or legislative act or judicial decision, resort must be had to the customs and usages of civilized nations, and, as evidence of these, to the works of jurists and commentators who by years of labor, research, and experience have made themselves peculiarly well acquainted with the

subjects of which they treat. Such works are resorted to by judicial tribunals, not for the speculations of their authors concerning what the law ought to be, but for trustworthy evidence of what the law really is.

The Supreme Court's *Paquete* decision remains the preeminent authority on the role of customary international law in the U.S. federal systems. The Court appears to state that the "customs and usages of civilized nations" will be controlling unless the president or Congress opts out of a particular norm through the legitimate exercise of their federal powers. Some have taken this to mean that neither the president nor Congress is truly bound by international law in so far as each has the implicit ability to contravene international norms. Others have argued that the president may only violate international law when authorized to do so by Congress. For instance, Congress gave the president authority to interpret aspects of the Geneva Convention under the Military Commissions Act of 2006. Still others remark that the U.S. Constitution places special emphasis on treaties, thereby excluding customary law from the type of international norms that the founding fathers wished to incorporate into U.S. law. Undoubtedly, the precise role of customary international law will continue to be of interest to scholars and policy makers alike well into the future.

Though the legal force of customary law is well established, defining its content has never been an easy task, even for the most well-studied jurists. The technical requirements for establishing a customary international law are commonly said to be two: a "material" element in certain past uniformities in behavior and a "psychological" element, or *opinio juris*, certain subjectivities of legal "oughtness" attending the uniformities in behavior (for example, an expectation that something is legally appropriate or required). In the *North Sea Continental Shelf* case (1969),[3] which pitted the Federal Republic of Germany against Denmark and the Netherlands concerning norms applicable to delimit the continental shelf in dispute, the ICJ pointed out that "an indispensable requirement" to "the formation of a new rule of customary international law" is that "State practice... including that of States whose interests are specially affected, should have been both extensive and virtually uniform... and should moreover have occurred in such a way as to show a general recognition that a rule of law or legal obligation is involved."[4] The court elaborated further:

> Not only must the acts concerned amount to a settled practice, but they must also be such, or be carried out in such a way, as to be evidence of a belief that this practice is rendered obligatory by the existence of a rule of law requiring it. The need for such a belief, i.e., the existence of a subjective element, is implicit in the very notion of the *opinio juris sive necessitatis*. The States concerned must therefore feel that they are conforming to what amounts to a legal obligation. The frequency or even habitual character of the acts is not in itself enough. There are many international acts, e.g., in the field of ceremonial and protocol, which are performed

almost invariably, but which are motivated only by considerations of courtesy, convenience or tradition, and not by any sense of legal duty.[5]

The application of both material and psychological requirements is, however, highly flexible. Uniformity is no more realistically required than unanimity.

The relevant patterns in behavior extend not only to the acts and utterances of transnational and national officials located at many positions in structures of authority but also to those of private individuals and representatives of nongovernmental organizations. Such acts diverge both in frequency of repetition and in duration of recurrence. The subjectivities of oughtness required for such patterns of behavior may relate to various systems of norms, including prior authority, natural law, reason, morality, or religion. The critical subjectivities are those of expectation of future uniformities in decision, regardless of the norms of justification; this is borne out by the practice of honoring law-creating consequences even of subjectivities initially asserted in contravention of prior authority. The evidence that decision makers may consult in order to ascertain past behavior and subjectivities ranges from such familiar items as international agreements, resolutions of international governmental organizations, public utterances by international and national officials, diplomatic correspondence and instructions, national court decisions, legislative measures, and the writings of publicists to "every written document, every record of act or spoken word which presents an authentic picture of the practice of states in their international dealings."[6]

Confusion often develops regarding the degree of uniformity required to establish customary international law. In the *Asylum* case (1950), involving Colombia's claim for unilateral competence to grant diplomatic asylum against Peru, the International Court of Justice first emphasized "a constant and uniform usage practiced by the States" as essential to customary international law.[7] The court rejected the Colombian claim by declaring:

> The facts brought to the knowledge of the Court disclose so much uncertainty and contradiction, so much fluctuation and discrepancy in the exercise of diplomatic asylum and in the official views expressed on various occasions, there has been so much inconsistency in the rapid succession of conventions on asylum, ratified by some States and rejected by others, and the practice has been so much influenced by considerations of political expediency in the various cases, that it is not possible to discern in all this any constant and uniform usage, accepted as law, with regard to the alleged rule of unilateral and definitive qualification of the offence.[8]

The requisite patterns in past behavior and subjectivities are generality, not universality. Article 38(1)(b) of the ICJ Statute thus speaks of "international custom" in terms of a "general" rather than "universal" practice. The express consent of every nation-state is not a prerequisite to the authority of a particular customary law. Whereas a keystone of the Westphalian concept of international law is the notion of consent, the function of customary international law is precisely to vitiate the requirement of specific consent as the basis of international obligation. The honoring of somewhat diffuse expectations generated by cooperative reciprocal behavior permits "sovereign" states—new as well as old—to be subject to international law without specific consent. Thanks to such a process of accommodation, nation-states can, without undue affront to their inflated notions of sovereignty, take account of their conditions of interdependence and reciprocity and cooperate in the pursuit of common goals and policies without explicit agreement. A customary prescription thus need not be unanimous; it need only be "applied by the overwhelming majority of states which hitherto had an opportunity to apply it."[9] Normally, this overwhelming majority would include all the major powers and the states especially affected by a particular customary prescription. No customary international law in outer space is conceivable, for example, without the participation of a major space power.

Another element relates to the length of time required to form customary international prescription. The time requirement is a function both of general community expectations and of circumstances in context. In establishing certain decision makers with competence to prescribe future policies, the world community attempts to secure prescription in accordance with contemporary expectations. The temporal requirement is calculated to make certain that these expectations are accurately ascertained. Understandably, the central concern of contemporary demands and expectations is to distribute values toward the future rather than the past. "Time-honored practice is not a necessary element in customary International Law,"[10] though it serves importantly as evidence, which may be otherwise provided, of contemporary expectations and demonstrates the stability of relevant patterns of expectation. In certain contexts the requisite degree of certainty about contemporary expectations has been ascertained by reference to past behavior and subjectivities of relatively short duration.

In any event, the significance of the traditional requirements of a flow of patterns in behavior and subjectivity through time can be understood only in their larger context. These historic emphases refer only to certain features of the broader process of communication by which customary expectations about policy, authority, and control are created. The full exposition of how customary expectations are created requires a thorough exploration of every feature of the process of communication involved. The relevant features include communicators and communicatees (both official and nonofficial) and the range of participation; participants' perceptions about the content of their communication and its relation to existing law; the geographical, temporal, institutional, and crisis factors of the situation; the knowledge, skill, and other resources possessed by participants; strategies in generating the flow of words and the flow of behavior; the degree of uniformity in words and behavior; and shared expectations about policy, authority, and control. These patterns can also be viewed in terms of intensity of demand or commitment as well as degree of sharing.

The Prescribing Role of International Governmental Organizations

The most striking recent development in the prescribing function relates to the growing role of international governmental organizations (IGOs). Contrary to the lingering myth that such organizations enjoy little direct prescriptive competence, they play an increasingly important role as forums for the flow of explicit communications and acts of collaboration that create expectations about authoritative community policy. This is especially true of the United Nations and its affiliated agencies.

International governmental organizations have played an increasingly large role in the development of international law following World War II. The first IGOs can be traced back to antiquity, when city-states created alliances for the purposes of peacekeeping and common defense. In modern times, IGOs took on increasing importance during the nineteenth century, especially in Europe, when nations established permanent conferences to address issues of common concern such as the maintenance and navigation of waterways and construction of railways and telephonic infrastructure.

The end of World War I led to the establishment of the League of Nations, with its mission of supporting global peace and stability. Although the League's tenure was short, it provided a foundation for the United Nations that followed. The founders of the United Nations drew on the League's experiences and made efforts to overcome some of its shortcomings. Importantly, the United Nations has been able to recruit sufficient member states to form a truly global body. Since that time, the United Nations has continued to grow in importance and influence and has given rise to a system of IGOs tasked with addressing a vast range of international problems.

The prescriptive power of IGOs challenges the notion that states are the sole legitimate subjects of international law. Quasi-governmental bodies such as the United Nations are equipped with an international legal personality and fundamental rights that have been affirmed by the International Court of Justice. This status allows them to participate as major players on the international stage. While IGOs are formed by states in order to pursue common interests, these organizations function independently of the host states in which they operate.

IGOs participate in the formulation of legal prescriptions that touch on every area of international law, both public and private.[11] Their efforts have contributed to an ever-growing body of rules and norms, including most significantly international treaties as well as mechanisms for resolving international disputes, between both nations and private parties. Moreover, there is a growing body of international law related to the governance of IGOs themselves. Many of the rules that bind nations and other participants in the international arena have been developed in consultation with IGOs that provide a measure of objectivity and subject-matter expertise necessary for their operation as legitimate intermediaries between states. Moreover, through their decision making and promotional efforts, IGOs have been influential in the development of what is called "soft law"—shared norms of appropriate conduct that exist even in the absence of formal written prescriptions. Though not binding, soft law is aspirational and has the potential to become authoritative through use over time. What was not authoritative at the outset may become so as soft norms are communicated between parties and take on the character of authority. That is to say, they begin to shape expectations of conduct through a process of identifying and clarifying common interests.

The Role of the U.N. General Assembly

The General Assembly, in particular, has adopted many resolutions that deal with major problems in international law. Each year, the General Assembly passes about three hundred resolutions concerning a wide range of issues of global import. The legal effect of these resolutions is debated among specialists. The availability of the General Assembly, coupled with the wide acceptance of the requirements of customary law, seems to point to a new modality of lawmaking. When resolutions enjoy the overwhelming support of the member states, including all the major powers, they would appear to have the force of law whether they are characterized as "instantaneous customary law," as "quasi legislation," or as something else. The crucial point is that there emerges a new institutional mode by which the peoples of the world can clearly communicate expectations of authority and control in relation to all problems and value processes. The traditional time requirement associated with the creation of customary law ensures that such expectations are widely shared and thus exist. With this new institutional modality of lawmaking, the time requirement recedes to a minimum.

This is not to suggest that all General Assembly resolutions are law. Some bear little resemblance to genuine expressions of what law is in terms of shared expectations. Whether a General Assembly resolution genuinely expresses community expectations about authority and control depends on every feature of the process of communication involved. One needs to know who voted for it or against it and how many participated in the flow of communication. One needs to know the content of the policy and its relation to the overriding goals of the community. One must know how deliberately the resolution was considered and how long and in what mode it was communicated. One needs to know how well decision makers were aware of past decisions and their bearing on the resolution adopted. One needs to know not only isolated communications but the total flow of communications both within and outside the United Nations. One must examine outcomes in communication: How clear was the policy specified, and what are shared expectations of authority and control?

Much controversy has been generated, as discussed in chapter 18 regarding the authoritative effect of both General Assembly resolutions on permanent sovereignty over natural resources and on the establishment of a new international economic order. The issue of expropriation has aroused particularly intense debate. The debate centers on the relative authority of General Assembly Resolution 1803 (paragraph 4), Permanent Sovereignty over Natural Resources (1962),[12] vis-à-vis Article 2(2)(c) of Resolution 3281, the Charter of Economic Rights and Duties of States (1974), and Resolution 3171 (paragraph 3) (1973).[13] Although Resolution 1803 emphasizes the payment of "appropriate compensation" in accordance with "international law" and settlement of the dispute "through arbitration or international adjudication," Article 2(2)(c) of the charter leaves it to the expropriating state to determine "appropriate compensation" by "taking into account its relevant laws and regulations and all circumstances" it "considers pertinent" and to settle any dispute, unless otherwise agreed on by all states concerned, under its "domestic law" and "by its tribunals." Paragraph 3 of Resolution 3171, similar to Article 2(2)(c), states that "the application of the principle of nationalization carried out by States, as an expression of their sovereignty in order to safeguard their natural resources, implies that each State is entitled to determine the amount of possible compensation and the mode of payment, and that any disputes which might arise should be settled in accordance with the national legislation of each State carrying out such measures." Resolution 1803 (paragraph 4) abides by international law, yet both Article 2(2)(c) of Resolution 3281 and Resolution 3171 (paragraph 3) rely on domestic law. Obviously the two positions are incompatible. Which one, then, is authoritative?

This issue was spotlighted in the arbitral award of *Texaco Overseas Petroleum et al. v. Libyan Arab Republic* (1977),[14] which involved claims against Libya for its nationalization of all of the rights, interests, and property of two international oil companies in Libya. The two oil companies relied heavily on Resolution 1803, but Libya strongly invoked, among others, Article 2(2)(c) of the charter (Resolution 3281) and Resolution 3171. The sole arbitrator, Rene-Jean Dupuy (appointed by the president of the ICJ), rejected Libya's claim that "any dispute relating to nationalization or its consequences should be decided in conformity with the provisions of the municipal law of the nationalizing State and only in its courts"[15] and delivered an award on the merits in favor of the companies. (Though Libya refused to take part in the arbitral proceedings, it set forth its position in a memorandum to the president of the court.)

Dupuy discussed the legal effect of U.N. General Assembly resolutions in general and that of the above-mentioned resolutions in particular. He noted that the "legal value" of U.N. resolutions "differs considerably depending on the type of resolution and the conditions attached to its adoption and its provisions."[16] Hence, in "appraising the legal validity of the above-mentioned Resolutions," he resorted to "the criteria usually taken into consideration, *i.e.*, the examination of voting conditions and the analysis of the provisions concerned."[17]

Noting that Resolution 1803 was "passed by the General Assembly by 87 votes to 2, with 12 abstentions," he stressed that the majority voting for this text included "many States of the Third World" and "several Western developed countries with market economies, including the most important one, the United States."[18] He pointed out, however, that the conditions under which Resolutions 3171 and 3281 were adopted were "notably different." The "specific paragraph concerning nationalization, disregarding the role of international law," as contained in Resolution 3171, "not only was not consented to by the most important Western countries, but caused a number of the developing countries to abstain."[19] Similarly, "paragraph 2(c) of Article 2 of the Charter, which limits consideration of the characteristics of compensation to the State and does not refer to international law, was voted by 104 to 16, with 6 abstentions, all the industrialized countries with market economies having abstained or having voted against it."[20]

Thus, "only Resolution 1803" was "supported by a majority of Member States representing all of the various groups." In contrast, the other resolutions mentioned above were "supported by a majority of States but not by any of the developed countries with market economies which carry on the largest part" of international trade. "On the basis of the circumstances of adoption mentioned above and by expressing an *opinio juris communis*," Dupuy concluded that Resolution 1803 "seems to this Tribunal to reflect the state of customary law existing in this field." He further stated that "the absence of any connection between the procedure of compensation and international law and the subjection of this procedure solely to municipal law cannot be regarded by this Tribunal except as a *de lege ferenda* formulation, which even appears *contra legem* in the eyes of many developed countries." This position is "further reinforced by an examination of the general practice of relations between States with respect to investment."[21]

The evolution of the Universal Declaration of Human Rights as "quasi legislation" and custom offers another instructive example. When the Universal Declaration was adopted unanimously in December 1948 by the General Assembly, the original shared expectation was that it represented only "a common standard of achievement" without direct legal authority and enforceability. But the authoritative nature of the Universal Declaration has grown in the six decades since then. It has been affirmed and reaffirmed by numerous resolutions of U.N. entities and related agencies, invoked and reinvoked by various participants, and incorporated into many international agreements and national constitutions; it has also found increasing expression in judicial decisions, both transnational and national. Today, the Universal Declaration is widely acclaimed as a Magna Carta of humankind, to be observed by all the participants in the world arena. The authoritative effect of the Universal Declaration is recognized in a number of ways: as the authoritative identification and clarification of human rights guaranteed under the U.N. Charter, as part of customary international law, as a vital component of *jus cogens*, and/or as an indispensable component of the developing global bill of human rights.[22]

A comparable evolution occurred with the Helsinki Accords (officially, the Final Act of the Conference on Security and Cooperation in Europe, now called the Organization for Security and Cooperation in Europe), an important instrument that once delimited East-West relations and contained the famous "basket three" concerned with human rights and humanitarian affairs. It was said to be a "nonbinding treaty."[23] But, given the frequency with which it was invoked and applied by officials and nonofficials alike, and the machinery established for periodic review, it was not surprising that the nonbinding treaty in due course generated and crystallized ample expectations in support of its authority.

Likewise, in the arena of international humanitarian law, officials and nonofficials look to the Geneva Conventions as representing customary expectations of conduct during times of war. The treaties' authoritative effect is evidenced by the degree to which they have been invoked by states as legitimate expressions of basic rights by both signatory and nonsignatory nations. Provisions outlawing practices, most notably torture, have attained status as *jus cogens* as the result of their widespread adoption and over the decades since the conventions' ratification.

Appraisal

The modalities of prescription do not mutually exclude; depending on context, one mode may be more economic and effective than another. The crucial point is not so much the modality of communication as the degree to which the policies projected become a part of the working expectations of the effective participants in the world community. Human expectations, or the demands and identifications with which they interlock, are not static. It cannot be taken for granted that the words of treaties or other written documents reflect community expectations without appropriate verification. As viewpoints are in flux, so is today's structure of expectation open to inevitable change, as new conditions arise and new suggestions are put forth.

International law has historically been made by articulated multilateral agreement and by unarticulated, habitual, cooperative behavior, from which expectations about authority and control are derived. United Nations practices have not only boosted these traditional modes of lawmaking but added a new dimension that more closely approximates parliamentary enactment. The activities of the General Assembly, through its committees and other subsidiary entities and supplemented by the activities of other intergovernmental organizations and the U.N. Specialized Agencies, have greatly rationalized prescription by multilateral agreement. The opportunities it provides for the representatives of many communities to articulate their conceptions of law and to incorporate them in formal resolutions have substantially eased the historic burden of identifying customary law and clarifying its content. This latter modality of General Assembly resolution, greatly foreshortening the requisite time to establish customary law and affording an economical mode to articulate consensus about common interest, increasingly bears the hallmarks of parliamentary enactment.

Thanks to the potentials of global communications and the availability of different modalities of lawmaking, the global prescribing process exhibits inclusivity, rationality, and effectiveness. An appropriate inclusivity is greatly fostered by the informal components in transnational prescribing process that permit expectations about policies, authority, and control to be created by cooperative behavior of both official and unofficial participants. Such processes represent a preferred policy of democracy and representativeness because they entail a constant accommodation of the interests and behavior of all actors affected by the prescriptions being created. Both groups and individuals may participate. The General Assembly and other structures of authority communicate to the worldwide audience, articulating and reflecting the expectations of the peoples of the world.

In spite of encouraging developments, difficulties remain. The world arena lacks a well-organized, centralized lawmaking institution; hence the continuing reliance on three modalities of lawmaking. Under the deliberate mode of prescription, states are not bound by a particular international agreement as an agreement unless they give express consent. Over time, an agreement may become customary law. For example, the 1982 Law of the Sea Convention was a goldmine of controversy over which parts represented customary law and which parts new formulations, until differences were resolved and the treaty implemented in 1994.

The parliamentary mode of prescription (lawmaking) is not necessarily democratic. It may be democratic in the sense that states are nominally equal (one state, one vote) but not in the sense that individuals participate democratically. The crude, cumbersome procedures in the General Assembly mean that prescription may be manipulated to serve special interests rather than common interests.

Although the least deliberate mode of prescription affords greater participation by groups and individuals, the process is extremely slow and fragmentary. In the absence of a centralized body empowered to prescribe and proclaim, whether and when a particular customary law has emerged is always controversial. Given the realities of the world's effective power process, there are limits to how effectively U.N. procedure and multilateral agreements can bind nation-states large and small.

Notes

1. RESTATEMENT (THIRD) OF THE FOREIGN RELATIONS LAW OF THE UNITED STATES §102(2) (1987).

2. Paquete Habana; The Lola, 175 U.S. 677 (1900).

3. North Sea Continental Shelf (Ger./Den.; Ger./Neth.), 1969 I.C.J. 3 (Feb. 20).

4. *Id.* at 43.

5. *Id.* at 44.

6. GEORGE A. FINCH, THE SOURCES OF MODERN INTERNATIONAL LAW 51 (Carnegie Endowment for Int'l Peace 1937) (quoting Walker).

7. Asylum (Colom./Peru), 1950 I.C.J. 266, 276 (Nov. 20).

8. *Id.* at 277.

9. Josef L. Kunz, *The Nature of Customary International Law*, 47 A.J.I.L. 662, 666 (1953).

10. ALF ROSS, A TEXTBOOK OF INTERNATIONAL LAW 89 (London 1947).

11. *See* JOSÉ ALVAREZ, INTERNATIONAL ORGANIZATIONS AS LAW-MAKERS (Oxford University Press 2005).

12. G.A. Res. 1803, ¶ 4, U.N. Doc. A/5217 (Dec. 14, 1962).

13. G.A. Res. 3281, U.N. Doc A/9631 (Dec. 12, 1974); G.A. Res. 3171, ¶ 3, U.N. Doc. A/9030 (Dec. 17, 1973).

14. Texaco Overseas Petroleum Company/California Asiatic Oil Company v. Libyan Arab Republic (U.S. v. Libya), Award on the Merits of Jan. 19, 1977, *reprinted in* 17 I.L.M. 1 (1978) [Eng. trans.].

15. *Id.* at 31.

16. *Id.* at 29.

17. *Id.* at 28.

18. *Id.*

19. *Id.* at 29.

20. *Id.*

21. *Id.* at 30.

22. *See* MYRES S. McDOUGAL, HAROLD D. LASSWELL, & LUNG-CHU CHEN, HUMAN RIGHTS AND WORLD PUBLIC ORDER 325–30 (1980) and references therein.

23. *See* Oscar Schachter, *The Twilight Existence of Nonbinding International Agreements*, 71 A.J.I.L. 296 (1977). The text of the Final Act is found in 73 DEP'T STATE BULL. 323 (1975) and *reprinted in* 14 I.L.M. 1292 (1975).

23 The Invoking Function

THE INVOKING FUNCTION refers to the provisional characterization of events in terms of community prescriptions. This function is a prelude to the applying function and sets an application in motion. An invocation ordinarily includes initiation, exploration of facts and potential policies, provisional characterization of the selected facts by reference to authoritative policies, and stimulation of applicative arenas. Like other claims to authority, an invocation involves assertions about facts, relevant policies (prescriptions), and appropriate remedies. People who invoke make allegations about what has happened, what policies have been violated, and what future action might remedy the wrong. Invocation thus serves as a bridge from prescription to application. A provisional characterization of events as deviations from prescribed norms, whether it sets the applying function into motion, may of itself entail significant value consequences.

The participants in invocation before transnational arenas include states, international governmental organizations, nongovernmental organizations and groups, and individuals. The objectives of invocation extend from obtaining the benefits of an informal appreciation of events to setting in motion a formal application by authoritative decision makers. Invocation may occur in situations laden with crises. In situations of a lesser degree of institutionalization, invocation is generally open to all effective participants; in arenas of a higher degree of institutionalization, access is available only through formal channels and may be highly restricted. The international process has both features, especially since individuals are often effectively locked out of formal decisional arenas but can help to shape attitudes and behavior.

The base values of invokers may vary greatly in relative strengths, abilities, skills, and resources. Invokers may employ strategies in the forum of private communications (letters, telegrams, and so on), the media, mass communication (editorial, reporting, letter writing, computer networking, picketing or demonstrating on camera, and so on), or highly formal procedures. Outcomes may involve changing public opinion, arousing the attention of selective elites, or initiating the process of application.

Broad access to and participation in invocation are indispensable to a global constitutive process designed to secure both minimum world order and optimum world order, especially human rights. Maintenance of minimum world order depends on timely invocation in response to breach of peace and other gross violations of international law. Respect for and confidence in processes of authoritative decision depend greatly on the ability of individuals and private groups to challenge unlawful deprivations. An effective public order of human dignity requires that representative organs of the general community be enabled to stimulate decision when imminent threats to public order or human dignity occur and when injured parties are unable to do so. A trend toward broader participation in the invoking function is evident, although current access to invocation is far from optimum. Individuals are increasingly accorded the competence to invoke processes of transnational decision to defend their rights.

Nation-states are historically the most important formal invokers in the world arena, responding to matters ranging from breaches of peace to violations of human rights, yet individuals and groups have always played at least informal roles. States request emergency meetings of the Security Council or the General Assembly to deal with serious threats to peace and security, global or regional. But complaints by states extend to a wide range of other matters.

In the area of human rights, state officials have traditionally played a vital role in invoking the customary international law of state responsibility to protect their nationals abroad. In addition, an important modality of invocation—the state-to-state complaint—has been institutionalized for the global and regional human rights programs.

The remedy of diplomatic protection of nationals, as discussed in chapter 12, is based on a nationality test but is otherwise discretionary. A state generally does not invoke transnational decision to protect nonnationals. Even with regard to its own nationals who have suffered deprivations imposed by other governments, a state may choose not to espouse claims because of either special policy considerations or ambiguous conceptions of nationality.

The state-to-state complaint system under the contemporary human rights movement is becoming increasingly important. A host of international human rights treaties, notably the International Covenant on Civil and Political Rights, the International Convention on the Elimination of All Forms of Racial Discrimination, the Convention against Torture and Other Cruel, Inhuman, or Degrading Treatment or Punishment, the International Convention on the Protection of the Rights of All Migrant Workers and Members of their Families, the International Convention for the Protection of All Persons from Enforced Disappearance, the Constitution of the International Labor Organization, the UNESCO Protocol Instituting a Conciliation and Good Offices Commission in Relation to the Convention Against Discrimination in Education, the European Convention on Human Rights, and the American Convention on Human Rights, explicitly authorize a state party to invoke transnational prescription against defaulting parties. Though the Convention of the International Labour Organization, the UNESCO Protocol, and the European Convention make the state-to-state complaint procedure mandatory, the International Covenant on Civil and Political Rights and the American Convention on Human Rights make it optional. The Convention on the Elimination of All Forms of Discrimination Against Women (CEDAW) requires states to submit disputes to arbitration, which may be followed by a referral to the International Court of Justice.

The usefulness of the state-to-state complaint procedure has been questioned because of its potentially harmful effects on friendly relations between states, its possible abuse from political motivation, and its likely infrequent use. But the experiences under the European Convention on Human Rights and under the International Labour Organization appear to support its value. In the words of Lady Gaitskell, "[t]he infrequency of complaints demonstrated the responsible attitude taken towards the procedure and its value; the procedure's very existence was a deterrent, serving to encourage a Government to remedy more quickly any abuse of human rights within its territory."[1]

In spite of its utility, state elites are undeniably reluctant to resort to the formal state-to-state complaint procedure to accuse other governments of human rights violations, lest they themselves become targets of complaints. The dynamics of reciprocity and retaliation in a decentralized world here operate to the detriment of world public order. Hence, invocation by individuals and private groups in human rights matters is imperative. Unless individuals and nongovernmental groups can invoke transnational authority for remedy on their own behalf or on behalf of other victims, the elaborate human rights prescriptions may become nothing more than illusory aspirations.

The increasing access of individuals and private groups to transnational arenas of decision, as described in chapter 7, is most notable in the area of human rights. Individuals, provided they are the victims or represent victims of human rights abuse, and private groups, such as nongovernmental organizations, are accorded access to the U.N. Human Rights Council, the Committee Against Torture, the Committee on the Elimination of Racial Discrimination, the European Court of Human Rights, and the Inter-American Commission on Human Rights. The Optional Protocol to the International Covenant on Civil and Political Rights allows petitions to the Human Rights Committee by individuals but not by private groups. The procedures for individual petition are, however, far from simple, open, or effective. Contemporary prescriptions create extraordinary obstacles to the effective exercise of the right of individual petitions, as illustrated by the procedures within the United Nations and the cumulative experience under the European Convention on Human Rights.

The facts of effective power suggest that petitions by individuals are not at present the most effective form of remedy for human rights deprivations. The discrepancy in effective power between an individual petitioner and a respondent state is simply too great. It appears crucial that, in addition to state-to-state complaints and individual petitions, some form of invocation, representative of the general community and backed by its strength, be made available. A promising alternative has at last appeared with the long-awaited creation of a U.N. High Commissioner for Human Rights. The high commissioner is an international ombudsperson charged with the responsibility of invocation on behalf of victims and the general community. The high commissioner, with a broad mandate, is able, for example, to deploy human rights officers to troubled areas to investigate suspected rights violations and prevent future ones.

The role of the representatives of the general community extends not only to human rights matters but to all aspects of international law. The role of the Secretary-General of the United Nations is particularly noteworthy. The secretary-general is empowered to call attention to crises that threaten world peace and security and to call for an emergency meeting of the Security Council or of the General Assembly. The effective role of this office could be greatly enhanced through strong leadership by calling world attention to matters of enormous importance affecting humankind.

The establishment of the International Criminal Court (ICC) has provided the international community with another forum in which to hold individuals accountable for injustices committed under the guise of state action. The ICC has been empowered with the authority necessary to apprehend and try defendants who are found within the jurisdiction of member states. Individuals who are outside the jurisdiction of the ICC must limit their movements if they wish to avoid being brought before the court. These real consequences give teeth to the invoking function in the context of the ICC and make it a more effective instrument for deterring and sanctioning violations of international law. This concept is explored further in chapter 29.

The foregoing emphasizes invocation in the context of formal decision arenas. To grasp the dynamics of the invoking function, however, one must take into account the flow of informal invocations that occur in a less institutionalized fashion. Specific and responsible allegations of violations of international legal norms, though falling short of mobilizing formal application by authoritative decision makers, could in the aggregate produce significant effects in ending lawless acts or in securing greater compliance with established international standards. World public opinion is the court of last resort for informal invocations, which can be undertaken day in and day out by nongovernmental groups, the media of mass communication, and concerned individuals. Publicity mobilizes support, support leads to action, and action alleviates abuses.

In the field of human rights, for example, exposing the dark side of governmental behavior is widely believed to be an effective and economical weapon. Many nongovernmental organizations undertake the important task of "monitoring," in the sense of reporting general conditions of human rights in many communities and in bringing to public attention instances of violations. Such informal invocations (sometimes accompanied by mass protests, rallies, letter-writing campaigns, publicity campaigns, and other tactics) often produce constructive results, for example, concessions by the government concerned in order to placate both external condemnation and internal opposition. The pointed finger of shame, especially when directed by a reputable organization known for its impartiality and independence, has often resulted in the stay of executions, commutation of death sentences, release of prisoners, discontinuation of torture, amelioration of prison conditions, permission for emigration, withholding of mass expulsion, or general improvement of human rights conditions.

In the field of environmental protection, the incident of the *Rainbow Warrior* in New Zealand in 1985 illustrates such informal invocation. The environmentalist pressure group Greenpeace International, in its concern for environmental safety regarding oceanic nuclear weapons testing, threatened to interrupt French nuclear tests in the Pacific Ocean by sailing its schooner into the test zone. French governmental intelligence officers, provoked by the group's frequent anti-French press statements expressing its intention to sail despite France's repeated warnings against such activity, turned to violence. They planted explosive charges on the Greenpeace vessel, the *Rainbow Warrior*, which flew a British flag, and detonated the explosives while the ship sat in the harbor of Auckland, New Zealand, killing a crew member and destroying the schooner. The French government first denied responsibility but soon confessed, thanks to a vigilant world press and world public opinion. The sequence of events, though tragic, did bring a strong opposition to the nuclear testing to world attention and exerted significant restraint on the French government. It not only led to successful mediation of the dispute between New Zealand and France by former U.N. Secretary-General Javier Perez de Cuellar but also culminated in an unprecedented international damages case arbitrated by agreement between a sovereign state and a nongovernmental organization (ordering France to pay more than $8 million in damages to Greenpeace).

Similarly, individuals and groups have attempted to place pressure on the government of Israel by challenging a naval blockade of the Gaza Strip. Beginning in 2010, activists on ships crossing the Mediterranean Sea made efforts to bypass the blockade in order to deliver humanitarian aid to Gaza. However, their efforts were thwarted several times by Israeli forces, who used force against the activists on some occasions, resulting in deaths. Such incidents helped draw attention to the campaigners' efforts and provide an opportunity to shed light on the conditions in Gaza and raise questions about the legality of the blockade. In 2011, a U.N. report stated that Israel's blockade was a legitimate measure to control the flow of arms to militants.[2] Nonetheless, Turkey registered its dissatisfaction with Israel for its refusal to apologize for the deaths of Turkish citizens traveling on a Gaza-bound ship the year before. In this way, the activists' informal efforts at invocation gave rise to state-to-state responses through formal channels.

Similarly, uprisings of the Arab Spring in the Middle East and North Africa—and the violent response of some regimes—brought intense scrutiny on governments in the region. Informal invocations in the form of popular protests led in turn to formal invocations by international bodies, including the United Nations, as well as nations. Examples included Security Council resolutions characterizing the situation in Libya as a threat to international peace and security and statements by world leaders condemning Syrian forces for carrying out violent crackdowns against protesters there. Such invocations hoped to bring an end to violence and place pressure on regimes to afford greater protections to their citizens.

Notes

1. 21 U.N. GAOR C. 3 (1415th mtg.) 223, U.N. Doc. A/C.3/SR.1415 (1966).

2. REPORT OF THE SECRETARY-GENERAL'S PANEL OF INQUIRY ON THE 31 MAY 2010 FLOTILLA INCIDENT (Sept. 2, 2011), *available at* http://www.un.org/News/dh/infocus/middle_east/Gaza_Flotilla_Panel_Report.pdf.

24 The Applying Function

THE APPLYING FUNCTION refers to a relatively final characterization of events by decision makers in terms of community prescription and the management of sanctioning measures to secure enforcement. In conventional usage, many imprecise terms are employed to describe constituent parts of, and varying approximations, to application. These labels include investigation, fact-finding, on-the-scene observation, reporting, commissions of inquiry, negotiation, good offices, mediation, conciliation, arbitration, and adjudication. Viewed comprehensively, application may embrace the following sequential features: exploration of potentially relevant facts, including the precipitating events and their larger context; exploration of potentially relevant policies; identification of significant facts; determination of the authoritative policies applicable; making of the decision, including the projection of future relations between the parties; enforcement; and review.

The application of prescriptions is the culmination of all other functions. Other functions are in some way designed to assist in securing rational, uniform, effective, and constructive applications. Unless such outcomes are obtained, the other functions are largely hortatory. As important as it is to challenge unlawful violations, it is equally urgent to secure applications that put basic community policies into controlling practice and mobilize a continuing consensus in support of both minimum world order and optimum world order.

Most applications of international law continue to be made by national officials in an ongoing process of unilateral determinations and reciprocal responses. This process goes forward from foreign office to foreign office, in internal and external arenas. Many applications are made by national courts, and some even by legislative bodies. National officials play important roles in application in all transnational arenas, often in concert with the officials of international governmental organizations. Such applications take place in normal diplomatic activities and occasional conferences, or in the more formal parliamentary, adjudicative, and executive structures existing on the global scale. Even nonofficials may partake in a range of equivalent activities. What appears to be private may in effect be a functional application of transnational prescriptions.

The chief objective in application is to put prescriptions into controlling practice. The demand for application is thus a demand to perform the sequence of activities that constitute an application, including exploring and characterizing facts and exploring and choosing policies. The exploration of policies characteristically entails three inter-related subgoals: interpretation of prescriptions to achieve the closest approximation to the communications made; supplementation by filling gaps and removing ambiguities; and integration, in the sense of policing and accommodating prescriptions in terms of priorities in community policies.

The transnational structures of authority involved in the applying function include diverse arenas. Diplomatic interaction is the scene of the bulk of official applications at the international level. Adjudicative arenas, including judicial and arbitral tribunals (both transnational and domestic), are noted for their specialization in application. Even parliamentary bodies, such as the General Assembly and the Security Council, cannot escape the task of characterizing particular instances in terms of prescriptions. The transnational arenas of application are increasingly open and are moving slowly toward some degree of compulsoriness. The base values (authority and effective control) at the disposal of various appliers differ immensely. A burgeoning body of transnational prescriptions is increasingly available to appliers in all arenas. Whereas the effective power of national officials depends on the overall power of their states and perceptions of common interest, that of international officials remains extremely modest. Strategies of application vary according to arena and to activity. The strategies of initiation and exploration in an adjudicative arena are markedly different from those in a diplomatic or an executive arena.

In the preenforcement phase, agencies undertake various activities to explore and characterize relevant facts and policies. The outcomes of application, as expressed in a continuing flow of characterizing instances in terms of community prescriptions, affect all patterns of value allocation and future behavior.

Where deviations from decision persist, community intervention is needed to enforce the determined allocation of values or projection of future policy. Enforcement may rely on inducement as well as coercion. Sanctioning measures may be tailored to the goals of prevention, deterrence, restoration, rehabilitation, reconstruction, and correction. In a dynamic process of interaction and decision under ever-changing conditions, no deci-sion is final. Each application is an experiment toward realization of projected goals that is tested through time and changing context by the responses of those affected and of the general community.

Ongoing review becomes necessary at different levels and through different modalities.

Exploration of Facts

In a decentralized legal system where auto-interpretation prevails, where state officials function as both claimants and judges, where no centralized structure has sufficient authority to compel recalcitrant parties to appear before it, ascertaining the facts of a dispute becomes the first indispensable step in application.

When a dispute arises, claimants commonly have different versions as to what had occurred. In the tragic incident of Korean Air Lines flight 007 of September 1983 (involving a Soviet SU-15 fighter shooting down a South Korean Boeing 747 jetliner that strayed into Soviet airspace and the death of all 269 people aboard), for example, the contending sides differed fundamentally on crucial facts (whether, for example, the civil aircraft was involved in some sort of spy mission). When relevant facts are perceived differently, legal arguments diverge. Without a decision maker to determine authoritatively what the relevant facts are, the disputants could simply go on arguing over alleged violations. Impartial fact-finding is crucial. If relevant facts could be ascertained through an impartial, third-party process, it would contribute significantly to settling a dispute.

Because exploring and ascertaining facts is integral to the dispute-settling process, it merits special attention. Much international effort toward application has been directed to achieve just that. The devices of investigation, fact-finding, on-the-scene observation, reporting, and commissions of inquiry all cater to this purpose. The underlying assumption is that once relevant facts are established by an impartial third party, dispute settlement can move from there.

Recourse to Direct Negotiations

The emphasis on "pacific" settlement of disputes through bilateral negotiations between "equal," "sovereign" states is understandable. Even in an interdependent world where the absolute supremacy inherent in the concept of sovereignty would appear archaic and absurd, nation-states do not hesitate to play up such rhetoric when it serves their purposes. The overriding concern of international law is neither to punish states nor to embarrass them but to secure compliance with international legal norms. When compliance can be secured through peaceful, noncoercive procedures, it enhances the effectiveness of international law under the principle of economy with minimal insult or embarrassment to states.

In the contemporary world of decentralization, as sustained by shared perception of common interest and reciprocity, participants are expected to act on their own to settle differences in a noncoercive manner with minimal involvement of inclusive authority. The most common procedure to settle differences and secure compliance is through diplomatic negotiations between contending states. Since most negotiations are conducted without drawing public attention, the achievement of ordinary diplomatic channels may not always be duly recognized. Numerous international agreements concerning the peaceful settlement of disputes confine their application to disputes that cannot be solved by diplomacy. Recognizing the importance of diplomatic negotiations as a form of application, the Permanent Court of International Justice declared that "before a dispute can be made the subject of an action at law, its subject matter should have been clearly defined by means of diplomatic negotiations."[1]

Direct bilateral negotiations can be successful between contending parties. But such negotiations may become deadlocked, hence the utility of such noncoercive devices as good offices, mediation, and conciliation. These devices inject into the application process a disinterested third party agreeable to both disputants, with varying degrees of authorized involvement, to facilitate peaceful settlement even for participants who have become too estranged to negotiate. The third party assists, not replaces, bilateral negotiations. The technical distinctions traditionally made regarding good offices, mediation, and conciliation reflect the degree of authorized involvement for the third party and do not affect the essence of bilateral negotiations. The ultimate settlement is contingent on the consent of the disputing parties.

These procedures have a long history in dispute settlement. Under the Hague Convention of 1899 for the Pacific Settlement of International Disputes, the signatory states, in consideration of the desirability of attempting pacific settlement, pledged to make such efforts and acknowledged the right of third parties to offer assistance in arriving at peaceful solutions. With the establishment of the League of Nations, permanent agencies were created to perform functions of good offices, mediation, and conciliation. These procedures are incorporated in the Charter of the United Nations. Commentators have sought to make technical distinctions among the procedures of good offices, mediation, and conciliation. But in practice these terms have been used with considerable flexibility. The tasks can be performed by a single third party but can also be done collectively. Their usefulness is limited in the sense that they cannot be successful, or even be initiated, without the cooperation of the disputants. But if such procedures do work toward composing differences and helping to secure compliance with international legal norms, so much the better.

Third-Party Decision Making

Arbitration and judicial settlement, as discussed in chapter 7, are typical modes of third-party decision making. The U.N. Charter explicitly includes both among the means of peaceful settlement of disputes. In arbitration and judicial settlement (through the International Court of Justice and other judicial tribunals), characterized by adverse proceedings with contending parties, the thrust of the emphasis differs from that prevailing in the previous phase of pacific settlement—with the third party playing the role the claimants want it to play.

During the nineteenth and early part of the twentieth centuries, arbitration was frequently used to settle international disputes. In order to facilitate and encourage its use, nation-states entered into bilateral and multilateral agreements for arbitration. In spite of the establishment of the Permanent Court of Arbitration in 1899, the procedure of arbitration is essentially ad hoc.

Widespread recognition of serious deficiencies in arbitral procedure led to the eventual establishment of the Permanent Court of International Justice, which was replaced by the International Court of Justice (ICJ), one of the principal organs of the United Nations. As discussed in chapter 7, however, because of a lack of compulsory jurisdiction—and in cases of acceptance of compulsory jurisdiction (by less than a third of the members of the United Nations), they are so highly qualified as to be more symbolic than substantial—the usefulness of judicial settlement by the court has not been maximized as contemplated. The U.S. withdrawal, in October 1985, of its previous acceptance of compulsory jurisdiction in reaction to the court's assumption of jurisdiction in the case of *Nicaragua v. United States* was an especially severe blow,[2] although the United States (as most states) is bound by several treaties recognizing special acceptance of the court's competence to interpret and apply such treaties. Special acceptance seems to be the preferred mode at present.

The chamber procedure the ICJ used in the *Gulf of Maine* case (1984)[3] has somewhat encouraged more use of this economical and effective procedure. In this case Canada and the United States invoked Article 27 of the ICJ Statute, which provides for use of a Special Chamber by agreement of the parties. A five-person panel was selected by consent of the parties to decide the disputed fisheries jurisdiction in the Gulf of Maine. Both agreed to submit drafts of their proposed methods for drawing the baselines and settling the dispute, which would determine each state's territorial waters and continental shelf rights. But by virtue of Article 27, both parties also agreed to abide by the decision of the panel without reservation. The Special Chamber, after accepting proposals from each party, independently determined the new line. The compulsory third-party decision-making mechanism of the Law of the Sea Convention has been another encouraging step toward the peaceful and lawful settlement of international disputes since it was implemented in 1994. Such dispute settlement processes are based on consent of the parties, and their involvement and participation in the decision process affords a greater chance of compliance.

Judicial adjudication has developed at the regional level—notably, the Court of European Communities, the European Court of Human Rights, and the Inter-American Court of Human Rights. The development of new forums to settle disputes peacefully increases the accessibility of various parties to effective arenas, thereby fostering greater compliance with community goals.

Recourse to International Governmental Organizations (Especially the United Nations)

When contending parties fail to settle disputes through either direct negotiations or third-party decision making, what can they do? Can they turn to international governmental organizations—most notably the United Nations—for help?

The United Nations is not designed to be a centralized agency for general law enforcement at the global level, though it is endowed with enormous responsibility to maintain international peace and security. The U.N. Charter encourages dispute settlement through noncoercive procedures outside the organization, expressing the policy of economy and effectiveness. The charter proclaims the basic principle of settling disputes by peaceful means in Articles 1(1) and 2(3). The charter's framers contemplated that most disputes should be settled by noncoercive methods and that settlement by organs of the United Nations should be resorted to only when other procedures fail. Article 33 thus obliges the member states to solve a dispute "by negotiation, enquiry, mediation, conciliation, arbitration, judicial settlement, resort to regional agencies or arrangements or other peaceful means of their own choice." In practice, member states tend to bring disputes before the Security Council without exhausting these peaceful means.

Although the United Nations is less than a general law enforcement agency, it is entrusted with the tremendous responsibility to maintain minimum world order. This has been especially the case in the past few years. As a whole, the charter is much more concerned with disputes that are likely to disrupt minimum order. Thus, the application of Chapter VI of the charter is expressly limited to disputes "the continuance of which is likely to endanger the maintenance of international peace." Violations of international law embrace a range of situations; a violation may or may not constitute a breach of such magnitude. Unless requested otherwise by the contenders, the Security Council or the General Assembly is empowered to recommend either procedures of peaceful settlement or terms of settlement only if a preliminary investigation indicates that the "dispute or situation is likely to endanger the maintenance of international peace and security" (Article 34). The noncoercive procedures of settlement set forth in the charter have been carefully designed to permit a gradual approach to each dispute—the competence of the United Nations is contingent on the seriousness of the dispute and the degree of danger to minimum world order. The United Nations would normally step in only when a dispute is likely to disrupt minimum public order. Even then the United Nations is confined to recommending only procedures or terms of settlement.

In addition to the framework for peaceful settlement of disputes, the United Nations is authorized to take enforcement measures. The Security Council is empowered, under Article 39 of the charter, to determine the existence not only of "an act of aggression" or "breach of the peace" but also "a threat to the peace" and to take proper enforcement measures. Any violation falling short of threatening the peace will be outside the scope of the Security Council's competence. The concept of what constitutes such a threat has been increasingly broadened in the recent past, however, with the Security Council becoming a much more active decision-making body since the end of the Cold War.

A significant development in the Security Council's efforts to contribute to global peace and stability was the release of the "An Agenda for Peace" Report in 1992.[4] The report was disseminated to highlight four distinct yet interrelated tasks: preventative diplomacy; peacemaking; peacekeeping; and postconflict peace-building. The report outlined a range of diplomatic and other measures available to the United Nations to discourage and resolve disputes with the goal of maintaining peace. These tools include the use of armed troops under the direction of the United Nations to stabilize conflict zones and prevent violent escalations between warring parties. The report also introduced the concept of postconflict peace-building, a process focused on encouraging the development of conditions and institutions that are essential to long-lasting peace. Finally, the report also called for the participation of regional organizations to support the efforts of the Security Council. The role of these organizations was explored in chapter 3.

How effective has the United Nations been in performing its sanctioning functions? The veto power of the permanent members of the Security Council has made it extremely difficult, if not impossible, to enforce effectively the measures provided by Chapter VII of the charter, even against a clearly identified challenge to minimum world order. This has continued to be true after the Cold War as witnessed by its failure leading up to the war in Bosnia and the difficulty in maintaining support from all the superpowers for past sanctions against nations such as Iraq and Iran. In a bold peacetime experiment, the Security Council undertook multilateral efforts to destroy Iraq's war-making capabilities through sanctions and on-site inspections. These sanctions, begun in 1990, were ultimately unsuccessful in preventing a new war in Iraq a decade later.

The General Assembly's formal authority in peacekeeping, as described in chapter 3, was greatly enlarged on November 3, 1950, with the passage of Resolution 377 A, otherwise known as the Uniting for Peace Resolution. At that time, the Security Council was paralyzed by disagreements among the permanent members, which had culminated in a boycott by the Soviet Union. The impasse prevented the Security Council from exercising its powers to intervene in the growing conflict in the Korean Peninsula. In response, under the leadership of U.S. Secretary of State Dean Acheson, the General Assembly adopted Resolution 377 A, giving itself the power to make recommendations on matters of international peace and security (an issue primarily reserved for the Council under the U.N. Charter). The resolution also permits the convening of emergency sessions at the request of the Security Council or a majority of the General Assembly's members. In February 1951, the General Assembly passed Resolution 498 (V), urging U.N. members to act to counter the People's Republic of China's aggressions in Korea.[5] Since 1950, the United Nations has called ten emergency sessions, most recently in regard to the Israeli occupation of Palestinian territories—a session that remains in effect more than a decade later. The International Court of Justice has opined on more than one occasion that the resolution validly changed the charter's balance of power between the General Assembly and the Security Council, further legitimizing the General Assembly's actions.

Resolution 377 A gave the General Assembly an enhanced role in adopting recommendations concerning international peace and security at a time when the Security Council found itself unable to act. Since then, the Security Council's members have improved their ability to cooperate and discharge the council's functions. Yet the resolution continues to empower the General Assembly to convene the global community in times of crisis. Nevertheless, the General Assembly remains handicapped. It continues to face limitations in performing the applying function to deal with a range of acts of lawlessness, especially in the very area that constitutes one of the organization's major goals. For example, the permanent members of the Security Council have veto powers which they can use to block a resolution by the General Assembly, thus protecting the council's primacy within the United Nations.

Recourse to Unilateral Measures of Self-Help

The U.N. Charter represents the general efforts of the organized community of nations to substitute effective collective measures for unilateral measures of nation-state self-help, which are highly susceptible to abuse. Yet the existing structures of authority and procedure provided by the charter are not sufficiently comprehensive and effective to enable the United Nations to function as a centralized organ for securing compliance with international law across the board. When states that are victims of all sorts of lawless acts cannot, despite their genuine efforts, secure justice or peace through either noncoercive methods or international governmental organizations, will they be permitted to resort to unilateral coercive measures in response to prior unlawful acts?

In the past, resort to unilateral coercive measures was a recognized means of enforcement. Enforceability of international law depended in large measure on such patterns of unorganized and uninstitutionalized remedies. Measures thus taken by states were generally labeled self-help, reprisal, retaliation, or measures short of war. "Self-help" would appear to be a generic term appropriate for the present purpose. Forcible self-help was regarded as permissible when it was reasonably necessary and taken in response to a prior unlawful act, including failure to carry out international obligations, when such act was imputable to the state against which the self-help measure was directed.

The U.N. Charter, with its general proscription of the threat or use of force, as contained in Article 2(4), has generated a continuing controversy about the permissibility of self-help involving the use of armed force. As elaborated in chapter 19, we have reluctantly concluded that absent effective machinery for collective law enforcement under the present world conditions, self-help, even involving military force, remains permissible as a measure of last resort, subject to the rigorous requirements of necessity and proportionality. The necessity for self-help will occur only when all good faith efforts in exhausting all available noncoercive means in response to a prior act of lawlessness have proved futile. The requirement of proportionality must be appraised by reference to all factors relevant in a particular context, considering especially the nature of the precipitating act of lawlessness and the harm it has caused, and the modality (military or nonmilitary) of the responding measure and the deprivation it may cause.

Self-help measures that are nonmilitary in nature can be permissible, provided the conditions of necessity and proportionality are met.

Toward Effective Management of Sanctioning Measures to Optimize Sanctioning Goals

The enforceability of international law is a long-standing question. To this day skeptics harbor the notion that international law is not law at all, because it lacks "enforceability" or has only "marginal enforceability." Such a view approaches the question of enforcement in terms of a centralized system of command and community coercion and fails to grasp the dynamics inherent in a decentralized legal system. It often confuses sanctions, moreover, with use of the military instrument without reference to the real-world impact of economic, diplomatic, and ideologic instruments.

Although it is sometimes suggested that enforcement and sanction be kept separate, they are often used interchangeably. For the present purpose, we adhere to the popular usage, but with a comprehensive dynamic orientation. In grappling with the question of enforceability, one must project a comprehensive set of sanctioning goals and mobilize all participants and available means of sanction, both coercive and noncoercive, taken from both short-term and long-term perspectives. The specific sanctioning goals are prevention, deterrence, restoration, rehabilitation, reconstruction, and correction.

Prevention aims both to develop in decision makers strong preferences to conform to international legal norms and to minimize the probabilities of violations and deprivations. It is a long-term goal, projected into the indefinite future. Prevention embraces a range of measures and activities designed to minimize violations and the probability of undesirable outcomes. The Canadian government, for example, in 1985 enacted the Waters Pollution Prevention Act, "a model attempt by one state to provide comprehensive environmental policing for its designated area of coverage."[6] The act prohibits and prescribes penalties for the deposit of "waste" in Arctic waters or on the islands or mainland under conditions that such waste may enter Arctic waters. Other nations have made differing arrangements in accordance with what they understand as the nature and scope of their pollution responsibility for their own waters and in regard to inclusive resources.

Deterrence, unlike prevention, is concerned with a potential violation that has emerged and been clearly posed. Deterrence is not a new goal in the field of sanction. Because of the "balance of terror" (or MAD, mutual assured destruction) brought about by the development of Cold War nuclear strategies, the term has gained not only a specific emphasis but a distinctive connotation. It is usually this connotation that commentators refer to when they speak of the "strategy of deterrence" nowadays. Deterrence, for the present purposes, is not to be understood in this distinctive sense but is more general in reference. It is designed to deter impending impermissible acts.

Once a violation takes place, the goal of restoration comes into play. Restoration aims at compelling the violator state to terminate its impermissible act.

Rehabilitation is concerned with immediate reparation of the values deprived or compensation for injury sustained and the facilitation of quick resumption of peaceful and normal interactions between the contenders. Violations of international obligations are generally assumed to result in the "duty to make reparation," one of the cardinal principles in the realm of state responsibility. Further, as Article 8 of the Universal Declaration of Human Rights makes clear, every human being has the right to an effective remedy for violations of his or her human rights.

The goal of reconstruction is to avoid the recurrence of impermissible acts by bringing about structural changes in the value processes of the violator state and to create and maintain conditions conducive to peaceful, normal interaction. Thus conceived, reconstruction may merge into prevention. Whereas prevention operates within existing structures and processes, reconstruction is concerned with long-term efforts to cause structural changes favorable to peaceful interactions among states. Furthermore, whereas prevention addresses all territorial communities, efforts for reconstruction are primarily directed to the identified violator state.

The goal of correction is directed to persons held responsible for conduct offensive to the conscience and decency of humanity, with a view toward changing their dispositions. With the establishment of the International Criminal Court, the goal of correction is becoming an increasingly prominent and effective aspect of international law. This concept is explored further in chapter 29.

Each of the sanctioning goals is distinct, yet all are related. The relative prominence of each is a function of context. After the context is analyzed, the arsenal of sanctioning measures must be tailored to these goals. This is not an ideal model of centralized sanction and enforcement in a highly organized legal system. But it is a more realistic approach in an essentially decentralized legal system—an approach that would inspire some confidence that much more can be done rather than generate the paralysis that results from a sense of futility.

The case of Iran demonstrates the difficulty of securing compliance with international legal prescriptions through sanctions. Both the United States and the United Nations have employed various measures against Iran in response to refusals to adhere to obligations under international law and to discourage the development of weapons of mass destruction. As a party to the Nuclear Non-Proliferation Treaty (NPT), Iran retains the right to develop civilian nuclear energy programs. However, it must also apply certain safeguards in connection with its nuclear programs and allow the International Atomic Energy Agency (IAEA) to inspect facilities to verify compliance with the treaty.

In 2005, the IAEA concluded that Iran had failed to properly report its nuclear assets under the NPT. In 2006, on the recommendation of the IAEA, the Security Council demanded that Iran suspend its nuclear enrichment activities and imposed sanctions under Resolution 1737.[7] However, Iran's President Ahmadinejad refused to act to suspend his country's activities. In March 2007, the Security Council voted to widen the scope of its existing sanctions against Iran with Resolution 1747.[8] In March 2008, the Security Council passed Resolution 1803, extending sanctions to cover a wider range of financial institutions, travel, and exports.[9] In June 2010, the Security Council passed Resolution 1929, imposing a complete arms embargo on Iran and travel bans on certain Iranian officials and banning Iran from trading in ballistic missiles.[10]

The acts listed here demonstrate many aspects of the decision functions taking place within various authoritative contexts, namely invocation and prescription. The outcomes of these processes, when directed toward a subject, whether a state or another entity, exemplify the applying function. And when such actions seek a change in conduct, they are rightly considered as sanctioning measures. In the case of Iran, the actions taken by the IAEA, the United Nations, and others fall within the scope of the prevention, deterrence, and restoration phases of the sanctioning process. Having identified conduct which is in violation of community expectations, the sanctioning bodies have devised a program to disincentive the continuation of the offending behaviors—or the adoption of new ones like them—while hastening the termination of the targeted policies.

After years of intensifying sanctions against Iran, a detente emerged following the election of a new Iranian president, Hassan Rouhani, in 2013. After diplomatic exchanges between Iran and the United States, including some held in secret, a much-watched summit was held in Geneva in November, where the five permanent members of the U.N. Security Council plus Germany signed an agreement with Iran to secure a temporary pause to some of its nuclear activities.[11] Iran also agreed to permit IAEA experts to visit its nuclear sites to ensure compliance with international standards. In exchange, Iran would receive immediate relief from some sanctions, giving it access to frozen financial assets and opening the door to limited direct flights between Iran and the United States, among other benefits. The six-month agreement was designed to permit time for further negotiations on the issues.

For the West, the breakthrough with Iran provided evidence of the effectiveness of sanctioning measures, although it is too soon to tell whether a sustainable agreement will be reached. Moreover, some observers noted that sanctions alone were not enough to bring Iran to the bargaining table without the addition of positive diplomacy and the promise of worthwhile economic rewards. Indeed, the Iranian situation provides a ripe example of the overlapping of the ideological, economic, and diplomatic instruments in practice. It also highlights the roles played by individual decision makers and elites whose actions prevent or promote the resolution of conflicts, often with enormous domestic implications. The appraisal of any outcome regarding Iran should depend both on the common interests of the world community expressed by the United Nations and the maintenance of minimum world order, which depends on the effective regulation of nuclear weapons. The practice of enforcement provides a means through which the international community may define and reinforce shared expectations of conduct through a communicative process of action and reaction. The desired long-term effect of enforcement—whether applied against nation-states or individuals—is the obtainment of minimum world order through greater awareness and acceptance of community policies.

Notes

1. Mavrommatis Palestine Concessions, (Greece v. Gr. Brit.), 1924, P.C.I.J. (ser. A) No. 2, at 15 (Aug. 30).

2. U.S. Department of State Letter and Statement Concerning the Termination of Acceptance of I.C.J. Compulsory Jurisdiction, *reprinted in* 24 I.L.M. 1742 (1985).

3. Delimitation of the Marine Boundary in the Gulf of Maine Area (Can./U.S.), 1984 I.C.J. 246 (Oct. 12).

4. An Agenda for Peace: Preventive Diplomacy, Peacemaking and Peace-keeping, U.N. Doc. A/47/277, S/24111 (June 17, 1992), *available at* http://www.un.org/Docs/SG/agpeace.html.

5. UNITED NATIONS AUDIOVISUAL LIBRARY OF INTERNATIONAL LAW, UNITING FOR PEACE GENERAL ASSEMBLY RESOLUTION 377 (V), http://legal.un.org/avl/ha/ufp/ufp.html.

6. Arctic Waters Pollution Prevention Act, R.S.C., 1985, c. A-12 (Can).

7. S.C. Res. 1737, U.N. Doc. S/RES/1737 (Dec. 27, 2006).

8. S.C. Res. 1747, U.N. Doc. S/RES/1747 (Mar. 24, 2007).

9. S.C. Res. 1803, U.N. Doc. S/RES/1803 (Mar. 8, 2008).

10. S.C. Res. 1929, U.N. Doc. S/RES/1929 (June 9, 2010).

11. Anne Gearan and Joby Warrick, *Iran, World Powers Reach Historic Nuclear Deal*, WASH. POST, Nov. 23, 2013, *available at* http://www.washingtonpost.com/world/national-security/kerry-in-geneva-raising-hopes-for-historic-nuclear-deal-with-iran/2013/11/23/53e7bfe6-5430-11e3-9fe0-fd2ca728e67c_story.html.

25 The Terminating Function

THE TERMINATING FUNCTION involves removing the authority of prescriptions, and of arrangements or processes affected under prescriptions, when prescriptions and arrangements cease to conform to demanded goals of world public order. Ending a prescription is itself a prescription, with the distinction that it is directed toward changing a prior prescription. Termination communicates that a prior prescription or arrangement is no longer authoritative. Conceived comprehensively, termination entails a sequence of activities, including initiating the function; investigating the facts about alleged obsolescence of a prescription or an arrangement; exploring community policy relevant to the end of such prescription or arrangement; canceling the prior prescription or arrangement; and ameliorating the loss caused by such termination.

When performed in an effective and timely fashion, the terminating function fosters expectations that change can be made in ways compatible with basic community goals and that a balance can be struck between stability and change. A public order that cherishes human dignity will continue to alter outmoded prescriptions to conform them to newly clarified goals of human dignity, while deferring to existing arrangements and the expectations created by such arrangements. It will further seek to minimize all losses and costs likely to result from necessary change and to lessen potentially disruptive impact through contextual scrutiny of relevant facts and policies. A hallmark of a functioning public order is sensitivity to the claims and expectations grounded in the manifold events of the past, present, and future.

The participants in the terminating function, as in the other functions, are those active in the effective power process, including officials of nation-states, officials of international governmental organizations, representatives of private associations and groups, and individuals. This function is maintained for two basic demands: to keep the prescriptions of the world community compatible with the goals of world public order, both minimum and optimum, and to strike a balance between necessary stability and dynamic change. The demand for change caused by the exigencies of radically different conditions is tempered by the demand to minimize potential deprivations attendant upon the obsolescence and more formal change of prescriptions. It is further disciplined by realistic expectations about the dynamics of intensifying interaction in an interdependent world.

Decisions about change occur in all structures of authority, both transnational and national, and even in the habitual interactions of nonofficial processes. The base values at the disposal of all participants embrace authority and all the value assets of effective power. "Authority" is found in a complex of prescriptions (both written and unwritten) about the termination of agreements, in specified requirements for customary change (desuetude), and in specific provisions for collective procedures. A significant base of effective power is the conspicuous mobilization of opinion and effort for change. (Witness, for example, the domino effect of reform throughout Eastern Europe and Russia, the dramatic demonstration of "people power" in the Philippines and, comparably, in South Korea, or most recently, the revolutions in Northern Africa and the Middle East.) The strategies of termination vary by type of prescription: multilateral agreements are ended by new agreements, by unilateral denunciation because of changed conditions, and by obsolescence or preemption through customary development; customary prescriptions are terminable either by appropriately comprehensive agreements or by the development of new customs; and finally, termination may occur through collective procedures maintained by the organized community within the framework of the United Nations. Its outcomes, as discussed in chapter 16, involve degrees of change, including amendment, modification, suspension, withdrawal, and termination of the prescription.

Perhaps the most dramatic recent example of the termination function occurred on December 8, 1991, when the leaders of Belarus, the Russian Federation, and Ukraine signed an agreement in Minsk to found a commonwealth of independent states, effectively proclaiming the end of the Union of Soviet Socialist Republics (USSR). The Minsk Agreement begins as follows:

Preamble
We, the Republic of Belarus, the Russian Federation and the Republic of Ukraine, as founder states of the Union of Soviet Socialist Republics (USSR), which signed the 1922 Union Treaty, further described as the high contracting parties, conclude that the USSR has ceased to exist as a subject of international law and a geopolitical reality.[1]

Egypt's ousting of former President Hosni Mubarak in January 2011 provides many illustrations of the terminating function. Mubarak's thirty-year-rule ended following eighteen days of mass protests, and control of Egypt was assigned to its military. After taking control, the Egyptian military dissolved parliament and suspended the constitution. A constitutional referendum was scheduled to draft constitutional amendments. While the interim government promised to honor its international commitments, it was unclear how serious the new government would take pledges made by its predecessor. For example, there was a question of whether Egypt, a predominantly Islamic nation, would observe its peace treaty with Israel. Similarly, the new government had the opportunity to appraise and terminate practices that were inimical to human dignity and that had contributed to the nation's popular uprising. This process of appraisal and termination will undoubtedly continue as Egypt transitions from a military to a civilian government.

The U.N. Charter anticipates the necessity of change by stipulating the amending process. Article 108 of the charter reads: "Amendments to the present Charter shall come into force for all Members of the United Nations when they have been adopted by a vote of two-thirds of the members of the General Assembly and ratified in accordance with their respective constitutional processes by two-thirds of the Members of the United Nations, including all the permanent members of the Security Council." Article 109 contemplates a general conference to review the charter for the purpose of charter revision but embodies the same amending requirement as Article 108: "Any alteration of the present Charter recommended by a two-thirds vote of the conference shall take effect when ratified in accordance with their respective constitutional processes by two-thirds of the Members of the United Nations including all permanent members of the Security Council." Evidently, the two-thirds requirement is compounded by the requisite unanimity of the five permanent members of the Security Council. Owing to this built-in veto in the amending procedure, change of charter provisions through formal amendment has been rare, although the United Nations has undergone profound constitutive development since its establishment, largely as a result of patterns of expectation and behavior outside any formal amending process. The only formal changes thus far relate to enlarging the membership of the Security Council and the Economic and Social Council and to corresponding changes in the requisite voting to make decisions, in light of the vast increase in the total U.N. membership.

The existing human rights prescriptions erect considerable barriers for termination, because they express, as discussed in chapter 12, the basic, most widely shared and intensely demanded policies for which the global constitutive process is maintained. Some human rights conventions do not contain withdrawal provisions; others do. Some do not contain denunciation provisions; others do. Most human rights conventions' provisions became customary in the 1990s, and some have even become *jus cogens*, or peremptory norms. The two most important treaties—the International Covenant on Civil and Political Rights (and its optional protocols) and the International Covenant on Economic, Social, and Cultural Rights—contain no provision for denunciation, nor does the Universal Declaration contemplate such a result. This ostensible omission is highly significant: it signifies that the human rights obligations stipulated in the covenants are not expected to be unilaterally disregarded. They are *obligatio erga omnes*, rights or obligations toward all. Article 56 of the Vienna Convention on the Law of Treaties is instructive:

1. A treaty which contains no provision regarding its termination and which does not provide for denunciation or withdrawal is not subject to denunciation or withdrawal unless:
   a. it is established that the parties intended to admit the possibility of denunciation or withdrawal; or
   b. a right of denunciation or withdrawal may be implied by the nature of the treaty.
2. A party shall give not less than twelve months' notice of its intention to denounce or withdraw from a treaty under paragraph 1.

Given the authoritative policy in support of the intense demand for global protection of human rights, and given the absence of explicit provision for denunciation, it would appear that the commitments incorporated in the two covenants were intended neither to admit the possibility of denunciation or withdrawal nor to imply a right of denunciation or withdrawal.

Furthermore, even provisions for denunciation contained in certain human rights conventions cannot easily be made effective. The denunciation clauses typically embody certain temporal constraints: barring an exercise of denunciation within a specified period (such as five or ten years), or barring the operative effect of a formal denunciation pending the lapse of a specified period (normally twelve months). Thus, an act of denunciation does not, immediately on notification, relieve the denouncing party of the obligations embodied in the denounced treaty, and the denouncing party may still be held accountable under the treaty obligations during the interim.

Above all, an act of denunciation does not exempt the denouncing party from obligations, which may parallel or reproduce those in the denounced convention, prevailing under general customary international law. The Vienna Convention on the Law of Treaties, in Article 43, states unequivocally: "The invalidity, termination or denunciation of a treaty, the withdrawal of a party from it, or the suspension of its operation, as a result of the application of the present Convention or of the provisions of the treaty, shall not in any way impair the duty of any State to fulfill any obligation embodied in the treaty to which it would be subject under international law independently of the treaty."

Termination is a legal right, and states generally have the right to control binding legal obligations.[2] There are different provisions that affect a state's ability to terminate an agreement. For example, the Article 10(1) of the Nuclear Non-Proliferation Treaty permits withdrawal only if a state can show "that extraordinary events, related to the subject matter of this Treaty, have jeopardized the supreme interest of its country." In contrast, the World Trade Organization and others permit unconditional withdrawal with six months' notice. For example, in 2007, Bolivia withdrew from the U.N. Convention on the Settlement of Investment Disputes—which required six months' notice—without legal ramifications.[3] These provisions generally outline the circumstances and restrictions under which legal termination can be made and/or provide procedures for which termination is to be executed. In other words, these provisions reduce or eliminate the legal consequences of the exiting state.[4]

Termination, otherwise, would be illegal because a state is violating a binding legal obligation, and generally, there are legal costs—such as reciprocity, retaliation and reputation[5]—that a violating state may face. Reciprocity is simply the withdrawal of the benefits that were awarded to a state through an agreement. By exiting the treaty, the state is giving up its right to benefit from the treaty. Reciprocity generally affects all exiting states and, thus, is more an effect of termination than a deterrent. On the other hand, retaliatory and reputational sanctions are deterrents against illegal exits. For example, the United States withdrew from the Optional Protocol to the Vienna Convention on Consular Relations, which did not include a withdrawal provision. (Generally, the lack of a withdrawal provision infers lack of a legal right to do so under Article 56 of the Vienna Convention on the Law of Treaties.) The United States was criticized for doing so, and its reputation suffered.[6] As with all sanctions, the effectiveness may be limited, but their existence may deter some states from illegal terminations.

The content of all treaties, including the U.N. Charter, naturally can be changed, as even national constitutions are changed, through the development of new customary law. This, however, is a complex process of communication involving a range of participants in continuous interaction. To ascertain whether the communications in past uniformities of behavior, with their attendant subjectivities about lawfulness, have crystallized into the expectations about content, authority, and control that constitute a new customary law requires a comprehensive inquiry. The relevant questions are: Who are the primary communicators and communicatees; what demands and expectations have been communicated; what patterns of general expectation are extant; what is the complex matrix of interaction in terms of spatial, temporal, institutional, and crisis features; what inferences can be drawn from the relative bases of power of the participants; what signs and behavior have been employed as strategies of communication; and what is the culminating mediation of expectations about future policy, authority, and control?

The same U.N. machinery used to expedite the prescribing function can also be used to expedite the terminating function. The making of a new custom—and hence a termination through customary development—can be expedited by contemporary collective procedures. The United Nations, particularly the General Assembly, furnishes a unique, and an exceptionally convenient, forum in which most of the world's peoples can be represented to articulate demands. The tempo of communication can be accelerated through institutional arrangements; the certainty of peoples' expectations about policy, content, authority, and control can be established without lengthy time lapses. Just as custom can now be created "instantaneously" through this new modality, so change and termination of prescription, if sufficiently demanded by the world's peoples, can now also be rapidly achieved.

Nevertheless, in this era of perpetual change, a vexing problem remains: the tension and uncertainty likely to be generated when an established norm is severely challenged and an emerging alternative has crystallized into a new authoritative norm. The controversy concerning the changing standard of compensation in the case of expropriation (nationalization) offers a prime example (see chapters 18 and 22).

The question of the width of territorial sea offers another excellent example.

Before 1982 an array of claims (ranging from three to two hundred miles) had jeopardized the customary rule of three-mile territorial sea and created tremendous confusion regarding the permissible width of territorial sea. The three-mile rule, as originated in the cannon-shot rule of the eighteenth century, became widely accepted in the nineteenth century. During the twentieth century, although the major maritime powers insisted on the three-mile rule, states increasingly departed from this norm, especially the new states that proliferated in the era of the United Nations. The insistence by the major powers on a narrow belt of territorial sea (and hence a wide domain allowing high seas freedom) clashed with the growing demands of the lesser powers to protect security and fishery interests. Failures to agree to the width of territorial sea by both the First and the Second United Nations Conferences on the Law of the Sea in 1958 and 1960 further aggravated the situation. By the early 1980s, of the 137 independent coastal states, only a minority of twenty-four still adhered to the three-mile rule, while an overwhelming majority of seventy-nine states claimed twelve miles, with the rest claiming either six miles or more than twelve miles and up to two hundred miles. The Law of the Sea Convention, adopted in 1982, settled this long-standing controversy by allowing coastal states to claim territorial sea not in excess of twelve nautical miles.

In the *Fisheries Jurisdiction* case between the United Kingdom and Iceland (1974),[7] which involved Britain's challenge of Iceland's unilateral competence to extend its fisheries zones from twelve to fifty miles, the International Court of Justice (ICJ) confronted conflicting claims about customary law governing a coastal state's fisheries rights. The ICJ declared that since 1960 there had developed a customary norm that permitted coastal states to claim exclusive fishery zones of twelve miles, including the territorial sea, but not zones of fifty miles. It stated that the coastal state enjoyed a preferential right of fishing in adjacent areas of sea beyond the twelve-mile limit, insofar as the coastal state, like Iceland, depended economically on local fisheries, but that it could not exclude other states from fishing in such areas, especially if they had traditionally fished there and economically depended on fishing there. In a joint separate opinion, Judges

Isaac Forster, Cesar Bengzon, Eduardo Jimenez de Arechaga, Nagendra Singh, and Jose Maria Ruda noted specially:

> If the law relating to fisheries constituted a subject on which there were clear indications of what precisely is the rule of international law in existence, it may then have been possible to disregard altogether the legal significance of certain proposals, declarations or statements which advocate changes or improvements in a system of law which is considered to be unjust or inadequate. But this is not the situation. There is at the moment great uncertainty as to the existing customary law on account of the conflicting and discordant practice of States. Once the uncertainty of such a practice is admitted, the impact of the aforesaid official pronouncements, declarations and proposals most undoubtedly have an unsettling effect on the crystallization of a still evolving customary law on the subject.[8]

As the above case illustrates, states' "proposals, declarations, or statements" can impact nonsettled customary international law because, as the world advances, customary international law evolves, incorporating new norms and standards of state engagement. However, once customary international law is settled and considered a norm, individual states' actions cannot so easily impact and change it.

Notes

1. The Agreement Establishing the Commonwealth of Independent States, (the Minsk Agreement), Dec. 8, 1991, *reprinted in* 31 I.L.M. 138 (1992).

2. *See* Duncan B. Hollis, *Why State Consent Still Matters—Non-State Actors, Treaties, and the Change Source of International Law*, 23 BERKELEY J. INT'L L. 137 (2005).

3. *See* News Release, Int'l Ctr. For Settlement of Inv. Disputes, Bolivia submits a Notice under Article 71 of the ICSID Convention (May 16, 2007), *available at* http://icsid.worldbank.org/ICSID/StaticFiles/Anouncement9.html.

4. Laurence R. Helfer, *Exiting Treaties*, 91 VA. L. REV. 1579, 1582 (2005).

5. ANDREW T. GUZMAN, HOW INTERNATIONAL LAW WORKS 33 (Oxford University Press 2008).

6. Timothy Meyer, *Power, Exit Costs, and Renegotiation in International Law*, 51 HARV. INT'L L.J. 379, 396 (2010).

7. Fisheries Jurisdiction (U.K. v. Ice.), 1974 I.C.J. 3 (July 25).

8. *Id.* at 48.

26 The Appraising Function

THE APPRAISING FUNCTION involves evaluating the decision process in terms of policy objectives of the larger community and identifying the participants responsible for past successes and failures. It is concerned with the adequacy of past decision in achieving postulated goals and widely shared and intensely felt expectations. It relies on the intelligence and promoting functions to determine how well the process of decision is functioning and how it can be improved. The sequence of activities involved in appraisal includes gathering the necessary information about the decision process and its outcomes; evaluating the economy, effectiveness, and consequences of decision; and disseminating findings and recommendations to relevant audiences.

To evaluate the constitutive process in terms of desired public order, appraisal must be both comprehensive and appropriately selective. Operating effectively, the appraising function will ascertain the successes and failures of demanded values, probe for the factors in all phases of the decision functions that affect successes and failures, and ascribe responsibility for such successes and failures as a strategy for improvement. Appraisal seeks to bring relevant intellectual skills (identifying and clarifying goals, surveying trends, analyzing conditions. projecting developments, and inventing alternatives) to bear on every feature of both constitutive process and public order. To ensure necessary independence and impartiality, appraisers must be insulated from immediate threats or inducements and self-appraisals scrutinized by other appraisers. Though intermittent appraisals may mobilize needed occasional attention and support, most sustained and creative effects are likely to transpire when the appraising function is continuously performed within stable structures capable of relating each detail to the set of community goals and the spectrum of conditions.

Generally speaking, participation in the appraising function is highly democratic. All participants in all structures and processes of authority, national and transnational, are to a degree always engaged in self-appraisal and appraisals of others, reviewing and assessing authoritative decision in terms of its content, economy, effectiveness, and consequences. Other participants interested in the quality of public order, including political parties, pressure groups, private associations, and individuals, are also constantly involved in appraisal, through political platforms, demands of pressure groups, private views, and so on. Intellectuals, both within and outside the academic community, play a special role in performing the difficult tasks of appraisal.

The basic objective of the appraising function is to secure a continuing reform of the decision process in the light of changing demands and expectations under ever-changing conditions. Although structures of authority may sometimes be specialized to the appraising function, appraisal is generally incidental to structures specialized for other functions. The task of formal appraisal tends to be more widely dispersed than concentrated, and more episodic than continuous. The structures are yet to be established to make systematic appraisal an important, continuing feature of the process of decision.

Most of the base values employed to gather, process, and disseminate information bear directly on appraisal. Capacities for appraisal have expanded greatly, thanks to the proliferation of information about world social process; the acquisition of new knowledge and skills to evaluate public order effects; the development of expertise in many fields to analyze the past and the present, and forecast the future; and the growth of interdisciplinary cooperation. Most of the strategies employed for intelligence and promotion are equally useful for the appraising function. The culminations of appraisal are a continuing flow of information and assessment and the ascertainment of responsibility regarding features of the decision process and its outcomes and effects.

The appraising function through institutional effort is amply reflected in provisions of the U.N. Charter, including Articles 15, 17, 24(3), 62(1), 64, 87, 88, and 98. The General Assembly is authorized under Article 15 to receive and consider annual and special reports from the Security Council and other U.N. organs. In dealing with budgetary matters under Article 17, the General Assembly is inevitably involved in evaluating past successes and failures as a guide for priorities and allocations. The bulk of the annual report of the Economic and Social Council deals comprehensively with economic, social, cultural, and humanitarian matters. The reporting has been greatly eased by the provision of Article 64:

1. The Economic and Social Council may take appropriate steps to obtain regular reports from the specialized agencies. It may make arrangements with the Members of the United Nations and the specialized agencies to obtain reports

on the steps taken to give effect to its own recommendations and to recommend matters falling within its competence made by the General Assembly.

2. It may communicate its observations on these reports to the General Assembly.

The Secretary-General of the United Nations occupies a unique position. The role of the office, extant and potential, in appraisal is worth special notice. The secretary-general is required by Article 98 to submit an annual report to the General Assembly on the work of the organization. When taken seriously and performed effectively, the secretary-general's annual report can provide not only essential information about the work of the United Nations but also an important occasion to appraise the state of the world community in all major fields and sectors. Given a unique vantage point and a continuing and comprehensive authority, as assisted by a substantial corps of international civil servants in the Secretariat, the secretary-general can contribute immensely through the annual report. It can highlight (without being polemic or strident) past successes and failures in matters of peace and security and in economic, social, cultural, human rights, and other fields and focus world attention on matters that deserve top priority or require continuing follow-up efforts, thereby eliciting the timely collaboration of all parties concerned (governmental and nongovernmental sectors alike) to enhance both minimum and optimum world order.

Appraisal can take many forms. The reporting system developed in the field of human rights has proven highly useful. Under this system, as originally instituted by the Economic and Social Council, U.N. member states, specialized agencies, and certain nongovernmental organizations submit periodic reports to the U.N. Human Rights Council. Though the reports submitted by governments tend to be perfunctory and self-serving, their quality and importance can be greatly enhanced if the council take their tasks of appraisal seriously rather than serve merely as transmitters of superficial information.

Nongovernmental organizations also play an important role in providing ongoing assessment of developments that are made objectively without the limiting perspective of individual states. Many of these organizations issue annual or semi-regular reports containing statistics and comparisons on issues such as human rights and economic development. For example, Freedom House produces annual assessments of democracy and freedom of the press in nations around the world, while Amnesty International and Human Rights Watch issue regular reports concerning threats to human rights, and the International Campaign to Ban Landmines issues an annual update on efforts to eliminate the use of landmines in war zones and to disarm existing landmines left over from previous conflicts.

The contemporary human rights conventions generally establish a reporting system designed to afford a continuing channel of appraisal. The list includes the International Covenant on Civil and Political Rights; the International Covenant on Economic, Social, and Cultural Rights; the International Convention on the Elimination of All

Forms of Racial Discrimination; the Convention on the Elimination of All Forms of Discrimination Against Women; the Convention on the Political Rights of Women; the Convention on the Rights of the Child; the Convention Relating to the Status of Refugees; International Convention on the Protection of the Rights of All Migrant Workers and Members of Their Families; the Convention Against Torture and Other Cruel, Inhuman or Degrading Treatment or Punishment; the European Convention on Human Rights; the European Social Charter; and the American Convention on Human Rights.

Committees of experts are often tasked with monitoring and appraising the implementation of nations' obligations under the treaties to which they are signatories. For example, the Human Rights Council developed the Universal Periodic Review (UPR) to monitor the human rights' records of all U.N. member states. Far from perfunctory, the UPR is an ongoing review process in which a country's human rights records are examined every four years. International agreements can also create obligations for states to self-report on the status of the implementation of their obligations. These reports serve functions including: providing the treaty bodies with an update on the states' progress under treaties, identifying shortcomings and obstacles to implementation, and laying out strategies for successfully upholding obligations. A committee may request further information or conduct its own inquiries before issuing its findings on a state's efforts. Moreover, in some cases, there may be opportunities for individuals, organizations, and states to submit formal complaints to the treaty bodies in order to draw attention to violations of international obligations. These statements may in turn lead to formal inquiries and reporting measures.

The International Labour Organization (ILO) provides the most successful example of sustained institutional appraisal through the reporting system. The ILO Constitution requires a member to submit an annual report to the International Labour Office, specifying the measures it has taken to give effect to the provisions of conventions to which it is a party. The report must conform, both in form and in substance, to the prescribed regulations of the governing body. Such reports, essential for application of ILO Conventions, add to realistic appraisal. To aid the applying and appraising functions, the director general must submit a summary of the governments' reports to each session of the International Labour Conference, and the member governments must transmit, in keeping with the unique, tripartite character of the ILO, copies of their annual reports to the representative organizations of employers and workers. These annual reports are closely examined by a committee of experts composed of independent persons of the highest standing, whose findings are reviewed by the Conference Committee on the Application of Conventions and Recommendations. The committee of experts takes its essential function of "criticism" seriously and draws up a report after a thorough examination. The Conference Committee executes its appraising task by reference to the summary of reports submitted by the director general, the report of the committee of experts, and the additional information provided by governments. At the

Conference Committee, governmental representatives can add desired observations or clarify any obscurities to which the committee of experts has drawn attention. Because the Conference Committee is tripartite in composition (representing governments, employers, and workers), nongovernmental interests are well represented in the appraising process. This unique character has proved to be a major asset of the long-standing reporting system of the ILO.

In addition to the continuing channels of established structures and procedures, formal appraisal can be performed through occasional international conferences devoted to a particular subject. Notable examples include the International Conference on Human Rights, the U.N. Conference on Environment and Development, the Beijing Women's Conference, the International Conference on Population and Development, and the World Food Conference. Conferences of this kind usually involve such multiple purposes as exchanging information and knowledge, making new proposals, and mobilizing support for action. A key purpose is appraisal. For instance, the International Conference on Human Rights, convened in Tehran in 1968, aspired, among other things, to evaluate "the effectiveness of methods and techniques employed in the field of human rights at the international and regional levels."[1] Unfortunately, its achievements in this regard were less than impressive, but the efforts to build on the principles of the U.N. Charter and the Universal Declaration on Human Rights are continuing, as could be seen at the World Conference on Human Rights held in Vienna in 1993, which produced both short- and long-term plans of action.

The World Conference of the International Women's Year, convened in Mexico City in 1975, was fairly successful in appraising the process of decision for the advancement of women; the conference also adopted plans of action for the years to come, calling for efforts at all community levels (global, regional, and national) and in all sectors (governmental and nongovernmental). Ten years later, in July 1985, the U.N. Decade for Women Conference was held in Nairobi to praise the Decade for Women. In spite of divergent assessments and political wrangling, the conference ended on a note of unity and a shared sense of purpose and formulated "Forward-Looking Strategies" for advancement of women toward the year 2000 and beyond.[2] In 1995 the Fourth United Nations Conference on Women was held in Beijing, demanding the eradication of discrimination against and violence toward women, reaffirming the right to equal education and freedom of association and speech, and appraising achievements toward goals proclaimed at Nairobi. And, despite efforts by the Chinese authorities to discourage activism, the conference was able to issue a Declaration and Platform for Action providing a blueprint for every country regarding ways to enable the participation of women in society as full citizens.[3]

The U.N. Conference on Environment and Development (UNCED) in Rio de Janeiro in 1992 laid the groundwork for a global program for sustainable development and environmental protection. The resulting action plan, Agenda 21, called for improvements in the availability data on nation's progress to meet sustainable development goals, especially in the developing world. The agenda identified key local, national, and international indicators that offered a framework for monitoring and coordinating initiatives aimed at improving shared values related to economic and social development and the environment.[4]

The persistent financial and other crises confronting the United Nations have kindled a sense of urgent need to make a comprehensive appraisal of the functioning of the organization itself. Even though the U.N. Charter, in Article 109, contemplated a general conference of member states to review the charter in due course, such a conference did not materialize for a long time. The Report of the Joint Inspection Unit on Personnel Problems in the United Nations, known as the Bertrand Report, submitted to the United Nations in 1971,[5] showed devastatingly the absence of any effective appraising function for most of the United Nations' political and technical programs. When the United Nations commemorated its fortieth anniversary in a somber mood amid the gathering storms, the General Assembly established a group of high-level intergovernmental experts to undertake a comprehensive review of the efficiency of U.N. administrative and financial functions.[6] The group of eighteen lost no time in carrying out its task and submitted a report to the General Assembly in time for consideration at the forty-first assembly session, commencing in September 1986. The report, dealing with the intergovernmental machinery of the United Nations and its subsidiary organs, the structure of the Secretariat, the personnel policy of the organization, activities related to coordination, monitoring, evaluation, and inspection, and the planning and budget procedure, contained numerous recommendations. It noted that as the U.N. agenda had grown, so had the intergovernmental machinery to sustain it. Agendas and work had become duplicated, particularly in the economic and social fields, and efficiency had suffered.[7]

Perceiving the report as a beginning of a long, continuing process of reform rather than an end, the General Assembly in December 1986 accepted for implementation the recommendations of the group of eighteen and adopted a set of principles to guide the U.N. planning, programming, and budgeting process.[8] Pursuant to one of the recommendations, the Economic and Social Council in February 1987 established a special commission to evaluate U.N. functions and structure in the economic and social fields.[9] The task of effective appraisal was long overdue and the agenda lengthy, but the challenging task was begun.

By 1995, an independent working group on the future of the United Nations convened at the request of Secretary-General Boutros Boutros-Ghali issued a report titled "The United Nations in Its Second Half-Century."[10] The report appraised the changing role of the United Nations at a time of sweeping transformation in the world's political, social, and economic order, in communications, and in the environment. The report divided its appraisal and recommendations into four areas: security, the economic sphere, the social fabric, and the U.N. leadership.

Goals were set for the next fifty years in all these areas. Chief among the report's recommendations for "refitting" the good vessel was a major restructuring of the

U.N. machinery to create three interrelated councils: an Economic Council and a Social Council, each to function in the same way as the Security Council. The Economic and Social Council (ECOSOC) would be dissolved. In addition, recommendations were made for the expansion of Security Council membership; a more streamlined General Assembly with a smaller agenda; reorganization of the Secretariat to oversee the restructuring of the U.N. central core into the three-council arrangement; and new options and sources of funding not dependent on internal spending cuts.

In addition, An Agenda for Peace and An Agenda for Development, which were issued in 1992 and 1994 respectively by Boutros Boutros-Ghali, appraised the U.N. achievements and made recommendations to meet the challenges posed by changing times. The former broadens the agenda for peace to embrace preventative diplomacy, peacemaking, peacekeeping, and postconflict peacebuilding—each is distinct and fortified, yet interrelated. The latter has spotlighted "sustainable development" in the agenda for development.

Under the leadership of Kofi Annan, the United Nations continued Boutros Boutros-Ghali's legacy and began to shift its development approach from focusing on states to focusing on people. This shift was marked by the Millennium Declaration, delivered in September 2000, which affirmed the United Nations' commitment to reducing global poverty, increasing access to primary education, reducing maternal mortality, reducing the rate of HIV infection and other preventable diseases, and improving the lives of slum-dwellers. With the Millennium Declaration came the Millennium Development Goals (MDGs), which outline eight major themes in world development and provide a matrix of specific goals for global human development. As discussed in chapter 18, the aim of the MDGs was to galvanize the global community to address the needs of the world's poor and devise lasting solutions. Kofi Annan took the appraising function seriously regarding the work and future of the United Nations. Notable among his many reports are (1) In Larger Freedom: Towards Development, Security, and Human Rights for All (Report of the Secretary-General, 21 March 2005), and (2) Report of the High-Level Panel on Threats, Challenges, and Change: A More Secure World: Our Shared Responsibility (1 December 2004). Together they have clearly and strongly articulated the shared responsibility of member states and the peoples of the world to collaborate in the task of development, security, and human rights for all.

Secretary-General Ban Ki-moon continues in the footsteps of his predecessors and has reaffirmed the United Nations' commitment to the MDGs. In 2008, the secretary-general convened a high-level summit on the MDGs, which rallied world leaders around hunger, poverty, and disease. In 2010, the Summit on Millennium Development Goals brought together world leaders to build initiatives aimed at further combating hunger, poverty, and disease, ending with the development of a global action plan. In this connection, the secretary-general could play a leading role in calling the attention of the world's citizens through an annual "State of the World Message," perhaps to be broadcast by global TV networks, such as CNN, BBC, and Al Jazeera. Commanding a worldwide bully pulpit, the secretary-general is in a unique position of influence to inform and educate the citizens of the world, raising their collective consciousness toward the goals of maintaining minimum world order and achieving optimum world order, thereby establishing a world community of human dignity and human security.

It may be hoped that the reinvigorated world organization, fortified by renewed commitment and support from its members, can continue to perform its appraising function with all seriousness and turn the present crises into opportunities for the twenty-first century.

On the national level, nation-states are constantly involved, in one form or another, in the appraising function regarding events occurring within their borders, for internal or transnational consumption. It is equally urgent that the processes of appraisal in light of the paramount goals of securing minimum and optimum world order be pressed forward simultaneously at national and local levels. The appraising function is also open to nongovernmental participants. Requiring no institutional or representative authority, nongovernmental organizations and individuals play an important role in appraisal, beyond the more familiar roles of intelligence and promotion. For example, they can assess the content and efficiency of authoritative decision and quality of public order and provisionally ascribe responsibility. Mass communication media, such as official news sources or social networking cites, play a vital role in appraisal, with varying degrees of deliberateness. The intellectual community, in the form of opinion makers, contributes both individually and collectively to appraisal. The importance attached to scholarly appraisal is most vividly demonstrated in Article 38 of the Statute of International Court of Justice, which includes "the teachings of the most highly qualified publicists of the various nations" as a "subsidiary means for the determination of rules of law" for the court. Ultimately, of course, the aggregate of individuals provide the final review or appraisal through an interacting process of shaping attitudes and behavior. A multiplicity of appraisers (governmental and nongovernmental) democratizes and adds rich diversity to the process of appraisal and serves certain policing functions in the common interest.

The appraising function, viewed as a whole, however, seems sporadic, fragmentary, and unorganized. A more centralized, systematic structure, with adequate authority and effective bases of power, is needed. Though organized appraisal is ultimately reviewable by all participants, an organized process can usefully guide, stimulate, and effectuate both minimum and optimum order. Given the tremendous potentials of modern technology, a proper balance between systematic and sporadic, centralized and decentralized, and organized and unorganized appraisal would vastly upgrade the quality of performance of the function, thereby contributing to the efficiency of all other functions and indeed of the global constitutive process of authoritative decision.

Notes

1. Final Act of the International Conference on Human Rights, Tehran, Iran, Apr. 22–May 13, 1968, U.N. Doc. A/CONF.32/41 (May 13, 1968).

2. G.A. Res. 40/108, 40 U.N. GAOR Supp. (No. 53) at 223, U.N. Doc. A/40/53 (Dec. 13, 1985).

3. Beijing Declaration and Platform for Action, Rep. of the Fourth World Conference on Women, Sept. 4–15, 1995, U.N. Doc. A/CONF.177/20/Rev.1 (1996).

4. United Nations Conference on Environment and Development, Rio de Janeiro, Braz., June 3–14, 1992, Rio Declaration on Environment and Development, U.N. Doc. A/CONF.151/26/Rev.1 (Vol. I), Annex I (Aug. 12, 1992).

5. U.N. Joint Inspection Unit, Report of Personnel Problems in the United Nations, U.N. Doc. JIU/REP/71/7 (1971) (by Maurice Bertrand).

6. G.A. Res. 40/237, U.N. Doc. A/40/L.42/Rev. (Dec. 18, 1985).

7. Rep. of the Group of High Level Governmental Experts to Review the Efficiency of the Administrative and Financial Functioning of the United Nations, U.N. Doc. A/41/49; GAOR Supp. No. 49 (1986).

8. G.A. Res. 41/213, U.N. Doc. 41/RES/213 (Dec. 19, 1986).

9. UN CHRONICLE, Vol. 24, No. 2, May 1987, at 57.

10. THE REPORT OF THE INDEPENDENT WORKING GROUP ON THE FUTURE OF THE UNITED NATIONS (1995), *available at* http://www.library.yale.edu/un/images/un-second-half-century.pdf.

VIII Effects

27 Succession of States

A NATION-STATE IS like a living organism, having a life cycle of its own—from birth, through growth and maturity, to demise. Just as change is a fact of life for a human being, so it is for a nation-state. Changes for a territorial community are manifested in various ways, relating to each of the important features of its community process. Changes may occur in patterns of participation, involving both effective elites and established officials. They may involve perspectives, as manifested in fundamental constitutional policies and in ideological orientation. Changes may relate to the aggregate situation of interaction, especially changes in structures of government. They may occur in the aggregate bases of power, in terms of control over territory, resources, and people. Changes may be manifested in the strategies employed, in terms of relative emphasis on persuasion and coercion and management of differing instruments of policy. Finally, changes may relate to outcomes in the performance of various decision functions, especially prescriptions and applications.

These changes occur in differing degrees and combinations. Some are relatively insignificant, leaving a territorial community virtually as it was before. Some may be so fundamental as to give birth to a new territorial community. In response to such changes, territorial communities have made certain distinctive claims, traditionally under the labels of "state" and "governmental" succession.

Central to the distinction between state and governmental succession is whether a change fundamentally affects the legal identity and continuity of a territorial community as a nation-state. When changes involve only the government itself—notably changes in leadership (effective elites or established officials), basic constitutional policy, internal or external policies, or structures of government—the question of governmental succession arises, entailing no effect on the legal identity and continuity of the state it represents. This involves no change in territorial domain. When changes involve continuity or discontinuity in authoritative and effective control over territory, people, and resources, the question of the legal identity and continuity of statehood is seriously implicated, giving rise to the question of state succession.

Sometimes such a distinction is far from easy to draw. After the Bolshevik Revolution of 1917, for example, the new government claimed itself to be not only a new government but also a new state and hence not responsible for the international obligations assumed by the previous regime. Other states rejected such claims, holding the Union of Soviet Socialist Republics (USSR) responsible for those obligations. After the dissolution of the USSR in 1991, the Russian Federation, existing as a successor state to the former Soviet Union, voluntarily assumed legal responsibility for all treaty and international obligations of its predecessor. At any rate, the traditional distinction between changes in state and changes in government, with its inordinate emphasis on the territorial factor, has been increasingly attacked.

The present focus, nevertheless, is the question of state succession. This question historically arose in the transfer of territory from one nation to another through cession, annexation of colonial territories, federation, or dissolution of a federation. Since the establishment of the United Nations, thanks to the process of decolonization, a predominant phenomenon has been the emergence of new states via the independence of colonial territories and peoples. As decolonization runs its course, problems of succession arise in other contexts, including secession, the dismemberment of existing states, and the formation of unions of states.

Among the important questions raised are: To what extent does a successor state acquire the treaty rights and obligations of its predecessor? Does the successor inherit its predecessor's membership in international governmental organizations? Do the inhabitants of the transferred territory become nationals of the successor? To what extent does the predecessor's state property pass to the successor? What state is to be held liable for public debts of the predecessor? Where do the state archives of the predecessor go?

Basic Community Policy

Two theoretical constructs for state succession have historically contended: universal succession and outright nonsuccession.

Universal succession, posited by Hugo Grotius, was the earliest theory and lingered until the twentieth century. This view, derived from an analogy to the Roman law of testamentary succession, held that all rights and obligations of the predecessor state passed to the successor state automatically on the former's extinction, since its legal personality continued on. Certain absolute natural rights, once established, were deemed to attach to the state, as defined by its territorial domain, and were inherited even though rulers may subsequently have changed. Arrangements undertaken by the sovereign in a public capacity, including debts, treaties, and contracts, descended to the successor state. The universal succession theory was a general response to the frequent political and boundary changes caused by wars and other upheavals in Europe during the eighteenth and nineteenth centuries.

The nonsuccession theory gained support in the late nineteenth century. Moving to the polar opposite of universal succession, negative theorists maintained that all rights and obligations of the predecessor state were to lapse on succession. Law was conceived of as an expression of "sovereign will"; the substitution of a sovereign necessarily implicated a change in will and a change in the legal order. In treaty matters, as will be described below, the negative theory did allow certain exceptions to the rule.

Neither of these polar views—universal succession and automatic nonsuccession—can be expected to secure the common interest in accommodating the need for stability and the demand for change in the contemporary world. The complementary policies sought by the larger community here, as in the field of international agreements, are that of maintaining a reasonable stability of expectations of people and that of fostering peaceful change, responsive to changing demands, expectations, and conditions. To strike a proper balance between the two is no mean task; it requires a contextual scrutiny of all relevant factors by reference especially to the overriding goals of minimum and optimum order.

Trends in Decision and Conditioning Factors

During the colonial era, the law of state succession largely mirrored the progress of empires: rise, struggle, and fall. The law of state succession was just another branch of law that reflected the permissibility of the use of force to acquire territory through conquest and other coercion.

In the contemporary era of decolonization and self-determination, state succession has been linked most closely to the birth of independent states newly freed from colonial bondage. New problems have developed that cannot be adequately dealt with by customary law. This has proved even more true with the post–Cold War creation of new states in the former Soviet Empire. Current practice is as diverse as it is confusing. The need to clarify the common interests involved and formulate workable guidelines has been evident.

In recognition of this need, the International Law Commission has undertaken the task, culminating in the conclusion of the Vienna Convention on Succession of States in

Respect of Treaties of 1978 (hereafter the Treaty Succession Convention) and the Vienna Convention on Succession of States in Respect of State Property, Archives, and Debts of 1983 (hereafter the Other Succession Convention).

The Treaty Succession Convention is patterned after the Vienna Convention on the Law of Treaties, and seeks to maintain continuity with it. The International Law Commission, in designing the Treaty Succession Convention, deemed it important to incorporate language paralleling the earlier convention. The Treaty Succession Convention applies only to the effects of a succession occurring "in conformity with international law." Hence, its prescriptions will not apply to transfers of territory through the use of force or in violation of the principle of self-determination, as in the case of South African Bantustans. The convention applies prospectively only, but states may on their own declaration have the convention apply in respect of their own succession occurring before the effective date of the convention, provided that other state parties to a treaty in question consent.

The Other Succession Convention deals with state succession in respect only to the categories listed—state property, archives, and debts—and is inapplicable to other subjects. Like the Treaty Succession Convention, the Other Succession Convention applies only to the effects of succession that occur lawfully in accordance with the principles of the U.N. Charter. Its application is prospective, extending only to the effects of succession that occur after the convention enters into force. Successor states may, however, declare that the convention shall apply to the effects of their own succession occurring before that time, in relation to another party to the convention, which by declaration accepts such retroactive application. It would thus appear that, in terms of time and space, the scope of application for the two succession conventions is limited. In 1999, the International Law Commission drafted the text of *Nationality of Natural Persons in Relation to the Succession of States*[1] and recommended the adoption, in the form of a resolution, to the General Assembly of the United Nations, with a view of such a convention in the future. The General Assembly is in the process of taking comments on the subject, including the form that might be given to the draft articles.

In the following sections, major aspects of state succession are highlighted in light of recent state practice as well as the new succession conventions.

INTERNATIONAL AGREEMENTS

The two major theories of state succession—universal succession and outright nonsuccession—have been particularly relevant to treaty matters.

According to the theory of universal succession, a successor state inherits the rights and obligations of its predecessor. This was the controlling theory until the later part of the nineteenth century, an age in which relatively few treaties were extant. As the number of international agreements multiplied, the inadvisability of the universal succession theory became increasingly apparent.

The negative theory of state succession evolved in the late nineteenth century and was highly influential in the early part of the twentieth century. It relied heavily on the contract principle that obligations contemplating personal performance are erased by the death of a party to the contract, owing to impossibility of performance. This theory also relied on the distinction between succession of government and succession of state: only in the latter are treaty obligations erased. This distinction has contributed significantly to the intellectual confusion in this area of law.

An important exception allowed by the negative school to its general theory of non-continuation of treaties concerns "dispositive" or "impersonal" treaties. This class of treaties consists of those which determine boundaries or establish servitudes and easements or other related rights of a permanent character (for instance, transit, navigation, and demilitarization).

The negative theory, furthermore, distinguishes total from partial succession: total succession involves extinction of the predecessor state, whereas partial succession involves only the cession of a portion of a state's territory, not the legal personality of the ceding state. In regard to total succession, the "clean slate" doctrine makes all treaty rights and obligations lapse automatically. In the case of partial succession, the "moving treaty frontiers" doctrine prevails: the predecessor's treaties cease to apply to the lost territory, but the successor state's treaties become applicable.

In recent decades, writers have espoused three major theories of state succession. Two represent reformulations of the traditional theories, and the third is an eclectic approach that incorporates elements of both.

The universalists point to the need for stability in international relations and the chaos that would result if every change of "sovereignty" became a pretext to repudiate treaty obligations. For support they rely heavily on the general practice of newly independent states.

The neonegativists, in contrast, assert that the issue of state succession is essentially a matter of policy rather than law. Under this theory, the entire issue of succession to treaties is itself viewed as a matter of treaty law rather than succession law. A treaty cannot be assumed to apply automatically to a successor state unless the intentions of the parties were that it would so apply, and even then the doctrine of *rebus sic stantibus* might well prevail.

The eclectic theory, which seeks a proper balance, has taken two forms. One approach relies on the special status of dispositive treaties, and state practice concerning them, and by analogy attempts to identify other types of treaties that should also be accorded automatic survival. These include, notably, extradition treaties and law-making, or legislative treaties. The latter group refers to treaties that codify customary international law or prescribe new standards for various activities having transnational effect. The other approach, termed the "Nyerere doctrine," involves a voluntary provisional period of application by a successor state of all the predecessor's treaties in force.

The modern practice of successor states as to treaties has been less than consistent. The traditional distinction between dispositive and personal treaties lingers: dispositive treaties are inheritable and personal treaties are not. Dispositive treaties have in general been considered to survive succession, under both state practice and international judicial decisions. The trend concerning multilateral conventions has also been toward continuity.

The main trouble area has been that of "personal treaties" between states. Whatever consistency is exhibited in this area depends largely on the specific type of state succession involved. In cases of annexations, cessions, and secessions, the treaties of the predecessor state have generally lapsed and those of the successor have taken over. In cases of succession involving union or federation, treaties have generally lapsed when they result in constitutional problems or inconsistent obligations.

Newly independent states—the predominant form of successor states in the post–World War II era—have employed diverse and inconsistent practices. These new states, plagued by bitter experiences of colonial rule, kindled by a new sense of pride, nationalism, and adventure, handicapped by relative inexperience and ignorance, and disciplined by the hard realities of a complex, interactive world, have been extremely assertive on the question of succession to the treaties of their predecessor states. Moving away from the general pattern developed in the era of European colonization, the new states have followed five paths:

1. *Total rejection*: This follows the negativist position by rejecting totally prior treaties under the doctrine of clean slate. A new state thus commences its national life unfettered by the treaties that had applied to its territories before independence. Notable examples are Israel, Algeria, and Upper Volta (Burkina Faso).

2. *Devolution agreements*: By virtue of a devolution agreement, a new state explicitly agrees to assume the rights and obligations of the treaties that the prior administering power had concluded for, and applied to, the territory of the new state. A British innovation, this device was used extensively in terminating all types of British dependencies. France and the Netherlands followed this practice to a lesser extent.

3. *Temporary application*: This in essence is the Nyerere doctrine, allowing pre-independence treaties to continue for an interim period pending review. When Tanganyika attained independence, President Julius Nyerere refused to conclude a devolution agreement with the United Kingdom. Instead, he declared that for a period of two years, all of the predecessor's treaties affecting Tanganyika would provisionally continue in force. During this period, Tanganyika would review each treaty individually, with a view to reaching an accord with the interested parties on continuing or modifying such treaties in a mutually agreeable manner. If Tanganyika took no action before the interim expired, preindependence treaties would lapse automatically. This formula has

been followed by such states as Botswana, Burundi, Kenya, Lesotho, Malawi, and Swaziland.

4. *Selective acceptance*: Under this approach, a new state simply picks and chooses, unilaterally declaring which of the predecessor's treaties it will honor and which it will disregard. Examples include the Congo (Brazzaville) and the Republic of the Congo (Leopoldville). (Earlier examples include the Soviet Union and the People's Republic of China; the independent former Soviet republics have not followed this approach.)

5. *Deferment of decision*: Some new states have found it more convenient not to take an immediate stand on the question of succession to treaties. They adopt a noncommittal posture by deferring a decision and prefer to deal with particular problems as they arise. A notable example is Madagascar (formerly Malagasy Republic).

Unlike "newly independent" states, the "separating" state's international legal identity is said to remain relatively constant. The separating successor state is obligated to maintain the international obligations of the predecessor state. The dissolution of the union of the United Kingdom of Sweden and Norway in 1905 illustrates state practice in cases of separation.

In the case of the former USSR, it has been suggested that its division into fifteen separate entities after the breakup makes these new republics "separating" states. Although the Russian Federation has voluntarily agreed to assume the obligations of the former Soviet Union, it has been pointed out that because the former republics may not satisfy the traditional understanding of the "dependent territory test" used to determine the status of new states, the new republics need not assume these former obligations. Under the "dependent territory test," former states that were not dependent upon a predecessor state for international relations are deemed to have consented to preexisting international agreements. In the case of the former Soviet republics, however, many may in fact have been essentially colonial states; and many of the agreements to which they are party may not have been consensual. Thus, conventional international law's static and rigid distinction between separate and newly independent states fails to address "hybrid" situations such as that of the former USSR.

It would appear, from the foregoing, that contemporary state practice is characterized by diversity and considerable freedom of choice.

The Treaty Succession Convention (the Vienna Convention on Succession of States in Respect of Treaties) was greatly influenced by the newly independent states' actions concerning their predecessor states' treaties. While reiterating "the principles of free consent, good faith and *pacta sunt servanda*," the convention also underscores the basic principles of international law embodied in the U.N. Charter, including self-determination, sovereign equality and independence of all states, noninterference in the domestic affairs of other states, nonuse of force, and protection of human rights. The outcome was considered more the development, rather than the codification, of law in this area.

The Treaty Succession Convention painstakingly sought to accommodate the complementary policies of stability and change (flexibility), giving partial expression to both major traditional theories on state succession. The policy differentiation is made contingent on the factual context of succession. Generally speaking, in the case of succession due to unification or separation of states, the policy is to continue the predecessor's treaties; in the context of newly independent states, the policy of clean slate prevails. Article 16 states: "A newly independent State is not bound to maintain in force, or to become a party to, any treaty by reason only of the fact that at the date of the succession of States the treaty was in force in respect of the territory to which the succession of States relates."

Much language in the convention can be traced to the Vienna Convention on the Law of Treaties, and, to the extent possible, the International Law Commission attempted to be consistent as to both conventions. Several situations are expressly excluded from the scope of the convention. They include state succession in violation of international law, successions in respect of international organizations, questions regarding treaties resulting from hostilities, and questions relating to military occupations.

A significant departure from previous law is found in Articles 11 and 12, which leave the continuity of dispositive treaties open to question. A succession of states "as such" is said not to affect such treaties, but there is no positive requirement that they be continued by successor states. This seems to be in keeping with the fact that the convention imposes no requirement that treaties continue in operation with regard to newly independent states.

An interesting and highly controversial provision of the convention appears in Article 7, dealing with the temporal application of the convention. Article 7(1) declares that, "except as may be otherwise agreed" between a successor state and a party to the convention, "the Convention applies only in respect of a succession of States which has occurred after the entry into force of the Convention." The problem with an absolute bar to retroactive application would have been that newly independent states would be precluded from taking advantage of the convention, since they could not become parties until after their succession. This problem was overcome in Article 7, paragraphs 2 and 3, whereby newly independent states are enabled to apply the convention retroactively to their own successions, once they agree to be bound by it, through declarations to this effect. Only those state parties accepting the successor state's declaration are bound as to the convention's applicability to the successor state's succession. The successor state is also able to apply the convention provisionally to its own succession before the convention's entry into force.

MEMBERSHIP IN INTERNATIONAL GOVERNMENTAL ORGANIZATIONS

A matter of related concern to newly independent states is their admission to membership in international governmental organizations, such as the United Nations, the

International Labour Organization, or the International Monetary Fund, or, as in the case of some Eastern European countries, membership in the European Union and NATO. The central issue is whether such organizations will readily extend admission opportunities to new states, or whether they will be extended membership by virtue of a predecessor's membership. Joining an organization as a new member or as a successor to the membership of an existing state can be of considerable significance. As a successor to an existing membership, for example, a state is expected to assume the burden of indebtedness for expenses and so on incurred by its predecessor or to inherit the benefits of standing credit.

The issue of state succession to membership in an international governmental organization is governed by the constitution and specific membership rules of each organization.

The United Nations addressed the issue of succession to membership when it considered Pakistan's membership on gaining independence by splitting from India in 1947. Pakistan claimed that it should be treated as an original member of the United Nations by virtue of India's membership in the organization. The Legal Committee of the U.N. Secretariat disagreed, concluding that Pakistan was a new state and as such must apply for admission as a new member. India, however, was said to have retained its legal identity and its membership as well. The committee declared that a state does not "cease to be a Member simply because its Constitution or frontier has been subjected to changes, and that the extinction of the State as a legal personality recognized in the international legal order must be shown before its rights and obligations can be considered thereby to have ceased to exist."[2]

The issue of succession to membership in the United Nations arose again following the collapse of the Soviet Union and the Socialist Federal Republic of Yugoslavia (SFRY), with two contrasting outcomes. Russia, in a letter to the secretary-general, claimed that it would maintain the Soviet Union's membership, including the permanent membership of the Security Council. In addition, the former members of the USSR, in the name of the Commonwealth of Independent States (CIS), formally announced their support of Russian succession to the USSR's membership, including permanent membership in the Security Council. The secretary-general circulated the request, and the member states did not object to Russia's succession. Although Russia's succession to the USSR's membership in the United Nations was fairly smooth, it was not without opposition. Some international lawyers questioned the legality of the succession, especially given the U.N. Charter in Article 23(1) specifies the Union of Soviet Socialist Republics, and not the Russian Federation, as a permanent member of the Security Council. The main legal issue was whether the Russian Federation was a new state or the continuation of the Soviet Union. The possibility of an amendment to the charter was not out of question, but the debate was overlooked because of its impracticability as no objections were raised by any member states. Thus, a political and realistic solution was reached, regardless of its potential illegality.

Immediately following the dissolution of the Socialist Federal Republic of Yugoslavia (SFRY), the new Federal Republic of Yugoslavia (FRY) claimed a right to succeed to its membership of the United Nations. In contrast to Russia, the Security Council, by an overwhelming vote of twelve in favor with three abstaining, decided that the Serb-dominated government of the FRY "cannot continue automatically the membership of the former Socialist Federal Republic of Yugoslavia in the United Nations."[3] Members of the Security Council explained that such a decision was mostly based on the lack of support from the former members of the SFRY. Shortly thereafter, the General Assembly followed the Security Council's lead, as 127 members voted congruently while only six dissented. The International Court of Justice also sided with the Security Council and the General Assembly as it dismissed a genocide action brought by the FRY against NATO in 1999. The court held that it did not have jurisdiction to hear the case because, at the time of filing, the FRY was not a member of the United Nations. In 2000, the FRY was admitted to the United Nations as a new state.

The Treaty Succession Convention, in Article 4, stipulates its applicability to treaties establishing international governmental organizations but "without prejudice to the rules concerning acquisition of membership and without prejudice to any other relevant rules of the organization."

NATIONALITY

Two distinct views on the effect of succession on the nationality of inhabitants of the predecessor state have been voiced. The dominant view holds that nationality changes automatically to that of the successor state: because it is not only the sovereign authority but also the duty of the successor state to confer nationality to a population localized on the territory concerned. The other view maintains that nationality is essentially a matter of domestic jurisdiction and hence it is up to the national law of the successor state to decide.

Following the dissolution of the USSR, Lithuania adopted the dominant view while Estonia and Latvia maintained that nationality was a matter of domestic jurisdiction. Lithuania adopted a policy to grant citizenship to all permanent residents who desired to obtain Lithuanian citizenship. In contrast, Estonia and Latvia adopted legislation which granted citizenship to only those persons who had citizenship prior to Soviet annexation and their descendants. Furthermore, their naturalization laws include a thorough language requirement, which has proven to be a high barrier for large percentages of Russian-speaking residents, who were mostly relocated to the territories during the annexation. The difference of policies between these nations is mostly credited to the ethnic makeup of the territories. At the collapse of the Soviet Union, more than 80 percent of the population of Lithuania was Lithuanian, whereas Estonians and Latvians made up only 52 percent and 61.5 percent of their nation's populations, respectively. As a result of their restrictive practices, about 15 percent of current Latvian residents and

10 percent of Estonian residents are listed as "noncitizens," the vast majority of whom are Russian. Noncitizens have limited rights, which include travel and employment, but do not include voting rights.

The International Law Commission was troubled by the practices of Estonia and Latvia, and thus the draft of *Nationality of Natural Persons in Relation to the Succession of States* commends the dominant view.[4] While the draft articles recognize that the matter of nationality is determined through domestic legislation, it points out that such matters raise international concerns and shall follow the limits of international law. Hence, domestic legislation on nationality shall guarantee the protection of human rights, namely an individual's right to the nationality of at least one of the states concerned. A corollary to the protection of human rights is the prevention of statelessness and the harms which follow. The draft articles suggest three general guidelines to achieve these goals:

1. Ensure that the circle of persons to whom that State grants its nationality include all persons that have an appropriate connection to the State. International law, in deference to human rights, requires that in order for the successor state to confer its nationality on the inhabitants of the predecessor territory there be an appropriate connection between those persons and the territory. Thus the nationality of the successor state can be conferred on nationals of the predecessor state only if they submit voluntarily to its jurisdiction, by virtue of an explicit declaration or voluntary return to their land of origin. This position was underscored in *United States ex rel. Schwarzkopb v. Uhl, District Director of Immigration* (1943),[5] where the court held that an Austrian national who had been resident in the United States when Germany annexed Austria had not acquired German nationality.

2. Enlarge the circle of persons entitled to acquire their nationality through providing a right of options, including the retention of the original nationality (where the predecessor state continues to exist). One example of such options is the Czech Republic Law No. 40/1993 on the acquisition and loss of citizenship Article 6, which grants an option for former citizens of Czechoslovakia, but not of the Czech Republic or Slovakia, to opt for citizenship of the Czech Republic by declaration. Another example is the Yugoslav Citizenship Law of 1996 Article 47, which allows a former citizen of the Social Federative Republic of Yugoslavia (SFRY), who is currently residing in the territory of Yugoslavia but had the citizenship of another republic of the SFRY, to acquire Yugoslav citizenship.

3. An agreement among concerned states of which the occurrence of statelessness would be precluded. Despite efforts to grant its nationality to those that establish an appropriate connection and to enlarge the circles of persons, a single nation's effectiveness in preventing statelessness is inadequate. Thus an

agreement among the concerned states provides a more effective solution that is also in accordance with international law. The experts of the Council of Europe have stated that two states involved in the succession have an international obligation to avoid statelessness. Such agreements to prevent statelessness would also be consistent with several multilateral treaties, including the 1930 Hague Convention, the Convention relating to the Status of Stateless Persons, and the Convention on the Reduction of Statelessness.

The International Law Commission draft articles on nationality also set forth detailed provisions for nationality in relation to states succession according to four specific categories:

1. *Transfer of part of the territory*: When one state transfers part of its territory to another state, the successor state shall grant its nationality to the habitual residents of the territory and the predecessor state shall withdraw its nationality from such persons, unless otherwise indicated by the right of option, which shall be granted to affected persons.
2. *Uniting of states*: In a uniting of states, all citizens of the predecessor state will be granted citizenship of the successor state.
3. *Dissolution of states*: When a state dissolves into two or more successor states, each successor state, unless otherwise indicated by the right of option, shall grant its nationality to those that have their habitual residence or an appropriate connection to its territory.
4. *Separation of part or parts of the territory of a state*: "When part or parts of the territory of a State separate from that State and form one or more successor States while the predecessor State continues to exist," a successor state, unless otherwise indicated by the right of option, shall grant its nationality to those that have their habitual residence or an appropriate connection to its territory.

State practice generally reflects the dominant view. When one state cedes a territory to another, the ceding state is traditionally deemed competent to transfer the allegiance of the inhabitants, and the successor state is required to confer its nationality on these inhabitants. This occasionally is tempered by considerations of self-determination and human rights. A plebiscite may be held to determine whether the territorial transfer accords with the wishes of a majority of the inhabitants.

STATE PROPERTY

According to the Other Succession Convention (Vienna Convention on Succession of States in Respect of State Property, Archives, and Debts), state property owned by the predecessor state shall pass, without compensation, to the successor state, unless otherwise agreed between the states concerned. "State property" includes all property that at the time of succession belongs to the predecessor state according to its law. When such property passes to a successor state under the convention's terms, all rights of the predecessor in the property are extinguished.

A succession has no effect, in and of itself, on the property of third states located in the predecessor state and identified as the third states by the predecessor's internal law. The predecessor state is obliged to prevent damage or destruction to property that will pass to a successor.

The convention, in Articles 14–18, sets forth detailed provisions for the succession of state property according to the specific category of state succession involved. There are five distinct categories:

1. *Transfer of part of the territory of a state*: When one state transfers part of its territory to another state, the passing of state property is settled by agreement. If no such agreement is reached, all immovable state property in the transferred territory goes to the successor, and all movable state property in that territory, connected with the predecessor's activities in that territory, also passes to the successor.

2. *A newly independent state*: When a successor state is a "newly independent state," all movable state property within its territory that belonged to the predecessor and was either originally the property of the territory in question or was used by the predecessor in connection with its activities there passes to the successor state. Other movable property "to the creation of which the dependent territory has contributed" also passes in proportion to that contribution. All immovable state property in the territory passes to the successor state.

3. *Uniting of states*: In a uniting of states, all state property of the predecessors passes to the successor state.

4. *Separation of part or parts of the territory of a state*: "When part or parts of the territory of a State separate from that State and form a successor State," unless otherwise agreed, the following state property of the predecessor state passes to the successor state: immovable state property within the territory; movable state property connected with the predecessor's activities in the territory; and equitable proportions of other movable state property located in the territory.

5. *Dissolution of states*: When a state dissolves into two or more successor states, unless those states agree otherwise, immovable property of the predecessor goes to the successor territory in which it is situated; immovable property of the predecessor located outside its territory passes to the successor states "in equitable proportions"; movable property of the predecessor state connected with its activities in a successor's territory goes to the successor state concerned; and other movable property passes to the successor states in equitable proportions.

In sum, these guidelines clearly take into account the nature, situs, and functions of property involved and the principle of equity. Throughout, the basic distinction is made between immovable and movable property. Immovable property of the predecessor state located within the successor state passes to the successor state. Movable property of the predecessor state connected with its activities in the successor state's territory passes to the successor state. Otherwise, the overriding concern is to effect equitable distribution.

STATE DEBTS

State debt, as defined in Article 33 of the Other Succession Convention, refers to "any financial obligation of a predecessor State arising in conformity with international law towards another State, an international organization or any other subject of international law." Debts to private persons are not covered. The modality by which state succession occurs becomes especially important in regard to state debts, as in the case of state property. If the successor state was created by either a transfer or separation of part or parts of the predecessor's territory, the predecessor's state debts are extinguished on succession and pass to the successor state. The obligation passes in equitable proportion to the accompanying property rights and interest received by the successor. Such a passing of state debt does not in itself affect the rights and obligations of creditors.

In the case of newly independent states, no state debt passes unless the predecessor and the new state reach an agreement otherwise. To buttress this point, the International Law Commission, in its report for the Thirty-third Session, invoked a prominent precedent: the United States did not succeed to any debt of Great Britain. Agreements with the predecessor state, Article 38(2) admonishes, "shall not infringe the principle of the permanent sovereignty of every people over its wealth and natural resources."

In all other forms of state succession, state debt passes in an equitable proportion unless the relevant states agree otherwise.

STATE ARCHIVES

The Other Succession Convention deals not only with state property and state debts but also with state archives. The initial provisions of the part concerned with state archives more or less mirror comparable provisions dealing with state property.

State archives refer to "documents of whatever date and kind" that "belonged to the predecessor State according to its internal law" and were held by the predecessor state in the exercise of its functions (Article 20). Absent specific agreement, state archives relating to the successor state's territory shall pass to the successor state. All rights of the predecessor in any archives that pass to a successor state are extinguished, and such passing is accomplished without compensation. Again, the succession of states has no effect on archives that, according to the predecessor's internal law, are the property of a third state.

A unique provision, Article 25, refers to the "preservation of the integral character of groups of State archives of the predecessor State." The convention exercises no control over any question relating to such issues. Again, the predecessor state is obliged to preserve state archives that pass to the successor.

The underlying policy consideration is to ensure that each resulting successor state procures all archives that deal with its territory. When archives deal with more than one territory, reproductions are to be made available so that all states interested in the information will have it at their disposal.

One issue dealt with in particular is archives concerning the delimitation of a successor state's territory, which must be furnished by a predecessor. Archives concerning history and cultural heritage are also emphasized. With regard to newly independent states, the separation of part or parts of a state's territory, or the dissolution of a state, the convention stipulates that an agreement concerning archives between the predecessor state and the successor state "shall not infringe the right of the peoples of those States to development, to information about their history, and to their cultural heritage."

Notes

1. G.A. Res. 55/153, U.N. GAOR, 55th Sess., Supp. No. 10, U.N. Doc. A/55/610 (Jan. 30, 2001).

2. Letter from the Chairman of the Sixth Committee to the Chairman of the First Committee, concerning legal problems in connexion with the question of the admission of Pakistan, U.N. GAOR, 1st Comm., 2nd Sess., Annex 14g, U.N. Doc. A/C.1/212, at 582 (Oct. 11, 1947); *see also The Succession of State in Relation to Membership in the United Nations, Memorandum Prepared by the Secretariat*, Doc. A/CN.4/149, *in* 2 YEARBOOK OF INTERNATIONAL LAW COMMISSION 101, 103 (1962).

3. S.C. Res. 777, ¶ 1, U.N. Doc. S/RES/777 (Sept. 19, 1992).

4. *See* G.A. Res. 55/153, *supra* note 1.

5. United States *ex rel.* Schwarzkopb v. Uhl, 137 F.2d 898 (2d. Cir. 1943).

28 Responsibility of States

NATION-STATES ARE EXPECTED to bear the consequences of their actions or inaction; they may be held responsible for what they do or fail to do. In playing their roles, in interacting with other actors, to pursue their objectives, through institutions, by using resources and employing strategies to perform decision functions, nation-states create complex relations with one another. Their activities in the aggregate generate important value consequences, some intended, some not. But, on the whole, they are held accountable for their actions or inaction, especially when foreseeable damage is involved. This is the area of concern known as "responsibility of states," or international responsibility.

In the vast literature this subject is traditionally discussed in terms of responsibility of states for injuries to aliens, with all the related doctrines of minimum international standard versus standard of national treatment, denial of justice, diplomatic protection, and so on. State responsibility in this restrictive sense, constituting the core of customary law in this area in the past, has been substantially dealt with in chapter 12. For present purposes, a larger focus is needed.

Viewed comprehensively, the question of state responsibility relates to every aspect of state activity. It brings all aspects of international law together. It is indeed a vast, complex area in which divergent views and approaches have vigorously contended.

State accountability can occur in many ways: a breach or nonperformance of treaty obligations; violations of international legal norms; failure to maintain internal order;

unintentional acts that foreseeably create harmful effects on others. Here is a quick list of examples:

- About five hundred Iranian militants seized the U.S. embassy in Tehran, taking ninety hostages (including sixty-six Americans).
- After repeated denials, the French government admitted that its agents sank an antinuclear protest ship belonging to Greenpeace, an international environmental group, in New Zealand.
- In December 1987, Pan Am Flight 103 exploded over Lockerbie, Scotland, allegedly the result of actions by Libyan terrorists, whom Libya subsequently refused to hand over for trial.
- The United States supplied the contras in Nicaragua with military supplies and a manual depicting illegal tactics.
- Cemex, a Mexican cement company, brought the Venezuelan government for arbitration before the International Centre for Settlement of Investment Disputes after the Venezuelan government nationalized it and the two sides could not agree on the compensation due.
- The island nation of Tuvalu threatened to sue the United States and Australia, claiming their carbon emissions contribute to rising sea levels that may drown the tiny nation.
- On April 26, 1986, the Chernobyl nuclear power station, about seventy miles north of Kiev, in Ukraine, exploded and burned, spewing radioactive particles into the atmosphere. The disaster spread radioactive fallout across much of Europe, contaminating farm vegetables and the forage of cows and sheep.
- Military operations, including missile strikes, by the United States and its allies in countries such as Iraq, Afghanistan, and Pakistan have been blamed for the deaths of innocent civilians.
- Nuclear material escaped from the crippled Fukushima power plant in Japan following a devastating earthquake and tsunami. Contamination was subsequently discovered in the air, soil, and water around the plant and may have spread beyond the region.

A proper focus would thus require locating the question of state responsibility in the context of a state's dealings with other actors, not only in terms of protection and treatment of aliens (which remains, of course, a vital aspect of this field) but in other areas of international law.

In the brief treatment of this vast and complex field, we are especially concerned with a range of questions involving "who does what to whom, how, under what circumstances, with what outcomes and effects, and what responses." More specifically: What action or inaction will trigger international responsibility for states? An internationally wrongful act? What is an internationally wrongful act? A breach of treaty obligations? A violation of international legal norms, customary or conventional? Failure to act? Is deprivation (actual and potential) required? What type of damage and harm? Are states held responsible for all acts of their state officials, or only when such acts occur under the authority or color of authority of the state? In other words, what acts are regarded as attributable, or imputable, to states and what acts are not? How about the acts of private parties and individuals? Acts of private armies? What standard of conduct is expected and required of states? Is negligence always required, or is the strict (no-fault) standard applicable? What procedures must victim states follow to seek a remedy, and what remedies are available?

Basic Community Policy

The paramount objective sought through the law of state responsibility is the minimization of all unauthorized coercions and deprivations. More specifically, as developed in chapter 24, this overriding goal can be described in terms of six subgoals: (1) prevention of violation of international legal norms, both customary and conventional, and of deprivations; (2) deterrence of impending violations or deprivations; (3) restoration of conditions altered by violations; (4) rehabilitation of resulting deprivations through reparation or compensation; (5) reconstruction of overall conditions in ways that would minimize future incidences of violations and deprivations; and (6) corrections directed at individual human actors, who are the ultimate driving force behind state actions.

Each goal is distinct yet closely related to the others. The relative weight of each is a function of the context involved.

Trends in Decision and Conditioning Factors

International law of state responsibility has historically been an outgrowth of customary law, centering on the subject of treating aliens and protecting nationals abroad and extending to other areas of international law. The development of customary law in this area—especially by Latin American countries and by the Soviet Union after the Bolshevik Revolution—has not gone unchallenged in the past.

The emancipation of peoples from the shackles of colonialism and the proliferation of new states after the establishment of the United Nations have had tremendous impacts on the development of contemporary international law. One area of contention has been the responsibility of states. Many newly independent nations assert that the customary law of state responsibility is a relic of colonialism and imperialism, a product of past Western domination, in the formulation of which they had played no part. Some would like to choose what customary prescriptions apply to them—which of course cannot be tolerated if minimum world public order is to be maintained.

The clarion call has been to codify international law of state responsibility, a call that came shortly after the International Law Commission began its work in the codification and progressive development of international law. Codification—providing workable guidelines in service of the common interest—in this complex area is no easy task, as the members of the International Law Commission have learned in abundance. Progress has been painfully slow, and the commission has had considerable difficulty in deciding what its focus should be—whether comprehensive or narrow. At its inception in 1949, the commission identified "the law of state responsibility" as a topic suitable for codification. In its early phase, when Francisco V. Garcia-Amador was the special rapporteur (1955–61), it focused on the responsibility of states for injuries to aliens. Garcia-Amador submitted six reports to the commission. Unfortunately, the commission was unable to devote its attention to these reports, which contained some very innovative ideas and proposals.

Instead, in 1963, the commission scrapped its old efforts and charted a new course on state responsibility. As Roberto Ago became the new special rapporteur, the commission shifted to a more comprehensive focus: dropping the subject of state responsibility for injuries to aliens and undertaking the subject of international responsibility of states in general, dealing with "general rules" and "general aspects." After Ago submitted many reports, the commission completed the first reading of part one of the Draft Articles on State Responsibility in 1980.

At long last, in 2001, the International Law Commission completed a final text of articles on state responsibility (hereinafter the ILC Text).[1] The final draft consists of four parts. Part one, which sets forth the substantive elements of internationally wrongful acts of a state, consists of five chapters titled "General principles," "Attribution of conduct to a State," "Breach on an international obligation," "Responsibility of a State in connection with the act of another State," and "Circumstances precluding wrongfulness." Part two, "Content of the international responsibility of a State," lays out the legal consequences for internationally wrongful acts, as set forth in part one. Available reparations include restitution, compensation, and satisfaction. Part three, "The implementation of the international responsibility of a State," describes the procedural mechanism for invoking state responsibility. Part three also sets forth the conditions under which an injured state may resort to countermeasures. Part four contains five "General Provisions" articles, which address topics such as the responsibility of an international obligation and individual responsibility.

In January 2002, the U.N. General Assembly adopted Resolution 56/83, in which it took note of the 2001 ILC Text and decided that it would consider at a future date convening an international conference of plenipotentiaries to consider the ILC Text and to attempt to conclude a convention on state responsibility.[2] This was the course of action the ILC had recommended the General Assembly to take.

WHAT ACT OR OMISSION: AN INTERNATIONALLY WRONGFUL ACT

State responsibility on the international plane is the consequence of a state's violation of its substantive legal obligations—namely, acts or omissions regarding treaty and customary law obligations. Thus, Article 1 of the 2001 ILC Text states: "Every internationally wrongful act of a State entails the international responsibility of that State."[3]

Under this formulation, an internationally wrongful act of a state consists of two elements:

1. An action or omission is attributable to the state under international law: this raises the question of state action in international law, traditionally discussed in terms of "attributability" or "imputability."
2. The action or omission involved constitutes a violation of an international obligation, customary or conventional.

A fundamental change of perspective is reflected in this new formulation, moving from the traditional damage-oriented approach to an obligation-centered approach. A violation of an international obligation, not the occurrence of damage, triggers international responsibility for a state. Even without damage, the mere fact that an international obligation has been violated will result in international responsibility.

This fundamental shift in perspective leads to the crucial question: At what moment is international responsibility triggered? The moment of violation, not when actual damage occurred, is determinative. Situations may exist in which a violation of an obligation cannot be determined without verifying the existence of damage. An example in point is transfrontier pollution insofar as the pollution-causing activity is not subject to any specific conduct-related norms of international law. In such a situation, damage is an unavoidable criterion for ascertaining conduct that violates international law. When action or failure to act is attributable to a state and internationally wrongful, then the question of possible remedies arises. This is reflected in Articles 20–26 of the 2001 ILC Text.

BY WHOM: THE CONCEPT OF STATE ACTION—IMPUTABILITY OR ATTRIBUTABILITY

International responsibility arises only when an act or omission is imputable to the state. A state is responsible for any breach of its international obligations through action or inaction by state organs, agencies and governmental officials, employees, and agents. This extends not only to conduct within the scope of governmental authority but also to conduct under color of such authority. The concept is broad: it matters little which branch of government—executive, legislative, judicial, or other—is involved. Similarly, governmental officials and employees, regardless of their position in governmental hierarchy, are within the reach of its broad concept of state action.

For state officials in the field of external affairs, such as heads of state, foreign ministers, and diplomats, their acts are easily imputable to the state because of their authority to represent the state according to its internal law. For governmental officials in the area of internal affairs, the determination of what is imputable may seem to pose a greater problem. But a basic community policy is that every state is expected to maintain its internal decision-making processes in such a way as to fulfill international obligations.

An excuse based on internal law is no defense. This is the essence of the supremacy of international law over national law.

When governmental officials act within the limits of their authority under internal law, their acts naturally are attributable to the state. A particularly controversial issue is whether unauthorized acts or acts deemed to be *ultra vires* under international law may give rise to state responsibility. Article 7 of the ILC Text resolved this question affirmatively, provided the entity or person was empowered to exercise some governmental authority: "The conduct of an organ of a State or of a person or entity empowered to exercise elements of the governmental authority shall be considered an act of the State under international law if the organ, person, or entity acts in that capacity, even if it exceeds its authority or contravenes instructions."

This is the appropriate view. In ascertaining the attributability of actions to the state the respective domains of international and domestic law are generally distinguished. Although reference is commonly made to national law to determine if an individual is competent to act on behalf of the state, the question of whether an outcome is attributable to the state is governed exclusively by international law. State responsibility is imputed only if an injury is inflicted in a wrongful manner under international law; a state may not plead principles of its domestic law in defense of an international claim.

Therefore, although the putative wrong may result from an *ultra vires* act, the official and the state will not be immune from legal consequences. It is sufficient that the act was taken pursuant to general or apparent authority—as in the use of measures appropriate to the actor's official character, which is distinguished from some personal independent act. The issue of individual criminal responsibility in international law is explored in detail in chapter 29.

STANDARD OF CONDUCT

The customary standard of state responsibility is based on the fault principle. A state is held responsible for an act performed with some degree of guilty knowledge or negligence that causes a proscribed result. The subjectivity underlying a particular conduct is significant. If, for example, a state expropriates a foreign investor's property for the purpose of political reprisal or other retaliation, such taking is deemed "arbitrary" and hence impermissible. But if a government takes private property pursuant to a genuine public purpose (for example, land reform or industrial nationalization) in a nondiscriminatory manner, such a taking is presumed lawful, provided just compensation is made.

Whether a state is at fault can also be presumed. A state is presumed responsible, for example, when injury results from a state's failure to exercise effective control over its territory or to maintain an effective system of justice. A most instructive example of the relation between a state's exercise of sovereign control and the imputation of culpable knowledge, and thus international responsibility, is the 1949 *Corfu Channel* case.[4] In that case, the International Court of Justice held Albania liable for damage incurred by British ships passing through Albanian territorial waters in which mines had been placed. Because Albania had exclusive control over these waters (and Britain the right to unobstructed passage), Albania was obligated to warn Britain of dangers known or reasonably foreseeable to Albania; its failure to do so—a reasonable inference was that it was wrongfully negligent—resulted in the imposition of international responsibility. Significantly, it was immaterial that a specific agent of Albania was not shown to be directly culpable: "Strictly, every breach of duty on the part of a state must arise by reason of the act or omission of one or more of the organs of the state, and since in many contexts the principle of objective responsibility applies, the emphasis is on causal connexion and the 'conduct appropriate' to a given situation."[5]

The adequacy of the fault principle in connection with activities that generate transnational pollution and damage the global environment has been increasingly questioned in recent years. The central issue is whether fault is required in order to find liability or whether the mere fact of transnational pollution-caused damage is sufficient.

At present, the fault principle remains the applicable general international standard. Neither case law nor practice recognizes the imposition of strict liability for occurrences of transnational pollution. As discussed in chapter 10, however, a trend toward the no-fault principle may be in the making. This is most evident in the area of so-called ultrahazardous activities (such as nuclear energy generation or spacecraft launching). Under the Convention on International Liability for Damage Caused by Space Objects (1972), for example, the launching state assumes absolute liability for damage caused by its space object on the surface of the earth. And the no-fault principle is incorporated in the Convention on the Liability of Operators of Nuclear Ships (1962).

It is crucial to determine when an activity is hazardous. Without such determination, any transnational damage due, for example, to pollution from a particular activity would not give rise to absolute or strict liability. However, if the extent of the damage is significant enough, the damage itself may serve as evidence that the activity is indeed ultrahazardous.

A further controversy relates to whether a state may be held strictly liable for transnational pollution damage resulting from private ultrahazardous activity. The better view is that in such a situation the control of the state may be presumed, and thus the state should be liable. As the state is presumed to benefit from the hazardous activity, so it should be held accountable for any associated transnational costs. It may even be that in a given case fault is provable.

With the growing expansion of ultrahazardous activities on an interdependent planet, it is increasingly urged that the concept of "responsibility" be kept distinct from that of "liability." Whereas responsibility is attached to an internationally wrongful act for violating an international obligation, liability may result from lawful activities that damage others. For the former, state responsibility is predicated on a violation of an international obligation rather than on damage; for the latter, damage is the basis of liability. In its work on state responsibility, the International Law Commission has maintained this distinction: state "responsibility" for internationally wrongful acts and international "liability" for the injurious consequences of activities that are lawful, activities that are not prohibited per se by international law but that have deleterious consequences.

JUSTIFIABLE DEFENSES

Even when the breach of an international norm is attributable to a state so as to make it internationally responsible, certain conditions, as stipulated in the ILC Text Articles 20–27, may justify the state's act or omission, thereby "precluding wrongfulness." These "circumstances precluding wrongfulness" are consent, self-defense, countermeasures in respect of an internationally wrongful act, *force majeure*, distress, and necessity. Some of these justifications are familiar from basic municipal law. Others, such as legal countermeasures, are unique to international law. Some of these defenses will be discussed in brief.

Force majeure in the sense of an "irresistible force" or "unforeseen external event" beyond a state's control may also justify a state's breach of an international obligation.[6] This defense would seem to be analogous to the impossibility of performance doctrine of treaty law. There is also a limited defense in situations of "distress" if the author of the otherwise internationally wrongful act had "no other reasonable way... of saving the author's life or the lives of other persons entrusted to the author's care."

"Necessity" as a justification for a state's breach of an international norm is highly restricted. Under Article 25 of the ILC Text, it may not be invoked unless the act taken was the only way the state could safeguard an "essential" interest from a "grave and imminent peril" and does not seriously impair an essential interest of the state or states to which the breached obligation was owed. Furthermore, necessity may not be invoked if the international obligation excludes necessity as a defense, or when "[t]he State has contributed to the situation of necessity."[7] In the situation of war, however, military necessity may be invoked to justify certain actions (such as seizure of alien ships within a state's jurisdiction) but not others (such as violations of the requirements of the Geneva Conventions not expressly limited by the principle of necessity).

The ILC Text also precludes a finding of wrongfulness if a state's would-be internationally wrongful act is a legitimate countermeasure. The conditions under which a countermeasure is considered legitimate are set forth in part three, chapter II of the ILC Text.

PROCEDURE FOR REMEDY

State responsibility may sometimes be characterized as "direct" or "vicarious." When a state imposes deprivation on another state, its wrongful act results in "direct" responsibility. The aggrieved state can thus make an international claim for remedy against the offending state without first submitting itself to the domestic legal procedure of the offending state. Where an alien suffers deprivation, the host state does not automatically become "responsible." International law, however, may require, given the nature of the deprivation, that the host state take some action to punish the wrongdoer and provide an appropriate remedy through its domestic courts or other agencies for the injured alien. Indeed, failure to do so would constitute a breach of the state's international obligations and result in its international responsibility. The responsibility of the state stems not from the wrong originally committed against the injured alien but from the state's failure to provide reasonable access to its courts and to afford an effective remedy for its wrong.

In regard to state responsibility arising from injuries to aliens, customary law has developed what is known as the doctrine of exhaustion of local remedies. Under this doctrine, before a protecting state may espouse, on behalf of its nationals, an international claim against another state for alleged injuries to its nationals, the injured party must first exhaust all remedies available under the domestic law of the defendant state. This includes the full use of all the state's procedural devices, such as the use of witnesses and the procuring of depositions and documentation.

An alien, in entering the host country, is presumed to submit voluntarily to the legal order there. Civil claims against him or her "follow the person" into the host territory. In addition, the doctrine of exhaustion of local remedies expresses the policy of effectiveness and economy, seeking to foster localization of dispute settlement and minimize international friction. Local remedies must be exhausted before a claim can be internationalized.

A key issue concerning the duty to exhaust "local judicial remedies" is the extent to which the private party must go in order to satisfy that duty. The test has been that of reasonableness. Reasonableness, as third-party decision makers may determine, can be ascertained by reference to judicial jurisdiction, the degree of independence of the judicial system concerned, available compensation, and temporal factors.

Will the courts of the host state hear the claim on its merits? Or would the local courts dismiss it on such grounds as a political question? When will continued efforts at local remedies become patently futile? If the case has already been heard at the trial level and the state's appellate courts may only address questions of law, a question of fact may remain in issue. If so, further attempts at redress may be futile. Similarly, if, due to political pressure and interference, the courts of the state are apparently in no position to perform their function independently and impartially, there may be no need to pursue local remedies. That a remedy exists on paper does not necessarily mean the presence of effective remedies, as international tribunals have often acknowledged. As a matter of practical wisdom, the costs of proceeding further on the local level are often balanced against the chances of eventual "satisfaction." Finally, a remedy that is not forthcoming within a reasonable time may be no remedy at all. Justice unduly delayed will be justice denied.

In the famous *Interhandel* case of 1959,[8] the Swiss company Interhandel had sought in vain, through litigation in American courts for more than a decade, the release of assets seized by the United States during World War II. The government of Switzerland, in extending diplomatic protection to its national company, urged the International Court of Justice to make an exception to the rule of exhaustion of local remedies in light of the protracted legal proceedings involved. The court, however, declared the case inadmissible for failure to exhaust local remedies and expressed confidence in the judicial system of the United States, especially its Supreme Court, to treat the matter in conformity with international law.

TYPES OF REMEDY AVAILABLE

The commission of an internationally wrongful act gives rise to state responsibility and commonly results in the duty to make some form of reparations. The purposes of reparations are not only to restore conditions altered by violations and to rehabilitate resulting deprivations but also to prevent and deter future incidences of violation. "[R]eparations must," in the words of the Permanent Court of International Justice in the *Chorzow Factory* (Indemnity) case (1928), "as far as possible, wipe out all the consequences of the illegal act and reestablish the situation which would, in all probability, have existed, if that act had not been committed."[9] Broadly conceived, this may take the form of restitution, compensation, punishment of responsible individuals, official apology, or other forms of satisfaction. The form of reparation in a particular case would depend largely on the injuries and damages involved and the demands of the injured state or other claimant.

Restitution, the preferred form of reparations, is essentially a return to the status quo ante and entails the performance of an obligation, revocation of an unlawful act, return of property wrongfully removed, or abstention from further wrongful conduct. Restitution includes two forms, legal restitution and restitution in kind. The former occurs when a tribunal refuses to recognize, or declares invalid, an act of the offending party. Restitution in kind, which is exceptional, is often not the most appropriate method of reparation; in many situations it is preferable to have a remedy that accommodates the internal authority of governments while redressing the injured party.

Indemnity or money payment should be made if restitution in kind is impossible. Generally, this should compensate for all damages that result from the unlawful act. Costs, interest, and even attorney fees are typically awarded by arbitral and domestic tribunals. In some instances even punitive or aggravated damages have been awarded to states and private litigants. In the case of Iraq, the Cooperation Commission, established in 1991 to administer and provide compensation to victims of Iraqi aggression in the Gulf War, has processed more than 2.6 million claims valued at more than $160 billion.

Finally, satisfaction is appropriate for nonwealth deprivations and takes the form of regrets, apologies, punishment of guilty officials, measures to prevent recurrence, or formal acknowledgment or judicial declaration regarding the wrong. The "year of the spy" (1985) in the United States reached its climax when a civilian counterintelligence analyst for the U.S. Navy was charged with selling military secrets to the Israelis for large amounts of money. It sent tremors through official Washington, causing shock or disbelief among Israel's friends and supporters. It raised, among other things, the question of the degree of ministerial responsibility for Israel's purported espionage operation in the United States, its staunchest ally. Was this an act of the government of Israel, or was it merely the work of a "loose cannon" in the Israeli intelligence apparatus? Who was to be held responsible? Under growing U.S. pressures and after some stutters of embarrassment, the Israeli government apologized for its espionage in the United States to the extent that it did take place. And the United States quickly welcomed Israel's apology and closed the book.

On July 3, 1988, the U.S. cruiser *Vincennes* shot down an Iranian civilian airbus (Iran Air Flight 655) en route to Dubai from Bandar Abbas with 290 people on board for having failed to respond to seven warnings on civilian and military radio channels. The United States shortly expressed "regret," though not an "apology," for the tragic incident and promised to pay compensation directly to the victims' families out of humanitarian concern and compassion, pending an authoritative determination of responsibility. The case was withdrawn from the International Court of Justice when both countries were able to reach an agreement settling all claims.

During NATO's campaign to force the Yugoslav army out of Kosovo, on May 7, 1999, U.S. warplanes inadvertently bombed the Chinese Embassy in Belgrade, killing three Chinese journalists and injuring more than twenty others. Despite President Clinton's apologies, the Chinese government rejected the official U.S. explanation that the embassy had been accidentally targeted, and mobs of angry demonstrators attacked and damaged the U.S. embassy in Beijing. On July 30, 1999, the two countries reached a partial settlement, and the United States agreed to pay China $4.5 million as compensation for the victims. In December 1999 the two countries reached a further agreement: the United States would pay $28 million for the destruction of the Chinese embassy in Yugoslavia, and China would provide $2.87 million to cover damages to the U.S. embassy and consulates in China caused by the angry demonstrators.

More recently, in July 2011, Syrian protesters vandalized the U.S. Embassy in Damascus with paint, rocks, and other objects, causing extensive damage to the exterior of the building. U.S. officials condemned the actions and faulted the Syrian government for its failure to contain the riots. The United States also said it intended to hold Syria accountable for providing compensation for the damage caused to the embassy by the demonstrators.

These examples highlight just some of the circumstances under which states may be held accountable to other states as a result of damages stemming from their action or inaction. Clarifying states' responsibility and the appropriate procedures for rectifying claims is an important step toward attaining goals such as compliance, compensation for victims, and the peaceful settlement of disputes while holding parties responsible for their actions under international law.

Notes

1. International Law Commission, Responsibility of States for Internationally Wrongful Acts (2001), *available a*t http://legal.un.org/ilc/texts/instruments/english/draft%20articles/9_6_2001.pdf]

2. G.A. Res. 56/83, U.N. Doc. A/RES/57/83 (Jan. 28, 2002).

3. Special Rapporteur on State Responsibility, *Addendum—Eighth Rep. on State Responsibility*, U.N. Doc. A1/CN.4/SER.A/1980/Add. 1 (Part 2) (Feb. 19 and June 10, 19, 1980) (by Roberto Ago).

4. Corfu Channel (U.K. v. Alb.), 1949 I.C.J. 4 (Apr. 9).

5. Ian Brownlie, Principles of Public International Law 433 (Clarendon Press, 2d ed. 1973).

6. *Supra* note 1, article 23.

7. *Supra* note 1, article 25.

8. Interhandel (Switz. v. U.S.), 1959 I.C.J. 6 (Mar. 21).

9. Chorzow Factory (Ger. v. Pol.) 1928, P.C.I.J. (ser. A) No. 9, at 31(Sept. 13).

29 Individual Criminal Responsibility

JUST AS A state can be held responsible for wrongful acts under international law, so can an individual be held criminally accountable for acts that violate international criminal law. As discussed in chapter 24, "The Applying Function," the purpose of correction as a sanctioning goal is to secure compliance with international law by holding an individual accountable for his or her actions.

The notion of individual criminal responsibility, largely nonexistent prior to World War II, has become a central principle of international law, especially within the realm of human rights. Beginning with the Nuremberg trials, and culminating, at least for the moment, with the establishment of the International Criminal Court (ICC), the belief that individuals are ultimately responsible for a state's actions has grown from a relative novelty to enjoy widespread acceptance. While it is remarkable that this field of international law has developed so rapidly over the course of just a few decades, there have also been bumps along the way. During the Cold War era, for example, international gridlock allowed a number of egregious international crimes to go unpunished by the international community. Nor has the concept of individual criminal responsibility gained complete acceptance. The ICC still faces a number of hurdles, including the lack of direct involvement by major world powers such as the United States and China, the difficulty of enforcement of the court's decisions, and the pending adoption of a definition for the crime of aggression. So too does international criminal law generally still face substantial challenges, such as the tension between criminal accountability and the historic reluctance to interfere with the internal affairs of sovereign states. Despite these challenges, however, great strides have been made in the area of individual criminal accountability—progress that is likely to continue for some time to come.

International Criminal Law Prior to World War I

Prior to the Nuremberg prosecutions, there was very little individual criminal responsibility under international law. In 1872, Guastav Moynier, a founder of the Red Cross, made the first attempt at creating an international criminal court in response to the horrors of the Franco-Prussian War. His proposal required a court to be automatically activated in the case of conflict between parties with the responsibility of determining guilt or innocence and imposing penalties. The proposed court would hold individuals criminally responsible for violations of the Geneva Convention, subject to criteria clearly defined in another instrument. However, Moynier's proposal was rejected and no vehicle was created in his lifetime.

Criminal responsibility remained essentially limited to violations of "the law of nations" and included two main categories of violations. The first was piracy, as it was in the interest of all states to ensure safe navigation of the high seas. Accordingly, any nation could prosecute domestically those accused of acts of piracy on the high seas. (This understanding was a precursor to contemporary conceptions of universal jurisdiction, which is discussed in chapter 14.)

Second, there was some individual criminal responsibility recognized for violations of *jus in bello*, or the law of war, which prohibited certain conduct in the course of waging battle. This body of international law was wholly customary until the 1850s, when attempts were made to codify it. While there was some success in doing so, in the form of the Hague Conventions of 1899 and 1907, there were major shortcomings in their ability to provide a legitimate means of imposing individual responsibility for violations of *jus in bello*. While the 1899 convention provided for individual responsibility, it did not provide a mechanism by which violators could be punished for their crimes. The 1907 convention did not provide for individual responsibility whatsoever. Rather, violations were to be punished by compensation paid by the state-violator to the state-victim. Finally, even if a state did wish to try a foreign war criminal in its domestic courts, the "act of state" defense generally immunized heads of state from criminal prosecution. Given these major shortcomings, the pre–World War I period, as embodied in the Hague Conventions of 1899 and 1907, can be seen as important first steps in the codification of individual criminal responsibility, but as more hortatory than substantive.

The Frustration of Attempts to Impose Individual Criminal Accountability in the Wake of World War I

The atrocities committed during the First World War led to a second attempt to create a regime for individual criminal responsibility. Like the earlier efforts embodied by Guastav Moynier and the two Hague Conventions, the new efforts were largely unsuccessful at cementing individual responsibility for violations of the law of war. Nonetheless, these efforts were significant in the precedent and groundwork they laid for the later efforts at Nuremberg.

Thirty nations, including the victorious Allied Powers, made initial efforts at the Paris Peace Conference of 1919 to assign individual accountability for violations of international law committed during the war. These nations established the Commission on the Responsibility of the Authors of the War and on Enforcement of Penalties, an international commission charged with cataloging various war crimes, assigning responsibility for the instigation of the war, and making recommendations on how to deal with the crimes committed.

The commission assigned primary responsibility for starting the war to Germany and Austria-Hungary, but also found that Bulgaria and Turkey had supported the German-Austrian war of aggression. The commission also found that representatives of each of the four Central Powers had committed war crimes, of which the commission documented thirty-two discrete offenses.

Significantly, the commission's final report seemed to distinguish between "war crimes" and violations of the "laws of humanity." Thus, the commission's catalog of offenses committed referred to violations of "the Laws and Customs of War and the Laws of Humanity." This latter category of offenses apparently referred to crimes committed by representatives of a state against their own subjects, such as crimes committed by Turkish forces against Armenians (who were Turkish subjects).[1] As will be discussed in the following section, American opposition kept the inclusion of violations of the laws of humanity from ultimately being included in the offense charged under the Treaty of Versailles. However, the commission's separation of the two crimes was an important first step toward the international community recognizing that international criminal law could be violated by a state against its own people. This initial recognition ultimately won acceptance at Nuremberg, where "crimes against humanity" were finally recognized and prosecuted.

The commission was also responsible for drafting a constitution and rules of procedure for an international tribunal that would be charged with prosecuting those responsible for war crimes and "authoring" the war. The commission's recommendation for such an international tribunal included the then-novel feature of recommending that heads of state be subject to prosecution for their own violations of international law.

Disagreement among the "Great Powers" (the United States, the United Kingdom, France, Italy, and Japan) led to a number of compromises being forged between the relatively strong position taken by the Commission on Responsibility, outlined above, and the much softer position favored by some states, including the United States. Thus, the Treaty of Versailles included some important provisions concerning individual accountability, but did not go so far as to adopt all of the commission's recommendations.

In one of the most important victories for individual criminal responsibility for gross violations of international law, Article 227 provided that a special tribunal would be established to try the former German Emperor, Kaiser Wilhelm, for "a supreme offense against international morality and the sanctity of treaties...." This was accomplished despite strong opposition from the United States and Japan. While the establishment of such a tribunal was a significant step toward holding accountable those who are often most responsible for the worst war crimes under international law, Queen Wilhelmina of the Netherlands refused to extradite the Kaiser, and he was never brought before the special tribunal envisioned in Article 227.

In other respects, however, the treaty reflected a weakened notion of individual criminal accountability. In Articles 228 and 229, the treaty provided for the use of military tribunals, as opposed to the establishment of an international criminal tribunal, to prosecute military leaders who committed acts violating the laws and customs of war. This was a step backward for individual criminal responsibility, in that an international criminal tribunal suggests the ultimate victim of international law crimes is the entire international community, whereas military tribunals, operated by individual state-victims, suggest that the victim is the state of nationality of the individual victim. This is much more reminiscent of the older notion of states, rather than individuals, as the ultimate actors and victims in international law. Likewise, the Americans won the day with the exclusion of prosecutions for violations of the "laws of humanity," which they argued violated the principle of *nullum crimen sine lege* (that there can be no crime without a preexisting law).

Despite the preferability of an international criminal tribunal over military tribunals, military tribunals would still have been capable of holding responsible those who committed the worst offenses. In Germany, however, domestic opposition to such tribunals led the Allies to agree to allow alleged war criminals to be tried by Germany in its own domestic courts. Out of a list of roughly 20,000 accused that had been identified by the commission, German officials brought only twelve defendants to trial. Of those twelve, only six were convicted, receiving modest sentences.

Events in Turkey followed a similar course. The preliminary peace treaty provided for an international criminal tribunal, but the final treaty called for amnesty for those accused of war crimes. Not only did the Allies agree to allow Turkey to try its own nationals accused of war crimes, but the end results were similar to the outcomes in Germany.

Thus, the events surrounding World War I were significant in terms of the development of several important concepts to individual criminal responsibility under international law, including the desire for a permanent international criminal court. An initial rejection of the act-of-state defense that had immunized heads of state from criminal prosecutions was perhaps the most important of these developments, although it did not lead to any criminal prosecutions of heads of state. Also significant was the move toward recognizing crimes against humanity. While there was far from universal agreement on this point, the initial recognition of this category of international crimes laid the groundwork for prosecution at the Nuremberg trials.

Nuremberg and Its Legacy

The International Military Tribunal (IMT), held at Nuremberg between October 1945 and July 1946, was a watershed moment in the imposition of individual criminal accountability for grave human rights abuses. The IMT, which tried twenty-two defendants for their roles in the Nazi war efforts and related human rights abuses, was established by the London Charter in the wake of the Allied victory over the Axis powers. It was composed of judges and prosecutors from the major Ally nations (the United States, the United Kingdom, Russia, and France). This was the first time that an international tribunal had been assembled to bring to justice those accused of major war crimes and mass human rights abuses and, as such, was a major victory for the supremacy of international law in this context.

The establishment of the IMT was quickly followed by creation of the Tokyo-based International Military Tribunal for the Far East (IMTFE), which oversaw the prosecution of thousands of Japanese military and political leaders for war crimes and other offenses committed in the Pacific during the war. The IMTFE was also significant for the development of individual criminal accountability under international law. However, because the IMT's trial at Nuremberg was the first of these two trials, the IMT is generally treated as the more revolutionary of the two. The importance of the IMTFE, however, should not be discounted.

The IMT at Nuremberg was also significant in that it laid the groundwork for subsequent international tribunals, such as the international criminal tribunals for the former Yugoslavia and Rwanda. Perhaps most important, though, the IMT reflected a changed perception of the nature of international criminal acts that is the cornerstone of individual criminal accountability under international law. As the IMT stated in its judgment, "Crimes against international law are committed by men, not by abstract entities, and only by punishing individuals who commit such crimes can the provisions of international law be enforced."[2]

Under the London Charter, the IMT had jurisdiction over three crimes: crimes against peace, war crimes, and crimes against humanity. These crimes were defined in Article 6 of the charter:

a. *Crimes Against Peace*: namely, planning, preparation, initiation or waging a war of aggression, or a war in violation of international treaties, agreements or assurances, or participation in a common plan or conspiracy for the accomplishment of any of the foregoing;

b. *War Crimes*: namely, violations of the laws or customs of war. Such violations shall include, but not be limited to, murder, ill-treatment or deportation to slave labor or for any other purpose of civilian population of or in occupied territory, murder or ill-treatment of prisoners of war or persons on the seas, killing of hostages, plunder of public or private property, wanton destruction of cities, towns or villages, or devastation not justified by military necessity;

c. *Crimes Against Humanity*: namely, murder, extermination, enslavement, deportation, and other inhumane acts committed against any civilian population, before or during the war, or persecutions on political, racial or religious grounds in execution of or in connection with any crime within the jurisdiction of this Tribunal, whether or not in violation of the domestic law of the country where perpetrated.

One of the primary defenses asserted before the IMT was that prosecution for these crimes was violative of the principle of *nullum crimen sine lege*. The Judgment of the Nuremberg Tribunal responded directly to this charge as to each of the three crimes charged. With respect to crimes against peace, the IMT found support in the Pact of Paris (1928) for its conclusion that aggressive war was a crime under international law in 1939:

> The General Treaty for the Renunciation of War of 27 August 1928, more generally known as the Pact of Paris or the Kellogg-Briand Pact, was binding on 63 nations, including Germany, Italy and Japan at the outbreak of war in 1939.... The nations who signed the Pact or adhered to it unconditionally condemned recourse to war for the future as an instrument of policy, and expressly renounced it.... In the opinion of the Tribunal, the solemn renunciation of war as an instrument of national policy necessarily involves the proposition that such war is illegal under international law; and that those who plan and wage such a war, with its inevitable and terrible consequences, are committing a crime in so doing.[3]

Beyond looking to international agreements, the IMT also looked to what it saw as the fundamental principles underlying the principle of *nullum crimen sine lege*. Focusing on abstract principles of justice, the IMT concluded:

> To assert that it is unjust to punish those who in defiance of treaties and assurances have attacked neighboring states without warning is obviously untrue, for in such circumstances the attacker must know that he is doing wrong, and so far from it being unjust to punish him, it would be unjust if his wrong were allowed to go unpunished....[4]

Thus, the IMT rejected the claim that the doctrine of *nullum crimen sine lege* barred it from convicting the defendants for crimes against peace.

With regard to war crimes, the IMT had little difficulty concluding that the offenses recognized by the London Charter as war crimes were already criminal prior to the war. The tribunal found that the acts were prohibited under the Hague Convention of 1907 and Geneva Convention of 1929. The IMT rejected the argument that the Hague Convention was inapplicable because Article 2 of that convention limited its application to conflicts in which all parties to the conflict were members to the convention, which was not the case in World War II. Rather, the IMT concluded, the Hague Convention of 1907 revised the then-existing laws and customs of war and that by 1939 the convention itself had become customary international law and so was enforceable even though not all belligerents were parties to it.[5]

The IMT generally avoided the question of whether the acts charged as crimes against humanity were criminalized under international law at the time they were alleged to have been committed. As noted above, American opposition prevented crimes against humanity from being included as prosecutable offenses in the Treaty of Versailles. Thus, there is at least some merit to the charge that prosecutions for crimes against humanity were violative of the principle of *nullum crimen sine lege*. Nonetheless, the tribunal's observations on crimes against peace, that the perpetrator must have known that what he was doing was wrong, is also persuasive in the context of crimes against humanity.

The IMT accepted the concept of crimes against humanity, but it sought to limit the scope of its application. The court found that, although crimes against humanity had undoubtedly been committed prior to the outbreak of the war, such crimes were not covered under the London Charter because they were not committed "in execution of, or in connection with, any crime within the jurisdiction of the Tribunal" as required under Article 6(c) of the charter. As to those acts committed after the outbreak of the war in 1939, however, the tribunal found:

> [W]ar Crimes were committed on a vast scale, which were also Crimes against Humanity; and insofar as the inhumane acts charged in the Indictment, and committed after the beginning of the war, did not constitute War Crimes, they were all committed in execution of, or in connection with, the aggressive war, and therefore constituted Crimes against Humanity.[6]

Applying this rationale, the IMT convicted defendants of crimes against humanity for the first time.

Many contemporary commentators were persuaded by the tribunal's arguments as to why its convictions were not barred by *nullum crimen sine lege*. While this debate is not unimportant, what is more significant is that all of the offenses prosecuted at Nuremberg, whether or not they were prohibited under international law at the time of the IMT, are now indisputably prohibited. In this way, the Nuremberg Trial contributed to defining substantive violations of crimes that are prosecutable under international criminal law.

Another significant and enduring contribution from the London Charter and the IMT is the rejection of several defenses that had previously been considered valid. In particular, the London Charter explicitly rejected as defenses the fact that a defendant was acting in an official capacity (including as head of state) or was following orders from a superior.[7] In rejecting the official capacity defense, the tribunal relied primarily on the charter's rejection of them, but also expanded somewhat on the justification for rejecting this defense, stating: "He who violates the law of war cannot obtain immunity while acting in pursuance of the authority of the state if the state in authorizing action moves beyond its competence under international law." Thus, to the extent that a state acted in violation of international law, so too did the individuals who carried out those acts. While this seems commonsensical today, at the time it was certainly not obvious that this should be so, especially in regard to heads of state. In addressing the defense of following orders, the IMT relied primarily on Article 8 of the charter, adding only that it was in accordance with the law of all nations that following orders should not relieve a person of criminal responsibility, although it may be considered as mitigating one's culpability.

Examples from the Cold War Era

Following World War II and the trials at Nuremberg and Tokyo, the Cold War began an almost fifty-year period in which there was essentially no progress on developing a regime of individual criminal accountability under international law. The East-West division that existed during this time prevented any agreement on international legal norms, with the end result being large-scale human rights abuses without any meaningful objection from the international community as a whole.

There were some early efforts by the international community to build on the successes of Nuremberg and Tokyo, but these were doomed to fail under the weight of the political divisions between the United States and the USSR. The creation of an international criminal court was contemplated, for example, in Article VI of the Convention on the Prevention and Punishment of the Crime of Genocide of 1948. Likewise, in 1948 the U.N. General Assembly charged the International Law Commission (ILC) with drafting both a code of international criminal law offenses and a statute for establishing an international criminal court. The ILC's efforts did produce a draft statute for an international criminal court. However, these efforts were ultimately abandoned because of disagreements on provisions within the criminal code, particularly the definition of the crime of aggression—disagreements that could not be overcome once the Cold War had begun.

The gridlock of the international community that stemmed from the Cold War resulted in mass human rights abuses committed with impunity. Under the rule of Pol

Pot and the Khmer Rouge in Cambodia, for example, approximately 1.7 million people were killed.[8] Many were massacred in the infamous "killing fields" by members of the Khmer Rouge, while others perished from starvation and forced labor. The response of the international community to the atrocities in Cambodia was initially characterized by indifference. Proposals for the use of the military instrument in the region were motivated not by a concern for egregious human rights abuses, but by geopolitics.

The lack of both military intervention and individual accountability in Cambodia was typical during the Cold War period. However, in recent years there has been significant progress toward holding these individuals responsible for their crimes under international law. Inspired by the International Criminal Tribunal for the Former Yugoslavia (ICTY) and the International Criminal Tribunal for Rwanda (ICTR) discussed in the following section, the Cambodian government and the United Nations took retroactive action and reached an agreement in 2003, after several years of negotiations, to create a tribunal to try those accused of perpetrating grave human rights abuses under the Pol Pot regime. The Extraordinary Chambers in the Court of Cambodia is a hybrid court that operates within the Cambodian justice system and consists primarily of Cambodian judges, although there are some international judges. The first trial held under this hybrid system resulted in the conviction of Kaing Guek Eav (also known as Kang Kek lew or Duch) in November 2009. Kaing had been the prison boss for the Khmer Rogue and accepted personal responsibility for the torture and deaths of more than 12,000 people. While the example of Cambodia during the Cold War illustrates the ineffectiveness of imposing individual criminal accountability during that time, Cambodia's more recent experience illustrates the willingness and relative effectiveness of efforts to impose individual criminal accountability in the post–Cold War period.

Post–Cold War: Establishment of Ad Hoc Tribunals

The end of the Cold War was significant to the imposition of individual criminal accountability for several reasons. First, the collapse of the Soviet Union, and the subsequent emergence of former Soviet republics as independent states, brought a period of previously unknown international cooperation. This was most remarkably so in the context of the U.N. Security Council, where the five permanent and veto-holding members were able to reach agreement and, for the first time in its history, act on their obligation to promote international peace and security.

Unfortunately, the progress made with respect to individual criminal accountability following the end of the Cold War also speaks to the relative turbulence of the time, and the need to address the corresponding rise in mass human rights abuses and deprivations that were witnessed in the midst of this political upheaval. The threat of mutual assured destruction (MAD) created a period of relative stability during the Cold War. This was largely so, in spite of large and violent proxy wars that were fought during the era, and is evidenced by the eruption of large-scale racial, ethnic, and religious conflicts soon after the collapse of the Soviet Union. With the end of the Cold War came a dramatic withdrawal of support that the United States and the Soviet Union had previously given to strong, often dictatorial regimes, which both sides had seen as necessary to ensure a block of friendly allies. A number of states—the former Yugoslavia, Rwanda, and Sierra Leone, to name just a few—saw internal religious and ethnic conflicts that had been previously suppressed boil over into large-scale armed conflicts. The resultant human rights abuses were met with the newfound spirit of cooperation within the Security Council that led to the first international criminal tribunals to be created since the IMT and IMTFE.

The former Yugoslavia and Rwanda are prototypical examples of the internal strife that has characterized the post–Cold War period. In the former Yugoslavia, which was made up of six republics (Serbia, Slovenia, Croatia, Bosnia, Macedonia, and Montenegro), Eastern Orthodox Serbs, Roman Catholic Croats, and Muslim Bosnians had coexisted in relative ethnic harmony throughout the dictatorial rule of Marshal Tito. With Tito's death, along with the end of the Cold War, ethnic conflict boiled over. Serbs, led by Slobodan Milosevich, sought to create a Serbian-dominated state consisting of Serbia and parts of Croatia and Bosnia with large Serbian populations. Grave human rights abuses were committed in the process, including the ethnic cleansing of non-Serbs from these areas. In Rwanda, ethnic differences that had been exploited under French colonialism, with the minority Tutsis given favored status over the majority Hutus, ultimately resulted in the Hutu-led genocide of Tutsi Rwandans. While estimates of the death toll vary, it is widely accepted that at least 500,000 Tutsis and moderate Hutus were killed. It was in response to these large-scale human rights deprivations in the former Yugoslavia and Rwanda that the Security Council, acting pursuant to its Chapter VII authority to respond to threats to the peace, created ad hoc tribunals to impose individual criminal responsibility.

The creation of the International Criminal Tribunal for the Former Yugoslavia (ICTY) was particularly important because it was the first international criminal tribunal conducted since the trials held at Nuremberg and Tokyo almost a half century earlier. It is significant that the ICTY was established while the armed conflict in the former Yugoslavia was still ongoing. This reflects the Security Council's belief that creating an international criminal tribunal could have an important deterrent effect. However, while deterrence was certainly a goal, it is also true that the Security Council created the ICTY because the international community was unable to agree on an alternative response, that is, a political or military one, to the atrocities that were being committed.

The ad hoc tribunals created to prosecute grave breaches of international criminal law in the former Yugoslavia and Rwanda built on the post–World War II international criminal tribunals. There were important differences, however, such as the crimes each tribunal was empowered to prosecute. Whereas the Nuremberg tribunal had been authorized to prosecute war crimes, crimes against humanity, and crimes against the peace, the ICTY was authorized to prosecute genocide, crimes against humanity, violations of the laws and customs of war, and grave breaches of the Geneva Conventions, which can be seen as a subset of war crimes. Similarly, the ICTR was authorized to prosecute genocide, crimes against humanity, and violations of Common Article 3 of the Geneva Conventions and the Additional Protocol II, which can also be seen as a subset of war crimes.

Thus, the ICTY and ICTR broke from their predecessors in two important ways regarding the crimes they prosecuted. First, the modern tribunals treated genocide as a distinct crime, whereas the IMT had treated genocide as a particular crime against humanity. This simply reflected the growing recognition in the post–World War II period that genocide, the attempt to systematically injure or destroy whole populations, was a uniquely grievous crime and ought to be treated as such. The second difference in the crimes charged at Nuremberg and by the ICTY and ICTR was that the latter tribunals did not prosecute crimes against peace as had been done of Nazi leaders at Nuremberg.

This second distinction is more significant for it reflects some of the difficulty international criminal law has had in responding to the changing nature of armed conflicts. "Crimes against the peace," as the term was used at Nuremberg, referred to the waging of aggressive war by one state against another. This crime was rooted in the concept of territorial integrity and the consensus among states that the infringement of one state's territorial integrity represented an unacceptable threat to the sovereignty of all states. In the post–Cold War era, however, the pattern of armed conflict has largely been of intra-state violence, usually based on ethnic, religious, and political divisions. Thus, international law has, thus far, failed to keep pace with the changing nature of armed conflicts in this respect.

In other ways, however, the ad hoc tribunals have done an excellent job of reflecting the changes in armed conflicts. One example of this is their broadening of the definition of "crimes against humanity." Whereas the IMT had limited prosecutions for crimes against humanity to acts taken after the commencement of hostilities (thus excluding crimes against humanity that were committed during the buildup to the war), the case law of both the ICTY and ICTR has eliminated the requirement that crimes against humanity be committed in the course of international conflict. Although Article 5 of the ICTY statute specifically refers to "crime[s]... committed in armed conflict," the Appellate Chamber has read this provision as requiring "nothing more than the existence of an armed conflict at the relevant time and place."[9] The Appellate Chamber has further concluded that this is merely a jurisdictional requirement, rather than a substantive element of the offense.

The ad hoc tribunals were also significant for having given gender-based crimes a significant emphasis within the offense of crimes against humanity. While rape and violence against women have historically been perpetrated in the conduct of war, such crimes were largely ignored by the London Charter and the IMT. The ad hoc tribunals, however, specifically include rape as a crime against humanity. Both tribunals have also successfully prosecuted acts of sexual violence as a genocidal act, as well as a war crime and a crime against humanity. Such prosecutions play an important role in the development of customary international law.

Another significant element of the ICTY and ICTR, and a distinction from the subsequent International Criminal Court (ICC), was that the ad hoc tribunals had primary jurisdiction, whereas the ICC has complementary jurisdiction. While the concept of complementary jurisdiction will be further discussed in the following section, it is sufficient here to say that under the complementary jurisdiction of the ICC, the relevant national criminal justice system must be either unwilling or unable to prosecute an offense before the ICC may do so. The ICTY and ICTR, by contrast, had primary jurisdiction over the offenses they were charged with prosecuting.

The relative successes of the ICTY and ICTR were crucial to the subsequent establishment of a permanent international criminal court. If not for those tribunals, it is very unlikely that the Rome Statute of the International Criminal Court (Rome Statute) would have been concluded in 1998.

The International Criminal Court (ICC)

In 1989, with the end of the Cold War (and prior to the creation of the ad hoc tribunals) the U.N. General Assembly revived its efforts from the 1950s to create a permanent international criminal court. At the request of the General Assembly, the ILC began work on a draft statute for an international criminal court, which was submitted to the General Assembly in 1993 and revised in 1994. The 1994 draft statute was remarkable for its relative success at accommodating the many competing interests, especially among the major powers.

The next important step in creating the ICC came in 1996, with the establishment of a Preparatory Committee on the Establishment of an International Criminal Court. The committee submitted a draft statute to the U.N. Conference of Plenipotentiaries on the Establishment of an International Criminal Court that was convened in Rome in June 1998 (Rome Conference). The draft submitted to the Rome Conference by the Preparatory Committee provided a wide range of options to the delegates. For example, the draft provided four alternatives for the definition of the war crime of using children to wage an armed conflict. While the inclusion of such a plenitude of choices was undoubtedly helpful to the diplomats negotiating at Rome, it is also reflective of the deep divisions that existed within the international community about what form an international criminal court should take.

Ultimately, the negotiators at Rome were able to reach substantial agreement and the Rome Statute was adopted on July 17, 1998. Adoption of the statute won the support of one hundred twenty states, with only seven voting against (the United States, China, Iraq, Israel, Libya, Qatar, and Yemen) and twenty-one abstaining. The statute entered into force on July 1, 2002, after a sufficient number of states had ratified the Rome Statute. As of 2013, 122 states had become parties to the Rome Statute. An additional thirty-one states had signed, but not ratified the statute—among these are two important global powers, including the United States and Russia. A third global power, China, neither signed nor ratified the statute.

KEY FEATURES OF THE ICC

The final draft of the Rome Statute reflects a number of compromises. In particular, several important concessions were made in the effort to win support from major powers, especially the United States. These compromises make up some of the most important features of the ICC and are worth discussing at some length.

Offenses Recognized

There are both important similarities and differences between the offenses over which the ICC has jurisdiction and those over which its predecessor special tribunals had jurisdiction. Article 5 of the Rome Statute limits the court's jurisdiction to the four "most serious crimes of concern to the international community as a whole": genocide, crimes against humanity, war crimes, and the crime of aggression. As discussed in chapter 17, the court's jurisdiction over the crime of aggression is subject to the ratification of an amendment to the Rome Statute by state parties after 2017. The amendment will define the crime of aggression along the lines of General Assembly Resolution 3314.

Article 6 of the Rome Statue defines "genocide" as any of five acts, taken with the intent to destroy, in whole or in part, a "national, ethnical, racial or religious group." Among the five prohibited genocidal acts are killing members of the group, causing serious bodily or mental harm on members of the group, deliberately inflicting group conditions designed to bring about their physical destruction, attempting to prevent births within the group, and forcibly transferring children of the group to another group. This definition is taken from Article 2 of the Genocide Convention, as it had been used by the ICTY and ICTR. This is distinct from Nuremberg and Tokyo, where "genocide" had been included under the umbrella of "crimes against humanity."

Article 7 of the Rome Statute defines "crimes against humanity." Paragraph 1 of this definition includes eleven prohibited acts (including a catch-all of "[o]ther inhumane acts of a similar character intentionally causing great suffering, or serious injury to body or to mental or physical health"), when such acts are committed as part of a "widespread or systematic attack directed against any civilian population." Included among the prohibited acts are murder, enslavement, deportation or forcible transfer, rape and other gender-based crimes, and enforced disappearance. Paragraph 2 defines an "attack directed against any civilian population" as the multiple commission of the acts prohibited by paragraph 1, when committed against any civilian population and "pursuant to or in furtherance of a State or organizational policy to commit such attack." Thus, the ICC, following the example of the ICTY and ICTR, parted from the requirement imposed by the IMT that crimes against humanity be committed in the course of an international armed conflict. This is significant because it reflects both the international community's recognition of the changing nature of armed conflict in the post–Cold War era and the changing conception of sovereignty discussed previously in chapter 12.

The final offense recognized in the Rome Statute is "war crimes," which is defined in Article 8. This is in some contrast to the ICTY, which had instead recognized grave breaches of the Geneva Conventions of 1949 and violations of the laws or customs of war, and the ICTR, which recognized violations of Article 3 of the Geneva Conventions and Additional Protocol II. Practically, though, the definition provided in the Rome Statute is functionally equivalent to that in the ICTY Statute, in that it specifically includes both grave breaches of the 1949 Geneva Conventions and "other serious violations of the laws and customs applicable in international law." (The ICTR had omitted the inclusion of customary law since Rwanda was a state party to the Geneva Conventions and Additional Protocol II.)

The Rome Statute required that these crimes have been committed after the Rome Statute came into force on July 1, 2002, or after the date the state became a signatory to the Rome Statute in order for the ICC to prosecute the offender.

Complementary Jurisdiction

Article 1 of the Rome Statute provides that the jurisdiction of the ICC "shall be complementary to national criminal jurisdictions." The principle of complementary jurisdiction means that, in the first instance, criminal prosecutions are to be conducted by domestic courts. Generally, it is only when the relevant domestic courts are unwilling or unable to effectively prosecute accused persons that would otherwise fall under the ICC's jurisdiction. This requires that a state's national judicial system be totally or substantially collapsed, or unavailable.

The complementary jurisdiction of the ICC reflects substantial respect for state sovereignty and is a departure from the earlier international criminal tribunals (the IMT, IMTFE, ICT, and ICTR), which exercised primary jurisdictions over crimes within their jurisdiction. In the case of the ad hoc tribunals at least, the primacy of the international tribunals was based, in large part, on a predetermination by the international community that the relevant domestic courts were unable or unwilling to effectively prosecute accused persons. The distinction in this respect between the ad hoc tribunals and the ICC is that the ICC is prospective, that is, it is intended to deal with crimes that have not yet been committed, and must therefore allow for the possibility that a state's domestic courts may be willing and able to prosecute offenses over which they have jurisdiction, whereas the ad hoc tribunals were intended to confront geographically and temporally limited situations that were capable of being judged for the willingness and ability of the relevant states to prosecute accused persons. As to the IMT and IMTFE, the primacy of jurisdiction that was bestowed upon the international tribunals largely reflected the strong desire for retribution felt by the international community over the atrocities committed during World War II, as well as the complete inadequacy of prosecutions carried out by domestic courts following World War I.

Personal Jurisdiction

Another important aspect of the jurisdiction of the ICC is also the result of a compromise achieved by negotiators at the Rome Conference over the question of which relevant state's ratification of the Rome Statute will confer jurisdiction on the court. During the Rome negotiations, South Korea advocated a relatively broad proposal, which would have allowed the court to exercise personal jurisdiction over a defendant if any one of four states was a state party to the Rome Convention: (1) the state of which the accused was a national; (2) the state of which the alleged victim was a national; (3) the state in which the offense charged was alleged to have been committed; or (4) the state in whose custody the accused was in. While this proposal had broad support, the United States rejected granting the court personal jurisdiction over any accused persons other than nationals of states parties. The end result was a compromise between the South Korean and U.S. proposals: the court may exercise its jurisdiction over nationals of states parties, regardless of where the crime is committed (as the United States supported), or where an individual commits a crime within the territory of a state party.

Significant Procedural Mechanisms

There are a number of significant features of the court's procedural operations worth discussing. First, there is the issue of how investigations or prosecutions are initiated. During the Rome negotiations, the United States urged a very narrow conception of how investigations or prosecutions should be initiated that would have limited such authority to the Security Council. Given the veto power of the five permanent members of that body, this would have meant that, as a practical matter, each of the five permanent members could have prevented the ICC from exercising its jurisdiction over any of its nationals (or anyone else it so chose to protect). This position was unacceptable to the vast majority of states. In the end, Article 13 of the statute recognizes three parties or bodies that can refer a situation to the prosecutor: (1) a state party; (2) the U.N. Security Council (acting pursuant to its Chapter VII peace-maintaining authority); and (3) the prosecutor who initiates an investigation *sua sponte*.

Since the Security Council may refer *any* situation to the prosecutor for investigation and subsequent prosecution, a referral from the Security Council will allow the ICC to assert jurisdiction over non-state parties. However, the statute does provide that the Security Council may use its Chapter VII authority to defer an investigation or prosecution (for an indefinitely renewable one-year term).

Once a situation is referred to, or initiated by, the Office of the Prosecutor, the prosecutor will seek permission from the Pre-Trial Chamber to initiate an investigation. The prosecutor will be allowed to do so unless the panel of judges determines that there is "no reasonable basis to proceed." (The ICC uses the term "situation" to refer to the state or region in which crimes within its jurisdiction are alleged to have been committed.) In this respect, the prosecutor serves somewhat of a dual role, fulfilling more of a police function during the investigatory phase (i.e., gathering and assessing evidence against individuals suspected of wrongdoing) and a prosecutorial function during the trial phase.

If the prosecutor is satisfied that there is sufficient evidence to bring charges, and all of the court's jurisdictional requirements are satisfied, he or she will seek an arrest warrant from the court's Pre-Trial Chamber. The Pre-Trial Chamber must only be satisfied that there are reasonable grounds to believe a crime within the court's competence has been committed to satisfy its burden. If an arrest warrant is issued and the accused is brought into custody, the charges against the accused must be confirmed by the Pre-Trial Chamber. During the confirmation of charges stage, both the prosecutor and the accused may present evidence, which may be rebutted by the opposing party. At this stage there is a more stringent burden of proof on the prosecutor. The Pre-Trial Chamber must be satisfied that there are "substantial grounds" to believe the accused has committed the offense(s) charged.

If charges against an accused are confirmed by the Pre-Trial Chamber, a three-member Trial Chamber is convened to try the accused. Article 66 provides that the accused must be presumed innocent until proven guilty. In order to convict the accused, the Trial Chamber must be convinced that he or she is guilty beyond a reasonable doubt. If the accused is found guilty, the Trial Chamber will also render a sentence. The sentence imposed may include imprisonment (in the general case for a period not to exceed thirty years, but up to a life sentence "when justified by the extreme gravity of the crime and the individual circumstances of the convicted person"), a monetary fine, or the forfeiture of proceeds, property, or assets derived from the convicted person's criminal acts. Property or money collected through fines or forfeiture may be directed to a victim's trust fund at the court's discretion. However, the ICC cannot impose a sentence of death for any criminal convictions

The ICC was the first court to recognize the participation of victims in the prosecutorial process. Victims are allowed to give prosecutors information that can be used to initiate an investigation or prosecution. During trial, victims have the right to examine the accused or appear for the prosecution as a witness. If the court allows it, victims may also present their views in person or through a legal representative.

The court also has an Appeals Chamber to which both the prosecutor and defense may appeal certain decisions made by the court during the trial, conviction, acquittal, or sentencing phases.

The ICC's Progress Since 2002

By January 2013, there were eight situations under investigation by the ICC representing twenty cases from the Democratic Republic of the Congo, the Central African Republic, Uganda, Darfur, Sudan, the Republic of Kenya, Libya, Côte D'Ivoire, and Mali.[10] Four of these situations were referred to the ICC by state parties and two were referred by the prosecutor *proprio motu*. In addition, the Security Council referred two situations involving non-state parties. The prosecutor's investigations in these situations led to criminal charges in approximately sixteen cases.

DEMOCRATIC REPUBLIC OF THE CONGO (DRC)

The situation in the Democratic Republic of the Congo (DRC) involved five cases against six defendants. In *Prosecutor v. Germain Katanga and Mathieu Ngudjolo Choi*,[11] the defendants were accused of a number of war crimes and crimes against humanity, alleged to have been committed in the course of their leadership of Congolese militia groups engaged in the Ituri conflict in northeastern DRC. On November 21, 2012, the Trial Chambers severed the charges against Katanga and Choi. The Chambers ultimately dismissed all charges against Choi on December 18, 2012, and he was released shortly after. In *Prosecutor v. Bosco Ntaganda*,[12] the defendant was accused of actively participating in the use of child soldiers by another militia group also involved in the Ituri conflict. The defendant in *Prosecutor v. Thomas Lubanga Dyilo*[13] was also accused of enlisting and conscripting children into the same militia as Bosco Ntaganda.

The *Lubanga* case was the first case before the ICC to go to trial and also illustrates some key features of the court. Ten days before the trial commenced in June 2008, the Trial Chamber ordered a stay of the proceedings in light of the prosecutor's inability to disclose to the defense a large amount of evidence because it had been obtained under Article 54(3)(e) of the charter, which permits the prosecutor to obtain evidence confidentially. The Trial Chamber found the prosecutor's broad reliance on this provision, which was used to keep hundreds of documents from the defense (most of which had been obtained from the United Nations), conflicted with the prosecution's obligation to disclose potentially exculpatory evidence (Article 67(2)). After staying the proceedings, the Trial Chamber ultimately concluded that a fair trial against Mr. Lubanga was impossible and ordered his release from ICC custody.

The prosecutor appealed this decision to the Appeals Chamber, where he won a partial victory. The Appeals Chamber concluded that while the Trial Chamber had been correct to stay the proceedings against Mr. Lubanga, it was wrong to conclude that a fair trial would not be possible. Rather, the Appeals Chamber said that it might be possible for a fair trial to proceed against Mr. Lubanga at some future time. Accordingly, the

Appeals Chamber remanded the matter back to the Trial Chamber to more thoroughly address whether it was appropriate to order Mr. Lubanga's unconditional release. The trial was subsequently commenced in January 2009.

Lubanga's case provided the ICC with its very first conviction. On March 14, 2012, he was found guilty of war crimes for enlisting, conscripting, and using children under fifteen years of age in hostilities. He was sentenced on July 10, 2012, to fourteen years' imprisonment. The conviction reinforced the court's purpose of ending "impunity for perpetrators of the most serious crimes of concern to the international community." However, some commentators criticized the court for the length of time the trial took to complete, which was almost three years.

CENTRAL AFRICAN REPUBLIC

The situation in the Central African Republic included one case, *Prosecutor v. Jean-Pierre Bemba Gombo*.[14] The defendant was accused of three counts of war crimes and two counts of crimes against humanity allegedly committed in the course of his leadership of the Movement of the Liberation of the Congo (MLC), a militia group that also fought in the northern DRC in 2002 and 2003. The trial started on November 22, 2010, and was still ongoing as of 2014. In November 2013, the ICC issued arrest warrants for Gombo, two members of his defense team, a defense witness, and a member of the Congolese parliament over allegations of conspiracy to present false evidence to the court.

UGANDA

In December 2003, Uganda was the first state party to make a voluntary referral to the ICC. The situation led to the issuance of arrest warrants for the five top members in the Lord's Resistance Army (LRA), a rebel group operating in northern Uganda—Joseph Kony, Vincent Otti, Okot Odhiambo, Dominic Ongwen, and Raska Lukwiya. (The case against Lukwiya was dismissed following the defendant's death.) Each of the defendants was accused of various crimes against humanity and war crimes. The arrest warrant enticed the LRA commander-in-chief, Joseph Kony, to participate in peace talks with Uganda. He demanded that the state withdraw its referral in exchange for the LRA's promise to end the violence. Uganda considered withdrawing its referral, but never made such a move because the LRA never signed a final peace agreement.

Subsequently, in 2012, Kony's atrocities in Uganda became highly publicized when a documentary called *Invisible Children* spread virally on the Internet. The documentary called for the international community to publicize Kony's actions and asked viewers to urge government officials to arrest Kony and bring him before the ICC to answer for his crimes. The situation received substantial support from the international community; however, the media attention was short-lived, and none of the defendants had been brought into custody as of 2014.

DARFUR, SUDAN

The situation in Darfur was referred to the prosecutor in 2005 to investigate large-scale human rights abuses against Black Sudanese by the Janjaweed, a nongovernmental Arab militia, with the support of the Sudanese government. This situation was unique in several important respects. First, the situation in Darfur was, at the time, the only situation that had been referred to the ICC by the Security Council. As with the Security Council decisions to establish ad hoc tribunals to prosecute large-scale human rights abuses in Rwanda and the former Yugoslavia, the Security Council's decision to refer the situation in Darfur to the ICC reflects a willingness on behalf of the Security Council to respond to grave human rights abuses that had been largely absent in the intervening decade.

The situation in Darfur is also remarkable, and has been somewhat controversial, for Prosecutor Luis Moreno Ocampo's decision to seek an arrest warrant for Sudanese President Omar al-Bashir, which was issued by a Pre-Trial Chamber in March 2009. Al-Bashir was charged with five counts of crimes against humanity (murder, extermination, forcible transfer, torture, and rape) and two counts of war crimes (pillaging and directing attacks against a civilian population or individual civilians not taking part in hostilities).

In addition to the case against al-Bashir, four other cases were opened in the Darfur situation. Ali Muhammad Ali Abd-al-Rahman, the alleged leader of the Janjaweed, was charged with fifty counts of crimes against humanity and war crimes and Ahmad Muhammad Harun, a high-ranking member of the Sudanese government, was charged with forty-two counts of crimes against humanity and war crimes.[15] Bahar Idriss Abu Garda, the leader of the United Resistance Front, a rebel group fighting against the Sudanese government, faced three counts of war crimes.[16] Abdallah Banda Abakaer Nourain, who headed an arm of the United Resistance Front, and Saleh Mohammed Jerbo Jamus, the previous Chief of Staff of the Sudan Liberation Army-Unity (SLA-Unity), were also charged with three counts of war crimes. Abdel Raheem Muhammad Hussein, Minster of National Defence, was charged with thirteen counts of crimes against humanity and war crimes.[17]

Both Banda and Jerbo appeared before the ICC in 2010, and the Pre-Trial Chamber confirmed the charges against them in 2011. The charges against Jerbo were dropped in October 2013, following his death. The case against Banda is expected to commence in late 2014. Following the prosecutor's actions, however, al-Bashir retaliated against the United Nations and stated Sudan would not comply with the ICC's warrants, urging allies to refuse to cooperate with the ICC. Fearing that executing the warrant would risk peace and stability within Darfur, Sudan's allies have thus far assisted in deferring the case. As a result, all of the remaining defendants are still at large (except for Abu Garda against whom the Pre-Trial Chamber declined to affirm the charges).

REPUBLIC OF KENYA

The situation in the Republic of Kenya stems from the violent 2007 presidential election in which over one thousand people were estimated killed and hundreds of thousands displaced. The prosecutor opened an investigation *proprio motu* in March 2010 and has charged six defendants with committing crimes against humanity. In the first case, William Samoei Ruto, the former Minister of Higher Education, Science and Technology, and Henry Kirpono Kosgey, a Member of Parliament, are both charged as indirect co-perpetrators with three counts of crimes against humanity.[18] However, the Pre-Trial Chamber II declined to confirm the charges against Kosgey. Joshuar Arap Sang, the head of operations at a radio station in Nairobi, is charged with contributing to the commission of three crimes against humanity.[19] The trial against Ruto and Sang began in September 2013. In the second case, Francis Kirimi Muthaura, the former Head of the Public Service and Secretary to the Cabinet, and Uhuru Muigai Kenyatta, the Deputy Prime Minister and former Minister of Finance, were both charged with five counts of crimes against humanity as indirect co-perpetrators.[20] Although Mohammed Hussein Ali, Chief Executive of the Postal Corporation, was charged as otherwise having contributed to five counts of crimes against humanity, the Pre-Trial Chamber II declined to confirm the charges.[21] In August 2013, an arrest warrant was issued for Walter Osapiri Barasa, a journalist, who was accused of attempting to corrupt witnesses in the Kenya cases.

Uhuru Kenyatta was subsequently elected to Kenya's presidency in March 2013. Although the charges against Kenyatta were confirmed by the ICC in January 2012, Kenya's parliament voted to withdraw from the court's jurisdiction in September 2013. The case continued nonetheless, with a postponement granted until February 2014.

LIBYA

The ICC opened an investigation into Libya in March 2011 following the U.N. Security Council's decision to refer the case to the ICC.[22] The situation in Libya arose from the Libyan military's crackdown on protesters across the country and resulted in mass human rights abuses and deaths.

This referral is significant for a number of reasons. First, the Security Council referred this case at the outset of the conflict, whereas in Darfur, the conflict had been ongoing for two years and required a strong recommendation from the U.N. International Commission in favor of the Security Council's referral. Furthermore, the Libyan referral was unanimous. The Security Council's actions show that its members, and the international community generally, are beginning to view the ICC as a legitimate and valuable institution that is willing and able to prosecute political and military leaders.

After the prosecutor's investigation, the ICC issued arrest warrants for former Head of State Muammar Mohammed Abu Minyar Gaddafi (now deceased) and also Saif Al-Islam Gaddafi, the honorary chairman of the Gaddafi International Charity and Development Foundation and the *de facto* prime minister, for committing two counts of crimes against humanity as indirect co-perpetrators. Saif, was captured in November 2011 by Lybian police in northwestern Libya. The ICC also issued an arrest warrant for Abdullah Al-Senussi, colonel of the Libyan Armed Forces, as an indirect perpetrator for two counts of crimes against humanity. Al-Senussi was captured in March 2012 and extradited to Libya.

After Gaddafi's death, his regime collapsed, and the ICC was presented with a unique issue. The ICC repeatedly requested that the new Libyan government surrender the two individuals for prosecution at The Hague. However, the Libyan government stated that it intended to prosecute Saif and al-Senussi in a Libyan court. In May 2013, the Pre-Trial Chamber insisted that Libya hand over Saif Gaddafi. However, later that year, in October, the Chamber deemed the case against al-Senussi to be inadmissible, as the case was already subject to a Libyan court, which was competent to oversee the trial.

CÔTE D'IVOIRE

The situation in Côte D'Ivoire arose from violence following the country's November 2010 elections, in which thousands of people were killed and grave human rights violations committed over a five-month period. Côte D'Ivoire, though not a party to the Rome Statute at that time (it became a state party in March 2013), submitted itself to ICC jurisdiction for the investigation. The investigation was expanded to cover the time period between September 19, 2002, and November 28, 2010, as well as future crimes that may be committed in relation to the elections. The prosecutor obtained two arrest warrants in connection with this situation. In *Prosecutor v. Laurent Gbagbo*, the defendant, Ivorian national and former president of Côte d'Ivoire, was charged with four counts of crimes against humanity as an indirect co-perpetrator. The defendant in *Prosecutor v. Simone Gbagbo* is an Ivorian national who was charged as an indirect co-perpetrator with four counts of crimes against humanity. The proceedings were ongoing as of 2014.

MALI

On July 13, 2012, the Government of Mali referred the situation in its territory to the Office of the Prosecutor. Six months later, the prosecutor opened an investigation into war crimes allegedly committed since January 2012. No arrest warrants had been requested as of 2014.

Appraisal

There were a number of criticisms leveled against the ICC following its establishment. Some critics pointed to the fact that the ICC had focused on African nations for its investigations and prosecutions. A second criticism was that the threat of prosecution made the resolution of ongoing conflicts less likely. Some have also argued that the ICC's procedures and mechanisms unfairly advantaged the prosecutor over defendants, for example, by not providing defendants with sufficient access to documentary evidence (by providing the defense with heavily redacted documents, for example) and by providing defense teams with smaller budgets.

The ICC has also been criticized for its shortcoming in enforceability of its arrest warrants and completion of trials. As of this writing, the ICC has only convicted one defendant and has at least eighteen cases pending. In addition, the ICC has issued over twenty arrest warrants and nine summonses, but very few individuals were in ICC custody. Notably, the ICC does not have its own police force and must rely on the cooperation of the state parties to enforce its warrants. However, in many cases, state parties have not been willing to cooperate with the ICC. Even where they did cooperate, their assistance was limited because ICC member states do not have power outside of their jurisdictional boundaries. Therefore, if a wanted individual fled to another state, the state party was prevented from enforcing the warrant within the other state without the Security Council's consent or authorization.

In addition to these specific criticisms of the ICC, a number of states objected to the mere existence of an international criminal court, at least in the form of the ICC. The United States was at one time one of the most outspoken opponents of the court. Among the United States' reasons for not ratifying the Rome Statute were that there were insufficient checks on ICC power; that the ICC was a threat to U.S. sovereignty; and that the ICC threatened fundamental democratic principles. However, under the Obama administration, the United States has softened its tone towards the court and has indicated greater support for its activities.

The ICC's involvement in the above situations illustrates the integral role of the prosecutors and the Security Council in assisting the ICC in accomplishing its goals. The manner in which the prosecutor and the Security Council dealt with these atrocities shaped the international community's perception of the ICC. In some cases, the prosecutor's decision on whom to prosecute caused the international community to question the court. However, with the successful completion of a prosecution and two referrals by the Security Council, the ICC has proven that it can be a legitimate means of addressing grave injustices throughout the world.

After ten years of operation, the ICC elected a new prosecutor, bringing the importance of the position into the spotlight. On December 12, 2011, the ICC elected Fatou Bensouda, former Deputy Prosecutor of the Office of the Prosecutor, Senior Legal Adviser at the ICTR, and Attorney General and Minister of Justice of the Republic of the Gambia, to replace Luis Moreno-Ocampo as the head of the Office of Prosecutor. The personnel change meant that the ICC had both a new public face and a new leader in its Office of the Prosecutor. It remains to be seen how Bensouda's experience in international law and ability to communicate with the international community and media will influence the types of cases the ICC will take and how the international community will view the ICC.

While it is too early to pass judgment on how successful Bensouda and the ICC as an institution will be over the long term, it can be said that the ICC has shown remarkable success in developing a workable concept of individual criminal accountability. Since its establishment, the ICC has completed two trials and, as of this writing, is currently rendering its second verdict. It has received two referrals from the Security Council—both of which resulted in arrest warrants for heads of state—and has several ongoing or preliminary investigations. These accomplishments have served to reinforce the ICC's reputation as the enforcer of international criminal law. Already, world leaders have shown a willingness to call on the court to address important cases.

Admittedly, the ICC's accomplishments have not come without criticisms of perceived deficiencies in the court's current procedures—most notably the lack of cooperation from state parties in executing its arrest warrants and the length of its earliest trial proceedings. The ICC's goal of obtaining justice for the victims can only be fulfilled if offenders can be brought to The Hague to answer for their crimes and can be expeditiously judged once there. Predictability and efficiency are worthy qualities that will enhance the ICC's reputation as well as the reputation of its judges and professional staff over time.

As for the international community, it is in the best interest of the community as a whole, including individuals and individual states, that human rights abuses be punished under international law. This is crucial to the effective deterrence of future human rights abuses. Perhaps most significant about the court is the fact that those who would commit the most egregious crimes—war crimes, crimes against humanity, genocide, and aggression against another state—are now on notice that they will not be able to do so with impunity. In just over sixty years, the international community has gone from having virtually no mechanism for holding individuals criminally accountable for their mass human rights deprivations, to establishing a permanent mechanism by which these criminals can be brought to account for their actions.

The goal of correction—holding individuals criminally responsible, no matter who the offender may be—is a vital part of securing compliance with international law. As discussed in chapter 24, a critical function of correction is to hold individuals responsible and to make them more aware of and responsive to the norms of the international law. The rise of individual criminal responsibility in the context of the ICC means that state officials will no longer be able to justify their actions under the guise of state action. This shift represents a huge advancement in civilization, offering a means to hold power elites accountable for wrongdoing. Rather, elites will be forced to take international human rights prescriptions seriously or face the risk of prosecution and increasing isolation from the international community.

Notes

1. *See* Theodor Meron & Jean Galbraith, *Nuremberg and Its Legacy, in* INTERNATIONAL LAW STORIES 13, 17 (John E. Noyes, Laura A. Dickinson, & Mark W. Janis eds., Foundation Press 2007).

2. Judgment of Nuremberg Tribunal, International Military Tribunal, Nuremberg (1946), 41 A.J.I.L. 172, 221 (1947).

3. *Id.*

4. *Id.*

5. *Id.*

6. *Id.*

7. London Agreement, Aug. 8 1945, art. 8, 59 Stat. 1544, E.A.S. No. 472, 82 U.N.T.S. 280.

8. *See Cambodian Genocide Program*, YALE UNIVERSITY, http://www.yale.edu/cgp/ (last visited Dec. 2011).

9. Prosecutor v. Seselj, Case No.:IT-03-67-AR72.1, Decision on the Interlocutory Appeal Concerning Jurisdiction, ¶ 4 (Int'l Crim. Trib. for the Former Yugoslavia Aug. 31, 2004).

10. INTERNATIONAL CRIMINAL COURT, ALL SITUATIONS, http://www.icc-cpi.int/en_menus/icc/situations%20and%20cases/situations/Pages/situations%20index.aspx.

11. Prosecutor v. Germain Katanga and Mathieu Ngudjolo Chui, Case No. ICC-01/04-01/07, Warrant of Arrest (July 2, 2007).

12. Prosecutor v. Bosco Ntaganda, Case No. ICC-01/04-02/06, Warrant of Arrest (Aug. 22, 2006).

13. Prosecutor v. Thomas Lubanga Dyilo, Case No. ICC-01/04-01/06, Warrant of Arrest (Feb. 10, 2006).

14. Prosecutor v. Jean-Pierre Bemba Gombo, Case No. ICC-01/05 -01/08, Warrant of Arrest (May 23, 2008).

15. Prosecutor v. Ahmad Muhammad Harun ("Ahmad Harun") and Ali Muhammad Ali Abd-Al-Rahman ("Ali Kushayb"), Case No. ICC-02/05-01/07, Warrant of Arrest (Apr. 27, 2007).

16. Prosecutor v. Bahar Idriss Abu Garda, Case No. ICC-02/05-02/09, Summons to Appear (May 7, 2009).

17. Prosecutor v. Abdel Raheem Muhammad Hussein, Case No. ICC-02/05-01/12, Warrant of Arrest (Mar. 1, 2012).

18. Prosecutor v. William Samoei Ruto, Henry Kiprono Kosgey and Joshua Arap Sang, Case No. ICC-01/09-01/11, Summonses to Appear (Mar. 8, 2011).

19. *Id.*

20. Prosecutor v. Francis Kirimi Muthaura, Uhuru Muigai Kenyatta and Mohammed Hussein Ali, Case No. ICC-01/09-02/11, Summonses to Appear (Mar. 8, 2011).

21. *Id.*

22. S.C. Res. 1970, U.N. Doc. S/RES/1970 (Feb. 26, 2011).

IX Prospects

30 Toward a World Community of Human Dignity

IT IS SOMETIMES lamented that, whereas most of humankind's problems are global in their reach, the processes of law maintained to cope with these problems are not. This, as amply demonstrated in the preceding chapters, would appear to be a profound misperception.

With ever-growing interdependence, the contemporary world arena does manifest a comprehensive process of authoritative decision. Although it has not yet achieved that high stability in expectations about authority and in degree of control over constituent members characteristic of the internal processes of mature national communities, this process does provide in more than rudimentary form the features essential to the effective making, application, and review of law on a global scale.

In recent decades, this dynamic process of authoritative decision has been expanding and improving itself at an accelerating rate, making itself more adequate to cope with global problems. The development of this ongoing process of authoritative decision wholly parallels, and is an integral part of, the larger development of world social process.

Historical Development

The basic features of a global constitutive process have been delineated only within relatively recent times. For millennia the conditions essential to the establishment and maintenance of larger community and decision processes were absent; the peoples of the world lived in isolated groupings with little physical contact, much less cooperative interaction in the pursuit of the common interest. As populations increased and interactions grew more frequent, institutional practices became differentiated and specialized, culminating in decision processes capable of sustaining stable contact and of restoring severed relations. The ancient civilizations of China, India, Greece, and Rome all recognized expectations of authority and control shared between different territorial communities as vital to clarify and protect common interest. Indeed, the Greek concept of a natural law shared by all humankind and the Roman notion of a *jus naturale* and a *jus gentium* shared by many peoples have for centuries exerted tremendous influence on the development of what is regarded as contemporary international law. Over many millennia the fragmentary practices in cooperation that began merely as exchanges of intermediaries have developed into a highly complex system of organized decision making, sustained by bilateral and multilateral arrangements. Many predispositions shaped in the primitive, preglobal arrangements of humankind continue to affect the configuration of contemporary decision making.

The universal decision institutions of the contemporary world are commonly regarded as having been shaped largely by the internal and external dynamisms of a Western Europe recovering from the centuries that followed the collapse of the Roman Empire and of feudalism in the West. As Europe's impact on peoples external to it gained momentum and international interactions accelerated and expanded, the world began to be molded into a single system of public order. In the seventeenth century, the relatively unipolar European system based on the supremacy of the pope and Christian unity began to develop into a multipolar state system. The loyalties of individuals shifted significantly from family, church, guild, and community to the nation-state, and the nation-state assumed a new authority to discharge security and other functions. This process of transformation climaxed in 1648, when the Peace of Westphalia ended the Thirty Years' War.

Spawned by the spiritual disunity in Christendom, the Peace of Westphalia marked a fundamental shift in the focus of power—from the church to the secular nation-state. A relatively centralized system of public order was transformed into a highly decentralized system, with many contending centers of power. Under this new system, a continuous balancing of power between changing alliances was crucial to maintain minimum public order and to effect the operation of the system.

The great writers regarded as the founding fathers of contemporary international law (Francisco de Vitoria, Hugo Grotius, Christian Wolff, Emmeric de Vattel, and so on) developed a framework of a law of nations appropriate to this new role. They drew on both the law of nature and custom as sources of substantive policy and conceived a process of decision, guided by practical considerations of reciprocity and retaliation, in which individual states were alternately both claimants and decision makers, thereby ensuring that claims be based on at least a modicum of common interest. Consequently, though the peoples of the world lived under the immediate authority of different territorial communities, they were "united in a larger legal community under the rule of a law higher in kind than the law of those bodies."[1] They enjoyed individual rights and had individual duties relating even to human rights or the "rights of man" or "mankind."

The formal institutional structures within the European-based constitutive process developed somewhat slowly. In the wake of the settlement of Vienna of 1815 and the Congress of Aix-la-Chapelle of 1818, a loose system of consultation among the great powers, known as the Concert of Europe, came into being to maintain a precarious peace under a delicate balancing of power. Although the Concert of Europe fell short of institutionalizing permanent structures of authority, it provided a framework for occasional great-power consultations and conferences, demonstrating that the European states shared a larger community interest. This community, with its developing constitutive process, expanded as European empire-building accelerated; its growth found further impetus in the Hague Conferences of 1899 and 1907, whose participants included non-European as well as European states, small as well as great powers.

With the establishment of the Pan-American Union near the end of the nineteenth century, followed by a series of inter-American conferences, the states of the Western hemisphere quickly became a distinctive subgroup within the larger multistate system. In the meantime, various nation-states, responding to the new needs and demands stimulated by the spread of modern science and technology and the new means of transnational communication and transportation, joined to create international governmental organizations specialized to particular values other than power. Both geographic and functional structures of authority gradually grew beyond the confines of the European territorial context to a larger world.

The structures of authority appropriate to a global constitutive process began to emerge only with the advent of the short-lived League of Nations and with its successor, the United Nations. The Covenant of the League of Nations sought to establish a relatively universal and permanent constitutional structure for the larger community of humankind. But the attempt failed; the reasons for the failure and the lessons to be learned have been recounted many times. The successor United Nations, building upon the league's experience, offers a vast and complex network of institutions. This interlocking network contains both highly centralized components to facilitate the making and application of law for multiple and universal purposes and more dispersed components to govern the workings of a host of regional and functional organizations for limited purposes. This immense maze of institutions within the United Nations, reinforced by many other relatively independent intergovernmental organizations, makes up the core structure of representative authority that gives form to the contemporary world constitutive process.

Recent trends in decision and practice suggest modest movement toward greater adequacy in global constitutive process. The end of the Cold War has made way for a new spirit of institutional cooperation and multilateralism. The number of states has increased tremendously, with a rapid expansion from European to non-European states and movement toward universality in participation. The number of democracies has increased. Non-state participants, including private associations specialized in many values, have multiplied and continue to play important roles (and now with increasing formal recognition). The perspectives of all these participants manifest demand not only for a minimum public order to reduce unauthorized coercion but also for an optimum public order to facilitate the largest production and widest possible sharing of all values. In a world of increasing globalization and interdependence, there appears a gradual expansion of identifications with the most inclusive community of human-kind and deepening perception of common interest. The arenas of decision have moved from loose institutionalization to a high degree of institutionalization; diplomatic and diplomatic-parliamentary arenas have been fortified by parliamentary, adjudicative, and executive arenas; sporadic interactions have been replaced by more permanent structures of authority; finally, the geographic distribution of arenas has been improved, ranging from local and national to regional and global.

Turning to bases of power, the trend has been from exclusive to inclusive authority, with erosion of the concept of domestic jurisdiction and expansion of the domain of international concern, and from exclusive to more inclusive control over other values. In relation to strategies, the customary modalities of creating expectations about authority by cooperation have been supplemented by deliberate lawmaking through explicit agreement, especially by parliamentary procedures. In terms of outcomes, the pristine unity of undifferentiated functions has developed into highly differentiated decision functions (that is, intelligence, promotion, prescription, invocation, application, termination, and appraisal), each of which is distinct yet related.

Recalling the myths and realities about international law that were raised in chapter 1, the point must be reiterated that international law is, in fact, law. While many of the preceding pages have documented examples of deviation from the dictates of international law, it is worth remembering that such deviations are the exception. In fact, compliance with international law is overwhelmingly the norm. It is simply that compliance with international law, or any other branch of law, for that matter, is, for obvious and understandable reasons, generally given less coverage, whether in the media or the academy. But this fact should not distract us from the reality that compliance with international law is the norm. Nor should we allow the occasional derivation from this drive us toward the myth that international law is not in fact law.

Achievements and Failures in the Pursuit of Public Order Goals

These trends are encouraging, but how well does the process function? Aside from each feature of the global constitutive process that maintains necessary institutions to perform indispensable functions and the apparent need to improve each feature, the effectiveness of the process must ultimately be judged by the products that flow out of, and are sustained by, it. That is, the effectiveness of the global constitutive process must be appraised not only by each of its operating features but, ultimately, by the flow of public order decisions, representing the aggregate quality of human life, that is achieved.

Public order decisions determine how human rights are protected or deprived; whether the making of community decisions is shared or monopolized; how resources are allocated and developed, and wealth produced and distributed; how information and knowledge are acquired and communicated or denied and impeded; how health, safety, and comfort are fostered or neglected; how acquisition and exercise of skills are promoted or slighted; how family or other intimate personal relations are fostered or neglected; and how norms of responsible conduct and universal justice are cultivated or ignored.

Public order decisions and the constitutive process constantly interact and reinforce each other. Thus, any meaningful appraisal must raise this fundamental question: To what extent are the overriding public order goals of minimum and optimum world order expressed in the ongoing flow of public order decisions that relate to different value processes?

The goals of both minimum and optimum world order, as discussed in chapter 6, have been clearly projected, in varying degrees of generality, to guide the making and application of international law. Minimum order, in the sense of minimizing unauthorized coercion and violence, is commonly expressed in terms of peace and security. Optimum order, in the sense of widest possible shaping and sharing of values, has been expressed in such equivalent terms as human dignity, justice, development, human rights, and quality of life.

The pursuit of minimum world order has been a magnificent obsession of humankind. Unhappily, the global constitutive process has failed to marshal and establish sufficient control over individual nation-states to preclude recourse to unauthorized coercion and violence. Although humankind has managed to avoid a third world war or a nuclear holocaust for the past six decades, the minimum order that exists is extremely precarious. Although it is widely assumed that war has no place under contemporary international law, armed conflicts and coercion of various scales (regional, national, and local) persist in many parts of the world. Witness, for example, the savagery of the conflicts in the former Yugoslavia, Rwanda, and Sudan. Likewise, the justifications for the invasion of Iraq in 2003 by the U.S.-led "coalition of the willing," as based on Security Council Resolutions 660, 678, and so on, have been highly controversial. "Just wars" of the past have been increasingly replaced by wars of religious and ethnic rivalry in our time. Terrorist activities have become alarmingly common and destructive in the past decade and have been carried out in locations that had previously been widely considered safe from such violence. Most notable are the attacks on the United States in September of 2001; the 2004 bombings in Madrid, Spain; the 2004 school siege in Belsan, North Ossetia; the 2005 bombings on London's mass transit system; the 2008 attack on a hotel in Mumbai, India; and the 2013 Boston Marathon bombing. These and other terrorist activities, regardless of their scale or the aspirations of their perpetrators, threaten not only specific targets but the innocent public writ large and have generated a considerable personal sense of "international anarchy."

In the pursuit of an optimum order, the peoples of the world, both elite and rank and file, have invoked, with varying intensity and specificity, various catchwords, including development, modernization, nation-building, quality of life, human rights, ecology, a new international economic order, a new world communication and information order, a humane order, and so on. Whatever their preferences in catchwords and whatever their differences in cultural traditions and institutional practices, the peoples of the world are today increasingly demanding the greater production and wider distribution of all basic values. They demand effective participation in the shaping and sharing of all basic values: respect, power, enlightenment, well-being, wealth, skill, affection, and rectitude. They demand a fundamental freedom of choice to participate in different value processes, equality that minimizes discrimination on grounds irrelevant to personal capabilities and maximizes effective opportunity, and a large domain of personal autonomy (respect). They demand full participation as persons in the processes of both authoritative decision making and effective power sharing (power). They seek freedom to acquire, to use, and to communicate information and knowledge (enlightenment). They seek health, safety, and comfort (well-being). They seek access to goods and services (wealth). They demand the freedom to discover, to mature, and to exercise latent talents (skill). They seek to establish and enjoy congenial personal relationships (affection). They demand freedom to form, express, and maintain norms of responsible conduct (rectitude). They demand, in the aggregate, human security.

But what are the contemporary realities? To what extent are their rising demands for protection and fulfillment satisfied? A cursory look at daily events around the world shows that deprivations and nonfulfillments continue to characterize the value-institutional processes of vast segments of the world's population. Though the nature, scope, and magnitude of the values at stake may differ from one community to another, the deprivations and nonfulfillments extend to every value sector.

Examples are dramatic. The demand for freedom of choice, for equality, and for personal autonomy meets with persistent discrimination on such invidious grounds as race, sex, religion, and political opinion, and the massive invasion of the civic domain of personal autonomy. The demand to share power meets with the persistence of totalitarian or authoritarian regimes, one-party rule and military dictatorships, martial "law," arbitrary arrest, detention, censure, imprisonment, and torture in many police states; restrictions on emigration and immigration; ethnic cleansing and mass and collective expulsion of aliens. The search for enlightenment encounters suppression of political dissent, widespread censorship by official elites, inadequate education for children and women, and systematic indoctrination as an instrument of policy. The search for well-being is blunted by overpopulation, hunger and starvation, and deprivations of life caused by war, oppression, terrorist activities, ecocide, and genocide. A striving for wealth faces poverty in developed as well as developing nations and the widening gap between rich and poor. The demand for skill development must cope with consequences of skill obsolescence due to technological advances, brain drain, unemployment, and underemployment. The quest for affection (family and other congenial personal relationships) encounters family disruptions, personal hostility, homelessness, and loneliness. Longings for a moral integrity meet with denial of freedom of worship, intolerance and persecution of religious minorities, and massacres and warfare involving religious fanatics. Demands for human security encounter the stark reality of pervasive insecurity and uncertainty in a turbulent world marked by rapid change and glaring disparities in the shaping of wealth, enlightenment, and other values.

The Arab Spring illustrates these conflicting processes. Encouraged by the largely nonviolent overthrow of the Ben Ali regime in Tunisia, popular movements spread throughout the Middle East and Northern Africa. While some of these movements sought reform within the existing structures of power, as in Bahrain, others have sought wholesale change in leadership, such as in Tunisia, Egypt, Libya, and Syria. Though difficult to generalize, at least one common feature unites them: there is a popular demand for greater shaping and sharing of power and other values. Perhaps more than any other factor, the differences between these movements have been dictated by the reactions of those whose power has been threatened. Also important to note, the degree of violence in each movement has been immense. In Tunisia and Egypt, the regimes of both Ben Ali and Mubarak were quick to relinquish power, despite having responded initially with violence. In Egypt, Mubarak's ouster at first begot mass celebrations; however, the administration of its next president, Mohamed Morsi, was overcome by fresh protests, and within a year, the Egyptian military seized power and suspended the country's newly adopted constitution. The military again resorted to violent means to suppress protesters who continued to press for reforms. Although the situation has stabilized, and plans have been envisioned for reinstating the constitution, it would appear that the people will continue to struggle for their goals in the immediate future. The Libyan revolution, by contrast, turned into a civil war requiring the aid of NATO to help oust Muammar Gaddafi, who was subsequently killed. The response in Syria has been similarly dramatic, with the military remaining loyal to President Bashar al-Assad and regularly resorting to violence to quash popular protests and opposition in what has become a protracted civil war. The Arab League has played a notable role in addressing the situation in Syria in conjunction with the United Nations, imposing sanctions and urging Syria's leadership to cease its crackdown. In 2013, an international outcry over the regime's use of chemical weapons against the opposition forces led to negotiations in which the Syrian government agreed to hand over its chemical weapons stockpiles. The weapons were planned to be destroyed under the supervision of the international community, led by a joint mission of the United Nations and the Organisation for the Prohibition of Chemical Weapons.

The Arab Spring can be used as a case study to understand both the achievements and failures in pursuing minimum and optimum world order. Regarding optimum world order, in countries that have overthrown long-standing authoritarian regimes, such as Tunisia, Egypt, and Libya, the potential exists for new power structures that are more respectful of their citizens' demands for dignity and a greater role in political participation and in the shaping and sharing of other values. However, officials' refusal to respond to the demands of the people presents an ongoing challenge in the movement toward democracy in the region.

In terms of minimum world order, the Arab Spring has led to significant deliberations over the appropriate use of coercion on the part of the international community. Though protests were many times quelled by state-backed violence, protesters largely refrained from engaging in violence themselves. And in a positive development for the establishment of minimum world order, in Libya, where the international community was heavily involved, intervention was only undertaken with the explicit endorsement of the U.N. Security Council (as well as the Arab League). At the present moment, however, a similar consensus has yet to emerge in regard to Syria, where equivocation on the part of some nations has prevented a unified military approach that could hasten the end of the country's civil war.

Conditions Affecting World Order

The conditions that have at times produced disparities between the rising common demands of people for human dignity values and the degree of their achievement are both environmental and predispositional. These sets of factors are in constant interplay.

Among the most important environmental factors are population, resources, and institutional arrangements and practices.

The explosive growth of the population is one of the most striking trends in human history. The population of the world today is characterized by massive numbers, continued high rates of growth, and uneven distribution, both globally and nationally. Whereas it took at least a million years for human numbers to reach the billion mark, it took only one hundred thirty years for the second billion and thirty years for the third billion. According to recent population projections, the world population of 4.8 billion in 1985 grew to 7 billion by 2012, and will increase to at least 9 billion by 2050.[2] The problem of numbers is compounded by the concentration of high growth rates in developing countries that are already congested, poor, and possessed of the least capacity and resources to absorb the increased population. More than two-thirds of today's people inhabit the developing regions, and more than 90 percent of the projected increases in the coming decades is expected in these regions. The implications of the population explosion are not confined to the Malthusian dimension of food supply but extend to the quality of life in every value sector. In the words of Professor Harold Lasswell:

> Uncontrolled population growth is expected to impair the aggregate output of values in every sector of society and to sharpen inequalities of distribution everywhere. An overcrowded world can be expected to swing between extremes of political conflict and massive apathy, and between exaggerated personal hostility and indifference. The control of values such as enlightenment, wealth, skill, and respect will be concentrated in the control of a few. From shortages of food and medicare will rise crises of malnutrition, disease, and defect. As numbers multiply and competition intensifies, human conduct will grow progressively egocentric and socially irresponsible.[3]

Although human numbers annually increase significantly, the amount of natural resources available to sustain the growing population, to eradicate mass poverty, and to improve the quality of human lives remains finite. Indeed, the natural resources of the world appear to be diminishing in quantity and deteriorating in quality, as dramatized by the energy and ecological crises. Resources are unevenly distributed, and discrepancies in the pattern of resource consumption are glaring. The energy crisis in past years and the host of problems it exacerbated (rampant inflation, monetary instability, uncontrolled deficit, mass unemployment) underscore the potential threats of impairment of resources on the enjoyment and fulfillment of all values. Similarly, massive diversion of resources for purposes of military overkill or oppression at a time of global ecological crisis dramatizes vividly the dangerous consequences of the mismanagement of resources. Military expenditures worldwide continue to reach mind-boggling figures, despite the Cold War's end. A steady flow of conventional arms continues to find its way to Third World countries, causing death and destruction, even as certain other countries reduce their military establishments. Yet without stronger efforts and expenditures toward methods for sustainable development, potentially disastrous consequences from global warming and deforestation loom on the horizon.

Confronted with the unprecedented challenges of our planetary ecosystem, the institutions and practices of humankind appear to be inadequate. Geographically, these value institutions and practices are too state-centered. Functionally, they are too tradition-bound to make timely responses and adjustments to the accelerated change, both in pace and dimension, as generated by the universalization of science and technology and the ever-intensifying global interdependence. The problems in the contemporary world are global in nature and scale, yet the basic organizational framework to deal with them continues to rest on the problem-solving capacities of separate and highly unequal states and thus remains essentially partial and fragmentary. The ascendancy of the nation-state has been such that the search for common interest is more often than not distorted by the inordinate emphasis on national "sovereignty."

Closely linked to the inadequacies of the institutional arrangements and practices in meeting the contemporary challenges in the pursuit of human dignity values are basic predispositional factors, which include the more fundamental demands, identifications, and expectations of the peoples of the world. And the aggregate pattern of demands, expectations, and identifications is deeply affected by the maximization postulate. According to this postulate, people act in social process, both consciously and unconsciously, in such a way as to maximize all basic values, and they adopt one course of action rather than another as guided by their expectations about net advantage.

The peoples of the world, whatever their differences in cultural traditions and institutional practices, are intensifying their demands to participate in shaping and sharing all basic values of human dignity. In a world marked by stark contrasts in rights and development, however, many popular demands tend to express special rather than common interests. Unable to clarify and agree on common interests, some peoples tend to be preoccupied with short-term, separate payoffs rather than long-term, aggregate consequences.

Attenuated conceptions of common interest are sustained by, and in turn foster, systems of identification that give primacy to national loyalties rather than to common humanity. The advent of cities broke the earliest syndromes of parochialism, reaching back to the family and the tribe, and facilitated identifications with the public order of civilized states. In recent times the nation-state has become the prime symbol around which collective identifications are fanned. With nationalism continuing to run high, nation-states, old and new alike, compete intensely to exact loyalties from individuals, and national identities have gained such primacy as often to inhibit the growth of more inclusive identities, especially those associated with common humanity. This vigorous syndrome of national parochialism has contributed not insignificantly to further fragmenting an already divided world.

Fragmented identifications have been sustained and fortified by persisting and widespread assumptions that, whether we like it or not, many conflicts will be settled by violence and coercion. Living under the perpetual threat of violence, most peoples (both elite and rank and file) are highly insecure, manifesting a pervasive sense of frustration over the inability to eradicate or deal effectively with armed conflicts, terrorism, and other forms of coercion. Too often measures that deprive individuals and groups and deny them fulfillment of basic values are justified and condoned because of chronic obsession with internal and external disorder. Gripped by anxieties and a keen sense of vulnerability, the effective elites are hypersensitive about openly initiating a change in world public order that would appear to subordinate them to other powers. They tend to be preoccupied with calculations of short-term payoffs and their own value positions rather than long-term aggregate gain. The peoples of the world exhibit varying degrees of realism about the conditions under which human dignity values can be fulfilled. They often fail to perceive the fact and the depth of contemporary interdependencies or to take them seriously and thus fail to explore, articulate, and implement common interests.

Indeed, the global interdependencies, in all their manifestations and dimensions, as they affect the aggregate pattern of human life on this planet, are still not sufficiently understood or taken seriously enough. Business as usual and obsolete institutions and practices are allowed to drift. The quality of life of every human now depends on many factors that operate beyond community and national boundaries. The interdependencies of peoples transnationally within a particular value process inexorably form a matrix with the interdependencies of peoples everywhere as between different value processes. In an earth-space arena in which the means of mass destruction threaten all civilization, no people can be secure in the shaping and sharing of values unless all peoples are secure.

Projections of Future World Order

Looking toward the future, what developments for world order are likely? What will the new trends be in the twenty-first century? Will there be few changes to life as we know it now? Or will the international community continue to advance and strive in its ultimate search for world peace and cooperation? Will the United States continue to play an even more active role in the international arena? And if so, will that be tolerated?

To contemplate the future is to allow the mind to assess possibilities in terms of probable occurrence. The trend, not the instance, is the distinctive emphasis in this projective thinking, concerned as it is with an estimate of the probability that significant features of a social context will stay the same or change in stated direction.

Probable developments cannot be realistically projected in terms of "inevitability" or of simple-minded extrapolation of the past. The continuation of past events depends on the total configuration of the many variables that may or may not support the direction and intensity of the trend. One useful tool is what Professor Lasswell has called "developmental constructs," which range through a broad spectrum of possibilities from the most optimistic to the most pessimistic.[4]

Central to our concern is whether future world order will move toward or away from the values, practices, and institutions of human dignity. To project most comprehensively, two basic constructs might be developed. The optimistic construct envisages a continuing progress toward a world public order of human dignity, which will foster, with minimal organized coercion and control, the wide shaping and sharing of power and other values, based on a more inclusive sense of identification and a deepening perception of the common interest. The pessimistic construct imagines a regressive movement toward a world public order of garrison-prison states that will be characterized by increasing power concentration, governmental regimentation, militarization, and Orwellian manipulation, as sustained by heavy coercion and control.

Which way will future world order move? Signals are somewhat mixed as judged by historic trends. From the trend away from caste societies, through the spread of urban civilization, to increasing globalization and interdependence, the tempo of change in human affairs has accelerated, due in no small measure to the universalization of science and science-based technology. Together they have contributed to a deepening shared perception about the common interest of all members of the human race in a common destiny and have inspired an abiding faith in the beneficent potential of science and technology and in the capacity of human intelligence and judgment.

But the drift toward a massive garrison state may be more than episodic; hierarchical barriers in power, wealth, and other value positions may become self-fulfilling and self-perpetuating, as fueled by continued expectations of violence. These expectations, fed by unyielding perceptions of threats and enemies from "across," "below," or "above," will continue to generate high levels of festering anxiety and personal insecurity for elites and nonelites alike. Instead of releasing the enormous potential of science and technology for constructive uses, people more often than not manipulate them so that they serve as instruments of control, oppression, and tyranny. Witness, for example, the growing threats to the individual in the form of physical, psychological, and data surveillance, as well as hacking and other invasions of privacy.

The mixed signals notwithstanding, the future clearly is not predetermined. The projection of future contingencies may help increase the likelihood that humankind can avoid the undesirable and achieve the desirable. The course of development depends on the constellation of factors, both predispositional and environmental, in the emerging context. It is largely within the power of people to make choices to shape the constellation of factors and to affect future developments in preferred ways. The actions and inactions of each actor will have consequences.

Alternatives for a World Order of Human Dignity: A Grand Strategy of Simultaneity and Total Mobilization

What alternatives are available to us for moving toward a world community of human dignity? Are the only options a world government or the mindless drifting of the status quo dominated by the "sovereign" nation-states? Professor Myres McDougal has incisively observed:

> There is of course no dearth in recommendation, either ancient or modern, about how global constitutive process and public order might be changed for the better. For centuries philosophers, clerics, and kings have proffered plans for perpetual peace, and contemporary proposals for world government, and lesser modifications of the existing anarchy, abound. Some of these proposals envisage grandiose transformations in the structures and processes of authoritative and effective power, others, in contrast, are characterized by concern for small changes about particular problems in incremental, cosmetic gimmickry. The difficulty with the grandiose approach is that its proponents seldom offer the hands and feet necessary to put the vast changes

they recommend into reality; the difficulty with the more humble approach is that the proponents of fragmented and anecdotal options offer little other than hands and feet, or isolated features of rule and procedure, without adequate relation to the larger processes of authoritative decision and effective power. Considered comprehensively most of the proposals share a but modest regard for the context of clarifying policies and conditions which affects both rationality and acceptability.[5]

Of the many proposals, the efforts of the World Order Models Project (WOMP), as represented by Richard A. Falk, Saul H. Mendlovitz, and others, were especially noteworthy.[6] The project, initiated in 1968, sought to promote a just world order by assembling scholars, intellectuals, and activists from various parts of the world to undertake research, publication, education, and other promotional activities. Perceiving the contemporary world as beset by such complex and interrelated problems as war, poverty, social injustice, ecological instability, and alienation, they employ an analytic-ethical scheme of inquiry, organizing around the basic themes of peace, economic well-being, social justice, ecological stability, positive identity, and meaningful participation. The project helped to transnationalize the world order inquiry, even though its inability to come to grips with the complex problems of transition has opened it to charges of idealism and utopianism. Instead of being preoccupied with the formal authoritative institutions rooted in the state-centric system, it has paid increasing attention to social movements and grassroots initiatives.

The choice open to humankind in future world order is by no means an either-or option. It is not one of simple dichotomy: either a world controlled solely by sovereign nation-states or a world government supplanting all the existing nation-states. The period of transition will be a continuing process, long and halting.

True, nation-states remain the predominant participants in the contemporary world arena. Yet it is well to remember that the "omnipotent" nation-state is but one of many structures that are created and maintained by human beings to protect and realize their interests. As a shield for individuals against the tyranny and exploitation of feudal lords, the nation-state was widely perceived to be the structure most appropriate for obtaining a more secure and fulfilling life for humankind. When the nation-state fails to serve adequately such common interest, its ongoing role cannot escape scrutiny in light of competing institutions.

Our world is one of pluralism and diversity. It is a global arena in which major powers, intermediate powers, small states, and mini-states coexist, along with a multiplicity of non-state actors operating at different community levels: global, regional, national, and local. States and non-state participants (groups and individuals) constantly interact under changing conditions. This has been and will be the course in the foreseeable future. The operations of the nation-states are modulated by the functional imperatives of interdependence, interdetermination, and human survival and by functional cooperation across state boundaries.

Even with the problems of imbalances caused by the explosive world population, unevenly distributed, in relation to the uneven distribution of limited resources, the present state of affairs can be improved, given the enormous potential released by advances and universalization of science-based technology in communication and other fields. The success in realizing the Millennium Development Goals (MDGs) will be a testimony to such collective human will and endeavor.

The marriage of the computer to communication technologies has given ordinary people access to an arsenal of gadgets from highly functional laptop and tablet computers to inexpensive smartphones that have obliterated the barriers of time and space and increasingly offered the individual portable and near limitless access to knowledge and information (making its acquisition a matter of private choice for a large number of the world's citizens) and participation in other value processes (such as wealth and power). The information revolution of our time, with the constant interplay of all the information media (aural, verbal, and visual), offers a step toward an abundance of information of universal availability, characterized by both massification and individualization of content. Increasingly, thanks to the Internet and digitization, a person can choose to draw his or her private stock of knowledge more easily and economically from the total information accumulated by humankind. New electronic storage systems interlinked globally provide not only accessibility but a renewed sense of the unity of humankind.

While advances in information technology have been distributed around the globe more equitably than other resources, there still remains a "digital divide" between developed and developing economies. This digital divide operates at numerous levels. At the most basic, access to newly emerging technologies is disparate and largely coincides with relative wealth. As a general rule, personal access to the Internet (i.e., home access) and other information technology advances is the rule in developed economies. While Internet access is generally available around the globe, in developing economies this access may be realized only in public settings, such as Internet cafes or community centers. Another element of the digital divide is speed of access, with the speed being substantially greater in developed economies with more advanced information technology infrastructures. Even within developed economies, such as the United States, speed of access is uneven, as for example the relative unavailability of high-speed Internet access in many rural areas.

Another important element of the digital divide is the relative freedom of access. Whereas factors relating to access generally correspond to the relative state of economic development, freedom of access to the Internet roughly corresponds to the availability of other personal freedoms (for example, democratic participation in the political process, freedom of speech, and freedom of the process). In many places, state-sponsored censorship of the Internet has severely curtailed the promise of advances in information technology. China's so-called Great Firewall has received the most attention in this respect, but many other states pursue similar Internet-blocking strategies.

To what extent can the potential benefits of the universalizing science and technology be shared by the whole of humankind? Decisions affecting institutional arrangements and practice are crucial. New technologies of communication and development, as in other areas, are inextricably connected with the pattern of human institutions and practice. In the face of the unprecedented challenge facing humankind, can the elites of the world transcend national parochialism and the demand of special interests (for example, monopoly of power in the guise of the public interest, or national interest) to act together for the common interest, from short-term, mid-term, and long-term perspectives? Will they even be surpassed as increased access and participation obviate some institutional arrangements?

The advance in science-based technology cannot be reversed; it reflects a general tendency toward universalization. There is no escape from technological advance. It is important to seize what science-based technology has offered humankind, not to retreat from it, and to make wise policy choices and necessary institutional adaptations in response to the pressing challenges of global interdependence. And the sooner the better. Demands for new world orders in economic development—in communication and information, in political development, in global environment, in human rights, and so on—have underlined the dynamics of global interdependencies and deepened the shared sense of interdependence. Can the traditional human institutions and practices centered on individual nation-states be modified to respond to these challenges? The choice is vital. The existing dependency, imbalance, and inequalities manifested in the contemporary global social process should be redressed, through concerted effort, so that viable communities with adequate resources can be maintained, affording optimum opportunities to shape and share values for all human beings, in whatever community (earth-based or in future space settings) they may live.

To enhance the wide shaping and sharing of values, amid the rising debate about the shape of world order to come, it is crucial that the fundamental freedom of choice to participate in all value processes be sustained and fortified. The increasing concern for the interests of particular states must not come at the expense of the classic concern for individual freedom and fulfillment and must make no mistake about the concern of officials who feign to represent the state at the expense of their people.

The way to foster a new and equitable world order is not to erode, dilute, or hamper this fundamental policy for freedom of choice and other human rights. The key, rather, is positive facilitation by making pertinent technology, knowledge, and resources available to all and by increasing the capacity of development and communication at every community level.

Recall that international law is a continuing process of authoritative decision through which the common interests of the members of the human community are clarified and reclarified, fashioned and refashioned. It impacts all members of the global community, elites and nonelites alike.

Confronted with the stark reality of the global effective power process, as punctuated by the tremendous disparities in the effective power of individual nation-states, the elites of the world must be made to realize that they have more to gain by cooperating with one another than by destroying one another. Education of ordinary people is equally important, because the differences in personality, class, interest, culture, and crisis experience are real, but the barriers can be overcome through genuine enlightenment and mutual understanding. This immense task is made increasingly feasible with the proliferation of technologies that multiply opportunities for individual contact. Facilitated by the Internet and the transmission of all forms of media, a new community of humankind is being mediated in double time by the vast flow of universalized symbols and globally shared experiences accessible to all.

What is required is a grand strategy of simultaneity that would mobilize all participants—groups and individuals—to the common task of human survival and fulfillment.

Human history cannot start from a clean slate (barring, of course, a nuclear holocaust). Humankind must build its future on past legacies and present conditions. Although grand visions and incremental improvement can accompany the perpetual process of transition, the ultimate task is to educate and mobilize all citizens of the world.

Just as control of weapons of mass destruction is too important to leave to politicians alone, so is international law too important to be a monopoly for international lawyers and decision makers. What is crucial is to mobilize all available technology and resources of enlightenment and communication, using every available network, forum, and opportunity, to wage a continuous worldwide citizenship education.

Genuine protection and fulfillment of human dignity values will be possible only when necessary conditions are created and maintained to enable individuals to be effective, active, equal participants in the social processes at different community levels and in different social settings. Most fundamentally, it requires education, not in the narrow construction of classroom teaching, but in the broadest possible sense. The people all over the world must be educated in ways that will enable them to make informed choices and judgments for participation so that they can interact meaningfully with others and participate in the community processes both as communicator and communicatee in ways that serve policy goals. Individuals must be educated in such a way as to allow them to participate meaningfully in the development and implementation of international law.

Individuals need not be the mere passive recipients of messages directed by the top elite; they must be able to think and speak for themselves. A new world order must move toward making the individual person a communicating being who can think, choose, participate, and express—think freely with adequate access to the stock of human knowledge and information; choose freely and intelligently; express opinions and ideas freely; and participate effectively in all other value processes. Citizens of the world must be made to think globally, temporally, contextually, and creatively.

Think globally to meet the challenge of global interdependence and interdetermination. The quest for a world order of human dignity that promotes both minimum and optimum world order requires sustained global thinking and collaboration.

Think temporally not only about the present generation but also about future generations. Responsible decision making, national as well as transnational, requires that concern be extended to long-term aggregate consequences as well as short-term effects for human survival and solidarity and for the totality of the global environment for this and succeeding generations.

Think contextually to relate decision making to all community levels and all value sectors of social interaction. No people can be secure until all peoples are secure, and no contemporary community can endure and thrive in seclusion and isolation from the rest of the world.

Think creatively in the common interest to mobilize all available intellectual skills toward solving problems in the pursuit of both minimum world order and optimum world order. Just as all human problems are created by human beings, so can they be managed and solved by human beings, no matter how formidable particular problems may be. The quest for the common interest of all humanity toward a world community of human dignity calls for ingenuity, goodwill, vigilant endeavor, and boundless creativity.

So too must elites be educated. Education of the elites must stress the importance of compliance with international law. As has already been stated, compliance with international law is the rule, noncompliance the exception. Elites must be made to appreciate that compliance with international law is in their own enlightened self-interest. Education of this sort takes place through the implementation of the sanctioning goals discussed in chapter 24. Especially significant in this respect has been the trend toward imposition of individual criminal accountability for breaches of international law, discussed in chapter 29.

Likewise, the education that is required under the grand strategy must not be narrowly focused only on individuals. Rather, it must also seek to raise collective consciousness. It is only through such collective education that parochial national interests will yield and a world community of human dignity will prevail.

A new world order should be a new order of human dignity, in which persuasion prevails over coercion and in which the wide shaping and sharing of all cherished values are secured and fulfilled. It should be a new world order embracing both minimum and optimum world order, in which human beings are at the very center, and where human security is supreme.

Notes

1. WALTER SCHIFFER, THE LEGAL COMMUNITY OF MANKIND 46 (2d ed. 1954).

2. Press Release: World Population to Exceed 9 Billion by 2050, United Nations Population Division, Mar. 11, 2009, *available at* http://www.un.org/esa/population/publications/wpp2008/pressrelease.pdf.

3. Harold Lasswell, *Population Change and Policy Science: Proposed Workshops on Reciprocal Impact Analysis, in* POLICY SCIENCES AND POPULATION 117, 118 (Warren F. Ilchman et al. eds., 1975).

4. *See* HAROLD LASSWELL, WORLD POLITICS AND PERSONAL INSECURITY (1935; 1965); HAROLD LASSWELL, A PRE-VIEW OF POLICY SCIENCES 67–69 (1971). *See also* Heinz Eulau, *H.D. Laswell's Developmental Analysis*, 11 W. POL. Q. 229 (1958).

5. Myres McDougal, *International Law and the Future*, 50 MISS. L.J. 259, 330–31 (1979).

6. *See, e.g.*, RICHARD FALK, A STUDY OF FUTURE WORLDS (1975); JOHAN GALTUNG, THE TRUE WORLDS: A TRANSNATIONAL PERSPECTIVE (1980); TOWARDS A JUST WORLD ORDER (Richard Falk, Samuel Kim, & Saul Mendlovitz eds., 1982).

Bibliography

PART ONE/DELIMITATION OF THE TASK

1. International Law in a Policy-Oriented Perspective

American Law Institute. *Restatement of the Law (Third): The Foreign Relations Law of the United States.* 2 vols. St. Paul, Minn.: American Law Institute, 1987.

American Society of International Law. *International Law in the Twentieth Century.* Edited by Leo Gross. New York: Appleton-Century-Crofts, 1969.

Arsanjani, Mahnoush H., Jacob Katz Cogan, Robert D. Sloane, and Siegfried Wiessner, eds. *Looking to the Future: Essays on International Law in Honor of W. Michael Reisman.* Leiden/ Boston: Martinus Nijhoff Publishers, 2011.

Bederman, David J. *Globalization and International Law.* New York: Palgrave Macmillan, 2008.

Biersteker, Thomas. *International Law and International Relations: Bridging Theory and Practice.* London: Taylor & Francis, 2007.

Bos, Maarten, ed. *The Present State of International Law and Other Essays.* Deventer, Netherlands: Kluwer, 1973.

Boyle, Alan and Christine Chinkin. *The Making of International Law.* New York: Oxford University Press, 2007.

Bradley, Curtis. *International Law in the U.S. Legal System.* New York: Oxford University Press, 2013.

Brierly, J. L. *The Law of Nations.* 6th ed. Edited by Sir Humphrey Waldock. New York and Oxford: Oxford University Press, 1963.

Brownlie, Ian. *Principles of Public International Law.* 5th ed. Oxford: Clarendon Press, 1998.

Brunnée, Jutta and Stephen Toope. *Legitimacy and Legality in International Law: An Interactional Account.* Cambridge: Cambridge University Press, 2010.

Buergenthal, Thomas and Sean D. Murphy. *Public International Law in a Nutshell.* 5th ed. St. Paul, Minn.: West, 2013.

Burley, Anne-Marie Slaughter. "International Law and International Relations Theory: A Dual Agenda." *American Journal of International Law* 87 (1993): 205.

Butler, William E., ed. *International Law in Comparative Perspective.* Alphen aan den Rijn, Netherlands: Sijthoffen Noordhoff, 1980.

Carter, Barry E. and Allen S. Weiner. *International Law.* 6th ed. New York: Aspen Publishers, 2011.

Cassese, Antonio. *International Law.* 2d ed. New York: Oxford University Press, 2005.

Cassese, Antonio. *International Law in a Divided World.* Oxford: Clarendon Press, 1994.

Charlesworth, Hilary and Christine Chinkin, *The Boundaries of International Law: A Feminist Analysis.* Manchester University Press, 2000.

Chen, Lung-chu. "Constitutional Law and International Law in the United States of America." *American Journal of Comparative Law, Supplement* 42 (1994): 453.

Cheng, Tai-Heng. *When International Law Works: Realistic Idealism After 9/11 and the Global Recession.* New York: Oxford University Press, 2012.

Chinkin, Christine and Alan Boyle. *The Making of International Law.* Oxford University Press, 2007.

Clapham, Andrew. *Brierly's Law of Nations: An Introduction to the Role of International Law in International Relations.* 7th ed. New York: Oxford University Press, 2012.

Conforti, Benedetto and Angelo Labella. *An Introduction to International Law.* Leiden/ Boston: Martinus Nijhoff, 2012.

Crawford, James. *Brownlie's Principles of Public International Law.* 8th ed. New York: Oxford University Press, 2012.

D'Amato, Anthony. *International Law: Process and Prospect.* Dobbs Ferry, N.Y.: Transnational Publishers, 1987.

Damrosch, Lori F., Louis Henkin, Sean D. Murphy, and Hans Smit. *International Law: Cases and Materials.* 5th ed. St. Paul, Minn.: West, 2009.

De Visscher, Charles. *Theory and Reality in Public International Law.* Rev. ed. Translated by P. E. Corbett. Princeton, N.J.: Princeton University Press, 1968.

Dixon, Martin. *Textbook on International Law.* 7th ed. New York: Oxford University Press, 2013.

Dunoff, J., and S. Ratner. *International Law: Norms, Actors, Process: A Problem Oriented Approach.* 3d ed. New York: Aspen Publishers, 2010.

Evans, Malcolm David. *International Law.* New York: Oxford University Press, 2006.

Falk, Richard A. *The Status of Law in International Society.* Princeton, N.J.: Princeton University Press, 1970.

Falk, Richard, Friedrich Kratochwil, and Saul H. Mendlovitz, eds. *International Law: A Contemporary Perspective.* Boulder, Colo.: Westview Press, 1985.

Guzman, Andrew T. *How International Law Works: A Rational Choice Theory.* New York: Oxford University Press, 2008.

Hathaway, Oona A. and Harold Hongju Koh. *Foundations of International Law and Politics.* New York: Foundation Press, 2004.

Head, John W. "Supranational Law: How the Move Toward Multilateral Solutions Is Changing the Character of International Law." *Kansas Law Review* 42 (1994): 601.

Henkin, Louis. *How Nations Behave: Law and Foreign Policy*. 2d ed. New York: Columbia University Press, 1979.

Higgins, Rosalyn. *Problems and Process: International Law and How We Use It*, Oxford University Press, 1995.

Higgins, Rosalyn. *Themes and Theories: Selected Essays, Speeches, and Writings in International Law*. 2 vols. Oxford University Press, 2009.

Janis, Mark W. *International Law*. 6th ed. New York: Aspen Publishers, 2012.

Janis, Mark W. and John Noyes. *International Law: Cases and Commentary*. 4th ed. New York: Foundation Press, 2010.

Jennings, Robert and Arthur Watts. *Oppenheim's International Law*. Vol. 1. 9th ed. Harlow, Essex, England: Longmans Group, 1992.

Johnstone, Ian. *The Power of Deliberation: International Law, Politics and Organizations*. New York: Oxford University Press, 2011.

Koh, Harold Hongju. "Why Do Nations Obey International Law? Review Essay: The New Sovereignty: Compliance with International Regulatory Agreements by Abram and Antonia Handler Chayes." *Yale Law Journal* 106 (1997): 2599.

Koh, Harold Hongju. "Is There a 'New' New Haven School of International Law?" *Yale Journal of International Law* 32 (2007): 559,

Kirgis, Frederic L. *The American Society of International Law's First Century, 1906–2006*. Leiden/Boston: Martinus Nijhoff Publishers, 2006.

Lasswell, Harold D. *A Pre-View of Policy Sciences*. New York: American Elsevier Publishing Co., 1971.

Lasswell, Harold D. and Myres S. McDougal. *Jurisprudence for a Free Society: Studies in Law, Science, and Policy*. 2 vols. New Haven, Conn.: New Haven Press; Dordrecht: Martinus Nijhoff, 1992.

Macdonald, R. St. J., and Douglas M. Johnston, eds. *The Structure and Process of International Law: Essays in Legal Philosophy, Doctrine, and Theory*. Dordrecht: Martinus Nijhoff, 1986.

McDougal, Myres S. and W. Michael Reisman. *International Law Essays: A Supplement to International Law in Contemporary Perspective*. Mineola, N.Y.: Foundation Press, 1981.

Murphy, Sean D. *Principles of International Law*. 2d ed. St. Paul, Minn.: West, 2012.

Nollkaemper, Andre and Janne Nijman. *New Perspectives on the Divide Between National and International Law*. New York: Oxford University Press, 2007.

Noyes, John E., Laura A. Dickinson, and Mark W. Janis. *International Law Stories*. New York: Foundation Press, 2007.

O'Connell, Mary Ellen. *The Power and Purpose of International Law: Insights from the Theory and Practice of Enforcement*. New York: Oxford University Press, 2008.

O'Connell, Mary Ellen, Richard F. Scott, and Naomi Roht-Arriaza. *The International Legal System: Cases and Materials*. 6th ed. New York: Foundation Press, 2010.

Paust, Jordan. *International Law as Law of the United States*. 2d ed. Carolina Academic Press, 2003.

Paust, Jordan J., Jon M. Van Dyke, and Linda A. Malone. *International Law and Litigation in the U.S.* 3d ed. St. Paul, Minn.: West, 2009.

Reimann, Mathias W., James C. Hathaway, Timothy L. Dickinson, and Joel H. Samuels. *Transnational Law: Cases and Materials*. St. Paul, Minn.: West, 2013.

Reisman, W. Michael. *Jurisprudence: Understanding and Shaping Law*. With Aaron M. Schreiber. New Haven, Conn.: New Haven Press, 1987.

Reisman, W. Michael. *International Law Essays*. Co-edited with Myres S. McDougal. Mineola, N.Y.: Foundation Press, 1981.

Reisman, W. Michael. *International Law in Contemporary Perspective*. 2d ed. With Mahnoush H. Arsanjani, Siegfried Wiessner, and Gayl S. Westerman. New York: Foundation Press, 2004.

Reisman, W. Michael. *The Quest for World Order and Human Dignity in the Twenty-First Century: Constitutive Process and Individual Commitment (General Course on Public International Law)*. Leiden/Boston: Martinus Nijhoff Publishers, 2012.

Reisman, W. Michael. *Toward World Order and Human Dignity: Essays in Honor of Myres S. McDougal*. Co-edited with Burns Weston. New York: Free Press, 1976.

Reisman, W. Michael and Andrew R. Willard, eds. *International Incidents: the Law that Counts in World Politics*. Princeton: Princeton University Press, 1988.

Scharf, Michael and Paul Williams. *Shaping Foreign Policy in Times of Crisis: The Role of International Law and the State Department Legal Adviser*. Cambridge: Cambridge University Press, 2010.

Shaw, Malcolm N. *International Law*. 6th ed. Cambridge University Press, 2008.

Slaughter, Anne-Marie *The Methods of International Law*. Edited with Steven R. Ratner. American Society of International Law Studies in Transnational Legal Policy, 2004.

Sloss, David, Michael Ramsey, and William Dodge. *International Law in the U.S. Supreme Court: Continuity and Change*. Cambridge: Cambridge University Press, 2011.

Tomuschat, Christian and Jean-Marc Thouvenin. *The Fundamental Rules of the International Legal Order: Jus Cogens and Obligations Erga Omnes*. The Hague: Martinus Nijhoff, 2006.

Triggs, Gillian. *International Law: Contemporary Principles and Practices*. LexisNexis Butterworths, 2006.

Weston, Burns H., Richard A. Falk, Hilary Charlesworth, and Andrew L. Strauss. *International Law and World Order: A Problem-Oriented Coursebook*. 4th ed. St. Paul, Minn.: West, 2006.

PART TWO/PARTICIPANTS

2. Nation-States

Agrawala, S. K., T. S. Rama Rao, and J. N. Saxena, eds. *New Horizons of International Law and Developing Countries*. Bombay: N. M. Tripathi, 1983.

Anand, R. P., ed. *Asian States and the Development of Universal International Law*. Delhi: Vikas, 1972.

Ando, Nisuke. "The Recognition of Governments Reconsidered." *Japanese Annual of International Law* 28 (1985): 29.

Bayefsky, Anne. *Self-Determination in International Law: Quebec and Lessons Learned — Legal Opinions*. The Hague: Martinus Nijhoff, 2000.

Buchheit, Lee C. *Secession: The Legitimacy of Self-Determination*. New Haven, Conn.: Yale University Press, 1978.

Cassese, Antonio. *Self-Determination of Peoples: A Legal Reappraisal.* Cambridge and New York: Cambridge University Press, 1995.

Chen, Lung-chu, ed. *Membership for Taiwan in the United Nations: Achieving Justice and Universality.* New York: New Century Institute Press, 2007.

Chen, Lung-chu. "Self-Determination as a Human Right." *Toward World Order and Human Dignity.* Edited by W. Michael Reisman and Bums Weston. New York: Free Press, 1976: 198–261.

Chen, Lung-chu and Harold D. Lasswell. *Formosa, China, and the United Nations: Formosa in the World Community.* New York: St. Martin's Press, 1967.

Chen, Lung-chu and W. M. Reisman. "Who Owns Taiwan? A Search for International Title." *Yale Law Journal* 81 (1972): 599.

Chiang, Y. Frank. "State, Sovereignty, and Taiwan." *Fordham International Law* Journal 23 (2000): 959.

Clark, Paul. "Taking Self-Determination Seriously: When Can Cultural and Political Minorities Control?" *Chicago Journal of International Law* 5 (2005): 737.

Cohen, Marc J and Emma Teng, eds. *Let Taiwan Be Taiwan: Documents on the International Status of Taiwan.* Washington, D.C: Center for Taiwan International Relations, 1990.

Coppieters, Bruno and Richard Sakwa, eds. *Contextualizing Secession: Normative Studies in Comparative Perspective.* New York: Oxford University Press, 2003.

Crawford, James. *The Creation of States in International Law.* 2d ed. New York: Oxford University Press, 2006.

Fan, Hua. "The Missing Link Between Self-Determination and Democracy: The Case of East Timor." *Northwestern University Journal of International Human Rights* 6 (2007): 176.

Franck, Thomas M. "The Emerging Right to Democratic Governance." *American Journal of International Law* 86 (1992): 46.

Galloway, L. Thomas. *Recognizing Foreign Governments: The Practice of the United States.* Washington, D.C.: American Enterprise Institute for Public Policy Research, 1978.

Grant, Thomas D. *Defining Statehood: The Montevideo Convention and Its Discontents.* *Columbia Journal of Transnational Law* 37 (1999): 403.

Hannum, Hurst. *Autonomy, Sovereignty, and Self-Determination: The Accommodation of Conflicting Rights.* Rev ed. Philadelphia: University of Pennsylvania Press, 1996.

Henckaerts, Jean-Marie, ed. *The International Status of Taiwan in the New World Order: Legal and Political Considerations.* London: Kluwer, 1996.

Knop, Karen. *Diversity and Self-Determination in International Law.* Cambridge: Cambridge University Press, 2000.

Koeck, Heribert Franz, Daniela Horn, and Franz Leidenmuehler. *From Protectorate to Statehood: Self-Determination v. Territorial Integrity in the Case of Kosovo and the Position of the European Union.* Cambridge: Intersentia, 2009.

Lauterpacht, Hersch. *Recognition in International Law.* Cambridge: Cambridge University Press, 1947.

Lee, Teng-hui. "Understanding Taiwan." *Foreign Affairs* (Nov.–Dec. 1999): 9–14.

Macedo, Stephen and Allen Buchanan, eds. *Secession and Self-Determination.* New York: New York University Press, 2003.

Musgrave, Thomas. *Self-Determination and National Minorities.* New York: Oxford University Press, 2000.

Orakhelashvili, Alexander. *Peremptory Norms in International Law.* New York: Oxford University Press, 2006.

Peterson, M. J. *Recognition of Governments: Legal Doctrine and State Practice, 1815–1995.* New York: Palgrave Macmillan, 1997.

Quigley, John. *The Statehood of Palestine: International Law in the Middle East Conflict.* Cambridge: Cambridge University Press, 2010.

Richardson, Henry J. III. "Failed States, Self-Determination, and Preventive Diplomacy: Colonialist Nostalgia and Democratic Expectations." *Temple International and Comparative Law Journal* 10 (1996): 1.

Roth, Brad. *Governmental Illegitimacy in International Law.* New York: Oxford University Press, 1999.

Schachter, Oscar. "The Decline of the Nation-State and Its Implications for International Law." *Columbia Journal of Transnational Law* 36 (1997): 7.

Schou, August and Arne Olav Brundtland, eds. *Small States in International Relations.* Stockholm: Almqvist & Wiksell; New York: John Wiley & Sons, 1971.

Simpson, Gerry. *Great Powers and Outlaw States: Unequal Sovereigns in the International Legal Order.* Cambridge: Cambridge University Press, 2004.

Suzuki, Eisuke. "Self-Determination and World Public Order: Community Response to Territorial Separation." *Virigina Journal of International Law* 16 (1976): 779.

Syatauw, J. J. G. *Some Newly Established States and the Development of International Law.* The Hague: Martinus Nijhoff, 1961.

Talmon, Stefan. *Recognition of Governments in International Law: With Particular Reference to Governments in Exile.* New York: Oxford University Press, 2001.

Tomuschat, Christian, ed. *Kosovo and the International Community: A Legal Assessment.* New York: Kluwer Law International, 2002.

Tomuschat, Christian, ed. *Modern Law of Self-Determination.* Dordrecht: Martinus Nijhoff Publishers, 1993.

Umozurike, Umozurike Oji. *Self-Determination in International Law.* Hamden, Conn.: Archon Books, 1972.

Water, Timothy William. "Contemplating Failure and Creating Alternatives in the Balkans: Bosnia's Peoples, Democracy." *Yale Journal of International Law* 29 (2004): 423.

Weller, Marc. *Contested Statehood: Kosovo's Struggle for Independence.* New York: Oxford University Press, 2009.

Yoo, John. "Fixing Failed States." *California Law Review* 99 (2011): 95.

Xanthaki, Alexandra. *Indigenous Rights and United Nations Standards: Self-Determination, Culture and Land.* Cambridge: Cambridge University Press, 2010.

3. International Governmental Organizations

Alagappa, Muthiah and Takashi Inoguchi, eds. *International Security Management and the United Nations.* Tokyo: United Nations University Press, 1999.

Alger, Chadwick F., ed. *The Future of the United Nations System: Potential for the Twenty-first Century.* Tokyo; New York; Paris: United Nations University Press, 1998.

Alvarez, José. *International Organizations as Lawmakers.* New York: Oxford University Press, 2006.

Alvarez, Jose E. "Judging the Security Council." *American Journal of International Law* 90 (1996): 1.

Amerasinghe, C. F. *Principles of the International Law of International Organizations.* 2d ed. Cambridge: Cambridge University Press, 2005.

Arend, Anthony Clark. "The United Nations, Regional Organizations, and Military Operations: The Past and Present." *Duke Journal of Comparative and International Law* 7 (1996): 3.

Armstrong, David E., Lorna Lloyd, and John Redmond. *From Versailles to Maastricht: International Organization in the Twentieth Century (Making of the 20th Century).* New York: Palgrave Macmillan, 1996.

Bailey, Sydney D. and Sam Daws. *The Procedure of the UN Security Council.* 3d ed. Oxford: Clarendon Press, 1998.

Bardow, Doug and Ian Vasquez, eds. *Perpetuating Poverty: The World Bank, the IMF, and the Developing World.* Washington, D.C.: Cato Institute, 1996.

Bennett, A. LeRoy. *International Organizations: Principles and Issues.* 3d ed. Englewood Cliffs: Prentice-Hall, 1984.

Bourantonis, Dimitris. *History and Politics of United Nations Security Council Reform.* London: Psychology Press, 2005.

Bowett, D. W. *The Law of International Institutions.* 4th ed. London: Stevens & Sons, 1982.

Chen, Lung-chu, ed. *Membership for Taiwan in the United Nations: Achieving Justice and Universality.* New York: New Century Institute Press, 2007.

Chesterman, Simon, Thomas M. Franck, and David M. Malone. *Law and Practice of the United Nations: Documents and Commentary.* New York: Oxford University Press, 2008.

Childers, Erskine. *Renewing the United Nations System.* With Brian Urquhart. Uppsala, Sweden: Dag Hammarskjold Foundation, 1994.

Claude, Inis L., Jr. *Swords into Plowshares.* 4th ed. New York: Random House, 1971.

Cogan, Jacob Katz. "Representation and Power in International Organization: The Operational Constitution and Its Critics." *American Journal of International Law* 103 (2009): 209.

Craig, Paul. *The Lisbon Treaty: Law, Politics, and Treaty Reform.* Rev. ed. New York: Oxford University Press, 2011.

Djikeul, Dennis. *The Management of Multilateral Organizations.* The Hague: Kluwer Law International, 1996.

Franck, Thomas. *Nation Against Nation: What Happened to the U.N. Dream and What the U.S. Can Do About It.* New York: Oxford University Press, 1985.

Goodrich, Leland M., Edvard Hambro, and Anne Patricia Simons. *Charter of the United Nations.* 3d rev. ed. New York and London: Columbia University Press, 1969.

Gorman, Robert F. *Great Debates at the United Nations: An Encyclopedia of Fifty Key Issues, 1945–2000.* Westport, Conn.: Greenwood Press, 2001.

Grant, Thomas. *Admission to the United Nations: Charter Article 4 and the Rise of Universal Organization.* The Hague: Martinus Nijhoff, 2009.

Gregg, Robert W. *About Face? The United States and the United Nations.* Boulder, Colo.: Lynne Rienner Publishers, 1993.

Gross, Leo. *Essays on International Law and Organization.* 2 vols. Dobbs Ferry, N.Y.: Transnational; The Hague: Martinus Nijhoff, 1984.

Hajnal, Peter I., ed. *International Information: Documents, Publications, and Electric Information of International Governmental Organizations*. 2d ed. Englewood, Colo.: Libraries Unlimited, 1997.

Hanlon, James. *European Community Law*. 3d rev. ed. London: Sweet & Maxwell, 2003.

Hawdon, James. *Emerging Organizational Forms: The Proliferation of Regional Intergovernmental Organizations in the Modern World-System*. Westport, Conn.: Praeger, 1996.

Higgins, Rosalyn. *The Development of International Law Through the Political Organs of the United Nations*. London: Oxford University Press, 1963.

Higgins, Rosalyn. *United Nations Peacekeeping: Documents and Commentary*. 4 vols. New York: Oxford University Press, 1969–1981.

Horwitz, Betty. *The Transformation of the Organization of American States: A Multilateral Framework for Regional Governance*. London/New York: Anthem Press, 2011.

Hurd, Ian. *International Organizations: Politics, Law, Practice*. Cambridge: Cambridge University Press, 2010.

Jenks, C. Wilfred. *International Immunities*. Dobbs Ferry, N.Y.: Oceana, 1961.

Kelsen, Hans. *The Law of the United Nations: A Critical Analysis of Its Fundamental Problems*. Clark, N.J.: The Lawbook Exchange, 2000.

Kirgis, Frederic L. *International Organizations in the Legal Setting: Documents, Comments, and Questions*. St. Paul, Minn.: West, 1977.

Kleinsorge, Tanja E. J., ed. *Council of Europe*. Kluwer Law International, 2010.

Krasno, Jean, ed. *The United Nations: Confronting the Challenges of a Global Society*. Boulder, Colorado: Lynne Rienner Publishers, 2004.

Mathijsen, P. S. R. F. *A Guide to European Union Law*. 11th ed. London: Sweet & Maxwell, 2013.

Mendlovitz, Saul H. and Bums H. Weston, eds. *Preferred Futures for the United Nations*. Irvington-on-Hudson, N.Y.: Transnational Publishers, 1995.

Michaels, David B. *International Privileges and Immunities*. The Hague: Martinus Nijhoff, 1971.

Morton, Jeffrey. *The International Law Commission of the United Nations*. Columbia, S.C.: University of South Carolina Press, 2000.

Portmann, Roland. *Legal Personality in International Law*. Cambridge: Cambridge University Press, 2010.

Reichard, Martin. *The EU-NATO Relationship: A Legal and Political Perspective*. London: Ashgate, 2006.

Roberts, Adam and Benedict Kingsbury, eds. *United Nations, Divided World. The United Nations' Roles in International Relation*. 2d ed. Oxford: Clarendon Press, 1994.

Sands, Philippe and Pierre Klein. *Bowett's Law of International Institutions*. 6th ed. London: Sweet & Maxwell, 2009.

Sarooshi, Dan. *International Organizations and Their Exercise of Sovereign Powers*. New York: Oxford University Press, 2005.

Schachter, Oscar and Christopher C. Joyner, eds. *United Nations Legal Order*. 2 vols. New York: Cambridge University Press, 1995.

Scharf, Michael P. and Paul R. Williams. *The Law of International Organizations: Problems and Materials*. 3d ed. Durham, N.C.: Carolina Academic Press, 2013.

Schermers, Henry G. and Niels M. Blokker. *International Institutional Law: Unity within Diversity*. 5th rev. ed. Lieden: Hotei Publishing, 2011.

Sean, Blain. *United Nations General Assembly Resolutions in Our Changing World*. Ardsley-on-Hudson, N.Y.: Transnational Publishers, 1991.

Shelton, Dinah and Paolo G. Carozza. *Regional Protection of Human Rights*. 2d ed. New York: Oxford University Press, 2013.

Simma, Bruno, Daniel-Erasmus Khan, Georg Nolte, and Andreas Paulus, eds. *The Charter of the United Nations: A Commentary*. 3d ed. New York: Oxford University Press, 2013.

Trifunovska, Snezana. *North Atlantic Treaty Organization*. London: Kluwer Law International, 2010.

United Nations. *The United Nations at Forty: Foundation to Build On*. New York: United Nations, 1985.

United Nations Department of Public Information. *Basic Facts About the United Nations*. New York: United Nations, 1998.

United Nations Department of Public Information. *The United Nations Today*. New York: United Nations, 2008.

Weiss, Thomas G. and Sam Daws, eds. *The Oxford Handbook on the United Nations*. New York: Oxford University Press, 2007.

Wellens, Karel. *Remedies against International Organisations*. Cambridge: Cambridge University Press, 2007.

4. Nongovernmental Organizations and Associations

Alston, Philip. *Non-State Actors and Human Rights*. New York: Oxford University Press, 2005.

Barnet, Richard J. and John Cavanaugh. *Global Dreams: Imperial Corporations and the New World Order*. New York: Simon and Schuster, 1993.

Barnet, Richard J. and Ronald E. Muller. *Global Reach: The Power of the Multinational Corporations*. New York: Simon and Schuster, 1974.

Berman, Maureen R. and Joseph E. Johnson, eds. *Unofficial Diplomats*. New York: Columbia University Press, 1977.

Bianchi, Andrea. *Non-State Actors and International Law*. London: Ashgate, 2009.

Charnovitz, Steve. "Two Centuries of Participation: NGOs and International Governance." *Michigan Journal of International Law* 18 (1997): 183.

Chiang, Pei-heng. *Non-Governmental Organizations at the United Nations: Identity, Role, and Function*. New York: Praeger, 1981.

Da, Xinyuan. *International Institutions and National Policies*. Cambridge: Cambridge University Press, 2007.

Eaton, Joshua P. "The Nigerian Tragedy, Environmental Regulation of Transnational Corporations and the Human Right to a Healthy Environment." *Boston University International Law Journal* 15 (1997): 261.

Forsythe, David. *The Humanitarians: The International Committee of the Red Cross*. Cambridge: Cambridge University Press, 2005.

Goldman, Ralph M. *Transnational Parties: Organizing the World's Precincts*. Lanham, Md.: University Press of America, 1983.

Hurwitz, Deena R., Margaret L. Satterthwaite, and Douglas B. Ford, eds. *Human Rights Advocacy Stories*. New York: Foundation Press, 2008.

Keohane, Robert O. and Joseph S. Nye. *Power and Interdependence: World Politics in Transition*. Boston: Little, Brown, 1977.

Lawson, Kay, ed. *Political Parties and Linkage: A Comparative Perspective*. New Haven, Conn.: Yale University Press, 1980.

Lindblom, Anna-Karin. *Non-governmental Organizations in International Law*. Cambridge: Cambridge University Press, 2005.

Martens, Kerstin. *NGOs and the United Nations: Institutionalization, Professionalization and Adaptation*. New York: Palgrave Macmillan, 2005.

Merrill Betsill, Michele. *NGO Diplomacy: The Influence of Nongovernmental Organizations in International Environmental Negotiations*. Cambridge, Mass: Massachusetts Institute of Technology Press, 2008.

Nanda, Ved P., James R. Scarritt, and George W. Shepherd, Jr., eds. *Global Human Rights: Public Policies, Comparative Measures, and NGO Strategies*. Boulder, Colo.: Westview, 1981.

Nelson, Jane. *Building Partnerships: Cooperation between the United Nations System and the Private Sector*. New York: United Nations Publications, 2002.

Noortmann, Math. *Non-State Actor Dynamics in International Law*. London: Ashgate, 2010.

Peters, Anne, Lucy Koechlin, Till Forster, and Gretta Fennier Zinkernagel, eds. *Non-State Actors as Standard Setters*. Cambridge: Cambridge University Press, 2009.

Rammeloo, Stephan. *Corporations in Private International Law: A European Perspective*. New York: Oxford University Press, 2001.

Rossi, Ingrid. *Legal Status of Non-governmental Organizations in International Law*. Cambridge: Intersentia, 2010.

Rubin, Seymour J. and Gary Clude Hufbauer, eds. *Emerging Standards of International Trade and Investment: Multinational Codes and Corporate Conduct*. Totowa, N.J.: Rowman and Allanheld, 1984.

Soroos, Marvin S. *Beyond Sovereignty: The Challenge of Global Policy*. Columbia: University of South Carolina Press, 1986.

Wallace, Cynthia Day. *Legal Control of the Multinational Enterprise*. The Hague: Martinus Nijhoff, 1982.

"We the Peoples": Civil Society, The United Nations and Global Governance: Report of the Panel of Eminent Persons on United Nations-Civil Society Relations. United Nations, 2004.

Weiss, Thomas G. and Leon Gordenker, eds. *NGOs, the UN, and Global Governance*. Boulder, Colo.: Lynne Rienner Publishers, 1996.

White, Lyman Cromwell. *International Non-Governmental Organizations*. New Brunswick, N.J.: Rutgers University Press, 1951.

Willetts, Peter, ed. *"The Conscience of the World": The Influence of Non-Governmental Organizations in the UN System*. Washington, D.C.: Brookings Institution Press, 1996.

5. The Individual

Higgins, Rosalyn. "Conceptual Thinking About the Individual in International Law." *New York Law School Law Review* 24 (1978): 11.

Lauterpacht, Hersch. *International Law and Human Rights*. Hamden, Conn.: Archon Books, 1968.

McDougal, Myres S., Harold D. Lasswell, and Lung-chu Chen. *Human Rights and World Public Order: The Basic Policies of an International Law of Human Dignity*. New Haven, Conn.: Yale University Press, 1980.

Nijman, Janne Elisabeth. *The Concept of International Legal Personality: An Inquiry into the History and Theory of International Law.* The Hague: T.M.C. Asser Press, 2004.

Parlett, Kate. *The Individual in the International Legal System: Continuity and Change in International Law.* Cambridge: Cambridge University Press, 2011.

PART THREE/PERSPECTIVES

6. Minimum World Order and Optimum World Order

Abass, Ademola. *Regional Organisations and the Development of Collective Security: Beyond Chapter VIII of the UN Charter.* Oxford: Hart Publishing, 2004.

Ando, Nisuke, ed. *Japan and International Law: Past, Present, and Future: International Symposium to Mark the Centennial of the Japanese Association of International Law.* The Hague: Kluwer Law International, 1999.

Angihe, Antony, Bhupinder Chimni, Karin Mickelson, and Obira Okafur, eds. *The Third World and International Legal Order: Law, Politics and Globalization.* Leiden: Martinus Nijhoff, 2004.

Borgen, Christopher. "Whose public, whose order? Imperium, Region, and Normative Friction." *Yale Journal of International Law* 32 (2007): 331.

Burger, Suzanne and Ronald Dore, eds. *Convergence or Diversity? National Models of Production and Distribution in a Global Economy.* Working Paper. Cambridge, Mass.: Massachusetts Institute of Technology Industrial Performance Center, 1994.

Cohen, Jerome A. and Hungdah Chiu. *People's China and International Law.* Princeton: Princeton University Press, 1974.

Commission on Human Security. *Human Security Now.* New York: United Nations, 2003.

Dore, Isaak I. *International Law and the Superpowers: Normative Order in a Divided World.* New Brunswick, N.J.: Rutgers University Press, 1984.

Dunoff, Jeffrey and Joel Trachman. *Ruling the World? Constitutionalism, International Law, and Global Governance.* Cambridge: Cambridge University Press, 2009.

Falk, Richard. *On Humane Governance: Toward a New Global Politics.* University Park: Pennsylvania State University Press, 1995.

Falk, Richard, Jacqueline Stevens, and Balakrishnan Rajagopal, eds. *International Law and the Third World: Reshaping Justice.* New York/Abingdon: Routledge-Cavendish, 2008.

Ferencz, Benjamin B. *New Legal Foundations for Global Survival: Security Through the Security Council.* New York: Oceana Publishers, 1994.

Greider, William. *Who Will Tell the People? The Betrayal of American Democracy.* New York: Simon and Schuster, 1992.

Guiora, Amos N. *Freedom from Religion: Rights and National Security.* 2d ed. New York: Oxford University Press. 2013.

Higgins, Rosalyn. *Conflict of Interests: International Law in a Divided World.* Chester Springs, Penn.: Dufour Editions, 1965.

Ku, Charlotte and Harold Karan Jacobson. *Democratic Accountability and the Use of Force in International Law.* Cambridge: Cambridge University Press, 2003.

Lebow, Richard Ned and Thomas Risse-Kappen, eds. *International Relations Theory and the End of the Cold War.* New York: Columbia University Press, 1995.

Lipson, Leon. "Peaceful Coexistence." *Law and Contemporary Problems* 29 (1964): 871.

Mahmood, Saba. *Politics of Piety: The Islamic Revival and the Feminist Subject.* Princeton, N.J.: Princeton University Press, 2005.

Manusama, Kenneth. *The United Nations Security Council in the Post–Cold War Era: Applying the Principle of Legality.* The Hague: Martinus Nijhoff, 2006.

Marks, Susan, ed. *International Law on the Left: Re-Examining Marxist Legacies.* New York/Cambridge: Cambridge University Press, 2008.

Matam Farral, Jeremy. *United Nations Sanctions and the Rule of Law.* Cambridge: Cambridge University Press, 2009.

McDougal, Myres S. and Harold D. Lasswell. "The Identification and Appraisal of Diverse Systems of Public Order." *American Journal of International Law* 53 (1959): 1.

Mgbeoji, Ikechi. *Collective Insecurity: The Liberian Crisis, Unilateralism, and Global Order.* Vancouver, B.C.: University of British Columbia, 2004.

Muzaffer, Chandra. "Human Rights and the New World Order." *American Journal of International Law* 88 (1994): 852.

Österdah, Inger. "The Exception as the Rule: Lawmaking on Force and Human Rights by the UN Security Council." *Journal of Conflict & Security Law* 10 (2005): 1.

Pauwelyn, Joost. *Optimal Protection of International Law: Navigating between European Absolutism and American Voluntarism.* Cambridge: Cambridge University Press, 2008.

Ramcharan, B. G. *The International Law and Practice of Early-Warning of Preventive Diplomacy: The Emerging Global Watch.* Dordrecht: Martinus Nijhoff Publishers, 1991.

Reisman, W. Michael. "International Law After the Cold War." *American Journal of International Law* 84 (1990): 859.

Ribbelink, Oliver. *Beyond the UN Charter: Peace, Security and the Role of Justice.* The Hague: Hague Academic Press, 2008.

Schreuer, Christopher. "The Waning of the Sovereign State: Towards a New Paradigm for International Law?" *European Journal of International Law* 4 (1993): 447.

Stahn, Carsten. "Enforcement of the Collective Will After Iraq." *American Journal of International Law* 97 (2003): 804.

Tunkin, Grigorii Ivanovich. *Theory of International Law.* Translated by William Butler. Cambridge, Mass.: Harvard University Press, 1974.

PART FOUR/ARENAS

7. Establishment of and Access to Arenas of Authority

Anand, Ram P. *International Courts and Contemporary Conflicts.* New York: Asia Publishing House, 1974.

Arend, Anthony Clark, ed. *The United States and the Compulsory Jurisdiction of the International Court of Justice.* Lanham, Md.: University Press of America, 1986.

Bell, Andrew. *Forum Shopping and Venue in Transnational Litigation.* New York: Oxford University Press, 2003.

Brown, Chester. *A Common Law of International Adjudication.* New York: Oxford University Press, 2009.

Charney, Jonathan I. "The Implications of Expanding International Dispute Settlement Systems: The 1982 Convention on the Law of the Sea." *American Journal of International Law* 90 (1996): 69.

Collier, John and Vaughan Lowe. *The Settlement of Disputes in International Law: Institutions and Procedures.* New York: Oxford University Press, 1999.

Darnrosch, Lori Fisler, ed. *The International Court of Justice at a Crossroads.* Dobbs Ferry, N.Y.: Transnational, 1987.

Falk, Richard A. *Reviewing the World Court.* Charlottesville, Va.: University Press of Virginia, 1986.

Giorgetti, Chiara, ed. *The Rules, Practice, and Jurisprudence of International Courts and Tribunals.* Leiden: Martinus Nijhoff, 2012.

Gross, Leo, ed. *The Future of the International Court of Justice.* 2 vols. Dobbs Ferry, N.Y.: Oceana Publications, 1976.

Hamilton, P. H.C. Requena, L. van Scheltinga, and B. Shifman, eds. *The Permanent Court of Arbitration: International Arbitration and Dispute Resolution.* The Hague: Kluwer Law International, 1999.

Helfer, Laurence and Anne-Marie Slaughter. "Why States Create International Tribunals: A Response to Professors Posner and Yoo." *California Law Review* 93 (2005): 899.

Homi Kaikobad, Kaiyan. *Interpretation and Revision of International Boundary Decisions.* Cambridge: Cambridge University Press, 2007.

International Court of Justice. *The International Court of Justice.* 4th ed. The Hague: ICJ, 1996.

Jenks, C. Wilfred. *Prospects of International Adjudication.* Dobbs Ferry, N.Y.: Oceana Publications, 1964.

Jennings, Robert. "The UN at Fifty: The International Court of Justice After Fifty Years." *American Journal of International Law* 89 (1995): 493.

Jonkman, Hans and Bette E. Shifman. "The Role of the Permanent Court of Arbitration in the United Nations Decade of International Law and the Peaceful Settlement of Disputes, 1990–1999 and Beyond." In Najeeb al-Nauirni and Richard Meese, eds. *Collected Essays: International Legal Issues Arising Under the United Nations Decade of International Law.* The Hague: Martinus Nijhoff Publishers, 1995.

Kaikobad, Kaiyan H. and Michael Bohlander, eds. *International Law and Power: Perspectives on Legal Order and Justice Essays in Honour of Colin Warbrick.* Leiden: Martinus Nijhoff, 2009.

Katz, Milton. *The Relevance of International Adjudication.* Cambridge, Mass.: Harvard University Press, 1968.

Keith, Kenneth J. *The Extent of the Advisory Jurisdiction of the International Court of Justice.* Leiden: A.W. Sijthoff, 1971.

Lauterpacht, Elihu. *Aspects of the Administration of International Justice.* Vol. 9, *The Hersch-Lauterpacht Memorial Lecture Series.* Cambridge, England: Grotius Publications, 1991.

Lillich, Richard B., ed. *The Iran–United States Tribunal, 1981–1983.* Sokol Colloquium Series. Charlottesville, Va.: University Press of Virginia, 1985.

Lowenfeld, Andreas F. *International Litigation and Arbitration.* St. Paul, Minn.: West Publishing, 1993.

MacDonald, Ronald J. St., Franz Matscher, and Herbert Petzold. *The European System for the Protection of Human Rights.* The Hague: Martinus Nijhoff Publishers, 1993.

Mackenzie, Ruth, Philippe Sands, Cesare Romano, and Yuval Shany. *The Manual on International Courts and Tribunals.* 2d ed. New York: Oxford University Press, 2010.

Merrills, J. G. *International Dispute Settlement*. 4th ed. Cambridge: Cambridge University Press, 2005.

Mistelis, Loukas A. and Julian D. M. Lew, eds. *Pervasive Problems in International Arbitration*. Kluwer Law International, 2006.

Nollkaemper, Andre. *National Courts and the International Rule of Law*. New York: Oxford University Press, 2011.

Palmer, Geoffrey. "The Difficulties of Third-Party Adjudication for Political People." *American Society of International Law Proceedings* 97 (2003): 289.

Permanent Court of Arbitration, ed. *Redressing Injustices Through Mass Claims Processes: Innovative Responses to Unique Challenges*. New York: Oxford University Press, 2006.

Petrochilos, Georgios. *Procedural Law in International Arbitration*. New York: Oxford University Press, 2004.

Posner, Eric and John Yoo. "Judicial Independence in International Tribunals," *California Law Review*. 93 (2005): 1.

Reisman, W. Michael. *Nullity and Revision: The Review and Enforcement of Judgements and Awards*. New Haven, Connecticut: Yale University Press, 1971.

Reisman, W. Michael. *Systems of Control in International Adjudication and Arbitration: Breakdown and Repair*. Durham, N.C.: Duke University Press, 1992.

Reisman, W. Michael et al. *International Commercial Arbitration: Cases, Materials, and Notes on the Resolution of International Business Disputes*. New York: Foundation Press, 1997.

Romano, Cesare P. R., ed. *The Sword and the Scales: The United States and International Courts and Tribunals*. Cambridge: Cambridge University Press, 2009.

Rosenne, Shabtai. *The Law and Practice of the International Courts, 1920–2005*. 4th ed. Leiden/Boston: Martinus Nijhoff, 2006.

Rosenne, Shabtai. *The World Court: What It Is and How It Works*. 3d rev. ed. Leiden: A. W. Sijthoff; Dobbs Ferry, N.Y.: Oceana, 1973.

Rosenne, Shabtai, ed. *Documents on the International Court of Justice*. 2d ed. Alphen aan den Rijn, Netherlands: Sijthoff and Noordhoff; Dobbs Ferry, N.Y.: Oceana, 1979.

Schreuer, Christoph H., Loretta Malintoppi, August Reinisch, and Anthony Sinclair. *The ICSID Convention: A Commentary*. 2d ed. Cambridge: Cambridge University Press, 2009.

Shany, Yuval. *Assessing the Effectiveness of International Courts*. New York: Oxford University Press, 2014.

Spiermann, Ole. *International Legal Argument in the Permanent Court of International Justice: The Rise of the International Judiciary*. Cambridge: Cambridge University Press, 2010.

Tams, Christian J. and James Sloan. *The Development of International Law by the International Court of Justice*. New York: Oxford University Press, 2013.

Teitel, Ruti and Robert Howse. "Cross-Judging: Tribunalization in a Fragmented But Interconnected Global Order." *New York University Journal of International Law & Politics* 41 (2009): 959.

Thirlway, Hugh. *The Law and Procedure of the International Court of Justice*. New York: Oxford University Press, 2013.

Tuerk, Helmut. "The Contribution of the International Tribunal for the Law of the Sea to International Law." *Penn State International Law Review* 26 (2007): 289.

Webb, Phillipa. *International Judicial Integration and Fragmentation*. New York: Oxford University Press, 2013.

Zimmermann, Andreas, Christian Tams, Karin Oellers-Frahm, and Christian Tomuschat, eds. *The Statute of the International Court of Justice: A Commentary*. 2d ed. New York: Oxford University Press, 2012.

PART FIVE/BASES OF POWERS

8. Control over Territory

Castellino, Joshua. *Title to Territory in International Law: A Temporal Analysis*. London: Ashgate, 2003.

Chen, Lung-chu and Harold D. Lasswell. *Formosa, China, and the United Nations: Formosa in the World Community*. New York: St. Martin's Press, 1967.

Chen, Lung-chu and W. M. Reisman. "Who Owns Taiwan? A Search for International Title." *Yale Law Journal* 81 (1972): 599.

Franck, Thomas M. "The Stealing of the Sahara." *American Journal of International Law* 70 (1976): 694.

Hoffman, Fritz L. and Olga Mingo Hoffman. *Sovereignty in Dispute: The Falklands/Malvinas, 1493–1982*. Boulder, Colo.: Westview, 1984.

Jennings, R. Y. *The Acquisition of Territory in International Law*. Manchester: Manchester University Press; Dobbs Ferry, N.Y.: Oceana, 1963.

Knoll, Bernhard. *The Legal Status of Territories Subject to Administration by International Organisations*. Cambridge: Cambridge University Press, 2008.

Makau wa Mutua. "Why Redraw the Map of Africa: A Moral and Legal Inquiry." *Michigan Journal of International Law* 16 (1995): 1113.

Ratner, Steven R. "Drawing a Better Line: Uti Possidetis and the Borders of New States." *American Journal of International Law* 90 (1996): 590.

Shaw, Malcolm N. "The Western Sahara Case." *British Yearbook of International Law* 49 (1978): 118.

Shaw, Malcolm N. "The Heritage of State: The Principle of *Uti Possidetis Juris* Today." *British Yearbook of International Law* 67 (1996): 75.

Shaw, Malcolm. *The International Law of Territory*. New York: Oxford University Press, 2009.

Song, Yann-huei. "Managing Potential Conflicts in the South China Sea: Taiwan's Perspective." EAI Occasional Paper No. 14. East Asian Institute, National University of Singapore, Singapore University Press, 1999.

Wilde, Ralph. *International Territorial Administration: How Trusteeship and The Civilizing Mission Never Went Away*. New York: Oxford University Press, 2008.

9. Control and Use of the Sea

Anand, R. P. *Origin and Development of the Law of the Sea*. The Hague: Martinus Nijhoff, 1983.

Annick de Marffy-Mantuano. "The Procedural Framework of the Agreement Implementing the 1982 United Nations Convention on the Law of the Sea." *American Journal of International Law* 89 (1995): 814.

Attard, David J. *The Exclusive Economic Zone in International Law*. Oxford: Clarendon Press, 1987.

Benvenisti, Eya I. "Collective Action in the Utilization of Shared Freshwater: The Challenges of International Water Resource Law." *American Journal of International Law* 20 (1996): 384.

Brown, E. D. *Sea-Bed Energy and Minerals: The International Legal Regime*. The Hague: Martinus Nijhoff Publishers, 2001.

Caminos, Hugo. *Law of the Sea*. London: Ashgate, 2001.

Charney, Jonathan I. "U.S. Provisional Application of the 1994 Deep Seabed Agreement" (Law of the Sea Forum: The 1994 Agreement on Implementation of the Seabed Provisions of the Convention on the Law of the Sea). *American Journal of International Law* 88 (1994): 705.

Charney, Jonathan I., ed. *The New Nationalism and the Use of Common Spaces: Issues in Marine Pollution and the Exploitation of Antarctica*. Totowa, N.J.: Allanheld, Osmun, 1982.

Churchill, Robin R. and Alan Vaughan Lowe. *The Law of the Sea*. 3d ed. Manchester: Manchester University Press, 1999.

Cook, Peter and Chris M. Carleton, eds. *Continental Shelf Limits: The Scientific and Legal Interface*. New York: Oxford University Press, 2000.

Elferink Oude, Alex and Donald Rothwell. *Oceans Management in the 21st Century: Institutional Frameworks and Responses*. The Hague: Martinus Nijhoff, 2004.

Gavouneli, Maria. *Functional Jurisdiction in the Law of the Sea*. The Hague: Martinus Nijhoff, 2007.

Geiss, Robin and Anna Petrig. *Piracy and Armed Robbery at Sea: The Legal Framework for Counter-Piracy Operations in Somalia and the Gulf of Aden*. New York: Oxford University Press, 2011.

Klein, Natalie. *Dispute Settlement in the UN Convention on the Law of the Sea*. Cambridge: Cambridge University Press, 2009.

Klien, Natalie. *Maritime Security and the Law of the Sea*. New York: Oxford University Press, 2011.

Kraska, James. *Maritime Power and the Law of the Sea: Expeditionary Operations in World Politics*. New York: Oxford University Press, 2010.

Lagoni, Rainer and Daniel Vignes. *Maritime Delimitation*. Martinus Nijhoff, 2006.

"Law of the Sea Forum: The 1994 Agreement on Implementation of the Seabed Provisions of the Convention on the Law of the Sea." *American Journal of International Law* 88 (1994): 687.

McDougal, Myres S. and William T. Burke. *The Public Order of the Oceans: A Contemporary International Law of the Sea*. New Haven, Conn.: Yale University Press, 1962.

Norchi, Charles. "The Gulf of Maine Judgment at Twenty-Five." *Ocean and Coastal Law Journal* 15. No 2, (2010).

Nordquist, Myron, John Norton Moore, and Kuen-Chen Fu, eds. *Recent Developments in the Law of the Sea and China*. The Hague: Martinus Nijhoff, 2005.

Noyes, John. "U.S. Policy and the United Nations Convention on the Law of the Sea." *George Washington University International Law Review* 39 (2007): 621.

O'Connell, D. P. *The International Law of the Sea*. Oxford: Clarendon, 1982.

Oda, Shigeru. *The Law of the Sea in Our Time*. 2 vols. Leiden: Sijthoff, 1977.

Ong, David. "Joint Development of Common Offshore Oil and Gas Developments: 'Mere' State Practice or Customary International Law." *American Journal of International Law* 93 (1999): 771.

Oxman, Bernard. "Does the International Tribunal for the Law of the Sea Have Jurisdiction over Disputes with Taiwan?" *Taiwan International Law Quarterly* 2 (2005): 205.

Oxman, Bernard. "The International Tribunal for the Law of the Sea." *Bringing New Law to Ocean Waters.* 285 Edited by D. D. Caron and H. N. Scheiber. Berkeley: Law of the Sea Institute, 2004.

Oxman, Bernard. "The Territorial Temptation: A Siren Song at Sea." *American Journal of International Law* 100 (2006): 830.

Oxman, Bernard. *Transit of Straits and Archipelagic Waters by Military Aircraft, Singapore Journal of International and Comparative Law.* L. 4 (2000): 377.

Payoyo, Peter Bautista, ed. *Ocean Governance: Sustainable Development of the Seas.* Tokyo: United Nations University Press, 1994.

Posner, Eric and Alan Sykes. "Economic Foundations of the Law of the Sea." *American Journal of International Law* 104 (2010): 569.

Reisman, W. Michael. *Straight Baselines in International Maritime Boundary Delimitation.* With Gayl Westerman. St. Martin's Press, 1992.

Roach, J. A. and Robert W. Smith. *United States Responses to Excessive Maritime Claims.* 3d ed. The Hague: Martinus Nijhoff Publishers, 2012.

Sohn, Louis B. "The 1994 Agreement on Implementation of the Seabed Provisions of the Convention on the Law of the Sea: International Law Implications of the 1994 Agreement." *American Journal of International Law* 88 (1994): 696.

Sohn, Louis B. and Kristen Gustafson. *The Law of the Sea in Nutshell.* St. Paul, Minn.: West, 1984.

Song, Yann-huei. "A Pathfinder on the Law of the Sea and Marine Policy." *Ocean Development and International Law* 24 (1993): 205.

Song, Yann-huei. "Marine Scientific Research and Marine Pollution." *Ocean Development and International Law* 20 (1990): 601.

Stokke, Olav Schram. *Governing High Seas Fisheries: The Interplay of Global and Regional Regimes.* New York: Oxford University Press, 2003.

Tanaka, Yoshifumi. *The International Law of the Sea.* Cambridge: Cambridge University Press, 2012.

Totten, Christopher and Matthew Bernal. "Somali Piracy: Jurisdictional Issues, Enforcement Problems and Potential Solutions." *Georgetown Journal of International Law* 41 (2010): 377.

Van Dyke, Jon M., Durwood Zaulke, and Grant Hewison, eds. *Freedom for the Seas in the 21st Century: Ocean Governance and Environmental Harmony.* Washington, D.C.: Island Press, 1993.

Vicuna, F. O. *The Exclusive Economic Zone: Regime and Legal Nature Under International Law.* Cambridge: Cambridge University Press, 1989.

10. Control and Use of Other Resources

Arsanjani, Mahnoush. *International Regulation of Internal Resources: The Study of Law and Policy.* Charlottesville, Virgina: University of Virginia Press, 1981.

Birnie, Patricia, Alan Boyle, and Catherine Redgwell. *International Law and the Environment.* 3d ed. New York: Oxford University Press, 2009.

Boisson de Chazournes, Laurence. *Fresh Water in International Law.* New York: Oxford University Press, 2013.

Dempsey, Paul Stephen. "Aviation Security: The Role of Law in the War Against Terrorism." *Columbia Journal of Transnational Law* 41 (2003): 649.

DiMento, Joseph. *The Global Environment and International Law*. Austin, Tex.: University of Texas Press, 2003.

Esmaeili, Hossein. *The Legal Regime of Offshore Oil Rigs in International Law*. London: Ashgate, 2001.

Freeland, Steven. "Up, up and... back: The Emergence of Space Tourism and Its Impact on the International Law of Outer Space." *Chicago Journal of International Law* 6 (2005): 1.

Freestone, David and Charlotte Streck. *Legal Aspects of Carbon Trading: Kyoto, Copenhagen and Beyond*. New York: Oxford University Press, 2009.

Gillespie, Alexander. *International Environmental Law, Policy and Ethics*. New York: Oxford University Press, 2000.

Goyal, Anupam. *The WTO and International Environmental Law: Towards Conciliation*. New York: Oxford University Press, 2006.

Guzman, Andrew T. *Overheated: The Human Cost of Climate Change*. New York: Oxford University Press, 2013.

Haanappel, Peter. *The Law and Policy of Airspace and Outer Space*. London: Kluwer Law International, 2003.

Handl, Gunther. *Human Rights and Protection of the Environment*. In *Economic, Social, and Cultural Rights: A Textbook* (A. Eide et al., eds.). 2d ed. Martinus Nijhoff, 2001.

Handl, Gunther. *Sustainable Development: General Rules versus Specific Obligations*. In W. Lang, ed. *Sustainable Development and International Law*. London: IWA Publishing, 1995.

Hertzfeld, Henry and Frans von der Dunk. "Bringing Space Law into the Commercial World: Property Rights Without Sovereignty." *Chicago Journal of International Law* 6 (2005): 81.

Hull, Eric. "Crude Injustice in the Gulf: Why Categorical Exclusions for Deepwater Drilling in the Gulf Mexico Are Inconsistent with U.S. and International Ocean Law and Policy." *UCLA Journal of Environmental Law & Policy* 29 (2011): 1.

Lyall, Francis and Paul Larsen. *Space Law: A Treatise*. London: Ashgate, 2009.

Matte, Nicolas Mateesco. *Treatise on Air-Aeronautical Law*. Montreal: ICASL, 1981.

McAdam, Jane. *Climate Change, Forced Migration, and International Law*. New York: Oxford University Press, 2013.

McDougal, Myres S., Harold D. Lasswell, and Ivan A. Vlasic. *Law and Public Order in Space*. New Haven, Conn.: Yale University Press, 1963.

Myhre, Jeffrey D. *The Antarctic Treaty System: Politics, Law, and Diplomacy*. Boulder, Colo.: Westview, 1986.

Nanda, Ved P., ed. *Climate Change and Environmental Ethics*. Ardsley, NY: Transnational Publishers, 2011.

Rajamani, Lavanya. *Differential Treatment in International Environmental Law*. New York: Oxford University Press, 2006.

Rich, Bruce. *Mortgaging the Earth: Crisis of Development*. Boston: Beacon Press, 1994.

Sands, Phillip, ed. *Greening International Law*. New York: New Press, 1994.

Schachter, Oscar. *Sharing the World's Resources*. New York: Columbia University Press, 1977.

Schneider, Jan. *World Public Order of the Environment: Towards an International Ecological Law and Organization*. Toronto: University of Toronto Press, 1979.

Schoenbaum, Thomas I. "International Trade and Protection of the Environment:The Continuing Search for Reconciliation." *American Journal of International Law* 91 (1997): 268.

Shrewsbury, Stephen. "September 11th and the Single European Sky: Developing Concepts of Airspace Sovereignty." *Journal of Air Law and Commerce* 68 (2003): 115.

Stephens, Tim. *International Courts and Environmental Protection.* Cambridge: Cambridge University Press, 2009.

Weiss, Edith Brown. "Trade and Environment: Environment and Trade as Partners in Sustainable Development: A Commentary." *American Journal of International Law* 86 (1992): 728.

Weiss, Edith Brown, Daniel B. Magraw, and Paul C. Scasz. *International Environmental Law: Basic Instruments and References.* The Hague: Martinus Nijhoff, 1992.

Zhukov, Grennady and Yuri Kolosov. *International Space Law.* Translated by Boris Belitzky. New York: Praeger, 1984.

11. Control of People: Nationality and Movement

Anaya, S. James. *Indigenous Peoples in International Law.* New York: Oxford University Press, 1996.

Betts, Alexander, ed. *Global Migration Governance.* New York: Oxford University Press, 2011.

Blay, Sam, and Andreas Zimmerman. "Recent Changes in German Refugee Law: A Critical Assessment." *American Journal of International Law* 88 (1994): 361.

Fitzpatrick, Joan. "Temporary Protection for Refugees: Elements of a formalized Regime."*American Journal of International Law* 94 (2000): 279.

Foster, Michelle. *International Refugee Law and Socio-Economic Rights: Refuge from Deprivation.* Cambridge: Cambridge University Press, 2009.

Gammeltoft-Hansen, Thomas. *Access to Asylum: International Refugee Law and the Globalisation of Migration Control.* Cambridge: Cambridge University Press, 2011.

Garcia-Mora, Manuel R. *International Law and Asylum as a Human Right.* Washington, D.C.: Public Affairs Press, 1956.

Goodwin-Gill, Guy S. *International Law and the Movement of Persons Between States.* Oxford: Clarendon Press, 1978.

Goodwin-Gill, Guy S. *The Refugee in International Law.* Oxford: Clarendon Press, 1983.

Grahl-Madsen, Atle. *The Status of Refugees in International Law.* 2 vols. Leiden: A. W. Sijthoff, 1966, 1972.

Grahl-Madsen, Atle. *Territorial Asylum.* Stockholm: Almqvist and Wiksell International; Dobbs Ferry, N.Y.: Oceana, 1980.

Hadda, Emma. *The Refugee in International Society: Between Sovereigns.* Cambridge: Cambridge University Press, 2008.

Hathaway, James. *The Rights of Refugees under International Law.* Cambridge: Cambridge University Press, 2005.

Henckaerts, Jean-Marie. *Mass Expulsion in Modern International Law and Practice.* The Hague: Martinus Nijhoff Publisher/Kluwer Law International, 1995.

Higgins, Rosalyn and Maurice Flory, eds. *Terrorism and International Law.* Routledge, 1997.

Hurwitz, Agnès. *The Collective Responsibility of States to Protect Refugees.* New York: Oxford University Press, 2009.

Lambert, Hélène. *International Refugee Law*. London: Ashgate, 2010.

McAdam, Jane. *Complementary Protection in International Refugee Law*. New York: Oxford University Press, 2007.

Nafziger, James A. R. "The General Admission of Aliens Under International Law." *American Journal of International Law* 77 (1983): 804.

Newmark, Robert L. "Non-Refoulement Run Afoul: The Questionable Legality of Extraterritorial Repatriation Programs." *Washington University Law Quarterly* 71 (1993): 833.

Newton, Michael, Charles Garraway, Elles van Sliedregt, Simon Butt, and Anton du Plessis. *Terrorism: International Case Law Reporter 2011*. New York: Oxford University Press, 2013.

Phuong, Catherine. *The International Protection of Internally Displaced Persons*. Cambridge: Cambridge University Press, 2010.

Plender, Richard O. *International Migration Law*. Leiden: A. W. Sitjhoff, 1972.

Shearer, I. A. *Extradition in International Law*. Manchester: Manchester University Press; Dobbs Ferry, N.Y.: Oceana, 1971.

Sinha, S. Prakash. *Asylum and International Law*. The Hague: Martinus Nijhoff, 1971.

Sohn, Louis B. and Thomas Buergenthal, eds. *The Movement of Persons Across Borders*. Studies in Transnational Legal Policy, no. 23. Washington, D.C.: American Society of International Law, 1992.

Vasak, Karel and Sidney Liskofsky, eds. *The Right to Leave and to Return*. New York: American Jewish Committee, 1976.

Weis, P. *Nationality and Statelessness in International Law*. 2d ed. Leiden: A. W. Sijthoff, 1979.

Wiessner, Seigfried. "Blessed Be the Ties That Bind: The Nexus Between Nationality and Territory." *Mississippi Law Journal* 56 (1986): 447.

12. Protection of People: From Alien Rights to Human Rights

Alston, Philip, ed. *The Best Interests of the Child: Reconciling Culture and Human Rights*. Oxford: Clarendon Press, 1994.

Brewer-Carías, Allan. *Constitutional Protection of Human Rights in Latin America: A Comparative Study of Amparo Proceedings*. Cambridge: Cambridge University Press, 2008.

Buergenthal, Thomas, Dinah Shelton, and David Stewart. *International Human Rights in a Nutshell*. 4th ed. St. Paul, Minn.: West Publishing, 2009.

Chinkin, Christine *U.N. Human Rights Council Fact-Finding Missions: Lessons from Gaza*. In Arsanjani et al., eds. *Looking to the Future: Essays on International Law in Honor of W. Michael Reisman*. Martinus Nijhoff, 2010.

Clapham, Andrew. *Human Rights Obligations of Non-State Actors*. New York: Oxford University Press, 2006.

Davidson, Scott. *The Inter-American Human Rights System*. Aldershot, England/Brookfield, Vt.: Dartmouth, 1997.

Davis, Jeffrey. Justice Across Borders: The Struggle for Human Rights in U.S. Courts. Cambridge: Cambridge University Press, 2008.

Dawson, Frank G. and Ivan L. Head. *International Law, National Tribunals, and the Rights of Aliens*. Syracuse, N.Y.: Syracuse University Press, 1971.

Eide, Asbjorn, Catarina Krause, and Allan Rosas, eds. *Economic, Social, and Cultural Rights: A Textbook*. The Hague: Martinus Nijhoff, 1995.

Evans, Gareth. *The Responsibility to Protect: Ending Mass Atrocity Crimes Once and For All.* Washington, D.C.: Brookings Institute Press, 2008.

Evans, Malcolm and Rachel Murray, eds. *The African Charter on Human and Peoples' Rights: The System in Practice, 1986–2006.* 2d ed. Cambridge: Cambridge University Press, 2010.

Fredman, Sandra, Philip Alston, and Gráinne Búrca. *Discrimination and Human Rights: The Case of Racism.* New York: Oxford University Press, 2001.

Freeman, Marsha A., Christine Chinkin, and Beate Rudolf, eds. *The UN Convention on the Elimination of All Forms of Discrimination Against Women.* New York: Oxford University Press, 2012.

Gallagher, Anne. *The International Law of Human Trafficking.* Cambridge: Cambridge University Press, 2010.

Garcia-Amador, F. V. *Recent Codification of the Law of State Responsibility for Injuries to Aliens.* Dobbs Ferry, N.Y.: Oceana; Leiden: A. W. Sijthoff, 1974.

Gearty, Conor. *Can Human Rights Survive?* Cambridge: Cambridge University Press, 2006.

Goodale, Mark, ed. *Human Rights at the Crossroads.* New York: Oxford University Press, 2012.

Hannum, Hurst. *Guide to International Human Rights Practice.* 2d ed. Philadelphia: University of Pennsylvania Press, 1992.

Henkin, Louis. *The Age of Rights.* New York: Columbia University Press, 1990.

Henkin, Louis. "U.S. Ratification of Human Rights Conventions: The Ghost of Senator Bricker." *American Journal of International Law* 89 (1995): 341.

Henkin, Louis, Sarah H. Cleveland, Laurence R. Helfer, Gerald L. Neuman and Diane F. Orentlicher. *Human Rights.* 2d ed. St. Paul, Minn.: West, 2009.

Hestermeyer, Holger. *Human Rights and the WTO: The Case of Patents and Access to Medicines.* New York: Oxford University Press, 2008.

Joseph, Sarah and Melissa Castan. *The International Covenant on Civil and Political Rights: Cases, Materials, and Commentary.* 3d ed. New York: Oxford University Press, 2013.

Kamminga, Menno and Martin Scheinin, eds. *The Impact of Human Rights Law on General International Law.* New York: Oxford University Press, 2009.

Koh, Harold Hongju. "The Case Against Military Commissions." *American Journal of International Law* 96 (2002): 337.

Koh, Harold H. *Deliberative Democracy and Human Rights.* With Ronald C. Slye. Yale University Press, 1999.

Koh, Harold H. *The International Human Rights of Persons with Intellectual Disabilities: Different but Equal.* With Stanley Herr and Lawrence Gostin, eds. Oxford University Press, 2002.

Lautenbach, Geranne. *The Concept of the Rule of Law and the European Court of Human Rights.* New York: Oxford University Press, 2013.

Lauterpacht, Sir Hersch. *An International Bill of the Rights of Man.* New York: Oxford University Press, 2013.

Lauterpacht, Hersch. *International Law and Human Rights.* Hamden, Conn.: Archon Books, 1968.

Likosky, Michael. *Law, Infrastructure and Human Rights.* Cambridge: Cambridge University Press, 2006.

Lillich, Richard B. *The Human Rights of Aliens in Contemporary International Law.* Manchester: Manchester University Press, 1984.

Lillich, Richard B., ed. *International Law of State Responsibility for Injuries to Aliens.* Charlottesville, Va.: University Press of Virginia, 1983.

Mayer, Ann Elizabeth. "Universal versus Islamic Human Rights: A Clash of Cultures or a Clash with a Construction?" *Michigan Journal of International Law* 15 (1994): 307.

McDougal, Myres S., Harold D. Lasswell, and Lung-chu Chen. *Human Rights and World Public Order: The Basic Policies of an International Law of Human Dignity.* New Haven, Conn.: Yale University Press, 1980.

Meron, Theodor, ed. *Human Rights in International Law: Legal and Policy Issues.* Oxford: Clarendon Press, 1984.

Merrills, J. G. *The Development of International Law by the European Court of Human Rights.* 2d ed. New York: Manchester University Press, 1993.

Moeckli, Daniel, Sangeeta Shah, and Sandesh Sivakumaran, and David Harris. *International Human Rights Law.* New York: Oxford University Press, 2010.

Nmehielle, Vincent O. O. *The Africa Human Rights System: Its Laws, Practice, and Institutions.* The Hague: Martinus Nijhoff, 2001.

Nowak, Manfred. *UN Covenant on Civil and Political Rights, CCPR Commentary.* 2d rev. ed. Kehl am. Rhen: Engel, 2005.

Ouguergouz, Fatash. *The African Charter on Human and Peoples' Rights: A Comprehensive Agenda for Human Dignity and Sustainable Democracy in Africa.* The Hague: Martinus Nijhoff, 2003.

Pasqualucci, Jo M. *The Practice and Procedure of the Inter-American Court of Human Rights.* Cambridge: Cambridge University Press, 2003.

Pattison, James. *Humanitarian Intervention and the Responsibility to Protect: Who Should Intervene?* New York: Oxford University Press, 2010.

Ramcharan, B. G., ed. *The Principle of Legality in International Human Rights Institutions.* The Hague: Martinus Nijhoff Publishers, 1997.

Ramcharan, Bertrand G. *The UN High Commissioner for Human Rights: The Challenges of International Protection.* The Hague: Martinus Nijhoff, 2002.

Ratner, Steven, Jason Abrams, and James Bischoff. *Accountability for Human Rights Atrocities in International Law: Beyond the Nuremberg Legacy.* 3d ed. New York: Oxford University Press, 2009.

Reisman, W. Michael. "Sovereignty and Human Rights in Contemporary International Law." *American Journal of International Law* 84 (1990): 866.

Robertson, A. H. *Human Rights in the World.* Manchester: Manchester University Press, 1996.

Roth, Andreas H. *The Minimum Standard of International Law Applied to Aliens.* Leiden: A. W. Sijthoff, 1949.

Rowe, Peter. *The Impact of Human Rights Law on Armed Forces.* Cambridge: Cambridge University Press, 2006.

Ruddick, Elizabeth E. "The Continuing Constraint of Sovereignty: International Law, International Protection, and the Internally Displaced." *Boston University Law Review* 77 (1992): 429.

Sathanapally, Aruna. *Beyond Disagreement: Open Remedies in Human Rights Adjudication.* New York: Oxford University Press, 2012.

Schabas, William. *Genocide in International Law: The Crimes of Crime.* Cambridge: Cambridge University Press, 2000.

Schabas, W., ed. *The Universal Declaration of Human Rights: The Travaux Preparatoires.* Cambridge: Cambridge University Press, 2013.

Shelton, Diane. *Remedies in Human Rights Law.* New York: Oxford University Press, 2006.

Shelton, Dinah, ed. *The Oxford Handbook of International Human Rights Law.* New York: Oxford University Press, 2013.

Shelton, Dinah and Paolo G. Carozza. *Regional Protection of Human Rights.* 2d ed. New York: Oxford University Press, 2013.

Sieghart, Paul. *The International Law of Human Rights.* Oxford: Clarendon Press, 1983.

Sinha, S. Prakash. *Asylum and International Law.* The Hague: Martinus Nijhoff, 1971.

Stavropoulou, Maria. "The Right Not to Be Displaced." *American University Journal of International Law and Policy* 9 (1994): 689.

Steiner, Henry J., Phillip Alston, and Ryan Goodman. *International Human Rights in Context: Law, Politics, Morals.* 3d ed. New York: Oxford University Press, 2007.

Teitel, Ruti. *Humanity's Law.* New York: Oxford University Press, 2011.

United Nations Department of Public Information. *The United Nations and Human Rights, 1945–1995.* New York: United Nations, 1995.

Van der Heijden, B. and B. Tahzib-Lie, eds. *Reflections on the Universal Declaration of Human Rights: A Fiftieth Anniversary Anthology.* New York: Springer, 1998.

Vasak, Karel. *The International Dimensions of Human Rights.* 2 vols. Westport, Conn.: Greenwood Press; Paris: UNESCO, 1982.

Victims Unsilenced: The Inter-American Human Rights System and Transitional Justice in Latin America. Due Process of Law Foundation, 2007.

Viljoen, Frans. *International Human Rights Law in Africa.* New York: Oxford University Press, 2012.

Weissbrodt, David. *The Human Rights of Non-Citizens.* New York: Oxford University Press, 2008.

Wiessner, Siegfried and Andrew R. Willard. "Policy-oriented Jurisprudence and Human Rights Abuses in Internal Conflict: Toward a World Public Order of Human Dignity." *American Journal of International Law* 93 (1999): 316.

Woods, J. and H. Lewis. *Human Rights and the Global Marketplace: Economic, Social, and Cultural Dimensions.* Brill, 2005.

Young, Kirsten A. *The Law and Process of the U.N. Human Rights Committee.* Leiden: Hotei Publishing, 2002.

13. Vertical Allocation of Authority

Breen, Claire. "The Necessity of a Role for the ECOSO in the Maintenance of International Peace and Security." *Journal of Conflict & Security Law* 12 (2007): 261.

Farral, Jeremy Matam. *United Nations Sanctions and the Rule of Law.* Cambridge: Cambridge University Press, 2009.

Franck, Thomas. "Collective Security and UN Reform: Between the necessary and the possible." *Chicago Journal of International Law* 6 (2006): 597.

Franck, Thomas M. "The Powers of Appreciation. Who Is the Ultimate Guardian of UN Legality?" *American Journal of International Law* 86 (1992): 519.

Gassama, Ibrahim J. "Safeguarding the Democratic Entitlement: A Proposal for United Nations Involvement in National Politics." *Cornell International Law Journal* 30 (1997): 287.

Howard, Lise Morjé. *UN Peacekeeping in Civil Wars*. Cambridge: Cambridge University Press, 2007.

King, Faiza Patel. "Sensible Scrutiny: The Yugoslavia Tribunal and Development of Limits on the Security Council's Powers Under Chapter VII of the Charter." *Emory International Law Review* 10 (1996): 509.

Murphy, Sean D. *Humanitarian Intervention: The United Nations in an Evolving Order*. Philadelphia: University of Pennsylvania Press, 1996.

Orakhelashvili, Alexander. *Collective Security*. New York: Oxford University Press, 2011.

Rajan, M. S. *The Expanding Jurisdiction of the United Nations*. Bombay: N. M. Tripathi; Dobbs Ferry, N.Y.: Oceana Publications, 1982.

14. Horizontal Allocation of Authority

Cameron, Iain. *The Protective Principle of International Criminal Jurisdiction*. Dartmouth Publishing, 1994.

Chehtman, Alejandro. *The Philosophical Foundations of Extraterritorial Punishment*. New York: Oxford University Press, 2010.

Dickinson, Andrew, Rae Lindsay, and James P. Loonam. *State Immunity: Selected Materials and Commentary*. New York: Oxford University Press, 2004.

Fox, Hazel and Philippa Webb. *The Law of State Immunity*. 3d ed. New York: Oxford University Press, 2013.

Franck, Thomas M. and Gregory M. Fox. *International Law Decisions in National Courts*. Irvington-on-Hudson, N.Y.: Transnational Publishers, 1996.

Gowlland-Debbas, Vera. "Relationship of the International Court of Justice and the Security Council in Light of Lockerbie." *American Journal of International Law* 88 (1994): 643.

Knox, John. "A Presumption Against Extrajurisdictionality." *American Journal of International Law* 104 (2010): 351.

Koh, Harold Hongju. "Why Transnational Law Matters." *Penn State International Law Review* 24 (2006): 745.

Langer, Máximo. "The Diplomacy of Universal Jurisdiction: The Political Branches and the Transnational Prosecution of International Crimes." *American Journal of International Law* 105 (2011): 1.

Lowenfeld, Andreas F. "The Cuban Liberty and Democratic Solidarity (Libertad) Act: Congress and Cuba: The Helms-Burton Act." *American Journal of International Law* 90 (1996): 419.

Lowenfeld, Andreas F. *International Litigation and the Quest for Reasonableness: Essays in Private International Law*. Oxford: Oxford University Press, 1996.

Lutz, Ellen L. and Caitlin Reiger, eds. *Prosecuting Heads of State*. Cambridge: Cambridge University Press, 2009.

Milanovic, Marko. *Extraterritorial Application of Human Rights Treaties: Law, Principles, and Policy*. New York: Oxford University Press, 2011.

O'Keefe, Roger and Christian J. Tams, eds. *The United Nations Convention on Jurisdictional Immunities of States and Their Property: A Commentary*. New York: Oxford University Press, 2013.

Paust, Jordan J. "Extradition and United States Prosecution of the *Achille Lauro* Hostage-Takers: Navigating the Hazards." *Vanderbilt Journal of Transnational Law* 20 (1987): 235.

Paust, Jordan. "Suing Karadzic." *Leiden Journal of International Law* 10 (1997): 91.

Randall, Kenneth C. "Universal Jurisdiction Under International Law." *Texas Law Review* 66 (1988): 785.

Reydams, Luc. *Universal Jurisdiction: International and Municipal Legal Perspectives.* New York: Oxford University Press, 2003.

Roht-Arriaza, Naomi. *The Pinochet Effect: Transnational Justice in the Age of Human Rights.* Philadelphia, Pa.: University of Pennsylvania Press, 2006.

Ryngaert, Cedric. *Jurisdiction in International Law.* New York: Oxford University Press, 2008.

Schreuer, Christoph. *State Immunity: Some Recent Developments.* Cambridge: Grotius, 1988.

PART SIX/STRATEGIES

15. The Diplomatic Instrument

Amerasinghe, Chittharanjan. *Diplomatic Protection.* New York: Oxford University Press, 2008.

Ashman, Chuck and Pamela Trescott. *Diplomatic Crime.* Toronto: PaperJacks, 1988.

Bundy, McGeorge, William J. Crowe, Jr., and Sidney D. Drell. *Reducing Nuclear Danger: The Road Away from the Brink.* New York: Council on Foreign Relations Press, 1993.

Carter, Barry E. "Immunity for Foreign Officials: Possibly Too Much and Confusing as Well." *American Society of International Law Proceedings.* 99 (2005): 230.

Denza, Eileen. *Diplomatic Law: Commentary on the Vienna Convention on Diplomatic Relations.* New York: Oxford University Press, 2008.

Higgins, Rosalyn. "The Abuse of Diplomatic Privileges and Immunities: Recent United Kingdom Experience." *American Journal of International Law* 79 (1985): 641.

Jacovides, Andrew. *International Law and Diplomacy.* The Hague: Martinus Nijhoff, 2011.

Klotz, Audie. *Norms in International Relations: The Struggle Against Apartheid.* Ithaca, N.Y.: Cornell University Press, 1995.

Ku, Julian and John Yoo. *Taming Globalization: International Law, the U.S. Constitution, and the New World Order.* New York: Oxford University Press, 2012.

Lauren, Paul Gordon, Gordon Craig, and Alexander George. *Force and Statecraft: Diplomatic Challenges of Our Time.* 4th ed. New York: Oxford University Press, 2006.

Lee, Luke and John Quigley. *Consular Law and Practice.* 3d ed. New York: Oxford University Press, 2008.

Melissen, Jan and Ana Mar Fernández. *Consular Affairs and Diplomacy.* The Hague: Martinus Nijhoff, 2011.

Ramcharan, B. G. *The International Law and Practice of Early-Warning of Preventive Diplomacy: The Emerging Global Watch.* Dordrecht: Martinus Nijhoff Publishers, 1991.

Roberts, Ivor, eds. *Satow's Diplomatic Practice.* 6th ed. New York: Oxford University Press, 2011.

Schrag, Philip G. *Global Action: Nuclear Test Ban Diplomacy at the End of the Cold War.* Boulder, Colo.: Westview Press, 1992.

Sen, B. *A Diplomat's Handbook of International Law and Practice.* The Hague: Martinus Nijhoff, 1979.

Shelton, Dinah, ed. *International Law and Domestic Legal Systems: Incorporation, Transformation, and Persuasion.* New York: Oxford University Press, 2011.

Van Ham, Peter. *Managing Non-Proliferation Regimes in the 1990s: Power Politics and New Policies*. London: The Royal Institute of International Affairs/Council on Foreign Relations Press, 1994.

Vicuna, Francisco Orrego. "The Status and Rights of Refugees Under International Law: New Issues in Light of the Honnecker Affair." *University of Miami Inter- American Law Review* 25 (1994): 35l.

Wilson, Clifton E. *Diplomatic Privileges and Immunities*. Tucson, Az.: University of Arizona Press, 1967.

16. International Agreements

Aust, Anthony. *Modern Treaty Law and Practice*. 2d ed. Cambridge: Cambridge University Press, 2013.

Bederman, David J. "Revivalist Canons and Treaty Interpretation." *UCLA Law Review* 41 (1994): 953.

Bell, Christine. "Peace Agreements: Their Nature and Legal Status." *American Journal of International Law* 100 (2006): 373.

Cannizzaro, Enzo. *The Law of Treaties Beyond the Vienna Convention*. New York: Oxford University Press, 2011.

Chen, Lung-chu. "Constitutional Law and International Law in the United States of America." *American Journal of Comparative Law, Supplement* 42 (1994): 453.

Churchill, Robin and Geir Ulfstein. "Autonomous Institutional Arrangements in Multilateral Environmental Agreements: A Little-Noticed Phenomena in International Law." *American Journal of International Law* 94 (2000): 623.

Dorr, Oliver and Kirsten Schmalenbach, eds. *The Vienna Convention on the Law of Treaties: A Commentary*. New York: Springer, 2011.

Elias, T. O. *The Modern Law of Treaties*. Dobbs Ferry, N.Y.: Oceana Publications; Leiden: A. W. Sijthoff, 1974.

Fitzmaurice, Malgosia, Olufemi Elias, and Panos Merkouris. *Treaty Interpretation and the Vienna Convention on the Law of Treaties: 30 Years On*. The Hague: Martinus Nijhoff, 2010.

Gardiner, Richard. *Treaty Interpretation*. New York: Oxford University Press, 2008.

Garvey, Jack I. "Trade Law and Quality of Life in Dispute Resolution Under the NAFTA Side Accords on Labor and the Environment." *American Journal of International Law* 89 (1995): 439.

Gordon, Edward. "The World Court and the Interpretation of Constitutive Treaties." *American Journal of International Law* 59 (1965): 794.

Hathaway, Oona. "Treaties' End: The Past, Present, and Future of International Lawmaking in the United States." *Yale Law Journal* 117 (2006): 1236.

Henkin, Louis. *Foreign Affairs and the United States Constitution*. 2d ed. New York: Oxford University Press, 1996.

Linderfalk, Ulf. *On the Interpretation of Treaties: The Modern International Law as Expressed in the 1969 Vienna Convention on the Law of Treaties*. New York: Springer, 2007.

Martin, Francisco Forrest. *The Constitution as Treaty: The International Legal Constructionalist Approach to the U.S. Constitution*. Cambridge: Cambridge University Press, 2012.

McDougal, Myres S., Harold D. Lasswell, and James C. Miller. *The Interpretation of Agreements and World Public Order: Principles of Content and Procedure*. New Haven, Conn.: Yale University Press, 1967.

Orakhelashvili, Alexander. *Peremptory Norms in International Law*. New York: Oxford University Press, 2006.

Rogoff, Martin A. "Interpretation of International Agreements by Domestic Courts and the Politics of International Treaty Relations: Reflections on Some Recent Decisions of the U.S. Supreme Court." *American University Journal of International Law & Policy* 1 (1996): 559.

Rosenne, Shabtai. *The Law of Treaties: A Guide to the Legislative History of the Vienna Convention*. Leiden: A. W. Sijthoff; Dobbs Ferry, N.Y.: Oceana Publications, 1970.

Rozakis, Christos L. *The Concept of JUS COGENS in the Law of Treaties*. Amsterdam: North-Holland, 1976.

Sinclair, Sir Ian McTaggart. *The Vienna Convention on the Law of Treaties*. 2d ed. Manchester: Manchester University Press, 1984.

Sloss David, ed. *The Role of Domestic Courts in Treaty Enforcement: A Comparative Study*. Cambridge: Cambridge University Press, 2009.

Steinberg, Richard H. "Trade and Environmental Negotiations in the EU, NAFTA, and WTO: Regional Trajectories of Rule Development." *American Journal of International Law* 91 (1997): 231.

Szasz, Paul. *International and Expert Monitoring of Treaties*. Ardsley, N.Y.: Transnational, 1999.

Vagts, Detlev. "The United States and Its Treaties: Observance and Breach." *American Journal of International Law* 95 (2001): 277.

Villiger, Mark E. *Commentary on the 1969 Vienna Convention on the Law of Treaties*. Lieden: Brill, 2009.

17. The Ideological Instrument

Baderin, Mashood. *International Human Rights and Islamic Law*. New York: Oxford University Press, 2003.

Besson, Samantha and John Tasioulas, eds. *The Philosophy of International Law*. New York: Oxford University Press, 2011.

Chen, Lung-chu. "Human Rights and the Free Flow of Information." *New York Law School Journal of International and Comparative Law*, 4 (1982): 37.

Dickinson, Laura. *International Law and Society*. London: Ashgate, 2007.

Hamson, Francoise I. "Incitement and the Media: Responsibility of and for the Media in the Conflicts in the Former Yugoslavia." Papers in the Theory and Practice of Human Rights, no. 3. Essex, England: Human Rights Centre, University of Essex, 1993.

Farer, Tom. *Confronting Global Terrorism and American Neo-Conservativism: The Framework of a Liberal Grand Strategy*. New York: Oxford University Press, 2008.

Foster, Francis H. "Information and the Problem of Democracy: The Russian Experience." *American Journal of Comparative Law* 44 (1996): 243.

Franck, Thomas. *The Empowered Self: Law and Society in an Age of Individualism*. New York: Oxford University Press, 2000.

Klabbers, Jan, Anne Peters, and Geir Ulfstein. *The Constitutionalization of International Law*. New York: Oxford University Press, 2011.

Kymlicka, Will. *Multicultural Odysseys: Navigating the New International Politics of Diversity*. New York: Oxford University Press, 2009.

Marks, Susan. *The Riddle of All Constitutions: International Law, Democracy, and the Critique of Ideology*. New York: Oxford University Press, 2003.

McDougal, Myres S. and W. Michael Reisman, eds. *Power and Policy in Quest of Law : Essays in Honor of Eugene Victor Rostow*. The Hague: Martinus Nijhoff, 1985.

Metze, Jamie Frederic. "Rwanda Genocide and the International Law of Radio Jamming." *American Journal of International Law* 91 (1997): 628.

Murty, B. S. *Propaganda and World Public Order: The Legal Regulation of the Ideological Instrument of Coercion*. New Haven, Conn.: Yale University Press, 1968.

Perritt, Henry H., Jr. "Jurisdiction in Cyberspace." *Villanova Law Review* 41 (1996): 41.

Rubi, Alfred. *Ethics and Authority in International Law*. Cambridge: Cambridge University Press, 2007.

Sau, Ben. *Defining Terrorism in International Law*. New York: Oxford University Press, 2006.

Schmitt, Michael N., ed. *Tallinn Manual on the International Law Applicable to Cyber Warfare*. Cambridge: Cambridge University Press, 2013.

Tomuschat, Christian. *Human Rights: Between Idealism and Realism*. New York: Oxford University Press, 2008.

Weeramantry, C. G. *Universalising International Law*. The Hague: Martinus Nijhoff, 2004.

18. The Economic Instrument

Arup, Christopher. *The World Trade Organization Knowledge Agreements*. 2d ed. Cambridge: Cambridge University Press, 2008.

Brown Weiss, Edith. *Fresh Water and International Economic Law*. New York: Oxford University Press, 2005.

Carter, Barry E. *International Economic Sanctions: Improving the Haphazard U.S. Legal Regime*. Cambridge: Cambridge University Press, 1988.

Cass, Deborah. *The Constitutionalization of the World Trade Organization: Legitimacy, Democracy, and Community in the International Trading System*. New York: Oxford University Press, 2005.

Choi, Won-Mog. *"Like Products" in International Trade Law Towards a Consistent GATT/WTO Jurisprudence*. New York: Oxford University Press, 2003.

Childers, Erskine and Brian Urquhart. *Renewing the United Nations System*. Uppsala, Sweden: Dag Hammarskjold Foundation, 1994.

Damrosch, Lori F., ed. *Enforcing Restraint: Collective Intervention in Internal Conflicts*. New York: Council on Foreign Relations, 1993.

Dolzer, Rudolf and Christoph Schreuer. *Principles of International Investment Law*. New York: Oxford University Press, 2013.

Doxey, Margaret P. *International Sanctions in Contemporary Perspective*. New York: St. Martin's Press, 1987.

Guzman, Andrew. *Cooperation, Comity, and Competition Policy*. New York: Oxford University Press, 2010.

Hufbauer, Gary Clyde, Jeffrey J. Schott, and Kimberly Ann Elliott. *Economic Sanctions Reconsidered*. 2d ed. Washington, D.C.: Institute for International Economics, 1990.

Jackson, John H. *Legal Problems of International Economic Relations*. St. Paul, Minn.: West, 1977.

Lang, Andrew. *World Trade Law After Neoliberalism: Reimagining the Global Economic Order*. New York: Oxford University Press, 2011.

Lillich, Richard B., ed. *Economic Coercion and the New International Economic Order.* Charlottesville, Va.: Michie, 1976.

Lowenfeld, Andreas. *International Economic Law.* 2d ed. New York: Oxford University Press, 2008.

Lowenfeld, Andreas. *Trade Control for Political Ends.* 2d ed. New York: Matthew Bender, 1983.

Meagher, Robert F. *An International Redistribution of Wealth and Power: A Study of the Charter of Economic Rights and Duties of States.* New York: Pergamon, 1979.

Nanda, Ved P., George W. Shepherd, Jr., and Eileen McCarthy-Arnolds, eds. *World Debt and the Human Condition: Structural Adjustment and the Right to Development.* Westport, Conn.: Greenwood Publishing Group, 1993.

Oesch, Matthias. *Standards of Review in WTO Dispute Resolution.* New York: Oxford University Press, 2004.

Paust, Jordan et al., eds. *The Arab Oil Weapon.* Dobbs Ferry, N.Y.: Oceana Publications, 1977.

Proctor, Charles. *The Law and Practice of International Banking.* New York: Oxford University Press, 2010.

Rammeloo, Stephan. *Corporations in Private International Law: A European Perspective.* New York: Oxford University Press, 2001.

Revesz, Richard, Philippe Sands, and Richard Stewart. *Environmental Law, the Economy and Sustainable Development: The United States, the European Union and the International Community.* Cambridge: Cambridge University Press, 2008.

Sauvant, Karl P., ed. *Yearbook on International Investment Law and Policy 2011–2012.* New York: Oxford University Press, 2013.

Schachter, Oscar. "Compensation for Expropriation." *American Journal of International Law* 78 (1984): 121.

Schill, Stephan. *The Multilateralization of International Investment Law.* Cambridge: Cambridge University Press, 2009.

Siegel, Deborah. "Legal Aspects of the IMF/WTO Relationship: The Fund's Articles of Agreement and the WTO Agreements." *American Journal of International Law* 96 (2002): 531.

Thomas, Chantal and Joel Trachtman. *Developing Countries in the WTO Legal System.* New York: Oxford University Press, 2009.

Trachtman, Joel P. *The Economic Structure of International Law.* Cambridge, Mass.: Harvard University Press, 2008.

Weiss, Thomas G., David Cortright, George A. Lopez, and Larry Minear. *Political Gain and Civilian Pain: Humanitarian Impacts of Economic Sanctions.* Lanham, Md.: Rowman and Littlefield, 1997.

Weston, Bums H. "The Charter of Economic Rights and Duties of States and the Deprivation of Foreign-Owned Wealth." *American Journal of International Law* 75 (1981): 437.

19. The Military Instrument

Alston, Philip and Euan Macdonald. *Human Rights, Intervention, and the Use of Force.* New York: Oxford University Press, 2008.

Arms Project of Human Rights Watch/Physicians for Human Rights. *Landmines: A Deadly Legacy.* St. Louis, Mo.: Saint Louis University Law School, 1993.

Blix, Hans. *Aggression, Neutrality and Sovereignty*. Stockholm: Almqvist and Wiksell, 1970.

Bowett, D. W. *Self-Defence in International Law*. Clark, N.J.: The Lawbook Exchange, 2009.

Brownlie, Ian. *International Law and the Use of Force by States*. Oxford: Clarendon Press, 1963.

Caron, David D. "The Legitimacy of the Collective Authority of the Security Council" *American Journal International Law* 87 (1993): 552.

Chayes, Abram. *The Cuban Missile Crisis: International Crises and the Role of Law*. New York: Oxford University Press, 1974.

Cryer, Robert and Neil Boister. *Documents on the Tokyo International Military Tribunal: Charter, Indictment and Judgments*. New York: Oxford University Press, 2008.

Cullen, Anthony. *The Concept of Non-International Armed Conflict in International Humanitarian Law*. Cambridge: Cambridge University Press, 2010.

Damrosch, Lori. *Enforcing Restraint: Collective Intervention in Internal Conflicts*. New York: Council on Foreign Relations Press,1993.

Damrosch, Lori. *Law and Force in the New International Order*. Co-edited with David J. Scheffer. Westview Press, 1991.

Dickinson, Laura. "Military Lawyers on the Battlefield: An Empirical Account of International Law Compliance." *American Journal of International Law* 104 (2010): 1.

Dinstein, Yoram. *War, Aggression and Self-Defence*. 4th ed. Cambridge: Cambridge University Press, 2005.

Draper, G. I. A. *The Red Cross Conventions*. London: Stevens, 1958.

Falk, Richard A. *Legal Order in a Violent World*. Princeton, N.J.: Princeton University Press, 1968.

Falk, Richard A., ed. *The Vietnam War and International Law*. 4 vols. Princeton, N.J.: Princeton University Press, 1968–76.

Ferencz, Benjamin B. *Defining International Aggression: The Search for World Peace*. 2 vols. Dobbs Ferry, N.Y.: Oceana Publications, 1975.

Fleck, Dieter, ed. *The Handbook of International Humanitarian Law*. 3d ed. New York: Oxford University Press, 2013.

Fletcher, George P. and Jens David Ohlin. *Defending Humanity: When Force Is Justified and Why*. New York: Oxford University Press, 2008.

Gardam, Judith. *Necessity, Proportionality and the Use of Force by States*. Cambridge: Cambridge University Press, 2011.

Garvey, Jack. *Nuclear Weapons Counterproliferation: A New Grand Bargain*. New York: Oxford University Press, 2013.

Gray, Christine. *International Law and the Use of Force*. 3d ed. New York: Oxford University Press, 2008.

Henckaerts, Jean-Marie and Louise Doswald-Beck, eds. *Customary International Humanitarian Law*. International Committee of the Red Cross, 2005.

Lillich, Richard B., ed. *Humanitarian Intervention and the United Nations*. Charlottesville, Va.: University Press of Virginia, 1973.

Lubell, Noam. *Extraterritorial Use of Force against Non-State Actors*. New York: Oxford University Press, 2010.

Maier, Harold G., ed. "Appraisals of the ICJ's Decision: *Nicaragua* v. *United States* (Merits)." *American Journal of International Law* 81 (1987): 77.

Matheson, Michael J. "The Opinions of the International Court of Justice on the Threat or Use of Nuclear Weapons." *American Journal of International Law* 91 (1997): 417.

McDougal, Myres S. and Florentino P. Feliciano. *Law and Minimum World Public Order*. New Haven, Conn.: Yale University Press, 1961.

Meessen, Karl. "Unilateral Recourse to Military Force Against Terrorist Attacks." *Yale Journal of International Law* 28 (2003): 341.

Melzer, Nils. *Targeted Killing in International Law*. New York: Oxford University Press, 2008.

Meron, Theodor. *The Humanization of International Law*. Leiden: Brill, 2006.

Moir, Lindsay. *The Law of Internal Armed Conflict*. Cambridge: Cambridge University Press, 2002.

Moore, John Norton, ed. *Law and the Civil War in the Modern World*. Baltimore: Johns Hopkins University Press, 1974.

Murphy, John F. *The United Nations and the Control of International Violence: A Legal and Political Analysis*. Totowa, N.J.: Allanheld, Osmun, 1982.

Murphy, Sean. *Humanitarian Intervention: The United Nations in An Evolving World Order*. Philadelphia: University of Pennsylvania Press, 1996.

Paust, Jordan. *Beyond the Law: The Bush Administration's Unlawful Responses in the "War" on Terror*, Cambridge University Press, 2007.

Pearson, Graham S. "The Prohibition of Biological Weapons: Current Activities and Future Prospects." *International Review of the Red Cross* 318 (1997): 270.

Reinold, Theresa. "State Weakness, Irregular Warfare, and the Right to Self-Defense Post-9/11." *American Journal of International Law* 105 (2011): 244.

Reisman, W. Michael. *The Laws of War: A Comprehensive Collection of Primary Documents on International Laws Governing Armed Conflict*. With Chris T. Antoniou. Vintage Press, 1994.

Reisman, W. Michael and Kristen Eichensehr, eds. *Stopping Wars and Making Peace*. Leiden: Martinus Nijhoff, 2009.

Roberts, Adam and Richard Guelff. *Documents on the Laws of War*. 3d ed. New York: Oxford University Press, 2000.

Rodin, David. *War and Self-Defense*. New York: Oxford University Press, 2005.

Rodley, Nigel and Matt Pollard. *The Treatment of Prisoners under International Law*. 3d ed. New York: Oxford University Press, 2011.

Natalino, Ronzitti. Rescuing *Nationals Abroad Through Military Coercion and Intervention on Grounds of Humanity*. New York: Springer, 1985.

Ruys, Tom. *"Armed Attack" and Article 51 of the UN Charter: Evolutions in Customary Law and Practice*. Cambridge: Cambridge University Press, 2011.

Shiner, Phil and Andrew Williams, eds. *The Iraq War and International Law*. Portland: Hart Press, 2008.

Slaughter, Anne-Marie and William Burke-White. "An International Constitutional Moment." *Harvard International Law Journal* 43 (2002): 1.

Song, Yann-huei. "China's Missile Tests in the Taiwan Strait: Relevant International Law Questions." *Marine Policy* 23 (1999): 81.

"Special Feature-Restraints on the Unilateral Use of Force: A Colloquy." *Yale Journal of International Law* 10 (1985): 261.

Stone, Julius. *Aggression and World Order: A Critique of United Nations Theories of Aggression*. Berkeley/Los Angeles: University of California Press, 1958.

Stone, Julius. *Legal Controls of International Conflict*. London: Stevens, 1954.

Stromseth, Jane, David Wippman, and Rosa Brooks. *Can Might Make Rights? Building the Rule of Law after Military Interventions*. Cambridge: Cambridge University Press, 2006.

Thuo Gathii, James. *War, Commerce, and International Law.* New York: Oxford University Press, 2009.

Trooboff, Peter D., ed. *Law and Responsibility in Warfare: The Vietnam Experience.* Chapel Hill, N.C.: University of North Carolina Press, 1975.

Walker, George K. "Anticipatory Collective Self-Defense in the Charter Era: What the Treaties Have Said." *Cornell International Law Journal* 31 (1998): 321.

Weller, Marc. *Iraq and the Use of Force in International Law.* New York: Oxford University Press, 2010.

Wiessner, Siegfried and Myres S. McDougal. "Law and Minimum World Public Order: Introduction to the Reissue." In Myres S. McDougal & Florentino P. Feliciano, *The International Law of War: Transnational Coercion and World Public Order.* New Haven: New Haven Press (1994): xix–lxxxii.

PART SEVEN/OUTCOMES

20. The Intelligence Function

Avenhaus, Rudolf. *Verifying Treaty Compliance: Limiting Weapons of Mass Destruction and Monitoring Kyoto Protocol Provisions.* New York: Springer, 2006.

Bar-Yaacov, Nissim. *The Handling of International Disputes by Means of Inquiry.* New York: Oxford University Press, 1974.

Bassiouni, M. Cherif. "Appraising UN Justice Related Fact Finding Missions." *Washington University Journal of Law and Policy* 5 (2001): 35.

Boutruche, Théo. "Credible Fact-finding and Allegations of International Humanitarian Law Violations: Challenges in Theory and Practice." *Journal of Conflict & Security Law* 16 (2011): 105.

Chesterman, Simon. "Secrets and Lies: Intelligence Activities and the Rule of Law in Times of Crisis." *Michigan Journal of International Law* 28 (2007): 553.

Collins, David. "Institutionalized Fact-Finding at the WTO." *University of Pennsylvania Journal of International Economic Law* 27 (2006): 367.

Grando, Michelle. *Evidence, Proof and Fact-Finding in WTO Dispute Settlement.* New York: Oxford University Press, 2009.

Kazazi, Mojtaba. *Burden of Proof and Related Issues: A Study of Evidence Before International Tribunals.* New York: Springer, 1996.

Keeley James and Robert Neil Huebert. *Commercial Satellite Imagery, and United Nations Peacekeeping: A View from Above.* London: Ashgate, 2004.

Roberts, Alasdair. *Blacked Out: Government Secrecy in the Information Age.* Cambridge: Cambridge University Press, 2008.

Shore, William I. *Fact-Finding in the Maintenance of Peace.* Dobbs Ferry, N.Y.: Oceana Publications, 1970.

21. The Promoting Function

Action for Equality, Development, and Peace (Beijing, China, September 1993). *Emory International Law Review* 10 (1996): 695.

Alston, Philip. "The United Nations High Commissioner for Human Rights." *American Society of International Law Newsletter,* Sept. 1995.

Barrett Scott. *Environment and Statecraft: The Strategy of Environmental Treaty-Making.* New York: Oxford University Press, 2003.

Ewumbue-Monono, Churchill and Carolo von Flue. "Promotion of International Humanitarian Law Through Cooperation between the ICRC and the African Union." *International Review of the Red Cross* 85 (2003): 749.

Gasser, Hans-Peter. "For Better Protection of the Natural Environment in Armed Conflict: A Proposal for Action." *American Journal of International Law* 89 (1995): 637.

Hohman, Harold, ed. *Basic Documents of International Environmental Law.* Vol. 1, *The Important Declarations;* Vols. 2 and 3, *The Important Agreements.* London: Kluwer/Graham & Trotman, 1992.

Kohen, Marcelo. *Promoting Justice: Human Rights and Conflict Resolution through International Law.* The Hague: Martinus Nijhoff, 2006.

Posner, Michael H. "Reflections on the Vienna Conference." *American Society of International Law Newsletter,* Sept. 1993.

Prantl, Jochen. *The UN Security Council and Informal Groups of States: Complementing or Competing for Governance?* New York: Oxford University Press, 2006.

Purvis, Nigel. "The Case for Climate Protection Authority." *Virginia Journal of International Law* 49 (2009): 1007.

Sullivan, Donna J. "Women's Human Rights and the 1993 World Conference on Human Rights." *American Journal of International Law* 88 (1994): 152.

Trachtman, Joel. *International Law and Politics.* London: Ashgate, 2008.

Tully, Stephen. *Corporations and International Lawmaking.* The Hague: Martinus Nijhoff, 2007.

Willetts, Peter, ed. *Pressure Groups in the Global System.* London: Frances Pinter, 1982.

Zillman, Donald, Alistair Lucas, and George Pring. *Human Rights in Natural Resource Development: Public Participation in the Sustainable Development of Mining and Energy Resources.* New York: Oxford University Press, 2002.

22. The Prescribing (Lawmaking) Function

Aljaghoub, Mahasen. *The Advisory Function of the International Court of Justice: 1946–2005.* New York: Springer, 2006.

Alvarez, José. *International Organizations as Lawmakers.* New York: Oxford University Press, 2006.

Buergenthal, Thomas, ed. *Human Rights, International Law and the Helsinki Accord.* Montclair, N.J.: Frances Schram, 1977.

Buergenthal, Thomas. *Law-Making in the International Civil Aviation Organization.* Charlottesville, Va.: University of Virginia Press, 1969.

Castaneda, Jorge. *Legal Effects of United Nations Resolutions.* Translated by Alba Amoia. New York: Columbia University Press, 1969.

Charney, Jonathan I. "International Agreements and the Development of Customary International Law." *Washington Law Review* 61 (1986): 971.

Cheng, Bin. *General Principles of Law as Applied by International Courts and Tribunals.* Cambridge: Cambridge University Press, 2006.

Falk, Richard. *The Role of Domestic Courts in the International Legal Order.* Syracuse, N.Y.: Syracuse University Press, 1964.

Harrison, James. *Making the Law of the Sea: A Study in the Development of International Law.* Cambridge: Cambridge University Press, 2011.

Henckaerts, Jean-Marie, Louise Doswald-Beck, and the International Committee of the Red Cross. *Customary International Humanitarian Laws: Rules.* Cambridge: Cambridge University Press, 2005.

Higgins, Rosalyn. *The Development of International Law Through the Political Organs of the United Nations.* New York: Oxford University Press, 1963.

Jansen, Nils. *The Making of Legal Authority: Non-legislative Codifications in Historical and Comparative Perspective.* New York: Oxford University Press, 2010.

Johnstone, Ian. "Legislation and Adjudication in the UN Security Council: Bring Down the Deliberative Deficit." *American Journal of International Law* 102 (2008): 275.

Lauterpacht, Hersch. *The Development of International Law by the International Court.* London: Stevens and Sons, 1958.

LeBlanc, Lawrence J. *The Convention on the Rights of the Child: United Nations Lawmaking on Human Rights.* Lincoln, Neb.: University of Nebraska Press, 1995.

Lee, Martin Lishexian. "The Interrelation Between the Law of the Sea Convention and Customary International Law." *San Diego International Law Journal* 7 (2006): 405.

McDougal, Myres S. and W. Michael Reisman. "The Prescribing Function in the World Constitutive Process: How International Law Is Made." *Yale Studies of World Public Order* 6 (1980): 249.

McWhinney, Edward. *United Nations Law Making: Cultural and Ideological Relativism and International Law Making for an Era of Transition.* New York and London: Holmes and Meier; Paris: UNESCO, 1984.

Meron, Theodor. *Human Rights and Humanitarian Norms as Customary Law.* Oxford: Clarendon, 1989.

Noortmann, Math and Cedric Ryngaert. *Non-State Actor Dynamics in International Law: From Law-Takers to Law-Makers.* London: Ashgate, 2010.

Onuf, Nicholas Greenwood, ed. *Law-Making in the Global Community.* Durham, N.C.: Duke University Press, 1982.

Parisi, Francesco and Vincy Fon. *The Economics of Lawmaking.* New York: Oxford University Press, 2008.

Paust, Jordon I. "The Complex Nature, Sources and Evidences of Customary Human Rights." *Georgia Journal of International and Comparative Law* 25 (1995–96).

Perreau-Saussine, Amanda and James Bernard Murphy. *The Nature of Customary Law.* Cambridge: Cambridge University Press, 2007.

Ramcharan, B. G. *The International Law Commission: Its Approach to the Codification and Progressive Development of International Law.* The Hague: Martinus Nijhoff, 1977.

Sands, Philippe and Pierre Klein. *Bowett's Law of International Institutions.* 6th ed. London: Sweet & Maxwell, 2009.

Sarooshi, Dan. *International Organizations and Their Exercise of Sovereign Powers.* New York: Oxford University Press, 2007.

Schweigman, David. *The Authority of the Security Council under Chapter VII of the UN Charter: Legal Limits and the Role of the International Court of Justice.* The Hague: Martinus Nijhoff, 2001.

Sinclair, Ian. *The International Law Commission.* Cambridge: Grotius, 1987. *Trade/Development.* Vols. 5 and 5(a), *Earth Space Environment.* Irvington-on Hudson, N.Y.: Transnational Publishers, 1994.

United Nations. *Making Better International Law: The International Law Commission at 50.* New York: United Nations, 1998.

Watts, Arthur. *The International Law Commission, 1949–1998.* New York: Oxford University Press, 1999.

Wood, Sir Michael and Arnold Pronto. *The International Law Commission, 1999–2009.* New York: Oxford University Press, 2011.

Zacher, Mark W. *Governing Global Networks: International Regimes for Transportation and Communications.* Cambridge: Cambridge University Press, 1996.

23. The Invoking Function

Anderson, Kym and Richard Blackhurst, eds. *The Greening of World Trade Issues.* Ann Arbor, Mich.: University of Michigan Press, 1992.

Arnold, Roberta. *The ICC as a New Instrument for Repressing Terrorism.* The Hague: Martinus Nijhoff, 2004.

Bayefsky, Anne. *How to Complain to the U.N. Human Rights Treaty System.* New York: Springer, 2003.

Bodansky, Daniel, John Crook, and Edith Brown Weiss. "Invoking State Responsibility in the Twenty-First Century." *American Journal of International Law* 96 (2002): 798.

Carey, John. *UN Protection of Civil and Political Rights.* Syracuse, N.Y.: Syracuse University Press, 1970.

Chiedu Moghalu, Kingsley. *Rwanda's Genocide: The Politics of Global Justice.* New York: Palgrave Macmillan, 2005.

Duxbury, Allison. *The Participation of States in International Organisations: The Role of Human Rights and Democracy.* Cambridge: Cambridge University Press, 2011.

Gassama, Ibrahim J. "The United Nations, NGOs and Apartheid." *Fordham International Law Journal* 19 (1996): 1464.

Ghazi, Bahram. *The IMF, the World Bank Group and the Question of Human Rights.* The Hague: Martinus Nijhoff, 2005.

Guest, Iain. *Behind the Disappearances: Argentina's Dirty War Against Human Rights and the United Nations.* Philadelphia: University of Pennsylvania, 1990.

Huffines, Jeffrey. "United States Ratification of Human Rights Treaties: The Role of NGOs in United States Ratifications of Human Rights Treaties." *ILSA Journal of Comparative Law* 3 (1992): 641.

Murphy, Craig. *The United Nations Development Programme: A Better Way?* Cambridge: Cambridge University Press, 2006.

Robertson, A. H. *Human Rights in the World.* 2d ed. New York: St. Martin's Press, 1982.

Vandenhole, Wouter. *The Procedures before the U.N. Human Rights Treaty Bodies: Divergence or Convergence?* Cambridge: Intersentia, 2004.

Weston, Bums H. "Human Rights." *Human Rights Quarterly* 6 (1984): 257.

Williamson, Richard L., Jr. "Law and the H-Bomb: Strengthening the Non-Proliferation Regime to Impede Advanced Proliferation." *Cornell International Law Journal* 28 (1995): 1030.

Young, Kirsten A. *The Law and Process of the U.N. Human Rights Committee.* Leiden: Hotei Publishing, 2002.

24. The Applying Function

Bantekas, Ilias. "The International Law of Terrorism Financing." *American Journal of International Law* 97 (2003): 315.

Barkun, Michael. *Law Without Sanctions: Order in Primitive Societies and the World Community.* New Haven, Conn.: Yale University Press, 1968.

Berns, Andrew and Jane Connors. "Enforcing the Human Rights of Women: A Complaints Procedure for the Women's Convention? Draft Optional Protocol to the Convention on the Elimination of All Forms of Discrimination Against Women." *Brooklyn Journal of International Law* 21 (1996): 679.

Bilder, Richard B. "International Dispute Settlement and the Role of International Adjudication." *Emory Journal of International Dispute Resolution* 1 (1987): 142.

Carter, Barry E. *International Economic Sanctions: Improving the Haphazard U.S. Legal Regime.* Cambridge: Cambridge University Press, 2008.

Chinkin, Christine. "Alternatives to Economic Sanctions." In Gowlland-Debbas, Vera, ed. *United Nations Sanctions and International Law.* Kluwer Law International, 2001.

Coleman, Katharina. *International Organisations and Peace Enforcement: The Politics of International Legitimacy.* Cambridge: Cambridge University Press, 2007.

Conlon, Paul. *United Nations Sanctions Management: A Case Study of the Iraq Sanctions Committee.* Leiden: Brill, 2000.

Cortright, David and George A. Lopez. *The Sanctions Decade: Assessing UN Strategies in the 1990s.* Boulder, Colo.: Lynne Rienner, 2000.

Crawford, Emily. *The Treatment of Combatants under the Law of Armed Conflict.* New York: Oxford University Press, 2010.

Damrosch, Lori. *Enforcing International Law Through Non-Forcible Measures.* In *Collected Courses of the Hague Academy of International Law.* The Hague: Martinus Nijhoff, 1997.

Due Process and Targeted Sanctions: An Update of the "Watson Report. Watson Institute for International Studies at Brown University. Providence: 2012.

Duffy, Helen. *The "War on Terror" and the Framework of International Law.* Cambridge: Cambridge University Press, 2005.

Fisher, Roger. *Improving Compliance with International Law.* Charlottesville, Va.: University Press of Virginia, 1981.

Forowicz, Magdalena. *The Reception of International Law in the European Court of Human Rights.* New York: Oxford University Press, 2010.

Katselli, Elena. *The Problem of Enforcement in International Law: Countermeasures, the Non-Injured State and the Idea of International Community.* London: Routledge, 2009.

Merrills, J. G. *International Dispute Settlement.* 5th ed. Cambridge: Cambridge University Press, 2011.

Nino, Carlos S. "The Duty to Punish Past Abuses of Human Rights Put in Context: The Case of Argentina." *Yale Law Journal* 100 (1991).

O'Connell, Mary Ellen. *The Power and Purpose of International Law: Insights from the Theory and Practice of Enforcement.* New York: Oxford University Press, 2008.

Oellers-Frahm, Karin and Norbert Wuhler, comps. *Dispute Settlement in Public International Law: Texts and Materials.* Berlin: Springer Verlag, 1984.

Orenlichter, Diane F. "Settling Accounts: The Duty to Prosecute Human Rights Violations of a Prior Regime." *Yale Law Journal* 100 (1991): 2537.

Orford, Anne. *Reading Humanitarian Intervention: Human Rights and the Use of Force in International Law.* Cambridge: Cambridge University Press, 2007.

Ratner, Steven R. "The Civilian Impact of Economic Sanctions." In Lori F. Damrosch (ed), *Enforcing Restraint: Collective Intervention in Internal Conflicts.* New York: Council on Foreign Relations Press, 1993.

Reisman, W. Michael. *Foreign Investment Disputes: Cases Materials and Commentary.* With Doak Bishop and James Crawford. Kluwer Law International, 2005.

Reisman, W. Michael. *International Commercial Arbitration: Cases, Materials and Notes on the Resolution of International Business Disputes.* With W. Laurence Craig, William Park, and Jan Paulsson. Foundation Press, 1997.

Reisman, W. Michael. *Systems of Control in International Adjudication and Arbitration: Breakdown and Repair.* Duke University Press, 1992.

Rosenne, Shabtai. *Provisional Measures in International Law: The International Court of Justice and the International Tribunal for the Law of the Sea.* New York: Oxford University Press, 2005.

Schulte, Constanze. *Compliance with Decisions of the International Court of Justice.* New York: Oxford University Press, 2005.

Sohn, Louis B. *Broadening the Role of the United Nations in Preventing, Mitigating or Ending International or Internal Conflicts That Threaten International Peace and Security.* Washington, D.C.: International Rule of Law Center, George Washington University Law School, 1997.

Strengthening Targeted Sanctions Through Fair and Clear Procedures. Watson Institute for International Studies at Brown University. Providence: 2006.

Tzanakopoulos, Antonios. *Disobeying the Security Council: Countermeasures against Wrongful Sanctions.* New York: Oxford University Press, 2011.

Wilson, Richard Ashby. *Human Rights in the "War on Terror."* Cambridge: Cambridge University Press, 2005.

Zalaquett, Jose. "Balancing Ethical Imperatives and Political Constraints: The Dilemma of New Democracies Confronting Past Human Rights Violations." *Hastings Law Journal* 43 (1992): 1425.

Zoller, Elisabeth. *Peacetime Unilateral Remedies: An Analysis of Countermeasures.* Dobbs Ferry, N.Y.: Transnational, 1984.

25. The Terminating Function

Brilmayer, Lea and Isaias Yemane Tesfalidet. "Treaty Denunciation and 'Withdrawal' from Customary International Law: An Erroneous Analogy with Dangerous Consequences." *Yale Law Journal Online* 120 (2011): 217.

Dallin, Alexander and Gail W. Lapidus, eds. *The Soviet System: From Crisis to Collapse.* Boulder, Colo.: Westview, 1995.

David, Arie E. *The Strategy of Treaty Termination: Lawful Breaches and Retaliations.* New Haven, Conn.: Yale University Press, 1975.

Gomaa, Mohammed M. *Suspension or Termination of Treaties on Grounds of Breach.* The Hague: Martinus Nijhoff Publishers, 1996.

Helfer, Laurence. "Existing Treaties." *Virginia Law Review* 91 (2005): 1579.

Jinks, Derek and David Sloss. "Is the President Bound by the Geneva Conventions?" *Cornell Law Review* 90 (2004): 97.

Kontou, Nancy. *The Termination and Revision of Treaties in the Light of New Customary International Law*. Oxford: Clarendon Press, 1994.

Lantis, Jeffrey. *The Life and Death of International Treaties: Double-Edged Diplomacy and the Politics of Ratification in Comparative Perspective*. New York: Oxford University Press, 2008.

Mendelbaum, Michael. "Coup de Grace: The End of the Soviet Union." *Foreign Affairs* 71 (1991): 164.

Miron, George. "Did the ABM Treaty of 1972 Remain in Force after the USSR Ceased to Exist in December 1999?" *American University International Law Review* 17 (2002): 189.

26. The Appraising Function

Arnold, Roberta. *International Humanitarian Law and Human Rights Law: Towards a New Merger in International Law*. The Hague: Martinus Nijhoff, 2008.

Bellinger III, John and Vijay Padmanabhan. "Detention Operations in Contemporary Conflicts: Four Challenges for the Geneva Conventions and Other Existing Law." *American Journal of International Law* 105 (2011): 201.

Bratspies, Rebecca. "Rethinking Decision-making in International Environmental Law: A Process-Orient Inquiry." *Yale Journal of International Law* 32 (2007): 363.

Carter, Barry. *International Economic Sanctions: Improving the Haphazard U.S. Legal Regime*. Cambridge: Cambridge University Press, 2008.

Cohen, Ronald, Goran Hayden, and Winston P. Nagan, eds. *Human Rights and Governance in Africa*. Gainesville, Fl.: University Press of Florida, 1993.

Cullet, Philippe. "Liability and Redress for Human-Induced Global Warming: Towards an International Regime." *Stanford Journal of International Law* 43A (2007): 99.

Economides, Spyros. *United Nations Interventionism, 1991–2004*. Cambridge: Cambridge University Press, 2007.

Footer, Mary. *An Institutional and Normative Analysis of the World Trade Organization*. The Hague: Martinus Nijhoff, 2005.

Fox, Gregory. *Humanitarian Occupation*. Cambridge: Cambridge University Press, 2008.

Freestone, David, ed. *The Law of the Sea: Progress and Prospects*. New York: Oxford University Press, 2006.

Holzgrefe, J. L. and Robert Keohane, eds. *Humanitarian Intervention: Ethical, Legal and Political Dilemmas*. Cambridge: Cambridge University Press, 2003.

Langer, Máximo and Joseph Doherty. "Managerial Judging Goes International, But Its Promise Remains Unfulfilled: An Empirical Assessment of the ICTY Reforms." *Yale Journal of International Law* 36 (2011): 242.

Lasswell, Harold D. "Toward Continuing Appraisal of the Impact of Law on Society." *Rutgers Law Review* 21 (1967): 645.

Lowe, Vaughan, Adam Roberts, Jennifer Welsh, and Dominik Zaum. *The United Nations Security Council and War: The Evolution of Thought and Practice Since 1945*. New York: Oxford University Press, 2008.

Martinez, Jenny S. "Towards an International Judicial System." *Stanford Law Review* 56 (2003): 429.

Reisman, W. Michael. "The Constitutional Crisis in the United Nations." *American Journal of International Law* 87 (1993): 83.

Report of the Group of High-Level Intergovernmental Experts to Review the Efficiency of the Administrative and Financial Functioning of the United Nations. United Nations General Assembly, Official Records: Forty-first Session, Supplement no. 49 (A/41/49). 1986.

Simeon, James. *Critical Issues in International Refugee Law: Strategies Toward Interpretative Harmony.* Cambridge: Cambridge University Press, 2010.

Underdal, Arild and Kenneth Hanf, eds. *International Environmental Agreements and Domestic Politics: The Case of Acid Rain.* London: Ashgate, 2000.

The United Nations in Its Second Half-Century: Report of an Independent Working Group on the Future of the United Nations. 1996.

van Ginkel, Bibi and Frans-Paul van der Putten, eds. *The International Response to Somali Piracy. Challenges and Opportunities.* Martinus Nijhoff, 2010.

Wippman, David and Matthew Evangelista, eds. *New Wars, New Laws? Applying the Laws of War in 21st Century Conflicts.* Ardsley, N.Y.: Transnational, 2005.

PART EIGHT/EFFECTS

27. Succession of States

Beato, Andrew M. "Newly Independent and Separating States' Succession Treaties: Considerations on the Hybrid Dependency of the Republics of the Former Soviet Union." *American University Journal of Law and Policy* 9 (1994): 525.

Bühler, Konrad. *State Succession and Membership in International Organizations: Legal Theories versus Political Pragmatism.* The Hague: Martinus Nijhoff, 2001.

Chen, Lung-Fong. *State Succession Relating to Unequal Treaties.* Hamden, Conn.: Archon Books, 1974.

Cheng, Tai-Heng. *State Succession and Commercial Obligations.* Ardsley, NY: Transnational Publishers, 2006.

Coppieters, Bruno and Richard Sakwa. *Contextualizing Secession: Normative Studies in Comparative Perspective.* New York: Oxford University Press, 2003.

Craven, Matthew. *The Decolonization of International Law: State Succession and the Law of Treaties.* New York: Oxford University Press, 2009.

Dumberry, Patrick. *State Succession to International Responsibility.* The Hague: Martinus Nijhoff, 2007.

Kohen, Marcelo, ed. *Secession: International Law Perspectives.* Cambridge: Cambridge University Press, 2006.

Kritz, Neil J., ed. *Transnational Justice: How Emerging Democracies Reckon with Former Regimes.* 3 vols. Washington, D.C.: United States Institute of Peace Press, 1995.

McWhinney, Edward. *The United Nations and a New World Order for a New Millennium: Self-Determination, State Succession, and Humanitarian Intervention.* New York: Springer, 2000.

Mullerson, Rein. "New Developments in the Former USSR and Yugoslavia." *Virginia Journal of International Law* 33 (1993): 299.

O'Connell, D. P. *State Succession in Municipal Law and International Law.* 2 vols. Cambridge: Cambridge University Press, 1967.

O'Keefe, Roger. "The Admission to the United Nations of the Ex-Soviet and Ex-Yugoslav States." *Baltic Yearbook of International Law* 1 (2001): 167.

State Succession in Matters of Property and Debts. Institut de Droit International. Grez-Doiceau: 2001.

Tomuschat, Christian, ed. *Modern Law of Self-Determination.* Dordrecht: Martinus Nijhoff Publishers, 1993.

28. Responsibility of States

Amerasingh, C. F. *Local Remedies in International Law.* Cambridge: Grotius, 1990.

Arsanjani, Mahnoush H. and W. Michael Reisman. "The Quest for an International Liability Regime for the Protection of Global Commons." In Karel Wellens, ed. *International Law: Theory and Practice. Essays in Honor of Eric Suy.* The Hague: Martinus Nijhoff, 1998: 469–92.

Bales, Jennifer S. "Transnational Responsibility and Recourse for Ozone Depletion." *Boston College International and Comparative Law Review* 19 (1996): 259.

Brownlie, Ian. *System of the Law of Nations: State Responsibility, Part 1.* Oxford: Clarendon Press, 1983.

Crawford, James. *The International Law Commission's Articles on State Responsibility: Introduction, Text and Commentaries.* Cambridge: Cambridge University Press, 2002.

Crawford, James, Allen Pellet, and Simon Olleson, eds. *The Law of International Responsibility.* New York: Oxford University Press, 2010.

Dickinson, Andrew, Rae Lindsay, and James Loonam. *State Immunity: Selected Materials and Commentary.* New York: Oxford University Press, 2004.

Fitzmaurice, Malgosia and Danesh Sarooshi, eds. *Issues of State Responsibility before International Judicial Institutions.* Portland, Oregon: Hart Publishing, 2004.

Fox, Hazel. *The Law of State Immunity.* New York: Oxford University Press, 2008.

Haesler, Thomas. *The Exhaustion of Local Remedies: Rule in the Case Law of International Courts and Tribunals.* Leiden: A. W. Sijthoff, 1968.

Handl, G. "Liability as an Obligation Established by a Primary Rule of International Law." *Netherlands Yearbook of International Law* 16 (1985): 49.

Handl, G. "State Liability for Accidental Transnational Environmental Damage by Private Persons." *American Journal of International Law* 74 (1980): 525.

Handl, Gunther. "International Accountability for Transboundary Environmental Harm Revisited: What Role for State Liability?" *Environmental Policy and Law* 37 (2007):116.

Jørgensen, Nina. *The Responsibility of States for International Crimes.* New York: Oxford University Press, 2003.

Kamminga, Menno T. *Inter-State Accountability for Violations of Human Rights.* Philadelphia: University of Pennsylvania Press, 1992.

Koh, Harold H. *Transnational Legal Problems.* With Henry Steiner and Detlev Vagts. 4th ed. Foundation Press, 1994.

Lillich, Richard B. ed. *The United Nations Compensation Commission.* Irvington, N.Y.: Transnational Publishers, 1995.

Lillich, Richard B. and David B. Magraw. *The Iran–United States Claim Tribunal: Its Contribution to the Law of State Responsibility.* Irvington, N.Y.: Transnational Publishers, 1996.

Nollkaemper, Andre. "Internationally Wrongful Acts in Domestic Courts." *American Journal of International Law* 101 (2007): 760.

Okowa, Phoebe. *State Responsibility for Transboundary Air Pollution in International Law.* New York: Oxford University Press, 2001.

Provost, René. *State Responsibility in International Law.* London: Ashgate, 2002.

Ragazzi, Maurizio, ed. *International Responsibility Today:* Essays in Memory of Oscar Schachter. Leiden: Martinus Nijhoff, 2005.

Rosenne, Shabtai. *The International Law Commission's Draft Articles on State Responsibility.* The Hague: Martinus Nijhoff, 1991.

Shelton, Dinah. "Private Violence, Public Wrongs, and the Responsibility of States." *Fordham International Law Journal* 13 (1990): 1.

Shelton, Dinah. "Righting Wrongs: Reparations in the Articles on State Responsibility" *American Journal of International Law* 96 (2002): 833.

Trapp, Kimberley. *State Responsibility for International Terrorism.* New York: Oxford University Press, 2011.

Turley, Jonathan. "'When in Rome': Multinational Misconduct and the Presumption Against Extraterritoriality." *Northwestern University Law Review* 84 (1990): 598.

Xue, Hanqin. *Transboundary Damage in International Law.* Cambridge: Cambridge University Press, 2009.

29. Individual Criminal Responsibility

Arsanjani, Mahnoush. "The Rome Statute of the International Criminal Court." *American Journal of International Law* 93 (1999): 22.

Arsanjani, Mahnoush and W. Michael Reisman. "The Law-in-Action of the International Criminal Court." *American Journal of International Law* 99 (2005): 385.

Bassiouni, M. C. *The Legislative History of the International Criminal Court.* Ardsley, N.Y.: Transnational Publishers, 2005.

Bassiouni, M. Cherif and Ved P. Nanda, eds. *A Treatise on International Criminal Law.* 2 vols. Springfield, Ill.: Charles C. Thomas, 1973.

Berg, Bradley E. "The 1994 International Law Commission Draft Statute for an International Criminal Court: A Principled Appraisal of Jurisdictional Structure." *Case Western Reserve Journal of International Law* 28 (1996): 221.

Bloomfield, Louis M. and Gerald F. Fitzgerald. *Crimes Against Internationally Protected Persons: Prevention and Punishment.* New York: Praeger, 1975.

Broomhall, Bruce. *International Justice and the International Criminal Court: Between Sovereignty and the Rule of Law.* New York: Oxford University Press, 2004.

Cassese, Antonio and Paola Gaeta. *Cassese's International Criminal Law.* 3d ed. Oxford University Press, 2013.

Dinstein, Yoram. *The Defence of "Obedience to Superior Orders" in International Law.* New York: Oxford University Press, 2012.

Ellis, Mark. *Sovereignty and Justice: Creating Domestic War Crimes Courts within the Principle of Complementarity.* New York: Oxford University Press, 2013.

Goldstone, Richard and Janine Simpson. "Evaluating the Role of the International Criminal Court as a Legal Response to Terrorism." *Harvard Human Rights Journal* 16 (2003): 13.

Hall, Christopher Keith. "The First Two Sessions of the UN Preparatory Committee on the Establishment of an International Criminal Court." *American Journal of International Law* 91 (1997): 177.

"The International Law Commission's Draft Code of Crimes Against the Peace and Security of Mankind: An Appraisal of the Substantive Provisions." *Criminal Law Forum* 5 (1994).

Linton, Suzannah, ed. *Hong Kong's War Crimes Trials*. New York: Oxford University Press, 2013.

Meron, Theodor. *The Making of International Criminal Justice: A View from the Bench.* New York: Oxford University Press, 2011.

Ohlin, Jens David. "Applying the Death Penalty to Crimes of Genocide." *American Journal of International Law* 99 (2005), 747.

Paust, Jordan and Bassiouni, M. C. *International Criminal Law—Cases and Materials.* Carolina Academic Press, 1996.

Paust, Jordan and Bassiouni, M. C. et al. *Human Rights Module: Crimes Against Humanity, Genocide, Other Crimes Against Human Rights, and War Crimes.* Carolina Academic Press, 2001.

SáCouto, Susana and Katherine Cleary. "The Gravity Threshold of the International Criminal Court." *American University International Law Review* 23 (2008): 807.

Safferling, Christoph. *International Criminal Procedure*. New York: Oxford University Press, 2012.

Schabas, William. *The International Criminal Court: A Commentary on the Rome Statute.* New York: Oxford University Press, 2010.

Schabas, William. *An Introduction to the International Criminal Court.* 3d ed. Cambridge: Cambridge University Press, 2007.

Schabas, William. *The UN International Criminal Tribunals: The Former Yugoslavia, Rwanda and Sierra Leone.* Cambridge: Cambridge University Press, 2006.

Scheffer, David. "The United States and the International Criminal Court." *American Journal of International Law* 93 (1999): 12.

Schlütter, Birgit. *Developments in Customary International Law: Theory and the Practice of the International Court of Justice and the International ad hoc Criminal Tribunals for Rwanda and Yugoslavia.* The Hague: Martinus Nijhoff, 2010.

Schwebel, Stephen. *Justice in International Law: Selected Writings.* Cambridge: Cambridge University Press, 2008.

Shahabuddeen, Mohamed. *International Criminal Justice at the Yugoslav Tribunal: The Judicial Experience.* New York: Oxford University Press, 2013.

Shany, Yuval. *The Competing Jurisdictions of International Courts and Tribunals.* New York: Oxford University Press, 2003.

van Alebeek, Rosanne. *The Immunity of States and Their Officials in International Criminal Law and International Human Rights Law.* New York: Oxford University Press, 2008.

Van Sliedregt, Elies. *Individual Criminal Responsibility in International Law.* New York: Oxford University Press, 2012.

Wexler, Leila Sadat. "The Proposed Permanent International Criminal Court: An Appraisal." *Cornell International Law Journal* 29 (1996): 665.

Zappala, Salvatore. *Human Rights in International Criminal Proceedings.* New York: Oxford University Press, 2003.

PART NINE/PROSPECTS

30. Toward a World Community of Human Dignity

Aaronson, Susan Ariel and Jamie Zimmerman. *Trade Imbalance: The Struggle to Weigh Human Rights Concerns in Trade Policymaking*. Cambridge: Cambridge University Press, 2007.

Aceves, William and Charles Hunnicut. *The Future of International Law: Proceedings of the 101st Annual Meeting, March 28–31, 2007, Washington, D.C.* American Society of International Law, 2007.

Alston, Philip and James Crawford. *The Future of UN Human Rights Treaty Monitoring*. Cambridge: Cambridge University Press, 2000.

Arsanjani, Mahnoush H., Jacob Katz Cogan, Robert D. Sloane, and Siegfried Wiessner, eds. *Looking to the Future: Essays on International Law in Honor of W. Michael Reisman*. Leiden/Boston: Martinus Nijhoff Publishers, 2011.

Bederman, David J. *International Law in Antiquity*. Cambridge: Cambridge University Press, 2001.

Bull, Hedley, Benedict Kingsbury, and Adam Roberts, eds. *Hugo Grotius and International Relations*. Oxford: Clarendon Press, 1992.

Cass, Deborah, Brett Williams, and George Barker. *China and the World Trading System: Entering the New Millennium*. Cambridge: Cambridge University Press, 2003.

Cavallaro, James and Stephanie Brewer. "Reevaluating Regional Human Rights Litigation in the Twenty-first Century: The Case of the Inter-American Court." *American Journal of International Law* 102 (2008): 768.

Clark, Grenville and Louis Bruno Sohn. *World Peace Through World Law*. 3d ed. Cambridge, Mass.: Harvard University Press, 1966.

Cohen, Jean L. *Globalization and Sovereignty: Rethinking Legality, Legitimacy, and Constitutionalism*. Cambridge: Cambridge University Press, 2012.

Damrosch, Lori. *Beyond Confrontation: International Law for the Post–Cold War Era*. Co-edited with Gennady Danilenko and Rein Müllerson. Westview Press, 1995.

Donnelly, Jack. *Human Rights in the 1990's: Promise or Peril? International Human Rights*. Boulder, Colo.: Westview Press, 1993.

Falk, Richard. *The End of World Order*. New York: Holmes and Meier, 1983.

Falk, Richard. *Law in an Emerging Global Village: A Post- Westphalian Perspective*. Ardsley, N.Y.: Transnational Publishers, 1998.

Falk, Richard. *Study of Future Worlds*. New York: Free Press, 1980.

Fassbender, Bardo, Simone Peter, and Daniel Hogger. *The Oxford Handbook of the History of International Law*. New York: Oxford University Press, 2013.

Ferencz, Benjamin B. *PlanetHood: The Key to Your Survival and Prosperity*. Coos Bay, Ore.: Vision Books, 1985.

Focarelli, Carlo. *International Law as Social Construct: The Struggle for Global Justice*. New York: Oxford University Press, 2012.

Galtung, Johan. *The True Worlds: A Transnational Perspective*. New York: Free Press, 1981.

Gong, Gerrit W. *The Standard of "Civilization" in International Society*. Oxford: Clarendon Press, 1984.

Greenburg, Melanine, John Barton, and Margaret McGuinness. *Words over War: Mediation and Arbitration to Prevent Deadly Conflict*. Lanham, Md.: Rowman & Littlefield, 2000.

Grossman, Claudio and Daniel B. Bradlow. "Are We Being Propelled Toward a People-Centered Transnational Legal Order?" *American University Journal of International Law and Policy* 9 (1993): 1.

Hurrell, Andrew. *On Global Order: Power, Values, and the Constitution of International Society.* New York: Oxford University Press, 2007.

Lachs, Manfred. *The Teacher in International Law.* The Hague: Martinus Nijhoff, 1982.

Lasswell, Harold D. *World Politics and Personal Insecurity.* New York: The Free Press; London: Collier-Macmillan Limited, 1965.

Lasswell, Harold D. and Myres S. McDougal. *Jurisprudence for a Free Society: Studies in Law, Science, and Policy.* 2 vols. New Haven, Conn.: New Haven Press; Dordrecht: Martinus Nijhoff, 1992.

McDougal, Myres S. "International Law and the Future." *Mississippi Law Journal* 50 (1979): 259.

Murphy, John Francis. *The Evolving Dimensions of International Law: Hard Choices for the World Community.* Cambridge: Cambridge University Press, 2010.

Nussbaum, Arthur. *A Concise History of the Law of Nations.* New York: Macmillan, 1954.

Nye, Joseph and John Donahue, eds. *Governance in a Globalizing World.* Brookings Institute Press, 2000.

Reisman, W. Michael. *Jurisprudence: Understanding and Shaping Law.* With Aaron M. Schreiber. New Haven, Conn.: New Haven Press, 1987.

Ruddy, Frank S. *International Law in the Enlightenment: The Background of Emmerich de Vattel's Le droit des Gens.* New York: Oceana Publications, 1975.

Sarfaty, Galit. "Why Culture Matters in International Institutions: The Marginality of Human Rights at the World Bank." *American Journal of International Law* 103 (2009): 647.

Seita, Alex Y. "Globalization and the Convergence of Values." *Cornell International Law Journal* 30 (1997): 429.

Slaughter, Anne-Marie. *A New World Order.* Princeton, N.J.: Princeton University Press, 2004.

Stone, Julius. *Visions of World Order: Between State Power and Human Justice.* Baltimore: Johns Hopkins University Press, 1984.

Vicuña, Francisco Orrego. *International Dispute Settlement in an Evolving Global Society: Constitutionalization, Accessibility, Privatization.* Cambridge: Cambridge University Press, 2004.

Wittes, Benjamin. *Law and the Long War: The Future of Justice in the Age of Terror.* Penguin, 2009.

Table of Select Treaties

The available information concerning the state parties to a particular treaty derives mainly from the United Nations, Multilateral Treaties Deposited with the Secretary-General, the U.S. Department of State Treaties in Force publication, and the organization where the written instrument has been deposited.

The texts of most of these treaties can be obtained from official sources that assure authenticity—e.g., governments, regional organizations, intergovernmental organizations, and nongovernmental organizations. The American Society of International Law offers a handy Electronic Resource Guide that provides instructions on how to locate the text and status of treaties mentioned in this book, as well as others. The Resource Guide is available at: www.asil.org/resources/electronic-resource-guide-erg. Additionally, information about many treaties is available from the United Nations Treaty Collection at treaties.un.org. Where possible, the status of each treaty listed below has been updated as of 2014. To obtain the current status of a treaty, including the number of signatories, state parties, and other historical information, readers may consult a variety of online resources. Treaties without page numbers are provided here as examples, although not discussed in the book.

Year		Page Reference
1864	Geneva Convention for the Amelioration of the Condition of the Wounded and Sick in Armed Forces in the Field (First Geneva Convention), *done* Aug. 22, 1864 (*entered into force* June 22, 1865). There were 57 signatories to the convention.	510

Year		Page Reference
1895	Treaty of Shimonoseki, *done* Apr. 17, 1895 (*entered into force* May 8, 1895). There were two state parties to this treaty.	48
1899	Convention for the Pacific Settlement of International Disputes, *signed* at The Hague, July 29, 1899, 32 Stat. 1779, T.S. No. 392, 1 Bevans 230 (*entered into force* Sept. 4, 1900). Revised in 1907 at the Second Hague Peace Conference. There are 112 state parties to one or both conventions.	137, 394, 407, 450, 510, 511, 537
1907	Convention Respecting the Laws and Customs of War on Land and its annex: Regulation concerning the Laws and Customs of War on Land, The Hague, Oct. 18, 1907, 36 Stat. 2277, T.S. No. 539, 1 Bevans 631. There are 37 state parties to this convention.	394, 510, 511, 515, 537
1919	Convention on the Regulation of Aerial Navigation, Paris, 11 L.N.T.S 174.	193
	Treaty of Versailles of 1919 (Treaty of Peace between the Allied and Associated Powers and Germany), *signed* June 28, 1919 (*entered into force* Jan. 10, 1920). There were 28 signatories to the treaty.	511–12, 515
	Covenant of the League of Nations, *adopted* June 28, 1919, [1919] U.K.T.S. 4 (Cmd. 153)/ [1920] A.T.S. 1/ [1920] A.T.S. 3 (*entered into force* Jan. 10, 1920). There were 63 member states of the League of Nations.	61, 153, 271, 378, 431, 450, 537
1920	Statute of the Permanent Court of International Justice, *concluded* Dec. 13, 1920, 6 L.N.T.S. 379, 390, 114 BFSP 860, 17 A.J.I.L. Supp. 115 (1923) (*entered into force* Aug. 20, 1921). There were 46 signatories to the statute.	134
1921	Convention on the Regime of Navigable Waterways of International Concern, *adopted* Barcelona Apr. 20, 1921, 7 L.N.T.S 35 (*entered into force* Oct. 31, 1922). There are 31 state parties to this convention.	191
1923	Convention on the Statute on the International Regime of Maritime Ports, *done* Dec. 9, 1923, 58 L.N.T.S. 285 (*entered into force* July 26, 1926). There are 43 state parties to this convention.	167
1925	Protocol for the Prohibition of the Use in War of Asphyxiating, Poisonous, or Other Gases, and of Bacteriological Method of Warfare, June 17, 1925, 26 U.S.T. 571, T.I.A.S. No. 8061, 94 L.N.T.S 65 (*entered into force* Feb. 8, 1928). There are 113 state parties to this protocol (13 state parties have deposited objections).	393

Year		Page Reference
1928	General Treaty for the Renunciation of War as an Instrument of National Policy (Kellog-Briand Pact; Pact of Paris), *adopted* at Paris Aug. 27, 1928, 46 Stat. 2343, 94 L.N.T.S. 57. There are 69 state parties to this treaty.	102, 308, 379, 514
1929	Geneva Convention relative to the Treatment of Prisoners of War (Geneva Convention of 1929), *done* July 27, 1929 (*entered into force* June 19, 1931). There were 53 state parties to this convention.	515
1930	Convention on Certain Questions Relating to the Conflict of Nationality Laws, *done* Apr. 12, 1930, 179 L.N.T.S. 89 (*entered into force* July 1, 1937). There are 22 state parties to this convention.	214, 223–24, 226, 492
	Protocol Relating to a Certain Case of Statelessness, *done* Apr. 12, 1930, 179 L.N.T.S. 115 (*entered into force* July 1, 1937). There are 24 state parties to this protocol.	223, 224, 492
	Protocol Relating to Military Obligations in Certain Cases of Double Nationality, *done* Apr. 12, 1930, 178 L.N.T.S. 227 (*entered into force* May 25, 1937). There are 26 state parties to this protocol.	227
1933	Convention of Rights and Duties of States (Montevideo Convention), *done* Dec. 26, 1933, 49 Stat. 3097, T.S. No. 881, 3 Bevans 145, 165 L.N.T.S. 19 (*entered into force* Dec. 26, 1934). There are 16 state parties to this convention.	26
	Convention Relating to the International Status of Refugees, *signed* Oct. 28, 1933, 159 L.N.T.S. 199. There are eight state parties to this convention.	231
1936	Convention Concerning the Use of Broadcasting in the Cause of Peace, *done* Sept. 23, 1936, 186 L.N.T.S. 301, 197 L.N.T.S. 394, 200 L.N.T.S. 557 (*entered into force* Apr. 2, 1938). There are 32 state parties to this convention.	347
1944	Convention on International Civil Aviation, *done* at Chicago Dec. 7, 1944, 61 Stat. 1180, T.I.A.S. No. 1951, 3 Bevans 944, 15 U.N.T.S. 295 (*entered into force* Apr. 4, 1947). There are 191 state parties to this convention.	193
	International Air Services Transit Agreement, *signed* at Chicago Dec. 7, 1944, 59 Stat. 1693, 3 Bevans 916, 84 U.N.T.S. 389 (*entered into force* Jan. 30, 1945). There are 129 state parties to this agreement.	193
	International Air Transport Agreement, *opened for signature* at Chicago Dec. 7, 1944, 59 Stat. 1701. There are 17 state parties to this agreement. (The United States accepted it on Feb. 8, 1945, and withdrew in 1947 due to a lack of international interest.)	193–94

Year		Page Reference

European Social Charter, *adopted* Oct. 18, 1961, ETS 35   472
(*entered into force* Feb. 26, 1965). There are 47 state parties to
the charter. The European Social Charter was revised in 1996.

Optional Protocol to the Vienna Convention on Diplomatic   136
Relations Concerning the Compulsory Settlement of
Disputes, *done* Apr. 18, 1961, 500 U.N.T.S. 241 (*entered into
force* Apr. 24, 1964). There are 69 state parties to this protocol.

Vienna Convention on Diplomatic Relations, *done* Apr. 18,   302, 303, 304, 305,
1961, 23. U.S.T. 3227, T.I.A.S. No. 7502, 500 U.N.T.S. 95   307, 318
(*entered into force* Apr. 24, 1964). There are 190 state parties to
this convention.

1962   Convention on the Liability of Operators of Nuclear Ships,   503
signed at Brussels May 25, 1962 (*not yet entered into force*),
reprinted in 57 A.J.I.L. 268 (1963). The convention requires the
ratification of at least one licencing state and one other state.

Protocol Instituting a Conciliation and Good Offices   441
Commission to be responsible for seeking a settlement of
any disputes which may arise between State Parties to the
Convention against Discrimination in Education, *adopted*
Dec. 10, 1962, *reprinted in* United Nations, Human Rights–A
Compilation of International Instruments 95–103, U.N. Doc.
ST/HR/1/Rev.3 (1988) (*entered into force* Oct. 24, 1968). There
are 35 state parties to this protocol.

1963   Convention on Offenses and Certain Other Acts Committed   282
on Board Aircraft (Tokyo Convention), *done* Sept. 14, 1963,
20 U.S.T. 2941, T.I.A.S. No. 6768, 704 U.N.T.S. 219 (*entered
into force* Dec. 4, 1969). There are 185 state parties to this
convention.

European Convention on Reduction of Cases of Multiple   227
Nationality and Military Obligation in Cases of Multiple
Nationality, European T.S. No. 43 (1963). There are 12 state
parties to this convention.

Optional Protocol to the Convention on Consular Relations   313, 465
Concerning the Compulsory Settlement of Disputes, *done* at
Vienna Apr. 24, 1963, 21 U.S.T. 325, T.I.A.S. No. 6820, 596
U.N.T.S. 487 (*entered into force* Mar. 19, 1967). There are 50
state parties to this protocol.

Treaty Banning Nuclear Weapons Tests in the Atmosphere,
in Outer Space, and under Water, 14 U.S.T. 1313, T.I.A.S. No.
5433, 480 U.N.T.S. 43 (*entered into force* Oct. 10, 1963). There
are 125 state parties to this treaty.

Year		Page Reference
1972	Agreement on Cooperation in the Field of Environmental Protection between the United States of America and the Union of Soviet Socialist Republics, *signed* May 23, 1972, 23 UST 845 (*entered into force* May 23, 1972). There were two state parties to this agreement.	411
	Convention on the International Liability for Damage Caused by Space Objects, *done* at Washington, London, and Moscow Mar. 29, 1972, 24 U.S.T. 2389, T.I.A.S. No. 7762 (*entered into force* Sept. 1, 1972). There are 90 state parties to this convention.	195, 503
	Convention on the Prohibition of the Development, Production, and Stockpiling of Bacteriological (Biological) and Toxin Weapons and on Their Destruction, Apr. 10, 1972, 26 U.S.T. 585, T.I.A.S. No. 8062. There are 170 state parties to this convention.	393
	European Convention on State Immunity, *done* at Basel May 16, 1972, *reprinted in* 11 I.L.M. 470 (1972) (*entered into force* June 11, 1976). There are eight state parties to this convention.	290
	Treaty on the Limitation of Anti-Ballistic Missile Systems (ABM Treaty), *signed* at Moscow May 26, 1972, 23 U.S.T. 3435, T.I.A.S. No. 7503 (*entered into force* Oct. 3, 1972).	334
	U.S.–U.K. Extradition Treaty of 1972, *adopted* June 8, 1972, 28 UST 227, 1049 U.N.T.S. 167 (*entered into force* Jan. 21, 1977). There were two parties to this treaty. The 1972 treaty was replaced by the U.S.–U.K. Extradition Treaty of 2003, S. Treaty Doc. 108-23.	235
1973	Convention on the Prevention and Punishment of Crimes against Internationally Protected Persons, Including Diplomatic Agents, *adopted* Dec. 14, 1973, 1035 U.N.T.S. 167 (*entered into force* Feb. 20, 1977). There are 176 state parties to this convention.	236
	International Convention on the Suppression and Punishment of the Crime of Apartheid, *adopted* Nov. 30, 1973, 1015 U.N.T.S. 244 (*entered into force* July 18, 1976). There are 109 state parties to this convention.	286
1974	Convention on Registration of Objects Launched into Outer Space, *adopted* Nov. 12, 1974, G.A. Res. 3235, 29 U.N. GAOR Supp. (No. 3) at 16, U.N. Doc. A/9631 (1973), *and opened for signature* Jan. 14, 1975, 1023 U.N.T.S. 15, 28 U.S.T. 695, T.I.A.S. No. 8480 (*entered into force* Sept. 15, 1976). There are 62 state parties to this convention.	196, 282

Year		Page Reference
1975	Final Act of the Conference on Security and Co-Operation in Europe, *adopted* Aug. 1, 1975, 73 State Dept. Bull. 323 (Sept. 1975), *reprinted in* 14 I.L.M. 1292 (1975). The act was signed by 35 heads of state or government.	45, 81, 140, 434
1977	Protocol Additional to the Geneva Conventions of 12 August 1949, and Relating to the Protection of Victims of Non-International Armed Conflict (Protocol II), *adopted* June 8, 1977, *reprinted in* 16 I.L.M. 1442 (1977) (*entered into force* Dec. 7, 1978). There are 167 state parties to this protocol.	83–84, 394, 519
	Protocol to the Geneva Conventions of 12 August 1949, and Relating to the Protection of Victims of International Armed Conflict (Protocol I), *adopted* June 8, 1977, *reprinted in* 16 Int'l Legal Materials 1391 (1977) (*entered into force* Dec. 7, 1978). There are 174 state parties to this protocol.	83–84, 394
1978	Vienna Convention on Succession of State in Respect of Treaties, *concluded* Aug. 23, 1978, U.N. Doc. A/CONF. 80/31, 1946 U.N.T.S. 2 (*entered into force* Nov. 6, 1996). There are 22 state parties to this convention.	483–84, 488, 490
1979	Agreement Governing the Activities of States on the Moon and Other Celestial Bodies (Moon Treaty), *adopted* Dec. 5, 1979, G.A. Res. 34/68, 34 U.N. GAOR Supp. (No. 46) at 77, U.N. Doc. A/34/36 (1979) (*entered into force* July 11, 1984). There are 16 state parties to this agreement.	104, 196–97
	Convention on the Elimination of All Forms of Discrimination against Women, *adopted* Dec. 18, 1979, U.N. Doc. A/RES/34/180, 1249 U.N.T.S. 13 (*entered into force* Sept. 3, 1981). There are 188 state parties to this convention.	127, 257, 407, 418, 441, 472
	International Convention Against the Taking of Hostages, *adopted* Dec. 17, 1979, G.A. Res. 34/146, 34 U.N. GAOR Supp. (No. 46) at 24, U.N. Doc. A/34/36 (1979), *opened for signature* Dec. 18, 1979 (*entered into force* June 3, 1983). There are 173 state parties to this convention.	236
1981	African Charter on Human and Peoples' Rights (Banjul Charter), *adopted* June 27, 1981 in Nairobi, OAU Doc. CAB/LEG/67/3/Rev.5 (1981), *reprinted in* 21 I.L.M. 59 (1982) (*entered into force* Oct. 21, 1986). There are 53 state parties to this charter.	131, 253, 257
	Treaty Establishing the Organization of Eastern Caribbean States, *done* June 18, 1981, *reprinted in* 20 I.L.M. 1166 (1981). There are nine state parties to this treaty.	325

Year		Page Reference
1982	United Nations Convention on the Law of the Sea (LOS Convention), *concluded* at Montego Bay Dec. 10, 1982, U.N. Doc. A/CONF. 62/122 and Corr. 1 to 11 (1982), 1833 U.N.T.S. 3 (*entered into force* Nov. 16, 1994); *reproduced in* United Nations, The Law of the Sea, U.N. Pub. Sales No. E. 83, V.5 (1983). There are 166 state parties to this convention.	29–30, 104, 116, 124, 138–39, 165–69, 171–73, 176–79, 181–82, 183–86, 204–5, 284–85, 410, 436, 451, 466
1983	Vienna Convention on Succession in Respect of State Property, Archives and Debts, *adopted* Apr. 7, 1983, U.N. Doc. A/CONF.117/14 (*not yet in force*), *reprinted in* 22 I.L.M. 306 (1983). There are seven state parties to this convention. Fifteen are required for this convention to enter into force.	484, 487, 492–95
1984	Convention against Torture and Other Cruel, Inhuman or Degrading Treatment or Punishment, *adopted* Dec. 10, 1984, U.N. Doc. A/RES/39/46, 1465 U.N.T.S. 85 (*entered into force* June 26, 1987). There are 155 state parties to this convention.	127, 254, 418, 440, 472
1986	Convention on Assistance in the Case of a Nuclear Accident or Radiological Emergency, *adopted* Sept. 26, 1986, 1457 U.N.T.S. 133 (*entered into force* Feb. 26, 1987). There are 111 state parties to this convention.	407
	Convention on Early Notification of a Nuclear Accident, *adopted* Sept. 26, 1986, 1457 U.N.T.S. 133 (*entered into force* Oct. 27, 1986). There are 116 state parties to this convention.	407
	Vienna Convention on the Law of Treaties between States and International Organizations or between International Organizations, *adopted* Mar. 21, 1986, 25 I.L.M. 543 1986 (*not yet in force*). There are 31 state parties to this convention.	321
1987	Treaty Between the United States of America and the Union of Soviet Socialist Republics on the Elimination of Their Intermediate-Range and Shorter-Range Missiles (INF Treaty), *signed* Dec. 8, 1987, Dep't State Bull., Feb. 1988, at 22–33 (*entered into force* June 1, 1998).	395
1988	Bilateral Agreement between the Republic of Afghanistan and the Islamic Republic of Pakistan on the Principles of Mutual Relations, in particular of Non-Interference and Non-Intervention (Afghanistan Agreement), *done* at Geneva, Apr. 14, 1988, *reprinted in* Dep't State Bull., June 1988, at 56–60 (*entered into force* May 15, 1988).	72
	Canada-U.S. Arctic Cooperation Agreement, *adopted* Jan. 11, 1988, 1852 U.N.T.S. 59 (*entered into force* Jan. 11, 1988). There are 2 state parties to this treaty.	170

Index